International Law, Politics and Security in Central Asia

Sergey Sayapin
Editor

International Law, Politics and Security in Central Asia

Studies on Transformation and Development in the OSCE Region

Springer

Editor
Sergey Sayapin
School of Law
KIMEP University
Almaty, Kazakhstan

ISBN 978-3-032-17817-6 ISBN 978-3-032-17818-3 (eBook)
https://doi.org/10.1007/978-3-032-17818-3

This work was supported by Organization for Security and Co-operation in Europe.

This Springer imprint is published by the registered company Springer Nature Switzerland AG
The registered company address is: Gewerbestrasse 11, 6330 Cham, Switzerland

Preface

The present volume seeks to open a sustained conversation about the role of Central Asia in the theory and practice of international law. Since the independence of Kazakhstan, Kyrgyzstan, Tajikistan, Turkmenistan, and Uzbekistan in 1991, the region has entered the international legal order not merely as a geographical periphery of Eurasia but as a distinct normative space. In the decades that have followed, Central Asian states have ratified a wide range of multilateral treaties, joined international organizations, contributed to debates on the development of customary rules, and gradually positioned themselves as active participants in shaping international law. Yet the scholarship documenting and critically evaluating this process has remained limited, fragmented, and often overshadowed by Eurocentric narratives. This book is an attempt to correct that imbalance by assembling diverse perspectives on the theory, institutions, and applications of international law in Central Asia.

The volume brings together contributions from scholars of different backgrounds, including academics based in the region and international experts with a comparative lens. This combination allows the reader to perceive Central Asia not simply as a passive recipient of international norms but as a dynamic site where international law is interpreted, contested, and transformed. The opening chapters in Part I set the conceptual stage. Sergey Sayapin's chapter highlights the region's trajectory in terms of international legal development since 1991. His analysis demonstrates how Central Asian states have relied on international law to consolidate sovereignty and participate in global governance. Rustam Atadjanov adds a critical dimension by interrogating positivist approaches to international law, showing how a purely doctrinal outlook often fails to account for the political and historical contexts of the region. Together, these contributions underline the necessity of a pluralist and historically conscious methodology for studying Central Asia in international law. This framework resonates with Anja Mihr's discussion of transitology, which contextualizes Central Asia's transition to sovereignty and democracy within the global processes of political change. Sultan Sakhariyev's chapter on international organizations demonstrates that Central Asia has served not only as a venue for the implementation of international law but also as a laboratory for new forms of regional cooperation, ranging from the Shanghai Cooperation Organization to the Eurasian Economic Union. Akbar Rasulov's essay positions Central Asia in the broader dialectics between the 'Second' and the 'Third Worlds', urging us to rethink how socialist legacies and postcolonial critiques converge in this region. Taken together, these chapters establish that the region cannot be understood through a simple lens of importation of foreign models. Rather, Central Asia has developed a hybrid identity in international law, simultaneously shaped by Soviet legacies, regional particularities, and global transformations.

The next thematic cluster in Part II explores international law as a factor in Central Asian politics. Sébastien Lafrance, Nik Khakhar, and Ayazhan Kazybekova analyze how the implementation and effectiveness of international law in the region depends on both formal mechanisms and informal practices, often revealing gaps between ratification and enforcement. Abay Abylaiuly's contribution on the International Law Commission brings Central Asia into the debates of one of the most authoritative global bodies in the codification of international law.

The subsequent chapters in Parts III–VIII bring international law 'down to earth' through concrete case studies. Nicolás Zambrana-Tévar explores the international legal implications of the January 2022 events in Kazakhstan, illustrating the tension between sovereignty and democracy promotion. Muslim Khassenov analyses labor law reforms in Central Asia, linking them to international labor standards and human rights commitments. Farkhod Fazilov discusses Uzbekistan's efforts to combat money laundering, situating domestic reforms within global regulatory frameworks. Sherzod Shadikhodjaev examines the WTO Agreement on Fisheries Subsidies, highlighting its unexpected relevance for landlocked Central Asian members of the WTO. These chapters demonstrate that international law is not an abstract set of rules imposed from outside, but a living practice that intersects with political economy, governance, and security in the region. The global meets the local in ways that both constrain and empower Central Asian states, producing outcomes that are sometimes paradoxical but always revealing of the law's contested nature.

A rich discussion emerges from Alberto Pecoraro's analysis of stabilization clauses in natural resource contracts. His chapter reveals the tension between economic sovereignty and investor protection, situating Kazakhstan and Uzbekistan within broader debates on constitutional law, international investment law, and sustainable development. These insights are complemented by Maria Baideldinova's study of international standards of animal welfare, which underscores how WTO rules and global trade practices increasingly shape domestic agricultural policies. Taken together, these contributions highlight the delicate balance Central Asian states must maintain between asserting sovereign control over their resources and integrating into the global economy under international legal commitments. They also show how international law offers both opportunities and constraints, creating space for agency but also exposing states to external pressures.

The environmental dimension is explored in depth by Kamila Mateeva, Kanykei Kasybekova, and Begaiym Esenkulova. Their chapter identifies systemic challenges in implementing international environmental law in Kazakhstan, Kyrgyzstan, and Uzbekistan, focusing on emblematic cases such as the Western Tien Shan, the Aral

Sea, and the Taldykol lakes. They argue that, while Central Asian states have formally ratified major environmental treaties, actual implementation often falters in the face of economic priorities and weak enforcement mechanisms. The discussion powerfully illustrates the intersection between environmental law and human rights, as environmental degradation has direct consequences for the wellbeing of populations.

The book concludes with Julia Emtseva's chapter on the teaching of international law in Central Asia. By comparing syllabi, textbooks, and professional backgrounds across private and public universities, she reveals a striking duality: private, Western-oriented institutions often adopt globalized curricula, while public universities continue to follow Soviet-influenced frameworks. This analysis is not only relevant for the region itself but also contributes to the broader literature on international legal education, raising questions about epistemological diversity, decolonization, and the transmission of legal knowledge. The significance of this closing chapter lies in its forward-looking perspective. If the future of international law depends on the next generation of lawyers, then the pedagogical choices made in Central Asia will profoundly shape how the region positions itself in the global legal order. Education thus becomes both a mirror of past legacies and a tool for shaping future agency.

What emerges from this volume is a complex picture of Central Asia as neither a passive recipient nor a fully autonomous producer of international law, but rather as a region engaged in an ongoing negotiation between global norms and local realities. The chapters collectively demonstrate that Central Asia matters for international law in at least three ways. First, the region highlights the continuing relevance of sovereignty. From alleged color revolutions to resource contracts, Central Asian states constantly assert their sovereignty while simultaneously navigating international commitments. This tension is not unique to the region, but it is illustrated in Central Asia in particularly vivid ways. Second, Central Asia exemplifies the role of international organizations and institutions as mediators of legal integration. Whether through the International Law Commission, the WTO, or regional organizations, Central Asian participation is both shaped by and shaping these bodies, contributing perspectives that challenge established assumptions. Third, the region illustrates the importance of pluralizing international law. By examining animal welfare, labor rights, environmental protection, and education, the book demonstrates that the scope of international law in Central Asia extends far beyond traditional doctrines of state responsibility and use of force. It encompasses socio-economic rights, human security, and environmental sustainability. These findings resonate with global debates about the need to pluralize international law, moving beyond Eurocentric narratives to recognize diverse sources of legitimacy and authority. Central Asia is not a periphery but a frontier where these debates are taking place in concrete, often contested ways.

This book is the product of two years of intellectual collaboration and collective effort. It would not have been possible without the dedication of all the contributors, whose chapters reflect deep expertise, critical insight, and commitment to advancing knowledge about international law in Central Asia. I am sincerely grateful to each of them for their generosity, collegiality, and intellectual rigor. Special thanks are due to the OSCE Academy in Bishkek, whose generous support enabled this volume to be published open access, ensuring that scholars and practitioners around the world can engage with its findings freely, and to Ms Alessandra Sztrimbely for her meticulous and thoughtful proofreading of the entire manuscript. I also warmly thank the Centre for International Law at the National University of Singapore, where I am currently serving as a Distinguished Visiting Global Scholar, and where the book has reached completion. Finally, I wish to express my appreciation to Springer for their exceptional professionalism throughout the editorial and production process. Their support has been crucial to bringing this project to fruition and in ensuring that the volume reaches the widest possible audience.

I hope that this book will serve as both a reference point and an inspiration for future research, teaching, and policy making. Central Asia has much to teach us about the evolving nature of international law, and it is my conviction that the voices assembled here will contribute meaningfully to the global dialogue.

Almaty–Singapore
November 2025

Sergey Sayapin

Contents

Part I Context and Development

1 **International Law in Central Asia: A Critical Overview** 3
Sergey Sayapin

2 **A Critical Reflection on Positivist Approaches Toward International Law in Central Asia** 31
Rustam Atadjanov

3 **Transitional Justice and Transitology in the Post-Soviet Space** 65
Anja Mihr

4 **International Organizations and the Development of International Law in Central Asia** 83
Sultan Sakhariyev

5 **Between the Second and the Third Worlds: The Legal Postcoloniality of Central Asia** 101
Akbar Rasulov

Part II International Law as a Factor in the Central Asian Politics

6 **The Implementation and Effectiveness of International Law in Central Asia** 137
Sébastien Lafrance, Nik Khakhar, and Ayazhan Kazybekova

7 **On the Necessity of Responding to the Findings of the International Law Commission** 171
Abay Abylaiuly

Part III International Law and Security

8 **Were the Events of January 2022 in Kazakhstan a Failed Colour Revolution?** 203
Nicolás Zambrana-Tévar

Part IV Human Rights

9 Labour Law Reforms in Central Asian Countries within the Context of International Labour Standards: A Comparative Analysis 227
Muslim Khassenov

Part V International Criminal Law

10 Uzbekistan's Experience in Combating Money Laundering 269
Farkhod Fazilov

Part VI International Trade and Investment Law

11 The Agreement on Fisheries Subsidies and Implications for Central Asian WTO Members as Landlocked Countries 293
Sherzod Shadikhodjaev

12 Stabilization Clauses and Subsoil Use: Economic Development, Sovereignty, and International Law in Central Asia 313
Alberto Pecoraro

Part VII International Environmental Law

13 International Legal Standards of Animal Welfare 331
Maria Baideldinova

14 International Environmental Law in Central Asia: Implementation Challenges and Limitations 347
Kamila Mateeva, Kanykei Kasybekova, and Begaiym Esenkulova

Part VIII International Law as an Academic Discipline

15 The Two Worlds of Teaching International Law in Central Asia ... 375
Julia Emtseva

Editor and Contributors

About the Editor

Dr. Sergey Sayapin (s.sayapin@kimep.kz) is Professor of Law at KIMEP University (Almaty, Kazakhstan). In 2000–2014, he held a few positions at the ICRC Regional Delegation in Central Asia (Tashkent, Uzbekistan). Professor Sayapin has published extensively on international institutions, conflict and security law, human rights, international criminal law, post-Soviet and Central Asian approaches to international law, and the international legal aspects of Russia's war against Ukraine. He is sub-editor for Central Asia of the *Encyclopedia of Public International Law in Asia* (Brill) and a member of the Executive Council of the Asian Society of International Law.

Contributors

Abay Abylaiuly Associate Professor in International Law, Maqsut Narikbayev University, Astana, Kazakhstan

Rustam Atadjanov School of Law, KIMEP University, Almaty, Kazakhstan

Maria Baideldinova Law School, KIMEP University, Almaty, Kazakhstan

Julia Emtseva HEC Paris, Paris, France

Begaiym Esenkulova AUCA Law Program Faculty, Bishkek, Kyrgyzstan; American University of Central Asia Law Program, Bishkek, Kyrgyzstan

Farkhod Fazilov Tashkent State University of Law, Tashkent, Uzbekistan

Kanykei Kasybekova AUCA Law Program Faculty, Bishkek, Kyrgyzstan; American University of Central Asia Law Program, Bishkek, Kyrgyzstan

Ayazhan Kazybekova Maqsut Narikbayev University, Astana, Kazakhstan

Nik Khakhar Toronto, ON, Canada

Muslim Khassenov Maqsut Narikbayev University, Astana, Kazakhstan;
Harvard University, Cambridge, MA, USA

Sébastien Lafrance Tashkent State University of Law, Tashkent, Uzbekistan

Kamila Mateeva Law Division of the American University of Central Asia, Bishkek, Kyrgyzstan;
American University of Central Asia Law Program, Bishkek, Kyrgyzstan

Anja Mihr OSCE Academy, Bishkek, Kyrgyzstan;
The Center on Governance Through Human Rights, Berlin Governance Platform, Berlin, Germany

Alberto Pecoraro Maqsut Narikbayev University, Astana, Kazakhstan

Akbar Rasulov School of Law, University of Glasgow, Glasgow, Scotland

Sultan Sakhariyev KIMEP University, Almaty, Kazakhstan

Sergey Sayapin School of Law, KIMEP University, Almaty, Kazakhstan

Sherzod Shadikhodjaev KDI School of Public Policy and Management, Sejong City, Republic of Korea

Nicolás Zambrana-Tévar KIMEP University School of Law, Almaty, Kazakhstan

Part I
Context and Development

Chapter 1
International Law in Central Asia: A Critical Overview

Sergey Sayapin

Abstract Since their independence in 1991, the states of Central Asia (Kazakhstan, Kyrgyzstan, Tajikistan, Turkmenistan, and Uzbekistan) have become increasingly important as regional and international actors. They have joined the United Nations (UN) as well as regional organizations, such as the Commonwealth of Independent States (CIS), the Collective Security Treaty Organization (CSTO), the Shanghai Cooperation Organisation (SCO), and the Eurasian Economic Union (EAEU). International law has played an important role in the processes of state-building and integration these countries have undergone, yet it has not always been consistently accepted as a policy tool and academic discipline. In particular, building a stable nexus between the practice of international law and academic research on the subject remains a challenge. This chapter provides an overview of Central Asian practices and doctrines of international law with a focus on international peace and security, international organizations, international environmental law, human rights, international humanitarian and criminal law, and international investment arbitration. It concludes with recommendations for more successful promotion and implementation of international law in the region.

Keywords Central Asia · International law · International organizations · Kazakhstan · Kyrgyzstan · Tajikistan · Turkmenistan · Uzbekistan

This chapter is a revised and updated version of Sayapin (2022a). Permission to reproduce published material is gratefully acknowledged.

S. Sayapin (✉)
School of Law, KIMEP University, Almaty, Kazakhstan
e-mail: s.sayapin@kimep.kz

S. Sayapin (ed.), *International Law, Politics and Security in Central Asia*,
https://doi.org/10.1007/978-3-032-17818-3_1

1.1 Introduction

During the Soviet period, the Central Asian states (Kazakhstan, Kyrgyzstan, Tajikistan, Turkmenistan, and Uzbekistan) were only nominally sovereign.[1] In 1991, they became full-fledged members of the international community of states and have been developing their respective schools of international law ever since.[2] Over the past 30 years, international law has been instrumental in dealing with regional politico-legal challenges, such as border issues, regional security, drug trafficking, human trafficking, disputes over water, and international terrorism. Developing their approaches to international law has also been fundamental for the consolidation of the newly independent states' sovereignty amid the competing interests of China, Russia, the United States, and the European Union in the region.[3] Yet, local populations, and even some legal professionals and policymakers, are still largely unfamiliar with the norms and instruments of international law and their implications for domestic legal orders. Based on such troubled nexuses, this chapter argues for a paradigmatic shift toward a more consistent role for international law in the Central Asian states.

Today, it is fundamentally important to bridge the gaps and reinforce the nexuses between the theory and practice of international law in Central Asia, as well as to further raise the prestige of international law as part of the (domestic) legal profession. To achieve this, public and private international law could, for instance, be made a mandatory part of the qualification exams for all legal professions, and in-service training on international law could be offered to legal professionals in the public and private sectors. A crucial step would be for Central Asia's international law schools to overcome their current academic isolation—especially their confinement to the Russian-speaking space—and enter the international academic scene. The world's leading international law associations—whether in America, Europe, or Asia—would benefit from the expertise of Central Asian scholars. Equally, scholars in the region have a lot to learn from international law doctrines beyond the Russian-speaking world.

According to Atadjanov, the 'longtime absence of discussion and review of international law-related issues in the constitutional justice discourse points toward a

[1] Cf. Article 3 of the 1924 Constitution of the USSR, Article 15 of the 1936 Constitution of the USSR, Article 76 of the 1977 Constitution of the USSR.

[2] In Kazakhstan, notable international law schools include the M. Narikbayev KAZGUU University, KIMEP University, Narxoz University, Kazakh National University (KazNU) named after Al-Farabi, and Eurasian National University (ENU) named after L. N. Gumilev. In Kyrgyzstan, some of the leading international law experts work at the American University of Central Asia (AUCA), International Alatoo University, Kyrgyz-Russian Slavonic University (KRSU), Kyrgyz State Law Academy, and Kyrgyz National University named after Zh. Balasagyn. In Tajikistan, the Tajik National University and the Russian-Tajik (Slavonic) University (RTSU) are leading establishments in teaching and researching international law. In Turkmenistan, international law is taught at the Institute of International Relations of the Ministry of Foreign Affairs. In Uzbekistan, Tashkent State University of Law (TSUL), Westminster International University in Tashkent (WIUT) and the University of World Economy and Diplomacy (UWED) train international lawyers for the public and private sectors.

[3] See Sayapin (2021a, pp. 169–170).

lack of interest and understanding of the significance of international law implementation at the country level.'[4] It is this systemic issue and the (need for stronger) synergies between the theory and practice of international law in Central Asia that is the key question and leitmotif of the present chapter. In other words, although legal professionals in Central Asia have been formally drawing on international law for 30 years, the problems of its practical relevance and of the role of international lawyers in policymaking are still not fully resolved. This chapter argues that Central Asian states and societies alike would benefit from the inclusive worldview and cooperative approaches of scholars of international law and that the involvement of the latter in the formulation of relevant policies should become more systematic. All of these are feasible goals, but attaining them requires significant effort.

This chapter is based on the laws and practices of the states of Central Asia, with due regard to the practice of relevant (domestic and international) institutions, selected publications written by Central Asian scholars of international law, and the author's own academic and practical observations. With a few exceptions, the focus has been on perspectives 'internal' to Central Asia, instead of 'external' views and opinions,[5] with the aim of better understanding the political and academic dynamics within the region. The thematic scope of the chapter is limited to the author's research interests. The chapter starts by considering the position of international law in the legal systems of the Central Asian states, moving on to discuss its role in a few key areas—such as international peace and security, international organizations, international environmental law, human rights, international humanitarian and criminal law, and international investment arbitration—to exemplify the successes and challenges in Central Asia's practices and doctrines of international law. It concludes with recommendations for the more successful promotion and implementation of international law in the region.

1.2 Troubled Nexuses Between International Law and the (International) Legal Profession in Central Asia

At first glance, the international legal profession appears to have an important status all over the region since international law is formally recognized as a source of law in all Central Asian states.[6] Article 4(1) of the Constitution of Kazakhstan stipulates that 'international agreements and other commitments of the Republic' are a part of the functioning law in the Republic of Kazakhstan. It may be assumed that 'other commitments' include, in particular, customary international law and the law of the various international organizations of which Kazakhstan is a member. Article 4(3) continues that 'international agreements ratified by the Republic have primacy over

[4] See Atadjanov (2021a, p. 31).

[5] For an interesting external perspective on political and normative developments in Central Asia, see Aidarkhanova (2021).

[6] Sayapin (2021a, pp. 170–171).

its laws. The legislation of the Republic determines the procedure and conditions of operation of international agreements in the territory of the Republic of Kazakhstan to which Kazakhstan is a party.' Article 6(1) of Kazakhstan's Law on Legal Acts of 6 April 2016 contains an analogous rule.

In addition to treaties, Article 6(3) of the Constitution of the Kyrgyz Republic refers to 'generally recognized principles and norms of international law.'[7] Presumably, such principles and norms include, at least, the principles expounded in the UN Friendly Relations Declaration of 1970 and general international law. A similar provision can be found in the second paragraph of Article 9 of the Constitution of Turkmenistan.[8] By contrast, the third paragraph of Article 10 of the Constitution of Tajikistan reflects a more positivist approach in that it refers only to 'international legal acts recognized by Tajikistan' but not to any other sources of international law.[9] Notably, the same constitutional provision stipulates explicitly that international legal acts have primacy over the sources of domestic law.[10]

Finally, the Constitution of Uzbekistan contains at least three separate provisions related to international law. First, in the preamble of the Constitution, the 'generally accepted norms of the international law' are referred to. Further, Article 17 of the Constitution stipulates that the Republic of Uzbekistan 'shall have full rights in international relations. The foreign policy of Uzbekistan shall be based on the principles of sovereign equality of the states, non-use of force or threat to use force, inviolability of frontiers, peaceful settlement of disputes, non-interference in the internal affairs of other states, and other generally recognized principles and norms of international law.' Next, Article 18 lays down that the Republic 'shall pursue a peaceful foreign policy aimed at the comprehensive development of bilateral and multilateral relations with states and international organizations. The Republic of Uzbekistan may enter into alliances, join commonwealths and other intergovernmental institutions, as well as withdraw from them, on the basis of the supreme interests of the state, the people,

---

[7] Cf. Article 6(3) of the Constitution of the Kyrgyz Republic: 'Treaties that entered into force in the manner prescribed by law, to which the Kyrgyz Republic is a party, as well as generally recognized principles and norms of international law, are an integral part of the legal system of the Kyrgyz Republic.

The procedure and conditions for the application of treaties and universally recognized principles and norms of international law are determined by laws.'

[8] See Article 9 of the Constitution of Turkmenistan, second paragraph: 'Turkmenistan recognizes the priority of universally recognized norms of international law.' Notably, this provision refers only to 'norms' but not 'principles' of international law, which are universally recognized. Probably this is because such principles are already listed in the first paragraph of the same article: 'Turkmenistan, as a full member of the world community, adheres to the principles of permanent neutrality in foreign policy, non-interference in the internal affairs of other countries, refusal to use force and participation in military blocs and alliances, and contributes to the development of peaceful, friendly, and mutually beneficial relations with the countries of the region and all countries of the world.'

[9] Cf. Article 38 of the Statute of the International Court of Justice (ICJ).

[10] See Article 10 of the Constitution of Tajikistan, third paragraph: 'International legal acts recognized by Tajikistan are an integral part of the legal system of the republic. In case of inconsistency of the laws of the republic with recognized international legal acts, the norms of international legal acts shall apply.'

its welfare and security.' Since Articles 17 and 18 deal with the role of international law in foreign policy, it appears to suggest that Uzbekistan approaches international law from a dualist perspective. All states of Central Asia have enacted laws on treaties,[11] which regulate the order of their conclusion, observance and application, domestic implementation, amendments and modifications, invalidity, suspension, or termination of their operation, etc., with due regard to the Vienna Convention on the Law of Treaties.

However, in practice, international law is confined to the foreign policies of the Central Asian states and does not seem to have a systemic impact on their domestic legal orders. For example, Kazakhstan's Legal Policy Concept for 2020–2030 relates to international law only in a brief section entitled 'The Legal Provision of Foreign Policy and Foreign Economic Activity,'[12] and even there, the limited focus is on 'further integration into the world economy through the use of tools of economic diplomacy, promotion and protection of state interests in international organizations and multilateral economic integration associations.' No mention is made of a direct application of treaties in accordance with Article 6(2) of the Law On Legal Acts.[13] Notably, the same section of the draft Legal Policy Concept reads that 'in the course of planning and at the subsequent stages of concluding international treaties, it is important to proceed from the *national interests* of the Republic of Kazakhstan, carefully assess their sectoral feasibility, and predict possible socioeconomic and political consequences. A qualitative study of the conclusion of treaties directly affects the level of protection of *State interests* in the international arena' (emphasis added). The cautious tone of these state-centered provisions seems to suggest that the state's intention is to restrict the application of international law for the purpose of protecting its own interests, in a similar manner to that which has been observed in the Russian Federation.[14] In line with this assumption, during a parliamentary debate on the draft Legal Policy Concept, it was stated that 'following the example of other neighboring countries, we probably need to establish (possibly in the Constitution) *some restrictions on the application of the norms of international agreements*. Significant losses in foreign arbitrations are driving such extraordinary decisions' (emphasis added).[15] Obviously, if the proposed restrictions were ever introduced, this would be the start of Kazakhstan's alienation from international law, with far-reaching adverse consequences for the international legal profession. Moreover, given Kazakhstan's influence in the region, the other Central Asian states might follow its example.

---

[11] Kazakhstan adopted a law on treaties on 30 May 2005, Kyrgyzstan on 24 April 2014, Tajikistan on 23 July 2016 (new edition), Turkmenistan on 10 May 2010, and Uzbekistan on 6 February 2019 (new edition).

[12] The text of the Legal Policy Concept is available at https://adilet.zan.kz/rus/docs/U2100000674#z336.

[13] Article 6(2) of Kazakhstan's Law 'On Legal Acts' reads: 'Treaties ratified by the Republic of Kazakhstan have priority over its laws and are applied directly, except for cases when it follows from a treaty that's application requires the publication of a law.'

[14] See Ioffe (2020).

[15] See Senate (2020).

Since the early 1990s, the Central Asian doctrines of international law have been evolving along two main trajectories.[16] The first generation of Central Asia's international lawyers were trained in the Soviet Union (mainly in Russia) and still maintain close working relations with Russian counterparts. Like a significant number of senior scholars of international law in the Russian Federation, many, if not most, senior Central Asian international lawyers lack knowledge of English and other foreign languages, and thus belong to a 'separate epistemological community' of Russian-speaking scholars of international law, 'tied together by a common language, history, and geographical space in the former USSR.'[17] This probably suggests the persistence of postcolonial trends in Central Asian doctrines of international law.[18] The second and third generations of Central Asian international lawyers, in contrast, were trained in sovereign Central Asian states, and their main representatives have quite different professional philosophies. Usually well versed in several foreign languages, as well as their mother tongues and Russian, and therefore exposed to a variety of scholarly doctrines, skilled younger international lawyers from Central Asia are increasingly gaining authority in the academic community, both within the region and internationally. Some hold academic and administrative posts at leading international law schools in Central Asia, South Korea, Finland, Germany, and the United Kingdom, and others work for international intergovernmental and non-governmental organizations, consultancies, and private law practices.

With due regard to the region's political priorities (see *supra* 3.1), Central Asian scholars are contributing to the doctrine in various areas of international law. In addition to several textbooks and manuals on international law,[19] Central Asian authors have produced studies dealing with the history of international law,[20] international legal personality and statehood,[21] state succession,[22] regional security,[23] human

[16] Sayapin (2021a, pp. 171–172).

[17] See Mälksoo (2015, p. 87).

[18] See Akbar Rasulov's chapter in this volume.

[19] See Adilkariyev (2003), Aidarbayev (2019), Lukashuk and Saidov (2006), Sarsembayev and Sarsembayev (2009), and Sayapin (2026).

[20] See Sarsembayev (2011) and Hakimov (2013).

[21] See Mansurov (2019) and Hakimov (2012).

[22] See Hakimov (2008).

[23] See Rahmonov et al. (2018).

rights,[24] international humanitarian law,[25] and international criminal law.[26] Important monographs on regional integration,[27] international economic law,[28] international criminal law,[29] and international conflict and security law[30] have been released by leading international law publishers. In 2026, an English-language *Central Asia Yearbook on International Law* is set to be published.

Yet, these early academic successes are not yet systematic or comprehensive. First of all, it is not clear whether Central Asian academics who work outside Central Asia still subjectively associate themselves with the region or whether they already consider themselves to be 'foreign' scholars with Central Asian origins. Within Central Asia, in turn, international law scholarship suffers from a number of systemic issues. International law scholarship rests on the enthusiasm and academic ambitions of individual authors rather than on demand or support from the state itself, and it is also underfunded. Certain forms of regular public-private partnership between states and academic circles might help resolve these issues. Formally, international law associations exist in Kazakhstan and Uzbekistan, but not in the other Central Asian countries, and even these two associations do not seem to carry out regular activities. There are only a few Central Asian members of the Asian, European, and American Associations of International Law. Most significantly, the practice of international law is largely detached from its scholarship, and states could call on advice and support from international law scholars more regularly. To achieve this, the ministries of foreign affairs (responsible for the implementation of international law) and ministries of justice (responsible for the regulation of the legal profession) could work together more closely. As explained below, the Central Asian states have accomplished important work in various areas of international law, but involving academics would help fill the existing gaps more successfully.

1.3 Central Asian Practices of International Law

The states of Central Asia have been active in various international formats, including universal and regional organizations, and have proposed several important international initiatives. This section highlights some key practices in select thematic fields, identifies related troubled nexuses in the implementation of international law, and serves as a basis for concluding observations and policy recommendations.

---

[24] See Hakimov (2006).

[25] See Rajabov (2006) and Hakimov (2007).

[26] See Rahmonov et al. (2017) and Sandibayev and Hakimov (2013).

[27] See Kembayev (2009).

[28] See Daulenov (2016), Rasulov and Haskell (2020), Saidov (2008), Saidov (2015), Saidov (2021), Shadikhodjaev (2009, 2018). See also Sherzod Shadikhodjaev's chapter in this volume.

[29] See Atadjanov (2019) and Sayapin (2014).

[30] See Sayapin and Tsybulenko (2018) and Sayapin et al. (2022).

1.3.1 International Peace and Security

The states of Central Asia have proposed several important international security initiatives. To name a few examples (in chronological order): on 12 December 1995, the General Assembly of the United Nations reaffirmed the permanent neutrality of Turkmenistan, which was subsequently reflected in Article 2 of the Constitution of Turkmenistan:

> Turkmenistan has the status of permanent neutrality, recognized by the world community, and secured by law.
>
> In the resolutions of the General Assembly on the 'permanent neutrality of Turkmenistan' of 12 December 1995 and 3 June 2015, the United Nations recognizes and supports the status of permanent neutrality proclaimed by Turkmenistan, calls on the Member States of the United Nations to respect and support this status of Turkmenistan, also respecting its independence, sovereignty, and territorial integrity.
>
> The permanent neutrality of Turkmenistan is the basis of its domestic and foreign policy.

Notably, not only is Turkmenistan the only state in Central Asia with the status of permanent neutrality, but its constitution is also unique in Central Asia in that it makes direct reference to the UN. Further, in 1997, Tashkent hosted an international conference entitled 'Central Asia—a zone free of nuclear weapons,' after which the Central Asian Nuclear-Weapon-Free Zone (CANWFZ) treaty was signed on 8 September 2008 and, following ratification by all Central Asian states, entered into force on 21 March 2009.[31] In accordance with Article 3(1)(a) of the treaty, each party generally undertakes 'not to conduct research on, develop, manufacture, stockpile or otherwise acquire, possess or have control over any nuclear weapon or other nuclear explosive device by any means anywhere.' The subsequent substantive provisions reinforce this general obligation through rules pertaining to the transit of foreign ships, aircraft, and ground transportation (Article 4), the testing of nuclear weapons (Article 5), environmental security (Article 6), the use of nuclear energy for peaceful purposes (Article 7), and the physical protection of nuclear material and equipment (Article 9). The procedural provisions pertain to cooperation with the International Atomic Energy Agency (IAEA) and consultative meetings (Articles 8 and 10, respectively). Central Asia has thus become one of the world's five Nuclear-Weapon-Free Zones (NWFZs).[32]

In 2010, Kazakhstan was the first Central Asian and post-Soviet state to chair the Organization for Security and Co-operation in Europe (OSCE).[33] In his speech of 14 January 2010, the first president of Kazakhstan, Nursultan Nazarbayev, described his vision for Kazakhstan's OSCE Chairmanship as follows:

> The motto of Kazakhstan's Chairmanship will be four Ts, namely, 'Trust', 'Tradition', 'Transparency', and 'Tolerance'. The first T refers to the trust that is necessary for all of us.

---

[31] The original English text and ratification status of the Treaty is available at https://treaties.unoda.org/t/canwfz.

[32] See United Nations (2025).

[33] See OSCE (2010a).

> The second one refers to our commitment to the fundamental principles and values of the OSCE. The third one conveys maximum openness and transparency in international relations, free from 'double standards' and 'dividing lines,' as well as a focus on constructive co-operation in order to address challenges and threats to security.
>
> Finally, the fourth T reflects global trends towards a strengthening of intercultural and inter-civilizational dialogue, which is gaining major importance in today's world.[34]

Kazakhstan's performance as OSCE Chair received mixed reviews. In early 2011, *Eurasianet* commented on the outcomes of the 2010 OSCE Summit in Astana as follows:

> The summit descended into disarray amid disagreements over the final declaration, with conflicts in the South Caucasus the chief stumbling block. The agreement was eventually watered down and the accompanying action plan discarded altogether.
>
> For Astana, though, the fact that it persuaded leaders to sign the declaration at all was a diplomatic victory – as was widespread praise at the summit for its smooth running of the chairmanship and its role in defusing last year's political crisis in Kyrgyzstan.
>
> Neighbouring Uzbekistan, however, used the summit to attack the OSCE's reaction to June's ethnic clashes in southern Kyrgyzstan as ineffective, and ongoing delays in deploying a planned OSCE police mission there have also drawn fire.[35]

On 10 September 2012, Law ZRU-330 On the Concept of the Foreign Political Activity of the Republic of Uzbekistan was promulgated by the first president of Uzbekistan. At the time of writing, it was not possible to retrieve the law from the national legislation database Lex.Uz. However, the main tenets of the concept, reported in 2012, are as follows:

> 1) Uzbekistan reserves the right to enter into alliances, join commonwealths and other interstate formations, as well as withdraw from them, guided by the highest interests of the state, the people, their welfare and security, priority areas for the modernization of the country, current national legislation, and accepted international obligations;
>
> 2) Uzbekistan pursues a peaceful policy, does not take part in military-political blocs, and reserves the right to withdraw from any interstate entity in the event of its transformation into a military-political bloc;
>
> 3) Uzbekistan takes political, economic, and other measures to prevent its involvement in armed conflicts and hotbeds of tension in neighbouring states, and also does not allow the deployment of foreign military bases and facilities on its territory;
>
> 4) In accordance with the Constitution, the Law 'On Defence', and the military doctrine, the armed forces of Uzbekistan are created solely to protect the state sovereignty and territorial integrity of the country, the peaceful life and security of its population, and the latter do not take part in peacekeeping operations abroad.[36]

In line with this policy, Uzbekistan suspended its membership in the CSTO in 2012. Notably, membership in the CSTO could not prevent armed clashes between Kyrgyzstan and Tajikistan from 28 April to 1 May 2021 and then again in January and

---

[34] See OSCE (2010b).

[35] See Lillis (2011).

[36] See Gazeta.Uz (2021).

September 2022.[37] This probably suggests that the CSTO peace-making machinery requires further fine tuning. As one of Afghanistan's closest neighbors, Uzbekistan hosted two high-level conferences on regional security cooperation (in 2018) and on challenges and opportunities for Central and South Asia (in 2021). Another international conference on Afghanistan took place in Tashkent on the 25th and 26th of July 2022. As reported by the Ministry of Foreign Affairs of Uzbekistan, 'the main goal of the event is to develop a set of measures and proposals for the world community to promote stability, security, and post-conflict reconstruction in Afghanistan, and the country's integration into regional cooperation processes in the interests of the multinational Afghan people and the whole world.'[38]

Due to its strategic location, there was considerable potential for conflict in Central Asia long before the Great Game of the nineteenth century,[39] and this remains the case today. At present, the maintenance of peace and security in the region is dependent on the successful management of numerous security concerns, and on cooperation both among the Central Asian states and between them and powerful external actors such as China, Russia, North America, and the European Union. International law plays a central role in these processes in that, since 1991, regional security alliances have been formed, foreign military bases have been established (in Kyrgyzstan and Tajikistan) and dismantled (in Kyrgyzstan and Uzbekistan), armed conflicts (in Tajikistan) and situations of violence have taken place (in Kyrgyzstan, Kazakhstan, and Uzbekistan) raising serious human rights concerns, and significant efforts have been made to combat international terrorism and transnational organized crime. The problems of corruption, energy, international supply chains, and the secondary effects of international sanctions imposed on the Russian Federation for its continued aggression against Ukraine are now adding to the complex mosaic of regional security. Central Asian international lawyers ought to continue analyzing these developments, impartially and objectively, and make recommendations on relevant domestic and international policies. As sensitive as these topics are, constructive dialogue between policymakers and the academic community will ultimately be useful.

1.3.2 Universal International Organizations[40]

The Central Asian states have been cooperating with universal international organizations since the early years of their independence. Initially, it was both a matter of prestige and a way of manifesting their newly acquired state sovereignty. The ensuing cooperation between universal international organizations and their members in Central Asia has yielded valuable results. The Central Asian states were admitted

---

[37] See RFE/RL (2022a, 2022b).

[38] See Kun.Uz (2022).

[39] Cf. Peter Hopkirk, *The Great Game: The Struggle for Empire in Central Asia* (Kodansha International, Tokyo, 1992).

[40] For more details, see Sultan Sakhariyev's chapter in this volume.

to the United Nations on 2 March 1992 and are also members of the UN specialized agencies. Uzbekistan has had five locations placed on UNESCO's World Heritage List, and no fewer than six of the country's cultural traditions have been recognized as Intangible Cultural Heritage.[41] The early years of Tajikistan's independence were marked by a violent non-international armed conflict,[42] and the UN's peacebuilding efforts were important.[43] In 1995, Turkmenistan had its permanent neutrality recognized by the UN General Assembly,[44] and in 2007, the United Nations Regional Centre for Preventive Diplomacy for Central Asia (UNRCCA) was established.[45] In 2017–2018, Kazakhstan was a non-permanent member of the UN Security Council, and used this status to, among other things, promote its campaign against nuclear weapons, raise international awareness of the security situation in and around Afghanistan, and to consolidate its role in UN peacekeeping operations.[46] For this purpose, the Almaty-based Peacekeeping Training Centre (Partnership for Peace) under the Ministry of Defence of the Republic of Kazakhstan is instrumental.

These and other examples of practices of the Central Asian states as members of the UN could help showcase the importance of general international law for Central Asia and reinforce its relevance both as a policy tool and an academic discipline. Such practices are relevant for general international law courses as well as to courses dealing specifically with international peace and security, international humanitarian law, and diplomacy. Students of international law would greatly benefit from regular guest lectures by UN experts, as their practical insights would be a valuable addition to students' theoretical training, improve their linguistic skills, and help at least some of them choose their career paths. In some Central Asian contexts, academic contact with foreign experts might be limited by national security considerations. For the sake of providing quality education, it would thus be advisable to reconsider such policies and facilitate regular and free opportunities for communication between students and scholars, on the one hand, and with representatives of the UN and its specialized agencies, on the other.

1.3.3 Regional Organizations[47]

Since 1991, several regional organizations have been established in which Central Asian members play key roles. The Commonwealth of Independent States (CIS),[48]

---

[41] See Permanent Delegation of Uzbekistan to UNESCO (2025).

[42] See Atadjanov (2021b).

[43] See Ministry of Foreign Affairs of the Republic of Tajikistan (2019).

[44] See Constitutional Law of Turkmenistan on Permanent Neutrality of Turkmenistan (27 December 1995), available at https://www.refworld.org/pdfid/405ab3d14.pdf.

[45] See UNRCCA (2025).

[46] See Sanchez (2019).

[47] For more details, see Sultan Sakhariyev's chapter in this volume.

[48] Sayapin (2021a, pp. 183–184).

the largest post-Soviet regional organization, was founded on 8 December 1991 by the Republic of Belarus, the Russian Federation (RSFSR), and Ukraine whereby they jointly declared that the USSR had 'ceased to exist as a subject of international law and a geopolitical reality' (cf. the first preambular paragraph of the Agreement on the Establishment of the Commonwealth of Independent States). On 21 December 1991, the leaders of Azerbaijan, Armenia, Belarus, Kazakhstan, Kyrgyzstan, Moldova, the Russian Federation, Tajikistan, Turkmenistan, Uzbekistan, and Ukraine signed a protocol to that agreement which effectively established the CIS. The CIS Statute was adopted on 22 January 1993.

The CSTO[49] grew out of a Collective Security Treaty, which was signed in Tashkent (Uzbekistan) on 15 May 1992 on behalf of Armenia, Kazakhstan, Kyrgyzstan, the Russian Federation, Tajikistan, and Uzbekistan. In 1993, Azerbaijan, Belarus, and Georgia also joined. The treaty entered into force on 20 April 1994 and was effective until 1999 when Azerbaijan, Georgia, and Uzbekistan withdrew from the treaty, and the other state parties agreed to automatically prolong the treaty's validity for subsequent five-year periods. On 14 May 2002, the treaty was transformed into an intergovernmental organization whose statute was approved on 7 October 2002 and registered at the UN Secretariat in 2003. In 2004, the CSTO was granted observer status at the UN General Assembly. Current members of the CSTO include Armenia, Belarus, Kazakhstan, Kyrgyzstan, Russia, and Tajikistan (Uzbekistan renewed its membership in 2006 and suspended it in 2012).

On 15 June 2001, Kazakhstan, China, Kyrgyzstan, Russia, Tajikistan, and Uzbekistan announced the establishment of the Shanghai Cooperation Organisation (SCO).[50] According to its website, the SCO's main goals include 'strengthening mutual trust and neighborliness among the member states; promoting their effective cooperation in politics, trade, the economy, research, technology and culture, as well as in education, energy, transport, tourism, environmental protection, and other areas; making joint efforts to maintain and ensure peace, security and stability in the region; and moving toward the establishment of a democratic, fair and rational new international political and economic order.'[51] The SCO Charter was adopted in June 2002 and entered into force on 19 September 2003. As of 2025, the SCO has ten member states—the founding members plus India and Pakistan (admitted in 2017) as well as Iran and Belarus (admitted, respectively, in 2023 and 2024)—making it the world's largest regional intergovernmental organization in terms of territory and population. Afghanistan and Mongolia have observer status, whereas Azerbaijan, Armenia, Bahrain, Cambodia, Egypt, Kuwait, the Maldives, Myanmar, Nepal, Türkiye, Qatar, Saudi Arabia, Sri Lanka, and the United Arab Emirates are SCO dialogue partners. The SCO Regional Anti-Terrorist Structure (RATS) is located in Tashkent.[52]

[49] Sayapin (2021b).

[50] Sayapin (2021c). See also Tsybulenko and Platonova (2022).

[51] See SCO (2025).

[52] See RATS SCO (2025).

For its part, the Eurasian Economic Union (EAEU) is a regional economic organization with elements of supranational competences.[53] The Treaty on the EAEU entered into force on 1 January 2015. The current EAEU membership comprises Armenia, Belarus, Kazakhstan, Kyrgyzstan, and Russia. On 11 December 2020, Uzbekistan and Cuba were granted observer status at the EAEU.

The number and intensity of the challenges currently facing Central Asia, however, seem to require even closer regional integration. For many years, Uzbekistan had a visa regime with most of its Central Asian neighbors, and Turkmenistan's visa policy is still very strict, including with respect to nationals of Central Asian states. In April 2021 and September 2022, unresolved border issues led to armed conflicts between Tajikistan and Kyrgyzstan.[54] Water scarcity is another problem, which, if unresolved, will aggravate the situation in the future.[55] The Aral Sea environmental disaster has been affecting the region for decades. These and other problems could be resolved more effectively if all Central Asian states were to make even more concerted efforts. As early as 2007, the first president of Kazakhstan, Nursultan Nazarbayev, suggested establishing a Central Asian Union but so far this opportunity for integration has not been seized. In May 2021, the prospects of Central Asian integration were discussed at an expert roundtable in Almaty. According to Professor H. Saidov (Russian-Tajik Slavonic University), 'each [Central Asian] state has colossal opportunities for development. Kazakhstan is the most advanced country in Central Asia, Uzbekistan is a giant with enormous opportunities, Turkmenistan has a positive international status, Kyrgyzstan is famous for its democratic transformation, and Tajikistan has powerful hydro resources. These efforts need to be combined.'[56] The next major step in the regional integration process was on 21 July 2022 when the presidents of Kazakhstan, Kyrgyzstan, and Uzbekistan signed a Treaty of Friendship, Good Neighborliness and Cooperation for the Development of Central Asia in the twenty-first century.[57] The President of Tajikistan signed the Treaty on 28 August 2025. If the Central Asian Union project ever materializes, it will indeed contribute to the region's sustainable development and to the welfare of all Central Asian societies.[58]

Given the distinct advantages of regional institutions—less bureaucracy, greater dynamism, and a better understanding of regional issues, for instance—their role is likely to grow in the future. Regional institutions help contextualize international law, thus making it more attractive and efficient. Based on my own experience of teaching international law in Central Asia, I have two further observations with respect to the contextualization of international law. First, students perceive the relevance of international law more readily if they are shown its role in the context of responding to the challenges their region faces.[59] Second, teaching mixed groups of students majoring

[53] See Daulenov (2021) and Antsygina and Quigley (2022).

[54] See Pozdnyakova (2021) and Furlong (2022).

[55] See Pannier (2021).

[56] See Sputnik Kazakhstan (2019).

[57] See Fergana News (2022).

[58] See Starr (2019).

[59] Cf. Julia Emtseva's observations in her chapter in this volume.

in international law and international relations is especially effective. Law students help students of international relations better grasp the role of law and other rules in domestic and international politics, and students of international relations encourage lawyers to consider the application of rules in practical international contexts and take account of dynamic relationships between the rules of law and non-legal factors, such as economics, politics, power, religion, etc.

1.3.4 International Environmental Law

Central Asia's major environmental problem—indeed, one of global significance—is the man-made desertification of the Aral Sea.[60] Due to predatory policies around irrigation, the Aral Sea level declined by an average of 0.2 m per year in the 1960s, by 0.6 m per year in the 1970s, and by as much as 0.85 m per year in the 1980s. In 1987, the water level reached 36.4 m, which is 16.6 m lower than the average long-term level before 1961. The resulting ecosystem collapse had devastating effects on the environment, public health, and the economy. In February 1992, the Agreement on Cooperation in Joint Management, Use and Protection of Interstate Water Resources was signed in Almaty, and the Interstate Commission for Water Coordination (ICWC) was established. In 1993, the International Foundation to Save the Aral Sea (IFAS) was founded. Since 1994, three Aral Sea Basin Programs (ASBP) have been implemented with financial support from various countries, the United Nations Development Programme (UNDP), the World Bank, the United States Agency for International Development (USAID), the Asian Development Bank (ADB), and other donors. Moreover, UNESCO has supported several scientific projects to develop policy recommendations and capacity building. As a result of the construction of the Kokaral Dam, between 2003 and 2005, the water salinity in the North Aral Sea decreased and positive microclimate changes have been reported.[61] As the condition of the South Aral Sea continued deteriorating, the IFAS suggested in 2018 that the South Aral Sea's environmental degradation might be lessened through the construction of an artificial delta of the Syr Darya River.[62]

As convincingly shown by Dinara Ziganshina,[63] the problem of Central Asia's transboundary water security reaches far beyond the region and is multidimensional in that it requires ecological, economic, technical, healthcare, and other solutions. At this stage, a credible possibility is the conclusion of a convention on the Aral Sea by the states of the region, with the option of other states and international organizations joining at a later stage. The convention would be based on relevant scientific data, place limits on the use of the Amu Darya and Syr Darya Rivers for irrigation and other purposes, regulate cooperation in the areas of healthcare, the economy, and

[60] See Sayapin (2021d). For more details, see the chapter by Kamila Mateeva et al. in this volume.

[61] See Columbia University (2007).

[62] Ibid.

[63] See *passim* Ziganshina (2014).

environmental protection, and establish an international expert monitoring mechanism. As such, the convention would unite experts from various disciplines with international lawyers and politicians and serve a practical and measurable common goal, whereby lawyers would translate data from various fields of science into the language of legally binding rules. Although obviously not an easy undertaking, the project would result in tangible economic, environmental, and humanitarian results in Central Asia and beyond.

1.3.5 International Human Rights Law

The Central Asian states are parties to the key human rights treaties.[64] In 2008, the Office of the High Commissioner on Human Rights (OHCHR) for Central Asia was established in Bishkek (Kyrgyzstan). It covers all Central Asian countries.[65] In accordance with the OHCHR mandate, the Regional Office cooperates with 'Governments, intergovernmental organizations, civil society, the private sector as well as relevant United Nations partners, to formulate and implement programs and activities for the promotion and protection of all human rights in the countries of Central Asia.'[66] It also 'works with countries in the region to strengthen the capacity of national governments, national human right institutions, non-governmental organizations, human rights defenders and civil society activists to increase compliance of national laws and practices with human rights standards and improve protection against human rights violations, in particular violations relating to fundamental freedoms, non-discrimination, freedom from torture, the right to a fair trial and independence of judges and lawyers.'[67] Other pressing human rights issues include the independence of trade unions,[68] freedom of religion, domestic violence, freedom of assembly, LGBTQ+ rights, the rights of refugees,[69] freedom of the press, and others.[70]

Windows of opportunity for improving the human rights situation in some of the Central Asian states opened up just a few years ago, and much work remains to be done. Most notably, Kazakhstan and Uzbekistan announced law enforcement reforms. With due regard to developments in Uzbekistan, *The Economist* opined in December 2019 that 'no other country has advanced that far,' and named Uzbekistan

[64] For an overview of Central Asian states' commitments under international human rights law, see OHCHR (2025a).

[65] OHCHR (2025b).

[66] Ibid.

[67] Ibid.

[68] See Khassenov (2022). See also his chapter in this volume.

[69] On the rights of refugees in Central Asia, see Azhigulova (2022).

[70] For a country-by-country overview of the human rights situation in Central Asia, see Human Rights Watch (2025). See also Sayapin (2021e).

'country of the year.'[71] In order to reinforce this trend and to improve the quality of human rights protection in the region, above all, the independence of the judiciary should be strengthened.[72] To achieve this, judges and law enforcement officials at the local and central levels ought to be trained on international human rights instruments, in cooperation with the UN and academics. Where this has not yet been done, Constitutional Courts should be established, and citizens should be given access to them. Regular dialogue between the states and human rights NGOs would also be worthwhile. In other words, the time seems to be right for Central Asian countries to realize that compliance with international human rights law is not 'harmful' to the state, and will, in the language of Uzbekistan's new Human Rights Strategy, contribute to 'further strengthening the country's authority in the international arena, in particular, [to] improving the position [of the State] in economic, political, and legal rankings and indices.'[73]

1.3.6 International Humanitarian Law

Established in 1992,[74] the Regional Delegation of the International Committee of the Red Cross (ICRC) for Central Asia has been supporting the states of the region in the implementation of international humanitarian law (IHL) ever since.[75] In particular, provisions related to the repression of war crimes were integrated in the criminal codes of Central Asian states, laws on the use and protection of the red cross and red crescent emblems were adopted,[76] and Tajikistan and Turkmenistan adopted laws on the legal status of their respective National Red Crescent Societies. Humanitarian principles and the basics of IHL were integrated into the curricula of selected secondary school subjects in Kyrgyzstan, Tajikistan, and Uzbekistan, and a few leading Central Asian universities started teaching IHL to students of jurisprudence, international law and relations, and journalism and pedagogy. In 2000–2010, competitions on IHL were held for students in the region, and a similar competition was organized in January 2016, with the support of the ICRC, for students at KIMEP University. In 2005–2007, the ICRC held a series of national IHL courses, IHL essay contests, and three Central Asian courses on IHL given by internationally renowned lecturers. A few Central Asian students and junior lecturers participated in

[71] The Economist (2019).

[72] See Sayapin (2019a, 2019b).

[73] See Decree No. UP-6012 On the Approval of the National Strategy of the Republic of Uzbekistan on Human Rights of 22 June 2020 (in Russian) available at https://lex.uz/ru/docs/4872357, 4th preambular paragraph.

[74] An overview of the ICRC action in Central Asia is available at https://www.icrc.org/en/where-we-work/europe-central-asia/uzbekistan.

[75] An overview of Central Asian states' obligations under IHL is available at https://ihl-databases.icrc.org/ihl.

[76] Having ratified the Third Additional Protocol to the 1949 Geneva Conventions so far, Kazakhstan and Kyrgyzstan also regulate the use of the 'red crystal' emblem.

the Warsaw courses on IHL organized by the Polish Red Cross. A number of alumni of the ICRC program for scholars went on to become prominent academics, lawyers, and civil servants. The program was gradually reduced and had virtually closed by the mid-2010s.

The ICRC has also been actively engaging with the Central Asian states' ministries of defense for the purpose of training officers at various levels on the law of armed conflict (LOAC). In Kazakhstan, a manual on the law of peace support operations was developed for Kazakhstani peacekeepers.[77] In Uzbekistan and Kyrgyzstan, the ICRC has been liaising with the ministries of interior, with a view to training their personnel on international human rights law (IHRL). In terms of protection and assistance, the ICRC was involved in the delivery of humanitarian aid to victims of a non-international armed conflict in Tajikistan (1992–1997), and in the aftermath of situations of violence in Kyrgyzstan (in 2005 and 2010). In early 2020, Uzbekistan announced the completion of mine clearance along its border with Tajikistan. Given that, since 2000, a total of 374 Tajik citizens had been killed by anti-personnel landmines and another 485 people injured,[78] this development is hugely important from a humanitarian perspective.

With due regard to modern technological developments, it would now be beneficial for the Central Asian states to continue equipping their military personnel with skills related to cyberwarfare, and to modernize domestic laws accordingly. While measures have already been taken to combat a few transnational cybercrimes,[79] rules of international law pertaining to *jus ad bellum* and *jus in bello* must now urgently be implemented in domestic legislation[80] to better respond to novel security threats. Similarly, leading international law schools ought to introduce courses on cyberspace law or law and technology. Ideally, such courses should be interdisciplinary and be co-taught by lawyers and IT experts.

1.3.7 International and Transnational Criminal Law

Although the states of Central Asia have been working on the implementation of international criminal law (ICL) since the early 1990s, this work reached a qualitatively new level in the 2010s. Conceivably, this was, to a great extent, due to the publication of a Russian translation of *Principles of International Criminal Law* by Professor Gerhard Werle,[81] which became a leading reference text on ICL in the CIS.

---

77 See Sayapin (2016a).

78 The Tashkent Times (2020).

79 See Chapter 7 in the Special Part of the Criminal Code of the Republic of Kazakhstan, Chapter 42 of the Criminal Code of the Kyrgyz Republic, Chapter 28 of the Criminal Code of the Republic of Tajikistan, Chapter 33 of the Criminal Code of Turkmenistan, and Chapter XX-1 of the Criminal Code of the Republic of Uzbekistan.

80 For a general account, see Schmitt (2017).

81 See Werle (2011).

The influence of this treatise is especially visible in the new editions of the criminal codes of Kazakhstan (adopted in 2014 and enacted in 2015) and Uzbekistan (in development since 2018).[82] The criminal codes of the Central Asian states now penalize all 'core' crimes under international law, except crimes against humanity,[83] as well as some transnational crimes. The general part of ICL has been quite satisfactorily implemented.[84] However, there is no case law involving crimes under international law in Central Asia,[85] and judges and law enforcement officials are likely to require substantial training on the subject. Among all the Central Asian states, Tajikistan is the only state party to the Rome Statute of the International Criminal Court (ICC).[86]

As far as transnational crime is concerned, the United Nations Office on Drugs and Crime (UNODC), which has been present in Central Asia since 1993, lists the following areas of priority in the region:

1. Strengthening member states' capacities to confront threats from transnational organized crime.
2. Supporting member states in implementing a balanced, comprehensive and evidence-based approach to the world drug problem that addresses both supply and demand.
3. Strengthening crime prevention and building effective criminal justice systems.
4. Tackling corruption and its catastrophic impact on societies.
5. Countering terrorism, including through implementation of the 19 international legal instruments against terrorism.[87]

With due regard to these priorities, UNODC provides national authorities with technical assistance:

> Some of the current UNODC activities include efforts to counter cybercrime and anti-money laundering; assistance to respective national drug control agencies on capacity development through training, infrastructure, and intelligence-led policing. Further support is being provided to improve prevention of evidence-based drug use, treatment, and rehabilitation programmes. Support is being provided for forensics, strengthening of criminal justice system, and crime prevention. Prevention of violent extremism and radicalization [as well as] legislative reforms related to terrorism prevention are an integral part of UNODC's work in the region. All these efforts are carried out in close cooperation with the local governments, international partners and donors.[88]

---

[82] See Sayapin (2022b).

[83] See Sayapin (2020a). As such, crimes against humanity are penalized only in Kyrgyzstan.

[84] See Sayapin (2019c).

[85] In the post-Soviet space, some notable case law involving public international law issues has been produced in Ukraine since 2014. See, for example, Sayapin (2018, 2020b).

[86] The current ratification status of the Rome Statute is available at https://asp.icc-cpi.int/en_menus/asp/states%20parties/Pages/the%20states%20parties%20to%20the%20rome%20statute.aspx. Russia, an influential actor in Central Asia, 'unsigned' the Rome Statute in 2016, see Sayapin (2016b).

[87] UNODC (2025).

[88] Ibid.

Given the range of current security threats, Central Asian states ought to continue taking measures to reinforce their security, including the implementation of the relevant rules of ICL. According to Atadjanov, such measures should specifically involve the 'introduction of separate *corpus delicti* (dispositions) of crimes against humanity as well as more inclusive formulations of war crimes and revised definitions of the crime of aggression into Central Asian criminal codes.'[89] The best international practices—such as the German *Völkerstrafgesetzbuch*—could be helpful resources for conducting such legislative reforms.

1.3.8 International Investment Arbitration

There have been some notable developments pertaining to international investment arbitration in Central Asia. All states of the region are parties to the 1958 New York Convention on the Recognition and Enforcement of Foreign Arbitral Awards.[90] The 1966 International Centre for Settlement of Investment Disputes (ICSID) Convention has been ratified by Kazakhstan, Kyrgyzstan, Turkmenistan, and Uzbekistan. Tajikistan is not a signatory state.[91] Domestic legislation on international arbitration is in place in all Central Asian states.[92] On 7 December 2015, Kazakhstan adopted a Constitutional Law On the Astana International Financial Centre (usually abbreviated as the AIFC), Article 9(1)(1) of which established an International Arbitration Centre (IAC).[93] Article 14 of the Constitutional Law stipulates with respect to the IAC:

1. The International Arbitration Centre shall hear disputes in case of the existence of an arbitration agreement between the parties.
2. The International Arbitration Centre shall be established and act in accordance with the resolution of the Council [for the management of the Centre] 'on the International Arbitration Centre'.
3. Awards of the International Arbitration Centre shall be recognized and enforced in the Republic of Kazakhstan in the same way, and on the same terms, as arbitration awards issued by arbitration institutions in the Republic of Kazakhstan. The translation of the awards of the International Arbitration Centre into the Kazakh

---

89 See Atadjanov (2021a, p. 31).

90 The list of Contracting States of the 1958 New York Convention is available at https://www.newyorkconvention.org/countries.

91 The Database of ICSID Member States is available at https://icsid.worldbank.org/about/member-states/database-of-member-states.

92 The Law 'On Arbitration Courts in the Kyrgyz Republic' was adopted on 30 July 2002. Turkmenistan's Law 'On International Commercial Arbitration' was adopted on 16 August 2014. Tajikistan adopted a Law 'On International Commercial Arbitration' on 18 March 2015. Kazakhstan's current Law 'On Arbitration' was adopted on 8 April 2016. Uzbekistan's Law 'On International Commercial Arbitration' was adopted in 2020 and signed by the president on 16 February 2021.

93 An English translation of the Constitutional Law is available at https://aifc.kz/files/legals/7/file/constitutional-statute-with-amendments-as-of-30-december-2019.pdf.

or Russian language shall thereby be ensured in accordance with the procedure determined by the acts of the Centre.

4. Arbitral awards shall be recognized and enforced in the territory of the Centre in accordance with legislation of the Republic of Kazakhstan.

According to the 2023 Annual Report, '[t]he AIFC Court and International Arbitration Centre have rapidly gained the business community's trust as premier international dispute resolution institutions in Central Asia protecting legal rights and adhering to international standards, handling a record 755 cases in 2023.'[94] The total number of cases handled by the AIFC Court and IAC has exceeded 2400.[95] Despite this progress, some Kazakhstani lawyers have criticized the alleged incompatibility of the AIFC's legal basis with the Constitution of Kazakhstan.[96] A comprehensive scholarly commentary on the AIFC Constitutional Law would probably help overcome such criticisms.

For his part, on 5 November 2018, the President of Uzbekistan signed a decree establishing the Tashkent International Arbitration Centre (TIAC). According to the TIAC website, 'the TIAC Court of Arbitration is a fully autonomous organ within the TIAC ('Centre') and is the only body within the Centre's structure that administers disputes according to the TIAC Rules of Arbitration in complete independence from the Centre, its founders, the Director or any other entities [...].'[97] Over time, the TIAC could become a viable alternative to the AIFC, depending on the development of the business climate in both countries.

According to UN Conference on Trade and Development (UNCTAD), Kazakhstan has been a respondent in no fewer than 20 investor-state dispute settlement (ISDS) arbitral proceedings,[98] Kyrgyzstan in no fewer than 18 of such proceedings,[99] Turkmenistan in 17,[100] Tajikistan in two,[101] and Uzbekistan in nine.[102] Given Central Asia's considerable investment potential,[103] and that there will be more such proceedings in the future, domestic commercial lawyers ought to be trained in international commercial arbitration. To achieve this, leading Central Asian law schools ought to introduce undergraduate and postgraduate courses on international commercial arbitration in cooperation with leading law firms as well as international and domestic arbitral institutions.

---

[94] AIFC (2023, p. 12).

[95] Ibid., p. 3.

[96] Shaikenov and Shaikenov (2017).

[97] See TIAC (2025).

[98] UNCTAD (2025a).

[99] UNCTAD (2025b).

[100] UNCTAD (2025c).

[101] UNCTAD (2025d).

[102] UNCTAD (2025e).

[103] See Pecoraro (2022).

1.4 Conclusion

As the foregoing analysis shows, the relationship between the doctrines and practices of international law in Central Asia remains quite complex. Although international law is formally a source of law in all states of the region, its regulatory potential is obviously underexploited and could be restricted further. Likewise, Central Asia has considerable intellectual capacity in terms of international law, but thus far this capacity has not been used consistently. To bring about constructive change, a few measures could be taken.

First of all, it is commendable that all Central Asian states have already enacted foreign policy concepts where the specific role of international law in foreign policy is discussed.[104] Among other things, these policy documents provide for an ongoing political dialogue on threats to peace and security in Central Asia, propose workable solutions based on international law, and will hopefully contribute to closer regional integration, which might ultimately culminate in the establishment of a Central Asian Union.

Second, a regular expert dialogue between the community of international law scholars and the Central Asian states is required. The ministries of foreign affairs ought to more systematically involve international law scholars in drafting and providing expert opinions on treaties, other texts of international law, and relevant acts of domestic law. The ministries would thus benefit from academic expertise, and academics could enrich their teaching with empirical data. Strategically, the Central Asian states might consider nominating competent national academics for membership in the International Law Commission.

Crucially, regular in-service training on international law could be provided to experts working in the legal departments of various ministries, parliaments, and national human rights institutions. This would expose them to the applicable international standards and help implement such standards in the relevant domestic legal acts and practices. Judges and law enforcement agents should also receive in-service training on international law, as this would help improve the quality of law enforcement and ultimately, reduce the number of complaints submitted against the respective states to international human rights monitoring bodies.

The teaching of international law at Central Asia's universities should relate to those challenges in the region which international law could help address. International law would thus be contextualized, which would cultivate a sense of social responsibility among the current students of international law in the region. More local textbooks on international law (in national languages, English, and Russian)

---

[104] The President of Kazakhstan approved a Foreign Policy Concept for 2020–2030 by his Decree No. 280 of 6 March 2020. The Foreign Policy Concept of the Kyrgyz Republic was enacted by the President's Decree UP No. 37 of 11 March 2019. The Foreign Policy Concept of the Republic of Tajikistan was approved by the President's Decree No. 332 of 27 January 2015. On 27 December 1997, the Halq Maslahaty (parliament) of Turkmenistan adopted the Foreign Policy Concept of Turkmenistan as a Neutral State. Uzbekistan's Law 'On the Concept of the Foreign Political Activity of the Republic of Uzbekistan' was promulgated on 10 September 2012, and proposals to amend the Concept were introduced in 2021.

ought to be produced. Such textbooks would raise and discuss regional issues, propose suitable solutions, and help develop the international law terminology in Central Asian languages. In addition to their respective state languages, junior international lawyers in Central Asia should also seek to master English, Russian, and other European and Asian languages. Such language skills would also be useful for participating in moot court competitions on international law (e.g., Jessup, Vis, Nuremberg, and others). Universities could usefully establish academic partnerships with international organizations and invite their representatives to give guest lectures in international law classes. This would motivate students to learn foreign languages, help them understand how international law applies in practical political contexts, and enable them to make informed decisions regarding their future professional paths. Students should also be encouraged to apply for internships in international organizations' country offices and abroad.

Finally, international law scholars in Central Asia ought to develop and maintain academic dialogue with colleagues in various parts of the world and consider joining international scholarly associations. National associations of international lawyers ought to be established or, where they exist, strengthened. Crucially, Central Asian international law scholars should submit more articles to reputed international law journals and participate in international research projects to make their respective doctrines better known abroad and thus gradually integrate the Central Asian schools of international law into the international academic community.

References

Adilkariyev HT (2003) Mezhdunarodnoye pravo [International law]. Tashkent State Law Institute, Tashkent

Aidarbayev SZ (2019) Mezhdunarodnoye publichnoye pravo [Public international law]. Zhety Zhargy, Almaty

Aidarkhanova E (2021) Regionalism and regional order in Central Asia: an interview with Filippo Costa Buranelli. https://voicesoncentralasia.org/regionalism-and-regional-order-in-central-asia-an-interview-with-filippo-costa-buranelli/. Accessed 17 Sept 2025

AIFC (2023) Annual report on the activities of the Astana International Financial Centre. https://aifc.kz/annual-reports/aifc-annual-report-2023/. Accessed 17 Sept 2025

Antsygina E, Quigley J (2022) The Eurasian integration process: whether political will is enough to keep alive the Eurasian Economic Union. In: Sayapin S, Burnashev R (eds) Central Asian yearbook of international law and international relations. Eleven, The Hague, pp 204–226

Atadjanov R (2019) Humanness as a protected legal interest of crimes against humanity: conceptual and normative aspects, T. M. C. Asser Press, The Hague

Atadjanov R (2021a) Challenges for the implementation of international law in Central Asia: contributing factors and possible solutions. Central Asia Bus J 12:25–34

Atadjanov R (2021b) Non-International armed conflict in Tajikistan. In: Lee S et al (eds) Encyclopedia of public international law in Asia, vol III. Central & South Asia. Brill, Leiden, pp 207–208

Azhigulova K (2022) Central Asian states' compliance with international refugee and human rights law: the case of Chinese uyghur asylum seekers. In: Sayapin S, Burnashev R (eds) Central Asian yearbook of international law and international relations 2022. Eleven, The Hague, pp 267–287

Columbia University (2007) The Aral sea crisis. http://www.columbia.edu/~tmt2120/environmental%20impacts.htm. Accessed 17 Sept 2025
Daulenov M (2016) Przeplyw osob, uslug, towarow i kapitalu w umowach miedzynarodowych Unii Europejskiej, Adam Marszalek, Toruń
Daulenov M (2021) Eurasian Economic Union (EEU). In: Lee S et al (eds) Encyclopedia of public international law in Asia, vol III. Central & South Asia. Brill, Leiden, pp 185–187
Fergana News (2022) Dogovor o druzhbe na sammite stran Tsentralnoy Azii podpisali tri prezidenta iz pyati [Three out of five presidents signed friendship treaty at the summit of Central Asian countries]. https://fergana.agency/news/127082/. Accessed 17 Sept 2025
Furlong R (2022) Tanks, firing, and evacuations amid Kyrgyz-Tajik clashes. https://www.rferl.org/a/tajikistan-kyrgyzstan-clashes/32037529.html. Accessed 17 Sept 2025
Gazeta.Uz (2021) V Kontseptsiyu vneshnepoliticheskoy deyatelnosti planiruyetsya vnesti izmeneniya [Plans for the amendment of the concept of foreign political activity]. https://www.gazeta.uz/ru/2021/01/19/foreign-policy/. Accessed 17 Sept 2025
Hakimov R (2006) Detstvo: problemy i perspektivy [Childhood: problems and prospects]. O'zbekiston, Tashkent
Hakimov R (2007) Mezhdunarodnoye gumanitarnoye pravo [International humanitarian law] O'zbekiston, Tashkent
Hakimov R (2008) Problemy pravopreemstva gosudarstv v mezhdunarodnom prave [Issues of state succession in international law]. Yangi asr avlodi, Tashkent
Hakimov RT (2012) Mezhdunarodnaya pravosubyektnost: voprosy istorii, teorii i praktiki [International legal personality: Issues of history, theory, and practice]. Fan, Tashkent
Hakimov R (2013) Mezhdunarodnoye pravo (Bibliografiya 1895 – 2012 gg) [International law (A Bibliography 1895–2012]. Yangi asr avlodi, Tashkent
Human Rights Watch (2025) Europe/Central Asia. https://www.hrw.org/europe/central-asia. Accessed 17 Sept 2025
Ioffe Y (2020) The amendments to the Russian constitution: Putin's attempt to reinforce Russia's isolationist views on international Law. https://www.ejiltalk.org/the-amendments-to-the-russian-constitution-putins-attempt-to-reinforce-russias-isolationist-views-on-international-law/. Accessed 17 Sept 2025
Kembayev Z (2009) Legal aspects of the regional integration processes in the post-Soviet area. Springer, Berlin, Heidelberg
Khassenov M (2022) Collective bargaining systems in Germany and Kazakhstan. In: Sayapin S, Burnashev R (eds) Central Asian yearbook of international law and international relations 2022. Eleven, The Hague, pp 130–162
Kun.Uz (2022) Tashkent to host an international conference on Afghanistan on July 25. https://kun.uz/en/17472591! Accessed 17 Sept 2025
Lillis J (2011) Kazakhstan: experts give Astana mixed review on OSCE chairmanship. https://eurasianet.org/kazakhstan-experts-give-astana-mixed-review-on-osce-chairmanship. Accessed 17 Sept 2025
Lukashuk II, Saidov AH (2006) Hozirgi zamon xalqaro huquqi nazariyasi asoslari [The theoretical fundamentals of modern international law], Adolat, Tashkent
Mansurov UA (2019) Mezhdunarodnaya pravosubyektnost Respubliki Tadjikistan, Chast 1: Pravo na chlenstvo v mezhdunarodnyh organizatsiyah [The international legal personality of the Republic of Tajikistan, Part 1: The right to membership in international organizations]. Russian-Tajik (Slavonic) University, Dushanbe
Mälksoo L (2015) Russian approaches to international law. Oxford University Press, Oxford
Ministry of Foreign Affairs of the Republic of Tajikistan (2019) Tajikistan—UN Cooperation. https://mfa.tj/en/main/view/195/tajikistan-and-united-nations-specialized-agencies-and-organizations. Accessed 17 Sept 2025
OHCHR (2025a) Europe and Central Asia region. https://www.ohchr.org/EN/Countries/EnacaRegion/Pages/EnacaRegionIndex.aspx. Accessed 17 Sept 2025

OHCHR (2025b) OHCHR—Central Asia Regional Office. https://www.ohchr.org/EN/Countries/EnacaRegion/Pages/CentralAsiaSummary.aspx. Accessed 17 Sept 2025

OSCE (2010a) Kazakhstan takes over OSCE Chair, seeks to strengthen organization and advance dialogue on future European security architecture. https://www.osce.org/cio/51810. Accessed 17 Sept 2025

OSCE (2010b) Text of the video address by President Nursultan Nazarbayev on the occasion of Kazakhstan's assumption of the Chairmanship of the OSCE January 2010. https://www.osce.org/files/f/documents/d/c/41121.pdf. Accessed 17 Sept 2025

Pannier B (2021) Central Asian heat wave and drought creating water shortages, crop failures. https://www.rferl.org/a/central-asian-drought-water-shortages/31324012.html. Accessed 17 Sept 2025

Pecoraro A (2022) MFN in BITs: the deconstruction of state consent to dispute settlement. In: Sayapin S, Burnashev R (eds) Central Asian yearbook of international law and international relations 2022. Eleven, The Hague, pp 111–126

Permanent Delegation of Uzbekistan to UNESCO (2025) Intangible Cultural Heritage. http://uzunesco.org/. Accessed 17 Sept 2025

Pozdnyakova N (2021) Konflikt Tadjikistana i Kyrgyzstana: voda, narkotiki, zemlya? [Conflict between Tajikistan and Kyrgyzstan: Water, drugs, land?]. https://www.dw.com/ru/konflikt-tadzhikistana-i-kyrgyzstana-voda-narkotiki-zemlja/a-57392981. Accessed 17 Sept 2025

Rahmonov AS et al. (2017) Osnovy protivodeystviya terrorizmu i ekstremizmu po zakonodatelstvu Rossiyskoy Federatsii i Respubliki Tadjikistan [The foundations of countering terrorism and extremism in the legislation of the Russian Federation and the Republic of Tajikistan]. Russian-Tajik (Slavonic) University, Dushanbe

Rahmonov AS et al. (2018) Pravovye osnovy obespecheniya natsionalnoy bezopasnosti, protivodeystviya ekstremizmu i terrorizmu Rossiyskoy Federatsii [The legal foundations of reinforcing national security, countering terrorism and extremism of the Russian Federation], Russian-Tajik (Slavonic) University, Dushanbe

Rajabov SA (2006) Implementatsiya norm mezhdunarodnogo gumanitarnogo prava v Respublike Tadjikistan: problem teorii i praktiki [The implementation of rules of international humanitarian law in the Republic of Tajikistan: issues of theory and practice]. Institute of State and Law under the Academy of Sciences of the Republic of Tajikistan, Dushanbe

Rasulov A, Haskell J (2020) International economic law: new voices, new perspectives. Series: European yearbook of international economic law, Springer Nature Switzerland, Cham

RATS SCO (2025) The Regional Anti-terrorist Structure of Shanghai Cooperation Organisation (RATS SCO). https://ecrats.org/en/. Accessed 17 Sept 2025

RFE/RL (2022a) Cease-fire halts deadly clashes along Kyrgyz-Tajik border. https://www.rferl.org/a/kyrgyz-tajik-border-shootout-batken/31674508.html. Accessed 17 Sept 2025

RFE / RL (2022b) Kyrgyz officials say death toll in border violence with Tajikistan rises to 36. https://www.rferl.org/a/kyrgyzstan-tajikistan-border-clashes-death-toll/32039417.html. Accessed 17 Sept 2025

Saidov D (2008) The law of damages in international sales: the CISG and other international instruments. Hart Publishing, Oxford

Saidov D (2015) Conformity of goods and documents: the Vienna sales convention. Hart Publishing, Oxford

Saidov D (2021) The law of damages in international sales: the CISG and other international instruments, 2nd edn. Hart Publishing, Oxford

Sanchez WA (2019) Analyzing Kazakhstan's first tenure at the UN Security Council: as the first Central Asian state to sit on the UNSC, what did Kazakhstan achieve? https://thediplomat.com/2019/03/analyzing-kazakhstans-first-tenure-at-the-un-security-council/. Accessed 17 Sept 2025

Sandibayev N, Hakimov R (2013) Xalqaro jinoyat sudi [International Criminal Court], Yangi ast avlodi, Tashkent

Sarsembayev M (2011) Mezhdunarodnoye pravo v istorii Kazakhstana i Sredney Azii [International law in the history of Central Asia], Foliant, Astana

Sarsembayev MA, Sarsembayev KM (2009) Mezhdunarodnoye pravo [International law], Zhety Zhargy, Almaty
Sayapin S (2014) The crime of aggression in international criminal law: historical development, comparative analysis and present state. T. M. C. Asser Press, The Hague
Sayapin S (2016a) Legal aspects of peace support operations/Pravovyye aspekty operatsiy po podderzhaniyu mira, ICRC Regional Delegation in Central Asia, Tashkent
Sayapin S (2016b) Russia's withdrawal of signature from the Rome statute would not Shield its nationals from potential prosecution at the ICC. http://www.ejiltalk.org/russias-withdrawal-of-signature-from-the-rome-statute-would-not-shield-its-nationals-from-potential-prosecution-at-the-icc/#more-14774. Accessed 17 Sept 2025
Sayapin S (2018) A curious aggression trial in Ukraine: some reflections on the *Alexandrov and Yerofeyev* case. J Int Crim Just 16:1093–1104
Sayapin S (2019a) Critical analysis, strict discipline and personal responsibility: some reflections on strengthening the independence of judiciary in Central Asia. Law and State 84(3):18–27
Sayapin S (2019b) Réflexions sur le renforcement de l'indépendance de la magistrature en Asie centrale [Reflections on strengthening the independence of the judiciary in Central Asia]. Les Cahiers De La Justice 14:657–665
Sayapin S (2019c) The general principles of international criminal law in the criminal code of the Republic of Kazakhstan. Asian J Int Law 9:1–9
Sayapin S (2020a) Why a crimes against humanity convention from a perspective of post-Soviet states? Afr J Int Crim Justice 6:125–135
Sayapin S (2020b) The *Yanukovych* trial in Ukraine: a revival of the crime of aggression? Israel Yearbook on Human Rights 50:63–79
Sayapin S (2021a) State report overview. In: Lee S et al (eds) Encyclopedia of public international law in Asia, vol III. Central & South Asia. Brill, Leiden, pp 169–173
Sayapin S (2021b) Collective Security Treaty Organization (CSTO). In: Lee S et al (eds) Encyclopedia of public international law in Asia, vol III. Central & South Asia. Brill, Leiden, pp 184–185
Sayapin S (2021c) Shanghai Cooperation Organisation (SCO). In: Lee S et al (eds) Encyclopedia of public international law in Asia, vol III. Central & South Asia. Brill, Leiden, pp 188–189
Sayapin S (2021d) The Aral sea. In: Lee S et al (eds) Encyclopedia of public international law in Asia, vol III. Central & South Asia. Brill, Leiden, pp 198–199
Sayapin S (2021e) Human rights in the Post-Soviet Central Asia. In: Leontiev L, Amarasinghe P (eds) Thirty years looking back: state-building, rule of law, good governance and human rights in the post-Soviet space. Routledge, Abington, pp 135–149
Sayapin S (2022a) International law in Central Asia: practices and doctrines. Rev Central East European Law 47:322–351
Sayapin S (2022b) The impact of professor Werle's doctrine of international criminal law in the post-Soviet Central Asia. In: Jessberger F, Vormbaum M, Burghardt B (eds) Festschrift für Gerhard Werle. Mohr Siebeck Verlag, Tübingen, pp 271–277
Sayapin S (2026) A Central Asian perspective on international law. Hart Publishing, Oxford
Sayapin S, Tsybulenko E (2018) The use of force against Ukraine and international law: Jus Ad Bellum, Jus in Bello, Jus Post Bellum. T. M. C. Asser Press, The Hague
Sayapin S et al. (2022) International conflict and security law: a research handbook. T. M. C. Asser Press, The Hague
Schmitt MN (2017) Tallinn manual 2.0 on the international law applicable to cyber operations, 2nd edn. Cambridge University Press, Cambridge
SCO (2025) About SCO. http://eng.sectsco.org/about_sco/. Accessed 17 Sept 2025
Senate (2020) Tekst vystupleniya otnositelno proyekta Kontseptsii pravovoy politiki (KPP prezentovan MinYustom) [Text of a statement regarding the draft Legal Policy Concept (LPC presented by the Ministry of Justice]. https://senate.parlam.kz/ru-RU/blog/934/news/details/23151. Accessed 17 Sept 2025

Shadikhodjaev S (2009) Retaliation in the WTO dispute settlement system. Kluwer Law International, London

Shadikhodjaev S (2018) Industrial policy and the World Trade Organization: between legal constraints and flexibilities. Cambridge University Press, Cambridge

Shaikenov A, Shaikenov V (2017) Konstitutsionen li MFCA i pomogut li popravki v Konstitutsiyu? [Do the AIFC constitutional, and will amendments to the constitution help?] Available at https://forbes.kz//process/expertise/konstitutsionen_li_mftsa_i_pomogut_li_popravki_v_konstitutsiyu/. Accessed 17 Sept 2025

Sputnik Kazakhstan (2019) Tsentralnoazatskiy Soyuz – byt ili ne byt? [A Central Asian Union—To be or not to be?]. *Sputnik* May 23, available at https://ru.sputnik.kz/politics/20190523/10232256/central-asia-soyuz.html. Accessed 17 Sept 2025

Starr SF (2019) Is this Central Asia's ASEAN moment? On November 29, Central Asia re-emerged as a world region. https://thediplomat.com/2019/12/is-this-central-asias-asean-moment/. Accessed 17 Sept 2025

The Economist (2019) Which nation improved the most in 2019? https://www.economist.com/leaders/2019/12/21/which-nation-improved-the-most-in-2019. Accessed 17 Sept 2025

The Tashkent Times (2020) Uzbekistan completes mine clearance of its border with Tajikistan. https://tashkenttimes.uz/national/4816-uzbekistan-completes-mine-clearance-of-its-border-with-tajikistan. Accessed 17 Sept 2025

TIAC (2025) About TIAC. https://www.tiac.uz/about-tiac-court-of-arbitration. Accessed 17 Sept 2025

Tsybulenko E, Platonova A (2022) Legal instruments of the Shanghai Cooperation Organisation: a case of missed opportunities? In: Sayapin S, Burnashev R (eds) Central Asian yearbook of international law and international relations 2022. Eleven, The Hague, pp 252–266

UNCTAD (2025a) Kazakhstan. investmentpolicy.unctad.org/investment-dispute-settlement/country/107/kazakhstan. Accessed 17 Sept 2025

UNCTAD (2025b) Kyrgyzstan. investmentpolicy.unctad.org/investment-dispute-settlement/country/113/kyrgyzstan. Accessed 17 Sept 2025

UNCTAD (2025c) Turkmenistan. investmentpolicy.unctad.org/investment-dispute-settlement/country/215/turkmenistan. Accessed 17 Sept 2025

UNCTAD (2025d) Tajikistan. https://investmentpolicy.unctad.org/investment-dispute-settlement/country/206/tajikistan. Accessed 17 Sept 2025

UNCTAD (2025e) Uzbekistan. investmentpolicy.unctad.org/investment-dispute-settlement/country/226/uzbekistan. Accessed 17 Sept 2025

United Nations (2025) Overview of nuclear-weapon-free zones. https://www.un.org/nwfz/content/overview-nuclear-weapon-free-zones. Accessed 17 Sept 2025

UNODC (2025) About UNODC in Central Asia. https://www.unodc.org/roca/en/About-unodc-roca/about-unodc-roca.html. Accessed 17 Sept 2025

UNRCAA (2025) United Nations Regional Centre for Preventive Diplomacy for Central Asia. https://unrcca.unmissions.org/. Accessed 17 Sept 2025

Werle G (2011) Printsipy mezhdunarodnogo ugolovnogo prava [Principles of international criminal law], TransLit, Odesa

Ziganshina D (2014) Promoting transboundary water security in the Aral Sea basin through international law. Brill, Nijhoff, Leiden

Chapter 2
A Critical Reflection on Positivist Approaches Toward International Law in Central Asia

Rustam Atadjanov

Abstract This chapter critically examines the influence of positivist approaches on the development and application of international law within Central Asian contexts, encompassing Kazakhstan, Kyrgyzstan, Tajikistan, Turkmenistan, and Uzbekistan. Through a meticulous review of existing legal frameworks, including constitutions and laws concerning international treaties, this essay aims to uncover the significant trends shaping the region's legal landscape. It will delve into the evolution of these laws to uncover local decision-makers' attitudes toward international law and its domestic enforcement. By exploring the prevailing perceptions of law both at the state and societal levels, the chapter seeks to illuminate how these attitudes have shaped the understanding and reception of international legal principles, norms, and key concepts such as rule of law and human rights in Central Asia. The essay's critical analysis will focus on the impact of positivist views on the evolution and enforcement of international law within domestic settings, highlighting both the beneficial and detrimental effects of such perspectives on the dynamics of international law's implementation in the region. This examination promises to offer insightful reflections on the interplay between positivist approaches and international law, contributing to a deeper understanding of its implications for Central Asian countries.

Keywords Legal positivism · Central Asia · International law and domestic law · Dualism and monism · Treaty implementation

R. Atadjanov (✉)
School of Law, KIMEP University, Almaty, Kazakhstan
e-mail: r.atadjanov@kimep.kz

S. Sayapin (ed.), *International Law, Politics and Security in Central Asia*,
https://doi.org/10.1007/978-3-032-17818-3_2

2.1 Introduction

2.1.1 Purpose and Scope of the Chapter

To begin with, and before turning to a more detailed analytical engagement, it is crucial to clarify that this chapter seeks to critically examine a persistently overlooked—yet increasingly consequential—feature of legal thinking and practice in Central Asia: the region's markedly positivist orientation in matters of international law. While much has been said, often in formalistic or celebratory terms, about constitutional frameworks and treaty ratification mechanisms in the post-Soviet space,[1] what remains less interrogated is the underlying conceptual approach driving the way legal drafters, policymakers, and sometimes even judicial bodies engage with international legal norms. This chapter, therefore, does not simply describe how international law is formally incorporated, or not, into domestic systems; rather, it aims to expose and reflect upon the intellectual, ideological, and practical manifestations of positivism that do or do not shape such processes.

In doing this,[2] the chapter underscores the need to treat the region not merely as a passive 'receiver' of international law but as an active, selective, and at times strategically resistant participant in shaping its domestic application. The choice of a positivist legal lens predominantly focused on textuality, state consent, and legal sources narrowly defined has not only determined how international law is perceived but also how it is implemented, delayed, or circumvented altogether. Particularly in legal regimes where discretionary executive power remains extensive and public legal consciousness is still in flux, such a narrow framework introduces risks that are neither abstract nor avoidable: they are real, structural, and unfolding as we speak.

At this point in time, and especially in view of recent regional attempts to recalibrate or 'modernize' certain constitutional and legislative provisions, the critical importance of questioning the prevailing legal philosophies cannot be overstated. The fact that international law, and particularly its more normatively charged domains such as human rights or environmental law, is often reduced to mere statutory compliance is telling of a deeper, unresolved tension between global legal norms and local legal mentalities. Domestic and international lawyers working in and on Central Asia's five constituent states can no longer afford to ignore the implications of these positivist tendencies. To do so would be to miss the very mechanisms through which international legal principles are filtered, recast, and occasionally stripped of their intended normative force.

Thus, the chapter's scope extends beyond mere doctrinal comparison; I will review and analyze the constitutional texts, treaty-related domestic legislation, and broader legal-political discourse in Kazakhstan, Kyrgyzstan, Tajikistan, Turkmenistan, and

---

[1] See, for example, Newton (2007, pp. 215–235).

[2] And without suggesting that Central Asia is unique in its adoption of dualist or formally positivist legal frameworks.

Uzbekistan. While each state exhibits its own specific legal dynamics, the comparative approach adopted here allows for the identification of region-wide patterns and shared legal assumptions. By highlighting how positivist approaches (however 'technically neutral' they may appear) contribute to constraining the transformative potential of international law, the chapter calls for a more reflective and, ultimately, more constructive regional conversation about legal reform, legal education, and the future of international law's domestic vitality in Central Asia.

2.1.2 Contextual Background: Central Asia and International Law

To properly grasp the domestic reception of international law in Central Asia, it is essential to begin with a frank acknowledgment: the five states comprising the region—Kazakhstan, Kyrgyzstan, Tajikistan, Turkmenistan, and Uzbekistan—have all formally accepted, at least on paper, the foundational legal instruments of public international law. They have not only acceded to the 1969 Vienna Convention on the Law of Treaties (or VCLT)[3] but also enacted domestic treaty laws that are, to varying degrees, reflective of the Convention's structure and principles. However, behind this veneer of formal alignment lies a more complex and somewhat contradictory reality—one that reveals a persistent and region-wide tendency to view international law through a narrow, state-centric, and, indeed, overwhelmingly positivist lens. The gap between formal ratification and effective implementation, i.e., between the declaratory provisions of national constitutions and the often inert or selectively applied practice, remains a telling marker of this tendency.

As becomes evident when one examines both diplomatic and substantive international law domains in the region, the national legislative frameworks of all five states treat international treaties as hierarchically significant yet procedurally constrained sources of law. Constitutional provisions often declare that ratified treaties form part of the law of the land (Kazakhstan, for instance, explicitly accords primacy to ratified treaties over national legislation[4]), but these declarations are counterbalanced by procedural norms that tightly control the terms, modalities, and consequences of such domestic legal integration. Moreover, as analyzed elsewhere, including in this author's study on diplomatic privileges and immunities,[5] the legislative and regulatory instruments dealing with treaty law tend to be exhaustive in form and overly cautious in spirit, thus revealing a deeper discomfort with the more open-ended

[3] Vienna Convention on the Law of Treaties, adopted 23 May 1969, entered into force 27 January 1980, United Nations Treaty Series, vol 1155, p. 331.

[4] Constitution of the Republic of Kazakhstan, adopted 30 August 1995, arts 4 and 8(2), full text in Russian available at https://online.zakon.kz (last accessed 12 April 2025).

[5] Atadjanov (2023), *passim*.

and value-laden aspects of international law such as customary norms or soft-law principles.[6]

permeates theThat cautious and often overly textual approach is even more pronounced in the criminal law context. As detailed in my separate study on crimes against humanity in Central Asia, none of the five states has fully implemented this category of international crimes in their domestic penal codes.[7] Tajikistan remains the only country to have ratified the Rome Statute of the International Criminal Court, yet even there, the domestic legislation does not reflect the substance of Article 7 of the Statute in a sufficiently precise or independent manner.[8] The absence of any definition or enumeration of crimes against humanity in the criminal codes of Kazakhstan, Kyrgyzstan, Turkmenistan, and Uzbekistan speaks volumes not only about the structural limitations of their domestic legal systems[9] but also about the prevailing doctrinal and ideological resistance to normatively charged international obligations. The unwillingness to define and prosecute such crimes domestically may be read as a symptomatic reflection of the broader, positivist culture of legal formalism that permeates the region.

In the field of treaty law specifically, the Central Asian states have all adopted specific laws on international treaties that are in structural conformity with the VCLT, as noted in comparative scholarly analysis.[10] Yet these laws clearly embody dualist conceptions, whereby international legal obligations must be transformed into domestic legal norms before they can be invoked or enforced in national courts. The very existence of detailed treaty laws—often more elaborate than those found in many other regions—testifies to a deep-seated belief in state sovereignty and procedural control as prerequisites for normativity. In Kazakhstan, for example, the Ministry of Foreign Affairs must approve treaty-making plans for up to three years in advance, and treaties affecting private entrepreneurs must be cleared through national expert councils.[11] Similarly, in Kyrgyzstan, even inter-parliamentary agreements are subject to procedures reinforcing the dualist framework and safeguarding the sovereignty of state organs in the treaty-making and implementation processes.[12]

Thus, when viewed together, these normative patterns and legislative frameworks provide more than just an institutional or doctrinal picture—they point to a shared regional ethos. That ethos, while not necessarily monolithic, exhibits a significant tilt toward legal positivism: a belief in the supremacy of written law, the centrality of state consent, and the limited role of judicial or interpretive discretion in applying international norms. The consequences of this ethos are tangible: from the inertia in implementing core international criminal law norms to the limited judicial engagement with international human rights treaties. More broadly, it reflects a prevailing

[6] Carty (2007, pp. 112–115).
[7] Atadjanov (2022).
[8] Ibid.
[9] And certain other internal factors impeding or restraining the implementation processes.
[10] Sayapin (2022).
[11] Ibid.
[12] Ibid.

attitude in the region whereby international law is accepted when convenient, tolerated when neutral, and domesticated, if at all, only when clearly subordinated to national legal and political interests. It is precisely this context that the present chapter seeks to illuminate, in the hope of encouraging a more critical, self-reflective, and normatively rich approach to international legal engagement in Central Asia.

2.1.3 Methodological and Analytical Approaches

In approaching the legal analysis offered in this chapter, the method I employed is primarily doctrinal and interpretive, albeit with contextual and comparative elements interwoven where necessary to ground the inquiry in the lived realities of Central Asia's legal systems. At the core of the doctrinal method lies the close reading and critical analysis of constitutional texts, laws on treaties, legislative acts on the implementation of international law, and relevant judicial or quasi-judicial interpretations where available. By treating these sources not simply as neutral legal instruments but as reflections of deeper ideational commitments and assumptions, my chapter aims to move beyond descriptive or mechanical comparison and toward an understanding of how legal texts embody and reinforce positivist worldviews, both conceptually and in practice.

At the same time, the analysis also retains a purposefully regionalist perspective, one that treats the Central Asian states not as isolated legal entities but as part of a post-Soviet legal-cultural formation marked by common institutional legacies, legal mentalities, and state-society relations. This important aspect should not be ignored. Hence, while individual country sections will scrutinize the relevant domestic legal instruments on their own terms, the comparative logic underpinning the structure of the chapter is explicitly designed to reveal shared patterns, recurrent omissions, and certain mutual reinforcing tendencies. That analytical choice is guided not only by the substance of the laws themselves but also by the conceptual affinity observable in the legal-political discourse surrounding international legal obligations across the region. Methodologically, this means reading legal provisions not merely in their literal wording but also through the prism of policy choices, institutional design, and implementation practices that render international law either a functional tool or an inert reference point.

Finally, the chapter draws upon a critical legal lens to interrogate the implications of these observed tendencies, particularly the dominance of positivist reasoning, for the broader trajectory of international law's domestic vitality in Central Asia. Here, the focus is not only on how international norms are formally adopted or interpreted, but also on what they are made to signify within the domestic legal order: are they perceived as external impositions, political risks, normative 'aspirationalities,' or as binding legal duties co-equal with domestic law? By asking such questions, my chapter engages not only with legal texts but also with legal consciousness and the discursive constructions of normativity within national systems. This approach ultimately aims to foreground the interpretive politics and structural constraints that shape the uneven reception of international law in the region, offering a layered and critical account that is both grounded in legal detail and attentive to the broader implications of legal method and ideology.

2.1.4 Structure of the Chapter

This chapter opens with a conceptual section that explains what is meant by the 'positivist approach' in international law. It outlines the basic features of legal positivism, including its focus on formal legal sources, the role of state consent, and the emphasis on written law. The section also briefly contrasts this approach with other schools of legal thought, such as natural law or policy-based reasoning, to clarify why positivism tends to dominate legal thinking in many post-Soviet systems. This opening section sets the stage for the rest of the chapter by showing why this approach matters, not only in theory but also in how laws are written, interpreted, and applied in practice.

The next section provides a general overview of how international law is treated within the constitutional and legal systems of the five Central Asian states. It looks at the relevant constitutional clauses, laws on international treaties, and broader legislative frameworks that deal with international legal obligations. All five countries adopt a dualist approach, meaning that international treaties must go through a specific legal process before they can have domestic effect. This section shows that, while the constitutions may give a formal place to international law, the detailed procedures and legal hierarchies often limit its actual influence (read: 'norms and principles') in practice.

Following this regional overview, the third section turns to a more detailed, country-by-country analysis. Each of the five sub-sections examines one Central Asian state, focusing on its constitution, treaty law, and relevant domestic legislation. The author's aim here is to identify and explain how each country's legal system reflects a positivist mindset. Special attention is paid to how laws are drafted, how treaties are processed, and how state officials interpret their international obligations. These examples will help reveal both common trends and specific national differences in how positivist thinking shapes domestic law.

After the individual case studies, the fourth section takes a step back to look at broader patterns across the region. It compares the five states and draws out the key themes that emerge from their legal frameworks and practices. This part of the chapter explores how and why a formal, state-centered view of international law continues to shape regional legal thinking. It also reflects on how these attitudes affect not only legal drafting but also the way courts, lawyers, and the broader public understand international law, especially in sensitive areas like human rights, judicial independence, or state responsibility.

The final section offers the main conclusions of the chapter. It sums up the key findings and reflects on the implications of the current situation for the future of international law in Central Asia. While recognizing the logic behind a positivist approach, especially in transitional legal systems, the chapter also highlights the risks this approach brings, such as a narrow understanding of legal obligations and a reluctance to engage with evolving international norms. The conclusion encourages a more balanced legal culture, one that remains grounded in legal certainty but also open to the deeper values and functions of international law in a changing global environment.

2.2 Understanding the Positivist Approach in International Law

2.2.1 Definition and Key Characteristics of Legal Positivism in International Law

To begin with, and perhaps more importantly in this context than in others, it must be clarified that legal positivism in international law is not merely a theoretical position concerning the source or structure of legal norms but also a deeply embedded mode of reasoning and 'rationalizing,' one that has come to shape the way states and legal actors define, invoke, but also contest international legal obligations. Unlike moralist or natural law approaches that ground the authority of law in universal values or ethical imperatives, positivism asserts that international law derives its validity from sources recognized by states as law: treaties, custom, general principles, and in more recent times, even acts of international organizations. In other words, what matters is not the justice of a norm but its formal source and procedural pedigree. This source-based logic, codified in Article 38(1) of the ICJ Statute,[13] is often viewed as the doctrinal bedrock of modern international law. Yet it is also a double-edged sword: it lends coherence and structure to the system, but at the cost of reducing normativity to formality.

Historically, and perhaps unavoidably, legal positivism in international law emerged from a desire to bring order and predictability to a fragmented legal landscape shaped by power, diplomacy, and conflict. Thinkers such as Hobbes, Pufendorf, and later Vattel laid the groundwork by emphasizing sovereignty, state consent, and *pacta sunt servanda* as foundational principles.[14] In their wake, jurists like Austin and, much later, Kelsen and Hart provided the formal vocabulary and structure for a positivist international legal theory.[15] Kelsen's pure theory was particularly influential in attempting to cleanse international law of ideological or moralistic contamination; his notion of a *Grundnorm* anchoring the international legal order sought

[13] Statute of the International Court of Justice, adopted 26 June 1945, entered into force 24 October 1945, United Nations Charter, annex; available at https://www.icj-cij.org/en/statute (last accessed 12 April 2025).

[14] Hobbes (1996, pp. 226–229), Pufendorf (1991, Book II, Ch 6), and de Vattel (1916, Book II, §§ 154–155).

[15] Austin (1995, pp. 3–33), Kelsen (1967, pp. 193–202), and Hart (1994, pp. 213–237).

to establish a legal science detached from politics.[16] But even within this supposedly neutral system, the role of the state remained dominant. Norms existed only to the extent that they could be traced back to acts of states or other entities explicitly authorized by them. That intellectual lineage, although revised in various ways, still informs much of how international law is understood and practiced today.

At its core, then, legal positivism in the international context is defined by three interrelated features. First, *a formal source theory of law*: only norms deriving from a recognized source—such as treaty or custom—can be considered international law. Second, *the centrality of state consent*: no rule binds a state unless that state has expressly or tacitly agreed to be bound. And third, a *preference for normativity over values*: the question is not whether a rule is just or fair, but whether it exists and is binding under the relevant legal system. These features can, and often do, lead to a legal landscape in which norms with strong moral authority (like those concerning human rights or environmental protection) are weakened or sidelined if they cannot be shown to originate from clear, state-approved sources. This is especially visible in regions such as Central Asia, where the formalism (or formalistic nature) of legal positivism provides both a shield against external normative pressure and a tool of internal political control.

It is no coincidence that in practice, many governments, especially in semi-authoritarian or post-authoritarian settings, gravitate toward legal positivism as a means of reinforcing their sovereign prerogatives and limiting the reach of contested or value-laden norms. When law is understood strictly as the command of a sovereign or the product of state will, the distinction between legal rule and political power becomes blurred. In such systems, arbitrary rule may be masked by formal legality: a law passed through regular procedure, even if oppressive in substance, is still law, provided it conforms to the form. In international law, this dynamic often manifests in how states approach human rights treaties, universal jurisdiction, or customary rules: acceptance is partial; implementation is delayed, narrowly interpreted, incomprehensive, or is simply ignored; and domestic courts rarely, if ever, invoke international norms unless clearly and unequivocally transformed into domestic statutes. The preference for textuality, precision, and procedural regularity, while not inherently problematic, becomes troubling when it leads to the systematic exclusion of evolving or unwritten norms.

Finally, and returning to a point that must be stressed throughout this chapter, the appeal of legal positivism in international law lies not only in its doctrinal clarity, but also in its political utility. In regions like Central Asia, where legal development has been tightly interwoven with state-building projects and centralized authority, positivism offers a comfortable framework: it allows international law to be embraced without conceding normative authority to external actors. Yet, as this chapter aims to show, the cost of this approach is high. By reducing law to what is merely written and ratified, by insisting on form over substance, states risk constructing legal systems that are formally coherent but normatively hollow. For international law to fulfill its role, not just as a language of order, but also of justice, this positivist reductionism

[16] Kelsen (1967, pp. 193–202).

must be critically reassessed, especially in contexts where the line between legality and arbitrariness remains dangerously thin.

2.2.2 Positivism vs. Other Approaches

In comparison to the natural law tradition, legal positivism in international law is distinguished first and foremost by its strict adherence to source-based validity rather than moral content. While natural law theorists, from classical thinkers like Aquinas and Grotius to modern proponents, see law as inherently tied to universal principles of justice and reason, positivism remains unconcerned with such moral evaluations. Within the international legal order, this means that a norm is not legally binding because it is just or humane, but because it stems from a recognized source such as a treaty or custom accepted by states. This divergence is particularly visible in debates surrounding peremptory norms (*jus cogens*), where natural law arguments emphasize their moral superiority, whereas positivist reasoning insists on tracing them to accepted legal practice and *opinio juris*. Nevertheless, the tension between these perspectives is sometimes overstated, as both ultimately rely on reason, though they channel it through different methods of validation.

Legal realism, by contrast, moves away from both the normative abstractions of natural law and the source-anchored certainty of positivism. In its classical American form, realism challenges the idea that law can be fully understood through texts or doctrines and emphasizes instead the role of actual decision-making practices, judicial behavior, and political context. In international law, this translates into an approach that views treaties, resolutions, and even customary rules as instruments whose application depends on broader geopolitical interests and institutional dynamics. Unlike positivism, which assumes that legal norms can be studied and applied independently of the political motivations behind them, realism draws attention to the indeterminacy of rules and the strategic behavior of states. While positivism seeks coherence and systematization through recognized sources, realism embraces uncertainty, treating law more as a language of diplomacy than a self-contained system of obligations.

From the standpoint of sociological jurisprudence, particularly in its Durkheimian or Weberian variants, law is viewed as a social institution embedded in normative structures that go beyond formal sources.[17] In international law, sociological approaches highlight the role of shared expectations, legitimacy, and institutional culture in shaping state behavior. Legal positivism, by contrast, often brackets these sociological dimensions in favor of textual certainty and doctrinal clarity. Thus, while a sociologist of international law might focus on how the norm against aggression has developed as a collective social belief reinforced by institutions like the UN Security Council, a positivist would instead emphasize the specific treaty provisions and binding resolutions that codify this prohibition. Yet, these views are not mutually

[17] Durkheim (2014, pp. 70–88) and Weber (1978, pp. 311–358).

exclusive; indeed, positivist doctrine has increasingly acknowledged the relevance of practices and expectations particularly when identifying the existence of customary international law.

Psychological and intuitive theories of law, such as those formulated by Petrażycki or echoed in parts of contemporary behavioral jurisprudence,[18] differ from positivism in that they conceptualize law as emerging from individual and collective mental states (experiences of duty, fairness, or moral intuition) rather than from formally adopted norms. In international law, this perspective would suggest that legal obligations exist not only because of formal treaties but also because states and actors perceive certain behaviors as legally necessary. Positivism, however, is concerned less with internal belief and more with outward expression of consent through formal acts. Nonetheless, overlaps may occur in areas like *opinio juris*, where the subjective belief in legal obligation is relevant. Even so, the positivist framework seeks to validate such belief only when paired with consistent state practice, thus maintaining its emphasis on empirical verification and institutional grounding.

Finally, in contrast with the libertarian theory of law which sees legal norms as vehicles of individual autonomy and formal equality, positivism in international law is generally silent on the purpose or justice of law, focusing instead on its systemic legitimacy through recognized sources. The libertarian approach, as developed in more recent philosophical traditions, tends to evaluate law based on its capacity to secure personal freedoms and uphold procedural fairness. By contrast, positivism would consider such an evaluative function as lying outside the proper scope of legal analysis. This divergence becomes relevant in international human rights law, where libertarian theorists may emphasize universal personal entitlements, while positivist lawyers focus on the specific instruments and ratification statuses that determine binding obligations. That said, the two approaches often intersect in practice, especially where treaty-based guarantees reinforce values also cherished in liberal legal theory.

2.2.3 Relevance and Implications of Positivist Thinking for International Legal Implementation

In order to grasp the relevance of legal positivism for the actual implementation of international law, one must begin with the recognition that positivist thinking brings with it certain conceptual and practical strengths, particularly in the areas of legal clarity, systemic coherence, and procedural legitimacy.[19] International law, by its nature, operates across a pluralistic and often politically fragmented landscape, where the establishment of binding obligations requires careful articulation and consensus among sovereign states. Within this context, positivism's insistence on recognized

[18] Petrażycki (1955, pp. 12–31) and Sunstein (2005).

[19] This is stated not with a purpose to underestimate the disadvantageous aspects of legal positivism but to provide a fairer and more comprehensive explanation of it.

sources such as treaties, custom, and general principles of law, acts as a stabilizing mechanism. It helps prevent legal uncertainty by clearly delineating what counts as law and what does not, thereby reducing the interpretive ambiguity that might otherwise paralyze implementation efforts at the domestic level. This is especially important for state organs like legislatures, executive authorities, and courts that must rely on precise formulations to give international norms domestic legal effect.

Moreover, the formalist nature of positivist legal reasoning, that is, its emphasis on textual analysis, structured hierarchy of norms, and logical consistency, makes it particularly compatible with the internal logic of many civil law systems, including those of the Central Asian states. For legal practitioners and policymakers in these jurisdictions, positivism offers a familiar framework within which international law can be received and applied. It enables a method of engagement that does not necessarily require internalizing abstract values or rethinking constitutional principles but instead focuses on procedural conformity and legal alignment. This can have a normalizing effect: states are more likely to implement treaty obligations when those obligations are framed in legal terms that mirror their own domestic legislative processes. In this sense, positivism serves as a functional bridge between the international and national legal orders.

At the same time, however, the implications of positivist thinking are not limited to technical matters of incorporation and legal drafting / legal technique. They also shape how states perceive their obligations: how seriously they take them, how they prioritize them, and how willing they are to subject them to judicial review or public scrutiny. In systems where legal positivism dominates, international law tends to be viewed through the lens of formal validity rather than normative aspiration. This means that the ratification of a treaty, for example, may be seen as the end point of a legal obligation rather than the beginning of an ongoing process of internalization, interpretation, and enforcement. As a result, there is a risk that international law becomes an inert symbol of compliance which is present in constitutional texts but largely absent in practice. Yet, even here, the positivist method offers certain opportunities: its focus on rules and procedure can be harnessed to push for institutional reform, capacity-building, and better rule-definition in domestic settings.

Finally, and this is perhaps the most important point for post-Soviet and developing legal systems, positivist thinking provides a common language for engaging with the international legal community. It permits legal systems that are otherwise hesitant to adopt international norms wholesale to nevertheless participate in the global legal order through agreed formal channels. Through treaty-making, ratification procedures, and legislative harmonization, states can fulfill their international obligations without necessarily overhauling their legal cultures. While this may appear limited or even reluctant, it also reflects a pragmatic route to integration—one in which the formal mechanics of international law are respected, even if the normative content is selectively embraced. In this way, I must admit, positivism functions not only as a legal philosophy but also as a technique of legal diplomacy, shaping how states both resist and conform to international legal expectations.

2.3 Constitutional and Legal Foundations for International Law in Central Asia

2.3.1 Overview of Constitutional References to International Law in the Five Central Asian States

Although outwardly diverse in their political organization and constitutional histories, the five post-Soviet states of Central Asia, i.e., Kazakhstan, Kyrgyzstan, Tajikistan, Turkmenistan, and Uzbekistan, share a number of features with regard to how international law is situated in their domestic legal orders. Most significantly, all five operate, either explicitly or implicitly, within the framework of dualism, wherein international treaties and norms require domestic incorporation in order to attain legal effect. And yet, despite the shared Soviet legacy and enduring positivistic legal cultures, the constitutional texts of these states nonetheless provide meaningful insights into how their decision-makers view the status, priority, and applicability of international legal instruments. These constitutional references, often brief but revealing, help identify not only the degree of normative openness toward international law, but also the stylistic choices that reflect each state's respective ideological posture toward global legal frameworks.

In the case of Kazakhstan, the Constitution clearly articulates the primacy of ratified international treaties over conflicting national legislation. Article 4 stipulates that international treaties ratified by the Republic form part of the applicable law and take precedence over domestic laws that contradict them. This formulation is further reinforced by Article 8, which affirms Kazakhstan's commitment to international legal norms and to peaceful dispute resolution.[20] Importantly, however, the Constitution does not elaborate on self-executing norms or the direct applicability of non-treaty-based international law, thus reinforcing a formalistic and hierarchical understanding consistent with positivist dualism.

The Constitution of Kyrgyzstan, revised in 2021, similarly acknowledges the role of international law, but does so with a slightly more guarded formulation. Article 6 explicitly recognizes the binding force of international treaties and 'generally recognized principles and norms of international law' as part of the legal system, albeit with the important caveat that their applicability must be governed by domestic legislation.[21] In this sense, while there is constitutional recognition of international law's normative authority, the state reserves discretion over its implementation, underscoring a cautious and 'sovereigntist' interpretation that remains tethered to the state-centric logic of legal positivism.

Tajikistan has adopted an even more affirmatively worded approach in its Constitution. Article 10 provides that international legal instruments recognized by Tajikistan

---

[20] Constitution of the Republic of Kazakhstan, adopted 30 August 1995, arts 4 and 8. Full text in Russian available at https://online.zakon.kz (last accessed 12 April 2025).

[21] Constitution of the Kyrgyz Republic, adopted 5 May 2021, arts 6(3) and 18. Full text in Russian available at https://cbd.minjust.gov.kg (last accessed 12 April 2025).

are an integral part of the legal system and that, in the event of a normative conflict, the international legal norms shall prevail over national laws.[22] Such an explicit prioritization of international law is rare among the Central Asian constitutions and may, at least formally, suggest a more progressive orientation. Nevertheless, as with the other states, this textual openness does not necessarily translate into seamless domestic enforcement, given the broader legislative practices that remain firmly embedded in legalistic positivist traditions.

In the Constitution of Turkmenistan, one finds a relatively brief but telling reference in Article 9, which proclaims the state's recognition of the primacy of universally recognized norms of international law.[23] The provision, however, stops short of granting treaties or norms direct applicability or supremacy over domestic law. The formulation reflects a declarative and symbolic commitment to international legality rather than a functional one. Combined with the overall centralized governance model and a tightly controlled legal environment, the constitutional framework continues to subordinate international law to state-driven interpretations, in line with positivist orthodoxy.

Finally, the recently revised Constitution of Uzbekistan (2023) offers a clearer constitutional stance than in its previous iterations. Article 15 confirms that international treaties and generally accepted principles and norms of international law are part of Uzbekistan's legal system and, in case of a contradiction with domestic legislation, the treaty norms shall apply.[24] This clause aligns Uzbekistan with the group of formally dualist but conditionally open states in the region. Nonetheless, much like in Kazakhstan and Kyrgyzstan, the operative mechanisms for ensuring the direct enforceability of international law remain undeveloped, and the constitutional primacy of treaties functions more as a legal ideal than a practical tool.

2.3.2 Dualist Legal Tradition in the Region: Formal Mechanisms and Practical Realities

The constitutional and legislative frameworks of the five Central Asian states demonstrate, with some jurisdictional variation, a predominant commitment to the dualist approach in matters of international law. As is well understood in public international legal theory, dualism refers to the doctrine whereby international law and domestic law are seen as two distinct legal systems, each operating autonomously and requiring a formal act of transformation for international norms to acquire domestic legal force. This distinction, grounded historically in the writings of Heinrich Triepel and later

[22] Constitution of the Republic of Tajikistan, adopted 6 November 1994, art 10. Full text in Russian available at https://mmk.tj (last accessed 12 April 2025).

[23] Constitution of Turkmenistan, adopted 18 May 1992 (as amended), arts 9 and 10. Full text in Russian available at https://mejlis.gov.tm (last accessed 12 April 2025).

[24] Constitution of the Republic of Uzbekistan, adopted 8 December 1992 (as amended), arts 15 and 19. Full text in Russian available at https://lex.uz/ru/docs/20596 (last accessed 12 April 2025).

reiterated by leading positivist theorists such as Anzilotti and Fitzmaurice, presumes that a state's obligations under international law do not, by themselves, alter domestic law unless they are expressly incorporated through legislative or equivalent normative acts.[25]

In the context of Central Asia, this doctrinal model has proven particularly influential, both conceptually and structurally. Each of the five post-Soviet republics—Kazakhstan, Kyrgyzstan, Tajikistan, Turkmenistan, and Uzbekistan—has enshrined in their constitutions certain formulations that recognize international law but do not permit its automatic self-execution without a procedural act of ratification or implementation. While these constitutions may declare that ratified treaties are part of the legal system, the enabling laws on international treaties impose specific requirements for ratification, publication, and sometimes even expert review. The resulting legal picture is that of a formally dualist, and at times selectively monist, approach that combines declaratory constitutional language with procedural safeguards reinforcing domestic legal sovereignty.

In practice, dualism in the region operates not only as a technical method of legal incorporation but also as a structural mechanism for preserving legislative discretion. International treaties, once ratified, are generally ranked above ordinary laws in hierarchy, yet they are rarely treated as self-executing unless expressly designated as such. This implies that, for international rules to be invoked in courts or administrative bodies, there must exist a corresponding national law or legal reference. Courts tend to apply international norms only when they are explicitly transformed into domestic legal instruments, and in most cases, they refrain from citing international sources in isolation.[26] As such, the dualist method serves both to maintain legal clarity and to limit judicial discretion, a feature that is particularly consistent with the legal culture of the region (as understood by this author).

From the perspective of administrative and legislative design, the dualist model enables states to exercise a high degree of procedural control over the domestic life of international law. Ratification processes often require parliamentary approval or presidential assent, and implementation may be delegated to specific ministries or executive agencies. In Uzbekistan, for example, treaties must not only be ratified but also officially published[27]; in Kazakhstan, the Law on International Treaties requires legal review by the Ministry of Justice before ratification is possible.[28] These mechanisms, while in theory ensuring compliance with domestic constitutional standards, also underscore a prevailing emphasis on state sovereignty and procedural regularity over normative immediacy.[29]

---

[25] Triepel (1899, pp. 7–29), Anzilotti (1928, pp. 48–53), Cassese (2005, pp. 213–215) and Fitzmaurice (1957).

[26] Conforti and Labella (2012).

[27] Law of the Republic of Uzbekistan on International Treaties, adopted 6 February 2019, No. ЗРУ-518, art 29. Full text in Russian available at https://lex.uz/ru/docs/4194256 (last accessed 12 April 2025).

[28] Law of the Republic of Kazakhstan on International Treaties, adopted 30 May 2005, No. 54-III, art 3. Full text in Russian available at https://adilet.zan.kz (last accessed 12 April 2025).

[29] Bantekas, Oette 2020, *passim*.

As this author sees it, it is within this formalized and sovereignty-conscious environment that the Central Asian model of international legal incorporation must be understood. Rather than treating dualism as a doctrinal constraint, the regional systems have effectively utilized it as a policy tool, one that permits selective engagement with international law while preserving constitutional and political discretion. Whether this approach fosters or inhibits long-term legal harmonization remains an open question. However, what is clear is that dualism in Central Asia is not merely a legal formality; it is a structural expression of how these states position themselves between international obligations and domestic priorities, a positioning that will be explored in more detail in the country-specific sub-sections that follow.

2.3.3 General Patterns in Treaty Ratification, Transformation, and Application in Domestic Law

In all five Central Asian states, the process of treaty ratification, transformation, and domestic application reflects a shared emphasis on structured legal formalism, procedural rigor, and executive control—hallmarks of the region's post-Soviet legal culture. The laws on international treaties adopted in Kazakhstan, Kyrgyzstan, Tajikistan, Turkmenistan, and Uzbekistan provide detailed procedural frameworks that govern every stage of a treaty's life: from negotiation and signing to ratification, publication, and termination. The overarching pattern is seemingly one of cautious incorporation: ratified treaties form part of the domestic legal system, but only after being subjected to internal constitutional and statutory filters, including mandatory expert review and parliamentary or executive approval. In each case, the transformation of treaty obligations into binding domestic law is not automatic, but it is definitely mediated through codified national mechanisms.[30]

A notable commonality across the region lies in the classification of treaties and the assignment of ratification authority. All five states differentiate between treaties signed by heads of state, governments, parliaments, and ministries depending on the subject matter and the level of legal or political significance. For instance, Kazakhstan's 2005 Law on International Treaties explicitly establishes thresholds for which treaties require parliamentary ratification (Article 11) versus executive-level approval (Articles 15–17).[31] Similarly, Kyrgyzstan's 2014 treaty law requires that international agreements on international peace and collective security and military issues, human rights, certain financial issues, and more, be submitted to the *Jogorku Kenesh* (Kyrgyz Parliament) for ratification, while other agreements may be concluded by ministries or agencies with executive authorization.[32] These

[30] See *passim* Waters (2020).

[31] Law of the Republic of Kazakhstan on International Treaties, adopted 30 May 2005, No. 54-III, arts 11, 15–17. Full text in Russian available at https://adilet.zan.kz (last accessed 12 April 2025).

[32] Law of the Kyrgyz Republic on International Treaties, No. 64, adopted 24 April 2014, art 11. Full text in Russian available at https://cbd.minjust.gov.kg (last accessed 12 April 2025).

formal distinctions mirror a broader regional logic of compartmentalized governance, wherein treaty obligations are categorized not only by content but by institutional jurisdiction.

Another important shared element is the role of legal and policy review prior to ratification (or accession). Most of the regional laws mandate expert legal evaluation to ensure consistency with constitutional norms[33] and existing legislation. In Tajikistan and Uzbekistan, for instance, the Ministries of Justice and Foreign Affairs are required to assess the treaty text for both legal conformity and political appropriateness before the instrument may be presented to the President or Parliament for approval.[34] This approach, while emphasizing legal compatibility, also reveals an implicit hierarchy where domestic coherence is prioritized over international uniformity. The cumulative effect of such procedures is to ensure that international commitments are absorbed into the domestic order only after being reconciled with national law and policy.

Finally, although all five states affirm in their constitutions or treaty laws that ratified treaties are binding and, in case of conflict, take precedence over ordinary legislation, the practical implementation of this principle tends to remain formalistic. Ratified treaties are generally published and registered, yet courts and administrative bodies often refrain from directly invoking international law unless it has been explicitly transformed into or referenced by national legislation. This is particularly evident in the absence of sustained judicial practice or constitutional case law applying treaty norms autonomously. In this sense, treaty law in the Central Asian republics operates primarily through a dualist and positivist matrix, where the rule of law is equated with procedural legitimacy and institutional authorization.[35] While this system ensures legal certainty and state control, it also conditions the domestic legal effect of international norms on their formal domestication.

[33] Which does appear logical and justified.

[34] Law of the Republic of Tajikistan on International Treaties, adopted 2004, art 4. Full text in Russian available at https://mmk.tj (last accessed 12 April 2025); Law of the Republic of Uzbekistan on International Treaties, adopted 6 February 2019, No. ЗРУ-518, arts 10–11. Full text in Russian available at https://lex.uz/ru/docs/4194256 (last accessed 12 April 2025).

[35] Klabbers (2021).

2.4 State-By-State Analysis: Legal Frameworks and Positivist Approaches

2.4.1 Kazakhstan

2.4.1.1 Constitutional Treatment of International Law

The Constitution of the Republic of Kazakhstan articulates its stance on international law through several key provisions. Article 8 underscores the nation's commitment to the principles and norms of international law, emphasizing policies of cooperation, good-neighborly relations, equality among states, non-interference in domestic affairs, peaceful dispute resolution, and a renunciation of the first use of military force.[36] In my view, this articulation not only reflects Kazakhstan's dedication to fostering harmonious international relations but also serves as a declarative statement aimed at positioning the country as a responsible member of the global community.

However, the practical implications of Article 8 warrant closer examination. While it sets a foundational ethos for foreign policy, the article's broad language may lead to interpretative challenges in its application. The emphasis on non-interference and equality among states, for instance, aligns with traditional Westphalian notions of sovereignty but may be tested in scenarios requiring collective international action or humanitarian intervention. Thus, while Article 8 establishes an aspirational framework, its operationalization depends significantly on the interpretative approaches adopted by Kazakhstan's legislative and executive branches.

Article 4 of the Constitution delineates the hierarchy and applicability of legal norms within Kazakhstan. It states that the law in force includes the Constitution itself, laws corresponding to it, other regulatory legal acts, international treaties and other commitments of the Republic, as well as regulatory resolutions of the Constitutional Council and the Supreme Court.[37] Importantly, it asserts that international treaties ratified by Kazakhstan have priority over its laws and are to be directly implemented unless the application of a treaty requires the promulgation of a law; the procedure and conditions for the operation on the territory of the Republic of Kazakhstan of international treaties to which Kazakhstan is a party are determined by the legislation of the Republic.[38] This provision ostensibly positions international agreements above domestic legislation, facilitating their integration into the national legal framework.

[36] Constitution of the Republic of Kazakhstan, adopted 30 August 1995, art 8. Full text in Russian available at https://online.zakon.kz (last accessed 12 April 2025).

[37] Ibid., art 4.

[38] Constitution of the Republic of Kazakhstan, adopted 30 August 1995, art 4(3). Full text in Russian available at https://online.zakon.kz (last accessed 12 April 2025).

Nonetheless, the practical application of Article 4 introduces complexities. The clause allowing for the necessity of additional legislation to implement certain international treaties introduces a layer of domestic discretion that can affect the immediacy and efficacy of international obligations. According to this author, such a dynamic underscores a nuanced balance between honouring international obligations and maintaining constitutional supremacy within Kazakhstan's legal system.

2.4.1.2 Law on International Treaties and Practice

Kazakhstan's procedural approach to international treaties is governed by the Law on International Treaties of the Republic of Kazakhstan, enacted on 30 May 2005. This comprehensive legislation outlines the processes for negotiating, signing, ratifying, executing, and terminating international agreements. It assigns significant roles to various state organs, notably empowering the Ministry of Foreign Affairs to coordinate treaty-related activities, including registration, accounting, and storage of international agreements, as well as serving as the depositary for multilateral treaties.[39] This centralized approach aims to ensure consistency and adherence to national interests in Kazakhstan's treaty practices.

2.4.1.3 Positivist Features in Legislative and Judicial Attitudes

Kazakhstan's legal system exhibits strong positivist characteristics, emphasizing the supremacy of written law and formal legal sources. The judiciary operates strictly within the confines of enacted legislation and ratified international treaties, adhering to the principle that justice is administered solely by the courts, as enshrined in the Constitution. This positivist stance ensures that judicial decisions are grounded in codified law, reflecting a commitment to legal certainty and predictability. However, it also implies a limited scope for judicial discretion, potentially hindering the adaptation of legal interpretations to evolving societal contexts.

While international treaties hold precedence over domestic laws once ratified, their application is contingent upon formal incorporation into the national legal system. This requirement underscores the procedural rigor characteristic of Kazakhstan's legislative and judicial practices. The emphasis on formalism ensures that all legal norms undergo thorough scrutiny before gaining domestic applicability, reinforcing the stability and coherence of the legal system. Nonetheless, this approach may also result in rigidity, posing challenges in responding swiftly to international developments and integrating emerging global legal standards.

[39] Law of the Republic of Kazakhstan on International Treaties, adopted 30 May 2005, No. 54-III, arts 2–2, 3, 6. Full text in Russian available at https://adilet.zan.kz (last accessed 12 April 2025).

2.4.2 *Kyrgyzstan*

2.4.2.1 Constitutional and Legislative Framework

The Constitution of the Kyrgyz Republic, adopted by referendum in 2021, contains multiple references to international law, some explicit and others more implicit. Article 6 states: 'Generally recognized principles and norms of international law, as well as international treaties that have entered into force in accordance with the legislation of the Kyrgyz Republic, are an integral part of the legal system of the Kyrgyz Republic. The procedure and conditions for the application of international treaties and generally recognized principles and norms of international law are determined by law.'[40] This provision—clearly, as I see it—places both ratified treaties and general principles of international law within the hierarchy of domestic sources. However, the Constitution does not define the precise legal status of these international norms in relation to national legislation nor specify how potential conflicts should be resolved.

While the language of Article 6 suggests a certain openness to international law, especially with its mention of general principles and norms, it is also careful to tie that applicability to a procedural formalist requirement: the conditions for the application of international treaties and generally recognized principles and norms of international law are determined by law. This indicates a dualist foundation wherein international law becomes applicable only after being transformed or endorsed through domestic mechanisms. The Constitution, in this respect, combines normative recognition with procedural filtering, a formulation that is cautious but consistent with the broader regional pattern of sovereignty-preserving legal integration. That, in the author's view, is a rather obvious pattern.

The legislative elaboration of this framework is found in the 2014 Law on International Treaties of the Kyrgyz Republic. This law meticulously regulates the process of negotiation, ratification, registration, and termination of international treaties. Article 1 affirms that all such processes must be carried out in accordance with the Constitution, domestic legal acts, and the treaties themselves, reiterating a layered legal hierarchy.[41] Moreover, Article 13 requires that the ratification of international treaties take the form of a law adopted by the *Jogorku Kenesh* and signed by the President, thereby embedding treaty obligations into the legislative domain of domestic law.[42]

Significantly, the law mandates legal reviews of draft treaties, provides for temporary applications under specific conditions, and even includes a mechanism for constitutional compatibility assessment (Article 19). Together, these provisions highlight a

---

[40] Constitution of the Kyrgyz Republic, adopted 5 May 2021, art 6(3). Full text in Russian available at https://cbd.minjust.gov.kg (last accessed 12 April 2025).

[41] Law of the Kyrgyz Republic on International Treaties, No. 64, adopted 24 April 2014, art 1. Full text in Russian available at https://cbd.minjust.gov.kg (last accessed 12 April 2025). While this article mentions 'the generally recognized principles and norms of international law' even before the Constitution, the 'provisions of the treaties themselves' are placed last in the enumeration.

[42] Ibid, art 13(1).

legislative system that is structurally committed to detailed internal oversight over the reception of international legal obligations. While such rigor undoubtedly reinforces legal certainty and institutional responsibility, it also embeds international law into a framework that favors formalization over spontaneous judicial or administrative application.

2.4.2.2 Role and Limits of International Law Domestically

The constitutional and legislative framework of Kyrgyzstan formally integrates international treaties and recognized principles of international law into the national legal system. In theory, this means that, once a treaty is ratified and enters into force, it becomes enforceable domestically. However, the actual legal practice is shaped by additional normative conditions. Article 21 of the Law on Treaties states that if a treaty contains provisions requiring changes to the Constitution, the treaty may only be ratified after corresponding constitutional amendments have been made.[43] This reinforces a strict hierarchy, where the supremacy of the Constitution is preserved even in the face of binding international obligations.

At the same time, there is no clear constitutional provision on whether ratified treaties override conflicting domestic statutes. This ambiguity can create interpretive uncertainties in cases of (possible) legal collision. Moreover, in practice, courts and other legal institutions tend to prioritize domestic law unless international norms have been explicitly implemented through legislation. As a result, international law often operates indirectly, filtered through the medium of domestic legal acts. This reflects the country's commitment to sovereignty-preserving dualism, where international obligations are welcomed but tightly managed within established national procedures.[44]

2.4.2.3 Interpretation and Evidence of Positivist Approaches

As shown above, the Kyrgyz legal system, both in its structure and institutional behavior, reflects many characteristics of legal positivism. First, the emphasis on clearly defined procedures for the incorporation of international law through legislative ratification and publication reveals a preference for formally adopted legal norms as the exclusive basis for enforceability. Judicial reliance on the letter of the law, rather than on broader normative reasoning, further underlines this positivist posture. Courts generally refrain from applying international legal norms unless those norms are expressly incorporated into national legislation or explicitly referenced in the constitutional text.

[43] Law of the Kyrgyz Republic on International Treaties, No. 64, adopted 24 April 2014, art 21. Full text in Russian available at https://cbd.minjust.gov.kg (last accessed 12 April 2025).

[44] Also arguably indicating, once again, an departure from being the only 'island of democracy' in the region and a move toward becoming a more traditional or typical Central Asian legalistic state.

This is further evidenced by the practice of classifying international agreements by type such as interstate, intergovernmental, and interdepartmental, as well as assigning their approval to different state organs depending on their perceived importance. The intricate mechanisms for approval, expert review, and constitutional assessment, while intended to protect national interests, also serve to insulate the legal system from the dynamic influence of international law unless filtered through domestic procedures. Thus, the Kyrgyz approach reveals a deliberate choice: international law is valued as a source of legal authority, but its legitimacy and applicability are validated only through procedural channels that affirm sovereign control of the state over its normative commitments.

2.4.3 Tajikistan

2.4.3.1 Constitutional Framework and Legal Hierarchy

The Constitution of the Republic of Tajikistan contains some of the clearest constitutional references to international law among the five Central Asian states. Article 14 explicitly states that 'rights and freedoms of a person and citizen are regulated and protected by the Constitution, laws of the republic, and international legal acts recognized by Tajikistan.'[45] In addition, it provides that these rights and freedoms are directly applicable and define the aims and content of the work of all branches of power. This provision is significant not only for its explicit mention of international instruments but for the way it ties their authority to the normative structure of domestic law. Rather than treating international norms as a secondary or supplementary source, the Constitution incorporates them into the legal reasoning of public institutions.

Equally notable is the hierarchy implied by Article 10 of the Constitution, which states that 'if the republican laws do not conform to recognize international legal acts, the norms of international law shall apply.'[46] This explicit prioritization of international law in case of conflict is uncommon in the region and would, at least on paper, suggest a strong monist tendency. However, practical implementation tends to be more complex. As elsewhere in Central Asia, the operation of international legal norms still depends on legislative incorporation and political interpretation. The theoretical supremacy of international law is mediated through institutional practice and legal culture, both of which remain marked by cautious engagement with external legal commitments.

---

[45] Constitution of the Republic of Tajikistan, adopted 6 November 1994, art 14(1). Full text in Russian available at https://mmk.tj (last accessed 12 April 2025).

[46] Ibid, art 10(3).

2.4.3.2 Treaty-Related Domestic Legal Mechanisms

Tajikistan's 2016 Law on International Treaties provides a detailed legal and institutional framework for the negotiation, ratification, implementation, and termination of international agreements. The law applies uniformly to intergovernmental, interministerial, and interstate agreements, and its scope includes everything from treaty registration and publication to procedures for suspension and denunciation. Articles 4 and 5 assign leading roles to the Ministry of Foreign Affairs and the Ministry of Justice in the legal review and political appraisal of treaties.[47] These reviews assess both the external feasibility and the constitutional and legal compatibility of the treaties under consideration.

Crucially, the law confirms that treaties requiring ratification must pass through Parliament (or *Majlisi Oli*) and receive presidential assent before acquiring domestic force. Moreover, Article 6 stipulates that treaties may only be ratified if they conform to the Constitution, and in cases of conflict, ratification must be preceded by constitutional amendment. These mechanisms collectively reflect a dualist legal approach whereby international law is not self-executing and must be filtered through a nationally determined legislative process. While Tajikistan's constitutional language appears normatively open, the practical incorporation of international law depends on national procedures that reflect both legal formalism and sovereignty-preserving caution.

2.4.3.3 Positivist Inclinations in Legal and Policy Reasoning

The legal order of Tajikistan demonstrates a strong inclination toward positivist reasoning, particularly in its treatment of legal sources and the formal hierarchy of norms. The Constitution recognizes only those international legal acts that have been 'recognized by Tajikistan,' thereby leaving the status of customary law or unratified treaties undefined. This is a typical feature of positivist systems, where the legitimacy of a norm is based, not on its moral or universal value, but on its procedural acceptance by the state. Courts in Tajikistan tend to rely almost exclusively on codified domestic legislation and rarely refer to international legal sources unless those sources have been explicitly ratified and incorporated.

Policy-making in the field of treaty law is similarly shaped by formalistic and institutional logic. The requirement for legal and foreign policy expertise prior to the ratification of treaties, as well as the central role of presidential authority in treaty-making, reinforces a top-down approach in which international obligations are only internalized if deemed politically and legally suitable. This structure appears to minimize ambiguity and enhance legal clarity, but it also limits the flexibility of the courts and administrative bodies in applying international law directly. As such, Tajikistan's approach to international legal integration reflects a coherent, though

[47] Law of the Republic of Tajikistan on International Treaties, adopted 2004, arts 4 and 5. Full text in Russian available at https://mmk.tj (last accessed 12 April 2025).

cautious, application of dualist-positivist principles that prioritize formal approval mechanisms over normative spontaneity.

2.4.4 Turkmenistan

2.4.4.1 Constitutional Stance on International Law

The Constitution of Turkmenistan, as last amended in 2023, offers a restrained yet notable reference to international law. While it does not contain a standalone article addressing the status or priority of international treaties in the domestic legal system, certain provisions indirectly indicate the country's orientation toward external legal obligations. For instance, Article 16 outlines the state's support for international cooperation in science, education, and culture, and more generally, positions Turkmenistan as an actor open to engaging in the global legal order.[48] The absence of an explicit hierarchy between international and national law, however, suggests a model where such relationships are determined not by constitutional supremacy but by legislative and administrative acts.

In this silence, the Constitution seemingly defers the regulation of international law's domestic status to statutory law, namely the Law on International Treaties. This legislative reliance confirms Turkmenistan's fundamentally dualist constitutional position. International treaties do not enjoy automatic domestic effect unless incorporated via ratification or approval. The Constitution thus leaves considerable discretion to the executive and legislature in determining whether, and how, to implement treaty obligations. From a positivist perspective, this deference to formal legislative channels reinforces a strictly source-based conception of law, where normative validity arises only through recognized state action.

2.4.4.2 State Control and Selective Implementation

The 2010 Law on International Treaties of Turkmenistan codifies a highly centralized and stratified treaty-making process. According to Articles 5 to 16 of the Law, the President and Cabinet of Ministers play dominant roles in initiating, negotiating, approving, and terminating international treaties.[49] The Majlis (Parliament) retains the authority to ratify treaties of particular political or legal significance including those affecting national security, territorial integrity, or requiring legislative amendments, while other categories of treaties may be approved solely by the President or relevant executive organs. This tiered system of treaty classification reflects a

[48] Constitution of Turkmenistan, adopted 18 May 1992 (as amended), art 16. Full text in Russian available at https://mejlis.gov.tm (last accessed 12 April 2025).

[49] Law of Turkmenistan on International Treaties, adopted 1993 (amended), arts 5–16. Full text in Russian available at https://mejlis.gov.tm (last accessed 12 April 2025).

model of executive control whereby the state retains broad discretion over the legal significance of international instruments.

Moreover, Article 4 of the law stipulates that, if an international treaty contains provisions contrary to domestic legislation, the treaty's provisions shall prevail.[50] While this appears to suggest a progressive stance, the reality is that such conflicts are generally pre-empted through pre-ratification scrutiny, which ensures conformity or legal adjustment before ratification proceeds. In practice, the state filters treaty content carefully to preserve coherence with domestic law and political priorities. This reinforces the idea of selective incorporation not in the sense of rejecting international law, but of shaping its domestic effects according to a controlled legal script. Such an approach exemplifies the primacy of sovereignty in legal reasoning, in line with a positivist tradition of centralized legal validation.

2.4.4.3 Legislative Formalism and Positivist Logic

Turkmenistan's treaty law exhibits the hallmarks of legislative formalism. The treaty ratification process is governed by specific statutory rules defining the types of agreements subject to parliamentary approval and the legal instruments required for them to take effect. Article 11 enumerates the categories of treaties that must be ratified by law, such as those involving human rights, national borders, or security arrangements.[51] This structured legalism ensures that only those treaties deemed significant by the state pass through the full legislative apparatus. Other treaties, particularly intergovernmental or inter-ministerial ones, may enter into force through administrative approval without parliamentary involvement.

This procedural design reflects a positivist logic that prizes formal hierarchy, legislative authority, and institutional order over interpretive openness. International law, under this model, is not rejected but is tightly managed through codified mechanisms that affirm the state as the exclusive validator of legal obligations. As such, Turkmenistan's approach to treaty law exemplifies state-centric positivism, in which the legal value of international norms depends not on their inherent content but on their procedural alignment with the domestic legal order. Judicial or administrative bodies are unlikely to apply treaty norms unless they are first explicitly transformed into national legal instruments, a pattern that further underscores the proceduralist ethos of Turkmenistan's legal system.

[50] Ibid, art 4(2).

[51] Ibid, art 11(1).

2.4.5 *Uzbekistan*

2.4.5.1 Constitutional and Treaty Law Analysis

The 2023 Constitution of the Republic of Uzbekistan contains several articles that define the place of international law within the domestic legal order. Article 17 affirms that Uzbekistan is a full-fledged subject of international relations, while Article 16 establishes the supremacy of the Constitution and mandates that all laws and regulations be based on and conform to it.[52] Most critically, Article 15 of the Constitution states that 'International treaties of the Republic of Uzbekistan, along with generally recognized principles and norms of international law, are an integral part of the legal system of the Republic of Uzbekistan.' It further clarifies that if a treaty contains provisions that differ from those in national law, the treaty's provisions shall prevail.[53]

This clause, clear and direct, is more normatively assertive than in some neighboring jurisdictions looked at above, yet the practical implications require a more cautious reading. The supremacy of international treaties over domestic legislation is affirmed only with respect to already ratified treaties. There is no indication that unratified treaties or customary international norms may be invoked in domestic legal processes. Moreover, the Constitution avoids characterizing international law as self-executing. In this respect, while the textual clarity is notable, the constitutional design remains in alignment with a dualist framework: international law becomes binding domestically not by its own force, but by virtue of incorporation and ratification through national legal channels.

2.4.5.2 Recent Reforms and Positivist Continuity

Uzbekistan's 2019 Law on International Treaties further clarifies the country's procedural approach to treaty law. It codifies the requirements for negotiation, ratification, implementation, and termination of treaties. Article 3 reiterates that treaties, once properly concluded, are a part of the legal system, alongside the general principles and norms of international law.[54] However, this inclusion is conditional upon proper entry into force through national procedures. Importantly, Article 2 provides that if a treaty prescribes rules different from domestic legislation, the treaty prevails[55]; but again, this effect follows only after the treaty's formal ratification.

---

[52] Constitution of the Republic of Uzbekistan, adopted 8 December 1992 (as amended), arts 17(1) and 16. Full text in Russian available at https://lex.uz/ru/docs/20596 (last accessed 12 April 2025).

[53] Ibid, art 15.

[54] Law of the Republic of Uzbekistan on International Treaties, adopted 6 February 2019, No. ЗРУ-518, art 3. Full text in Russian available at https://lex.uz/ru/docs/4194256 (last accessed 12 April 2025).

[55] Ibid, art 2(3).

These reforms signal greater coherence in Uzbekistan's international legal commitments, especially as part of broader legal modernization efforts since 2017. However, they do not alter the country's fundamentally positivist posture. Legal validity is still grounded in formal acts of recognition and codification. Ratification remains a condition for domestic applicability, and courts tend to interpret international norms conservatively unless they have been clearly domesticated. Thus, while procedural structures have become more detailed and perhaps more efficient, the deeper logic of legal positivism, normativity derived from formal source recognition, remains intact in both constitutional and treaty law.

2.4.5.3 Legislative Caution and Adherence to Formal Legalism

The legislative and administrative practices in Uzbekistan reflect a deep-rooted culture of legal formalism. The classification of treaties by level such as state-to-state, intergovernmental, and interagency, is matched by differentiated approval mechanisms. For example, treaties concluded on behalf of the Republic itself are approved by the president, while those at the intergovernmental level may be ratified by the Cabinet of Ministers. This structured system is reinforced by procedural steps involving the Ministry of Foreign Affairs and Ministry of Justice, both of which must review and coordinate implementation proposals for treaty provisions requiring new legislation.

Such procedures are not merely bureaucratic, as they may first appear on surface: they are manifestations of a legal worldview that equates legal legitimacy with institutional authorization. Even where international norms are substantively aligned with constitutional values, their domestic effect is conditioned on procedural regularity. The obligation to register all treaties in a centralized state registry and the stipulation that implementation laws must be adopted as necessary reflect a system that prioritizes order, hierarchy, and textual precision. As such, Uzbekistan exemplifies a modernizing yet still traditionally positivist model of international legal integration, one in which domestic law does not reject international norms but assimilates them on its own formal and sovereign terms.

2.5 Regional Synthesis and Critical Reflections

2.5.1 Cross-Cutting Trends in the Region's Constitutional and Legislative Treatment of International Law

Throughout the five Central Asian republics, the general pattern of constitutional and legislative engagement with international law reveals a cautious and structured incorporation of treaty-based obligations. While nearly all states—Kazakhstan,

Kyrgyzstan, Tajikistan, Turkmenistan, and Uzbekistan—affirm the place of international law in their legal systems, the extent of that incorporation is explicitly conditioned on domestic legislative and constitutional procedures. Ratified treaties generally enjoy a formally superior or equal status to national legislation, yet none of the five states recognizes the automatic applicability of customary international law, and all rely on legislative mechanisms to control implementation.

In my view, this shared reliance on dualist or semi-dualist frameworks is not surprising when viewed through the lens of the region's legal heritage and political structure. In each state, international obligations are filtered through the language of sovereignty and legal certainty, with institutional mechanisms established to screen and review treaty commitments prior to ratification. Laws on international treaties, often detailed and procedurally dense, underscore the degree of normative control exercised by executive and legislative authorities. Such legalistic filtering reveals a broader trend: the regional preference for clarity, hierarchy, and control over interpretive or flexible integration.

Taken together, the region's constitutional and legislative treatment of international law reflects an overarching concern with managing the interface between national sovereignty and global legal norms. While openness to international cooperation is frequently emphasized in declarative terms, the actual integration of international law remains procedural, state-centric, and often bureaucratized. Yet this approach, though at times rigid, has contributed to legal consistency and, arguably, to a more stable legal environment, even if it sometimes delays or constrains the fuller reception of evolving international legal standards.

2.5.2 Positivism as a Shared Legal-Cultural Tendency in Post-Soviet Central Asia

The sustained influence of legal positivism in the post-Soviet Central Asian republics is not merely a technical or theoretical preference; it is deeply rooted in legal culture, historical experience, and institutional habit. The Soviet legacy has left an enduring mark on legal thinking across the region, where law was long understood as an instrument of state power, not as a reflection of justice or a framework for individual rights. Even in the current constitutions, although liberal legal values are asserted, the regulatory and codified nature of law, that is, *lex* rather than *ius*, continues to dominate both legislative design and judicial interpretation.

This legal-cultural tendency is also connected to broader phenomena such as legal nihilism and low legal awareness—challenges that have been reviewed in some regional legal scholarship including by this author.[56] When law is perceived more as a formalistic obligation or administrative burden than a system of enforceable rights and mutual accountability, legal positivism fills a familiar conceptual space. It provides order, hierarchy, and predictability, but also risks formalism devoid of

[56] For example, in Atadjanov (2021).

normative commitment to justice. In such contexts, law's instrumental function may overshadow its aspirational role, reinforcing compliance rather than engagement.

Nevertheless, positivism has offered certain institutional benefits for the region. The emphasis on legal certainty, formal validity, and clear legal procedures has helped stabilize treaty-making practices and provided structure to otherwise fragmented legal systems. While it may at times constrain more dynamic interpretations of international law, especially in fields such as human rights, it also furnishes a coherent internal logic that supports domestic legal development. In that sense, legal positivism continues to function not as an obstacle but as a framework within which legal evolution, albeit gradual, can still take place.

2.5.3 Impacts on the Understanding of International Legal Principles

One of the more visible effects of positivist influence in Central Asia is the selective and often cautious engagement with broad international legal principles, particularly those derived from soft law, customary international law, or human rights doctrines. In the absence of explicit ratification or incorporation, such norms are seldom invoked in national jurisprudence or policy discourse. Courts and administrative bodies typically refrain from applying general principles of international law unless expressly authorized to do so by domestic statutes or constitutional provisions. This restricts the normative reach of international legal standards, especially in dynamic areas such as human rights protection.

The treatment of human rights in particular reveals this tension. On paper, all five constitutions endorse a wide range of civil, political, economic, and social rights, often modelled on international frameworks. However, the actual invocation of international human rights instruments, such as the ICCPR or CAT,[57] in domestic legal processes is rare, unless these treaties have been specifically implemented through national legislation. The reluctance to acknowledge customary or general international law as directly binding reflects the broader positivist posture: what is not written in domestic sources is generally deemed non-binding.

Yet this posture does not preclude future engagement with broader international legal principles. The gradual development of treaty-related jurisprudence, the professionalization of the judiciary, and increasing exposure to global legal debates may, in time, foster a more receptive attitude. For now, the emphasis remains on legal sources that are clearly codified, formally ratified, and hierarchically situated, principles that reflect both the strengths and limitations of the positivist tradition in Central Asia's international legal identity.

[57] International Covenant on Civil and Political Rights, adopted 16 December 1966, entered into force 23 March 1976, United Nations Treaty Series, vol 999, p. 171; Convention against Torture and Other Cruel, Inhuman or Degrading Treatment or Punishment, adopted 10 December 1984, entered into force 26 June 1987, United Nations Treaty Series, vol 1465, p. 85.

2.5.4 Societal and Institutional Attitudes Toward International Legal Obligations

The reception of international law in Central Asia is not shaped solely by formal legislative structures or constitutional texts; it is also deeply influenced by prevailing institutional cultures and public legal consciousness. In many cases, international legal obligations are perceived as distant or abstract, relevant mainly to state actors or elite diplomatic circles but disconnected from everyday legal practice. This detachment is reinforced by a legal education system that tends to emphasize national codification, formal sources, and a hierarchical concept of law, leaving limited space for comparative, human-rights-based, or policy-oriented perspectives.

Institutionally, international legal obligations are typically framed as matters of foreign policy rather than domestic legal reform. Ministries of Foreign Affairs and Justice handle treaty processes, while courts and law enforcement agencies remain largely internal-facing and normatively cautious. This division reinforces a 'siloed' approach to law, in which international norms are implemented only when domestically convenient or legally compelled. Within such frameworks, treaty obligations risk being treated as symbolic rather than functional, and international law becomes a register of compliance rather than a tool of transformation.

Overcoming these limitations will require deeper institutional commitment and societal engagement. International law must be taught, debated, and applied not just as an external system, but as a meaningful part of the domestic legal identity. This involves not only legal reform but also public education, judicial training, and clearer legislative strategies for implementation. Without such internalization, international legal norms—even when formally ratified—are unlikely to achieve their full normative or democratic potential in the region.

2.5.5 Implications for Future Development of International Law Domestically in Central Asia

Looking forward, the key challenge for Central Asia is to develop a legal culture where international law is not merely received but internalized, where it coexists with, and gradually reshapes, domestic legal traditions. Legal positivism, while valuable in maintaining clarity and sovereignty over norm development, must be balanced with interpretive flexibility and normative openness if the region is to evolve toward a meaningful rule-of-law framework. This does not require a rejection of positivism, but rather its integration with other traditions, particularly those that prioritize individual rights, social justice, and institutional accountability.

This author is of 0firm opinion, that a critical shift in this regard involves the reconceptualization of the concept of state sovereignty itself. If the current model of sovereignty (as absolute and largely inviolable) continues to dominate legal thinking, international legal obligations will remain subordinate to perceived national interests.

For international law to contribute to democratic transformation and legal modernization, sovereignty must increasingly be seen not as a conceptual shield but as a functional tool: one that serves the development of human dignity, rights, and freedoms, rather than merely the preservation of state prerogatives. This shift in perspective is foundational to the long-term legitimacy and integration of international law in domestic settings.

Admittedly, achieving such transformation will be immensely difficult under current global conditions. The international system itself is undergoing significant normative strain, with the erosion of multilateralism, the politicization of human rights, and growing skepticism toward global governance. These trends reinforce insular legal thinking and may further entrench positivist tendencies in transitional legal systems. Yet, even amid these headwinds, the effort to reimagine the role of international law within national frameworks remains essential, especially if the Central Asian republics are to pursue meaningful democratization and move beyond procedural legality toward a genuine state of law.

2.5.6 Opportunities and Challenges for Harmonizing with Global Legal Standards

The question of harmonization with global legal standards presents both opportunity and risk for the Central Asian states. On the one hand, engagement with international treaties, acceptance of technical legal assistance, and participation in multilateral institutions offer avenues for legal modernization and integration into global norms. On the other, harmonization efforts can sometimes lead to superficial compliance, where international standards are formally adopted but remain inert in practice. The challenge lies in ensuring that harmonization is not only textual but also substantive, that it reflects genuine legal transformation rather than symbolic alignment.

To this end, opportunities exist in areas such as judicial cooperation, treaty implementation, and the development of transnational legal expertise. International legal institutions and donor agencies can support this process by adapting their approaches to regional realities and offering not just legal models but also culturally sensitive capacity-building programs. More importantly, domestic actors such as lawmakers, judges, educators, and civil society, must take ownership of international legal norms and reframe them as tools of local empowerment, not just obligations imposed from abroad.

Still, the path ahead remains uneven. The dual legacies of legal formalism and institutional centralization continue to weigh heavily on reform prospects. Yet, if approached strategically and incrementally, legal harmonization offers a way to bridge normative gaps and facilitate legal development without undermining state agency. For that to happen, Central Asian legal systems must continue to evolve toward a model in which international law is not viewed as a foreign imposition, but as a shared language of justice, rights, and governance, one that complements, rather than contradicts, the pursuit of a lawful and democratic state.

2.6 Conclusion

2.6.1 Summary of Key Findings

This chapter has offered a regionally grounded, doctrinal, and interpretive examination of how international law is referenced and treated within the legal systems of Kazakhstan, Kyrgyzstan, Tajikistan, Turkmenistan, and Uzbekistan. By reviewing constitutional provisions and laws on international treaties in each of these states, and by situating them within their broader legal-political context, it has been shown that the five Central Asian republics display significant structural similarities in their normative approaches to international law. These include formal recognitions of ratified treaties, lack of clear status for customary norms, and a pronounced reliance on procedures of incorporation and legislative filtering prior to domestic applications.

Despite variations in constitutional formulations and institutional procedures, a shared legal trajectory becomes evident: each state retains a strong commitment to state sovereignty, legislative hierarchy, and codified sources of law. International obligations are not denied, but they are carefully managed, treated less as normative imperatives and more as contractual undertakings requiring validation through state will and formal processes. This shared approach is rooted, not only in the design of legal texts, but also in the prevailing legal mentality across the region: cautious, structured, and oriented toward legal certainty rather than normative fluidity.

What emerges from this analysis is a regional legal model shaped by a form of state-centric dualism, where the integration of international law into domestic systems remains formally possible, yet substantively constrained. While constitutions may affirm treaty priority, and laws on treaties may codify procedures for engagement, the practical implementation of international law continues to rely on domestic discretion filtered through national interests, legal formalism, and institutional control.

2.6.2 Reflections on the Strengths and Limitations of Positivist Approaches in the Region

Legal positivism, in the Central Asian context, has functioned as more than a theory of legal sources; it has become an organizing principle for legal systems in transition. It provides a coherent, predictable, and hierarchically ordered framework within which international legal obligations can be evaluated, domesticated, or delayed. In states emerging from the ideological rigidity of Soviet legality, this return to formal legal mechanisms, such as ratification, publication, and approval, has helped reassert state authority over the legal process and introduced a sense of legal continuity amid political flux. In this respect, the positivist model has supported legal stability and preserved national legislative autonomy.

This stability, however, has come at a cost. The same commitment to source-based validity and procedural rigor often leaves little room for substantive engagement with the evolving principles of international law, particularly those derived from non-treaty-based sources such as general principles or customary norms. This is most apparent in the field of human rights, where treaty commitments are acknowledged in form, but implementation is often partial, selective, or delayed. Courts seldom apply international law unless it is explicitly codified in domestic legislation, and administrative bodies remain reluctant to treat international norms as binding unless a domestic norm authorizes them to do so.

At a deeper level, the positivist approach in the region reflects and reinforces a legal culture that privileges obedience over interpretation, formality over justice, and order over autonomy. It discourages critical engagement with legal norms and marginalizes value-based reasoning, both in judicial decisions and in legal education. While positivism itself is not to blame for these outcomes, its dominance within post-Soviet legal consciousness has created a framework in which the potential of international law to serve as a transformative legal force remains, for the most part, unrealized.

2.6.3 Final Thoughts on the Prospects for International Law's Role in Central Asian Legal Development

If international law is to play a meaningful role in the legal and constitutional development of Central Asia, it must be more than merely acknowledged in legislation or referenced in preambles. It must become part of the region's evolving legal consciousness accepted not only as a legal source but as a framework for rethinking sovereignty, rights, and the role of law itself. For this to happen, legal positivism must not be abandoned but rebalanced. Its core strengths, i.e., legal clarity, hierarchy, and procedural discipline, can and should be preserved. But they must be complemented by more normatively open approaches: those that allow for judicial reasoning, the application of general principles, and an active engagement with global legal trends.

One of the key conceptual shifts required involves rethinking the meaning of state sovereignty. So long as sovereignty is understood to be an impermeable shield against external norms, international law will remain subject to political discretion and legal gatekeeping. If sovereignty can be reinterpreted as functional rather than metaphysical—as a framework for enabling rather than limiting rights—then international law may begin to serve not merely as a source of obligations for the state, but as a legal language through which individuals assert and protect their freedoms. This would mark a gradual but important evolution from state-centered to person-centered legal thinking.

Of course, such a transformation cannot be achieved easily, especially given the broader geopolitical and institutional challenges facing the region. The international legal system itself is under pressure, and many of the universal principles it once championed are now contested or politicized. Yet if the democratic project in Central Asia is to retain any future viability (if the region is to move toward not only formal but functional legal states), then international law must be part of that evolution. It cannot do so from the margins. It must be internalized, interpreted, and, where necessary, adapted, but certainly never ignored. The coexistence of international legal principles with domestic sovereignty, and of positivist frameworks with liberal legal traditions, is not only possible—it is essential.

References

Anzilotti D (1928) Corso di Diritto Internazionale, vol 1, 4th edn. Athenaeum, Rome
Arjomand SA (ed) (2007) Constitutionalism and political reconstruction. Brill Nijhoff, Leiden
Atadjanov R (2021) Building the State of Law (Rechtsstaat) in the countries of Central Asia: an unachievable dream or realistic objective? Law & State 3(92):52–70
Atadjanov R (2022) Domestic implementation of crimes against humanity in Central Asia. Asian J Comp Law 17(2):268–285. https://doi.org/10.1017/asjcl.2022.17
Atadjanov R (2023) Diplomatic privileges and immunities: central Asian Law and practice. In: Asian yearbook of international law. Brill Nijhoff, Leiden. https://doi.org/10.1163/9789004687202_005
Austin J (1995) The province of jurisprudence determined (ed: Rumble WE). Cambridge University Press, Cambridge
Bantekas I, Oette L (2020) International human rights law and practice, 3rd edn. Cambridge University Press, Cambridge
Cassese A (2005) International law, 2nd edn. Oxford University Press, Oxford
Carty A (2007) Philosophy of international law. Edinburgh University Press, Edinburgh
Conforti B, Labella A (2012). An introduction to international law. Brill Nijhoff, Leiden
de Vattel E (1916) The law of nations; or, Principles of the law of nature applied to the conduct and affairs of nations and sovereigns (trans: Fenwick CG). Carnegie Institution of Washington, Washington, DC
Durkheim É (2014) The division of labour in society, 2nd edn. Free Press, New York
Fitzmaurice G (1957) The general principles of international law considered from the standpoint of the rule of law. Recueil des Cours 92(II):1–227
Hart HLA (1994) The concept of law, 2nd edn. Oxford University Press, Oxford
Hobbes T (1996) Leviathan, Rev. student edn (ed: Tuck R). Cambridge University Press, Cambridge
Kelsen H (1967) Pure theory of law, 2nd edn (trans: Knight M). University of California Press, Berkeley
Klabbers J (2021) International law, 3rd edn. Cambridge University Press, Cambridge
Newton S (2007) Constitutional reform and international law in Central Asia. In: Arjomand SA (ed) Constitutionalism and political reconstruction. Brill Nijhoff, Leiden, pp 215–235
Petrażycki L (1955) Law and morality (trans: Babb HW, ed: Hartogm HLA). Harvard University Press, Cambridge, MA
Pufendorf S (1991) On the duty of man and citizen according to natural law (ed: Tully J, trans: Silverthorne M). Cambridge University Press, Cambridge

Sayapin S (2022) International law in Central Asia: Practices and doctrines. Rev Cent East Eur Law 47(3–4):322–351. https://doi.org/10.1163/15730352-bja10072
Sunstein CR (2005). Moral heuristics. Behav Brain Sci 28:531–573
Triepel H (1899) Völkerrecht und landesrecht. C.F. Müller Verlag, Karlsruhe
Waters C (2020) The normative role of treaties in domestic legal systems. Oxford University Press, Oxford
Weber M (1978) Economy and society, vol 1 (eds: Roth G, Wittich C). University of California Press, Berkeley

Chapter 3
Transitional Justice and Transitology in the Post-Soviet Space

Anja Mihr

Abstract Over twenty new countries among the former Soviet satellites and republics experienced dramatic political transitions and transformations in the 1990s. Many of these regime changes led to long-term violent conflicts and wars, such as those in former Yugoslavia, the Caucasus region, Central Asia, and, most recently, Ukraine. Conversely, others, such as the Baltic States, succeeded in establishing and consolidating democratic institutions. This was also seen to a much lesser extent in countries like Kyrgyzstan, Georgia, and Moldova. In this chapter, I will contribute to the extensive literature on these topics and argue that another factor affecting the abilities of these countries to complete the democratic transition process relates to the level of inclusiveness or exclusiveness with which they have implemented transitional justice measures. I contend that, firstly, during the early transition and institution-building phase of the 1990s, most of the new leadership in countries such as Kazakhstan, Belarus, and Russia came directly from the communist-socialist nomenclature, with very limited transitional justice measures put in place. In contrast, the Baltic States, Moldova, Georgia, and Armenia, which had already voted to leave the Soviet Union prior to the March 1991 referendum, later experienced mass protests in their capitals advocating for independence, sovereignty, and democracy, making it impossible for their leaders to retain the Soviet frameworks and forcing a more thorough transition. Whenever governments have implemented transitional justice measures in their transitions, democratic institution-building has had a better chance to succeed and become more resistant to anti-democratic movements.

Keywords Transitology · Transitional justice · Post-Soviet countries · Post-communist socialism · Democracy

---

A. Mihr (✉)
OSCE Academy, Bishkek, Kyrgyzstan
e-mail: a.mihr@osce-academy.net

The Center on Governance Through Human Rights, Berlin Governance Platform, Berlin, Germany

S. Sayapin (ed.), *International Law, Politics and Security in Central Asia*,
https://doi.org/10.1007/978-3-032-17818-3_3

3.1 Introduction

It is often argued that, during the Soviet era from 1922 to 1991, the Latvian, Lithuanian, and Estonian republics experienced more freedom than other Soviet republics. They also had the advantage of transitioning more rapidly and smoothly from totalitarian rule to democracy in the 1990s, which helped them successfully join the European Union in 2006. While this may be true, they still had fewer freedoms and less self-governance than Soviet satellite states like Hungary, Poland, or Yugoslavia, which did not transition to democracy quickly or at all, unlike the Baltic States (Libanidze 2020). Therefore, the hypothesis that the Baltic States were privileged under Soviet rule cannot stand alone, nor can it be the only reason for their successful democratic transition in the 1990s. I argue that the pace and success of democratic transition depend on how well these nations combine democratic institution-building with Transitional Justice measures and methods.

Today, many former Soviet satellite states or independent communist-socialist countries are less democratic than Estonia or Latvia. Hungary, Croatia, and Poland score significantly lower in democratic performance compared to the Baltic nations. Therefore, the level of freedom a former Soviet republic had did not determine its success or failure in completing democratization. There must be some other factor that influences the success of establishing democratic institutions. Another aspect of successful versus unsuccessful transitions to democracy is how these countries managed the numerous human rights abuses and totalitarian dictatorships. Damsa argues that the political agendas of some transitional post-communist Central European and Soviet countries did not focus on retributive justice, which involves condemning and prosecuting former communist leaders. Instead, they prioritized measures of distributive justice, such as converting communist property into private property (Damşa 2016). As a result, a clear lustration and vetting process to prevent former communist leaders from holding office in new democratic regimes did not take place. Many of these former oppressors became 'democratic leaders' overnight without ever taking responsibility for their violations of international and domestic laws. Consequently, establishing the rule of law became nearly impossible in these countries.

Deciding whether to implement instruments and mechanisms of Transitional Justice, such as vetting procedures, trials, compensation, or security sector reforms, is one of many factors that can influence whether a country becomes democratic over a longer period. The Baltic States introduced some forms of Transitional Justice during their democratic transition, but others, like Belarus, Azerbaijan, or Tajikistan, did not at all. Rather than such implementation, we mostly see memorials or other forms of commemoration in the post-Soviet space, without any actions taken to address the root causes of the terror and totalitarian regimes of that era.

Over twenty countries from the former Soviet sphere, as well as its satellites and republics, underwent dramatic regime changes in the 1990s. Many of these changes resulted in long-lasting violent conflicts and wars, such as those in the former Yugoslavia, the Caucasus region, Central Asia, and, most recently, Ukraine. In contrast, some countries, such as the Baltic States, have successfully established and strengthened democratic institutions, while others, including Kyrgyzstan, Georgia, and Moldova, have seen less progress.

In this chapter, I aim to contribute to the extensive literature on these issues and argue that another factor influencing some of these countries' ability to complete the democratic transition relates to how inclusive or exclusive they have been in implementing transitional justice measures. I will argue that, first, during the early transition and institution-building phase of the 1990s, most of the new leaders in countries like Kazakhstan, Belarus, and Russia came directly from the communist-socialist nomenclature. This was evident in the March 1991 referendum, when all citizens of the Soviet Union were invited to vote on whether to stay in or leave the Russian Federation, with over 80% voting in favor of remaining. The Baltic States, Moldova, Georgia, and Armenia had already declared their independence and did not participate. Later, they experienced mass protests in their capitals calling for independence, sovereignty, and democracy, making it impossible for their leaders to stay part of the Russian Federation.

The fact that, in many post-Soviet republics and satellite states, the majority of the new political elite emerged from the Soviet-trained nomenclature contributed to their reluctance to distance themselves from and clarify their connections to the violent and unjust past of Soviet wrongdoings. While the Central Asian states of Kazakhstan, Uzbekistan, Kyrgyzstan, Tajikistan, and Turkmenistan, as well as Azerbaijan in the Caucasus and Belarus in Europe, sought to strengthen their relationships with Russia, Ukraine, instead, was divided, with the eastern part overwhelmingly favoring alignment with Russia and the western part opposing it (White and Feklyunina 2014).

However, regardless of the referendum's result, the shift in political power in Moscow shortly afterward allowed all former Soviet republics to become independent nations in 1991. While the core region of the former empire, the Russian Federation, remained a clear successor to what was once the Soviet Union, the other former republics have managed their Soviet pasts very differently since gaining independence (Bilgic 2012).

A similar divide exists in other Eastern and Central European countries, including former Yugoslavia, Hungary, Poland, Slovakia, and East Germany, where most supported independence and a democratic government but opposed transitional justice. Strong resistance came from those who preferred to stay under authoritarian socialist-communist rule, as it seemed to meet their basic needs (Akchurina and Della Sala 2023). Others, however, favored the old regime because of the privileges they had enjoyed under it. This has since developed into a resilient opposition characterized by anti-Western and anti-European sentiments (Arel 2018). Trials of former KGB officers or security sector members have not systematically taken place in these countries, nor have the former communist elites openly admitted responsibility for past wrongdoings. Blame was usually placed on external powers, like Western countries or NATO, or on deceased individuals, such as Stalin.

Secondly, the lack of a comprehensive and inclusive Transitional Justice process—including tools and mechanisms like systematic trials, parliamentary hearings and inquiries, reparations, compensation, educational reforms, public dialogues, as well as vetting, lustration, and security sector reforms—has caused a failure to hold the past and the autocratic communist regimes accountable. Instead, shortly after the fall of the totalitarian regimes in the post-Soviet region, many people started to idolize that era, mixing ignorance with nostalgia. However, Transitional Justice methods could have helped confront the brutal and repressive history of the Soviet Union, delegitimize it, and at the same time legitimize new democratic leaders and institutions, such as an independent judiciary, the rule of law, and fair elections (Adler and Petrovic 2018).

Moreover, the active civil society that supported regime change during the Glasnost (openness) and Perestroika (restructuring) movements of the 1980s, as well as the democratic institution-building efforts of the 1990s, often abandoned these countries after the regime changes. The significant brain drain and migration flows in the 1990s contributed to the halt in further democratic progress. This lack of sustained civil society became one of the biggest hurdles for the newly independent states. There was not enough pro-democratic civil society to oppose the shift backward to autocratic practices. Around 2010, as a new generation of political leaders came into power, two distinct patterns emerged: some leaders, such as those in Ukraine, Kyrgyzstan, and Armenia, pushed for more democracy through pro-democracy movements and revolts; others, including those in Azerbaijan, Belarus, and Kazakhstan, aimed to strengthen authoritarian rulership. For many observers, this period marked the 'era of backsliding' in democracy and the second 'wave of autocratization' since World War II (Lührman and Lindberg 2019).

3.2 Dealing with the Past

The Soviet Union and its satellite states experienced significant human rights violations and crimes against humanity, often occurring within the framework of authoritarian governance, political repression, and systemic abuse from 1922 to 1991. Most remain undetected to this day, undermining the democratization and consolidation processes. In many countries, first and foremost in the Russian Federation itself, there has been no break from the totalitarian regimes, and the autocratic, suppressive bureaucracy of the Soviet era remains unchanged. The rule of law was undermined to serve the interests of the Communist Party, and today serves a corrupt authoritarian political cast, leading to arbitrary arrests, unfair trials, and widespread torture. The regimes' policies consistently prioritized political control over social welfare, resulting in severe impacts on citizens' health, education, social mobility, and overall well-being. Communism's centralized economy led to inefficiencies for large segments of the population, resulting in food shortages, medical supply shortages, and a scarcity of essential goods.

During the Stalin era, from 1922 to 1953, repressive policies, purges, and state-sponsored violence left a legacy that affected the nation until 1991, including the satellite states. The most severe phase was the Great Purge between 1936 and 1938, when Stalin's government continued arresting and executing hundreds of thousands of perceived political enemies, often accusing them of being 'class enemies' or

'spies'. Ethnic minorities such as Crimean Tatars, Volga Germans, Chechens, Poles, and others were deported to Siberia or Central Asia, with many facing starvation and death. This practice persisted after the war. Millions died due to food shortages and poor economic management. The major famines in Kazakhstan and Ukraine caused millions of deaths from starvation and have even been labeled genocides by some officials. Millions were forced into inhumane labor camps (Gulag), where overcrowding, lack of food, and brutal treatment were common. Although the Gulag system was somewhat reduced after Stalin's death, forced labor camps continue to exist today.

Stalin's successor, Khrushchev, who ruled from 1953 until 1964, publicly denounced Stalin's excesses in a secret speech at the 20th Congress of the Communist Party in 1956, acknowledging the purges, the system of terror, and other injustices. However, many victims of Stalin's purges were never granted full restitution, and that is part of the collective memory to this day in the wider post-Soviet sphere. Political repression continued in more subtle ways. Khrushchev targeted intellectuals, writers, and artists who diverged from the party line, especially those pushing for greater political freedom or criticizing Soviet policies. During protests in places like East Germany (1953), Hungary (1956), and Czechoslovakia (1968), the Soviet Union used military force to quash dissent, violating the rights of those seeking more autonomy or reform. Leonid Brezhnev's leadership (1964–1982) kept up the pattern of repressing dissidents and human rights activists—notable figures, such as Andrei Sakharov, a nuclear physicist and human rights advocate, faced persecution.

This period was characterized by systematic surveillance and censorship by the Committee for State Security (KGB). The KGB extensively monitored individuals suspected of being 'anti-Soviet'. It enforced severe religious persecution, especially against the Russian Orthodox Church, other Christian denominations, Jews, and Muslims in Central Asia and the Caucasus. The Andropov era, until the early 1980s, intensified restrictions on cultural expression and the political independence of non-Russian ethnic groups, along with deportations and discrimination against various ethnic communities. Eventually, the new chairman of the Politburo from 1985 to 1991, Mikhail Gorbachev, introduced the concepts of glasnost and perestroika. However, his government also carried out brutal crackdowns on peaceful protesters, as seen in Georgia (1989) and Lithuania (1991). By the time the USSR dissolved in 1991, Gorbachev's reforms had failed to prevent the state's collapse. Due to the lack of an organized civil society (except for Memorial) and a mass pro-democratic movement capable of mobilizing citizens to hold perpetrators accountable, a comprehensive transitional justice process was never carried out in Russia.

Instead, a mindset of 'irresponsibility' cultivated under the Russian and, later, Soviet Empires in the nineteenth and twentieth centuries now dominates. Key Russian and Soviet stakeholders have rarely faced accountability for their actions and have seldom taken responsibility for their wrongdoings. Mechkova et al. argue that the culture of irresponsibility fostered a climate of impunity throughout the 1990s transition period (Mechkova et al. 2017, p. 168). This created an environment of mistrust, conspiracy, and insecurity, exacerbating the security dilemma and contributing to the persistence of authoritarian rule to this day.

Despite this, the Gorbachev era permitted some modest freedoms and encouraged engagement with civil society. Thousands of political prisoners were released, and previously banned works by dissidents were made available for publication. There was also a limited introduction of transitional justice measures, such as the establishment of the Russian NGO Memorial (1987–2023), which prompted greater public scrutiny and awareness of the extent of the Soviet state's abuses. However, despite these modest efforts, there was never an attempt to implement a comprehensive transitional justice process in Russia. By 2015, there was not a single state-sponsored commemorative plaque in Moscow honoring the victims of Stalinism. Although a Gulag Museum opened that year, and in 2017, President Putin unveiled the Wall of Sorrow to commemorate the victims of Stalin's terror, he noted, at the same time, that the country should, by all means, avoid transitional justice as it would reignite confrontations by 'settling scores' (Stan and Nedelsky 2023, p. 531). This example shows that Putin was acutely aware of, yet also afraid, that any deeper form of transitional justice would expose the past, thereby increasing social unrest and shedding light on the uninterrupted continuity between the gruesome and unheroic techniques of the Soviet past and those of his present government.

The unresolved issues from the past and the absence of inclusive transitional justice processes led to many violent conflicts and wars during the post-Soviet era. Azerbaijan and Armenia fought their first war over territory in Karabakh from 1988 to 1994, followed by a civil war in Chechnya starting in 1994. The former satellite state of Yugoslavia fell into a decade-long, devastating civil war from 1992 to 1999, which caused the country's complete fragmentation. Tajikistan experienced a brutal civil war from 1992 until 1997, fueled by political, ethnic, religious, and territorial struggles after the Soviet Union collapsed. Border conflicts among Tajikistan, Uzbekistan, Kyrgyzstan, Azerbaijan, Armenia, Georgia, and Russia, as well as between Russia and Ukraine, still frequently occur today and escalate into full-scale wars. Many of these conflicts stem from a common struggle for national unity and a shared sense of national identity.

Only in the Baltic States, East Germany, and, to some extent, Croatia, Poland, Georgia, Ukraine, and the Czech Republic, did full-scale transitional justice processes begin after regime change to address their traumatic periods of injustice. However, many of these processes were established by foreign countries or international organizations, such as the United States, the United Kingdom, or Germany, as well as by the Council of Europe (CoE), the European Union (EU), or the OSCE in their areas of operation (Akchurina and Della Sala 2023).

3.3 Transitional Justice in Post-Communist Countries

To illustrate why the intertwining effect between transitional justice measures and democratic institution-building is crucial for successfully establishing democracy, it is important to understand the democratic deficits or backsliding occurring in many post-Soviet and post-independence countries in Eurasia today. The UN defines transitional justice measures and processes as a range of judicial and non-judicial tools and mechanisms, including trials, truth commissions, vetting and lustration processes, memorials, reparations, restitution, compensation, and even amnesty and rehabilitation laws (Palmer and Watene 2020).

The measures aim to address the legacy of widespread human rights abuses that occur during or after wars, forced occupations, dictatorships, corrupt regimes, and other violent and oppressive conflicts. They involve criminal, historical, and political procedures and actions (Mihr 2020). When implemented systematically and inclusively, these transitional justice measures can lead to institutional reforms, including in the security sector, vetting of former perpetrators, and the development of legal and democratic constitutions. TJ can also promote civil or political initiatives and strengthen civil society during the transition and transformation of political regimes and institutions. A primary goal of TJ is to change the political and legal culture from authoritarianism to democracy (Gready and Simon 2022; Teitel 2014).

In light of the democratic transitions that occurred globally between 1991 and 2010 in the post-Soviet space, the UN General Assembly adopted general guidelines on transitional justice in 2006. It also declared 2009 as the 'International Year of Reconciliation', urging member states to implement transitional justice measures to promote democratization, even in less severe contexts and post-war situations. However, neither the UN guidelines nor the year of reconciliation fully resonated with policymakers in Ukraine, for example, disregarding them (Mihr 2019).

In the post-Soviet and post-independent countries after 1991, the only initiatives taken to confront the past include notable efforts by various non-governmental organizations (NGOs), including USAID, Japanese aid organizations, German political foundations, the British Council, GIZ, the OSCE, the ODIHR, EU programs, the International Center for Transitional Justice (ICTJ), and the Open Society Institute (OSI), also known as the George Soros Foundation, among others. These entities have been active throughout the decades.

In 1990, Estonia enacted laws and measures to address individuals involved in crimes, including war crimes, committed between 1940 and 1991. This targeted both Nazi (if still alive) and Soviet-KGB perpetrators, resulting in the prosecution of dozens. Along with building democratic institutions, reforms in schools and textbooks, numerous memorials, history commissions, reparations, and vetting and lustration procedures have been implemented (Stan and Nedelsky 2023, p. 210ff).

Unlike in Estonia, in Georgia, after initial reluctance and several unsuccessful attempts to pass any legislation on past wrongdoings, in 2010, the parliament made a significant attempt to pass the Liberty Charter package. It included TJ measures addressing the Nazi-atrocities (between 1939 and 1945) and the Soviet past until

1991 alike. The parliament voted it down in 2011, and instead, it invested the Ministry of Internal Affairs with the power over lustration. It was a politicized attempt, doomed to be abused and thus ineffective, never fulfilling the purpose of strengthening democratic institutions (Stan and Nedelsky 2023, p. 240).

The Czech Republic, on the other hand, enacted a Law on Judicial Rehabilitation in 1990 for former political prisoners and those who were expropriated and tortured. This initiated a long-term vetting process, similar to what East Germany experienced after reunification that same year, through a comprehensive set of laws and legislation, including the '*Stasi-Unterlagengesetz*' for vetting procedures related to the secret security service and the repression apparatus, the Stasi, between 1949 and 1989. Anyone collaborating with the former secret services and strongholds of authoritarian regimes, such as the Stasi in Germany, the Securitate in Romania, or the KGB in Russia, would be evaluated individually. Those who did not pass the vetting would be barred from holding political or public office under the new democratic government. Such vetting legislation has proven crucial in starting a vetting and lustration process to prevent former officials, communist elites, perpetrators, and anti-democratic thinkers from regaining political power and influence, thereby paving the way for the development of democratic institutions (Kravchenko 2016).

Besides the hesitation to fully implement a thorough TJ process, most researchers or investigators trying to access documents and archives from that period face practical challenges, such as language barriers and the fact that many Soviet-era archives remain closed to research or inaccessible for the foreseeable future. For a comprehensive investigation and an effective TJ process, domestic and international actors need to be fluent in the national languages while maintaining independence and neutrality. How many judges, researchers, and investigators—including international ones—can speak fluent Russian, Tajik, Serbo-Croatian, Azerbaijani, Hungarian, Estonian, Georgian, Kyrgyz, or Turkmen to fully understand the issues? The fact that almost all Politburo and KGB documents are stored in Moscow and remain inaccessible further complicates matters.

External and international actors have limited influence over this process due to political and legal barriers; however, they can provide incentives. For example, the Council of Europe's Court of Human Rights (ECtHR) cannot act retroactively regarding the Soviet period, despite Russia and some former Soviet states joining the Court in the 1990s, and Russia's subsequent exit from the Council in 2022.

However, specific property rights cases from the Soviet Union's expropriation period have been addressed in Eastern Europe, the Balkans, and the Caucasus. Most cases, however, as in the Baltic States, have focused on freedom of expression, fair trials, freedom from torture, and political liberties during the transition period after 1991. The International Court of Justice (ICJ), a UN-led court of interstate jurisdiction, has also handled numerous cases concerning border conflicts between former Soviet countries and their satellite states. These cases usually involve issues of state sovereignty, territorial disputes, human rights, international law, and the use of force, such as Kazakhstan v. Kyrgyzstan (1998), Uzbekistan v. Kyrgyzstan (1999), Georgia v. Russian Federation (2008), Ukraine v. Russia (2017), and Armenia v. Azerbaijan (2021). They mainly address unresolved interstate territorial disputes—a shared legacy of the Stalin era across the region—and issues of reparations. While these cases at the ICJ or ECHR can help initiate further domestic trials and reparations, they cannot replace a comprehensive transitional justice process within the countries. The same applies to the International Criminal Court (ICC), established in 2002, which has investigated a limited number of crimes against humanity and serious human rights violations linked to the Soviet period, mainly in regions of the Caucasus, Central Asia, and most prominently in Ukraine. In 2023 and 2024, the ICC issued arrest warrants against Russian President Putin and some of his high-ranking military officials for crimes of aggression against Ukraine (Kasianov 2022).

Generally, these courts have limited jurisdiction over nations unless the cases involve war crimes, crimes against humanity, violations of customary international law, or breaches of the Geneva Conventions on humanitarian law. Universal jurisdiction is essential for transitional justice in the post-Soviet context but is most effectively enforced in domestic courts if they can operate independently (Mihr 2024).

Many additional transitional justice measures have been adopted, primarily in former Soviet republics such as Uzbekistan, Kazakhstan, Georgia, and Ukraine. These include symbolic acts such as returning stolen artifacts to their rightful owners or countries after periods of occupation, as well as creating historical films, memorials, documentaries, literature, and novels featuring victims, heroes, perpetrators, or bystanders. Education reforms have also occurred, often marked by the opening of Gulag museums, 'Walls of Sorrow', or 'cemeteries of the fallen'. Furthermore, there has been a revival of churches, mosques, and synagogues, along with the reappearance of donor-funded Islamic madrasas—frequently sponsored by Qatar, Turkey, or the UAE—and Orthodox Christian convents and other faith-based educational institutions. Most of these efforts show little focus on addressing the political accountability related to the Soviet past, instead focusing on the sorrows, victimhood, and struggles of that period.

Today, the reluctance of governments to confront the past is often replaced by private initiatives, social media, blog posts, influencers, and AI-generated data. Influencers and civil society play a crucial role in quickly exposing wrongdoing, including issues related to the Soviet past and those connected to it. Students and NGOs gather narratives, identify perpetrators and victims, and even 'retell' historical events on smartphones—often with little to no government response (Akchurina and Della Sala 2023). In Russia today, challenging the official Kremlin narrative about the Soviet past in such ways can lead to persecution and imprisonment.

3.4 Transitology in Former Communist and Socialist Countries

There will be no democratic transition or regime change without a national, bottom-up catharsis. In their analysis of data from 1900 to 2006, Chenoweth and Stephan (2011) found that catharsis-driven nonviolent resistance succeeded 53% of the time in pro-democratic movements, compared to just 26% for violent resistance. One main argument is that nonviolent campaigns tend to attract a broader and more diverse range of participants, and a consolidated majority of three-quarters of the population. Such mass movements enhance the legitimacy of pro-democratic regime change and could lead to a 'pacted' and peaceful democratic transition process that includes all parties. This creates a foundation for a culture of consensus-building, which is vital for a functioning democracy. The Baltic States achieved this in the late 1980s and early 1990s. Such widespread involvement also increases the movement's social power and makes it harder for authoritarian regimes to enforce repression (Libanidze 2020).

Dankwart Rustow observed similar developments in the post-WWII era and coined the concept of Transitology to describe the different paths and stages toward democracy. The period of the second wave of democratization, which began in 1945 and concluded in 1965 in Western Europe, and later continued into the Third Wave, lasting from the 1970s into the 1990s, also affected the former Soviet republics and satellite states (Huntington 1991). Even today, the similarities between transition processes during previous waves of democratization and this third wave are striking. Transitology helps us understand the rise and fall of young democracies in Central Asia and Europe. For him, the critical pattern of this democratic transition is when:

> People who were not in conflict about some rather fundamental matters would have little need to devise democracy's elaborate rules for conflict resolution. And the acceptance of those rules is logically a pact of the transition process rather than its prerequisite. (Rustow 1970, p. 362)

His, Chenoweth's, and Stephan's findings show that external support often benefits nonviolent movements more than violent ones, as it can pressure oppressive regimes without justifying violence. The authors found that in all successful nonviolent pro-democratic campaigns, such as those in Ukraine, at least 3.5% of the population needed to initiate protests, including strikes, boycotts, campaigns, or other peaceful actions, to spark a movement and gain one-third popular support and more once the movement is ongoing. These actions cause widespread disruption, build momentum, and generate significant political pressure that can lead to the widespread movement necessary to reach the critical mass of about two-third of the adult population for successful change (Chenoweth and Stephan 2011).

Therefore, the chances of successful democratization depend on a peaceful, bottom-up, civil society-led approach driven by the people and their citizens. Imposed, top-down democratic institution-building will not succeed in the long run. It is an act of political usurpation, imposing a democratic constitution that is not supported by the majority of the population, as seen in the Central Asian countries after 1991. Such usurpation, as desirable as it might seem, has little chance of achieving real democracy. After examining a series of post-war and post-revolution democracies, Rustow concluded that (1) wars, social conflicts, and, most importantly, inequalities are drivers for democratization, not the end; (2) a bottom-up, cooperative approach involving various political elites, civil society, and stakeholders is essential for mobilization in favor of democratization; and (3) even when democratic institutions like elections or civil society are established, democracy remains an ongoing struggle for the people and competing interests. Therefore, he predicted that the transition from autocracy to democracy in post-independent countries can only occur if at least two-thirds of the population is united in support of democracy, rather than against it. Where that is not the case, democracy will most likely not be seen as an alternative vis-à-vis authoritarian modes of governance.

While most of the conditions mentioned earlier were common in many Soviet republics around 1990, not all pro-democratic activists had the support of the citizens to organize and mobilize their constituencies. For example, the five Central Asian countries lacked a pro-democratic movement, with over 80% of the population voting in the 1991 referendum to stay part of the newly formed Russian Federation, the successor to the Soviet Union (Akchurina and Della Sala 2023). Ultimately, it was Russian President Boris Yeltsin who urged them to become independent states, to some extent against the will of their respective governments, in 1991.

However, following the concept of Transitology, more is required than widespread societal dissatisfaction with fundamental matters and injustice, such as Stalin's terrors, the dysfunctional economy, or national identities. Without fatigue for autocratic leadership and a desire for a more participatory political system, change will not happen. Without a national catharsis, there will be no political change.

A movement to confront the fundamental inequality and injustice of the Soviet Union, and to organize a proactive civil society, occurred in Latvia and Lithuania, and later in Ukraine and Georgia, as well as in East Germany, Poland, Romania, Hungary, and Czechoslovakia. However, this was not true in most of the other countries, as seen in Belarus, Russia, Azerbaijan, and the Central Asian states.

Many of the shortcomings of the democratic institution-building process of the 1990s only became visible in the early 2000s. Sometimes, these led to protests, revolts, and even revolutionary strikes in countries that failed to democratize in the 1990s. The pro-democratic Orange Revolution in Ukraine in 2006 marked the start not only of open and transparent elections but also of a transitional justice process dealing with the Soviet past (Pop-Eleches and Robertson 2018). In Kyrgyzstan, following a period of political violence and ethnic clashes in 2010 and a subsequent change in government, the president established the 'Muras' (Heritage) Foundation in 2012 to independently study and evaluate the national tragedy of the mass killings known as the 'Urkun' during the Russian Empire in 1916. During that time, Kyrgyz people opposed the expansion of the Russian (and later Soviet) Empire(s), as well as the recruitment of Kyrgyz soldiers for World War I. According to international observers, however, the causes of the April 2010 Revolution in the aftermath of the ethnic clashes between Kyrgyz and Uzbek civilians in Southern Kyrgyzstan were addressed only inadequately. The UN had to send a special envoy to report on it and demand more fair trials. Given the sensitivity of the situation and the fact that these clashes were directly linked to the unresolved past and territorial borders of the Soviet Union, transitional justice was externalized to international forums. Most notably, the UN and the OSCE demanded greater transparency regarding these clashes. The UN rapporteur, however, faced expulsion after submitting his report about the massacres to the government in 2010 (Stan and Nedelsky 2023, p. 347).

Another example is Ukraine. Although a series of transitional justice measures was implemented as early as 1991, they proved inadequate. The lack of systematic vetting and lustration of the former Soviet elite fostered a Soviet-style political culture that required obedience to Moscow's directives. The absence of vetting and lustration laws allowed former Soviet elites to regain power and positions, corruption was high, and citizens' trust in state institutions was low. This contributed to widespread mobilization and political violence against pro-Russian leaders during the Orange Revolution in 2006 and the rise of a national catharsis in 2014, during the Euromaidan protests and so-called 'Revolution of Dignity'.

In 1991, the Ukrainian parliament established a rehabilitation commission, which, although biased and exclusive, reviewed over three hundred thousand cases, banned the Communist Party, reformed the security sector, and issued numerous commemorative acts related to the suffering of the Soviet past. Specifically, Stalin's repressions and the subsequent famine-genocide known as the Holodomor in the 1930s were central to Ukrainian civil society and politics. However, a vetting and lustration process to exclude those loyal to the autocratic practices of the Soviet regime and responsible for many crimes did not happen inclusively. De facto amnesties were more common than holding people accountable. As a result, this nomenclature and its anti-democratic and often corrupt practices persisted in much of Ukraine's leadership, hampering the country's path to full democratization (Stan and Nedelsky 2023, pp. 622–225).

It was similar in Georgia, where the parliament was never equipped with the necessary tools, like vetting laws, to prevent Soviet nostalgic and anti-democratic political actors from assuming presidencies, leading to political violence over the decades, culminating in 2024.

Many citizens in post-Soviet states have only recently realized that one reason they revert to authoritarianism is society's and government's inability or reluctance to confront the painful Soviet past. However, in satellite states like Romania and Bulgaria, not least because of a free popular culture that promoted films, novels, and other works illustrating the political violence under socialist rule, commissions of inquiry and trials were encouraged, and past wrongdoings came to light. Along with incentives to join the European Union in 2007, these often-triggered trials, memorials, reparations, or compensations lead to what Rustow calls 'pro-democratic catharsis'.

Although nearly all post-Soviet and satellite states that pursued a democratic path have notable flaws and low levels of democratic performance, those that advanced beyond 2010 are still in development. Even Hungary, with its widespread democratic weaknesses and its downgrade from a liberal democracy to an electoral democracy in 2022 by the European Parliament, has not fully abandoned democracy. One reason, among many, is the strong memory of the autocratic communist regime as a common story in Hungary. This shows that when democratic institutions are strengthened and most people adopt and practice civic culture, it is unlikely to fully revert to authoritarianism, as democratic norms, practices, and institutions become deeply rooted and stable. However, most societies have yet to achieve this, which is why only a few democracies are fully consolidated worldwide.

Poland's Solidarity movement, a labor union formed in the Eastern Bloc in 1981 and led by Lech Wałęsa, for example, was the first major civil society organization to emerge, becoming a powerful force for change and inspiring thousands across the Soviet empire. Similar groups emerged throughout the region, including the Civic Forum in Czechoslovakia, the Hungarian Democratic Forum, and various dissident groups in East Germany. As a result, the democratic transition was not uniform across the region, with some countries facing greater challenges than others. Countries with a tradition of organized civil societies, such as Poland, Hungary, Estonia, Slovenia, Romania, and East Germany—and to some extent Ukraine, Croatia, Georgia, and Albania—had a stronger start in 1991 and during the pro-democracy protests after 2010 than countries lacking organized civil society.

3.5 Incomplete Transitology: A Path to Re-Autocratization

According to Roderick (1999), six key political issues in Transitology and democratic transition within the post-Soviet space went wrong. First, there was the issue of how the new elites handled past perpetrators and atrocities, such as whether there were trials and vetting. Second, the lack of effort in regime legitimation and in developing a 'civic culture' that could support new political institutions was critical. Third, the complete formation of national political parties, which did not occur, would have been necessary to build coherent political platforms and connect national and local political goals. Fourth, there was an imbalance of power between the executive and the legislature. Fifth, there has been almost no decentralization of authority, and instead, there has been a refusal to share responsibility with local actors.

In most post-Soviet countries, the decline of democratic institutions became increasingly evident after two legislative cycles at the start of the 2000s. Russia's President Putin was officially elected in 2000, marking the beginning of a re-centralization of the political regime. Under his leadership, aiming to 're-unite' the former Soviet states, Russia invaded Georgia in 2008 and annexed Ukraine's Crimean Peninsula in 2014. As the leader of the Soviet successor state, with no break in political practices, he openly claimed that further democratization was unnecessary in exchange for economic aid and debt relief, which had always been conditions set by the EU and other external stakeholders. Putin revived Soviet nostalgia and introduced the concept of '*Russkij Mir*' as a quasi-ideology promoting Russian supremacy that former Soviet republics should aspire to.

The return to autocracy was also driven by both new and established hegemons in Eurasia, including China, Russia, Iran, India, the UAE, and Turkey. These nations have played a significant role in the ongoing process of democratic backsliding or consolidation in the post-Soviet region, especially in the Caucasus and Central Asia. By the turn of the millennium, democratic erosion had begun, coinciding with Putin's first term as president, which began in 2000.

While most post-Soviet and independent transition countries made democratic progress during the early years of regime change, little of that progress remained after the second legislative term (between 1995 and 2000) because neither politicians, civil stakeholders, nor businesses followed democratic rules or played a fair political game. Instead, the re-autocratization of political practice took hold, and oligarchs and organized crime groups gained control of the economic and security sectors. Russia, Tajikistan, Azerbaijan, and Belarus are examples of this. Building resilient institutions, an independent judiciary, a multi-party parliamentary system, and supporting a strong civil society remain a challenge for most countries today. Those who claim to adopt democracy often turn into populist leaders aiming to recreate a centralized, paternalistic presidential system.

After Georgia's defeat and loss of de facto control over its territories of South Ossetia and Abkhazia following the 2008 Russia-Georgia war, China and Russia began engaging in risky policy maneuvers, such as dividing the Caucasus and Central Asian countries into their spheres of influence. Small and weak democracies like Kyrgyzstan or Georgia have little resilience against such influence. China's anti-democratic Belt and Road Initiative, launched symbolically in Kazakhstan in 2012, confirmed this trend. It culminated, among other events, in the war between Azerbaijan and Armenia from 2021 to 2024, and Russia's ongoing aggressive war against Ukraine since 2014 (Kornely et al. 2022).

China's new leadership role in many post-Soviet states exploited the countries' democratic weakness. At the same time, the leadership in Beijing positioned itself as the new hegemon, investor, and modernizer across much of Eurasia, especially in Central Asia, without clear democratic incentives. Consequently, any further democratic transition is currently paused, marking the second wave of autocratization and significant democratic backsliding since 2010. Merkel contends that the representative institutional role of political and civil actors depends on the proper use or wrongful abuse of the norms established in the constitution since 1991. A civic culture, let alone resilient institutions, was nowhere to be seen after two legislative terms (Merkel 1999).

Today, many of these states have become de facto Mafia and deep states, governed by a patronage system that many treat as organized crime. 'Elected Businessmen', 'security councils', and 'council of elders' are claiming to restore 'traditional values' often linked to faith and religion, or in the case of Russia, a vision of ethnic supremacy such as Russki Mir. They promote nostalgia, patriarchy, and nationalist identity politics instead of pursuing democratic freedoms, equality, and diversity as their main goals. According to Przeworski's game theory, such interest groups—or deep state—have intensified and radicalized political behavior at different stages of the transition process (Brückner 2019). One reason for this is that the autocratic practices of the Soviet past have never been fully delegitimized or demystified through a transitional justice process.

3.6 Conclusion

While many former communist-socialist countries in Eastern Europe have made significant progress in establishing democratic systems, the transition remains uneven across the post-Soviet states, with the exception of the Baltic countries. Accession and benefits by the European Union certainly played a role but are not the primary reason for successful democratization. Rather, countries that have implemented transitional justice measures, strengthened their rule of law, and allowed their civil society to grow independently and freely, successfully democratized. The more inclusively and systematically these countries employed TJ methods, such as vetting, lustration, trials, and security sector reforms, during their democratization process, the more democratic they are today. Conversely, the less they engage in these processes, the more likely they are to revert to autocratic rule.

For some, such as Kyrgyzstan, the linkage between TJ and democratic institution-building in the 1990s came to a halt in and around 2010. For others, such as Ukraine, it began with the Orange Revolution in 2006 and led to the pro-democratic shifts in 2014.

In many Central Asian countries and in Russia, Lenin's statues were never removed, Soviet laws are still enforced, and acknowledgment of Soviet terror remains hidden. The Great Patriotic War and Nazi Germany's victory in 1945 continue to be unifying symbols, although in some nations, the 9th of May is today more of a public holiday than an official remembrance. In countries like Kazakhstan, Russian-style military parades for commemoration have stopped, but festivities continue, replaced by an 'Immortal Regiment' march ('*Batyrlarga tagzym*'), which has been given a Kazakh name. Ukraine eliminated the 9th of May as a public holiday in 2023, creating a new set of commemorative events and days in response to the full-scale Russian invasion in 2022 (Mihr 2024). This does not mean these countries no longer honor WWII victims or remember the crimes committed by Nazi Germany. However, they no longer subscribe to the Soviet unifying narrative of the 'Great Fatherland' and ceremonies promoted by Russia.

In light of the above, what is noteworthy is that when governments implement transitional justice measures, connecting them to the development of democratic institutions, including civil society and the free media, democratic institution-building in the context of Transitology has a better chance to succeed, become stronger, and resist anti-democratic movements and attempts to re-autocratize the society and the regime.

References

Adler N, Petrovic V (eds) (2018) Understanding the age of transitional justice: crimes, courts, commissions, and chronicling genocide, political violence, and human rights. Rutgers University Press, London

Akchurina V, Della Sala V (2023) The European Union, Russia and the Post-Soviet space shared neighbourhood, battleground or transit zone on the New Silk Road? Routledge, London

Arel D (2018) How Ukraine has become more Ukrainian. Post-Soviet Aff 34(2–3):186–189. https://doi.org/10.1080/1060586X.2018.1445460

Bilgic A (2012) Towards a new societal security dilemma: comprehensive analysis of actor responsibility in intersocietal conflicts. Rev Int Stud 39(6–2013):185–208. https://doi.org/10.1017/S0260210512000095

Brückner J (2019) Transformation and transition research: an introduction. In: Merkel W, Kollmorgen R, Wagener HJ (eds) The handbook of political, social, and economic transformation, pp 1–13. Online edn, Oxford Academic. https://doi.org/10.1093/oso/9780198829911.003.0006. Accessed 21 Mar 2019

Chenoweth E, Stephan M (2011) Why civil resistance works: the strategic logic of nonviolent conflict. Columbia University Press, New York

Damşa L (2016) Post-communist property transformations and transitional justice. some historical, legal, and philosophical issues. In: The transformation of property regimes and transitional justice in central eastern Europe. Stud Hist Law Justice 8:21–52. https://doi.org/10.1007/978-3-319-48530-0_2

Gready P, Simon R (eds) (2022) From transitional to transformative justice. Cambridge University Press, Cambridge

Huntington SP (1991) The third wave: democratization in the late twentieth century. University of Oklahoma Press, Norman

Kasianov G (2022) War of the past. Zeit Online. https://www.zeit.de/2022/31/georgiy-kasianov-ukraine-krieg-geschichte. Accessed April 2025

Kornely K, Tracey CG, Stephen FJ (eds) (2022) Georgia's foreign policy in the 21st century: challenges for a small state. Bloomsbury Publishing, London

Kravchenko V (2016) Fighting soviet myths: the Ukrainian experience. Harvard Ukrainian Stud 34(1–4):447–484

Libanidze B (2020) Russia, the EU, and the Post-Soviet democratic failure. Springer, Wiesbaden

Lührmann A, Lindberg S (2019) A third wave of autocratization is here: what is new about it? Democratization 26(7):1095–1113

Mechkova V, Lührmann A, Lindberg S (2017) How much democratic backsliding? J Democracy 28(4):162–169. https://doi.org/10.1353/jod.2017.0075

Merkel W (1999) Systemtransformation Eine Einführung in die Theorie und Empirie der Transformationsforschung, UTB. Leske & Budrich

Mihr A (2019) Regime consolidation and transitional justice, comparative case studies of Germany, Spain, and Turkey. Cambridge University Press, Cambridge

Mihr A (2020) Transitional justice research in post-totalitarian societies in the OSCE region. In: Mihr A (ed) Transformation and development. Springer, Cham, pp 147–154

Mihr A (2024) Transitional justice in Ukraine. In: Mihr A, Pierobon C (eds) Polarization, shifting borders, and liquid governance. Springer, Cham, pp 409–427

Palmer E, Watene K (2020) Reconciliation, transitional and indigenous justice. Taylor & Francis, London

Pop-Eleches G, Robertson G (2018) Identity and political preferences in Ukraine—before and after the Euromaidan. Post-Soviet Aff 34(2–3):107–118. https://doi.org/10.1080/1060586X.2018.1452181

Roderick M (1999) Political transformation. Transforming Management in Central and Eastern Europe. Online edn, Oxford Academic. https://doi.org/10.1093/acprof:oso/9780198775690.003.0002. Accessed 3 Oct 2011

Rustow D (1970) Transitions to democracy: toward a dynamic model. Comparative Polit 2(3):337–363

Stan L, Nedelsky N (eds) (2023) Russia, encyclopaedia of transitional justice, 2nd edn. Cambridge University Press, Cambridge

Teitel RG (2014) Globalizing transitional justice. Oxford University Press, Oxford

White S, Feklyunina V (2014) Ukraine and 'Europe': elite discourses. In Identities and Foreign Policies in Russia, Ukraine, and Belarus. Palgrave Macmillan, London. https://doi.org/10.1057/9781137453112_5

Chapter 4
International Organizations and the Development of International Law in Central Asia

Sultan Sakhariyev

Abstract This chapter examines how international organizations shape the making and practice of international law in Central Asia since 1991, against the backdrop of the region's strategic geopolitics and diverse development challenges. Using historical, and legal analysis, it maps the interventions of global and regional bodies, including the United Nations, the International Committee of the Red Cross, the Collective Security Treaty Organization, the Eurasian Economic Union, the OSCE, and others, across security, human rights, trade, governance, and environmental agendas. The analysis shows that international organizations simultaneously enable and constrain state action: they diffuse standards, build capacity, and open markets, while at times narrowing domestic policy space, entrenching dependencies, and sidelining local legal orders and practices. Attention to selective sovereignty and legal pluralism illustrates how Central Asian states adapt, negotiate, or resist imported templates amid shifting power hierarchies. The chapter concludes that durable legal development in the region requires context-sensitive engagement, participatory norm-setting, and scholarship that reconciles universal commitments with local traditions—so that Central Asian states act not merely as subjects of international law but as co-authors of its future.

Keywords International organizations · Central Asia · International law · Sovereignty · Human rights · Trade · Security · Environmental governance · OSCE · EAEU · CSTO · CIS

4.1 Introduction and Research Question

Since gaining independence from the Soviet Union in 1991, the Central Asian republics of Kazakhstan, Kyrgyzstan, Tajikistan, Turkmenistan, and Uzbekistan have undergone dramatic transitions in their legal, political, and economic systems. As

S. Sakhariyev (✉)
KIMEP University, Almaty, Kazakhstan
e-mail: s.sakhariyev@kimep.kz

S. Sayapin (ed.), *International Law, Politics and Security in Central Asia*,
https://doi.org/10.1007/978-3-032-17818-3_4

relatively new members of the international community, these states have actively engaged with international organizations to facilitate nation-building and institutional development. In doing so, they have become embedded in global legal regimes that both support and constrain their sovereignty.

International organizations—ranging from global entities such as the United Nations, the World Bank, and the World Trade Organization to regional bodies like the Shanghai Cooperation Organisation (SCO) and the Eurasian Economic Union (EAEU)—have played a pivotal role in shaping the development of international law in Central Asia. These actors have introduced legal frameworks and standards that affect human rights, trade, public governance, security, and regional cooperation.[1] This chapter examines how international organizations have influenced the development of international law in Central Asia. It critically assesses the normative impact of these organizations on legal institutions, law-making processes, and regional legal integration. Drawing on Third World Approaches to International Law (TWAIL), this study views law not merely as a tool for technical reform but as a historically contingent and politically charged domain in which power asymmetries are reproduced or challenged.

The chapter is structured as follows: it outlines the theoretical foundations of TWAIL and explains its relevance to post-Soviet statehood, provides an overview of how legal sovereignty evolved in Central Asia following independence, explores the role of key international organizations in legal norm development, and reflects on the region's legal future and the possibilities for decolonial engagement with international law through the work of international organizations.

4.2 TWAIL and Postcolonial International Law

Third World Approaches to International Law (hereinafter—'TWAIL') emerged as a critical movement in response to the Eurocentric foundations of international law and its colonial legacy. TWAIL scholars argue that international law has historically served as a justification for conquest, the imposition of unequal treaties, and the marginalization of non-European legal systems.[2] TWAIL challenges the narrative of international law as a neutral and universal system by exposing its embedded structures of inequality.

Central to TWAIL is the critique of sovereignty. TWAIL scholars contend that the sovereignty granted to postcolonial states is often formal rather than substantive. This 'conditional sovereignty' is constrained by legal regimes and economic structures imposed by global institutions. TWAIL highlights the tension between formal independence and continued subordination through international law, often in the form

[1] Rankin (2025).

[2] Anghie (2005).

of development conditionalities, trade rules, and human rights enforcement mechanisms.[3] TWAIL also emphasizes resistance and the possibility of emancipatory legal reform. It recognizes that international law is not monolithic; within its structure lie opportunities for reinterpretation, norm contestation, and legal pluralism. Postcolonial states can use international legal frameworks to assert their agency and challenge dominant narratives.

For Central Asia, TWAIL provides an analytical lens to understand how post-Soviet states have navigated legal modernity under the shadow of external control. The region's colonial history under Russian and Soviet rule, followed by rapid integration into global legal regimes, mirrors the experiences of other postcolonial regions. However, Central Asia's unique geostrategic position and inherited socialist legal traditions complicate conventional TWAIL narratives. Scholars such as Antony Anghie and Obiora Okafor have argued that sovereignty in postcolonial contexts must be viewed as a negotiated legal space. In Central Asia, international organizations have intervened in constitution-making, legal education, judicial reform, and trade regulation.[4] These interventions, though often framed as neutral technical assistance, reflect power hierarchies in which donor priorities shape domestic legal orders.

Moreover, TWAIL critiques the technocratic rationality of international organizations, which tends to depoliticize law. Legal reforms are often presented as apolitical modernization, ignoring the historical and cultural specificities of recipient states. TWAIL calls for a more pluralistic, dialogic, and context-sensitive approach to legal development, particularly in postcolonial regions. The TWAIL framework is particularly attentive to the normative contradictions embedded in international law. On the one hand, it serves as a source of legitimacy for postcolonial states to assert equal membership in the international system; on the other, it remains anchored in rules and institutions historically crafted by and for dominant powers. TWAIL thus insists on a double move: critique and reconstruction. It seeks not only to expose the structural inequalities of the international legal order but also to propose alternative approaches grounded in local experience and transnational solidarity.[5]

Central Asia presents a fertile terrain for applying TWAIL analysis. Despite the region's relative absence from early TWAIL scholarship, recent contributions have begun to situate Central Asia within global postcolonial dynamics. For instance, scholars have pointed to the region's experience of 'double colonialism'—first under the Russian Empire, then Soviet socialism—and its contemporary subjection to international conditionalities as evidence of enduring colonial patterns. The legal dimensions of this continuity are visible in trade law, human rights law, environmental law, and economic regulation. In light of these dynamics, this chapter adopts a TWAIL perspective to critically examine the mechanisms through which international law is produced, implemented, and contested in Central Asia. It seeks to trace how legal norms are transmitted, translated, and sometimes transformed within the region.

[3] Chimni (2006).

[4] Rankin (2025).

[5] Mutua (2000).

It also considers how Central Asian states strategically engage with international organizations to navigate between global expectations and domestic priorities.

4.3 Central Asia's Legal Sovereignty Post-1991

4.3.1 From Nominal Independence to Legal Contestation

The dissolution of the Soviet Union in 1991 formally emancipated the Central Asian republics from a multinational imperial formation. Yet this independence did not equate to legal or institutional autonomy in the fullest sense. Unlike former colonies in Africa or South Asia, Central Asian states did not inherit constitutional traditions forged in anti-colonial struggle, nor did they reject Soviet legal systems wholesale. Instead, they entered the post-Soviet international order as *de-facto* dependent states, compelled to engage with international law under conditions of asymmetrical power. While sovereignty was internationally recognized, it remained substantively incomplete. Each state lacked mature legal institutions, constitutional consensus, and the normative infrastructure necessary to exercise full agency within the global legal order. Their admission into the United Nations and accession to major treaties marked symbolic thresholds, but the actual content of law—civil, constitutional, administrative, environmental, and trade—remained heavily shaped by external actors. This paradox illustrates what Antony Anghie describes as the 'colonial genealogy of sovereignty', where sovereignty itself is a product of hierarchical legal relations between the core and periphery.

4.3.2 Legal Sovereignty in a Postcolonial Eurasian Context

The TWAIL framework is helpful in understanding how sovereignty in Central Asia was both conferred and constrained through legal mechanisms. Formal independence allowed for participation in global legal fora, yet the modalities of that participation—treaty ratification, loan conditionality, technical assistance—often translated into the importation of foreign legal templates. This process echoes what BS Chimni termed 'the civilizing mission of international law', where law becomes the vector for external reform rather than internal transformation.[6] For example, in the early 1990s, Kazakhstan undertook sweeping constitutional reform with assistance from the Venice Commission and the OSCE, producing a hybrid legal system that retained Soviet elements while incorporating liberal-democratic norms. Yet the resulting institutions, particularly the executive-heavy presidency, reflect a selective internalization of external legal models. Meanwhile, the Kyrgyz Republic, often hailed as the most

[6] Chimni (2006).

liberal polity in the region, embraced an open constitutional process but remained dependent on foreign aid for implementation.[7] These cases suggest that the emergence of post-Soviet constitutionalism was less an expression of decolonial agency than a negotiated compromise between global norms and domestic consolidation of power.

4.3.3 Legal Reform Through External Templates

The legal codes of all five states—civil, criminal, and administrative—were drafted or revised with significant support from international organizations. These reforms rarely emerged from local legislative traditions. Rather, they were modeled on European civil codes, North American constitutional doctrines, and transnational governance standards, as well as Soviet traditions.

4.3.4 Selective Sovereignty and Norm Internalization

Central Asian states have demonstrated both compliance and resistance in their legal engagements with international organizations. Turkmenistan, for instance, has ratified major human rights treaties but delays implementation of its obligations in relation to core political and civil rights. Kazakhstan, meanwhile, embraced multivector diplomacy not only in geopolitics but also in law. It has signed treaties with the European Union, participated in SCO-led legal harmonization, and positioned itself as a norm entrepreneur in environmental and trade law. Yet this flexibility comes at the cost of systemic incoherence, as competing legal norms—from civil law, Islamic traditions, and authoritarian executive doctrines—coexist uneasily. These strategies illustrate selective sovereignty—a form of legal pragmatism wherein states accept certain norms for strategic benefit while resisting others that challenge domestic power structures.[8]

4.3.5 Sovereignty Beyond the State: Informal Legal Orders

Another dimension of Central Asia's legal sovereignty lies outside state institutions. Throughout the region, informal governance structures such as *aksakal* councils (elders), neighborhood communities, and tribal networks coexist with formal law, and are sometimes introduced in legislation. While international legal reform efforts

[7] Venice Commission (2021).

[8] Mutua (2000).

typically overlook these systems, they are crucial to understanding the actual operation of law on the ground. In many Central Asian states informal dispute resolution mechanisms continue to adjudicate property disputes or family conflicts. For TWAIL, such hybrid legalities are not merely artifacts of underdevelopment—they are expressions of local agency, often more legitimate than imported norms. In Kazakhstan, for example, voices are heard for reestablishment of nomadic laws in national legislation. Nevertheless, the coexistence of these systems with formal law presents challenges. Legal pluralism can entrench patriarchal or exclusionary practices, particularly in areas such as gender rights or minority protections. Yet the outright rejection of these systems by international organizations often leads to normative dissonance and implementation failure.

4.3.6 A Region in Legal Transition

Three decades after independence, Central Asia remains in legal transition. Its sovereignty is continuously renegotiated through treaty commitments, technical cooperation, and regional legal harmonization. While some international organizations have enabled legal capacity-building, others have also perpetuated structural asymmetries and normative dependency. The region's experience underscores the TWAIL claim that international law is neither neutral nor universal; it is a contested site where sovereignty is reconstructed under conditions of legal and political hierarchy. Central Asia's legal sovereignty is best understood as a layered condition—formally recognized, structurally constrained, and contextually hybrid. By situating the region within a postcolonial framework, we can better analyze how law functions both as a vehicle for emancipation and as an instrument of regulation. As the next section demonstrates, international organizations have played a pivotal role in shaping this paradoxical legal order.

4.4 International Organizations and Legal Development in Central Asia

International organizations have played a pivotal role in shaping the trajectory of legal development in post-Soviet Central Asia. These institutions—multilateral, regional, and issue-specific—have engaged with the region through instruments ranging from treaty ratification and technical assistance to normative harmonization and institutional capacity-building. While many of these engagements have facilitated modernization and legal reform, they have also reproduced asymmetries in normative authority and institutional dependency, echoing the concerns raised by TWAIL scholars about the hegemonic functions of international law.

4.4.1 The United Nations: Human Rights and Legal Reform

The United Nations has been deeply involved in Central Asia's legal development since the early 1990s. Upon gaining independence, each republic joined the UN and subsequently acceded to its major human rights treaties. These included the International Covenant on Civil and Political Rights (ICCPR), the Convention Against Torture (CAT), and the Convention on the Elimination of All Forms of Discrimination Against Women (CEDAW). Through its treaty bodies and special procedures, the UN system has exerted normative influence over constitutional design, criminal justice reform, and rights-based governance.[9] In Central Asian states, it helped to strengthen human rights protections and minority inclusion, as well as the adoption of legislation on gender equality, anti-torture safeguards, and child protection. However, local enforcement mechanisms remain weak, and the transposition of international norms into domestic law often proceeded without institutional buy-in. Such reforms risk becoming performative rather than transformative—fulfilling reporting obligations while leaving structural conditions unchanged.[10] For example, it took a series of high-profile criminal cases on violence against women in Kazakhstan to improve legal protections for women against gender-based violence. It was only after a publicly streamed court case in 2024 that Saltanat's Law (i.e., a series of amendments to legislation enacting harsher criminalization of gender-based violence named after a victim of such violence) was adopted.[11]

4.4.2 The Organization for Security and Cooperation in Europe (OSCE): Democratization and Rule of Law

The OSCE has been particularly active in Central Asia, combining diplomatic presence with legal and political engagement. Its Office for Democratic Institutions and Human Rights (ODIHR) has provided legislative reviews, election monitoring, and rule of law training across the region. In Kyrgyzstan, the OSCE has provided legal advice on electoral law, civil society legislation, and freedom of expression. Notably, its support during the 2010–2011 constitutional process helped entrench proportional representation and judicial review mechanisms. Yet these reforms coincided with volatile political transitions, and critics argue that the OSCE's emphasis on formal legal changes underestimated the embedded nature of informal power networks. In Uzbekistan and Kazakhstan, the OSCE promoted media law reform and judicial transparency. However, its normative agenda—rooted in liberal-democratic values—was frequently resisted by political elites who viewed it as externally driven. In Turkmenistan, OSCE efforts have been limited by the government's refusal to allow

[9] Sayapin (2022).

[10] Mutua (2000).

[11] Drobny (2024).

substantial political liberalization. The OSCE has still successfully supported various human rights related projects in Central Asia, for example human rights summer school in Kazakhstan, not to mention the creation of the OSCE Academy in Bishkek, Kyrgyzstan.

From a TWAIL perspective, the OSCE exemplifies the export of Euro-Atlantic normative frameworks into postcolonial contexts. Its work on capacity-building and dialogue facilitation, as well as general legal framework improvement has been successful. However, it often replicates the assumption that liberal norms are universally applicable, regardless of historical and cultural specificities.

4.4.3 The World Trade Organization: Trade Law and Market Liberalization

Kyrgyzstan was the first post-Soviet country to accede to the World Trade Organization (WTO) in 1998, followed by Kazakhstan in 2015. Uzbekistan has been in the accession process since the early 1990s. WTO accession necessitates comprehensive legal changes, including amendments to customs law, intellectual property regimes, competition policy, and sanitary standards.

For Kyrgyzstan, the rapid implementation of WTO rules brought both benefits and vulnerabilities. On the one hand, accession improved access to international markets and attracted limited foreign direct investment. On the other, it imposed obligations that many domestic producers—particularly in agriculture—could not meet due to the sudden exposure to global competition. Legal harmonization in this context deepened economic inequalities and weakened the state's ability to regulate in the public interest. Kazakhstan's accession process was more measured, involving multi-year negotiations and staged reforms. New laws were enacted on investor protection, anti-monopoly regulation, and technical standards. The legal system was brought into closer alignment with WTO rules, including dispute resolution procedures. However, critics argue that these changes benefited multinational investors more than local firms, as complex compliance requirements excluded many domestic actors.

TWAIL critiques emphasize the WTO's role in privileging strong states and corporations. The Dispute Settlement Body, while celebrated for its rule-based processes, disproportionately favors actors with legal expertise and financial resources. For Central Asian states, WTO membership offers legal predictability but also curtails policy space. Such legal liberalization without developmental safeguards risks entrenching dependency rather than promoting agency.[12]

[12] Shaffer (2003) and Rodrik (2007).

4.4.4 The Shanghai Cooperation Organisation: Security and Legal Cooperation

The Shanghai Cooperation Organisation (SCO) is often described as a post-Western regionalism initiative. Founded by China and Russia alongside the Central Asian states, the SCO has promoted legal cooperation in counterterrorism, cybercrime, and transborder security. While it does not operate a supranational legal system akin to the EU, it has fostered normative convergence through declarations, joint protocols, and technical working groups. Kazakhstan, Uzbekistan, and Tajikistan have adopted SCO-aligned legal provisions criminalizing extremism, enhancing border surveillance, and regulating digital communication. Critics have raised concerns that these laws, though formally legalistic, enable political repression and violate civil liberties. For instance, in Uzbekistan, counter-extremism laws have been used to detain political dissidents and restrict religious expression. Similarly, Kazakhstan's cybersecurity laws—aligned with SCO frameworks—have expanded state surveillance under the pretext of national security.

TWAIL scholars would interpret the SCO as both a counter-hegemonic and hegemonic actor. On the one hand, it resists Western dominance by promoting regional security governance. On the other, it replicates authoritarian legal models under the guise of sovereignty. The SCO represents 'authoritarian regionalism'—a legal order premised on stability over rights and unity over diversity.

4.4.5 The Eurasian Economic Union: Legal Harmonization and Economic Sovereignty

The Eurasian Economic Union (EAEU), led by Russia and joined by Kazakhstan and Kyrgyzstan, represents a more structured legal integration project. It creates a common market and legal space governed by a supranational court, the Eurasian Economic Commission, with harmonized regulations. For Kazakhstan, EAEU membership required aligning laws on customs, labor mobility, technical standards, and dispute settlement. While these changes improved intra-regional trade flows, they also limited legislative autonomy. National parliaments had to transpose EAEU directives without substantial modification, raising concerns about democratic accountability. Kyrgyzstan's accession to the EAEU in 2015 followed extensive legal revisions. Laws on phytosanitary measures, migration, and financial regulation were harmonized with EAEU standards. However, the legal transition was costly, requiring institutional restructuring and compliance with complex protocols. Local industries faced challenges adjusting to new regulatory environments. The EAEU is thus a legal arrangement where formal independence is maintained, but substantive policymaking is ceded to regional bodies. While EAEU integration supports South-South cooperation in theory, it also entrenches Russia's normative dominance, leaving smaller states with limited bargaining power.

4.4.6 *Summary: IOs as Architects of Legal Sovereignty*

International organizations have profoundly shaped the legal architecture of post-Soviet Central Asia. Their roles range from lawmaking (WTO, EAEU), to norm promotion (UN, OSCE), to institutional design. While they have contributed to legal modernization and institutional capacity-building, they have also imposed models that prioritize conformity over contextual legitimacy. These engagements illustrate how law becomes a medium of governance that reflects and reinforces global hierarchies. International organizations have not only facilitated the legal development of Central Asian states but have also circumscribed their sovereignty, often under the rubric of technical neutrality. The next section explores this duality further, analyzing how international law acts simultaneously as a constraint and an enabler in the postcolonial condition.

4.5 Law as Constraint and Enabler in Postcolonial Central Asia

International law in Central Asia functions within a deeply ambivalent framework—simultaneously enabling legal modernization, institutional consolidation, and global integration, while also constraining sovereignty, reproducing dependency, and marginalizing local agency. This chapter explores the contradictory nature of international legal development, demonstrating how international law acts both as a tool of emancipation and a mechanism of global discipline in post-Soviet Eurasia.

4.5.1 *Negotiating Sovereignty in Unequal Legal Orders*

One of the defining features of post-Soviet legal reform in Central Asia has been the heavy reliance on international expertise. From WTO-aligned commercial reforms in Kyrgyzstan[13] and Kazakhstan[14] to UNDP-supported constitutional drafting in Kazakhstan, the legal norms adopted by Central Asian states have been overwhelmingly shaped by external templates. These include civil law codes modeled on European systems, human rights norms from UN treaties, and economic liberalization measures promoted by the World Bank and IMF. This model of reform reflects what TWAIL scholars describe as epistemic hierarchy—a structure in which knowledge production about law, governance, and development is concentrated in the Global North and exported as technical assistance to the Global South. International law's authority is not merely normative but epistemological: it defines what counts as 'modern law'

[13] WTO (2021), Trade Policy Review.

[14] WTO (2025), Trade Policy Review.

and who is qualified to author it. Central Asian legal development, in this sense, has been filtered through a global hierarchy of expertise that privileges imported knowledge over local legal traditions.

For example, the adoption of anti-corruption legislation based on Transparency International benchmarks in Kyrgyzstan is rarely accompanied by mechanisms that reflect local values or dispute resolution traditions.[15] Customary practices such as *aksakal* mediation councils in Kyrgyzstan, *mahalla* governance in Uzbekistan, or religious jurisprudence are often ignored or marginalized despite their functional importance and 'popular' legitimacy. Reform processes rarely include these mechanisms in meaningful ways, leaving legal systems formalistically sound but socially disconnected. This dynamic mirrors the TWAIL critique of 'legal imperialism': the tendency of international law to overwrite local legal cultures with universalist norms that reflect the values of powerful states or international organizations.

Despite the constraining effects of international legal engagements, Central Asian states are not passive recipients of global norms. Rather, they practice what has been termed selective sovereignty—the strategic adoption, adaptation, or resistance to international legal obligations based on domestic interests, regime security, or geopolitical positioning. It can be seen as a case of instrumental engagement, where postcolonial states use international law both to assert formal sovereignty and to legitimize domestic policies that may otherwise contradict global liberal norms.[16] Kazakhstan, for example, has actively used legal harmonization with WTO and EAEU standards to attract foreign investment and diversify its economy,[17] yet it has resisted international pressure on democratic reforms or political pluralism, revealing a selective approach to legal convergence. Similarly, Uzbekistan under President Mirziyoyev has implemented targeted human rights reforms—particularly around forced labor and judicial independence—to meet eligibility for trade benefits, while preserving tight control over political opposition.

Turkmenistan presents another instructive case. It has formally ratified key international treaties, including CEDAW and the Convention Against Torture (CAT), but implementation remains minimal. Civil society in the country is heavily restricted, and international legal standards often serve symbolic or declarative roles rather than facilitating genuine reform.[18,19] This occurs to the extent that some discriminatory provisions against women are directly provided in legislation and legislative amendments, and have not been repealed regardless of being previously highlighted by the relevant human rights mechanisms. These examples illustrate how legal hybridity in the region permits governments to reap the benefits of international legitimacy while insulating themselves from deeper normative transformation.

---

[15] TI (2024).

[16] Okafor (2007).

[17] WTO (2025), Trade Policy Review.

[18] Committee on the Elimination of Discrimination against Women (2024), Concluding observations on the sixth periodic report of Turkmenistan.

[19] Committee against Torture and Other Cruel, Inhuman or Degrading Treatment or Punishment (2025).

TWAIL scholarship emphasizes that this hybridity is not a failure of law but a manifestation of its political nature. International legal norms are not universally internalized; they are negotiated, co-opted, and at times resisted, especially by states operating under conditions of structural inequality and historical marginalization. Amid global and regional legal engagements, Central Asian societies have continued to rely on informal legal institutions, customary practices, and religious norms. These local systems coexist with formal legal codes but often operate under different logics: consensus over litigation, elders over judges, restitution over punishment. TWAIL scholarship argues that legitimacy is not derived from formality alone, but from cultural resonance and historical continuity. The marginalization of local legal systems in the name of universal human rights or technical efficiency risks undermining both legal legitimacy and efficacy.

Kyrgyzstan's *aksakal* courts Beyer (2015) and Uzbekistan's mahalla councils provide well-known examples of such enduring customary mechanisms. These institutions resolve civil disputes and local conflicts using traditional practices with significant community legitimacy. However, their place within the broader legal system is precarious. *Aksakal* courts, for instance, enjoy quasi-official status but often lack procedural safeguards and are criticized for gender bias and opaque decision-making. In Uzbekistan, *mahalla* courts have been partially formalized under state oversight, limiting their autonomy. Efforts to integrate informal justice mechanisms into formal systems have produced mixed results. While some actors view these systems as efficient and socially rooted, international organizations often treat them as peripheral to legal modernization. TWAIL's call for legal pluralism emphasizes the importance of inclusive norm production—where law is not imposed from above but co-created through participatory processes that validate multiple forms of legal reasoning.

4.5.2 Legal Reform, Conditionality, and Dependency

A central tension in Central Asia's legal development lies in the relationship between reform and dependency. International organizations such as the World Bank and IMF have conditioned their assistance on the adoption of specific legal reforms—commercial relations, property laws, anti-corruption statutes, and investment protections. These reforms have often prioritized market efficiency over social equity, exposing domestic economies to external volatility and weakening the state's redistributive capacities.

In Kyrgyzstan, IMF-backed structural adjustment led to the privatization of the energy and agricultural sectors, followed by increases in inequality and a weakening of local governance. In Tajikistan, World Bank funding for hydropower projects was contingent on environmental and commercial legal frameworks that privileged multinational corporate interests over local communities. These legal conditionalities constitute a form of submission to global government—a regime of legal rationalities, incentives, and obligations that disciplines postcolonial states through market-oriented governance. Legal compliance becomes a prerequisite for development assistance, and sovereign decision-making is effectively bounded by external expectations. Critically, the formal legality of these reforms does not shield them from contestation. Local actors, civil society groups, and even state institutions have expressed resistance to externally imposed legal models. This resistance often manifests not as outright rejection but as informal non-compliance, bureaucratic stalling, or alternative legal interpretations. TWAIL scholars view these forms of resistance as constitutive of postcolonial agency, even within constrained legal environments. While resistance of local NGOs to imported legal 'best-practices' sometimes adds to consideration of national or cultural features, it may also be used as a tool to create obstacles for the provision of protection by international legal standards. For example, the Kazakhstan Parents Association, an NGO working in the area of promotion of traditional family values in Kazakhstan, has conducted activities against the development of human rights protections for the LGBT community and women's rights on several occasions under the umbrella of protection of cultural heritage.[20]

4.5.3 Regionalism as Legal Strategy: SCO and EAEU

While global institutions like the UN and WTO have shaped Central Asia's legal landscape through treaty regimes and normative frameworks, regional institutions such as the SCO and EAEU have offered alternative pathways to legal development—albeit with their own constraints. The SCO, emphasizing principles of sovereignty, non-interference, and security cooperation, has promoted legal frameworks on terrorism, extremism, and cybercrime. These frameworks have enabled Central Asian states to pass domestic laws that align with regional priorities while resisting Western liberal norms. However, these same laws have also been used to suppress political dissent, restrict media, and limit religious freedoms—practices that contradict international human rights standards. The EAEU has fostered deeper legal harmonization through supranational regulatory bodies and binding legal instruments. Kazakhstan and Kyrgyzstan have adjusted national legislation on trade, customs, and labor migration to conform to EAEU norms. While this has enhanced regional integration and legal predictability, it has also reduced the domestic policy space, especially for smaller states with limited negotiating power.

TWAIL perspectives do not view regionalism uncritically. While South-South cooperation can be a means of resisting Western legal hegemony, regional institutions may replicate hierarchical structures under the leadership of more powerful states. Russia's dominance in the EAEU and China's normative influence in the SCO raise questions about whether these institutions truly offer emancipatory legal alternatives or merely shift the locus of legal authority.

---

[20] Mohireva (2025), The Village Kazakhstan (2023).

4.5.4 *Reclaiming Normative Agency*

Despite their structural vulnerabilities, Central Asian states are not excluded from the making of international law. Through participation in international organizations, regional bodies, and treaty negotiations, they contribute—albeit unevenly—to norm development. Kazakhstan's leadership in environmental governance within the SCO, Uzbekistan's engagement with WTO legal processes, and Tajikistan's advocacy for water rights in regional fora are all examples of normative agency. However, this agency remains constrained by global legal hierarchies, limited capacity, and geopolitical dependencies. TWAIL emphasizes the need to democratize norm creation—to ensure that formerly colonized and structurally marginalized states have a meaningful voice in shaping the legal regimes that affect them. For Central Asia, this means building legal institutions that reflect domestic priorities, promoting education and legal scholarship that decenters Western epistemologies, and forming regional alliances that advocate for equitable legal standards in global governance.

In Central Asia, international law operates as a double-edged instrument. It has contributed to state-building, rule-of-law reform, and global integration. At the same time, it has constrained sovereignty, entrenched normative dependency, and marginalized local agency. This paradox reflects a broader postcolonial condition in which the law is not merely a reflection of justice but a terrain of contestation, hierarchy, and negotiation. Understanding this complexity requires moving beyond simplistic dichotomies of compliance and resistance. As TWAIL suggests, postcolonial states engage international law strategically, instrumentally, and often creatively. They are not merely subject to global norms but co-producers of legal orders—if often under unequal conditions. By critically examining the enabling and constraining functions of law, we gain insight into the ways in which Central Asia navigates its post-Soviet, postcolonial trajectory. The final chapter turns to the normative implications of this analysis, asking what lessons the Central Asian experience offers for the future of international legal development.

4.6 Rethinking International Law Through Central Asia and the Work of International Organizations

The Central Asian republics—Kazakhstan, Kyrgyzstan, Uzbekistan, Tajikistan, and Turkmenistan—emerged from the collapse of the Soviet Union into a world already saturated with legal norms, institutional hierarchies, and powerful international organizations. Since 1991, their sovereign trajectories have been shaped not only by internal political dynamics but also by a dense web of international legal instruments, development agencies, regional alliances, and normative regimes.

Through sustained engagement with critical postcolonial perspectives—particularly Third World Approaches to International Law—it has become clear that international law in the region is not a neutral facilitator of justice but a complex architecture of influence. Law has enabled post-Soviet state-building, facilitated accession to global markets, and expanded institutional capacity. But it has also constrained domestic agency, entrenched external dependency, and obscured the epistemic hierarchies that govern legal reform.

International organizations such as the United Nations, the World Bank, the International Monetary Fund, the World Trade Organization, the OSCE, the Shanghai Cooperation Organisation, and the Eurasian Economic Union have each played roles in shaping legal development in the region. Their interventions have ranged from normative standard-setting and technical assistance to binding legal obligations and regional harmonization. These engagements have had transformative effects on constitutions, civil and commercial codes, judicial systems, human rights legislation, and administrative law. Yet the legal development fostered by these organizations has rarely been organic or locally driven. Legal codes have often been imported wholesale, reflecting the assumptions and priorities of donor states and institutions rather than the historical, cultural, and normative foundations of Central Asian societies. Technical assistance has privileged global 'best practices' over context-sensitive solutions, and legal compliance has frequently served to secure financial flows or political legitimacy rather than meaningful reform.

Despite these structural constraints, Central Asian states are not mere objects of international legal authority. They exercise strategic agency—selectively adopting, resisting, or reframing legal norms to protect regime interests, respond to public demands, or navigate geopolitical alliances. Kazakhstan's legal diplomacy, Uzbekistan's incremental reforms, Kyrgyzstan's experimentation with pluralism, Tajikistan's post-conflict legal evolution, and Turkmenistan's guarded isolation all reveal different strategies of engagement. These strategies underscore TWAIL's assertion that postcolonial states are both constrained by and active within international legal orders.

The role of regional institutions such as the SCO and EAEU is particularly instructive. They offer non-Western platforms for legal cooperation and norm production, allowing Central Asian states to diversify their legal alignments. However, they too are embedded in hierarchical dynamics, often dominated by Russia or China, and risk substituting one form of dependency for another. Thus, regionalism, while potentially emancipatory, must be critically assessed through the same lens as global institutions.

A central takeaway from this study is that legal development must be decolonized not only in form but in process. This means acknowledging the plurality of legal traditions, promoting participation in norm-setting, resisting one-size-fits-all technical models, and valuing legal knowledge produced within the region. It also means supporting regional legal scholarship, judicial dialogue, and civic legal empowerment that reflect Central Asian experiences and priorities.

At the same time, it is essential to recognize that international law and the work of international organizations remain indispensable instruments for the maintenance and affirmation of the independence and sovereignty of Central Asian states. Engagement with international legal regimes has enabled these states to assert their presence in global governance, secure recognition as equal sovereigns, and access frameworks for cooperation, dispute resolution, and institutional development. Rather than rejecting international norms outright, the more enduring challenge lies in harmonizing these universal legal values—such as human rights, rule of law, and accountability—with local legal traditions, cultural frameworks, and historical experiences. This process of normative reconciliation requires not only legal technicality but also epistemic humility: a recognition that international law must evolve through dialogical encounters with diverse legal cultures. For Central Asia, the path forward is not disengagement but the cultivation of a pluralistic legal order in which sovereignty is both preserved and meaningfully exercised through informed, context-sensitive engagement with international law. Ultimately, Central Asia's experience reflects a broader postcolonial legal condition—marked by formal sovereignty, structural constraints, and a perpetual negotiation between compliance and autonomy.[21] The study of legal development in this region contributes to a growing body of scholarship that calls for a more just and pluralistic international legal order, one in which formerly colonized and marginalized states are not merely recipients of law but recognized as co-authors of its future.

References

Anghie A (2005) Imperialism, sovereignty and the making of international law. Cambridge University Press, Cambridge. https://doi.org/10.1017/CBO9780511614262

Beyer J (2015) Customizations of law: courts of elders (Aksakal courts) in rural and urban Kyrgyzstan. PoLAR Polit Leg Anthropol Rev 38(1):53–61

Chimni BS (2006) Third world approaches to international law: A Manifesto. Int Commun Law Rev 8(1):3–27

Committee on the Elimination of Discrimination against Women (2024) Concluding observations on the sixth periodic report of Turkmenistan

Committee against Torture (2025) Concluding observations on the third periodic report of Turkmenistan

Drobny N (2024) Tokayev has signed the "Saltanat's Law", Orda.kz. https://orda.kz/tokaev-podpisal-zakon-saltanat-385129/

IDLO (2019) Practitioner brief: navigating complex pathways to justice: engagement with customary and informal justice systems. International Development Law Organization, Rome. https://www.idlo.int/sites/default/files/pdfs/publications/IDLO-Practitioner-Brief-Customary-and-Informal-Justice-Feb2019-LR.pdf

Mohireva A (2025) Parents Association has prevented feminist training in Almaty Again, Orda.kz. https://orda.kz/sojuz-roditelej-opjat-sorval-trening-feministok-v-almaty-398047/

Mutua M (2000) What is TWAIL? Proc Annu Meet (Am Soc Int Law) 94:31–38

Okafor OC (2007) The African Human Rights system, activist forces and international institutions. Cambridge University Press, Cambridge

Rankin J (2025) EU urged to put human rights centre stage at first Central Asia summit. The Guardian, Apr 4. https://www.theguardian.com/world/2025/apr/04/eu-urged-to-put-human-rights-centre-stage-at-first-central-asia-summit

Rodrik D (2007) One economics, many recipes: globalization, institutions, and economic growth. Princeton University Press, Princeton

Sayapin S (2022) International law in Central Asia: practices and doctrines. Rev CentL East Eur Law. https://doi.org/10.1163/15730352-bja10072

[21] Sayapin (2022).

Shaffer G (2003) Defending interests: public-private partnerships in WTO litigation. Brookings Institution Press, Washington, D.C.

TI (2024) Transparency International urges Kyrgyzstan's decision makers to withdraw law on "foreign representatives". https://www.transparency.org/en/press/transparency-international-urges-kyrgyzstans-decision-makers-to-withdraw-law-on-foreign-representatives

The Village Kazakhstan (2023) Parents Association has Identified LGBT Propaganda in Semey Children's Play. https://www.the-village-kz.com/village/city/news-city/32643-soyuz-roditeley-v-semee-uglyadel-lgbt-propagandu-v-detskom-spektakle-pro-druzhbu-malchika-s-gipoallerge

Venice Commission/Council of Europe (2021) Compilation of Venice commission opinions and reports in Central Asia. Council of Europe, Strasbourg. https://www.venice.coe.int/webforms/documents/default.aspx?pdffile=CDL-PI(2021)017-e

WTO (2021) Trade policy review. https://www.wto.org/english/tratop_e/tpr_e/s411_e.pdf

WTO (2025) Trade policy review. https://docs.wto.org/dol2fe/Pages/SS/directdoc.aspx?filename=q:/WT/TPR/S459R1.pdf&Open=True

Chapter 5
Between the Second and the Third Worlds: The Legal Postcoloniality of Central Asia

Akbar Rasulov

Abstract How can we understand the basic character of Central Asia's postcoloniality for international law purposes? What role have international institutions and international law scholarship played in clarifying or obfuscating this problem? The fall of the USSR 30 years ago brought an end to Russia's direct political rule over the region. The arrival of formal independence, however, was not matched by the parallel decoupling of legal and institutional modalities and traditions. Something similar, of course, had happened decades earlier in the former British and French colonies. What distinguishes the Central Asian case, however, was both the vector of the formal shift—Central Asian states gained independence from the preeminent power of the Second World, not the First World—and the rather distinct character of the post-independence transition processes. In many cases, these processes, choreographed and coordinated through a network of international institutions not existent at the time of the previous wave of decolonization, came to be shaped not just by the local aspirations toward independence but also an intense external pressure to adopt a particular combination of Western-style legal and political reform packages. A large part of what accounts for the way this pressure was realized in practice was the rise of a certain kind of international law imaginary: a combination of sanctioned ignorance, a firm belief in 'transition science', and a postmodern version of 'civilising mission'. The one crucial element that brought this ideological complex together was the consistent exoticization of Central Asia via the implicit denial of its postcolonial status. The structural shift that allowed this complex to turn into a practically active international law regime was the replacement of the classical modes of international coercion with modern-day techniques of 'adverse publicity'. As one set of colonial forms and dynamics gave way to another, the question of Central Asia's postcoloniality, already made politically opaque by the 'second-worldist' origins of the Soviet empire, receded ever further into the background. What exacerbated this process even more at the theoretical level was the persistent failure on the part of the international law discourse to maintain any degree of interest in the region. As the task of determining how international law and its institutions should approach and understand

A. Rasulov (✉)
School of Law, University of Glasgow, Glasgow, Scotland
e-mail: akbar.rasulov@glasgow.ac.uk

S. Sayapin (ed.), *International Law, Politics and Security in Central Asia*,
https://doi.org/10.1007/978-3-032-17818-3_5

Central Asia fell to non-lawyers, the resulting narratives about Central Asia and its place in the international legal arena took on increasingly neocolonialist overtones of the kind one would rarely see admitted in relation to other non-Western regions. The fact that the predominant mode of debating postcoloniality in international law in the post-Cold War era took on the form of 'Third World Approaches to International Law' certainly did not help either, as its inbuilt geographic imaginary of third-worldism implicitly relegated Central Asia even further beyond the limits of critical attention. This chapter is an attempt to push back against this trend. In critiquing the traditional international law conception of Central Asia that has emerged over the last thirty years and in rethinking the shape of Central Asia's legal postcoloniality, it offers reflections not only about the basic relationship between post-Sovietness and postcoloniality but also the broader challenge of conceptualizing decolonization, neocolonialism, and postcoloniality in contemporary international law.

Keywords Law and postcoloniality · Transitology · International economic law · Central Asia and international institutions · Standard of civilization · Informal international law

5.1 Introduction

Every discipline, Hayden White writes, is defined in the end as much by what it chooses to acknowledge and attend to in the world outside itself as by what it tries to ignore and pass over.[1] Looking at things from that perspective, the region of Central Asia must undoubtedly be recognized as one of the most character-defining blind spots in contemporary international law.

It is not obvious, to be fair, how international law should acknowledge and attend to Central Asia, rather that is to say, how international lawyers should view Central Asia and what they should know about it as international lawyers. That they must have *some* kind of idea about it and some kind of knowledge about it, seems relatively certain. Covering a territory of more than 4,000,000 square kilometers, home to some 83 million people and more than 120 different ethnic groups, Central Asia is not exactly so insignificant a piece of geopolitical reality that being ignorant of its existence can make basic pragmatic sense. And yet, curiously enough, the region, its history, politics, and economics, not to mention its record of past and present encounters with the broader international law system and its institutions,[2] have received

[1] See White (1978, p. 126).

[2] What would count as attention-worthy encounters is, of course, a matter of conjecture. But even without going as far back in history as Martti Koskenniemi does in *To the Uttermost Parts of the Earth*, one can easily identify a few solid candidates that most international lawyers would normally have an interest in: the manmade disaster in the Aral Sea (climate crisis, the law of the Anthropocene), Russian conquest and Soviet reconquest post-1918 (civilizing mission, colonialism), the Basmachi insurrection (anticolonial resistance, *jus in bello*), Silk Route trade (*lex mercatoria*, early global commodity chains), the role of international financial institutions in shaping the course of

virtually no mention in any of the leading international law textbooks published over the last three decades since it achieved its independence from Russia,[3] a fact that, one might add, puts Central Asia in stark contrast not only with the vast majority of the rest of the Asian continent but also with the rest of the former Soviet sphere.[4] Only a small handful of academic monographs and articles written by international law scholars from outside the region have made any effort to include within their ambit of inquiry any aspects of Central Asia's experience with international law; even fewer have made it part of their express focus.[5] Two hundred years after the infamously titled colonial adventure[6] first led Western imperial powers to a standoff on the slopes of the Pamir mountains, and nearly a quarter of a century since 'Operation Enduring Freedom' brought the first NATO troops into the valleys of Afghanistan,[7] Central Asia continues to remain an island of 'sanctioned ignorance' for the discipline of international law.

Still, behind every absence one can always find the trace of a presence. In the murky underside of an untroubled silence, a whole tradition of thought has grown up: a series of theories and knowledges about Central Asia, its present and its past, its place in history, and its relationship with international law. Even if international lawyers have not shown any real inclination to want to talk about Central Asia as international lawyers, there has still come into existence a large, well-developed body of discourse about Central Asia's place in the contemporary global legal arenas that has become practically operative in the sense that it has been taken up by the various institutions of the contemporary international legal system as the source of their common vision of what Central Asia 'is like' and 'what it can become'.

---

post-independence reforms (sovereign debt governance, expert rule), etc. Cf. Koskenniemi (2021) (retracing the story of Europe's encounters with what would end up becoming modern international law to 1300).

[3] See, e.g., Evans (2024), Von Arnauld (2023), Klabbers (2021), Crawford (2019), Combacau et Sur (2019), Dixon (2013), Cassese (2005), Dupuy (2004), Gardiner (2003), Malanczuk (1997). Not that the passage of time has brought any increase in attention. Compare Shaw (2003) (mentions Kazakhstan, Turkmenistan, and Tajikistan twice, though the latter is spelt differently on each occasion, and Kyrghyzstan (sic) and Uzbekistan once, when listing the names of those post-Soviet republics which agreed to abide by the EC Guidelines on the Recognition of New States in Eastern Europe and in the Soviet Union) with Shaw (2017) (same as before except that Turkmenistan now receives only one mention).

[4] Cf. Shaw (2017, pp. 161, 727–9) (repeatedly discussing the USSR's illegal annexation of the Baltic states and its implications for the way the law of state succession evolved). See also Shaw (2017, pp. 159, 189) (discussing Azerbaijan's experience with the lack of territorial contiguity and the legal implications of its conflict with Armenia over Nagorno-Karabakh).

[5] The only notable exceptions on this front are Newton (2017), Boyle (2003) Sievers (2002a) and (2002b).

[6] The name by which it is usually known in the Western tradition is the 'Great Game', a term whose authorship is usually attributed to one Arthur Connolly, a British spy executed by Bukharan authorities in 1842. Count Karl Nesselrode, Nicholas I's foreign minister, reportedly preferred a different designation: 'the tournament of shadows'. For a modern, unabashedly Eurocentric introduction to the subject, see Meyer and Blair Bryssac (1999).

[7] See CFR (2021).

At the heart of this vision lies a simple but powerful narrative that promises to make sense of the basic historical context shared by the five Central Asian states, their relationship with the rest of the world, and their place and trajectory in the contemporary legal and political arenas. Few international lawyers have ever acknowledged the existence of this narrative. None have subjected it to any degree of critical interrogation. And yet, the basic structure of imagination that this 'shadow narrative' projects, I want to argue, constitutes one of the most important factors that have influenced the way the contemporary international legal system and its institutions have approached and engaged Central Asia over the last thirty years: how they have come to view the five Central Asian states and their peoples; what they have come to believe them to be capable of, hopeful for, and predisposed to; and what place they decided they must occupy in the global political, legal, and economic arenas past and present. This structure of imagination to a very large extent still remains active today.

My aims in this chapter are essentially twofold. In the first place, I am going to try to uncover, critique, and problematize this thirty-year-old shadow narrative. In Sect. 5.2, I will map its main defining features. In Sects. 5.3 and 5.4, I will trace out and lay bare its implicit ideological messaging and the implications of this messaging. What sort of stance does it invite us to take toward Central Asia legally and politically? What sort of 'ethics' does it encourage us to assume in deciding how we should approach and engage Central Asia? With the descriptive and critical parts of the exercise completed, in the second stage, I am going to try to displace the basic structure of imagination that this shadow narrative has helped entrench by proposing another, alternative way of looking at Central Asia, its peoples, and its history from the standpoint of international law (Sects. 5.5 and 5.6).

The central point of contention that links these two alternative visions or interpretative frames—the basic question that separates them, in other words, but also connects them under the heading of a common theoretical problematic—is the question of *Central Asia's postcoloniality*. Should the five Central Asian states be regarded as postcolonial states, or is there another, more suitable category under which they can be meaningfully subsumed? What might the idea of postcoloniality even mean in this context? Can a post-Soviet state in international law also be regarded as postcolonial? To what extent can we consider Central Asia a part of the global South or the Third World? Bearing in mind Central Asia's Soviet past, that is to say, its previous membership of the paradigmatic Second World power, what do these questions tell us about the way these concepts have come to be operationalized in our thinking? What lessons does Central Asia have for contemporary international law and its politics of geopolitical imagination?

The indeterminacy of Central Asia's postcolonial status is certainly not an issue that is exclusive to international law. For good or ill, in most neighboring fields the state of the debate on the subject, however, appears by now to have reached a much more advanced stage.[8] If one were to hazard a guess as to what has prevented international lawyers from achieving the same measure of progress, the most plausible answer would be that the course of knowledge production in international law is not just decided in academic contexts. How the question of Central Asia's postcoloniality can be resolved in international law is a function not only of the way in which this question typically gets raised or framed in the academic legal debate but also of the patterns of treatment it receives in the official discourses of international legal practice, not least those of positive international law.

From this standpoint, the state of play could hardly seem more unfavorable for Central Asia. Even the shortest survey of the relevant sources will show that in the eyes of positive international law Central Asia has never been recognized as either an object of colonial annexation (by Russia and then the USSR) or a theater of anti-colonial struggle (on the part of the so-called '*Basmachis*'). The five ex-Soviet Central Asian republics have never been identified as non-self-governing territories for the purposes of Chapter XI of the United Nations Charter. The reach of the General Assembly Resolution 1514 was never extended to them. Even in the field of state succession, a virtually universal consensus right from the start has been to view the five Central Asian republics as the successor states of the former USSR rather than as 'newly independent states', a legal-political category originally applied to the formerly colonized states after World War II.[9]

Proceeding against such a background, the idea of trying to reorient how the discipline of international law constructs its 'idea' of Central Asia by problematizing the question of Central Asia's postcoloniality may not look like the most obvious solution. If one were to maximize the chances of generating a new intra-disciplinary consensus, surely a far more effective strategy would have been to choose a topic that has not been so persistently evaded in positive international law. Alas, for better or for worse, there does not seem to be much room for maneuvering in this case. The problem of Central Asia's postcoloniality *is* the central defining problem around which international law's ideological relationship with Central Asia revolves today. There is no getting around it: every question we as international lawyers can pose today about Central Asia sooner or later inevitably returns to it. One might call it, in this sense, international law's theoretical ground zero for Central Asia. For, like every ground-zero question, what it reflects in the end is not so much the actual starting point for the resulting body of knowledge as the basic condition of its possibility.

---

[8] See e.g., Kassymbekova and Chokobaeva (2021), Roche (2018), Abashin (2015), Northrop (2004), Myer (2002).

[9] For further discussion, see Rasulov (2003, pp. 154–65).

5.2 Central Asian Transitology as an Exercise in Historicized Exoticization: The Anatomy of a Narrative Strategy

A certain interpretative framework has emerged over the last three decades that has come to shape the way the contemporary international legal system and its institutions recognize, understand, and approach the five Central Asian states. At the core of this framework stands an easily recognizable narrative—a way of representing and depicting Central Asia—that operates simultaneously as a vehicle of expert knowledge, a policy vision, a normative agenda, and a carefully coded message about the personal politics of those who embrace its main starting premises.[10] From a literary-theoretical point of view, one might describe it as an ideologeme.[11] From the critical-legal point of view, its main function is the legitimization of a certain set of *international legal policies*.

Because of its close relationship with the sub-field of political science studies called transitology, one might call this narrative the narrative of *Central Asian Transitology (CAT)*. It is not my intention in these pages to review the full intellectual genealogy of the transitology field.[12] What needs to be noted, however, is that although CAT certainly represents a part of the broader field of post-Soviet transitology discourse, its political orientation and ideologematic dynamics remain highly distinctive. Without recognizing this distinctiveness, the role that the CAT tradition has come to play in the contemporary international legal imagination is impossible to appreciate.

Most writers and institutions that have contributed to the initial development and spread of the CAT discourse would not usually be regarded as participants in international legal debates.[13] But just as the evolution of historical narratives is not only shaped by the work of professional historians, so too the formation of the collective imaginary operationalized in the practice of international law and its broader institutional regime is not a product merely of self-professed international law scholars.

The basic vision of how international law should see and approach Central Asia that is propagated by the CAT narrative is not very complex. Structurally, every one

[10] A point of methodological clarification: the kind of narrative phenomena I am talking about in this chapter are products of inter-textual structuration. That is to say, while one can often find traces of their influence in scholarly and non-scholarly discourse, they do not necessarily 'exist' at the level of any individual text but can be better understood, rather, as composite objects that unfold across different textual sites, much in the same way as 'genres' or 'tropes'.

[11] See Bakhtin and Medvedev (1991, pp. 16–23), Jameson (2002, pp. 73, 102).

[12] But see Haskell (2016).

[13] For various book-length examples of CAT-driven scholarship, see Lempp and Mayer (2024), Spaiser (2018), Starr (2018), Cooley (2012), Cummings (2012), Warkotsch (2010), Lewis (2008), Collins (2006), Brill Olcott (2005), Jones Luong (2002). See also Blackmon (2021), Koch (2018), World Bank (2007), and sources cited at footnoted 16, 19, 31, 40 below.

of its formal features can be traced to one single fact: CAT's unwavering investment in what one might call the project of Central Asia's *historicized exoticization.*

What the CAT discourse essentially seeks to do to Central Asia in representational terms is to construct it as a thoroughly exoticized Other whose ultimate source of exoticism derives solely from its immediate historical experience rather than any metaphysical essence or primordial feature.[14] The immediate historical experience in question is the region's previous membership in the USSR. The specific nature of the exoticizing effect this experience brought to Central Asia was that it had left the five Central Asian states consistently and woefully unprepared—economically, politically, but above all institutionally—to (re-)join the modern family of nations following the USSR's demise.

Put differently, the general solution which the CAT narrative proposes to the problem of Central Asia's postcoloniality lies not so much in denying the relevance of this question as in substituting it with an alternative theoretical framing centered around the two closely related claims of *legal and political underdevelopment* and *post-communist normalization.*

The first claim—the idea that the single most noteworthy fact about the five Central Asian states is the fundamental underdevelopment of their legal and political cultures and institutional landscapes—acts as the main starting point of the whole narrative complex. Its function broadly is to pave the way for what essentially seems to be a version of Antony Anghie's classical dynamic-of-difference thesis[15]: to assert the presence of a fundamental defect in the new states' existing institutional structure so as to argue on that basis for a need to restrict the extent of their sovereign autonomy, until such time as that defect is successfully removed. In analytical terms, the argument unfolds as a sequence of three points:

(i) a serious gap exists between the legal and institutional culture of Central Asian states and what is commonly understood to be the international standard;
(ii) if Central Asian states are to assume full and effective membership of the international community, this gap needs to be overcome; and
(iii) what this means in practice is the necessity during a certain period of time for some form of international tutelage to help guide the Central Asian states on their path to reform.

The second claim—the idea that what the five Central Asian states are now looking at is a process of post-communist normalization—derives from the same initial premise: the notion of a fundamental defect in the basic institutional structure.

[14] This is not to say that there exists no room for this kind of discourse in the field of Central Asian studies. The idea that the best way to understand modern-day Central Asia begins with figuring out its primordial essence—the keys to which should be sought in Tamerlane's life story, Sufism, sultanism, Kazakh clan tribalism, etc. or some other decidedly exotic and premodern quality—has never quite gone out of fashion among Central Asianists. For illustrations, see Burghardt and Sabonis-Helf (2018), Kunysz (2012), Kangas (2002). Unlike CAT, however, this way of looking at Central Asia has not spilled over as much into the practices of the contemporary international law system and its institutions.

[15] See Anghie (2005, pp. 37, 188).

In rhetorical terms its contribution to what gives the CAT narrative its distinctive ideological flavor seems far more central. The reason why the five Central Asian states are not ready yet to assume the advantages of full sovereign autonomy, argues the CAT tradition, is because of their serious legal and political underdevelopment. The cause of this underdevelopment lies not in something that is inevitably intrinsic to whatever one might regard as their 'essential identity', but rather in their shared historical inheritance: their previous membership in the Soviet Union.[16]

Note what linking the dynamics-of-difference argument to the trope of post-communist normalization does for the CAT narrative. On the one hand, it allows it to frame the idea of proposed international tutelage in essentially 'neutral' terms: the need for the Central Asian states to agree to a relative restriction of their sovereignty is presented as a matter of *achieving normality*, i.e., of getting to the same place as everyone else. On the other hand, it also pushes us to see this need for sovereignty restriction as a consequence of their having suffered through the unenviable experience of living under the *Soviet political economy*. Note the two immediate effects that flow from this kind of framing. Firstly, linking the claim of Central Asia's legal and political underdevelopment to the idea of Soviet inheritance rather than, say, some kind of primordial feature unique to Central Asian civilizations or some metaphysical essence such as 'Islamic tradition', helps the CAT discourse deflect any potential accusations of neo-Orientalism and cultural imperialism—traditionally the main weak spot in all dynamic-of-difference narratives. Secondly, introducing the trope of *normalization* immediately helps also defuse the inevitable anxiety triggered by the idea of restricting sovereignty. What Central Asian states will have to do to eventually be able to enjoy the full measure of their sovereignty, goes the implied argument, is nothing more than what other states have to do to enjoy it as well. By being placed in this restricted mode, they are, in other words, neither being singled out nor penalized: they are just being asked to do what everyone else is asked to. The idea of 'international standards' (and through it the idea of international law *lato sensu*) performs in this context an absolutely critical function in the sense that it does not just help stabilize the CAT narrative rhetorically, but actually helps define its main political promise. Whatever restrictions of sovereignty Central Asian states are going to be subjected to—whatever form of international tutelage in other words they will be asked to accept in completing their path along post-independence reform—will have their basis, in the CAT universe, in universal international norms, not some subjective political theory, and thus will be argued for and justified accordingly.

It would hardly be an exaggeration to call this kind of framing a stroke of tactical genius. By presenting Central Asia's alleged underdevelopment as a case of repairable abnormality and locating its cause in the region's experience with a particular mode of economic production, the CAT discourse manages, on the one hand to assume the appearance of a basically technocratic enterprise, while on the other hand placing

---

[16] For a typical example of such framing extended to the study of Central Asian policing practices, see, e.g., Friesendorf (2022, pp. 1435–6). For an even more telling example of applying a CAT-style historicized exoticism approach to explain the interaction between Islam and state politics in Central Asia, see Hanks (2016).

itself within an ostensibly historico-materialist plane of debate—a distinctly non-Orientalist and theoretically non-reductionist discursive formation.[17] Furthermore, by channeling the conversation around Central Asia's post-independence journey into the plane of post-Soviet studies, it also successfully sidesteps the need to explore any potential parallels between Central Asia's escape from Russian rule and other, earlier waves of decolonization.

A different way of seeing it would be to say that, by compressing the discussion of Central Asia's post-independence trajectories into a problematic of legal and political underdevelopment and post-communist normalization, the CAT narrative has essentially managed to

(i) put forward the idea that the best way to understand the five Central Asian states—their place in the world, their relationship with other states, and their past and present trajectories in the global legal and political arenas—is to look at them in terms of what they have inherited from their shared Soviet past but not, say, their 'individual' histories or pre-Soviet past;
(ii) identify as the most important strand of this past its domestic politico-economic component (socialism), rather than its international (colonial conquest and annexation) or cultural (sweeping Russification of public life) dimensions;
(iii) inoculate the resulting body of discourse from potential accusations of reproducing crude Orientalist tropes;

and

(iv) construct the five Central Asian states as being a part of the so-called 'developing world' and thus requiring international assistance to graduate to full sovereign capacity.

What sort of implied geopolitical model arises from all this should not be hard to work out. On the one hand, unlike what would be the case with the more standard neo-Orientalist discourses, in the CAT discourse the five Central Asian states are presented as fully historicized entities. Whether the focus of the ensuing discussion falls on the post-independence education reforms, the evolution of local policing practices, or the struggle to end the use of child labor in state-owned agricultural complexes, at every step of the way Central Asian states are presented as both the *products* and the *inheritors* of their own history, the complex impacts of which, it is made clear, provide the main causal factors to explain their trajectory and present situation.[18] Indeed, if anything, one often gets the sense that the single most noteworthy fact about these

[17] The standard model of Orientalist discourse, of course, has little patience for any form of systematic historicization. For a classic introduction to the subject, see Said (1978).

[18] A common trope in CAT-shaped discourses is to preface any discussions, critiques, and observations with the seemingly innocent descriptive note that '[t]he five Central Asian republics as we know them today are a new form of political entity that has never existed before in this shape.' In addition to removing the scope for essentializing the Central Asian 'spirit', this sort of framing helps shrink the scope of what is implicitly considered to be the relevant historical horizon for understanding Central Asia. See Spaiser (2018, p. 20).

five states is just how much they seem to be caught up within the strictures of path dependence created by this history.[19]

At the same time, the actual *historical field* of which the five Central Asian states are shown to be a part of consistently also gets depicted as a highly truncated and selective affair. The only history that matters for understanding contemporary Central Asia, it appears, is the history of the last Soviet quarter-century. Anything beyond that seems irrelevant. Any parallels between Central Asian states and other non-Western countries that secured their independence from Western rule are not just dismissed but outright ignored. Any reflections on what impact the mode of Central Asia's initial entry into the Russo-Soviet sphere of influence may have had on the post-exist dynamics are similarly by and large passed over.

For most of the last two hundred years, the usual attribute of Western imperialist discourses has been the turn to civilizational models of geopolitics.[20] One of the most distinctive features of the CAT project over the last thirty years, by contrast, has been its consistent refusal to read Central Asia's international politics through any kind of culturalist or religion-centric lens or to subsume the five states in question within the same explanatory frame as other Muslim-majority countries, be it Iran, Pakistan, or Indonesia. Looking at things from this perspective, the consistent downplaying in the CAT discourse of the religious and cultural determinants of Central Asia's international relations may seem at first glance a marker of a critically progressive theoretical setup. And yet, on closer look, its actual ideological effects seem a lot more ambivalent than that. For, just as it insists on detaching the five Central Asian states from any broader Islamicate bloc, representing their legal and political trajectories as products solely of their shared post-Soviet legacy, the CAT tradition also actively insists on detaching them from the rest of the post-Soviet region. Building on the fact that, because of their geography the five Central Asian states never entered the broader European legal-institutional space—none of them joined the Council of Europe or the European Union—it consistently seeks to decouple Central Asia not only from the outer East European periphery of the former communist camp (Poland, Hungary, East Germany) but also from other ex-Soviet republics, not least the Caucasus and Russia itself.[21]

The underlying logic of this move may not seem immediately obvious. But placed side by side with the other truncations and decouplings listed earlier, its general effect seems unmistakable. Neither quite like the rest of the post-communist bloc nor really a part of the broader Muslim world, neither fully post-Soviet nor really postcolonial, neither quite Afro-Asian nor really East European—the five Central Asian states in the CAT universe are left looking decidedly *sui generis* and thus inexorably exotic.

What is more, by planting the notion that the five Central Asian states do not fully fit either in the post-Soviet space or in the broader post-colonial world, either in old Asia or in new Europe, the CAT tradition not only cuts Central Asia off from any broader historical totalities. It also, even if only as a by-product, achieves the feat of

---

19 See, e.g., Wooden and Stefes (2009).

20 For a classical recent illustration, see Huntington (1996).

21 See, e.g., Sievers (2003).

excluding Central Asia from the reach of what most internationalist disciplines today would recognize as the standard spatial extent of the 'Third World'. In a discipline like international law—where, because of the historical accidents of imagination, the only effective institutional expression of postcolonial criticism to date has been anchored precisely in that geopolitical category—that can ultimately mean only one thing.

It did not have to happen this way, but the stronger the claim laid by the Third World Approaches to International Law (TWAIL) tradition to represent the full horizon of postcolonial critical thought became in international law, the more ingrained its structural blinds pots became in international law's disciplinary imaginary. Being excluded from the spatial reach of the Third World has meant in this context yet another form of historicization for Central Asia, and yet another round of ideological inoculation for the CAT-inspired approach to thinking about Central Asia's encounters with the contemporary international legal system.

It should not be hard to guess where this argument goes next. In the absence of any real threat of exposure to critical scrutiny, what the CAT tradition has been able to bring to international law's imagination of Central Asia is essentially a classic case of a *neo-colonialist sensibility*. Not only, goes the argument, do Central Asian states suffer from a fundamental legal and political development gap because of their unique post-Soviet inheritance in a context conspicuously devoid of any decolonizational overtones. It is also the case that these states now have to find a way to close this development gap (catch up) or risk being seen to have failed to meet the norms expected of sovereign statehood.

In linking the obligation to catch up with the threat of being marked down as a failure in its most immediate expression, the CAT discourse may be a product of a relatively recent historical vintage, but the general model of geopolitics and a basic vision of law's relationship with politics which it gives voice to have a decidedly long pedigree in international law. Developed at that muddy intersection where the self-proclaimed science of good governance meets new institutional economics, the CAT tradition, in its most basic form, is essentially an attempt to bring back into international law what used to be known as *the doctrine of the 'standard of civilization'*.[22]

5.3 The Politics of CAT: The Idea of 'Legal and Political Physics' and Legitimation of Neocolonialism

Much of the modern discipline of economics, observes Philip Ball, has its origins in the early Enlightenment project of discovering a sociological equivalent of Newtonian physics: a set of universally applicable 'natural laws' of social life that hold true regardless of the immediate cultural or historical context.[23] The basic model behind

[22] For a general introduction to this topic, see Gong (1984).

[23] See Ball (2005, pp. 65–71).

CAT's implied vision of how international law ought to approach Central Asia in large measure can be described, in relation to this insight, as the search for a universally applicable 'physics' of post-communist transition. The two structural components of this physics were the idea of the 'basic principles' of democratic design—the legal and political physics of transitioning from a socialist political economy to smoothly functioning free market democracy—and what elsewhere in the literature came to be known as the 'liberal/democratic peace thesis'—the idea that liberal democracies, because of their internal structural setup, are inherently predisposed toward the paths of peace and friendly cooperation in foreign policy, and thus, the best way to ensure a lasting state of international peace and security is to ensure the spread of the liberal democratic model of governance globally, including in former communist countries.

The way the legal and political physics part of the argument played out in the CAT context, in a nutshell, could be presented as a sequence of four claims:

(1) all societies are governed by the same iron laws of legal and political physics that determine which legal and political forms will work in which economic and institutional contexts;
(2) the better we understand these laws, the more effectively we can close whatever legal and political development gaps we need to close;
(3) as it just so happens, Central Asia's underdevelopment gap comes down precisely to its lack of the understanding of these laws; conveniently, its international friends have made enormous progress in uncovering the knowledge of these laws and, rather than keeping this to themselves, are ready to share it in a spirit of good-neighborliness with the newly independent Central Asian states;
(4) streamlining the transmission of this knowledge and following up on its correct application on the proverbial ground is an important part of the challenge confronting Central Asia and its friends, and it is here that international law and its institutions can play their most effective role in helping Central Asia.

Note the clear echoes of the classical *mission civilizatrice* sensibility. The language of the 'white man's burden' may no longer be in fashion in international politics, but the paternalistic model of international legal policy it stood for remains very much alive in the world of the CAT discourse.

It would be nothing more than an act of altruism and philanthropy, argues the CAT narrative, to help the new (and still largely inexperienced) Central Asian states figure out which particular development targets they ought to adopt and to give them the roadmaps they ought to stick to in chasing these targets. To be sure, as independent states they would remain free, legally, to decide their own future, and no external force may interfere with their political or ideological choices.[24] But none of what these targets and roadmaps represent actually has anything to do with politics or ideology. All of it is really just a matter of understanding the basic principles of the universally valid legal and political physics and applying the right institutional solutions (good governance) these principles suggest.

---

[24] *Nicaragua v. United States*, Merits, ICJ Reports (1986), §263.

It should not be hard for an informed reader to recognize the dominant overtone behind this narrative. Like the rest of the post-Soviet transitology complex, the CAT narrative is essentially a product of the early post-Cold War ideological imaginary. The shadow of Ibrahim Shihata looms large over it,[25] but so also does that of the Paris Charter for a New Europe.[26]

It is not just the promotion of human rights, democracy, and the rule of law but also the 'transition to market economy by countries making efforts to this effect', declares the Paris Charter, that comprises a matter of legitimate international concern.[27] Insofar as the newly independent Central Asian states have confirmed their adherence to the Charter's goals and principles, when their Western partners now propose to share their knowledge of good governance techniques and ask Central Asian states to accept and implement this or that set of domestic legal or political reforms, there is, quite obviously, nothing illegitimate, interventionist, or self-serving about that. It is precisely what their international obligations require Central Asian states to do: '[domestic g]overnance issues [in Central Asia after all] are … more than [just the] "internal affairs" of the republics'.[28]

By the same token, there is also nothing illegitimate, interventionist, or self-serving about Western states' asking Central Asian states to build an effective rule of law system or specifying, given the latter's lack of experience in the matter, what this actually means in terms of specific institutional reforms. Further, given that the essential *raison d'etre* of international organizations is to serve the interests of the international community, it only stands to reason that in doing so the Western states should be able to rely on the help of these international organizations. Should the Central Asian states fail to put the advice they receive to use effectively, there is nothing wrong about these organizations reassuring them and, where necessary, perhaps even admonishing them.[29] For, indeed, if they fail to complete the correct transition reforms on time, the negative impact this will have on their overall 'state capacity' will inevitably trigger 'security threats across all … security dimensions' not just for themselves but also for their friends in the 'far neighbourhood[s]' like Western Europe.[30]

Stripped to its basic outline, the CAT vision for what Central Asia ought to expect from the international legal system may seem arrestingly offensive—if not for its brazenly imperialist logic, then for its openly patronizing tone. And yet what

---

[25] Ibrahim Shihata, the one-time general counsel of the World Bank group, is widely credited with developing and popularizing the argument that initiatives aimed at strengthening the rule of law and good governance are fundamentally nonpolitical in character. See Santos (2006, pp. 269–70).

[26] See CSCE (1990).

[27] See 'A New Era of Democracy, Peace and Unity', ibid.

[28] Spaiser (2018, p. 161).

[29] That Central Asian states are not unique among post-communist states in having been subjected to this kind of technocratic neocolonialism is an important point. Unlike with East European states, however, there has been a lot less wariness about how to frame the justifications for this kind of 'socialization' programme and a lot less carrot-usage in the proverbial sticks-and-carrots context. On how the socialization process worked out in East Europe, see, e.g., Schimmelfennig (2005).

[30] Spaiser (2018, pp. 28–40).

remains far more striking about this vision perhaps is just how well-established and widespread it has become across different discursive communities in and around international law.

Between the West and Central Asia, there are many 'significant differences in normative and institutional contexts', writes the Sudanese-American human rights scholar Abdullahi an-Naim at the turn of the millennium. Just as it would be right that the 'Muslims in France must [start to] formulate their demands … in [universalist] human rights terms', so too the Muslim-majority populations of Central Asian states must learn 'to adopt a human rights paradigm [in articulating] their Islamic identity.'[31] Of course, one could protest that imposing that sort of requirement may look like a form of cultural imperialism, since it would mean compelling Central Asian societies to 'accept the incorporation of an external normative system … into their own identity in order to claim that identity.' Nevertheless, notes an-Naim, such an incorporation must take place and be insisted on, since *any attempt to resist or delay it would be read as 'rejecting … today's interdependent world.'*[32]

As 'one of the most repressive … regions of the world', writes the German government official Olga Alinda Spaiser in 2018, Central Asia does not just look set to become 'the next tinderbox'.[33] It also finds itself in need of constant external support and guidance so as to overcome its 'democratic accountability' deficit. Obviously, it is not enough that this support only be limited to advice and consultation: the mechanisms of support delivery must be robust and backed up by a system of effective incentives. Thus, while it may not be the same in other regions, it is only right and proper, Spaiser concludes, that in Central Asia the EU's regional outreach policy should be channeled via institutional frameworks like the Rule of Law Initiative (RLI), a body that not only has the 'ability to review [any] developments in the sphere of legal reform' undertaken by Central Asian states but also the power to call out in public any fake 'Potemkin reforms [made only] in order to comply with international expectations'.[34] For ultimately, of course, in the long run such tough love will only benefit Central Asia itself: Without 'modernizing their [legal] systems' they would be unable not only to achieve a stronger 'capacity of legitimacy' but also to 'attract and secure' investment and foreign trade.[35]

Forget for the moment the basic legal-realist point that, given the radical informational asymmetry between private investors and the RLI, the actual capacity of Central Asian states to attract foreign investment and trade in this case would be at least as much impacted by the negative discourse coming from the RLI itself as by any perceived flaws in the domestic legal and institutional landscapes, and so it is not at all clear, in causal terms, who in fact undermines that capacity more: the Central Asian governments through their failure to 'modernize' their legal systems, or the EU by badmouthing them and creating adverse publicity. A far more telling insight

[31] An-Naim (2000, pp. 939–41).

[32] Ibid., p. 941 (italics added).

[33] Spaiser (2018, p. 32).

[34] Ibid., pp. 163–78.

[35] Ibid., pp. 32, 162.

into CAT's working philosophy comes from the vision statement included in the RLI Official Platform: 'The main goal of the RLI … is the promotion of European legal norms [to] help the countries of Central Asia to approximate their national judicial models, legislation, and practices with international (primarily European) standards.'[36]

An earlier generation of Western observers, writes Cornelius Friesendorf in the early 2020s, often assumed that the need for such external pressure and disciplining of Central Asia would only be temporary. Alas, he notes, the history of the last thirty years, has taught us otherwise: 'Central Asian governments [often] emulate Western formal models' but '[t]here are limits to how far [they] are willing to promote or tolerate [real] reform'.[37] Although many good international standards and best practices have emerged on any number of subjects, the spectre of Potemkinism remains. In the end, there is no getting around the need to maintain continual external oversight, since 'reform is perennial but not a teleological path toward democracy'.[38] Bridging the developmental gap is a long, potentially never-ending journey. If the international community wants Central Asia to succeed on this journey, it cannot trust Central Asians to manage this process themselves: neither the local civil society, nor the parliamentary institutions, nor '[e]ven the United States … officials' acting through bilateral diplomatic channels have been able to ensure that progress on the reforms remains genuine.[39] The need for tutelage by international institutions is unavoidable, and every attempt by the local governments to push back against that is only further evidence of their lingering inability and unwillingness to build a true democracy. What is more, even when locally-driven initiatives for democratization do somehow materialize, one should not be misled: left to their own devices, modern-day Central Asians rarely embrace actual democratism; where they gravitate instead is inevitably toward some form of 'consultative authoritarianism'.[40] Even when 'the space for reform [internally] broadened in Uzbekistan' to 'benefi[t] the Uzbek parliament' and 'parliamentary oversight', all that this led to in practice, argues Friesendorf, was just 'buttressing authoritarian modernization'.[41] However one looks at it, the conclusion of the necessity for a regime of continuous interventionism by the international community seems inevitable, and 'states with a stake' in seeing Central Asia's transition succeed—'namely, liberal democracies in Europe and North America'—must not hesitate to become 'assertive policy implementers' and make use of whatever 'means at their disposal': be these 'sponsoring research' or training and funding local activists 'to be more assertive toward Central Asian governments'.[42]

---

[36] Ibid., p. 165 (italics added).

[37] Friesendorf (2022, p. 1437).

[38] Ibid.

[39] Ibid., pp. 1437–9.

[40] See Knox and Sharipova (2024).

[41] Friesendorf (2022, p. 1442).

[42] Ibid., 1455–6.

Out of the pan and into the fire: having emerged from Russian imperial rule, the first order of business now that the five Central Asian states have gained admission to the sovereign club is to prove over and over that they, in fact, are not undeserving of it and that their use of it is not going to pose a threat to the West. Thus they must accept direct external oversight by international organizations to prove the government is not a Potemkinite con-artist; copy-paste European legal regimes to prove they are undergoing the kind of modernization that is needed to confirm their 'capacity of legitimacy' and are not a security threat to Europe or 'rejecting today's interdependent world'. Elsewhere in the international arena the idea of reinstituting a standard of civilization procedure may no longer be viewed as acceptable, but when it comes to Central Asia every operative part of it is firmly kept in place.

Whether advanced via institutional channels like the RLI or academic writings penned by lawyers and law-cosplaying political scientists, the two main effects which the quiet percolation of the CAT tradition into the collective imaginary of the international law system has enabled leave no doubt about its highly reactionary bias:

(i) a consistent *ideological isolation of Central Asia from the reach of any form of postcolonial critical inquiry*: the kind of things Western commentators have long ceased feeling comfortable they can say about African or Middle Eastern societies and cultures, they can still easily get away with saying when it comes to Central Asia;

and

(ii) a steady promotion of the idea that, in dealing with Central Asia the international law system ought to embrace not just the pompous paternalism of the standard of civilization doctrine but an *openly neocolonialist attitude*—it is we who decide what you should do or there will be no more trade or investment and you will be seen to have no 'capacity of legitimacy' and marked as a security threat.

The common view shared among the students of international legal history today is that the emergence of the standard of civilization doctrine at the end of the nineteenth century represents the high watermark in the acceptance of the principle of racial hierarchy as the official basis of international society. On its surface, CAT-shaped constructions of Central Asia may not seem as crass or crude, but they certainly do encourage the spread and entrenchment of a legal-political sensibility based around the notion of inter-state hierarchies, with Central Asian states invariably placed at the business end of it.

5.4 CAT and International Law: Rankings, Ostracism, and Adverse Publicity as a New Legal Paradigm

On its surface, the proposed act of catching-up that is expected from Central Asian states in CAT-shaped discourses is usually presented in decidedly neutral and formal terms: 'state-building', 'institutional reform', 'modernization', 'improving accountability', 'internationally agreed standards', etc. The overall effect is to conjure the image of a fundamentally technocratic process devoid of any political or cultural content, taking place within a single-track historical reality where the degree of a country's progression along the implied spectrum of developed-ness is essentially a matter of 'putting in the effort' and 'seeing things through'.

It will not come as a surprise to an informed reader that the actual programme of reforms and transformation the CAT tradition has been throwing its weight behind over the last thirty years is in fact nothing of the kind. At the macro level, the proposed single track of history, purportedly the only one possible, on closer inspection turns out to be both openly politicized, given the highly biased model of class relations it seeks to normalize, and not at all historically obvious, given that none of the states promoting it have in fact followed it themselves.[43] At the micro-level, the actual reform package prescribed by CAT advocates far more often than not also tends to be nothing more than a mix of second-generation Washington Consensus—strong property rights, independent judiciary, anti-corruption, corporate reform, etc.—and a selection of standard human rights platitudes, with a particular emphasis on the freedom of religion.[44]

None of this, of course, should come as a surprise. Although as a narrative complex CAT first began to emerge nearly three decades ago, the body of discourse it has inspired has seen very little ideological or imaginational evolution since—a fact that perhaps says more than most about how effectively the historicized exoticization move CAT has performed on Central Asia has ultimately insulated the mental and discursive spaces in which the international policy discourse about Central Asia takes place against any form of postcolonial critical inquiry.

One of the by-products of this insulation, as we have seen earlier, has been the active revival within the international legal imaginary of what in effect is a classical standard-of-civilization project. Another has been the remarkably totalizing nature of the obligation to catch up that the CAT discourse proposes ought to be imposed on the Central Asian states. Even where the actual reasons responsible for their apparent underdevelopment are acknowledged to lie objectively outside their control, the practical conclusion drawn by CAT still points toward the need to respond to these challenges via accepting the package of modernization reforms proposed by international institutions. Consider by way of illustration the way a mid-2000s

---

[43] More generally, for a critical overview of the development recipes typically advocated in the transitology discourse, see Rodrik (2007).

[44] On the second-generation Washington consensus and the place of human rights in it, see more generally Rittich (2006), Stiglitz (2008).

policy paper from the World Bank 'resolves' the relationship between trade and geography for Central Asia. A large part of what has prevented Central Asian states from increasing their trade with the outside world, explains a paper entitled 'The Cost of Being Landlocked', comes down to their essentially unfavorable geographical status as landlocked countries stuck in the middle of an enormous landmass. However, 'transport costs explain at best [only a] part of the high logistics costs', and so the best thing Central Asian states can do going forward—rather than, say, negotiating new sea-access routes internationally—is to reduce their government's role in regulating transit while also strengthening the protection of foreign property rights: 'broader governance reforms' aimed at 'reducing rent-seeking activities', 'reforming market structure', and 'enhanc[ing] supply chain predictability' are the *real* key to improving trade turnovers between Central Asia and the rest of the world.[45]

The hallmark of a legal system, famously says Hans Kelsen, is not the fact that it calls itself such but the fact that in the process of its operation it combines the functions of prescription and enforcement.[46] It is not enough that the legal system signals to its subjects what norms and standards it expects them to follow: an equally important part is complementing that with a threat of authorized coercion significant enough to cause noticeable detriment to the norm-breacher.

The replication of the standard-of-civilization doctrine—the twinning of the postulated development gap with the obligation to catch up and in doing so to prove oneself worthy of (retaining) one's sovereignty—forms the main substantive axis of what one might call CAT's international law philosophy. What turns this philosophy into a ready-for-implementation *legal regime* is the fact that this obligation is also backed up by an elaborate system of highly effective international enforcement mechanisms. That is where, ultimately, the problem of CAT's continuing proliferation in the murky underbelly of international law's collective imaginary crosses over from the domain of 'mere theory' into one of actual neocolonialism.

Like with previous iterations of the dynamics of difference project,[47] the obligation to catch up that CAT imposes on Central Asian states is not just posited and declared in the abstract. The moment it becomes accepted as a policy proposal—whether in a multilateral context like with the World Bank or a bilateral one like with the RLI—it immediately finds itself embedded within the large panoply of classical compliance-building procedures—from periodic reporting processes to in-country monitoring missions and expert recommendation panels—in which Central Asian states have become progressively enmeshed ever since achieving independence.[48] Any failure to follow these procedures in full is guaranteed to result in immediate censure. Any setback, delay, or deviation from the path of decided upon reforms is guaranteed to result in the immediate downranking of the respective state according to one or more internationally instituted transition assessment scales, the most serious consequences of which are the *refusal of commerce* and *designation as a 'failed state'*.

[45] Arvic et al. (2007, pp. 55–8).

[46] See Kelsen (1953, pp. 9–15).

[47] See Anghie (2005).

[48] The standard repertoire of these procedures is reviewed in Chayes and Chayes (1994).

The role of the last two mechanisms as tools of legal enforcement may not seem immediately obvious to a traditionally trained international lawyer. A number of institutional and ideological factors can make it difficult to recognize the connection or, more generally, the fact that the kind of international regime that is typically advocated for by rankings-focused transitology narratives, such as CAT, is not only basically neocolonial in its political orientation but also *fundamentally juridical in terms of its operative premise.* The first and the most salient among these factors is the tendency for most international lawyers to think of legal enforcement (compliance-inducing legal coercion) in terms of what is essentially a largely outdated, mid-twentieth century legal-theoretical outlook that combines elements of unreflective positivism (a penalty is that which is so named and regulated under positive law) and naïve formalism (positive law can only be created pursuant to a prescribed list of lawmaking procedures).

Inasmuch as the system of positive international law and the doctrinal international law discourse deriving from it have not yet recognized 'failed statehood', 'hardline autocracy', or 'predatory state' as *legally relevant statuses*, the idea that being publicly marked by one of these labels can constitute an act of compliance-inducing coercion does not usually enter the horizon of traditional international law analysis. By the same token, since in both positive law and the doctrinal international law discourse the power to refuse commerce—via trade boycotts, import restrictions, conditional market access, etc.—is typically framed as part and parcel of the refusing state's sovereign prerogative, the natural tendency for traditional international law analysis is to view this power more in terms of the refusing state exercising its discretionary rights than the refused state being deprived of access to those resources—say, foreign currency to purchase advanced technologies—that it may otherwise need. So long as no pre-existing legal relationship between the two states then requires the refusing state to have allowed any particular form of trade to occur between them, no question of coercion or compulsion can be said to arise in the eyes of international law.

The second factor is closely linked to the first. Not only are the refusal of commerce and designation as a failed state not recognized formally in positive international law as forms of enforcement action: they are also not regulated in terms of their 'procedural' implementation. Given the aforementioned tendency of knowledge production in international law to be dominated by discourses of legal practice, this lack of regulatory attention inevitably ends up playing an analytically debilitating role. How exactly may a state end up on the list of failed states, who monitors this list, what exact consequences may follow from being placed on this list, how can such placement be contested by the affected parties, what sort of access deprivations can cause serious enough economic hardship to justify trade remedies, what sort of remedies might those be—the fact that none of these questions have been formally discussed, let alone codified, in positive international law logically seems to suggest to the traditionally trained international lawyer that, insofar as international legal analysis is concerned, questions of 'statehood failure' and refusal of commerce and any related ranking exercises cannot possibly be legally relevant.

Yet, as every practicing lawyer well knows, the absence of legal codification or any other form of formal engagement between the legal system and a given class of political practices is not in itself an indication that no such engagement is in fact taking place. The power of the law, as legal realists remind us, is realized inasmuch as its exercise is *felt* by the subjects affected by it—recall the Holmesean bad man[49]—not insofar as its exercise is formally acknowledged as such by the lawmakers.

The idea that refusing to transact with someone who urgently needs access to the transacted object (desperate buyer scenario) or who cannot obtain it from any other sources (monopolistic seller scenario) constitutes a form of coercion that is no less effective than the imposition of criminal law penalties—and that it is the legal order itself that, ultimately, gives the refusing actor the power to exercise this coercion—has of course been long recognized in private law theory.[50] One does not have to invent particularly fanciful scenarios to see how this works: just think of the power an insulin seller has over a diabetic sufferer or the vulnerability that is felt by a developing state needing to secure a large-scale loan to acquire the kind of technology required to accelerate its industrialization process.

Mid-twentieth century international law tradition typically conceptualized the subject of compliance-inducing legal coercion in terms of a narrowly limited range of formal mechanisms centered around procedures like reprisals, countermeasures, and Chapter VII action by the UN Security Council, relegating all other forms of lawful coercion to the black-box category of 'retorsion'.[51] By the early 1990s, when the CAT narrative first began to take shape, the empirical realities accompanying the evolution of the general international law regime governing the relations between the developing and the developed worlds, however, had long since outgrown this simplistic framework. Driven in no small part by the consolidation of cross-institutional cooperation and lockstep linkages between players like the World Bank, the IMF, and the Paris Club,[52] this evolution signaled, among other things, the growing pre-eminence of *community ostracizing procedures*—exclusion from global political and economic intercourse via different forms of blacklisting—and the central role played in these procedures by the age-old mechanism which post-realist administrative law scholars had first theorized under the rubric of *'adverse publicity'* and civil society activists preferred to call *naming-and-shaming*, but which far more accurately perhaps can be simply best described as *legally admissible reputation-tarnishing*.[53]

The connection between the two—communal ostracism and adverse publicity—seems obvious but is also structurally central. Where the targeted subject is effectively invulnerable to the threat of the former, the latter often will not be effective. Where such vulnerability is present, however—which in the age of economic globalization

---

[49] Holmes (1897, p. 459).

[50] See, e.g., Hale (1923).

[51] For a general overview, see White and Abbas (2003).

[52] For background, see Cypher and Dietz (2009, p. 575), Cosio-Pascal (2010).

[53] Though there had been little conscious theorization of its systemic significance, the importance of community ostracizing as a tool of enforcement was not, of course, lost on all mid-twentieth century international lawyers. See, e.g., Schwarzenberger (1950, p. 294).

has become a much more unavoidable prospect—the targeting actor would hardly need to resort to any other tool of coercive action to be able to achieve the desired level of punitive or compliance-inducing effect.

As Ernest Gellhorn explains:

> When [government organs] focus [] adverse publicity on named parties, the consequences to such parties can be disastrous. Perhaps the most notorious examples of governmental abuse of adverse publicity occurred during the McCarthy era, when press releases and congressional committee hearings assailed with legal impunity the patriotism and integrity of many persons. …
>
> 'Adverse … publicity' … refers to affirmative measures taken by an agency which, by calling public attention to agency action, may adversely affect persons identified in the publicity. … Its rationale is generally stated as 'the public's right to know'. …
>
> Much agency publicity identifying individuals or firms and thus likely to have an adverse impact is intended only to warn or inform the public; the harm occurs because publicity is a 'gross' informational or warning tool. Occasionally [however] publicity which informs or warns also functions to punish [or] deter … conduct … In such cases, the adverse publicity functions as a sanction.[54]

No tool of communal ostracizing and adverse publicity-generation developed in the post-Cold War international practice has proved as crushingly effective and disenfranchising for the developing states as the discourse of state failure.

Originally a product of abstract scholarly debates in political science and international relations, the concept of failed statehood made the successful jump from being a mere academic theory to a burgeoning area of technocratic neocolonial expertise by the late 1990s.[55] In 2005, an American NGO called Fund for Peace began the practice of explicitly ranking non-Western states in terms of their failure potential by publishing an annually-updated *Failed States Index* (later renamed *Fragile States Index*).[56] The foundations for this had been laid several years prior, when the Center for International Development and Conflict Management at the University of Maryland began to compile ever-expanding datasets and 'interpretative methodologies' to equip what would eventually evolve into a CIA-funded project called State Failure Task Force (later renamed Political Instability Task Force). By the early 2000s, SFTF's evaluations of developing states—many of them based around the perceived rate and readiness with which states achieved externally agreed upon development markers and completed the required transition reforms—would come to claim a predictive accuracy of 70 to 80 percent.[57] Though ostensibly devoid of any formal legal implications, such listings were quickly coopted to inform policy and political responses by a growing range of international actors and institutions.

One does not have to be a card-carrying legal realist to be able to recognize what these ranking exercises amount to in practice. In a comparable context, the Indian Marxist international law scholar B. S. Chimni concludes that what non-Western

---

[54] Gellhorn (1973, pp. 1381–3).

[55] For an influential early formulation of the concept of failed statehood, see Jackson (1990).

[56] See 'Fragile State Index', *Fund for Peace*, available at https://fragilestatesindex.org.

[57] See Goldstone et al. (2000).

states such as the five Central Asian republics would find themselves being exposed to in this sort of situation is not just some vaguely defined political pressure but a fully regularized division of labor between Western states and Western-dominated international organizations on the one hand, and the various elements of the Western-funded global civil society on the other, all done in the service of advancing a carefully coordinated regime of neocolonial governance. The fact that the ranking exercises in question are performed by NGOs rather than foreign governments represents, in this view of things, neither a fluke nor a flaw but a design feature. What for reasons of diplomacy and legal restraints the latter cannot afford to do in the open is simply being delegated and outsourced to the former.[58]

Not that such outsourcing was in fact always necessary. As the example of the SFTF shows, even before the Fund for Peace started to publish its annual index, numerous Western government officials and diplomats began to routinely deploy the vocabulary of 'failed states' in the international institutional arena and in formal policy announcements.[59] A variety of international organizations, from the UN to the World Bank, likewise, began to make increasing use of the concept of state failure and its associated derivatives, feeding them into a growing range of new policy frameworks and programmatic visions, culminating most notoriously perhaps in the announcement of the so-called 'Responsibility to Protect' doctrine of the mid-2000s.[60] The fact that amidst all this the concept of state failure was not recognized in the eyes of positive international law as a formal legal doctrine, rather than being a sign of its juridical immaturity, became in this sense an integral element of how the broader system which made use of it was operationalized in practice.

What held true for state failure held true also for its various derivatives—'rogue regimes', 'fragile states', 'collapsed states', 'predatory states'—and the quasi-diagnostic categories that began to be added to them—'human freedom index', 'democracy index', 'Bertelsmann Transformation Index', 'corruption perception index', and, inevitably, 'ease of doing business index'.[61]

The increase in the number of transition assessment criteria these constructs came to signify translated into a corresponding surge and complexification in ranking exercises. Some of these constructs appeared to arrange themselves in a broadly hierarchical manner: the corruption perception index fed into the ease of doing business

---

[58] See Chimni (2004).

[59] A classic example here is the public lecture delivered by the then British foreign secretary, Jack Straw, at the University of Birmingham in 2002. In Straw's vision, the lessons of 9/11 required the international community to copy the medical profession, who 'look at a wide range of indicators to spot patients who are at high risk of certain medical conditions', and develop a similar litmus test for 'failed statehood' which would enable it to draw up a 'watch-list' and 'begin to place the states along a continuum of failure'. See Straw (2002). The text of the lecture, previously available on the ERI website, has since been taken down, but summaries of it can still be found in various secondary sources and in the scholarly literature. See, e.g., Lemay-Hebert (2010), Chandler (2007).

[60] For background, see Lambach (2004). More generally on the responsibility to protect, see Bellamy and Dunne (2016).

[61] There is a wealth of literature on the use of such indices in modern global governance and their relationship with international law. A good place to start would be Merry et al. (2015), Merry (2016).

index, 'fragile' seemed to be a precursor for or a less intense variation of 'failed', etc. Others appeared to be formally independent and unconnected with one another. The crucial fact, from the legal point of view, in any event has been that

(i) like state failure, none of these categories made entry into the discourse of positive international law, that is to say, the one plane of *international legal contestation*—the formal legal arena—in which non-Western states such as the five Central Asian republics would have been able, as Martti Koskenniemi notes, to count on having an even playing field between themselves and the West[62];
(ii) each of these categories formed the basis for some kind of *ranking exercise* which in turn served as the foundation for a related *coercive mechanism* by providing an objective excuse for the issuance of *adverse publicity* about the ranked states' performances;
(iii) the reputation tarnishing effects that followed from the failure to score highly under these ranking exercises inevitably led not just to significant *curtailments in political and economic opportunities* (denial of benefits) but also to various forms of *legalized communal ostracism* (withdrawal or refusal of cooperation), including the loss of access to Western markets, reduction in investment inflows, refusal of favorable loan conditions, increases in financial and political insurance premiums for doing business with the states in question, visa travel restrictions, denial of licences for the purchase of defense-related and dual-use technologies, etc.;
(iv) in terms of their legal significance, these ranking exercises not only connect the categories and indices in question to the neocolonialist standard-of-civilization, part of the new legal regime discussed earlier, but also help to operationalize for practical purposes the process of 'measuring' Central Asia's proposed development gap, thus rendering the enterprise of insisting that Central Asian states should meet internationally agreed upon development targets and roadmaps and comply with external oversight not only less visibly political but also objectively justifiable.

Legal systems, critical legal theory reminds us, often expose their actual political biases not at that point where they expressly impose any particular political programme but at those points where they 'choose' not to prevent those patterns of behavior that have considerable political implications from emerging and becoming entrenched. The failure of the legal order to do something in such cases, writes Duncan Kennedy, will usually be seen as 'lack of regulation' or the sign of a lamentable deficit of political will. A more accurate characterization will often be that the given system's blind-spots are, in fact, entirely a part of its design and reflect precisely the kind of political agenda the legal order in question seeks to defend and promote.[63]

---

[62] See Koskenniemi (2002, pp. 500–2).

[63] See Kennedy (1993, pp. 90–1).

Notice the interplay in this context between formalism and non-legalized juridified processes. Since what exactly makes a state 'failed', 'fragile', or 'unfree' has never been codified as a matter of *formal international law*, but the rankings based on these concepts are still treated as a product of *internationally agreed standards* and *objective norm application* and the consequences of appearing on any such list are (a) articulated as if they are *normatively necessitated*; and (b) remain *undeniably detrimental* to the states in question, the basic political effect of this arrangement in its application to Central Asia, in legal-realist terms, seems essentially neocolonialist. Unlike the classical neocolonialism of the mid-twentieth century, however, which had left a certain room for the decolonized countries to push back against the new imperial practices, this version of neocolonialism is defined by a particularly insidious form of ideological disablement. Not only does the general balance of power between the Western actors, who carry out (and pay for) the rankings, and the Central Asian states, on whom these rankings are imposed, end up leaning heavily in favor of the former, the entire process has also become insulated against any potential challenges by the latter—recall Koskenniemi's point about operative concepts not being placed within the formal legal arena while still being legitimated by being grounded in *a series of juridically-looking practices* involving international standards and norm application. Talk of having your pie and eating it too!

At different stages over the last thirty years the prospects of getting downranked in one or more of these ranking exercises would have, of course, risen and fallen differently for different Central Asian states. The important point in all of that, however, is that none of these states at any point have been able to escape the disciplining effects of these exercises, effects that, of course, remain entirely unknown even today for most Western states.[64] Despite their formal non-existence in the eyes of international law, the concept of failed statehood and its derivatives, one may thus conclude, have come to establish themselves as the single most significant mediating element between the theoretical plane of the CAT narrative and the actual international law policy it has encouraged the international community to institute in relation to Central Asia, the background international legal regime the CAT tradition seeks to put in place between the five Central Asian states, the West, and the international legal system and its institutions.

One of the defining features of any form of imperial governance is the essential impunity enjoyed by the imperial power in the eyes of the respective legal order. The ranking-ostracism-coercion governance mechanism promoted by CAT-style narratives exhibits this feature in a truly remarkable fashion. Take the World Bank's Doing Business survey. 'A change in a country's rankings' produced by the Bank, explains the Italian scholar Fernanda Nicola, can affect not only the scale of cooperation the Bank itself will be willing to offer, it can also 'have a huge impact on how much money [the country can] receive from foreign investors'. '[A] 1 percentage point improvement in [the] overall Doing Business score correlates with 250 million to

[64] Lempp et al. provide a telling summary of the consistent lowering of rankings over the late 2010s-early 2020s for all five Central Asian states under the Democracy Index run by the Economist Intelligence Unit. See Lempp et al. (2024, pp. 75–6).

500 million USD in additional foreign direct investment.'[65] Consider what sort of resources then would have been at stake and what sort of damage potentially inflicted when, between 2009 and 2010, its assessment of the ease of staring a new business took Uzbekistan from 71st to 92nd place, even as the number of procedures required to register a new business (7) and the length of time it took to do so (15 days) had not changed. The impact of this amount of red tape on Uzbekistan's economic capacity, the Bank calculated, was equivalent to 11.5 percent of GNI per capita, which went some way toward explaining why Uzbekistan would rank 150 in the overall 2010 ease of doing business score. By comparison, in Kyrgyzstan, where the number of registration procedures was 3 and the process lasted 11 days, the economic impact of red tape was hypothesized to be only 5.23 percent, earning Kyrgyzstan a ranking of 14 and 41st place in the overall ratings.[66]

A little more than a decade later, the news emerged that the Bank officials had been manipulating for years not just the data they fed into their ranking but also the resulting rankings themselves to help improve the scores for some states and lower them for others. Against the background of such allegations, in 2021 the Bank officially canceled the Doing Business project, acknowledging that important mistakes had been made and ... doing nothing else. None of the countries affected by its manipulated rankings received anything more from it nor was any sanction applied against the Bank itself. Indeed, a mere two years later, the Bank excitedly revived its ranking enterprise giving it a new catchier name: first, Business Enabling Environment,[67] then simply B-READY.[68]

The devil-in-the-detail moment in all of this, of course, is the fact that the score calculations in such rankings do not just come down to figures and numbers of red tape procedures. At the IMF, the assessed states, it has been consistently noted, receive much better ratings if they have lower corporate taxes and weaker labor regulations, i.e., pursue an economic policy with a distinctly pronounced class bias.[69] What is more, as Nicola notes, studies have also shown that 'the legal reforms favored by the [Bank] always appear biased in favor of [national legal] systems based on common law', and that it is enough for a state to be a part of the civil law tradition to get downranked across a whole number of metrics, including 'registering property'.[70]

---

65 See Nicola (2021).

66 See further World Bank (2009a) and (2009b).

67 See World Bank (2022).

68 See World Bank (2025).

69 See Stiglitz (2021).

70 See Nicola (2021). The conclusion, argues Nicola, is that the Doing Business Index appears to have been not so much aimed at assessing the efficiency of the business scene within the evaluated countries but to 'push [them] toward a shareholder-focused corporate and business model molded on US-style capitalism.'

5.5 The Peculiar Case of Central Asia: Third-Worldism, Its Blind Spots, and Their Implications for International Law

It is possible, of course, to find another explanation for Central Asia's continuing absence from the discursive planes of international law scholarship. A pattern of consistent silence in disciplinary settings is not always a product of an intellectual blind spot. It can also be an institutional form expressing the general conditions of that discipline's socio-political organization.

There is little doubt that the international law discipline experiences a great deal of theoretical confusion in the face of Central Asia and its history of various explicit colonial and neocolonial encounters. The struggle to identify a suitable organizing category under the rubric which can subsume these encounters, however, suggests a challenge that one might argue goes far beyond merely theoretical difficulties. As TJ Clark remarks elsewhere, it is not just the radical incommensurability of the Other that ultimately determines how the Self is going to perceive the Other but also the realization of some form of vague commonality between them.[71] It is out of this vaguely recognizable commonality, notes Clark, that ultimately comes the inclination for the Self to judge the Other by its own internal standards. It is also out of it that arises the tendency to view the Other as inherently untrustworthy and dangerous—that long-established archetype of 'the Other-that-is-ourself[:] familiar (yes, this creature is like me) but for that very reason [also] potentially deceptive, possibly treacherous, unrepresentable.'[72]

Vitoria's argument that, for all their dissimilarity to the Christian Spaniards, the Indians were, after all, the children of the same God may look to some like the early seeds of human rights universalism. But, as Anghie reminds us, it also proved central to justifying Spain's wars of colonial conquest, providing the pretext that the Indians in their actual social and political practices had not complied with their obligations under those universal laws that as God's children they had to observe.[73] The key insight, Anghie remarks, comes in that movement which takes us from the 'ontological universalism' of the Other to its 'historical particularism' and thence to the inevitable finding of non-compliance:

> [On the one hand,] the Indians belong to the universal realm like the Spanish and all other human beings because … they have the facility of reason … [On the other hand,] the Indian's specific social and cultural practices are at variance from the practices required by the universal norms … which are applicable to both Indian and Spaniard.[74]

The conclusion that follows from this, observes Anghie, seems as cynical as it is predictable: '[t]he discrepancy between the ontologically "universal" Indian and the socially, historically, "particular" Indian' cannot be let rest but 'must be remedied

---

[71] Clark (2013).

[72] Ibid., p. 11.

[73] Anghie (2005, pp. 21–2).

[74] Ibid., p. 22.

by the imposition of sanctions [to] effect the necessary transformation'—not just to enforce the rule of universal justice but to protect the interest of 'the Indians themselves'.[75]

As I have noted previously, it would not be hard to find an obvious parallel between this theoretico-ideological complex and the CAT tradition as detailed earlier. The point that has to be recognized, however, is that in tracing this pattern of ideological continuities, it is important also not to lose sight of the very last point Clark makes. The vague familiarity of the Other inevitably sets it up to be viewed as inherently dangerous and treacherous, but it also makes it essentially unrepresentable.

It is not for nothing that so much of the CAT discourse has come from the pens of writers and actors not traditionally regarded as direct contributors to international legal debates. The discipline of international law has yielded the field when it comes to equipping the international law system and its institutions with the basic building blocks they require to construct a general vision of Central Asia not just because international law scholars could not actually be bothered to say anything about the region and its peoples. Silence in such cases does not necessarily only signify indifference. Sometimes it can also indicate an inability to manage an analytical aporia or the fact of running up against the outer limits of one's operative vocabulary.

Things certainly did not need to turn out this way, but they have. The arrival of the five Central Asian states into the international law arena in the early to mid-1990s did not just take place against the background of the rise of transitology and good governance discourses, it also coincided, temporally if not politically, with the long-delayed entry of the postcolonial studies movement into international law academia.[76] The particular configuration that the idea of postcoloniality would go on to assume in the international law imaginary in the aftermath of this shift was in the end as contingent and non-self-evident as it was, essentially, understandable. The most influential group of voices that helped shape the initial political and intellectual agendas of the postcolonial studies movement in international law included a wide range of scholars from African, South Asian, Middle Eastern, and Latin American backgrounds, who inevitably ended up speaking to the various historical and lived experiences of international law prevalent in their regions. For reasons that perhaps had as much to do with convenience as nostalgia, most of these voices also came to favor the revival of Bandung-influenced categories like 'the Third World' and 'Third World approaches'. As their concerted attack on the mainstream international law traditions of the day met with greater and greater success, the entrenchment of these categories and the mental maps that were inscribed in them became a common shared feature of the broader intra-disciplinary international law imaginary, quickly crowding out any alternative models and ontologies. Whatever positive implications this may have led to otherwise, the steady mainstreaming of the TWAIL agenda within academic international law thus effectively went on to set Central Asia up for a kind of 'accidental' (but still entirely systematic) representational failure, making the

[75] Ibid.

[76] For the earliest examples, see Anghie (1993), Mutua (1996).

question of its postcoloniality not only essentially unresolvable but also essentially un-posable *within the terms of the newly reformed intra-disciplinary imaginary*.[77]

5.6 Rethinking International Law's Relationship with 'Central Asia': A Postcolonial International Law Beyond CAT and TWAIL

An ideologeme is an ideologically charged trope or cluster of tropes the exact political significance of which is neither pre-given nor historically fixed but can only be grasped through a close analysis both of its actual legitimating effects (political impact) and the structural differentiation that separates it from other such alternative tropes or clusters of tropes (its placing within the field of rival framings and interpretations). What makes both the CAT narrative *and* the idea of reducing the possibility of postcolonial critique in international law into TWAIL-style geographic framework ideologemes is not just the fact that each of them helps make a certain range of political outcomes in the relationship between the international legal system and a certain group of states or economic interests more likely and other outcomes less likely, but also the fact that in making use of these *artefacts* in their discourse, international lawyers also at the same time signal their rejection of other standardized narrative complexes that could be used in their stead, such as, say, old-school Orientalist narratives that cast Central Asian history as the epiphenomenal projection of some eternal Islamicate essence or liberal-internationalist narratives that insist on carving up the legal geography of international law in terms of liberal vs non-liberal states, rather than postcolonial vs non-postcolonial ones. It is the ideological messaging that comes from this kind of signaling—a messaging that is intended to say as much about us and our conception of ourselves as it does about how we actually understand the world—that really makes the task of understanding the impact which the CAT tradition and the TWAIL-inspired impoverishment of international law's geographic imaginary have had on the discipline of international law so important.

The unopposed continuation of the two-pronged dynamic that consists, on the one hand, of the CAT's enduring influence over the general practice of the international law imaginary and, on the other hand, of the uncritical reproduction of the TWAIL's 'monopolizing' claim over the project of postcolonial criticism in international law does not just impact the political relationship between the discipline and Central Asia, it also entrenches a certain model of self-understanding—that is to say, helps interpellate into existence a certain kind of political identity—within the international law profession itself.

What happens when the question of postcoloniality gets bypassed or becomes impossible to ask on account of some preconceived mental image? Much of the argument sketched out in the previous sections treads familiar ground. There is a

[77] On the mainstreaming of TWAIL over time, see Haskell (2014), Becker Lorca (2024).

good reason for this, of course. One can't get to talking about ways forward without understanding first what is wrong with remaining where one is.

The breathtaking neocolonialism of the CAT outlook, not to mention its sheer racialism, cries out for years if not decades of relentless and unforgiving denunciation, but the fact of its disciplinarily 'foreign' origin also presents a critical opportunity in the context of post-TWAIL-focused international legal thought: to honor Central Asia's uneasy path of decolonization by constructing a representational framework that would enable its recognition while also remaining, fully and clearly, a product of international legal analysis. The first step toward that, I would like to suggest, is to attend to the development of two analytically separate but closely intertwined practical narratives: one about the general place the national legal systems of the five Central Asian states occupy today in the broader global legal and political arena; the other about the politics of their ongoing relationship with the contemporary international law system and its institutions. With the TWAIL-inspired impoverishment of the discipline's legal-geographic imaginary, this is not going to be an easy task. One, however, must start somewhere.

The original sin of the CAT narrative was its selectively dehistoricizing construction of Central Asia. Bringing that sensibility to those mental and discursive spaces in which the terms of international law's encounter with Central Asia took shape has meant that not only were the actors and institutions leading that encounter on international law's side encouraged to turn a blind eye to Central Asia's basic postcolonial condition, as far as matters of international legal policy were concerned, but it also helped to decouple Central Asia from the rest of the decolonized world.

If the suppression of the broader question of Central Asia's postocoloniality was the source of the original problem, a simple willy-nilly readmission of this question into our collective discourse is not in itself necessarily going to be a sufficient solution. There is no doubt that, under terms that made historical sense at the time, before gaining their independence, the five Central Asian states formed a part of the Second World. There is also little doubt that today they do not. Does this mean that they should therefore be considered now to be a part of the Third World? The idea that a group of states which began as part of the Second World could then join the Third World, quite apart from the rather unhelpful analogies it evokes of sports team getting relegated at the end of a bad season, brings into question not only the essential logic of the concept of the Third World itself, it also destabilizes, through an extension of the same critical thrust, the broader category of postcoloniality itself. To the first point, the geopolitical phenomenon that this concept sought to express had a clearly defined historical ontology, whose basic framework no longer resonates with the existing realities. To the second, if the concept of the 'postcolonial world' can end up covering so many dissimilar groups of states and peoples—everything from Egypt to Cameroon to Kazakhstan—what is it really that they are all meant to have in common that would justify the retention of this and other related concepts as analytically effective categories? If somehow we manage to get rid of postcoloniality as an analytically effective category, how could we then tell the stories of those states and peoples that we would have previously labeled 'postcolonial' in a way that would not ignore or obfuscate the most basic realities of their historical experience the way, for example, that the CAT narrative has done to Central Asia?

I am not sure I have clear readymade answers to any of these questions, but I have a few hunches, and it is on that note that I want to finish this chapter:

- The five Central Asian states were once a part of the Second World. They are not now. That doesn't mean they are a part of the Third World. The idea of the Third World may constitute an occasionally helpful ideological trope, but as an analytical category it is devoid of any utility and often helps hide more than it can help clarify. The only condition on which its use can even be contemplated is if it expressly gets placed, in Derridean terms, *sous rature*.[78] However, most international lawyers do not read Derrida and do not use Derridean categories to organize their practice, so it is probably best if both the idea of the Third World itself and TWAIL as categories of international legal thought are simply put to rest.
- Central Asian states are postcolonial societies. The kind of postcoloniality they have experienced and are experiencing differs from that experienced by former British and French colonies, and downplaying this fact will lead to only marginally worse results than pretending, like the CAT tradition has, that Central Asia inhabits a *sui generis* legal and political reality that has little in common with the realities inhabited by other regions and countries that experienced Western colonialism.
- One of the ways in which Central Asia's distinctiveness in matters of postcoloniality manifests itself is in its complex relationship with what one might call for the sake of brevity the post-Soviet legal culture. The post-Soviet legal culture is a distinct mode of legal consciousness (in Duncan Kennedy's sense of the term)[79] that is exemplified, on the one hand, in the relatively uninterrupted continuation of Soviet-style institutional frameworks (such as the enduring prevalence of *prokuratura*) and patterns of legal practice (such as the insistence, wherever possible, to formulate the termination of employment relations as 'at one's own initiative' (*po sobstvennomu zhelaniiu*)) and, on the other hand, the organic persistence of a distinctly late-Soviet dual consciousness vis-à-vis the question of law's autonomy wherein, as during the late Soviet period, law for Central Asians today is somehow both *still* a Victorian-style science and a tool of political domination.
  - Like with the late-period Soviets, the ruling model for the idea of the legal science is found in German pandectism as refracted through a crude, simplified version of socio-legal jurisprudence. The general prevalence of such an orientation toward law inevitably supports the persistence, in the context of the mainstream legal-cultural position, of a strong fondness for Austinian-style legal positivism (in terms of the practical-legal sensibility) and a general predisposition in favor of a clearly articulated and stable 'vertical of power' (in terms of the practical-institutional consensus concerning what seems to be necessary to meet the legal-interpretational and law-enforcement needs of a

[78] See Powell (1997, pp. 46–7).

[79] See Kennedy (2006, pp. 19–23).

legal system built on these premises). Finally, the counterpoint to this sort of mainstream is then given the shape, within this mode of legal consciousness, of a quasi-moralist rights-centric and social justice-focused (but fundamentally apolitical) sensibility.

- A large part of what makes the CAT-inspired discourse not only neocolonial but also obscurantist has been its tendency to interpret the misalignment between the institutional vision encoded in the post-Soviet legal culture and the vision encoded in the post-Cold War Euro-American legal culture as evidence of Central Asia's fundamental legal-cultural underdevelopment and authoritarian biases rather than the sign of a basic imaginational discontinuity between rival legal-political paradigms.

References

Abashin S (2015) Sovestkii Kishlak: Mezhdu Kolonializmom i Modernizatsiey. Novoe Literaturnoe Obozrenie, Moscow

Anghie A (1993) 'The heart of my home': colonialism, environmental damage, and the Nauru case. Harv Int Law J 34:445

Anghie A (2005) Imperialism, sovereignty and the making of international law. Cambridge University Press, Cambridge

An-Naim A (2000) Human Rights and Islamic identity in France and Uzbekistan: mediation of the local and global. Hum Rights Q 22:906

von Arnauld A (2023) Völkerrecht, 5th edn. C.F. Müller, Heidelberg

Arvic JF et al. (2007) The cost of being landlocked: logistics costs and supply chain reliability. World Bank policy research working paper 4258. https://documents.worldbank.org/en/publication/documents-reports/documentdetail/987461468008762479/pdf

Bakhtin MM, Medvedev PN (1991) The formal method in literary scholarship: a critical introduction to sociological poetics. The Johns Hopkins University Press, Baltimore, MD

Ball P (2005) Critical mass: how one thing leads to another. Arrow Books, London

Becker Lorca A (2024) After TWAIL's success, what next? Eur J Int Law 34:779

Blackmon P (2021) After Karimov and Nazarbayev: change in Uzbekistan and Kazakhstan? CentL Asian Surv 40:179

Bellamy A, Dunne T (eds) (2016) The Oxford handbook of the responsibility to protect. Oxford University Press, Oxford

Boyle A (2003) Central Asian water problems: the role of international law. In: Cummings S (ed) Oil, transition and security in Central Asia. Routledge, London, pp 203–215

Brill Olcott M (2005) Central Asia's second chance. Carnegie Endowment for International Peace, Washington, DC

Burghart D, Sabonis-Helf T (eds) (2018) Central Asia in the era of sovereignty: the return of Tamerlane? Lexington Books, Lanham, MD

Cassese A (2005) International law, 2nd edn. Oxford University Press, Oxford

Chandler D (2007) The responsibility to protect? Imposing the 'liberal peace.' Int Peacekeeping 11:59

Chayes A, Handler Chayes A (1994) The new sovereignty: compliance with international regulatory agreements. Harvard University Press, Cambridge, MA

Chimni BS (2004) International institutions today: an imperial global state in the making. Eur J Int Law 15:1

Clark TJ (2013) Lucky hunter-gatherers. Lond Rev Books 35(6):11.
Collins K (2006) Clan politics and regime transition in Central Asia. Cambridge University Press, Cambridge
Combacau J, Sur S (2019) Droit international public, 13th edn. LGDJ, Paris
Conference on Security and Cooperation in Europe (CSCE) (1990) Charter of Paris for a New Europe. https://www.osce.org/files/f/documents/0/6/39516.pdf
Cooley A (2012) Great Games, local rules: the new great power contest in Central Asia. Oxford University Press, Oxford
Cosio-Pascal E (2010) Paris Club: intergovernmental relations in debt restructuring. In: Herman B et al (eds) Overcoming developing country debt crises. Oxford University Press, Oxford, pp 231–276
Council on Foreign Relations (CFR) (2021) Timeline: The US War in Afghanistan. https://www.cfr.org/timeline/us-war-afghanistan
Crawford J (2019) Brownlie's principles of public international law. Oxford University Press, Oxford
Cummings S (2012) Understanding Central Asia: politics and contested transformations. Routledge, London
Cypher J, Dietz J (2009) The process of economic development, 3rd edn. Routledge, London
Dixon M (2013) Textbook on international law, 7th edn. Oxford University Press, Oxford
Dupuy PM (2004) Droit international public, 7eme edn. Editions Dalloz, Paris
Evans M (ed) (2024) International law, 6th edn. Oxford University Press, Oxford
Friesendorf C (2022) Supporting democratic policing in Central Asia: limitations of the OSCE. Eur Asia Stud 74:1433
Gardiner R (2003) International law. Pearson, Harlow.
Gellhorn E (1973) Adverse publicity by administrative agencies. Harv Law Rev 86:1380
Goldstone J et al (2000) State failure task force report: phase III findings. https://www.raulzelik.net/images/rztextarchiv/uniseminare/statefailure%20task%20force.pdf.
Gong G (1984) The Standard of 'civilization' in international society. Oxford University Press, New York
Hale R (1923) Coercion and distribution in a supposedly non-coercive state. Polit Sci Q 39:470
Hanks R (2016) Narratives of Islam in Uzbekistan: authoritarian myths and the Janus-State Syndrome. Central Asian Surv 35:501
Haskell J (2016) Will the real transitology please stand up? Balt Yearb Int Law 15:62
Haskell J (2014) TRAIL-ing TWAIL: arguments and blind spots. Can J Law Jurisprud 27:383
Holmes OW (1897) The path of the law. Harv Law Rev 10:457
Huntington S (1996) The clash of civilizations and the remaking of world order. Simon & Schuster, London
Jackson R (1990) Quasi-States: sovereignty, international relations, and the third world. Cambridge University Press, Cambridge
Jameson F (2002) The political unconscious: narrative as a socially symbolic act. Routledge, London
Jones Luong P (2002) Institutional change and political continuity in post-soviet central Asia: power, perceptions, and pacts. Cambridge University Press, Cambridge
Kangas R (2002) Uzbekistan: the Karimov Presidency—Amir Timur revisited. In: Cummings S (ed) Power and change in Central Asia. Routledge, London, pp 130–149
Kassymbekova B, Chokobaeva A (2021) On writing soviet history of Central Asia: frameworks, challenges, prospects. Central Asian Surv 40:483
Kelsen H (1953) Théorie du droit international public. Recueil des Cours 84:1
Kennedy D (2006) Three globalizations of law and legal thought. In: Trubek D, Santos A (eds) The new law and economic development: a critical appraisal. Cambridge University Press, Cambridge, pp 19–73
Kennedy D (1993) Sexy Dressing Etc. Harvard University Press, Cambridge, MA
Klabbers J (2021) International law, 3rd edn. Cambridge University Press, Cambridge

Knox Cand Sharipova D (2024) Consultative authoritarianism in Central Asia. Eur Asia Stud 76:1120
Koch N (2018) Disorder over the border: spinning the spectre of instability through time and space in Central Asia. Central Asian Survey 37:13
Koskenniemi M (2021) To the uttermost parts of the Earth. Cambridge University Press, Cambridge
Koskenniemi M (2002) The gentle civilizer of nations. Cambridge University Press, Cambridge
Kunysz N (2012) From Sultanism to Neopatrimonialism? Regionalism within Turkmenistan. Centr Asian Surv 31:1
Lambach D (2004) The Perils of weakness: failed states and perceptions of threat in Europe and Australia. Conference Paper. https://www.researchgate.net/publication/272509903_The_Perils_of_Weakness_Failed_States_and_Perceptions_of_Threat_in_Europe_and_Australias
Lemay-Hebert N (2010) Trying to make sense of the contemporary debate on state-building: the legitimacy and the institutional approaches on state, state collapse and state-building. Conference Paper. http://pure-oai.bham.ac.uk/ws/files/6469815/PSA_Trying_to_Make_Sense.pdf
Lempp J, Mayer S (eds) (2024) Central Asia in a multipolar world. Springer, Wiesbaden
Lempp J et al (2024) The political system of Kyrgyzstan. In: Lempp J, Mayer S (eds) Central Asia in a multipolar world. Springer, Wiesbaden, pp 75–90
Lewis D (2008) The temptations of tyranny in Central Asia. Columbia University Press, New York
Malanczuk P (ed) (1997) Akehurst's Modern introduction to international law, 7th rev. edn. Routledge, London
Merry SE (2016) The seductions of quantification: measuring human rights, gender violence, and sex trafficking. The University of Chicago Press, Chicago, IL
Merry SE et al (eds) (2015) The quiet power of indicators: measuring governance, corruption, and rule of law. Cambridge University Press, Cambridge
Meyer K, Blair Brysac S (1999) Tournament of shadows: the great game and the race for empire in Central Asia. Basic Books, New York
Mutua M (1996) The ideology of human rights. VA J Int Law 36:589
Myer W (2002) Islam and Colonialism: Western perspectives on Soviet Asia. Routledge, London
Newton S (2017) The constitutional systems of the independent Central Asian states. Hart, Oxford
Nicola F (2021) Scandal involving World Bank's "doing business" index exposes problems in using Sportslike rankings to guide development goals. The Conversation. https://theconversation.com/scandal-involving-world-banks-ng-business-index-exposes-problems-in-using-sportslike-rankings-to-guide-development-goals-169691
Northrop D (2004) Veiled Empire: gender and power in Stalinist Central Asia. Cornell University Press, Ithaca, NY
Powell J (1997) Derrida for beginners. Writers and Readers Publishing, Danbury, CT
Rasulov A (2003) Revisiting state succession to humanitarian treaties: is there a case for automaticity? Eur J Int Law 14:141
Rittich K (2006) The future of law and development: second-generation reforms and the incorporation of the social. In: Trubek D, Santos A (eds) The new law and economic development: A critical appraisal. Cambridge University Press, Cambridge, pp 203–252
Roche S (2018) Knowledge production on Central Asia: transcultural approaches in Central Asian studies. J Transcultural Stud 9:1
Rodrik D (2007) One economics, many recipes: globalization, institutions, and economic growth. Princeton University Press, Princeton, NJ
Said E (1978) Orientalism (1978). Vintage Books, New York
Santos A (2006) The World Bank's uses of the "rule of law' promise in economic development. In: Trubek D, Santos A (eds) The new law and economic development: a critical appraisal. Cambridge University Press, Cambridge, pp 253–300
Schimmelfennig F (2005) The EU: promoting liberal-democracy through membership conditionality. In: Flockhart T (ed) Socializing democratic norms. Palgrave, London, pp 106–126
Schwarzenberger G (1950) The problem of an international criminal law. Curr Leg Probl 3:263
Shaw M (2017) International law, 8th edn. Cambridge University Press, Cambridge

Shaw M (2003) International law, 5th edn. Cambridge University Press, Cambridge
Sievers E (2002a) Transboundary jurisdiction and watercourse law: China, Kazakhstan, and the Irtysh. Texas Int Law J 37:1
Sievers E (2002b) Water, conflict, and regional security in Central Asia. NYU Environ Law J 10:356
Sievers E (2003) The Post-Soviet decline of Central Asia: sustainable development and comprehensive capital. Routledge, London
Spaiser OA (2018) The European Union's influence in Central Asia: geopolitical challenges and responses. Lexington Books, Lanham, MD
Starr SF (2018) The long game on the silk road: US and EU strategy for Central Asia and the Caucasus. Rowman & Littlefield, Lanham, MD
Stiglitz J (2008) Is there a Post-Washington consensus consensus? In: Serra N, Stiglitz J (eds) The Washington consensus reconsidered. Oxford University Press, Oxford, pp 41–56
Stiglitz J (2021) A coup attempt at the IMF. Project Syndicate. https://www.project-syndicate.org/commentary/coup-attempt-against-imf-managing-director-georgieva-by-joseph-e-stiglitz-2021-09
Straw J (2002) Failed and failing states. Speech delivered at the European Research Institute, University of Birmingham
Warkotsch A (ed) (2010) The European Union and Central Asia. Routledge, London
White H (1978) Tropics of discourse. The Johns Hopkins University Press, Baltimore, MD
White ND, Abbas A (2003) Countermeasures and sanctions. In: Evans M (ed) International law. Oxford University Press, Oxford, pp 505–528
Wooden A, Stefes C (2009) Multivaried and interacting paths of change in Central Eurasia. In: Wooden A, Stefes C (eds) The politics of transition in Central Asia and the Caucasus: enduring legacies and emerging challenges. Routledge, London, pp 249–263
World Bank (2007) Doing business 2008: Central Asia. https://documents.worldbank.org/en/publication/documents-reports/documentdetail/488201468016223313/pdf
World Bank (2009a) Doing Business 2010: Uzbekistan comparing regulation in 183 economies. https://documents.worldbank.org/en/publication/documents-reports/documentdetail/732001468127806268/ng-business-2010-uzbekistan-comparing-regulation-in-183-economies.
World Bank (2009b) Doing business 2010: Kyrgyz Republic comparing regulation in 183 economies. https://documents.worldbank.org/en/publication/documents-reports/documentdetail/334731468263685697/ng-business-2010-kyrgyz-republic-comparing-regulation-in-183-economies
World Bank (2022) Business enabling environment. Concept Note. https://thedocs.worldbank.org/en/doc/2250b12dfe798507f7b42064378cc616-0540012022/original/BEE-Concept-Note-December-2022.pdf
World Bank (2025) Business-Ready (B-READY). https://www.worldbank.org/en/businessready

Part II
International Law as a Factor in the Central Asian Politics

Chapter 6
The Implementation and Effectiveness of International Law in Central Asia

Sébastien Lafrance, Nik Khakhar, and Ayazhan Kazybekova

Abstract For international legal norms to be effective, they must be reflected and genuinely applied in the domestic law of a state. The main issue discussed in this chapter is two-fold. First, after discussing the Central Asian context, the authors examine the means and methods, more specifically the incorporation (monism) or the transformation (dualism) of international legal norms, that are privileged by one or another Central Asian country in implementing international legal norms, including what this entails and where the choice made for this or that approach comes from, from both a factual and legal perspective. Second, the authors turn their minds to the question of the hierarchical status of international law as provided by Central Asian constitutions. Overall, the implementation of international law is studied in the context in which it is most often used, the integration of human rights law into domestic law, with a focus on the Central Asian context.

Keywords International Law · Monism · Dualism · Constitutional Law · Human Rights · Central Asia · Implementation · Effectiveness · Soviet Legacy · Kazakhstan · Kyrgyzstan · Tajikistan · Turkmenistan · Uzbekistan

This work was prepared separately from Sébastien Lafrance's and Nik Khakhar's employment responsibilities at the Public Prosecution Service of Canada. The views, opinions, and conclusions expressed herein are personal to these authors and should not be construed as those of the Public Prosecution Service of Canada or the Canadian Federal Crown.

S. Lafrance (✉)
Tashkent State University of Law, Tashkent, Uzbekistan
e-mail: seblafrance1975@gmail.com

N. Khakhar
Toronto, ON, Canada

A. Kazybekova
Maqsut Narikbayev University, Astana, Kazakhstan

S. Sayapin (ed.), *International Law, Politics and Security in Central Asia*,
https://doi.org/10.1007/978-3-032-17818-3_6

6.1 Introduction

For international legal norms to be effective, they must be reflected and genuinely applied in the domestic law of a state.[1] The question of how international law is implemented within national legal systems is a complex issue.[2] The main issue discussed in this chapter is two-fold. First, after discussing the Central Asian context, the authors examine the means and methods[3]—more specifically the incorporation (monism)[4] or the transformation[5] (dualism) of international legal norms—that are privileged by one or another Central Asian country in implementing international legal norms, including what this entails and where the choice made for this or that approach comes from, from both a factual and legal perspective. In that respect, the attention of the authors is more focused on the implementation of international treaties in Central Asia than on the implementation of customary international law,[6] mostly because '[m]uch of the substantive content of contemporary international law is … found in formal treaties'.[7] Second, the authors turn their minds to the question of the hierarchical status of international law as provided by Central Asian constitutions, since these represent the 'fundamental or primary norm'[8] in any country, and more importantly, because 'the question of how norms of public international law are received into domestic legal systems is *largely* a matter of constitutional law.'[9] Overall, the implementation of international law is studied in the context it is 'most often used'—the integration of human rights law into domestic law[10]—with a focus on the Central Asian context.

[1] Monaco (1968, p. 250).

[2] Tursunova (2019, p. 64).

[3] Oralova and Rakisheva (2014, pp. 341–342) and Nogoibaeva and Myrsalieva (2009, p. 98).

[4] Mendez (2013, p 17): 'By incorporation what is meant … is that the treaty is considered to become [automatically] a binding part of domestic law.' Oralova and Rakhisheva, ibid: '[T]he difference between incorporation and transformation is that the former adopts international law into national law just because it is international law, whereas the later requires a deliberate act on the part of the state concerned.'

[5] Capotorti (1994, pp. 222–223). Oralova and Rakisheva (2014, p. 342): 'The doctrine of transformation … stipulates that rules of international law do not become part of national law until they have been expressly adopted by the State.'

[6] Tiunov (2009, p. 270): Even though 'history of international law shows that its most important provisions have [initially] developed in the form of customary law' [translated from Russian by Sébastien Lafrance].

[7] Brunnée and Toope (2002, p. 13); see, e.g., for Kyrgyzstan: Kadyralieva (2021, p. 182); see, e.g., for Uzbekistan: Rakhimova (2012, p. 146).

[8] Kelsen (1926, p. 258) [translated from French by Sébastien Lafrance].

[9] Van Ert (2010, p. 927) (italics added); Mirkine-Guetzévitch (1931, p. 355), Mosler (1957, p. 633), and Sperduti (1976, p. 388).

[10] Rakhimova (2012, p. 144).

6.2 What Is Central Asia?

It would be a mistake and oversimplification to summarily describe the five Central Asian countries through the prism of either the unofficial motto of Switzerland[11] or the motto of the three musketeers[12]: 'One for all, and all for one'. As Sayapin puts it, 'there is no single Central Asia'.[13] Each Central Asian country 'developed differently' following the collapse of the Soviet Union,[14] meaning, for instance, that '[i]n spite of adopting [sometimes] *identical* laws, the ways of implementing them [are different] from each other'.[15] Similarly, Central Asian countries have adjusted their respective constitutions over time in 'revealingly divergent ways',[16] including, for example, when it comes to how international law is implemented into their domestic law.

Mosler wisely wrote in 1957 that '[w]e cannot consider a legal order by ignoring the facts … regulated by this legal order.'[17] Therefore, inspired by some determining factors used by one author to tackle the issue of human rights in Kazakhstan,[18] the following section of this chapter uses the spirit of some of those factors which apply, in our opinion, to Central Asia as a whole and, more particularly, to better understand what Central Asia in the context of our analysis. These factors are: first, the influence of Russia on Central Asia, more specifically before, during and after the Soviet times; second, the relationship (and the tensions that exist) between the East and the West; and third, the situation of human rights in Central Asia.

6.3 Russia's Influence on Central Asia

A discussion of the implementation and enforcement of international law in Central Asia could hardly ignore the role of Russia in the region. Russia's influence on Central Asia is undeniable and pre-dates the birth of the Soviet Union following the October Revolution in 1917.[19] The tie between Central Asia and Russia remains strong even after the collapse of the latter. By analogy with the old adage, 'when the United States sneezes, the world catches a cold',[20] 'whatever law the Russian Federation adopts has a subsequent "chilling" effect on Central Asia.'[21] This is not only because of

[11] Usually used in Latin, i.e., *unus pro omnibus, omnes pro uno.*

[12] Dumas (1844).

[13] Sayapin (2023, p. 15) and Girshovich (2019, p. 701).

[14] Wittke and Rabinovych (2022, p. 251).

[15] Yunusov (2014, p. 2) (italics added).

[16] Newman (2017, p. 2).

[17] Mosler (1957, p. 629).

[18] Bisztyga (2015, p. 317).

[19] See generally, e.g., Glenn (1999).

[20] See, e.g., Read (2009, pp. 144–148) and Lafrance (2024).

[21] Toktogazieva (2024, p. 129) and Toktogazieva (2019, p. 318).

the geographical proximity of Central Asia to Russia—if so, the importance of their relations might not be any different than those of many neighbouring countries[22]—but also because of the historic and linguistic connections between the two. Russia is thus an inescapable partner in the region.[23]

6.3.1 The Importance of Historical Ties and of (Known and Unknown) Languages

While all of Central Asia was colonized by the Russian Empire starting in the mid-nineteenth century, and later Sovietized in the twentieth century, Kazakhstan experienced particular Russification.[24] In Kazakhstan, 'most of the population speaks Russian [and] only about half of ethnic Kazaks [*sic*] speak Kazak [*sic*] fluently.'[25] Some even go as far as claiming that Kazakhstan and Russia have 'a common destiny',[26] which, if true, could single out the former in one way or another from the other Central Asian countries. This view is, however, hardly unanimous in Kazakhstan.[27] What is not arguable is that '*Central Asia and Kazakhstan* was the standard Soviet designation for the region, emphasizing the distinctiveness of Kazakhstan.'[28] This specific feature does not preclude the fact that the Russian language still has, even after the collapse of the Soviet Union where it was the *lengua franca*,[29] a special status, not only in Kazakhstan, but also in two other Central Asian constitutions, namely those of Kyrgyzstan, which has 'a strong Soviet legacy',[30] and Tajikistan.[31] In addition, even though Uzbekistan, for example, does not give special status to the Russian language in its constitution, it still 'shares [a] significant legal tradition'[32] with Russia, as do other post-Soviet States.[33]

---

22 Bureau of Western Hemisphere Affairs 2024.

23 See, e.g., Ayupova (2015, p. 42).

24 Newman (2017, p. 32).

25 Ayupova (1998, p. 84).

26 See, e.g., Zotov (2022).

27 For example, Mehrara (2024).

28 Newman (2017, p. 32).

29 Against all odds, nowhere in the Constitution (Fundamental Law) of the Union of Soviet Socialist Republics of 1977 (the last in force) was Russian given a prominent status over any other languages of the other Soviet republics.

30 Sayapin (2023, p. 18).

31 Kazakhstan's Constitution of 1995, Article 7(2): 'Russian language shall be officially used on equal grounds along with the Kazakh language'; Kyrgyzstan's Constitution of 2010: 'The Russian language shall be used as the official language in the Kyrgyz Republic', Article 13(2), even though '[t]he Kyrgyz language is the State language of the Kyrgyz Republic', Article 13(1); Tajikistan's Constitution of 1994, Article 2: 'Russian shall be the language of inter-ethnic communication' without being, however, an official language.

32 Bantekas (2005, p. 18).

33 Tkatova (2010, p. 216).

The continuing impregnation of the Russian language in all Central Asian countries is not without consequences on how these countries approach the law in general, and international law in particular, including its implementation and enforcement. Even if we were to put aside for a moment the pure Soviet legacy in our analysis, the language barrier *alone*, caused by the predominance of the Russian language, combined with the lack of knowledge of the English language and other foreign languages,[34] in addition to the fact that most international treaties are not available in the national languages as an official translation,[35] and added to the fact that some unofficial translations contain sometimes ludicrous and questionable translations,[36] would have the effect of creating create a pernicious *intellectual shield* against the sharing of knowledge between Central Asia and the rest of the world.[37] This sharing could obviously go both ways since 'several principles formulated by Russia have become fundamental elements of international law',[38] such as the freedom of the seas, and so have some of the principles of Soviet foreign policy.[39] Why then should the intensity of the blooming and possible sharing of ideas be any different in Central Asia, now having five independent states?

6.3.2 Soviet Legacy in Central Asia: Same Old?

The Soviet Union experience is 'critical',[40] even after its fall, to understanding Central Asia today. As Wittke and Rabinovych state, 'the … practice of … international law in many post-Soviet countries will continue to be shaped by shared continuities inherited from the Soviet past.'[41] While it is true that '[t]he communist system and the communist ideology failed, and [that] their influence is insignificant',[42] as declared by Tajikistan's representative at the United Nations General Assembly in 1992, the Soviet legacy remains quite vivid, to various degrees, throughout Central Asia, and it still exists, for example, in the judiciary system, and more broadly in the legal field, where the 'old [Soviet] thinking [still] dominates'.[43]

[34] Atadjanov (2021, p. 29) and Sayapin (2021).

[35] See, e.g., for Uzbekistan: Umirdinov and Khamikov (2020, p. 234).

[36] See, e.g., Article 169 of the Penal Code of Kazakhstan, which describes 'ecocide' in its unofficial translation as the '[m]ass destruction of the *vegetable* or animal world' (italics added) wherein 'vegetable' should read 'vegetation'.

[37] Atadjanov (2021, p. 29).

[38] Krylov (1947, p. 411) [translated from French by Sébastien Lafrance].

[39] Ibid., p. 432.

[40] Kangas (2018, p. 32).

[41] Wittke and Rabinovych (2022, p. 267).

[42] Tajikistan. United Nations General Assembly, 47th Sess, 8 October 1992, p. 62; Newman (2017, p. 2).

[43] Kangas (2018, p. 39).

For the sake of clarity, what we refer to here is indeed the '*Soviet* way of thinking', and not what was put in place following the fall of the Soviet Union, such as the Community of Independent States (CIS),[44] 'a fairly loose organization of States',[45] whose power is not as compelling as was that of the Soviet Union. If one were to 'wonder whether membership in the CIS affects the domestic implementation of international law in the CIS States',[46] we could give the example of two of the five Central Asian States, who either signed (Kyrgyzstan) or ratified (Tajikistan) the 1995 Convention on Human Rights and Fundamental Freedoms of the Commonwealth of Independent States,[47] noting that this Convention's enforcement mechanisms are described, at least by one author, as being 'obsolete'.[48] Therefore, if the CIS was meant to somehow hide the 'invisible hand' of Russia, it would be fair to say that its power through this specific means would remain somewhat limited.

Atadjanov reported on the 'lack of interest and understanding of the significance of international law implementation at the country level'[49] in Central Asia, but the exact same observation can also be made for other parts of the world.[50] The lack of penetration of Western legal ideas and concepts in Central Asia cannot be, however, of any benefit for anyone. In that respect, Sayapin rightfully replied, agreeing with Atadjanov cited above, that there is 'a lot to learn from international law doctrines beyond the Russian-speaking world.'[51] This boils down to the question of how the above-mentioned intellectual shield continues live on after the fall of the Soviet Union. Newman observed that '[i]t has become customary for analyses of Central Asia … to invoke "Soviet legacies" [where it] chiefly seem[s] to refer to the obstinate persistence of Soviet political and administrative culture, attitudes and reflexes, after the demise of Soviet ideology.'[52] Let us recall (even if it may be obvious for many readers) that the Soviet 'culture' involved, among many other things, a 'distrust of

[44] It regroups most of the former Soviet Republics except the Baltic States and Ukraine.

[45] Danilenko (1999, p. 67).

[46] Ibid., p. 66.

[47] Council of Europe 2001 Resolution 1249.

[48] Mihr (2023, p. 32). This author wrote more precisely that 'the 1995 Convention on Human Rights and Fundamental Freedoms of the CIS has *neither monitoring nor enforcement mechanisms* and is therefore seen as obsolete' (italics added), but Article 34 of that Convention rather stipulates the existence of *monitoring* via the works of the Human Rights Commission of the Commonwealth of Independent States.

[49] Atadjanov (2021, p. 31); for Central Asian State officials specifically, see Lehner (2009, p. 49); for Uzbekistan, see, e.g., Umirdinov and Khamikov (2020, p. 233).

[50] See, e.g., the Canadian equivalent observation made by Brunnée and Toope (2002, pp. 9–10): '[S]ome of the difficulties experienced in the domestic application of international law appear to be rooted in a lack of familiarity with international law itself and in a resulting reluctance [by the courts] to engage in the identification of the applicable international law.'

[51] Sayapin (2022, p. 324).

[52] Newman (2017, pp. 84–85).

democracy'.[53] We should all be aware that democracy, including the strict observance of human rights,[54] is a fundamental feature of most modern Western countries.

Why then is the Soviet legacy never-ending, to various degrees, in Central Asia? The authors would like to attempt explaining this almost-indelible stain of the past, the answer to which may, at least partially, reside in (the remnants of) the tensions that were prevalent not only during the Cold War, but also pre-dating the October Revolution. These tensions thus have deeper roots in history, extending to before the twentieth century.

6.4 Conundrum of the Relationship Between the East and the West

The intrinsic tensions that exist between the West and the East are not new. The old opposition between Slavophiles and Pro-Westerners, best encapsulated in the seminal work of Berdyaev's 'The Russian Idea' where he wrote that '[t]he Russian people is not purely European and it is not purely Asiatic. ... It unites two worlds, and within the Russian soul two principles are always engaged in strife – the Eastern and the Western',[55] has been replaced in Central Asia, according to Tkatova, 'by antagonism between the Atlantists and Eurasists'.[56] One could thus argue that the more things change, the more they remain the same.

In the early 1990s, soon after the independence of each former Soviet republic, some, if not many, believed that the new states would almost undoubtedly move towards a democratic political regime.[57] The understanding of these optimistic people was that there was no way back to the former nor to any other form of authoritarian regime. This was the zeitgeist of the time. Fukuyama had written in 1989, year of the fall of the Berlin Wall, that the end of the Cold War marked 'the *end point* of mankind's ideological evolution and the *universalization of Western liberal democracy* as the *final* form of human government.'[58] It turned out, as we now all know, that the following years did not mark the end of history at all, and that 'democratization in the post-Soviet space has been much slower and uneven than what was predicted.'[59] In fact, the collapse of the Soviet Union and its satellite states paved the way for the next chapter of history, which unfolded in the reshuffling of the countries that are now the world's leading powers—the inexorable and unstoppable rise of socialist-led

53 Ayupova (2015, p. 43).

54 Danilenko (1998, p. 4).

55 Berdyaev (1948, p. 1) and Lafrance (2022b, pp. 27–38).

56 Tkatova (2010, p. 217).

57 Norling and Cornell (2016, p. 8).

58 Fukuyama (1989, p. 4) (italics added) and Fukuyama (1992).

59 Norling and Cornell (2016, p. 8).

China and against the continued, if relatively declining,[60] leading role of the United States on the world scene.

It is also true that Central Asian governments (with the exception of Turkmenistan's) had also, following their independence, 'flirted with the idea of using Western concepts of legal rights',[61] and beyond flirting, some states, like Kyrgyzstan, even directly 'sought foreign assistance ... from the West'.[62] However, 'attitudes changed [in Central Asia] as a result of the difficulties faced when putting [Western ideals] into practice.'[63] As a result, Central Asian states have been 'swinging between the application by "inertia" of the Soviet conception of international law, the difficulties of adapting the Western models and the quest for their own "Central Asian" way.'[64] This oscillation between these different approaches to international law shows that the battle for democracy should not be considered as being over, and there is no guarantee either, given the rise of illiberal regimes in the Western world, that the gains democracy has made so far in Central Asia will not eventually turn into a Pyrrhic victory.

6.5 What About Human Rights in Central Asia?

Even though the prevailing view is that a new state becomes subject to existing international law without having to formally recognize it,[65] all the Central Asian states felt the need to claim the status of subject of international law following their independence.[66] All of them accessed to or ratified the United Nations human rights treaties rather than succeeding to them.[67] For example, they all ratified the International Covenant on Civil and Political Rights (ICCPR).[68] Two questions thus caught our attention in our study of the implementation and effectiveness of human rights in Central Asia: first, the question of the universality of human rights, and second, the argument of Central Asian cultural uniqueness. These are examined in turn below.

---

[60] Stevenson (2023).

[61] Kangas, p. 37.

[62] Ibid., p. 39.

[63] Ibid., p. 27.

[64] Tkatova (2010, p. 206).

[65] Kelsen (1926, p. 305).

[66] Newman (2017, p. 15).

[67] Girshovich (2019, p. 704).

[68] Kazakhstan (2006), Kyrgyzstan (1994), Tajikistan (1999), Turkmenistan (1997) and Uzbekistan (1995).

6.5.1 The Universality of Human Rights

In line with our overarching topic regarding the interactions between international law and domestic law in Central Asia, it should be recalled that the '[u]niversal and *effective* recognition of rights and freedoms must be achieved through the interaction of international and national measures.'[69] For some, the superiority of international law should impose itself in that context both for practical and moral reasons.[70] With this backdrop in mind, and based on the candid premise that nobody is against virtue (from a Western-centric perspective), a perception existed in the 1990s—and maybe still does—that international human rights standards 'expressed "*universal* human values" shared by the *majority* of the international community.'[71] This was not the case. The failure of this concept of universal human rights can be shown with an example taken straight from Central Asia: the former Turkmen president, Saparmurat Niyazov, also known as Türkmenbaşy (the head of the Turkmen) rejected this concept in 1992.[72]

Nonetheless, one could counter-argue that Turkmenistan is, unlike other Central Asian States, 'profoundly authoritarian'[73] and that it has 'pursued a managed isolationism',[74] which might distinguish it from its sister states. Of note, Turkmenistan's regime remained 'largely intact' even after the death of Türkmenbaşy.[75] The situation in Turkmenistan should not be understood as a reflection of reality in all Central Asian countries where, in fact, their governments have not 'deliberately' backtracked on their commitments to international human rights, at least on paper.[76] For instance, all current Central Asian constitutions include provisions regarding the protection of human rights,[77] and some of these constitutions even recognized their universality.[78] The other side of this is that these rights may also be restricted by the state[79] (but so can they be under international law[80]). In that respect, one should keep in mind that

[69] Tiunov (2009, p. 282) (italics added) [translated from Russian by Sébastien Lafrance].

[70] Virally (1964, p. 490).

[71] Danilenko (1998, p. 5) (italics added).

[72] Helsinki Watch (1993), cited in Panico (1993). As a side note, it must be mentioned here that 'national leaders (Presidents) have played an important role in defining [states'] approaches towards international law': Girshovich (2019, p. 703).

[73] Omelicheva (2018, p. 66).

[74] Newman (2017, p. 24) and Radchenko (2017, p. 168).

[75] Newman, ibid., p. 25 and 29.

[76] Mihr (2023, p. 32).

[77] Article 12 of the Constitution of Kazakhstan 1995; Paragraph 23(1), 56 and 26 of the Constitution of Kyrgyzstan 2021; Article 14 of the Constitution of Tajikistan 1994; Article 25 of the Constitution of Turkmenistan 2008; Preamble and Article 19 of the Constitution of Uzbekistan 2023.

[78] Article 55 of the Constitution of Kyrgyzstan 2021; Preamble of the Constitution of Uzbekistan 2023; Article 25 of the Constitution of Turkmenistan 2008.

[79] Article 39 of the Constitution of Kazakhstan 1995; Paragraph 23(2) of the Constitution of Kyrgyzstan 2021; Article 14 of the Constitution of Tajikistan 1994; Article 65 of the Constitution of Turkmenistan 2008; Article 21 of the Constitution of Uzbekistan 2023.

[80] For example, see Article 19(3) ICCPR for the freedom of expression.

authoritarian tendencies in governments 'may render the constitutional provisions on international law irrelevant' where the letter of the law would simply not suffice.[81]

Different from Turkmenistan, Kyrgyzstan was called in the 1990s an 'island of democracy'.[82] Regardless, all Central Asian States are experiencing 'a converge of authoritarianism', even though some of them have 'less outlandish forms' of it.[83] Generally speaking, 'there is a certain correlation between the efforts to establish democracy following the defeat of an authoritarian or totalitarian system', like the Soviet Union, 'in a war or revolution and the "*opening*" of state constitutions to … international law.'[84] If the disconnection caused by the Soviet Union, which then included de facto Central Asia, from the rest of the world was only due to the Cold War, then the end of the latter would have meant, almost automatically, perhaps from a naïve perspective, the *full* opening of Central Asia, and not, as was the case, a *gradual* opening,[85] which 'has not always been transformed into reality'[86] for what concerns the application of human rights standards. A *full* opening would have also meant, in turn, the reception and a *strict* application, beyond the letter of the law, of most, if not all, core international legal norms in the domestic legal order. This includes, more specifically, the *genuine* application of human rights in Central Asia.[87] Human rights in Central Asia correspond, at least on paper, to 'the European constitutional catalogues of freedoms and human rights'.[88] As aptly noted by two authors, 'whether binding or non-binding, *action* rather than aspiration is the true determinant of successful implementation' of international legal norms.[89]

Central Asia, following their newly-acquired independence, welcomed a 'direct penetration of international principles and norms'[90] by 'accepting unreservedly the democratic way of development and the European vision of international law',[91] which is nothing new in general for newly-born states of the twentieth century.[92] This penetration, some would call it pervasiveness, of the influence of the West not only meant the inclusion, for instance, of Western-type human rights, but also took

---

[81] Danilenko (1998, p. 41).

[82] Asanbekova et al. (2021, pp. 267–268), Omelicheva (2018, p. 62), and Rhodes and Tscherne-Lempiainen (2002, p. 40).

[83] Radchenko (2017, p. 171).

[84] Danilenko (1998, p. 2) (italics added).

[85] Ibid., p. 1.

[86] Danilenko (1999, p. 69).

[87] See, e.g., for Kazakhstan, Buzurtanova (2019, p. 113): 'Kazakhstan is selective in terms of their domestic application' of human rights.

[88] Bisztyga (2015, p. 319).

[89] Duxbury and Tan (2019, p. 14) (italics added).

[90] Danilenko (1998, p. 5).

[91] Tkatova (2010, pp. 211–212).

[92] Mosler (1957, p. 636): '[T]he constitutions born in recent years in countries which only later became sovereign and equal members of the community of international law use *mutatis mutandis* the traditional forms of organization used in the European and American world' [translated from French by Sébastien Lafrance].

the form, for example, of using western-style language[93] in the drafting of their initial constitutions as independent states. Therefore, the West had an influence on both the form and the substance of Central Asia's legal development following their independence.[94]

But mimicking the West when it comes to the human rights model does not necessarily mean, for instance, that the intentions behind doing this were all devoid of self-interest and solely oriented towards a candid legal harmonization of Central Asia with the West. This can be illustrated by the example of Kazakhstan after its signature of the ICCPR in 2002 where debates were held domestically about its ratification. Some wanted Kazakhstan to make a reservation to a provision of the ICCPR that was inconsistent with its constitution while 'the opposite view [to ratify it without reservations] would reassure the world community of Kazakhstan's consistent course towards democratic reforms and human rights.'[95] The latter view prevailed.

Some Central Asian leaders tapped 'into their earlier legal traditions to find philosophical and historical justifications [for asserting their power], even if they continued [at the same time] to *parrot* international norms and practices.'[96] In short, while the five Central Asian constitutions would not be considered a 'sham',[97] as the Soviet Union constitution was, the fact remains that Central Asian constitutions are 'all to a significant degree instrumentalist.'[98] In that context, Atadjanov recalls, however, that the 'five Central Asian constitutional systems [may be] instrumentalist [but] ... these systems are still young.'[99] This seems to echo, voluntarily or not, what the former Kazakh president replied in an interview given in 2010 when he said, 'We're a young democratic state ... democracy for us is not the beginning of the path, it is the end.'[100] Something similar has also been written by the former Uzbek president Karimov.[101] Similarly to Atadjanov, Sayapin added that Central Asian States are 'still learning to apply international human rights law'.[102]

Central Asian countries only *half* opened the door to the reception in their domestic law of international legal norms following their independence, in contrast to the 'Soviet legal order [that] remained *closed* to international legal norms.'[103] For

93 Kangas (2018, p. 33).
94 See, generally, Tkatova (2010, p. 213).
95 Girshovich (2019, p. 724).
96 Kangas (2018, pp. 34 and 43) (italics added).
97 Newman (2017, p. 56).
98 Ibid., p. 3, 6 and pp. 27–28.
99 Atadjanov (2021, p. 30).
100 European Dialogue (2010).
101 Karimov (1996, p. 105): What has been achieved regarding democracy in Uzbekistan is only 'part of a long and difficult path to the goal we have set for ourselves.'
102 Sayapin (2023, p. 24).
103 Danilenko (1998, p. 53) (italics added).

the sake of clarity, this does not mean that the Soviet Union never ratified international treaties. It did. For example, the Soviet Union ratified the ICCPR in 1973,[104] but '[it] advocated a conception of human rights different from the notion of rights prevalent in the West.'[105] The Soviet conception of human rights is solely declarative, and not constitutive, in that it 'refused the individual the right to the formal, thus constitutional, protection of their rights.'[106] Importantly, Newman notes: 'The Soviet culture of rights remained singularly weak, and the procedural mechanisms for their assertion by citizens and their enforcement by courts were conspicuously undeveloped. These structural defects were carried over into the successor Central Asian systems and have continued to afflict them, to varying degrees.'[107]

Therefore not only is the practical application in Central Asia contrary to what an author contends in a different context is '[t]he value of international human rights ... demonstrated when nations incorporate the provisions of the major internationally-created human rights covenants into their own domestic legal systems'[108] but the theory should also be (better) reflected into the practice.[109] It is not because human rights are well protected on paper in Central Asia, as they are, that their effectiveness automatically follows suit. The ratification of an international treaty does not necessarily mean that its terms will properly be implemented and then applied in this or that state.[110]

While in countries like Canada, the Canadian Charter of Rights and Freedoms has made its nest in the heart of Canadians, who view it 'very favourably' and are enamoured' with it,[111] such a deep attachment to a legal instrument, called 'constitutional patriotism' by Newman, does not seem to have made its way to Central Asian countries where 'constitutionalism is [not] stitched into the fabric of national life and traditions.'[112] This emotional distance of Central Asians from their constitutions matters to the extent where '[c]onstitutions can flourish and succeed only if they are firmly planted in the cultural soil from which they gain legitimacy.'[113] Attempting to create such a bond between the general population and the State was perhaps, at least by analogy, what animated the current Kazakh president Tokayev to

---

104 See, e.g., Ciampi (2019, p. 53).

105 Patenaude (2012): More specifically, 'Western legal theory emphasized the so-called "negative" rights: that is, rights of individuals against the government. The Soviet system, on the other hand, emphasized that society as a whole, rather than individuals, were the beneficiaries of "positive" rights: that is, rights from the government.'

106 Bisztyga (2015, p. 318), Kangas (2018, p. 38), and Danilenko (1999, p. 2).

107 Newman (2017, p. 78).

108 Burns (1992, p. 108).

109 Sayapin (2022, p. 324), Rakhimova (2012, p. 143); see, generally, Lafrance (2022a, p. 6).

110 Tursunova (2019, p. 65).

111 Parkin (2002, p. 363) and Lafrance (2020, p. 73).

112 Newman (2017, p. 7).

113 Gordon (1999, pp. 530–531), cited in Harding and Bui (2016, p. 170). This is not without recalling the 'living tree' doctrine enunciated by Lord Sankey L.C. in Edwards v Attorney-General for Canada of 1930, p. 136, which, as subsequently applied in Canada, provides 'a continuing framework for the legitimate exercise of governmental power': Hunter v Southam Inc. 1984, p. 155.

adopt the concept of the 'listening state', which came to life in the context of human rights reforms.[114]

In any event, it is (unfortunately) true, *ceteris paribus*, that '[n]o State respects human rights perfectly'.[115] Among the things that all Central Asian States have in common is that 'fundamental rights and freedoms [are] endangered throughout the region',[116] even though 'there are marked differences between [them] in terms of the magnitude of [their] violations'.[117] Hannum created an analytical framework where he described three categories of human rights violations, categorized in terms of their seriousness. The first category of violations he identified corresponds to cases where 'violations are deliberate, based on a fundamental rejection of at least some universal human rights norms.'[118] Former Turkmen president Niyazov's rejection of the concept of universal human values that we mentioned previously would fall in the first category of this framework. Another example can be found in Kyrgyzstan where its former president, Almazbek Atambayev, 'allow[ed] Kyrgyzstan to legally disregard international rulings on alleged violations of individual rights within its borders.'[119]

The second category identified by Hannum corresponds to situations where 'a violation may be deliberate, but based on a different interpretation of human rights rather than a rejection of the right in question per se.'[120] This category takes form in situations where states act in ways that seem contrary to international law but do so under their own interpretation of international legal norms.[121] A violation that would fall in the second category could perhaps be somehow justified, to a certain extent, by the fact that '[t]he application of [human] rights always implies taking into account the context'.[122] This may be illustrated, to a certain extent, by some practices unique to Central Asia that could otherwise be 'interpreted by the West as human rights violations.'[123] Finally, Hannum mentioned a third category of violations. These 'may be unintentional, insofar as the violations reflect the imperfection of human behaviour and government implementation, rather than a conscious desire to contravene widely accepted international norms.'[124] Hannum's legal framework also underscores the idea that states are not simply bound by international law in an abstract fashion, but they instead engage in complex processes of interpretation and adaptation based on their own domestic structures.

---

[114] See, generally, for the concept of 'listening State', Kurmanov et al. (2024) and Sayapin (2023, p. 17).

[115] Hannum (2019, p. 139).

[116] Omelicheva (2018, p. 57).

[117] Ibid.; Sayapin (2023, p. 16).

[118] Omelicheva (2018, p. 57).

[119] Marat (2018, pp. 418–419).

[120] Hannum (2019, p. 139).

[121] Chen (2017, p. 287).

[122] De Schutter (2002, p. 24) [translated from French by Sébastien Lafrance].

[123] Sayapin (2023, pp. 15–16).

[124] Hannum (2019, p. 139).

6.5.2 Central Asian Cultural Uniqueness

The world remains 'very far from uniformity',[125] contrary to the Fukuyama quote cited above. Instead, 'the polarization of anti-Western propaganda, and hence anti-human rights propaganda, has increased in recent decades' in Central Asia.[126] This anti-Western sentiment has given rise to the blooming, 'over the past decade, [of] alternatives to Western notions of rule of law [that] have now become the norm'.[127] These alternatives are grounded on, among other things, the claim of the cultural uniqueness of Central Asian countries,[128] which has 'slowly worked its way in the Central Asian discourse'[129] since Imperial Russian and Soviet times. However, while Central Asians may share similar values,[130] the fact is that each Central Asian country has distinct cultures and other defining features that differentiate them.[131]

The argument pertaining to cultural uniqueness could perhaps be used to justify the stalling of the democratization process in Central Asia.[132] For example, the former Turkmen president Niyazov once said, 'People have forgotten how to think independently.'[133] This does not, however, stand the test of time. If this argument were true, then why should we not all have remained under the aegis of Middle Ages obscurantism since such absolutist monarchic regimes would also have led people to forget how to think independently. Nevertheless, this did not (thankfully) prevent the coming of the Age of Enlightenment in the eighteenth century. Closer to our times, the authors agree with the contention that 'the reception and development of the theory and *practice* of human rights is an integral component of the processes of modernization of Asia.'[134] Thus, the value of the Central Asian cultural uniqueness argument may be challenged in various ways. However, the use of this argument should not be surprising since, as Hannum has pointed out, the context of 'Asian values' applies by analogy to the argument of Central Asia 'cultural uniqueness', and 'most countries and regions [often] claim that they are "exceptional" in one respect or another.'[135]

The nature of the cooperation between Central Asian countries and other international partners may also be affected by the origin, cultural background, and political orientation of these partners. Indeed, major international actors such as China and Russia focus on security issues while the European Union emphasizes the promotion

[125] Tkatova (2010, p. 220).

[126] Mihr (2023, p. 35).

[127] Kangas (2018, p 46).

[128] Ibid.

[129] Ibid., p. 47; for the sake of completeness, there is 'no study of post-Soviet regimes in Central Asia [that] has made exclusively cultural arguments': Omelicheva (2018, p. 72).

[130] Ayupova (2015, p. 43).

[131] Atadjanov (2021, p. 25).

[132] Mihr (2023, pp. 33–34) and Ayupova (2015, p. 43).

[133] Washington Post (1993, p. A1).

[134] Yulan (1993, p. 105) (italics added), cited in Chen (2006, p. 487).

[135] Hannum (2019, p. 133).

of democracy and human rights.[136] Their competing interests can hardly be reconciled, and they are not deemed to be on equal footing, since 'the presence of Russia and China in Central Asia … serve[s] as a *barrier* to the EU's promotion of democracy.'[137] This is confirmed by the fact that Russia and China's focus on security issues 'has greatly contributed to an increase in human rights violations'.[138] The primacy of security issues over individual rights would be caught by the concept of 'Asian values',[139] which 'does not leave too much room for individual freedom'.[140] Thus, China and Russia's approaches to their cooperation with Central Asia may also fuel and reinforce the above-mentioned intellectual shield.

6.6 Monism and Dualism

Monism is a legal doctrine that asserts the automatic and imperative enforcement of international law within domestic legal systems. A '*true*' monist approach 'bring[s] together in an integral legal order the totality of the law in force',[141] i.e., international and domestic law. Conversely, dualism insists on the autonomy of the international and domestic legal orders,[142] requiring the formal transformation of international legal norms into the domestic legal order by way, for example, of enacting domestic legislation.[143]

The following section will, first, summarily recall the foundational principles of monism and dualism; second, examine some of the reasons supporting their current use; third, scrutinize the role and place played by international law in the Central Asian constitutions; and fourth, assess the concept of sovereignty as a political tool in that context.

136 Ayupova (2015, p. 36) and Kuşçu (2014, p. 99 and 106).

137 Ayupova, ibid., p. 42 (italics added).

138 Rhodes and Tscherne-Lempiainen (2002, pp. 41–42) and Omelicheva (2018, p. 72).

139 Hannum (2019, p. 133).

140 Bisztyga (2015, p. 317).

141 Walz (1937, p. 391) (italics added).

142 Mosler (1957, p. 633).

143 Monaco (1968, p. 250).

6.7 Monism and Dualism: Foundational Principles

From the standpoint of monism, 'international law enjoys *ultimate* supremacy over domestic law'.[144] Proponents of monism, Kelsen,[145] Mosler,[146] De Visscher,[147] and, closer to our times, Sayapin[148] in Central Asia, argue, in a nutshell, that international treaties should apply directly, and that they should not require formal incorporation or transformation into domestic law to become enforceable.[149] If formalities should still need to be followed to a certain extent, they should be kept to a bare minimum,[150] and exclude the requirement for any State legislative action to make the international legal norm part of the law of the land.[151] Therefore, treaties, according to the monist approach, should have a direct and automatic effect within the domestic legal order.[152]

Contrary to monism, the dualist theory contends that domestic law should prevail in cases of a conflict between domestic and international law.[153] Some prominent figures supporting the dualist approach, are Triepel,[154] who developed the dualist theory,[155] Anzilotti,[156] and Monaco.[157] The dualist theory argues that the international legal order, on the one hand, and, the domestic legal order, on the other, are 'fully independent'[158] or, said differently, 'coexist without being united'.[159] The norms applicable in one or the other order thus should be 'exclusive' to that order.[160] This strict separation between the two legal orders does not, however, preclude the possibility of any interactions between them.[161]

---

[144] Wittke and Rabinovych (2022, p. 250) (italics added), Virally (1964, p. 503), Mirkine-Guetzévitch (1931, p. 392). For Uzbekistan, see, e.g., Lukashuk and Saidov (2007, p. 111): 'Xalqaro huquqning ustunligi aksariyat davlatlarning konstitutsiyalarida, xususan O'zbekiston Respublikasi Konstitutsiyasining Muqaddimasida ham mustahkamlangan.' [The supremacy of international law is confirmed in the constitutions of most countries, especially in the Preamble of the Constitution of the Republic of Uzbekistan] [translated from Uzbek by Sébastien Lafrance].

[145] Kelsen (1926, pp. 291–292) and Walz (1937, p. 393).

[146] Mosler (1957, p. 631).

[147] De Visscher (1972, p. 24).

[148] Sayapin (2023, p. 25): "[I]nternational human rights treaties and constitutional provisions on human rights should be *directly* applicable in domestic legal systems" (italics added).

[149] Oralova and Rakhisheva (2014, p. 342).

[150] Mosler (1957, p. 637).

[151] Iwasawa (2022, p. 23).

[152] Ibid., p. 171.

[153] Toktogazieva (2024, p. 120) and Toktogazieva (2019, p. 276).

[154] Walz (1937, p. 385).

[155] See generally, Kirchmair (2024).

[156] Sperduti (1976, p. 337).

[157] Monaco (1968, pp. 247–249).

[158] Sperduti (1976, p. 335) and Van Panhuys (1964, p. 46).

[159] Krylov (1947, p. 445) and Capotorti (1994, p. 220).

[160] Monaco (1968, p. 249).

[161] Walz (1937, p. 381).

For dualism, the contention that 'domestic law and international law constitute two systems of rules independent of each other but *simultaneously valid* [raises] the possibility of an *insoluble* conflict between them'.[162] Such conflict may happen in a dualist context when, for instance, a domestic legal norm is not in line with its international counterpart.[163] Practically, such conflicts occur where the scope of the content of a fundamental right or freedom provided by domestic law is not be equivalent to the right or freedom at the international level[164] and these two rights or freedoms must be protected at both levels.[165] Additionally, such legal conflict may arise when a treaty, not yet entered into force, is deemed by a national court to be unconstitutional.[166,167] All five Central Asian republics have adopted provisions that are deemed to address situations of inconsistency between their national legislations and international treaties.[168] However, these provisions do not peremptorily solve the question of the correlation between domestic and international legal norms since '[i]t is not [always] clear which rule would apply in the case of their collision.'[169]

6.8 Monism and Dualism: Why We Should (Still) Care

This brings us to the question of whether monism or dualism should be preferred by states for the implementation of international law.[170] Some have claimed that 'nobody dares any longer rely on ... monism',[171] while others have claimed that the 'vast majority' of authors agree with the monist approach.[172] In addition, Crawford also notes that '[t]he relationship between international and national law is often presented

162 Kelsen (1926, p. 281) (italics added) [translated from French by Sébastien Lafrance].

163 Capotorti (1994, p. 221) and Morelli (1956, p. 484).

164 Mosler (1957, p. 654): '[T]he question of whether an international treaty overrides the fundamental rights of the constitution itself may arise'.

165 Almaz (2015, p. 114).

166 Iwasawa (2022, p. 187).

167 See, e.g., the possible outcome following the application of paragraph 72(3) and paragraph 74(1) of the Kazakh constitution or of paragraph 97(3) of the Kyrgyz constitution; for Kyrgyzstan, see also Nogoibaeva and Myrsalieva (2009, pp. 101–102); see also for Kyrgyzstan, European Commission for Democracy Through Law (Venice Commission) 2021, para 39.

168 Paragraph 4(3) of the Constitution of Kazakhstan 1995; Article 20, 'On International Treaties of the Kyrgyz Republic'; Article 10 of the Constitution of Tajikistan; Article 4, 'On International Treaties of the Republic of Turkmenistan' 2010; Article 15 of the Constitution of Uzbekistan 2023 and Article 2, 'On International Treaties of the Republic of Uzbekistan' 2019. Interestingly, a law on normative legal acts, such as the laws on international treaties, is something that was lacking in the Soviet Union: Newman (2017, p. 83). Therefore, their existence in some Central Asian States could be characterized as a sign of progress.

169 Nogoibaeva and Myrsalieva (2009, pp. 101–102).

170 Capotorti (1994, p. 219) [translated from French by Sébastien Lafrance].

171 Mosler (1957, p. 632) and Kelsen (1926, p. 275).

172 Virally (1964, p. 488).

as a clash at a level of high theory, usually between "dualism" and "monism".'[173] In practice, however, while international law norms must be adopted and applied by domestic jurisdictions in order to be enforced, it is also 'compelled, in many cases, to take into account the existence and the validity of State norms.'[174] In plain terms, international law and domestic law are communicating vessels, and '[t]he two approaches are by no means mutually exclusive, as many States combine elements of monism and dualism within their legal orders',[175] which seems to be the case for most Central Asian countries.[176]

Should this then be the end of the discussion (and this chapter)? As Bantekas notes, '[t]heorists have long argued as to whether international or domestic law should prevail over one another.'[177] Some have also even argued that this whole debate was 'apt to lose much of its moment',[178] and that the tensions engendered may perhaps explain the disaffection of many people for international law.[179] We disagree. We rather suggest that the study of the relationship between international law and domestic law remains 'of importance',[180] and that understanding whether a domestic legal system follows a dualist or monist approach or a blend of the two is 'central'.[181] We are reinforced in this view by the fact that this relationship has 'always' attracted the attention of international law experts,[182] and is not (and should not be) a thing of the past.

While some have also argued that the opposition between monism and dualism has lost some of its 'vigour',[183] we rather believe that 'this whole discussion [that] might have seemed to be dispelled will come to the fore again.'[184] We submit that this should be sooner than later since 'the problem with human rights in Central Asia lies with *implementation*'[185] where these rights are 'poorly implemented'.[186] Therefore, an examination of the issues of the implementation of human rights in Central Asia could perhaps explain, at least in part, why these countries have a 'poor human

[173] Crawford (2019, p. 45), Wittke and Rabinovych (2022, p. 250), and Morelli (1956, p. 481).

[174] Virally (1964, p. 491). See, for instance, the Permanent Court of International Justice (PCIJ) judgment in Certain German Interests in Polish Upper Silesia 1926, para 52, where the PCIJ acknowledged the *existence* of municipal laws as facts it may consider.

[175] European Commission for Democracy through Law (Venice Commission) (2014), p. 7; Wittke and Rabinovych (2022, pp. 250–251).

[176] Girshovich (2019, p. 718), see, e.g., for Uzbekistan specifically, see Bantekas (2005, p. 11).

[177] Bantekas (2005, p. 1).

[178] Van Panhuys (1964, p. 12).

[179] Virally (1964, p. 489).

[180] Van Panhuys (1964, p. 14).

[181] Rakhimova (2023, p. 143).

[182] Capotorti (1994, p. 219).

[183] Mosler (1957, p. 632).

[184] Van Panhuys (1964, p. 14).

[185] Lehner (2009, p. 49) (italics added).

[186] Mihr (2023, p. 32), Stoudmann (2003, p. 119), and Rhodes and Tscherne-Lempiainen (2002, p. 46).

rights record'.[187] As the common saying goes: 'Recognizing the problem is half of the solution.' The same unfortunate conclusion must also be drawn with respect to the *enforcement* of human rights in the Central Asian states who have 'acquired a reputation as laggard in their enforcement of those rights, as in their compliance with the concomitant international obligations'.[188] Thus, looking into the implementation and the enforcement of international human rights in Central Asia is far from being a futile theoretical exercise since, once an international legal norm is implemented in a state, it becomes binding and may then be enforced.[189]

6.9 Monism and Dualism: Central Asian Constitutional Tango

As Mirkine-Guetzévitch wisely put it, '[t]he rules of constitutional law ... are of the *greatest interest* for the study of the relationship between international law and domestic law.'[190] The examination of the content of the constitution of each Central Asian State is then crucial for elucidating the question of the implementation of international law in each one of them.

6.9.1 Relevant Soviet Legal Background

The 1977 Soviet Union Constitution,[191] then covering all five Central Asian former Soviet Republics,[192] provided that the ratification of treaties was not automatically enforceable in the Soviet domestic order,[193] making it a dualist state. Krylov wrote in the Soviet Doctrine of International Law that international law could become part of domestic law only 'if a State [*meaning here the Soviet Union*] has included in its legislation the terms of the international treaty it had signed.'[194] The Soviet position on the implementation of international law in domestic law was also 'particularly vociferous as regards human rights treaties',[195] meaning that they 'avoid[ed] implementing some or all of their provisions'.[196] Tkatova particularizes the Soviet

[187] Mihr, ibid., p. 34; Sayapin (2023, p. 22) and Newman (2017, pp. 214–215).

[188] Newman, ibid., p. 189; Omelicheva (2018, p. 57).

[189] Girshovich (2019, p. 716).

[190] Mirkine-Guetzévitch (1931, p. 365) (italics added) [translated from French by Sébastien Lafrance].

[191] This was the last constitution in force in the Soviet Union before its collapse.

[192] Girshovich (2019, pp. 713–714).

[193] Bantekas (2005, p. 2).

[194] Krylov (1947, p. 445).

[195] Bantekas (2005, p. 2).

[196] Danilenko (1998, p. 3).

approach, more specifically the Stalinist approach, to international law, as being '*monism ... built on the primacy of national law* over international law',[197] which seems, at first glance, to be in contradiction to our initial characterization of the Soviet Union as a dualist State. This monist approach, which represents a form of 'constitutional nationalism',[198] could find its roots in Kelsen's contention that, besides the monist argument that 'international law enjoys ultimate supremacy over domestic law',[199] 'it [would] equally [be] possible that the relationship between legal orders could be conceived on the basis of the *primacy of national law*'.[200] However, Morelli opines that monism with primacy of national law 'could not be qualified as monist', mostly because this theory would not bring together the domestic and international legal orders into one.[201] In fact, this theory would simply constitute a subcategory of dualism.

6.9.2 Different Approaches to the Implementation of International Law

As Danilenko has pointed out, '[m]any CIS countries', including in Central Asia, initially rejected 'the traditional Soviet dualist approach to implementation of international law in domestic legal systems'.[202] By adopting their first constitutions following the collapse of the Soviet Union, Central Asian countries adopted 'a radical constitutional change that ... "*opened*" [their] domestic legal system[s] to [the] direct penetration of international principles and norms.'[203]

6.9.2.1 Kyrgyzstan

The 2021 Kyrgyz constitution provides, under the first sentence of paragraph 6(3), that 'international treaties ... are an *integral part* of the legal system of the Kyrgyz Republic'. The wording of this sentence is similar to that of the 2010 version of the Kyrgyz constitution wherein the key qualifier 'integral' of the 2021 version should be given a similar meaning as the term 'constituent' from the 2010 version, which read, '[i]nternational treaties ... shall be a *constituent part* of the legal system of the Kyrgyz Republic.' If taken alone, these two respective sentences of the 2021 and 2010 versions of the Kyrgyz constitution would lead us to qualify both these constitutions as monist. Our contention is reinforced by the analogous fact that a

[197] Tkatova (2010, p. 210) (italics added).

[198] Mirkine-Guetzévitch (1931, p. 312).

[199] Wittke and Rabinovych (2022, p. 250) and Virally (1964, p. 503).

[200] Crawford (2019, p. 45) (italics added); Kelsen (1926, p. 298; 1955, p. 189).

[201] Morelli (1956, p. 480).

[202] Danilenko (1998, p. 1).

[203] Ibid., p. 5 (italics added).

similar wording was used under paragraph 15(4) of the 1993 Russian constitution, which was considered to adopt 'a more monistic approach'.[204]

However, a comparison of the last sentence of paragraph 6(3) of the 2021 and 2010 versions of the Kyrgyz constitution should be enough to shatter the illusion of the similarity of both paragraphs 6(3). The 2021 version includes the following clause, '[t]he *procedure and conditions* for the application of international treaties ... *shall be determined by law*', which is different in substance from the 2010 clause, which rather provided, '[t]he provisions of international treaties on human rights shall have *direct* effect and shall enjoy *precedence* over provisions of other international treaties.' The former clause poses a condition for the reception of the treaty into domestic law, while the latter prescribes a direct application of it in Kyrgyz domestic law.[205] This is a major distinction between the two versions: the former shows a dualist approach in its implementation of international law, while the latter indicates a monist approach.

Mosler wrote in 1957, one could say prophetically: 'Even if a State opens its [constitution] to international law *to the greatest extent possible* [and] even if it provides that *international law is superior to the provisions of the constitution*, it should not be forgotten that [the relevant] provision is also part of the constitution. [This provision] can be removed by amending the constitution.'[206] This is precisely what happened in Kyrgyzstan. The former 2010 Kyrgyz constitution opened wide its arms to international law, including international human rights, by allowing its direct application in domestic law, making it a monist constitution, but the 2021 provision now requires the approval of domestic legislation for an international treaty to become enforceable in Kyrgyzstan and also eliminates the human rights specifics of the previous version. This major change constitutes, as observed by some, a shift from a monist to a dualist approach to the implementation of international law.[207]

While some would be inclined to qualify this shift as 'alarming',[208] others could potentially counter-argue that the practice in Kyrgyzstan was already to follow a dualist approach.[209] This shift, and other similar shifts in Central Asia, are then not necessarily rooted, as one has suggested,[210] in Russian influence, but simply, perhaps, in the harmonization of theory with practice. In addition, one author puts the so-called tendency of Central Asian states leaning towards dualism in opposition to global constitutionalism, which would be, as described by this author, more in favour of 'a monistic approach to the relationship between international and domestic law'.[211] While this comparison is not far-fetched in the abstract, it must be recalled

---

[204] Kahn (2022).

[205] For a similar reasoning, see Girshovich (2019, p. 715).

[206] Mosler (1957, p. 640) (italics added) [translated from French by Sébastien Lafrance].

[207] Toktogazieva (2024, p. 123), Toktogazieva (2019, p. 278); European Commission for Democracy Through Law (Venice Commission) 2016, para 42.

[208] Toktogazieva (2019, p. 294; 2024, p. 128).

[209] Nogoibaeva and Myrsalieva (2009, p. 100).

[210] Toktogazieva (2024, p. 120).

[211] Toktogazieva (2019, p. 318; 2024, p. 128).

that some states around the world, who are known for their robust democracy, also follows a dualist approach for the implementation of international treaties.[212] Thus, while perhaps the Russian influence on this shift should not be discarded, especially in light of what was discussed earlier and what will be discussed under Sect. 2.3.4, other factors may also have contributed to this shift in lieu of or in addition to Russian influence.

6.9.2.2 Kazakhstan

Kazakhstan seems to have followed the same path as Kyrgyzstan. The first sentence of paragraph 4(3) of its 1995 constitution (revised in 2017) reads, '[i]nternational treaties ratified by the Republic shall have *priority* over its laws' while the second sentence of the same paragraph provides that '[t]he *procedure and conditions* of the application in the territory of the Republic of Kazakhstan of international treaties to which Kazakhstan is a party *are determined by the legislation of the Republic*.' Previously, the 1993 Kazakh Constitution stated under Article 4 that '*[i]nternational treaties* ratified by the Republic *take precedence over its laws* and are applied *directly*'. The same reasoning and conclusion reached for Kyrgyzstan should then also be reached here for Kazakhstan, i.e., it has thus shifted from a monist to a dualist approach.[213]

However, Article 20–1 of the 2005 Law of the Republic of Kazakhstan 'On the International Treaties of the Republic of Kazakhstan' *still* provides for a *direct* application, in most cases, of the international treaties ratified by Kazakhstan. There is thus an inconsistency between the current paragraph 4(3) of the Kazakh constitution and said Article 20–1. Any debate over this inconsistency might be, however, a tempest in a teacup when considering the domestic hierarchy of sources in Kazakhstan. As the constitution of Kazakhstan remains pursuant to its paragraph 4(2), the 'supreme' law of the land, any possible legal conflict between these two legal instruments may be moot.

6.9.2.3 Uzbekistan

Article 15 of the 2023 constitution of Uzbekistan provides that '[i]nternational treaties of the Republic of Uzbekistan … shall be an *integral part* of the legal system of the Republic of Uzbekistan.' Contrary to Kyrgyzstan and Kazakhstan, the Uzbek constitution does not include a caveat requiring the approval of domestic legislation for the implementation and enforcement of international treaties. Article 3 of the 2019 Law of the Republic of Uzbekistan 'On International Treaties of the Republic

---

[212] See, e.g. Barnett (2021, p. 4): 'Canada operates according to a dualist model, a treaty that has been signed and ratified by the executive branch still requires incorporation through domestic law to be enforceable at the national level.'

[213] Toktogazieva (2019, p. 288; 2024, p. 125), Girshovich (2019, p. 715).

of Uzbekistan' (LIT) is to the same effect.[214] Thus, contrary to Kazakhstan, there does not seem to exist an inconsistency between the Uzbek constitution and Article 3. With that backdrop in mind, one may conclude that Uzbekistan has a *monist* constitution.

However, as it was the case in the 1992 Uzbek constitution (revised in 2011),[215] the 2023 Uzbek constitution *still* provides that the constitution and Uzbek laws have '*absolute* supremacy' in Uzbekistan.[216] If 'international law [does] not generally have *priority* over Uzbek law'[217] as in the 1992 Uzbek constitution, how can we reconcile the '*absolute* supremacy' still present in the 2023 Uzbek constitution with the fact that international law is *now* clearly identified as an *integral* part of the Uzbek legal system?[218] This particular aspect of the role and place of international law in Uzbekistan thus requites further investigation from a broader perspective. As a source of heated debates in the doctrine, there are three main positions: the first contends that the preamble of the 1992 Uzbek constitution should lead to the conclusion that the priority of international treaties should be implied; the second alleges that neither international law nor domestic law should be given priority in light of the 1992 constitution, and that it should be examined on a case-by-case basis; and the third group claims that 'the role of international legal norms in the [Uzbek] domestic legal order is rather vague and that such norms are [then] not considered to be normatively equal to domestic laws.'[219]

By way of background, the mentions of international law in the 1992 constitution of Uzbekistan were mostly limited to matters of foreign policy[220] and to the question of foreign citizens and stateless persons.[221] Besides these mentions, the place of international law in terms of hierarchy of sources was not clearly identified in the 1992 Uzbek constitution. Consequently, because of the mention of foreign policy in that context, a few authors have suggested that Uzbekistan 'approache[d] international law from a *dualist* perspective',[222] even if Article 3 of the 2019 LIT already provided that '[i]nternational treaties … are an *integral* part of the legal system of the Republic of Uzbekistan', and even if Article 33 of the latter legal instrument 'indicate[s] the obligatory observance by the Republic of Uzbekistan of all international treaties in accordance with international law, which indicates the possibility of *direct* effect of the international treaty'[223] rather supporting the existence of a *monist* approach. In any event, we must acknowledge the fact that 'the 2019 LIT does not settle the issue

214 'International treaties of the Republic of Uzbekistan … are an *integral part* of the legal system of the Republic of Uzbekistan.'

215 Article 15 (1992).

216 Article 15 (2023).

217 Bantekas (2005, p. 5) (italics added).

218 Article 15 (2023).

219 Umirdinov and Khamikov (2020, p. 207).

220 Article 17. This Article remained intact in the 2023 Uzbek constitution.

221 Article 23.

222 Sayapin (2022, pp. 326–327) and Umirdinov and Khamikov (2020, p. 211).

223 Tursunova (2019, pp. 66–67).

of the order of international treaties in relation to the domestic legal order.'[224] In addition, there is also a gap between theory and practice in Uzbekistan where, even if Uzbekistan would 'nominally adopt a monist approach to international law by giving it precedence over domestic', the practice would tell otherwise.[225] Because of the underlying uncertainty regarding the current (and also past) status of Uzbekistan as either a monist or dualist state, another doctrinal war may be coming over this tricky question.

6.9.2.4 Tajikistan and Turkmenistan

Pursuant to Article 10 of the Tajik constitution, '[i]nternational legal acts recognized by Tajikistan are a *constituent part* of the legal system of the Republic.' What makes Tajikistan stand out in comparison with other Central Asian States is its 'positivist approach', as qualified by Sayapin, since its constitution refers to ' "international legal acts recognized by Tajikistan", but not to any other [specific] sources of international law.'[226] Article 7 of the Law of the Republic of Tajikistan 'On normative legal acts' confirms that international legal acts are 'part of the hierarchy of the sources of law' in the country. Since 'international legal *acts* … includ[e] the *making* of treaties',[227] but because they do not refer, at least directly, to the *content* of the treaties themselves, it may be difficult, in terms of legal interpretation, to determine whether 'international legal acts' are or include, in fact, treaties, even though some seem to have no difficulty equating one with the other.[228]

With respect to Turkmenistan, the task of assessing whether it is a monist or dualist state seems to be less arduous, at least in theory. Pursuant to Article 9 of the Turkmen constitution, the State 'shall recognize the *priority* of the *universally* accepted norms of international law.' Therefore, Tajikistan and Turkmenistan both qualify as monist states.

6.9.3 The Lack of Clarity on the Implementation of International Legal Norms

The ambiguity of international legal instruments can significantly affect how they are enforced or incorporated into domestic legal systems.[229] There does not seem to exist a consensus on the clarity of how international legal norms are or should be implemented into the domestic law of Central Asian States in spite of the existing

[224] Umirdinov and Khamikov (2020, p. 207).

[225] Ibid., p. 196.

[226] Sayapin (2022, pp. 326–327).

[227] McLachlan (2005, p. 282) (italics added).

[228] Kabilov (2017, p. 75).

[229] Iwasawa (2022, p. 151).

official positions and legal instruments.[230] The lack of a 'clearly defined Central Asian doctrine of international law' is no help either.[231] Therefore, the question how the rules of international law can be implemented in domestic legal orders remains pertinent,[232] particularly in Central Asia where one must keep in mind that the domestic legal infrastructures of its five independent republics vary significantly, including on the practice of international law. On the one hand, one cannot expect international law to address and foresee every single possible factual scenario that may need to be covered since 'there are … many problems that cannot be adequately regulated by law'[233]; on the other hand, international law and domestic law must both be sufficiently predictable in their application to be considered effective.[234]

6.9.4 Dualism in Central Asia and Sovereignty as a (Potential) Political Tool

In international law, State's sovereignty 'demands that nations decide how international legal obligations and rights are received into their own domestic legal systems'.[235] Paradoxically, 'the recognition of State sovereignty … achieves in the same movement autonomy and suppresses it.'[236] Therefore, a State is not 'totally free to revise or abandon whenever it sees fit the obligations to which it has subscribed.'[237] Contrary to these core principles, many Soviet international law academics insist 'on the principle of *unlimited* sovereignty of the State as *essential* to the relationship between the State and international law.'[238] This past understanding of the concept of sovereignty has found its way into contemporary Russia, which now advocates a 'classic and strong concept of State sovereignty',[239] and which has, at least among some Russian legal scholars, 'a specific *illiberal* meaning'.[240] This questionable meaning of sovereignty cannot easily be reconciled with the democratic principles implied or expressly stated by international law.

---

230 See, e.g., for Uzbekistan: Tursunova (2019, p. 65). See, e.g., for Kyrgyzstan: European Commission for Democracy Through Law (Venice Commission) (2021, paras 38–39).

231 Tkatova (2010, p. 216). Nevertheless, we would be remiss to not mention the relentless work accomplished for the propagation of international law in Central Asia by Professor Sergey Sayapin, for example: see, e.g., Wittke and Rabinovych (2022, p. 263).

232 Monaco (1968, p. 251).

233 Lowe (2015, p. 26).

234 See, e.g., Morioka (2024).

235 Butt (2014, p. 3).

236 De Frouville (2018, p. 145). The most common reference to sovereignty in international law is the one provided by paragraph 2(1) of the United Nations Charter, which provides for the principle of the sovereign equality of all States.

237 Dupuy (2002, p. 101) [translated from French by Sébastien Lafrance].

238 Kelsen (1955, p. 158) (italics added).

239 Toktogazieva (2019, p. 322; 2024, p. 130).

240 Mälksoo (2015, p. 100) (italics added).

Along the same lines, the dogma of the sovereignty, as described by Kelsen, i.e., where individuals cannot be a subject of international law, would lead to the absence of 'effective protection' of their rights by their own state.[241] This could perhaps explain, at least in part, alongside the specific circumstances of the Central Asian states, including their historical and current ties with the Russian sphere of influence, the choice of some Central Asian States to move forward with a dualist approach as this recalls how international law was understood under the Soviet Union, i.e., with a distorted dualist approach that misunderstands and misapplies the fact that '[d]ualism … lives and dies with the premise of the … sovereignty of the state'.[242] Are we then witnessing a resurgence of the Soviet model of implementation of international law? Maybe. Time will tell. What is an additional source of concern is that dualism, according to Mosler, may lead to a 'strict isolation of domestic law'[243] from international law. In such a case, moving from a monist to a dualist approach, as has happened in some Central Asian States, could reinforce the above-mentioned intellectual shield against external sources of law, namely international law standards as they are commonly understood in most other (democratic) locales.

6.10 Conclusion

Due to various factors stemming from the recent and distant past, the reality of Central Asia (both as a whole and considering each of its five republics independently) regarding the issue of the implementation of international law both complex and captivating. It brings to the fore and revives key issues deemed by some to have become relics. While some have identified the tendency for some Central Asian States to move from monism to dualism, or to revert, perhaps, to dualism as it was in force under Soviet rule, these states are still worth studying individually with respect to their implementation of international law as each is unique not only with respect to their specific approach to the question but also because of their factual and legal backgrounds. Alongside the multifactorial influence of the Russian sphere, other factors may also impact whether a Central Asian state decides to adopt a monist or a dualist approach, or to move from one to the other. What is common to all Central Asian countries, however, is the existence of an intellectual shield, which isolates them, to various degrees, from the intellectual traditions around international law in other parts of the world, and primarily from the West.

---

[241] Kelsen (1955, p. 179).

[242] Sperduti (1976, p. 335).

[243] Mosler (1957, p. 636) [translated from French by Sébastien Lafrance].

References

Алмаз У А [Almaz U A] (2015) Имплементация международных принципов и норм по защите прав человека в национальной системе кыргызской республики [Implementation of international principles and norms for the protection of human rights in the national system of the Kyrgyz Republic]. Известия вузов [universities news] 12:82–83

Asanbekova D, Osmonova A, Abdyldaev I, Begaliev E, Ashimov K, Nurmamatkyzy K, Narbaev O, Karimov S, Abdullaeva Z (2021) Political system in the sovereign Kyrgyzstan. Open J Pol Sci 11:266–272

Atadjanov R (2021) Challenges for the implementation of international law in Central Asia: contributing factors and possible solutions. Cent Asia Bus J 12(1):25–34

Ayupova Z (1998) Constitutional liberties in the Republic of Kazakhstan. Tulsa J Comp Int'l L 6:77–86

Ayupova S (2015) Democracy promotion in Uzbekistan: do values matters? L'europe En Form 1(375):36–54

Bantekas I (2005) The law and legal system of Uzbekistan. Juris Publishing Inc., Huntington

Barnett L (2021) Canada's approach to the treaty-making process. Parliamentary information, education and research services, Publication No 2008–45-E, Library of Parliament. Ottawa, Canada

Berdyaev N (1948) The Russian idea. The MacMillan Company, New York

Bisztyga A (2015) General characteristics of the constitutional regulation of the individual freedoms and rights in Kazakhstan. L Rev Kyiv Univ L: 317–320

Brunnée J, Toope SJ (2002) A hesitant embrace: the application of international law by Canadian Courts. Can Y B Int'l L 40:3–60

Bureau of Western Hemisphere Affairs (2024) U.S. relations with Mexico—bilateral relations fact sheet. https://www.state.gov/u-s-relations-with-mexico/. Accessed 24 Nov 2024

Burns WD (1992) Thailand and international law. Master in Law thesis, University of British Columbia, Canada

Butt S (2014) The position of international law within the Indonesian Legal System. Emory Int L Rev 28(1):1–28

Buzurtanova M (2019) On effectiveness of the UN human rights treaty and charter bodies: the case of Kazakhstan. Спектр (Spectrum) 2(88):113–120

Canadian Charter of Rights and Freedoms. The Constitution Act (1982) Schedule B to the Canada Act 1982 (UK) c 11

Capotorti F (1994) Cours général de droit international public [General Course of Public International Law]. Collected courses of the Hague academy of international law, vol 70. Martinus Nijhoff Publishers, Leiden, pp 9–344

Certain German interests in Polish Upper Silesia, German v Poland, Merits, Judgment (1926) PCIJ Series A no 7

Chen AHY (2006) Comparative reflections on human rights in Asia. In: Peerenboom R, Petersen CJ, Chen AHY (eds) Human Rights in Asia. Routledge, London, pp 487–516

Chen Y (2017) International law as mere obligations: supremacy of international law and a Chinese conception. Peking Univ L J 5(2):285–308

Ciampi A (2019) History, isolation and effectiveness of human rights. In: Ciampi A (ed) History and international law. Edward Elgar Publishing

Constitution (Fundamental Law) of the Union Soviet Socialist Republics of 1977

Convention on Human Rights and Fundamental Freedoms of the Commonwealth of Independent States (1995)

Council of Europe (2001) Resolution 1249: co-existence of the convention on human rights and fundamental freedoms of the commonwealth of independent states and the European convention on human rights. Parliamentary Assembly

Crawford J (2019) Brownlie's principles of international law, 9th edn. Oxford University Press

Danilenko GM (1999) Implementation of international law in CIS states: theory and practice. Eur J Int'l l 10:51–69
Danilenko GM (1998) Implementation of international law in CIS states: theory and practice. https://www.nato.int/acad/fellow/96-98/danilenk.pdf. Accessed 2 June 2024
De Frouville O (2018) Vers une théorie démocratique du droit international [Towards a democratic theory of international law]. In: Ruvanot MC (ed) La démocratie appliquée au droit international: de quoi parle-t-on? [Democracy applied to international law: what are we talking about?]. Éditions A. Pedone, Paris
De Schutter O (2002) Universalité des droits de l'homme et mondialisation: la question des valeurs asiatiques [Universality of human rights and globalization: the question of Asian values]. In: Marrès T, Servais P (eds) Droits humains et valeurs asiatiques—Un dialogue possible? [Human rights and Asian values—a possible dialogue?]. Bruylant
De Visscher P (1972) Cours général de droit international public [General Course of Public International Law]. Collected courses of the Hague academy of international law, vol 136. Martinus Nijhoff Publishers, Leiden, pp 1–202
Dumas A (1844) The three musketeers. D. Appleton and Company (published in English in 1894)
Dupuy PM (2002) L'unité de l'ordre juridique international: cours général de droit international public [The unity of the international legal order: general course of public international law]. Collected courses of the Hague academy of international law, vol 297. Martinus Nijhoff Publishers, Leiden, pp 9–496
Duxbury A, Tan H-L (2019) Assessing human rights implementation in Southeast Asia in can ASEAN TAKE HUMAN RIGHTS SERIOUSly? Cambridge University Press
Edwards v Attorney-General for Canada, [1930] A.C. 124 (P.C.)
European Commission for Democracy Through Law (Venice Commission) (2016) Kyrgyz Republic—joint opinion on the draft law "on introduction of amendments and changes to the constitution"
European Commission for Democracy Through Law (Venice Commission) (2021) Kyrgyzstan—joint opinion of the OSCE/ODIHR and the Venice commission on the draft constitution of the Kyrgyz Republic, 126th Plenary Session
European Commission for Democracy through Law (Venice Commission) (2014) Report on the implementation of international human rights treaties in domestic law and the role of courts (Study No. 690/2012, CLD-AD(2014)036)
European Dialogue (2010) Nazarbayev: "economy first, then politics". http://eurodialogue.org/osce/Nazarbayev-Economy-first-then-politics. Accessed 16 Aug 2024
Fukuyama F (1992) The end of history and the last man. MacMillan Inc., New York
Fukuyama F (1989) Have we reached the end of history? Nat Inter J 16(3):3–18
Glenn J (1999) The soviet legacy in Central Asia. Palgrave Macmillan, New York
Girshovich M (2019) Central Asian states (Chapter 29). (Chapter 6). In: Chesterman S, Owada H, Saul B (eds) The Oxford handbook of international law in Asia and the Pacific. Oxford University Press
Gordon R (1999) Growing constitutions. Univ Pennsyl J Const L 1:528–582
Hannum H (2019) Human rights (Chapter 6). In: Chesterman S, Owada H, Saul B (eds) The Oxford handbook of international law in Asia and the Pacific. Oxford University Press
Harding A, Bui NS (2016) Recent work in Asian constitutional studies: a review essay. Asian J Compar L 11(01):163–183
Helsinki Watch (A Division of Human Rights Watch) (1993) Human rights in Turkmenistan. https://www.hrw.org/reports/pdfs/u/ussr/ussr.937/ussr937full.pdf. Accessed 2 Oct 2024
Hunter v. Southam Inc., [1984] 2 SCR 145
Höynck W (2003) The OSCE in Central Asia—on the right track. Hels Monit 14(3):300–305
International Law Commission (2001) Draft articles on the responsibility of states for internationally wrongful acts
Iwasawa Y (2022) Domestic application of international law: focusing on direct applicability. Brill Nijhoff, Leiden

Kahn J (2022) Consistency and change in Russian approaches to international law. Lieber Institute—West Point. https://lieber.westpoint.edu/consistency-change-russian-approaches-international-law/. Accessed 18 Sep 2024

Kabilov F (2017) Local water management in Tajikistan: legal framework. Cent Asian J Wat Res 3(2):73–88

Кадыралиева Б Д [Kadyralieva B D] (2021) Общепризнанные принципы и нормы международного права и международные договоры как часть правовой системы Кыргызской Республики [Generally accepted principles and norms of international law and international contracts as part of the legal system of the Kyrgyz Republic]. Московский журнал международного права [Moscow J Int L] 2:171–185

Kangas RD (2018) Legal reform in Central Asia: moving past history (Chapter 2). In: Burghart DL, Sabonis-Helf T (eds) Central Asia in the era of sovereignty—the era of Tamerlane? Lexington Books, Lanham

Kazakhstan's Constitution of 1995 (revised in 2017)

Kelsen H (1926) Les rapports de système entre le droit interne et le droit international [System relations between domestic law and international law]. Collected courses of the Hague academy of international law, vol 14. Martinus Nijhoff Publishers, Leiden, pp 227–332

Kelsen H (1955) The communist theory of law. Frederick A Praeger, New York

Kirchmair L (2024) Dualism and Kelsenian Monism. In: Kirchmair L (ed) Rethinking the relationship between international, EU and national law. Cambridge University Press, pp 11–58

Krylov S (1947) Les notions principales du droit des gens (La doctrine soviétique du droit international) [Main Notions of *Jus Gentium* (The Soviet Doctrine of International Law)] In: Collected courses of the Hague academy of international law (vol 70). Martinus Nijhoff Publishers, Leiden, pp 407–476.

Kurmanov B, Selteyev U, Almaganbetov A (2024) 'Listening state?': Exploring citizens' perceptions of Open Government in Tokayev's Kazakhstan. Central Asian Survey 43(2):235–256

Kuşçu Bonnenfant I (2014) Normative power Europe in Central Asia: the case of Kazakhstan. USAK Yearbook of Politics and International Relations 6:93–119

Kyrgyzstan's Constitution of 2010

Kyrgyzstan's Constitution of 2021

Lafrance S (2020) The justice in judicial activism: jurisprudence of rights and freedoms in India and Canada. In: Khurshid S, Malik L, Singh YP (eds) The Supreme Court and the Constitution—an Indian discourage. Wolters Kluwer

Lafrance S (2022a) The reception and effectiveness of international fundamental rights in some selected ASEAN states (Conference Paper). University of Melbourne, Australia. https://law.unimelb.edu.au/__data/assets/pdf_file/0008/4356674/LAFRANCE_Sebastien.pdf. Accessed 12 Nov 2024

Lafrance S (2022b) Without Canada, no Perestroika and Glasnost? Another brick in the wall of the misunderstanding of the Russian Soul (Conference paper). Traditions and modernization in the politics and Law of Russia, China and Vietnam (International Conference Proceedings). Nhà xuất bản Khoa học xã hội [Social Sciences Publishing House], pp 27–38

Lafrance S (2024) Ten years after the Mexican constitutional energy reform: a chronicle of a death foretold? OGEL Energ L J 22(2):1–18

Lai C (1993) Fung Yulan anthology. Huaxia Press, Beijing, China

Lauterpacht H (1947) The international protection of human rights. Collected courses of the Hague academy of international law, vol 70. Martinus Nijhoff Publishers, Leiden, pp 1–108

Law of the Kyrgyz Republic (2014) "On International Treaties of the Kyrgyz Republic", № 64

Law of the Republic of Kazakhstan (2005) "On the International Treaties of the Republic of Kazakhstan", № 54

Law of the Republic of Tajikistan (2016) "On the International Treaties of the Republic of Tajikistan" № 1326. [Russian version]

Law of the Republic of Turkmenistan (2010) "On International Treaties of the Republic of Turkmenistan", № 2. [Russian version]

Law of the Republic of Uzbekistan (2019) “On International Treaties of the Republic of Uzbekistan”, № ZRU-518

Lehner O (2009) Respecting human rights in Central Asia: will this stabilize or destabilize the region. Secu Hum Rts 20(1):48–55

Lowe V (2015) The limits of law. Collected courses of the Hague academy of international law, vol 379. Martinus Nijhoff Publishers, Leiden, pp 9–34

Lukashuk II, Saidov AX (2007) Hozirgi zamon zalqaro huquqi nazariyasi asoslari [Theoretical basis of modern international law]. Publishing House of the National Society of Uzbek Philosophers [O‘zbekiston faylasuflari milliy jamiyati nashriyoti]. Tashkent, Uzbekistan

Mälksoo L (2015) Russian approaches to international law (English ed). Oxford University Press [Kindle Edition]

Marat E (2018) Kyrgyzstan’s experiments with democracy (Chapter 17). In: Burghart DL, Sabonis-Helf T (eds) Central Asia in the era of sovereignty—the era of Tamerlane? Lexington Books, Lanham

McLachlan C (2005) The principle of system integration and Article 31(3)(c) of the Vienna convention. Int Compar L Q 54(2):279–320

Mehrara M (2024) Newsweek. Putin trolled with Huge Ukraine Flag while visiting Russia’s neighbor—newsweek. Accessed 10 Dec 2024

Mendez M (2013) The legal effects of treaties in domestic legal orders and the role of domestic courts in the legal effects of EU agreements. Oxford University Press

Mihr A (2023) Human rights education in Central Asia. In: Mihr A, Wittke C (eds) Human rights dissemination in Central Asia: Human rights education and capacity building in the post-Soviet Space. Springer Briefs in Political Science. Springer

Mirkine-Guetzévitch B (1931) Droit international et droit constitutionnel [International Law and Constitutional Law]. Collected courses of the Hague academy of international law, vol 38. Martinus Nijhoff Publishers, Leiden, pp 307–466

Monaco R (1968) Cours général de droit international public [General course of public international law]. Collected courses of the Hague academy of international law, vol 125. Martinus Nijhoff Publishers, Leiden, pp 93–336

Morelli G (1956) Cours général de droit international public [General course of public international law]. Collected courses of the Hague academy of international law, vol 89. Martinus Nijhoff Publishers, Leiden, pp 437–604

Morioka S (2024) International court of justice judge speaks in importance of international law. Michigan Law, University of Michigan. https://michigan.law.umich.edu/news/international-court-justice-judge-speaks-importance-international-law. Accessed 9 Dec 2024

Mosler H (1957) L’application du droit international public par les tribunaux nationaux [The application of public international law by national courts]. Collected courses of the Hague academy of international law, vol 91. Martinus Nijhoff Publishers, Leiden, pp 619–712

Newman S (2017) The constitutional systems of the independent Central Asian States: a contextual analysis. Bloomsbury Publishing

Nogoibaeva EK, Myrsalieva NK (2009) Correlation between International law and national legislation in the Kyrgyz Republic. AUCA Acad Rev: 97–104

Norling N, Cornell S (2016) The role of the European Union in democracy-building in Central Asia and the South caucasus. International Institute for Democracy and Electoral Assistance (International IDEA), Stockholm, Sweden

Omelicheva MY (2018) Human rights and governance in Central Asia (Chapter 3). In: Burghart DL, Sabonis-Helf T (eds) Central Asia in the era of sovereignty—the era of Tamerlane? Lexington Books, Lanham

Oralova Y, Rakisheva A (2014) Implementation of international standards to the legislation of the Republic of Kazakhstan: definition and mechanisms. Life Sci J 11

Panico CJ (1993) Turkmenistan: UNAffECTED BY WINDS OF DEMOCRATIC CHANGE. RFE/RL Res Rep 2(4):6–10

Parkin A (2002) The charter and judicial activism: an analysis of public opinion. Windsor Y.B. Access Just 21:361–384

Patenaude BM (2012) Regional perspectives on human rights: the USSR and Russia, part one—the USSR. Freeman Spogli Institute for International Studies—Spice Digest. Stanford University. https://spice.fsi.stanford.edu/docs/regional_perspectives_on_human_rights_the_ussr_and_russia_part_one. Accessed 15 Nov 2024

Penal Code of Kazakhstan (2014) No. 226-V of the Law of the Republic of Kazakhstan

Radchenko S (2017) Turkmenistan: grasping for legitimacy. J Democr 28(3):168–172

Рахимова МА (Rakhimova MA) (2012) Международное и национальное право. Как они взаимодействуют в Узбекистане [International and national law. How they interact in Uzbekistan]. Евразийская интеграция: экономика, право, политика [Eur Integr Econ L Pol] 12:143–148

Read C (2009) American sneezes and the world catches a cold. Global Financial Meltdown, Palgrave MacMillan, pp 144–148

Republic of Tajikistan "On normative legal acts" (2009)

Rhodes A, Tscherne-Lempiainen P (2002) Human rights and terrorism in the Central Asian OSCE states. Hels Monit 13(1):37–50

Рысбеков Ю Х, Рысбеков А Ю [Rysbekov Yu Kh and Rysbekov A Yu] (2016) О некоторых вопросах имплементации глобальных Водных Конвенций в национальное законодательство (на примере Узбекистана) [About some issues regarding the implementation of global water conventions into national legislation (the example of Uzbekistan]. http://www.cawater-info.net/bk/water_law/pdf/rysbekov16-2.pdf. Accessed 29 June 2024

Sayapin S (2023) Human rights in Central Asia: challenges and perspectives. In: Mihr A, Wittke C (eds) Human rights dissemination in Central Asia. Springer Briefs in Political Science. Springer

Sayapin S (2022) International law in Central Asia: practices and doctrines. Rev Cent East Eur L 47(3–4):322–351

Sayapin S (2021) State Report Overview—Central Asia. In: Lee S (ed), Encyclopedia of Public International Law in Asia Online. Brill

Sperduti G (1976) Le principe de souveraineté et le problème des rapports entre le droit international et le droit interne [The principle of sovereignty and the issue of the relations between international law and domestic law]. Collected courses of the Hague academy of international law, vol 153. Martinus Nijhoff Publishers, Leiden, pp 319–410

SS 'Wimbledon', United Kingdom and others v Germany (1923) PCIK Series A no 1, ICGJ 235

Stevenson T (2023) America's undying empire: why the decline of US power has been greatly exaggerated. The Guardian. https://www.theguardian.com/us-news/2023/nov/30/americas-undying-empire-why-the-decline-of-us-power-has-been-greatly-exaggerated. Accessed 3 Nov 2024

Stoudmann G (2003) Turkmenistan, a human rights black hole. Hels Monit 14(2):117–124

Swenson DR (2005–2006) The search for the rule of law: judicial independence in the former Soviet Republics of Central Asia. Rev Comp L 10–11:23–48

Tajikistan's Constitution of 1994 (revised in 2016)

Tajikistan. United Nations General Assembly, 47th Sess., 8 October 1992

Тиунов О И [Tiunov O I] (2009) Влияние международных договоров и международно-правовых обычаев на национальное законодательство [The Influence of International Treaties and International Legal Customs on National Legislation]. Вестник РГГУ [Bull Russian State Univ Hum] 11:269–285

Tkatova R (2010) Central Asian states and international law: between post-Soviet culture and Eurasian civilization. Chin J Int L 9(1):205–220

Toktogazieva S (2019) Constitutional review in transition: Central Asian constitutional court in comparative perspective. PhD Thesis. Department of Legal Studies, Central European University, Budapest

Toktogazieva S (2024) Human rights adjudication in Central Asia (Chapter 7). In: Mihr A, Pierobon C (eds) Polarization, shifting borders and liquid governance—studies on transformation and development in the OSCE region. Springer

Triepel CH (1923) Les rapports entre le droit interne et le droit international [The relationship between domestic law and international law]. Collected courses of the Hague academy of international law, vol 1. Martinus Nijhoff Publishers, Leiden, pp 73–122

Turkmenistan's Constitution 2008 (revised in 2016)

Турсунова М У [Tursunova M U] (2019) Теоретические и практические вопросы имплементации международно правовых норм в национальное законодательство Республики Узбекистан [Theoretical and practical issues of the implementation of international legal norms in the national legislation of the Republic of Uzbekistan]. Вестник науки и образования [Bull Sci Educat] 18(72):64–69

Umirdinov A, Khamikov A (2020) Tensions between Domestic and International Law for Supremacy in Uzbekistan. KLRI Journal of Law and Legislation 10(2):195–245

United Nations Human Rights Committee (2021) Report of the special rapporteur on the promotion and protection of the right to freedom of opinion and expression, Irene Khan, A/HRC/56/53

United Nations (General Assembly) (1966) International Covenant on Civil and Political Rights. Treaty Series, 999:171

United Nations Human Rights Treaty Bodies. Ratification Status for CCPR—International Covenant on Civil and Political Rights

Uzbekistan's Constitution of 2023

Uzbekistan's Constitution of 1992 (revised in 2011)

van Ert G (2010) Dubious dualism: the reception of international law in Canada. Val u l Rev 44(3):927–934

Van Panhuys JHF (1964) Relations and interactions between international and national scenes of law. Collected courses of the Hague academy of international law, vol 112. Martinus Nijhoff Publishers, Leiden, pp 1–90

Vienna Convention on the Law of Treaties (1969) United Nations, Treaty Series, 1155:331

Virally M (1964) Sur un pont aux ânes: les rapports entre droit international et droits internes in Mélanges offerts à Henri Rolin, Problèmes de droit des gens, Paris, Éditions A. Pedone, pp 488–505

Walz GA (1937) Les rapports du droit international et du droit interne [Relations between International Law and Domestic Law]. Collected Courses of the Hague Academy of International Law, vol 61. Martinus Nijhoff Publishers, Leiden, pp 375–356

Washington Post (1993) Turkmenistan is forgetting the Soviets, March 31. https://www.washingtonpost.com/archive/politics/1993/04/01/turkmenistan-is-forgetting-the-soviets/0d0f11fc-0861-4461-80e4-d8a9458a37d6/. Accessed 8 Aug 2024

Wittke C, Rabinovych M (2022) Troubled nexus between international and domestic law in the post-Soviet space. Rev Cent East Eur L 47:249–267

Yunusov K (2014) The Development of legal systems of Central Asian States. Studii Europene 2:23–34

Zotov S (2022) Русские и казахи: народы общей судьбы [Russians and Kazakhs: peoples of a common destiny]. Военно-политическая аналитика [Military-political analysis], April 16. https://dzen.ru/a/YePs5ZIvOA8bL0EQ. Accessed 15 Nov 2024

Chapter 7
On the Necessity of Responding to the Findings of the International Law Commission

Abay Abylaiuly

Abstract This section is devoted to substantiating the necessity of responding to the work of the United Nations International Law Commission (ILC). The rationale is fourfold. First, the conclusions of the ILC are increasingly invoked as a subsidiary means for the determination of rules of international law under Article 38(1)(d) of the Statute of the International Court of Justice (ICJ). Second, in the Jurisdictional Immunities of the State case, the ICJ emphasized that States are expected to respond to the ILC's work, and failure to do so may be interpreted as evidence of opinio juris. Third, over the past decade, the ILC has accelerated its activities, producing outcomes three times faster than during its previous sixty years. Fourth, the ILC's recent outputs address particularly significant issues such as jus cogens norms, subsequent agreements, subsequent practice in the interpretation of treaties, subsidiary means for the determination of international law, and other matters. In many of these works, the ILC pursues an excessively progressive approach that may run counter to the traditional understanding of international law and the interests of States. The section further highlights the absence of any formal reaction by the Republic of Kazakhstan to the ILC's work and, in this regard, calls for Kazakhstan's active engagement.

Keywords International Law Commission · International Court of Justice · Jus cogens · Opinio juris · Subsidiary means · Subsequent agreements · Subsequent practice · Interpretation of treaties

---

A. Abylaiuly (✉)
Associate Professor in International Law, Maqsut Narikbayev University, Astana, Kazakhstan
e-mail: a_abylaiuly@kazguu.kz

S. Sayapin (ed.), *International Law, Politics and Security in Central Asia*,
https://doi.org/10.1007/978-3-032-17818-3_7

7.1 Introduction

The United Nations International Law Commission (ILC) plays a pivotal role in the progressive development and codification of international law. Established in 1947, the ILC serves as an expert body tasked with drafting legal instruments that clarify and systematize international legal norms, ensuring their coherence and adaptability to contemporary challenges. Through its rigorous methodology—incorporating state practice, judicial decisions, and doctrinal analyses—the ILC produces authoritative legal texts that influence treaty-making, judicial reasoning, and state behaviour. Its work provides a foundation for the stability and predictability of international law, making it indispensable in an increasingly complex global legal order. Given the ILC's growing efficiency and expanding scope, its findings demand serious engagement from states to ensure that emerging legal norms reflect diverse perspectives and interests.

The ILC's practice demonstrates a dynamic shift from traditional treaty-drafting to the formulation of non-binding instruments such as principles, conclusions, and guidelines. This evolution responds to challenges like low treaty ratification rates and the UN General Assembly's reluctance to convene diplomatic conferences. Despite criticisms that the ILC has retreated from hard law, its outputs remain influential, often serving as subsidiary means for determining international legal norms under Article 38(1)(d) of the UN International Court of Justice (ICJ) Statute. The ILC's increasing reliance on soft law mechanisms, however, raises critical questions about state participation. Many states, particularly from Asia, remain passive in responding to ILC drafts, risking the marginalization of their legal perspectives in the development of customary international law. Key concerns include the ILC's expansive interpretations of treaty provisions (e.g., recognizing state silence as acquiescence in treaty interpretation) and its identification of peremptory norms (*jus cogens*), where methodological inconsistencies and regional biases may emerge. Without active state engagement, the ILC's conclusions—though non-binding—may gradually crystallize into norms that do not fully reflect the practices and consent of all states.

The aim of this chapter is to provide a thorough understanding of the ILC's role in international law and to advocate for the necessity of state engagement with its findings. By analysing the ILC's practice, its influence on the ICJ, and the implications for Kazakhstan, the text seeks to bridge the gap between theoretical discussions of international law and practical considerations for states. It underscores the risks of passive observation and highlights how proactive participation can shape legal norms in ways that align with national and regional interests.

The chapter offers a comprehensive analysis of the role, practice, and impact of the ILC in the development and codification of international law. It also examines the implications of the ILC's work for states and underscores the importance of engaging with the ILC's findings. The chapter also argues that states must proactively engage with the ILC's work to safeguard their legal interests and contribute to the legitimacy of international law. As evidenced by the ICJ's jurisprudence, the absence of state objections to ILC findings can be construed as tacit acceptance, reinforcing the Commission's authority in determining customary norms. Kazakhstan and other Asian states, in particular, should prioritize participation in ILC discussions to ensure regional practices are adequately represented. This includes submitting comments on draft conclusions, challenging contentious interpretations (such as those concerning treaty bodies' pronouncements as subsequent practice), and advocating for clearer methodologies in identifying *jus cogens* norms. Active engagement is not merely a procedural formality but a strategic necessity to prevent the imposition of norms that may conflict with domestic legal systems or geopolitical realities.

In *Jurisdictional Immunities of the State*,[1] the ICJ extensively examined the ILC's work and emphasized with significant importance that the '...complete absence of contrary jurisprudence is also significant, as is the absence of any statements by States in connection with the work of the ILC...'[2] The ICJ acknowledged the pivotal role played by the ILC in the development of customary international law and assessed the actions (or inaction) of states in the preparation of ILC draft articles, particularly evaluating the role they play in determining *opinio juris*.

Since the adoption of this judgement, the ILC has produced eight sets of draft articles,[3] and as of today, the ILC is actively addressing eight issues.[4] The chapter investigates three of them. Notably, draft conclusions on subsequent agreements and subsequent practice in relation to the interpretation of treaties, draft conclusions on identification and legal consequences of peremptory norms of general international law (*jus cogens*), and ongoing work on subsidiary means for the determination of rules of international law.

The chapter is structured to first examine the UN International Law Commission's practice, analysing its evolving methodologies and shift from hard law treaties to soft law instruments like principles and guidelines, while highlighting the Commission's growing efficiency in producing influential legal outputs. Next, it explores the ILC's role as subsidiary means under Article 38(1)(d) of the ICJ Statute, demonstrating how the Court relies on ILC drafts to identify customary international law, and the implications of state silence in response to the Commission's findings. The subsequent section, Why Kazakhstan Must Respond to the ILC's Findings, presents strategic reasons for engagement, focusing on the ILC's influence on regional customary norms and the risks of non-participation, with subsections

[1] Germany v. Italy 2012.

[2] Ibid., para. 77.

[3] ILC (2025).

[4] Ibid.

critiquing the Draft Conclusions on Subsequent Agreements and Subsequent Practice (particularly its treatment of state silence and treaty body pronouncements), the Draft Conclusions on *Jus Cogens* Norms (assessing methodological flaws and regional representation gaps), and Subsidiary Means for Determining International Law (addressing concerns about the broad interpretation of Article 38(1)(d)). The chapter concludes by reinforcing the necessity of state engagement with the ILC and offering actionable recommendations for Kazakhstan to enhance its influence in shaping international legal norms.

7.2 UN International Law Commission's Practice

The ILC develops and codifies international law by preparing draft articles with detailed commentaries, including precedents, treaties, judicial decisions, and doctrinal analyses. After receiving governmental feedback, the ILC finalizes these drafts and submits a report with recommendations to the General Assembly. The recommendations may suggest no further action, note or adopt the report, recommend the draft for a convention, or convene a conference. Since its inception, the ILC has produced numerous influential instruments and guidelines, significantly contributing to the stability and consistency of international law through its systematic and consultative approach.[5] This may suggest that the ILC is no longer actively engaged in the progressive development of international law, and some indeed make this claim.[6] However, practice suggests otherwise.

ILC has systematically developed numerous influential texts, instruments, and final reports, significantly contributing to the codification and progressive development of international law. Key outputs include: Reports on customary international law and Nürnberg Principles 1950; Report on reservations to multilateral conventions 1951; Draft conventions on statelessness and offenses against peace 1954; Articles on the Law of the Sea 1956; Diplomatic intercourse and arbitral procedure articles 1958; Articles on consular relations, treaty law, and diplomatic couriers 1961–1982; Articles on jurisdictional immunities, watercourses, crimes against peace, and state responsibility 1989–1996; Articles on state succession, wrongful acts, transboundary harm, fragmentation of international law, diplomatic protection, and treaty reservations 1999–2011; and Articles on extradition, expulsion, disaster protection, treaty interpretation, customary international law, crimes against humanity, provisional treaty application, atmospheric protection, *jus cogens* norms, and environmental protection during armed conflicts 2014–2022.[7]

---

[5] Ibid.

[6] Đorđeska (2015, p. 55).

[7] Ibid.

Fig. 7.1 ILC findings (draft articles, reports, guides)[8]

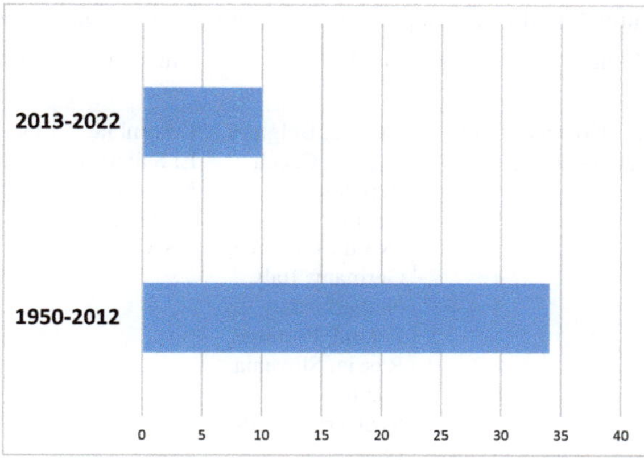

Upon detailed analysis, we can see that the ILC adopted 34 works from 1950 to 2012, and 10 works from 2013 to 2022. Thus, the ILC completed work on 34 issues in 62 years, and on 10 issues in the last 10 years. This indicates that the ILC is currently working three times faster (see Fig. 7.1) than previously.

If we analyse the practice of state participation in commenting on the eight most recent works of the ILC, we can see that European countries are the most actively engaged. Among the countries of the Americas, the United States demonstrates leadership, while Japan, Singapore, and South Korea are the most active participants from Asia. African and Oceanian countries show the least interest in participating in the discussion of the ILC's work. The table also shows that Kazakhstan has not submitted comments on any of the recent works of the International Law Commission (ILC). In fact, Kazakhstan has never commented on any of the ILC's work throughout all the years of its independence (see Table 7.1).

As of today, the ILC is actively addressing eight issues,[9] with questions such as Immunity of State Officials from Foreign Criminal Jurisdiction, Succession of States in Respect of State Responsibility, and Subsidiary Means for the Determination of Rules of International Law eliciting particular interest from states.

Since the turn of the millennium, the ILC has shifted its work product formats toward 'principles,' 'conclusions,' and 'guidelines.' Accordingly, the ILC no longer recommends convening conferences to conclude formal treaties or conventions. For example, in 2006, the ILC advised the General Assembly to endorse the *Draft Principles* on International Liability from Transboundary Harm and urge state action. In 2011, it recommended noting and disseminating the *Guide* to Practice on Reservations to Treaties. The 2006 *Guiding Principles* on Unilateral Declarations were merely commended to the Assembly's attention, and the 2008 Draft Conclusions on Customary International Law was similarly presented as '*draft conclusions.*'[10]

---

[8] ILC (2025).

[9] Ibid.

[10] Rim (2020, p. 30).

Table 7.1 ILC draft topics—state and institutional engagement[11]

Topic	Total states	Europe	Americas	Asia	Africa	Oceania
Jus Cogens (2016–2022)	30	Austria, Belgium, Cyprus, Czech Republic, Denmark (Nordic), France, Germany, Italy, Netherlands, Poland, Portugal, Russia, Slovenia, Spain, Switzerland, UK, Israel	Colombia, El Salvador, Mexico, Paraguay, USA	Japan, Singapore	South Africa, Morocco	Australia
Environment in Armed Conflicts (2022)	19	Belgium, Cyprus, Czech Republic, France, Germany, Ireland, Netherlands, Portugal, Slovenia, Spain, Switzerland, Sweden (Nordic), UK, Israel	Canada, Colombia, El Salvador, Paraguay	Japan, Lebanon	–	Micronesia
Atmosphere Protection (2021)	19	Austria, Belgium, Czech Republic, Estonia, Finland (Nordic), Germany, Netherlands, Portugal, Belarus, UK	Antigua and Barbuda, Argentina, Cuba, Mexico	Japan, Korea, Singapore	Togo	Micronesia

(continued)

[11] Ibid.

Table 7.1 (continued)

Topic	Total states	Europe	Americas	Asia	Africa	Oceania
Provisional Application of Treaties (2021)	34	Austria, Belarus, Czech Republic, Estonia, Finland (Nordic), Germany, Netherlands, Norway, Russia, Serbia, Slovenia, Spain, Switzerland, Turkey, UK	Argentina, Cuba, El Salvador, Mexico, Paraguay, USA	Bahrain, Korea, Singapore,	Botswana	Australia, Micronesia
Crimes Against Humanity (2019)	38	Austria, Belgium, Bosnia, Czech Republic, Estonia, Finland, France, Germany, Greece, Liechtenstein, Malta, Netherlands, Portugal, Spain, Sweden (Nordic), Switzerland, Ukraine, UK	Argentina, Brazil, Canada, Chile, Costa Rica, Cuba, El Salvador, Mexico, Panama, Peru, Uruguay, USA	Israel, Japan, Korea, Singapore	Morocco, Sierra Leone	Australia, New Zealand
Subsequent Agreements & Practice (2018)	15	Austria, Belarus, Czech Republic, Finland, Germany, Netherlands, Spain, Sweden, UK	El Salvador, Paraguay, USA	Uzbekistan	–	Australia
Customary International Law (2018)	24	Austria, Belarus, Belgium, Czech Republic, Denmark, Finland, Germany, Ireland, Netherlands, Russia, Switzerland, UK, Israel	Cuba, El Salvador, USA	China, Korea, Singapore, Uzbekistan	Botswana	New Zealand
Protection of Persons in Disasters (2016)	17	Austria, Belgium, Czech Republic, Finland, Germany, Netherlands, Switzerland, Turkey, UK	Cuba, El Salvador, Ecuador, Mexico, USA	Malaysia, Qatar	–	Australia

In addition, scholars have observed that, from 2008 to 2015, the ILC shifted from favouring hard law treaties to promoting gradually evolving soft law norms, responding to low ratification rates and the UNGA's reluctance to negotiate treaties, and believing that this shift could rejuvenate the ILC's relevance.[12] However, the impact of the ILC's work isn't solely measured by whether its outcomes become treaties approved by states. Even without clear indicators of state acceptance during negotiations, if ILC reports are heavily referenced by scholars and practitioners, they can influence state practices over time. While non-binding, ILC principles and guidelines serve as authoritative references for states addressing pertinent issues, potentially shaping international law development in the long run.[13]

Perhaps a new direction in the work of the ILC is the interpretation of international treaties that have entered into force. The ILC engages in the interpretation process through a structured approach that begins with agenda setting to identify legal areas requiring clarification, followed by the appointment of special rapporteurs who conduct research and prepare reports, which are then reviewed, discussed, and refined in plenary sessions, sometimes with the involvement of a Drafting Committee, ensuring a thorough, collaborative, and systematic development of legal interpretations before final approval.[14] For instance, the ILC has contributed to the interpretation of key provisions of the Vienna Convention on the Law of Treaties (VCLT) through various efforts, including the 2011 Guide to Practice on Reservations to Treaties,[15] which clarifies the permissibility and legal effects of treaty reservations under Articles 19–23; the 2018 Conclusions on Subsequent Agreements and Subsequent Practice,[16] which interpret Articles 31 and 32 by explaining how state practice influences treaty interpretation; the 2018 Draft Guidelines on Provisional Application of Treaties,[17] which elaborate on Article 25 regarding the legal status of treaties applied before formal entry into force; and the 2019 Draft Conclusions on *jus cogens*,[18] which define peremptory norms under Articles 53 and 64 and their impact on treaty law.

The ILC's increasing efficiency, expanding scope of work, and growing role in interpreting existing treaties indicate its rising influence in shaping international law. The shift from treaty-making to principles, conclusions, and guidelines, coupled with its structured approach to legal interpretation, suggests that the ILC's outputs will continue to guide state practice, judicial reasoning, and international legal discourse. As states engage with the ILC's evolving role, they must recognize its growing authority and respond proactively to its work.

---

[12] Cogan (2015, p. 286), Wood (2008, p. 377), Daugirdas (2014, p. 79), and Baylis (2019, p. 1008).

[13] Ibid.

[14] Azaria (2020, p. 200).

[15] ILC Yearbook (2011, p. 23).

[16] UN Doc A/73/10 2018.

[17] UN Doc A/76/10 2021.

[18] UN Doc A/77/10 2022.

7.3 UN International Law Commission's Work as Subsidiary Means

Article 38.1 of the ICJ Statute, which provides the most comprehensive list of sources of international law,[19] states: 'the Court, whose function is to decide in accordance with international law such disputes as are submitted to it, shall apply: (a) international conventions, whether general or particular, establishing rules expressly recognised by the contesting states; (b) international custom, as evidence of a general practice accepted as law; (c) the general principles of law recognised by civilised nations; (d) subject to the provisions of Article 59, judicial decisions and the teachings of the most highly qualified publicists of the various nations, as subsidiary means for the determination of rules of law.' Here, the phrase 'the teachings of the most highly qualified publicists' is of particular importance to us. It is noted that this wording is not restrictive in terms of which doctrines should be included. This category encompasses the work of the UN International Law Commission, including its articles, commentaries, and reports.[20]

The ILC promotes the progressive development and codification of international law by drafting conventions on unregulated legal issues and systematizing existing legal rules based on state practice, precedent, and doctrine.[21] It reviews proposals from UN members and agencies, collects input from governments and experts, and refines drafts before submitting them to the UN General Assembly.[22] Through this process, the ILC helps clarify international legal principles and contributes to the evolution of international law.[23]

The ICJ, while effectively participating in the process of law-making, may refer to the work of the ILC. By relying on these non-binding instruments, the Court fills gaps in international law, thereby actively contributing to the development of customary law norms.[24] The ICJ recognizes certain norms as customary international law or general principles of law by using the ILC's draft articles. The Court first referred to the work of the ILC in the *Gabčíkovo-Nagymaros Project* case. In determining the date of entry into force of an international treaty for Slovakia, the ICJ referred to the Commentaries to the Draft Articles on State Succession in respect of Treaties by the ILC[25] and concluded that 'Article 12 reflects a rule of customary international law.'[26] Furthermore, in the same case, the Court recognized the Draft Articles on State Responsibility as general principles of law.[27]

---

[19] Shaw (2017 p. 52).

[20] Crawford and Brownlie (2019, p. 40).

[21] ILC Statute (1947, Art 15).

[22] Ibid., Art 16.

[23] Ibid., Art 17.

[24] Đorđeska (2015, p. 9).

[25] UN Official Records 1980, p. 27, para. 2.

[26] Hungary v. Slovakia 1997, para 123.

[27] Ibid., paras 141, 147.

It should be noted that the ICJ may recognize rules as norms of international law even if the ILC's articles are not always supported by clear evidence of state practice or *opinio juris*. For example, in the *North Sea Continental Shelf* case, the ICJ relied on the work of the ILC when determining state practice and/or *opinio juris*. The Court noted that the principle of equidistance was not considered mandatory under customary international law and did not take precedence over alternative methods such as agreements between states or arbitration. The Commission's further hesitations and the lack of consideration of delimitation cases involving three or more states confirmed that the principle of equidistance had never been recognized as an inherent element of the continental shelf doctrine.[28] Thus, the ICJ's use of the ILC's work allows the Court to develop and affirm norms that have not yet gained widespread recognition among states but are deemed important for the evolution of international law.

At the same time, in *Jurisdictional Immunities of the State*,[29] the ICJ formulated important conclusions for the future of subsidiary means under Article 38 of the ICJ Statute. In this case, the ICJ analysed a conclusion of the ILC in which the ILC determined that the rule of state immunity is a 'general norm of customary international law, firmly rooted in contemporary state practice.'[30] Analysing state actions to determine *opinio juris* on matters of state immunity, the ICJ noted 'the almost complete absence of … any statements by States in connection with the work of the ILC regarding State immunity and the adoption of the United Nations Convention or, so far as the Court has been able to discover, in any other context asserting that customary international law does not require immunity in such cases.'[31]

From the above position of the ICJ, two important conclusions can be drawn. First, the ICJ believes that states should make statements regarding the work of the ILC, and the presence or absence of clear positions by states can affect the determination of *opinio juris*. Second, the ILC's works can serve as subsidiary means under Article 38(1)(d) of the ICJ Statute. These two conclusions are interconnected and complementary as the Court implies that, if the ILC determines a customary international law norm, a state wishing not to be bound by this norm must make specific statements; otherwise, the state's silence will signify consent. It is noteworthy that such a prominent role of the ILC did not encounter opposition during the ICJ's consideration of the case. In the case of Jurisdictional Immunities of the State, three separate opinions[32] and three dissenting opinions[33] were formulated by ICJ judges, and not a single judge objected to the conclusion that states should express their positions regarding the ILC's work on customary international law norms. Thereby,

---

[28] Germany v. Netherlands 1969, paras 48–63.

[29] Germany v. Italy 2012.

[30] ILC Yearbook (1980, p. 147).

[31] Germany v. Italy 2012, para 77.

[32] Germany v. Italy 2012, Koroma, Separate opinion; Germany v. Italy 2012, Keith, Separate opinion; Germany v. Italy 2012, Bennouna, Separate opinion.

[33] Germany v. Italy 2012, Trindade, Dissenting opinion; Germany v. Italy 2012, Yusuf, Dissenting opinion; Germany v. Italy 2012, Gaja, Dissenting opinion.

the ICJ considers the ILC's draft articles as clarifications of specific legal issues, as evidence of the existence of a rule of international law, or simply as *'the teachings of the most highly qualified publicists of the various nations'* within the meaning of Article 38(1)(d) of the ICJ Statute.

Overall, it should be noted that the number of cases in which the ICJ refers to the work of the ILC is increasing. While, as of 30 December 2018, the ICJ had explicitly referred to the Commission's work in 22 cases (3 advisory opinions and 19 decisions),[34] by March 2025, the ICJ had referred to the work of the ILC 9 times (1 advisory opinion and 8 decisions).[35] This reinforces the recognition of the ILC's important role in determining international law norms, the possibility of recognizing the ILC's work as subsidiary means, and the necessity for states to respond to the ILC's work or face significant implications. This is particularly true for states that do not respond to the ILC's work at all.

7.4 Why Kazakhstan Must Respond to the Findings of the ILC

There are many reasons why Kazakhstan and other Asian countries should respond to the ILC's work. First, when the ICJ and the ILC collaborate, the result directly impacts international law.[36] This has a solid foundation, as about one-third of the ICJ's fifteen judges were previously members of the ILC. The Court's practice underpins many of the Commission's key positions, from fundamental norms defining customary international law to conclusions such as the customary international law status of Article 31 of the Vienna Convention and the fundamental rule that a state's breach of an international obligation entails its responsibility.[37]

An example of this direct influence on international law is evident in the ICJ's positions in *Jurisdictional Immunities of the State*, where the Court emphasized that the presence or absence of clear state positions regarding the ILC's work can affect *opinio juris*, and cited the ILC's work as subsidiary means. Additionally, it was noted earlier that the ILC has become more active, producing one report annually, indicating a new direction in the development of international law. Thus, there is a necessity for a response to the ILC's work as it shapes contemporary international legal developments.

Furthermore, the ILC not only covers new areas of international law in its work but also examines (and revises when necessary) fundamental issues of international

[34] Azaria (2019, p. 1002).

[35] Advisory Opinion 2024; Azerbaijan v. Armenia 2024; Iran v. United States of America 2023; Chile v. Bolivia 2022; Gambia v. Myanmar 2022; Nicaragua v. Colombia 2022; Congo v. Uganda 2022; Ukraine v. Russian Federation 2019; India v. Pakistan 2019.

[36] Tladi (2022, p. 75).

[37] Ibid.

law. For instance, Special Rapporteur Michael Wood produced five reports,[38] and in 2018, the ILC drafted conclusions on identifying customary international law.[39] In 2019, Marcelo Vázquez-Bermúdez presented a report on the general principles of law,[40] and Dire Tladi presented a fourth report on peremptory norms (*jus cogens*), along with the ILC's adoption of 23 Draft Conclusions on *jus cogens*.[41] This analysis explores how ILC special rapporteurs have addressed sources of general (unwritten) international law.[42]

Moreover, Asian countries, including Kazakhstan, should respond to the work of the ILC. Firstly, norms of customary international law can emerge within a specific region,[43] including between two states.[44] Secondly, it is noted that the ILC may codify or propose the progressive development of international law despite clear divergences or inconsistencies in state practice, prioritizing regional practice within the European context.[45] In this regard, given that the ILC's work can influence the formation of customary law norms, Asian countries should take an active role.

Based on the above, the works of the ILC that deserve special attention are the Draft Conclusions on Subsequent Agreements and Subsequent Practice in Relation to the Interpretation of Treaties 2018,[46] the Draft Conclusions on Identification and Legal Consequences of Peremptory Norms of General International Law (jus cogens) 2022,[47] and the ongoing work on Subsidiary Means for the Determination of Rules of International Law.

7.4.1 Draft Conclusions on Subsequent Agreements and Subsequent Practice in Relation to the Interpretation of Treaties

The ILC adopted the Draft Conclusions on 'Subsequent Agreements and Subsequent Practice in Relation to the Interpretation of Treaties' and their accompanying commentaries[48] during its 70th session in New York (30 April–1 June) and Geneva (2 July–10 August) in 2018. The Draft Conclusions consist of 13 points covering the following topics: rules and means of interpretation, authentic means of interpretation, identifying and determining subsequent agreements and practices, treaty

---

[38] Wood (2013, 2014, 2015, 2016, 2018).

[39] ILC (2018b).

[40] Vázquez-Bermúdez (2019a).

[41] Tladi (2017, 2018c, 2019).

[42] Saganek (2019, p. 38).

[43] Colombia v. Peru 1950, pp. 266, 276 and Espiel (2001).

[44] El Salvador v. Honduras 1992, para 26.

[45] Barkholdt (2022, p. 184).

[46] ILC (2018a).

[47] ILC (2022a).

[48] ILC (2018a).

terms capable of evolving over time, decisions made within conferences of States Parties, constituent instruments of international organizations, and statements by expert treaty bodies.

Over multiple sessions of the International Law Commission, various governments and organizations provided input on the topic of 'Subsequent agreements and subsequent practice in relation to the interpretation of treaties. In 2015, Austria, Finland, Germany, the Netherlands, and the European Union submitted comments.[49] By 2016, contributions expanded to include Australia, the Czech Republic, Germany, Paraguay, Spain, and the International Labour Organization.'[50] In 2018, a broader range of states, including Belarus, the Czech Republic, El Salvador, Germany, Netherlands, Spain, Sweden, the United Kingdom, the United States, and Uzbekistan, had also provided feedback, reflecting continued international engagement with the subject.[51]

In commenting on the ILC's Draft, some states raised concerns about the:

- *Role of subsequent agreements and practice in treaty interpretation.* Several states emphasized the importance of clearly distinguishing between subsequent agreements and subsequent practice under Articles 31 and 32 VCLT. The Netherlands called for greater conceptual clarity and more precise terminology to prevent ambiguity.[52] The Czech Republic argued that Draft Conclusion 1 should explicitly clarify its scope concerning treaties between states and international organizations and criticized Draft Conclusion 2 for merging elements of Articles 31 and 32 VCLT.[53] The United States asserted that treaty interpretation should be based strictly on the practice of treaty parties rather than informal agreements or the positions of non-party entities, including international organizations.[54]
- *State silence as subsequent practice.* Uzbekistan, Belarus, and the Netherlands opposed the notion that state silence constitutes consent in treaty interpretation. Uzbekistan contended that silence may result from political considerations rather than *opinio juris,* and that only explicit state actions should be recognized as expressions of agreement.[55] Belarus similarly argued that a state's silence can only be regarded as acquiescence if the state is aware of its implications and has had an opportunity to object.[56] The Netherlands suggested incorporating a presumption against silence in Draft Conclusion 10, aligning it with Draft Conclusion 13, to ensure that silence is not automatically interpreted as consent.[57]

---

[49] ILC (2025, Comments by Governments).

[50] Ibid.

[51] Ibid.

[52] Netherlands (2018).

[53] Czech Republic (2018).

[54] United States (2018).

[55] Uzbekistan (2018).

[56] Belarus (2018).

[57] Netherlands (2018).

- *Role of conferences and international organizations.* Several states expressed concerns regarding the influence of international organizations and treaty bodies in treaty interpretation. Belarus insisted on limiting their role, asserting that the practice of international organizations should not be used to interpret their founding documents unless explicitly endorsed by member states.[58] The Netherlands acknowledged the relevance of Conferences of States Parties but highlighted the diversity of their practices, making broad generalizations difficult.[59] Uzbekistan supported the role of such conferences in treaty interpretation only where their decisions explicitly reflect state consent.[60] The United States warned against granting undue interpretative authority to non-party entities, including international organizations and the ICRC.[61]
- *Treaty bodies and non-state actors in interpretation.* The Nordic countries (Denmark, Finland, Iceland, Norway, and Sweden) acknowledged their relevance but emphasize that their pronouncements are not legally binding and cannot modify treaty obligations.[62] Germany highlighted the importance of treaty bodies but called for greater clarity on how their pronouncements fit within the framework of the VCLT, suggesting that they may qualify as supplementary means of interpretation under Article 32.[63] Uzbekistan asserted that expert opinions from treaty bodies do not constitute subsequent practice or agreements, with only state reactions to such acts being relevant for treaty interpretation.[64]
- *Need for conceptual and structural clarity in draft conclusions.* Austria, the Czech Republic, and the Netherlands called for greater precision in defining key terms and structuring the draft conclusions. Austria advocated for an inductive approach that differentiates between various types of immunities and called for a thorough examination of judicial case law to identify customary rules.[65] The Czech Republic criticized the structure of Draft Conclusion 2, arguing that the combination of elements from Articles 31 and 32 VCLT disrupts logical coherence, and calls for a clearer distinction between subsequent agreements and practice.[66] The Netherlands supported the reaffirmation that treaty interpretation is a 'single combined operation' but emphasized that Article 32 serves only as an aid to Article 31 and should not function as an independent interpretative tool.[67]
- *Specific legal terminology and interpretative presumptions.*
- The Netherlands recommended refining the terminology in the draft conclusions for greater precision, advocating for having 'taken a position' rather than 'assumed

[58] Belarus (2018).

[59] Netherlands (2018).

[60] Uzbekistan (2018).

[61] United States (2018).

[62] Nordic Countries (Denmark, Finland, Iceland, Norway, and Sweden) (2018).

[63] Germany (2018).

[64] Uzbekistan (2018).

[65] ILC (2015a, 2015b).

[66] Czech Republic (2018).

[67] Netherlands (2018).

a position.' It also cautioned against assuming that a 'manifest misapplication' of a treaty can always be easily determined. Additionally, it proposed addressing confidential protests in the commentary to ensure that silence is not misinterpreted as consent.[68] The Czech Republic criticized the rigidity of Draft Conclusion 3's presumption regarding subsequent agreements and advocated for a case-by-case approach.[69] The United States disagreed with the restrictive interpretation of informal agreements in Draft Conclusion 7 and challenges the definitions of 'subsequent agreement' and 'subsequent practice' in Draft Conclusion 4, arguing that the cited tribunal cases do not substantiate the conclusions drawn.[70]

Agreeing with the aforementioned positions, it is worth focusing separately on Conclusions 10 and 13. In Conclusion 10.2, the ILC states: 'The number of parties that must actively engage in subsequent practice in order to establish an agreement under article 31, paragraph 3 (b), may vary. Silence on the part of one or more parties may constitute acceptance of the subsequent practice when the circumstances call for some reaction.'[71] In its commentary to Conclusion 10, the ILC references the *Temple of Preah Vihear* case, where the International Court of Justice (ICJ) recognized the possibility of expressing agreement through silence or inaction, stating that '...it is clear that the circumstances were such as called for some reaction, within a reasonable period...' a state confronted with subsequent conduct by another party 'thereby must be held to have acquiesced.'[72]

However, this approach seems inapplicable to treaty bodies, primarily because they do not function as judicial institutions. Secondly, this approach could imply a departure from the original intentions of the treaty parties. For instance, the legal status of the Human Rights Committee's (HRC) views is not explicitly defined in the 1966 International Covenant on Civil and Political Rights (ICCPR) or its Optional Protocol. In General Comment No. 33, the HRC notes: 'the Views issued by the Committee under the Optional Protocol exhibit some of the principal characteristics of a judicial decision. They are arrived at in a judicial spirit, including the impartiality and independence of Committee members, the considered interpretation of the language of the Covenant, and the determinative character of the decisions.'[73] Additionally, 'the Views of the Committee under the Optional Protocol represent an authoritative determination by the organ established under the Covenant itself charged with the interpretation of that instrument.'[74] However, while the ICCPR does not specify the binding nature of the HRC's views, the adoption of General Comment No. 33 was seen as justifying '*the circumstances call for some reaction.*' The United States (US) provided their objection on the Draft General Comment

[68] Ibid.

[69] *Czech Republic* (2018).

[70] United States (2018).

[71] ILC (2022b).

[72] Cambodia v. Thailand 1962, para 23.

[73] General Comment No. 33 2009.

[74] Ibid., para 13.

No. 33, divided into two main points: (1) The US argues that the draft oversteps the HRC's mandate, implying judicial authority and binding treaty interpretations, whereas the US views the Committee as advisory and its opinions as non-binding. The US contests that ultimate treaty interpretation lies with States Parties; (2) The US disputes the notion that the Committee's opinions constitute 'subsequent practice' under the Vienna Convention on the Law of Treaties (VCLT), arguing that treaty interpretation should rely on state practice rather than expert bodies' opinions. The US recommends either withdrawing or significantly revising the draft, emphasizing that any expansion of the Committee's powers should be through formal treaty amendments, not interpretative declarations.[75] Following US feedback, General Comment No. 33 was adopted without recognizing the HRC's opinions as 'subsequent practice' for treaty interpretation under VCLT Articles 31 and 32.

In Conclusion 13.3, the ILC states: 'A pronouncement of an expert treaty body may give rise to, or refer to, a subsequent agreement or subsequent practice by parties under article 31, paragraph 3, or subsequent practice under article 32.' VCLT Article 31 allows treaty interpretation based on agreements between States or subsequent practice establishing the treaty's meaning. However, no such agreements exist concerning the binding nature of the HRC's opinions, and international practice does not support their binding force. There are a limited number of States in the world that have established special procedures for the implementation of treaty body views on individual complaints.[76] However, the existence of a special procedure does not necessarily mean that the Views have legal force. For example, In Slovakia, legislation guaranteeing the legal force of the HRC views was adopted in 2000.[77] The legislation obliged the government to refer a case to the Slovak Constitutional Court if the HRC ruled against Slovakia. Just two years later, the legislation was repealed because, as the ILA report says, the procedure 'was considered likely to lead to a violation of the principle of *res judicata*.'[78] The legislative practice of the Czech Republic provides that the Minister of Justice coordinates the implementation of the Views of the HRC. However, this act does not grant the courts any role in the implementation of the Views.[79] Law 288/96 of Colombia establishes the procedure for implementing the Views of the HRC and the decisions of the Inter-American Commission on Human Rights.[80] Specific cases of the HRC also support our observations. Austria, opposing the HRC's decision in *Weiss v. Austria*, stated that HRC's interim measures lack legal force.[81] Similarly, Canada's Ontario Court of Appeal ruled in *Ahani v. Canada* that the HRC's recommendations are non-binding.[82] Kazakhstan disregarded the HRC's

[75] Comments of the United States (2008).

[76] Ulfstein and Keller (2012, pp. 362–363).

[77] International Law Association (2004).

[78] Act No. 124/2002; Ulfstein and Keller (2012, p. 365).

[79] International Law Association (2004).

[80] La Ley 288 (1996).

[81] Weiss v. Austria 2002, para. 5.2–5.3.

[82] Ahani v. Canada 2002.

interim measures, extraditing Israil Arshidin to China.[83] Even in cases of 'gross violations' for non-cooperation, like *Piandiong v. the Philippines*,[84] states are not legally obliged to comply.[85]

Article 32 of the VCLT provides for additional interpretative means when Article 31 leaves a treaty ambiguous. Analysing the ICCPR's adoption context, it is evident that the ICCPR and its protocols were adopted in 1966 amid awareness of the binding 1950 European Convention on Human Rights. However, the creation of a universal mandatory individual complaints body was deemed unfeasible then due to post-war distrust and decolonization. This suggests that States did not intend for the HRC's opinions to be legally binding upon ratifying the ICCPR and its Optional Protocol.

7.4.2 *Draft Conclusions on Identification and Legal Consequences of Peremptory Norms of General International Law (Jus Cogens)*

The Draft Conclusions on Identification and Legal Consequences of Peremptory Norms of General International Law *(jus cogens)* 2022 (Draft Conclusions 2022) is the most recent work that, at the institutional level, has listed peremptory norms of international law. In the Draft Conclusions 2022, a non-exhaustive list of *jus cogens* norms is provided: (a) the prohibition of aggression; (b) the prohibition of genocide; (c) the prohibition of crimes against humanity; (d) the basic rules of international humanitarian law; (e) the prohibition of racial discrimination and apartheid; (f) the prohibition of slavery; (g) the prohibition of torture; (h) the right of self-determination.[86] As can be seen, the document presents eight types of peremptory norms which constitute the most extensive list of *jus cogens* norms in international law to date.

There are different approaches regarding the list and types of peremptory norms of international law. There have been warnings that overly broad uses of the concept may weaken its significance.[87] These cautions continue to be cited today as a reminder not to overestimate *jus cogens*.[88] Some scholars emphasize that this concept is primarily grounded in moral principles, and that, in today's world it is difficult to identify common values.[89] Others argue that criticism of attempts to extend the application of jus cogens beyond the realm of treaty law is based on an outdated perception of international public order.[90] Nevertheless, we have specific concerns regarding the

83 Arshidin Israil v. Kazakhstan 2011.

84 Piandiong et al. v. The Philippines 2000.

85 Abylaiuly (2017, p. 34).

86 ILC (2022c).

87 Weil (1983, p. 413); See Marocco's comments to the the Draft Conclusions, ILC (2002d).

88 Bianchi (2008, p. 505).

89 Shelton (2006, p. 323).

90 Dugard (1987, p. 142) and Orakhelashvili (2003, p. 24).

prohibition of crimes against humanity, the basic rules of international humanitarian law, and the right of self-determination.

7.4.2.1 Crimes Against Humanity

In international law, there is not yet a universally accepted and consistent recognition that the prohibition of crimes against humanity constitutes a peremptory norm (*jus cogens*), even though a growing body of practice and opinion supports this view. In its commentary to the Draft Conclusions on Identification and Legal Consequences of Peremptory Norms of General International Law *(jus cogens)*, the ILC references only the practice of the Supreme Court of Argentina, which found that the prohibition on crimes against humanity is a peremptory norm of international law.[91] In the 1998 case of *Aguilar Diaz v. Pinochet*, the Brussels Tribunal of First Instance held that, based on the *jus cogens* norm, universal jurisdiction over crimes against humanity exists, empowering national courts to prosecute and punish offenders under all circumstances.[92] In *Prosecutor v. Sesay, Kallon and Gbao*, the Special Court for Sierra Leone held that international law obliges states to prosecute *jus cogens* crimes; therefore, amnesty did not apply to genocide, crimes against humanity, or war crimes.[93] Under US law, courts have also issued judgments assigning civil liability for actions that violate *jus cogens* norms, such as genocide, war crimes, crimes against humanity, and torture.[94] In academic circles, Crawford and Brownlie argue that the least controversial *jus cogens* norms include the prohibition on the use of force, genocide, crimes against humanity, and the slave trade.[95] According to Bassiouni, crimes such as aggression, genocide, crimes against humanity, war crimes, piracy, slavery and related practices, and torture constitute *jus cogens* norms, as there exists a solid legal basis confirming their peremptory status under international law.[96] Cassese also holds that the duty of states to prosecute and punish those responsible for such crimes should itself be regarded as a *jus cogens* norm.[97] At the same time, Shaw lists as *jus cogens* norms only the unlawful use of force, genocide, slave trading and piracy, and the prohibition of torture.[98]

However, the recognition of the prohibition on crimes against humanity as a peremptory norm of international law poses difficulties due to challenges in defining a codifying international treaty that clearly delineates crimes against humanity as

[91] ILC Commentaries (2022b, p. 56).

[92] Aguilar Diaz et al. v Pinochet 1998.

[93] Prosecutor v Gbao 2004, para 10.

[94] Kadić et al. v Karadžić 1995; In re Estate of Ferdinand Marcos 1994; Xuncax et al. v Gramajo 1995.

[95] Crawford and Brownlie (2019, p. 581).

[96] Bassiouni (1996, p. 68).

[97] Cassese (2008, p. 419).

[98] Shaw (2017, p. 94).

a reflection of customary international law. For instance, the Charter of the International Military Tribunal for the trial and punishment of major war criminals of the European Axis Powers of 1945 (Nuremberg Charter) classifies crimes against humanity as 'murder, extermination, enslavement, deportation, and other inhumane acts committed against any civilian population, before or during the war, or persecutions on political, racial, or religious grounds in execution of or in connection with any crime within the jurisdiction of the Tribunal, whether or not in violation of the domestic law of the country where perpetrated.'[99] While acknowledging that this Charter first codified crimes against humanity, it lacks jurisdiction *ratione temporis* over such crimes committed after the end of World War II. Furthermore, the statutes of the International Criminal Tribunal for the former Yugoslavia 1993 (ICTY)[100] and the International Criminal Tribunal for Rwanda 1994[101] also have jurisdictional limitations *ratione materiae* and *ratione temporis* concerning the geography and timeframe of the crimes committed.

It is particularly noteworthy that the statutes of all the aforementioned tribunals allow for a broad interpretation of crimes against humanity. While the Nuremberg Charter uses the phrase 'and other inhumane acts committed against any civilian population,' the statutes of the tribunals for the former Yugoslavia and Rwanda employ the term 'other inhumane acts.' The application of such formulations could lead to an unjustifiably arbitrary expansion of the list of crimes falling under the category of peremptory norms of international law.

Referring to the universal codifying international treaty, the Statute of the International Criminal Court (ICC) from 1998, which lacks jurisdictional limitations like the aforementioned tribunals, we note that, in this Statute (Article 7), the list of crimes constituting crimes against humanity has been expanded. According to the Statute, crimes against humanity may include acts such as 'imprisonment or other severe deprivation of physical liberty in violation of fundamental rules of international law,' 'rape, sexual slavery, enforced prostitution, forced pregnancy, enforced sterilization, or any other form of sexual violence of comparable gravity,' and 'enforced disappearance of persons.'[102]

7.4.2.2 Basic Rules of International Humanitarian Law

The term 'basic rules of international humanitarian law (IHL)' allows for expansive interpretation and does not reflect widely accepted practice regarding the definition of war crimes. For instance, in the ICC Statute and ICTY Statutes, concepts such as 'grave breaches of the Geneva Conventions of 12 August 1949'[103] and 'violations

---

[99] Charter of the International Military Tribunal 1945.

[100] ICTFY Statute 1993.

[101] ICT Statute for Rwanda 1994.

[102] ICC Statute 1998.

[103] Ibid., Article 8.

of the laws or customs of war'[104] are used, enumerating specific criminal acts or omissions through which war crimes may be committed. Scholars rightly note that the Geneva Conventions already contain certain norms that can be considered *jus cogens, and they follow from the fundamental provisions of the Geneva Conventions.* Meron argues that the 'basic rights' enshrined in the Geneva Conventions, particularly Common Article 3 (the prohibitions on murder, mutilation, and torture mentioned in Article 3(1)(a)), constitute *jus cogens* norms.[105] Continuing this line of reasoning in the context of the 'grave breaches' provisions of the four Geneva Conventions, Navia-Nieto contends that many of the norms contained in these conventions do not meet the criteria necessary for recognition as *jus cogens*.[106] As Andrea Bianchi notes, the fact that the ICJ has never been particularly fond of *jus cogens* is further confirmed by its preference for using alternative notions, such as *erga omnes* obligations and 'intransgressible principles of humanitarian law,' in order to avoid referring explicitly to *jus cogens*.[107]

Indeed, IHL covers a wide range of rules regulating various aspects of armed conflict, including weapons, methods of warfare, and the protection of civilians and combatants, with some of these rules containing ambiguities in interpretation. Moreover, there is no clear and authoritative designation of specific IHL norms as *jus cogens* by the ICJ. This lack of explicit recognition complicates the definitive classification of these norms as peremptory. Additionally, further development of international humanitarian law may lead to the creation of new norms (basic rules), which could later raise questions about their recognition as peremptory norms of international law.

7.4.2.3 The Right to Self-Determination

The right to self-determination is a contentious issue when considering its status as a *jus cogens* norm. There are sharp disagreements among members of the Research School for Public and Private International Law at Maqsut Narikbayev University; one group emphasizes that it is a natural right of every people, while another group asserts that the right to self-determination is a discretionary principle that specific states may agree to observe in their relations with each other.[108] Overall, it is noted that similar uncertainty exists in the official positions of states regarding the recognition of this right as a peremptory norm of international law.[109]

Our conversations also concern other states. Japan expresses caution regarding the recognition of *jus cogens* norms through resolutions of international organizations or

---

[104] ICTFY Statute 1993, Art 3.

[105] Meron (1991, p. 31).

[106] Nieto-Navia (2016, p. 68).

[107] Bianchi (2008, p. 502).

[108] Maqsut Narikbayev University (2023).

[109] ILC Report 2022.

intergovernmental conferences.[110] Japan outlines three main concerns: Firstly, it is uncommon for an international organization to have the explicit or implied authority to establish a norm as *jus cogens*. Therefore, resolutions from organizations lacking such competence should not be considered evidence of *jus cogens*. Secondly, even organizations like the UN, despite their broad mandates, often declare actions as breaches of international law without invoking *jus cogens*. Thirdly, the acceptance and acknowledgement of *jus cogens* by states through their conduct in international organizations or conferences does not necessarily translate into resolutions. Regarding the work of expert bodies, Japan notes that, while the ILC is authorized to codify international law, including *jus cogens*, most other bodies lack the authority to determine *jus cogens* norms. Consequently, Japan calls on the ILC to clarify the criteria for selecting *jus cogens* norms, the reasoning behind specific formulations, and the exact scope of each norm listed.[111]

Singapore, in acknowledging the Commission's efforts, noted that it cannot support the draft conclusions as adopted on first reading. Singapore's primary concerns are twofold. First, not all users may grasp the importance of paragraphs (5) to (14) of the commentary, which contain critical nuances for understanding the non-exhaustive list of *jus cogens* norms. The relationship between the annex and these commentary paragraphs is unclear. Second, it is uncertain whether the Commission believes every item in the annex meets the methodology for determining *jus cogens* norms as outlined in the draft conclusions. If the intent is to compile relevant references, Singapore suggests listing these references separately with explanatory elements from the commentary, rather than incorporating them into Draft Conclusion 23 and its annex; this could be done in an annex or appendix without implying equal normative status with the Draft Conclusions.[112]

In its turn, the US noted that the ILC has shifted from primarily using 'draft articles' for its work products intended for conventions to formats such as 'principles,' 'conclusions,' and 'guidelines,' without clear reasons for these choices. The US notes a lack of state practice regarding peremptory norms of general international law, such as conflicting treaties or customary international law, with no cited examples of new treaties or acts contradicting *jus cogens*. The US disputes that international organization resolutions indicate that a norm is peremptory and questions whether the right to self-determination is a *jus cogens* norm, noting the ILC's inconsistent methodology and blurred distinctions between peremptory norms and obligations *erga omnes*.[113]

Overall, states have actively articulated their positions, though the number is limited; Asian countries are represented by only a few states. Notably, in the Draft Articles on *jus cogens* norms 2022, 26 states expressed their positions

[110] Japan (2021).

[111] Ibid.

[112] Singapore (2021).

[113] United States (2021).

and observations, with Japan and Singapore being the only Asian perspectives represented.[114]

7.4.3 *Subsidiary Means for the Determination of Rules of International Law*

The ILC included the topic 'Subsidiary means for the determination of rules of international law' in its long-term programme in 2021, with the General Assembly acknowledging this in resolution 76/111.[115] In 2022, the ILC formally added the topic in its work programme, appointing Charles Chernor Jalloh as Special Rapporteur and requesting a Secretariat memorandum on relevant past work and case law.[116] In 2023, the Special Rapporteur's first report examined the topic's scope, the history of Article 38(1)(d) of the ICJ Statute, and previous ILC work on subsidiary means. Following debates, the Commission provisionally adopted Draft Conclusions 1–3 and took note of draft conclusions 4 and 5.[117] By 2024, the second report focused on judicial decisions as subsidiary means, the role of precedent in international and domestic law, and the relationship between Articles 38(1)(d) and 59 of the ICJ Statute.[118] The Commission provisionally adopted Draft Conclusions 1–8, continuing its work in accordance with General Assembly resolutions.[119]

This work of the ILC was met without criticism from UN member states—even the United States, which typically voices objections, did not express any opposition to the ILC's work. Several states, including Sierra Leone,[120] the US,[121] Ireland,[122] the Netherland,[123] and the United Kingdom,[124] shared their practices regarding the application of international court decisions and doctrine by national courts. Only South Korea emphasized the need for a cautious approach when using international court decisions as subsidiary means for determining rules of international law. It cited the complexity of their interpretation and suggested minimizing reliance on controversial decisions, especially for states not directly involved in the cases.[125]

---

[114] ILC (2025).

[115] UN Doc A/76/10 2021, para. 302.

[116] Ibid., para. 240.

[117] Jalloh (2023).

[118] UN Doc A/CN.4/765 2024.

[119] Ibid.; ILC Report 2024.

[120] Republic of Sierra Leone (2023).

[121] United States (2023).

[122] Ireland (2023).

[123] Netherlands (2023).

[124] United Kingdom (2024).

[125] Korea (2023).

At the same time, Conclusions 2 and 5 should be carefully considered, as they may raise concerns regarding an overly broad or overly narrow understanding of subsidiary means for determining rules of law.

According to Conclusion 2, 'Subsidiary means for the determination of rules of international law include: (a) decisions of courts and tribunals; (b) teachings; (c) any other means generally used to assist in determining rules of international law.'[126] While judicial decisions and doctrine are recognized as subsidiary means for determining legal norms under Article 38 of the ICJ Statute, the phrase 'any other means generally used to assist in determining rules of international law' expands the scope of Article 38. In its commentary on Conclusion 2, the ILC notes that subsidiary means for determining rules of international law include 'any other means generally used to assist in determining rules of international law' and that this may encompass 'the works of expert bodies and the resolutions/decisions of international organizations.'[127]

At the same time, it is important to remember that states, as the primary subjects of international law, play a fundamental role in the creation of international legal norms, including the determination of subsidiary means. Even Article 38 of the ICJ Statute itself should be interpreted in accordance with the rules of the VCLT (Articles 31 and 32) and should not be construed beyond the ordinary meaning of its provisions and the intentions of UN member states. As Ian Brownlie notes, 'there is the principle that the general consent of states creates rules of general application.'[128] In practice, states voluntarily conclude international treaties and recognize international customs. Regarding subsidiary means, they acknowledge the role of the ILC in this process, as the ILC openly submits its work for discussion and expects feedback. Moreover, as noted in the *Jurisdictional Immunities of the State* case, states are now obliged to respond to the work of the ILC.

Regarding the role of expert bodies and resolutions of international organizations, caution should also be exercised. Certain concerns about treaty bodies were previously raised in the analysis of the Draft Conclusions on Subsequent Agreements and Subsequent Practice in Relation to the Interpretation of Treaties. As for the resolutions of international organizations, it should be noted that the ILC does not distinguish between different types of international organizations whose competence depends on constitutional provisions. Instead, they operate under the principle of speciality, meaning they only have the powers granted by the states that create them.[129] These powers are defined in their founding documents or may be implied if necessary for their functions. The ICJ has affirmed that organizations possess implied powers essential to fulfilling their responsibilities, even if not explicitly stated in their charters.[130] As can be seen, when it comes to the authority of international organizations, the key issue is determining the intentions of their member states—specifically, the

126 ILC Report 2024.

127 Ibid.

128 Brownlie (2008, p. 3).

129 Shaw (2017, p. 998).

130 Advisory opinion (1996, p. 66).

extent to which the organization's charter grants implied powers, including participation in the creation of subsidiary means for determining legal norms. Therefore, this suggests that the phrase 'any other means generally used to assist in determining rules of international law' is overly broad and lacks clear limits. This approach risks weakening a state-centric interpretation unless constrained by clear criteria.

The next conclusion that warrants attention is Conclusion 5, which states that, 'Teachings, especially those generally reflecting the coinciding views of persons with competence in international law from the various legal systems and regions of the world, are a subsidiary means for the determination of the existence and content of rules of international law.'[131] It is worth noting that the terms 'teachings,' *and* 'views of persons with competence in international law' should be understood separately. The wording 'teachings, especially those' gives us reason to believe that the ILC also interprets teachings broadly in the spirit of Article 38(1)(d) of the ICJ Statute. Otherwise, there would be no theoretical possibility of applying doctrines other than international legal doctrine, which would unduly restrict the scope of Article 38(1)(d) of the ICJ Statute by focusing solely on individuals with specific expertise. Article 38(1)(d) refers to *'the teachings of the most highly qualified publicists of the various nations,'* the literal meaning of which suggests that the provision's scope is not necessarily confined to legal doctrine alone. Furthermore, as already mentioned, international law recognizes that a customary norm may *emerge that binds only specific groups of states,* such as those in Latin America,[132] or even just two states,[133] reflecting the importance of respecting regional legal traditions.[134] Determining such local traditions may require not only legal doctrines but also historical perspectives, which in turn can serve as means of identifying legal norms. In this regard, it seems that the determining factor should not be an individual's expertise in international law per se but rather the quality of the doctrinal work and its applicability in identifying legal norms.

7.5 Conclusion

The ILC's findings increasingly serve as subsidiary means for determining international legal norms under Article 38(1)(d) of the ICJ Statute. The ICJ has repeatedly relied on ILC drafts to identify customary international law. Notably, the ICJ's jurisprudence in cases like *Jurisdictional Immunities of the State* suggests that state silence in response to ILC work may be interpreted as tacit acceptance of its conclusions. This creates a compelling incentive for states to actively engage with the Commission's drafts, as failure to do so could result in unintended legal consequences. The ILC's growing role as an authoritative interpreter of international law

[131] ILC Report (2024).

[132] Colombia v. Peru 1950, pp. 266, 276 and Espiel (2001).

[133] El Salvador v. Honduras 1992, para 26.

[134] Shaw (2017, p. 68).

underscores the necessity for states to scrutinize and respond to its work to ensure their positions are reflected in emerging norms.

A closer examination of key ILC outputs highlights several areas that merit careful consideration. The ILC's approach to treaty interpretation, particularly its treatment of state silence as potential acquiescence, may benefit from further discussion regarding its alignment with treaty parties' original understandings. Similarly, the process for identifying *jus cogens* norms could be strengthened through more consistent methodology and broader representation of diverse legal traditions. The interpretation of subsidiary means under Article 38(1)(d) also presents an opportunity for dialogue about maintaining an appropriate balance between expert contributions and state sovereignty. As the ICJ frequently references ILC work, Kazakhstan's active engagement—through thoughtful submissions, constructive critiques, and diplomatic participation—could help ensure these important legal developments fully incorporate perspectives from all regions, including Central Asia. Such participation would not only serve Kazakhstan's interests but also contribute to a more inclusive and representative international legal framework. Kazakhstan, as an emerging actor in international law, must adopt a proactive approach—submitting comments on draft conclusions, challenging problematic interpretations, and advocating for clearer methodologies in identifying customary and peremptory norms. Failure to do so risks allowing the ILC's findings to develop in ways that may not reflect the legal realities or interests of Kazakhstan. By actively participating in the ILC's processes, Kazakhstan can help shape a more balanced and inclusive international legal order, ensuring that its voice is heard in the evolution of global norms. The necessity of responding to the ILC's findings is not merely academic; it is a strategic imperative for safeguarding state sovereignty and influencing the future of international law.

References

Abylaiuly A (2017) Pravovoy kharakter soobrazheniy/resheniy dogovornykh organov OON v oblasti prav cheloveka. In: Pravovoy kharakter aktov dogovornykh organov OON v oblasti prav cheloveka. GU Institut zakonodatel'stva Respubliki Kazakhstan. Astana

Agreement for the Prosecution and Punishment of the Major War Criminals of the European Axis (1945) 82 UNTS 280

Ahani v. Canada (2002) UN Doc CCPR/C/80/D/1051/2002

Alleged Violations of Sovereign Rights and Maritime Spaces in the Caribbean Sea (Nicaragua v Colombia) [2022] ICJ Rep

Amendment to Act No. 38/1993, Coll. of Laws, Act No. 124/2002 (Czech Republic, 2002)

Application of the Convention on the Prevention and Punishment of the Crime of Genocide (The Gambia v Myanmar) [2022] ICJ Rep

Application of the International Convention for the Suppression of the Financing of Terrorism (Ukraine v Russia) [2019] ICJ Rep

Application of the International Convention on the Elimination of All Forms of Racial Discrimination (Azerbaijan v Armenia) [2024] ICJ Rep

Armed Activities on the Territory of the Congo (DRC v Uganda) [2022] ICJ Rep

Asylum Case (Colombia v Peru) [1950] ICJ Rep 266

Azaria D (2019) The International Law Commission's return to the Law of Sources of International Law. FIU L Rev 13:989–1002
Azaria D (2020) Codification by interpretation: the International Law Commission as an interpreter of International Law. Eur J Int L 31:171–200
Barkholdt J (2022) Is the International Law Commission taking regionalism seriously (enough)? Goettingen J Int L 12:153–184
Bassiouni MC (1996) International crimes: Jus cogens and obligatio erga omnes. L Contemp Prob 59(4):63–74. Duke University School of Law
Baylis E (2019) The International Law Commission's soft law influence. FIU L Rev 13:1007–1008
Belarus (2018) Последующие соглашения и последующая практика в связи с толкованием договоров. https://legal.un.org/ilc/sessions/70/pdfs/russian/sasp_belarus.pdf. Accessed 25 Mar 2025
Bianchi A (2008) Human rights and the magic of Jus Cogens. Eur J Int L 19:491–508
Brownlie I (2008) Principles of public international law, 7th edn. Oxford University Press, Oxford
Cassese A (2008) The human dimension of international law: selected papers of Antonio Cassese. Oxford University Press, Oxford
Certain Iranian Assets (Iran v USA) [2023] ICJ Rep
Cogan JK (2015) The changing form of the International Law Commission's Work. In: Evolutions in the law of international organizations. Brill Nijhoff, Leiden, pp 275–290
Comments by the Government of Japan (2021) ILC's draft conclusions on peremptory norms. https://legal.un.org/ilc/sessions/73/pdfs/english/jc_japan.pdf. Accessed 25 Mar 2025
Comments of the United States (2008) Human Rights Committee's draft general comment 33. https://2009-2017.state.gov/documents/organization/138851.pdf. Accessed 25 Mar 2025
Comments of the United States (2021) ILC's Draft conclusions on Jus Cogens. https://legal.un.org/ilc/sessions/73/pdfs/english/jc_us.pdf. Accessed 25 Mar 2025
Crawford J, Brownlie I (2019) Brownlie's principles of public international law. Oxford University Press
Czech Republic (2018) Comments on the ILC draft conclusions on subsequent agreements and subsequent practice. https://legal.un.org/ilc/sessions/70/pdfs/english/sasp_czech_republic.pdf. Accessed 25 Mar 2025
Daugirdas K (2014) The International Law Commission reinvents itself? Am J Int L Unbound 108
Dispute over the Status and Use of the Waters of the Silala (Chile v Bolivia) [2022] ICJ Rep
Đorđeska M (2015) The process of international law-making: The Relationship between the International Court of Justice and the International Law Commission. Int Compar L Rev 7
Dugard J (1987) Recognition and the United Nations. Grotius, Cambridge
El Salvador/Honduras Case [1992] ICJ Rep, para 26
Gabčíkovo-Nagymaros Project (Hungary/Slovakia) [1997] ICJ Rep 123
General Assembly (1947) Resolution 174 (II), amended by resolutions 485 (V), 984 (X), 985 (X), and 36/39
Germany (2018) Comments on subsequent agreements and subsequent practice. https://legal.un.org/ilc/sessions/70/pdfs/english/sasp_germany.pdf. Accessed 25 Mar 2025
Gros Espiel H (2001) La Doctrine du Droit International en Amérique Latine avant la Première Conférence Panaméricaine. J Hist Int L 3
Human Rights Committee (2000) Piandiong et al. v. The Philippines, UN Doc. CCPR/C/70/D/869/1999
Human Rights Committee (2002) Weiss v. Austria, UN Doc. CCPR/C/77/D/1086/2002
Human Rights Committee (2008) General Comment No. 33: obligations of states parties under the optional protocol to the international covenant on civil and political rights, UN Doc CCPR/C/GC/33
Human Rights Committee (2011) Arshidin Israil v. Kazakhstan, UN Doc CCPR/C/103/D/2024/2011
International Court of Justice (nd) Statute of the ICTY, Article 3. https://www.icty.org/x/file/Legal%20Library/Statute/statute_sept09_en.pdf. Accessed 25 Mar 2025

International Law Association (2004) Committee on international human rights law and practice, final report on the impact of findings of the United Nations Human Rights Treaty Bodies, para. 40
International Law Commission (1980) Yearbook of the International Law Commission, vol II(2), p 147, para. 26
International Law Commission (2011) Guide to practice on reservations to treaties, Yearbook of the International Law Commission, vol II(2):23
International Law Commission (2013) First report on formation and evidence of customary international law by Michael Wood, UN Doc A/CN.4/663, 17 May 2013
International Law Commission (2014) Second report on identification of customary international law by Michael Wood, UN Doc A/CN.4/672, 22 May 2014
International Law Commission (2015a) First report on formation and evidence of customary international law, UN Doc A/CN.4/663
International Law Commission (2015b) Third report on identification of customary international law by Michael Wood, UN Doc A/CN.4/682, 27 March 2015.
International Law Commission (2016) Fourth report on identification of customary international law by Michael Wood, UN Doc A/CN.4/695, 8 March 2016
International Law Commission (2017) Second report on Jus Cogens by Dire Tladi, UN Doc A/CN.4/706, 16 March 2017
International Law Commission (2018a) Draft conclusions on subsequent agreements and subsequent practice in relation to the Interpretation of Treaties, UN Doc A/73/10
International Law Commission (2018b) Fifth report on identification of customary international law by Michael Wood, UN Doc A/CN.4/717, 14 March 2018
International Law Commission (2018c) Third report on peremptory norms of general international law (Jus Cogens) by Dire Tladi, UN Doc A/CN.4/714, 12 February 2018
International Law Commission (2019a) First report on general principles of law by Marcelo Vázquez-Bermúdez, UN Doc A/CN.4/732, 5 April 2019
International Law Commission (2019b) Fourth report on peremptory norms of general international law (Jus Cogens) by Dire Tladi, UN Doc A/CN.4/727, 31 January 2019
International Law Commission (2022a) Draft conclusions on identification and legal consequences of peremptory norms of general international law (Jus Cogens), UN Doc A/77/10
International Law Commission (2022b) Draft conclusions on identification and legal consequences of peremptory norms of general international law (jus cogens), with Commentaries, UN Doc. A/77/10 (Advance version of 12 August 2022)
International Law Commission (2022c) Draft conclusions on identification and legal consequences of peremptory norms of general international law (jus cogens): commentary to article 14. UN Doc. A/77/10 (Advance version of 12 August 2022)
International Law Commission (2022d) Report on the work of its seventy-third session, UN Doc A/CN.4/755
International Law Commission (2023a) Report on the work of its seventy-fourth session, UN Doc A/78/10, ch VII, paras 15–16
International Law Commission (2023b) Report on the work of its sixty-sixth session, UN Doc A/78/10
International Law Commission (2024a) Report on the work of its seventy-fifth session, UN Doc A/79/10, ch 5
International Law Commission (2024b) Report on the work of the seventy-fifth session, UN Doc A/79/10
International Law Commission (ILC), United Nations. https://legal.un.org/ilc/. Accessed 27 June 2025
International Law Commission. Texts, Instruments and Final Reports. https://legal.un.org/ilc/texts/texts.shtml. Accessed 25 Mar 2025

International Law Commission. Comments by governments: analytical guide to the work of the International Law Commission—subsequent agreements and subsequent practice in relation to the interpretation of treaties. https://legal.un.org/ilc/guide/1_11.shtml. Accessed 27 June 2025
Ireland (2023) Submission on the use of subsidiary means for the determination of rules of international law. https://legal.un.org/ilc/sessions/75/pdfs/english/sm_ireland.pdf. Accessed 25 Mar 2025
Jadhav Case (India v Pakistan) [2019] ICJ Rep
Jalloh CC (2023) First Report on Subsidiary Means for the Determination of Rules of International Law, UN Doc A/CN.4/760
Jurisdictional Immunities of the State (Germany v Italy) [2012] ICJ Rep. Dissenting Opinion of Judges Gaja, Cançado Trindade, Yusuf, Bennouna, Keith, Koroma
Kingdom of the Netherlands (2023) Submission to the Office of Legal Affairs of the United Nations in Response to Note Verbale LA/COD/40 of 11 August 2022, 13 January 2023. https://legal.un.org/ilc/sessions/75/pdfs/english/sm_netherlands.pdf. Accessed 25 Mar 2025
La Ley 288 de 1996 (Colombia) Diario Oficial No. 42.826
Legal consequences arising from the policies and practices of Israel in the occupied Palestinian territory, including East Jerusalem (Advisory Opinion) [2024] ICJ Rep
Legal consequences of the policies and practices of Israel in the occupied Palestinian Territory [2024] ICJ Rep
Legality of the use by a state of nuclear weapons (advisory opinion) [1996] ICJ Rep 66, 78–79
Legality of the Use by a State of Nuclear Weapons [1996] ICJ Rep 66
Maqsut Narikbayev University (2023) Research seminar on the draft articles on the Jus Cogens Norms 2022, Astana, Kazakhstan, 11 October 2023
Meron T (1991) Human rights and humanitarian norms as customary law. Oxford University Press
Netherlands (2018) ILC draft conclusions on subsequent agreements and subsequent practice. https://legal.un.org/ilc/sessions/70/pdfs/english/sasp_netherlands.pdf/. Accessed 25 Mar 2025
Nieto-Navia R (2016) Are those norms truly peremptory? With special reference to human rights law and international humanitarian law. Global Community: Yearbook of International Law and Jurisprudence, 2015
Nordic Countries (2018) Written comments on subsequent agreements and subsequent practice. https://legal.un.org/ilc/sessions/70/pdfs/english/sasp_sweden_nordic.pdf. Accessed 25 Mar 2025
North Sea Continental Shelf (Germany/Netherlands) [1969] ICJ Rep, paras 48–63
Official Records of the General Assembly, seventy-sixth session, Supplement No. 10 (A/76/10)
Orakhelashvili A (2003) Peremptory norms and reparation for internationally wrongful acts. Baltic Yearbook of International Law 3:19–56
Republic of Korea (2023) Comments on subsidiary means for the determination of international law. https://legal.un.org/ilc/sessions/75/pdfs/english/sm_rok.pdf. Accessed 25 Mar 2025
Republic of Sierra Leone (2023) Submission on subsidiary means for the determination of international law. https://legal.un.org/ilc/sessions/74/pdfs/english/sm_sierra_leone.pdf. Accessed 25 Mar 202
Research Seminar (2023) Draft articles on Jus Cogens norms. Maqsut Narikbayev University, Astana
Response of Singapore (2021) ILC's draft conclusions on Jus Cogens. https://legal.un.org/ilc/sessions/73/pdfs/english/jc_singapore.pdf. Accessed 25 Mar 2025
Rim Y (2020) Reflections on the role of the international law commission in consideration of the final form of its work. Asian Journal of International Law 10:23–30
Rome statute of the international criminal court (1998, amended 2024)
Saganek P (2019) The sources of general international law in the recent works of the international law commission. Polish Yearbook of International Law 39:37–38
Shaw MN (2017) International law, 8th edn. Cambridge University Press, Cambridge
Shelton D (2006) Normative hierarchy in international law. Am J Int L 100(2):291–323

Special Court for Sierra Leone (2004) Prosecutor v Gbao (decision on preliminary motion on the invalidity of the agreement between the United Nations and the Government of Sierra Leone on the establishment of the special court) (Appeals Chamber), SCSL-2004-15-AR72(E)
Statute of the International Criminal Tribunal for Rwanda (1994) UNSC Res 955
Statute of the International Criminal Tribunal for the Former Yugoslavia (1993) UNSC Res 827
Statute of the International Law Commission 1947, Adopted by the General Assembly in resolution 174 (II) of 21 November 1947, as amended by resolutions 485 (V) of 12 December 1950, 984 (X) of 3 December 1955, 985 (X) of 3 December 1955 and 36/39 of 18 November 1981
Temple of Preah Vihear (Cambodia v Thailand) [1962] ICJ Rep, para 23. Separate Opinion of Judge Alfaro
Tladi D (2022) Representation, inequality, marginalization, and international law-making: the case of the international court of justice and the international law commission. UC Irvine J Int Trans Compar L 7:60–75
Tribunal of First Instance of Brussels, 1998. Aguilar Diaz et al v Pinochet, 6 November 1998 (Belgium)
Ulfstein G, Keller H (2012) UN human rights treaty bodies: law and legitimacy. Cambridge University Press, Cambridge
United Kingdom (2024) Comments on subsidiary means for the determination of international law. https://legal.un.org/ilc/sessions/75/pdfs/english/sm_uk.pdf. Accessed 25 Mar 2025
United Nations (1980) Official records of the United Nations Conference on Succession of States in Respect of Treaties, vol. III, doc. A/CONF.80/16/Add.2
United Nations (2024) Subsidiary means for the determination of rules of international law: memorandum by the secretariat, UN Doc A/CN.4/765
United Nations General Assembly (1947) Resolution 174 (II), 21 November 1947, as amended by rsolutions 485 (V) of 12 December 1950, 984 (X) of 3 December 1955, 985 (X) of 3 December 1955 and 36/39 of 18 November 1981
United States (2018) Comments on subsequent agreements and subsequent practice. https://legal.un.org/ilc/sessions/70/pdfs/english/sasp_usa.pdf. Accessed 25 Mar 2025
United States (2021) Comments on the international law commission's draft conclusions on peremptory norms of general international law (Jus Cogens) and Draft Annex, 30 June 2021. https://legal.un.org/ilc/sessions/73/pdfs/english/jc_us.pdf. Accessed 25 Mar 2025
United States (2023) Submission to the international law commission on the use of subsidiary means for the determination of rules of international law, 12 January 2023. https://legal.un.org/ilc/sessions/74/pdfs/english/sm_us.pdf. Accessed 25 Mar 2025
US court of appeals for the ninth circuit, 1994. In re Estate of Ferdinand Marcos, 25 F.3d 1467
US Court of appeals for the second circuit, 1995. Kadić et al v Karadžić, 70 F.3d 232
US district court for the District of Massachusetts, 1995. Xuncax et al v Gramajo, 886 F. Supp. 162
Uzbekistan (2018) По проектам выводов "Последующие соглашения и последующая практика". https://legal.un.org/ilc/sessions/70/pdfs/russian/sasp_uzbekistan.pdf. Accessed 25 Mar 2025
Weil P (1983) Towards relative normativity in international law? Am J Int L 77(3):413–442
Wood M (2008) The general assembly and the international law commission: what happens to the commission's work and why? In: International law between universalism and fragmentation. Brill Nijhoff, Leiden, pp 373–390

Part III
International Law and Security

Chapter 8
Were the Events of January 2022 in Kazakhstan a Failed Colour Revolution?

Nicolás Zambrana-Tévar

Abstract Colour revolutions are usually described as political processes which took place in former communist countries of Central and Eastern Europe, the Caucasus and Central Asia, during the early twenty-first century and which, using peaceful and festive mechanisms and involving NGOs and thousands of participants, managed or tried to oust corrupt and authoritarian governments in the context of rigged elections. Although the events in January 2022 in Kazakhstan share some of these characteristics, such as the authoritarian regime and the participation of many citizens, other features of the colour revolutions are not present, such as the peaceful nature of the protests or the elections. Confusing the two types of events may lead to putting forward inadequate solutions to improve the quality of democracy and the rule of law in Kazakhstan or in similar countries. Moreover, there are still many unanswered questions about the events of January 2022, such as the identity of those who instigated the riots and the violence and who really benefited from it.

Keywords Colour revolutions · Communism · Central Asia · Kazakhstan · Almaty · January 2022 · Democracy · Elections · Revolution · Qandy Qantar

8.1 Introduction

The January 2022 events—demonstrations, revolt, uprising, crisis—marked a turning point in Kazakhstan's recent political history. Rising fuel prices initially sparked protests in the West of the country, which quickly grew into nationwide demonstrations with broader anti-government sentiments. The protests were initially peaceful but soon escalated—particularly in Almaty, where violent clashes resulted in multiple deaths among demonstrators and policemen, as well as significant property destruction. The government responded with extreme measures, including a communications shutdown, a shoot-to-kill order, and an invitation for CSTO (Collective Security

N. Zambrana-Tévar (✉)
KIMEP University School of Law, Almaty, Kazakhstan
e-mail: n.zambrana@kimep.kz

S. Sayapin (ed.), *International Law, Politics and Security in Central Asia*,
https://doi.org/10.1007/978-3-032-17818-3_8

Treaty Organization) troops to intervene, leading to widespread criticism and fears of Russian interference just weeks before the invasion of Ukraine.

The January events took everybody by surprise in what was sometimes believed to be a country immune to the kind of revolutions and political processes which had taken place in the other post-socialist countries during the first two decades of the twenty-first century.[1] However, this chapter posits that it is probably a mistake to look at the events of January 2022 through the lens of so-called Colour Revolutions.[2] The events in Kazakhstan—often called *Qandy Qantar*—'Bloody January' or 'Tragic January' in Kazakh—share some features with those political phenomena, but also important differences. Trying to shoehorn the events in Kazakhstan into the category of the Colour Revolutions—or their successor, the 'Arab spring'—fails to capture these differences and does a disservice to the cause of the promotion of democracy and human rights.

8.2 Kazakhstan and the Colour Revolutions: Initial Comparison

As previously stated, the events in Kazakhstan commenced with peaceful and well-organized protests against the sudden rise of gas prices. This rise had been permitted by the government but had the potential to affect many workers and households. The protests started in the mining town of Zhanaozen, in the West of the country. However, unexpectedly, more protests—equally peaceful—sprouted in other parts of the country in support of the initial ones. What was even more surprising is that, together with the protests against the increase in gas prices, demonstrators around the country began to chant slogans which were more political than economic, denouncing the corruption of former president Nazarbayev and his entourage. It was only after this that the protests in some large cities—particularly in Almaty—became violent, with clashes with the police and a final mortality count of approximately 227 people, including around 25 police officers.

The official narrative of the events is that the demonstrations were a coup instigated by unnamed foreign agents and in which thousands of terrorists participated. However, the insistence on such an explanation may be seen solely as a way to justify the appeal to the troops of the CSTO. In the context of the impending invasion of Ukraine, the landing of a contingent of mostly Russian CSTO troops is what may have worried Western governments most, not the shooting of civilians during the demonstrations.

An alternative narrative, which also attempts to explain the mystery behind the January events and their unforeseen violence, is that, somehow, the original peaceful demonstrations were hijacked by *agent provocateurs* who were part of an intra-elite fight between members of the Nazarbayev clan and the Tokayev clan, i.e., the

[1] Niyazbekov (2018, pp. 401–425).

[2] Marat and Tumulu (2022).

clans of the former and the current presidents of Kazakhstan. The readjustment of positions of power and other assets after the events gives this alternative narrative some credibility, notably more so than the explanation that the country was being invaded by thousands of Islamic terrorists.

The Colour Revolutions, on the other hand, have, as their common denominator, the fact that they take place in former socialist countries around an electoral process in semi-democratic elections. Furthermore, opposition must exist and be unified and, with the help of well-trained NGO members and democratic activists, stage a colourful campaign to bring people to vote. Electoral observers then denounce various flaws and fraudulent behaviour in the elections but, nevertheless, the incumbent proclaims victory. The opposition subsequently challenges the results, and with the help of the abovementioned NGOs and activists, large numbers of citizens protest on the streets against the alleged electoral fraud. The courts or election authorities then call for a re-run of the elections or grant victory to the candidate of the opposition, forcing the incumbent to flee or accept defeat.[3]

This is a very basic account of the successful Colour Revolutions—those where the democratic opposition managed to come into power—in Serbia (2000), Georgia (2003), Ukraine (2004/5), and Kyrgyzstan (2005). However, there have also been unsuccessful attempts to replicate the same Colour Revolution paradigm in a number of post-Soviet countries like Armenia (2003/4), Azerbaijan (2005), Belarus (2006), and Russia (2011/12). The case of Serbia is often not referred to as a Colour Revolution because Serbia had not belonged to the Soviet Union, although it had indeed been a socialist country.

8.3 Society and Politics in Kazakhstan on the eve of the Protests

By January 2022, Kazakhstan had been suffering for years from economic inequality, unemployment, and rampant corruption. However, the government had failed to fulfil its promises of good governance and economic growth. Besides this, that same government was seen as divorced from the problems of society, living in a lavish parallel world. Moreover, by 2015–16, there was no real opposition which could give voice to these problems. To this we have to add the fact that, in a former socialist country, the population did in fact expect the government to cater to their needs.

The Kazakhstani regime itself could be characterized as one of 'authoritarian liberalism', whose only legitimacy was the promise of stability and welfare. This promise provided for the relative acceptance of a system where President Nazarbayev, his family, and political allies amassed vast amounts of wealth through corruption, without the people actually being able to voice their discontent through multiparty elections. Instead of a formal parliamentarian opposition, there were a variety of

[3] Gerlach (2014, pp. 33–39).

protesting groups, organized in loose political and labour union networks. The establishment of a real opposition was virtually impossible because labour unions and protestors were often labelled as hooligans, whose claims were illegitimate and whose leaders were harassed or imprisoned.

In retrospect, it is fair to say that the January events were just the last in a long series of protests, riots, and strikes in the country; however, these usually had very few participants or casualties, only a few of which are usually referred to in analysis of the history or politics of the country.

In December 2011 there were peaceful protests and a general strike in the oil-producing town of Zhanaozen in the West of the country, where workers occupied the town's main square to demand better working conditions. Similarly to what happened in Almaty in January 2022, violent provocateurs sequestered the protests and set fire to the city hall of Zhanaozen. The police fired on the demonstrators, with the actual number of victims still today being the subject of much controversy.

In July 2006 and 2008 there were also protests in the suburbs of Almaty—the largest city in the country—where the demonstrators asked for affordable housing. In February 2014, the sudden and painful devaluation of the national currency, the *tenge* on 'Black Tuesday' also led to protests. In April 2016, land reform was also the occasion of protests, as was the Kazakh spring of 2019 on the occasion of Nazarbayev's resignation.

Therefore, although the January events may have been unexpected because of their size, they can easily be put in the framework of a long line of similar, if smaller, protests without clear leaders or organizations, motivated by the harsh economic conditions for all but the luxury-enjoying elites who had gained by corrupt means.

8.4 The January 2022 Protests

As previously said, Nursultan Nazarbayev resigned unexpectedly as President in March 2019 but retained several important titles and thus many powers as well. For instance, Nazarbayev was able to elect several ministers and also to force the new interim president (by his own appointment), Kassym-Jomart Tokayev, to consult with him before making certain decisions and appointments.

In June 2019, Tokayev was elected president. In May 2020, Dariga Nazarbayeva, who had been appointed Speaker of the Senate the previous year, was dismissed from that position. In July 2021, evidence was released that the KNB, Kazakhstan's secret service, had been spying on Tokayev and some members of his government. Sometime afterwards, the head of the KNB, Kalmukhanbet Kasymov was dismissed by Tokayev. These replacements of top officials from Nazarbayev's entourage could well be interpreted as internal struggles between the different 'families' of Kazakhstan's deep state.

On 1 January 2022 there was a transition to electronic trading for Liquid Propane Gas and gas subsidies ended. Gas prices almost doubled in the Western regions of Kazakhstan where demand for liquid gas was high, for instance, by taxi drivers. On the morning of 2 January, citizens of Zhanaozen organized a rally and blocked roads into the city centre. Tokayev gave instructions to security forces to maintain public order. The protests spread quickly to the neighbouring city of Aktau.[4]

The Government commenced a dialogue with the peaceful protestors, gas prices were lowered, and an anti-trust investigation was launched against gas suppliers suspected of price collusion. Despite these measures, protestors increased their demands, now asking for political reforms and requesting that the government step down. Some well-known activists who participated in the protests were arrested.

From 4 to 6 January, the protests were seconded in Almaty, the biggest city in the country, where organizers began to call citizens to come out on the streets in support of the protests in Zhanaozen. The demonstrations in Almaty and in other cities did not have a clear leader but had apparently been instigated by political groups such as Oyan, Kazakhstan (Wake up, Kazakhstan) and the unregistered Democratic Party of Kazakhstan (DPK). Demonstrators initially gathered at the First President's Park and at the Almaty Arena and then marched to Republic Square in downtown Almaty, where clashes with the police began and continued over several days and nights. Internet and other communication services were disrupted by the government, as in previous occasions.[5]

Many of the initial activists and many of the ordinary people participating in the protests were detained and beaten up in police stations. It must be underlined that the initial protests were completely peaceful and that the violence in Almaty and other cities was probably caused by well-organized groups of thugs, which seemed to have received instructions and had clear goals and equipment like walkie-talkies, some guns, and petrol cans. It was these thugs who set fire to the Town Hall and other buildings of central Almaty, destroyed numerous shops, and who took control of the Almaty airport.

On 5 January, Tokayev accepted the resignation of his government, thus trying to shift the blame to others, as it is common in Kazakhstan. He also announced that Nazarbayev was no longer Chairman of the National Security Council. It was also reported that the Eurasian military alliance CSTO had approved sending troops to Kazakhstan, and that Karim Massimov, head of the National Security Committee, had been removed. CSTO troops began to arrive on 6 January. These troops came from Russia, Armenia, Belarus, Tajikistan, and Kyrgyzstan. Internet access was restored on 7 January. President Tokayev gave a televised address where he announced that the constitutional order had mostly been restored and that he had given orders to shoot without warning, calling protestors 'bandits and terrorists'. Samat Abish, the nephew of Nazarbayev and Deputy Head of the KNB was allegedly arrested in Almaty, and there were rumours that Nazarbayev had left the country. On 8 January, Massimov was also arrested on suspicion of treason. In the following days, other high-ranking officials of the KNB were dismissed, and other members of the Nazarbayev entourage either resigned or were removed from their political positions or their jobs in state companies.

---

[4] Kudaibergenova and Laruelle (2022, p. 8).

[5] Zhandayeva and Rosenberg (2022, pp. 4–7).

On 18 January, Nazarbayev appeared on television to support Tokayev and referred to himself as a mere 'pensioner'. Days later the Parliament approved the removal from Nazarbayev of his remaining positions and titles. By 19 January, CSTO troops had left the country. On 28 January, Nazarbayev also resigned from his post as head of the ruling Nur-Otan party. By that time, the worst aspects of the crisis seemed to have been averted by Tokayev.

8.5 The Government's Framing of the Crisis and its Aftermath

Tokayev's administration employed specific framing techniques to control the narrative of the January events. First, Tokayev assigned the blame for the violence, portraying the protestors as 'terrorists', 'bandits', and 'marauders', whose violence had been allegedly orchestrated by foreign elements aiming to destabilize Kazakhstan. This language was intended to dehumanize the protestors and justify aggressive countermeasures. By labelling the opposition as foreign-backed terrorists, Tokayev aimed to shift public perception away from government accountability, and instead towards an external threat to national stability.[6]

Tokayev also presented his own vision for restoring order and addressing the 'problem'. He claimed that the state's harsh measures were necessary to protect citizens and preserve peace. By framing the unrest as a security issue, rather than as a result of domestic grievances, the government legitimized its use of force and repression. Finally, Tokayev labelled participation in the protests as illegal and criminal and urged citizens to avoid provocations to rally the support of the public. His language conveyed a call for unity and patience, underlining the need to trust the state's actions as being in the best interest of public safety.

The communication shutdown, the shoot-to-kill order, and the CSTO intervention were still significant measures with high political and reputational costs. The internet and phone network shutdown began on 2 January via the state-controlled company *Kazakhtelecom*, hindering communication among protestors and preventing the organization of additional protests. The government justified this as an anti-terrorism measure under the National Security Law. Such tactics are common among authoritarian regimes, especially when control over the narrative is at stake.

On 5 January, Tokayev announced he had given a 'shoot-to-kill without warning' directive, authorizing lethal force against protestors. This decision sent a strong signal of the regime's commitment to restoring order, even at the cost of civilian lives. It also projected the image of a state willing to take drastic action to maintain stability, with the aim of thus suppressing resistance and deterring further unrest. This order, however, faced domestic and international criticism for violating human rights and exhibiting a disproportionate use of state power.

---

[6] Caron (2023, pp. 62–72).

The deployment of CSTO forces, which was the first such intervention by the Russian-led security alliance, served both practical and symbolic purposes. Practically, it helped stabilize strategic locations in Kazakhstan. Symbolically, it underscored regional solidarity with Tokayev's regime, deterring potential dissent and providing evidence for external endorsement of his leadership. Nevertheless, the intervention stirred public concerns about Kazakhstan's sovereignty and dependence on Russia.

Following the crisis, Tokayev initiated a series of constitutional reforms to distance his administration from the legacy of former President Nursultan Nazarbayev. Tokayev framed these reforms as efforts to establish a 'New Kazakhstan', characterized by accountability and a fairer political system. In the aftermath of Bloody January, Tokayev proposed fifty-six constitutional amendments aimed at limiting presidential power, strengthening parliament, and facilitating political pluralism. Key reforms included limiting the presidency to a single seven-year term, reducing the senate's power, and establishing local elections for mayors. These amendments, which were passed by popular referendum, were portrayed as essential to addressing the concentration of power that had characterized Nazarbayev's rule.

Despite the promises of reform, there remains scepticism regarding the authenticity of Tokayev's commitment to change. Critics argue that Tokayev's administration may revert to the same top-down, authoritarian model, simply under a different leadership. The January 2022 events, while providing Tokayev with an opportunity to consolidate power and redefine Kazakhstan's political landscape, also exposed the systemic fragility and dissatisfaction within Kazakhstani society. If the reforms fail to translate into genuine democratic progress and socio-economic improvements, the regime risks further unrest in the future.

8.6 Behind the January Events in Kazakhstan

One possible explanation for the violence which ensued from the initially peaceful protests is that violent criminals had indeed been unleashed by elements within the government who were dissatisfied with the arrival of Tokayev's political clique and the threat to the positions of power among Nazarbayev's clique in the government and in large and extremely lucrative government-owned corporations that this entailed.

It is also probable that some violent thugs were members of criminal gangs with links to the country's security services in the hands of individuals close to Nazarbayev, like Karim Massimov. It must also be taken into account that, at the initial stage of the clashes between the demonstrators and the police, the police seemed to offer very little resistance and even withdrew from police stations—and from the Almaty airport—allowing the opportunity for these to then be stormed by violent protestors in search of weapons. However, a competing narrative is that the police retreated because they did not receive back-up and were overwhelmed by the increasingly violent and armed protestors.

The theory of an 'internal revolt' against Tokayev may also be supported by the fact that Nazarbayev was stripped of the positions and titles he still retained and that several members of his entourage and his own family were arrested or were removed from their own positions in the government or in large government-related corporations both before and after the revolt.

Other possible theories or explanations about the January events do not describe them as a way to try to weaken Tokayev. On the contrary, they indicate that Tokayev could have at some point instigated, fuelled, or taken advantage of the protests to get rid of members of Nazarbayev's entourage and replace them with its own.[7]

Concerning accusations of Islamic extremism, there is only minor evidence for the presence of Islamist elements among violent protestors, but this, too, could be connected to Nazarbayev's allies through one of his nephews—Karait Satbaldy—who was linked to Islamist cells and had tried to organize a traditionalist religious party. However, even for those scholars for whom there is credible information about the participation of Islamist cells, they indicate that it cannot have been at the scale suggested by President Tokayev in his attempt to 'internationalize' the events and justify his appeal to the troops of the CSTO alliance, whose Article 4, paragraph 2, provides that:

> In case of aggression [...] toward any of the Member States, all the other Member States at the request of this Member State shall immediately provide the latter with the necessary help, including military aid.[8]

The members of the CSTO alliance are all post-Soviet States: Russia, Armenia, Belarus, Kazakhstan, Kyrgyzstan, and Tajikistan.

Nevertheless, the intervention of CSTO troops did little in terms of quenching the violence as the foreign soldiers did not actually engage the demonstrators. They had been called upon to provide protection for official buildings—a rather passive role. Nevertheless, the fact that Russia agreed to send in its troops for the first time in the history of this military alliance may have sent an important signal to any individuals and groups within the Kazakhstani government which were trying to oust Tokayev and recover their past influence: the signal that Putin and Russia supported Tokayev and that the Russian President was not willing to let him fall.[9]

Why Putin agreed to support Tokayev might well be explained by the impending invasion of Ukraine. If Russia has always tried to support authoritarian governments in the post-Soviet space in an effort to maintain stability in the region, the need for such stability in their 'backyard' was even more urgent on the eve of a major military operation.

Although Western media and governments were worried about what Tokayev may have promised Putin in return for his support in this crisis, Kazakhstan does not seem to have yielded yet to any demands from its powerful neighbour. For instance,

[7] Kudaibergenova and Laruelle (2022, p. 13).

[8] Collective Security Treaty of 15 May (1992), as amended by the Protocol of 10 December (2010), Kudaibergenova 12; Cornell (2022, p. 20), Emtseva (2022).

[9] Libman and Davidzon (2023, pp. 1296, 1306).

Kazakhstan refused to send CSTO troops to the war in Ukraine and has also vowed not to permit its country to be used to avoid complying with Western anti-war sanctions against Russia.[10]

The January 2022 protests marked a watershed moment in Kazakhstan's modern political history, shaking the image of stability that the government had long projected internationally. Following these events, Tokayev pledged reforms aimed at addressing the power imbalances and economic grievances that had triggered the protests. However, it remains uncertain whether these promises will lead to meaningful change or if they will be superficial adjustments meant to quell immediate unrest without addressing underlying systemic issues. The entrenched nature of the oligarchic power structure and the reliance on rentier capitalism complicate prospects for genuine reform.[11]

It can properly be said that a new culture of protest has emerged in Kazakhstan in the last decades, one that will likely persist, as long as socio-economic issues remain unaddressed. Despite the lack of unifying leadership, the protests have fostered a shared imaginary, tied to significant moments in Kazakhstan's history such as the 1986 protests, the Zhanaozen massacre of 2011, and the Kazakh Spring of 2019. These events contribute to a growing tradition of activism that may continue to challenge the country's authoritarian governance and demand a fairer, more transparent political and economic system.

8.7 The Colour Revolutions: Common Features

Fifteen years after the collapse of communism in Eastern Europe, much of the former Soviet Union faced deep-rooted kleptocracies, widespread corruption, and declining quality of life. The initial euphoria of the early 1990s gave way to disillusionment, as nations struggled to transition to democracy and build sustainable economies. The region remained immersed in economic stagnation, political authoritarianism, and poverty, with fraudulent elections undermining trust in governance.[12]

In this context, from late 2003 to mid-2005, a wave of protests began in Georgia, Ukraine, and Kyrgyzstan, collectively named the 'Colour Revolutions'. The 'classic' examples of these movements in the post-Soviet space are the Rose Revolution (Georgia, 2003), the Orange Revolution (Ukraine, 2004), and the Tulip Revolution (Kyrgyzstan, 2005). These movements arose in response to electoral fraud and were moved by a desire for more transparent governance and better leadership.

A defining feature of these revolutions was their reliance on nonviolent methods of protest and festive type events, drawing large crowds in capital cities. They are

[10] Cornell (2022, p. 9), Radio Free Europe (2022).

[11] Terzyan (2022, pp. 295–306).

[12] Mitchell (2012, pp. 17–43).

well known for their symbolic use of colours and names, which became unifying symbols for opposition movements.[13]

The Colour Revolutions lacked clear ideological motivations and were rather rooted in stolen elections and in a vague desire to become closer to the West and to Western institutions.[14] Georgia's parliamentary election in 2003 saw widespread fraud by Eduard Shevardnadze's government; Ukraine's 2004 presidential runoff was full of irregularities which favoured Viktor Yanukovych over Viktor Yushchenko; and Kyrgyzstan's 2005 parliamentary elections similarly sparked protests after pro-government candidates won through manipulation.

In each case, successful Colour Revolutions ousted well-established leaders and ushered in new governments initially perceived to be more democratic and pro-Western. However, these regimes often failed to consolidate democracy or meet public expectations in the long term. By 2010, the initial promise of the Colour Revolutions had largely dissipated. In Georgia, the Saakashvili government faced criticism for authoritarian tendencies. Ukraine saw Viktor Yanukovych, the very figure ousted in 2004, return to power in 2010. Kyrgyzstan's Kurmanbek Bakiyev, who rose to power after the Tulip Revolution, was later ousted amid allegations of corruption and nepotism. It would therefore be a mistake to equate these dramatic political moments with sustained democratic breakthroughs. While the Colour Revolutions were milestones in the struggle against authoritarianism, they often failed to foster enduring democratic institutions.

The Colour Revolutions also provided important lessons for democratization and key insights into the challenges of transitioning from authoritarian rule. First, they highlight the difficulty of moving from regime change to systemic reform. Second, they show how civil society, electoral processes, and external support can all play pivotal roles but often fail to sustain long-term democratization.

Concerning their political repercussions, the revolutions significantly impacted US-Russia relations. Moscow viewed these movements as Western-backed efforts to undermine Russian influence in the region. The post-revolutionary governments in Georgia and Ukraine aligned with NATO aspirations, intensifying tensions with Russia.

However, the three revolutions referred to above differed in their immediate triggers and outcomes. In Georgia, protests led to the resignation of Eduard Shevardnadze and the rise of Saakashvili, who championed modernization and pro-Western reforms. In Ukraine, the Orange Revolution resulted in the annulment of the fraudulent election and the eventual victory of Yushchenko in a subsequent re-run. In Kyrgyzstan, the Tulip Revolution ousted Askar Akaev, but the resulting government was plagued by similar issues of corruption and nepotism.

Thus, the Colour Revolutions were seen as democratic breakthroughs at the time, but their legacies were mixed. While they succeeded in ousting entrenched leaders,

---

[13] Ó Beacháin and Polese (2010, pp. 7–9).

[14] Baev (2011, pp. 10–11).

the subsequent governments often struggled to deliver on the promises of reform and democratization.[15]

Parallels can also be established between the Colour Revolutions and later uprisings, such as the Arab Spring in North Africa and the Middle East. Nevertheless, one should be careful not to conflate popular uprisings with democratic stability.

8.8 The Classic Colour Revolutions: Ukraine, Georgia, and Kyrgyzstan

Ukraine, Georgia, and Kyrgyzstan—the three classic examples of 'Colour Revolutions'—shared a 70-year history under Soviet rule. While their experiences varied, the centralization and authoritarian governance of the USSR had left a profound impact on their political and economic systems. The dissolution of the Soviet Union in 1991 marked a significant transition, but remnants of a Soviet-era governing style persisted in the form of entrenched bureaucracy, corruption, and centralized power.

The post-Soviet transition also saw economic collapse in all three nations. In Georgia, the breakdown of Soviet-era trade networks devastated the economy, leading to widespread unemployment and poverty. Ukraine struggled to modernize its industrial base, while Kyrgyzstan, which lacked natural resources, remained heavily reliant on remittances and international aid. Corruption permeated all levels of Government, undermining public trust and state legitimacy. In each case, the ruling elite exploited state resources for personal gain, exacerbating inequality and social discontent.

Electoral fraud became a hallmark of governance in all three countries, with ruling parties manipulating results to maintain power. These practices eroded trust in democratic institutions and galvanized opposition movements. Opposition forces began to coalesce in response to authoritarian governance. Civil society organizations, though limited in capacity, played critical roles in mobilizing public dissent and advocating for electoral reforms. Western governments and organizations supported democratization efforts through funding and training programmes for civil society groups. However, their influence varied across the three nations, depending on the strength of local political structures.

As previously said, in each of these three countries, the immediate cause of the Colour Revolutions was a 'stolen' election. Electoral fraud became the visible symbol of broader dissatisfaction with authoritarian governance and widespread corruption. The protests were not simply about electoral outcomes but were tied to grievances about governance failures, lack of accountability, and economic stagnation.

In Ukraine's 2004 presidential elections, the second round was widely viewed as fraudulent, favouring Viktor Yanukovych over opposition candidate Viktor Yushchenko. In Georgia's 2003 parliamentary elections, the results were manipulated for the benefit of the ruling party, prompting protests led by Mikheil Saakashvili and his allies. In Kyrgyzstan's 2005 parliamentary elections, electoral fraud occurred in a

[15] Mitchell (2022, pp. 435–444).

more repressive environment, with outcomes favouring pro-government candidates but igniting the Tulip Revolution.

Ukraine had been the second-largest Soviet republic and had played a central role in the USSR's economy and military. Its strategic importance and cultural ties to Russia created enduring political and social divisions. Its independence had been marked by economic hardships and political division between its pro-Western western regions and pro-Russian eastern regions. This split was exacerbated by the presence of a substantial Russian-speaking population in Crimea and eastern Ukraine. Leonid Kuchma, elected president in 1994, attempted to balance competing pressures from Russia and the West. His administration, however, became synonymous with corruption and political stagnation. Kuchma's presidency was marked by economic mismanagement, media suppression, and electoral fraud. Despite initial promises of reform, his government failed to address systemic corruption and inequality. Kuchma's support base in the industrialized east and Crimea was offset by growing opposition in Western Ukraine, where demands for closer ties with Europe increased.[16]

Georgia at the time could be described as a cultural and economic hub in the southern Caucasus, having maintained a distinct national identity despite Soviet dominance. Its relationship with Russia after the collapse of the Soviet Union oscillated between subjugation and collaboration. However, independence brought instability to the country. Eduard Shevardnadze, a former Soviet foreign minister, assumed power after the chaotic presidency of Zviad Gamsakhurdia, who had been ousted amid internal strife. The country also faced secessionist movements in Abkhazia and South Ossetia, exacerbated by the presence of Russian troops and local warlords. The state struggled to control the country, leaving much of it in disarray. Shevardnadze's tenure began with efforts to stabilize Georgia after the tumultuous early 1990s. However, his administration was known for being corrupt, inefficient and unable to deliver economic progress. By the late 1990s, widespread dissatisfaction with Shevardnadze's government created fertile ground for opposition movements, setting the stage for the Rose Revolution.[17]

Kyrgyzstan's identity as a modern polity had been shaped by the Soviet era, as it lacked a historical state structure. Its economy remained underdeveloped, reliant on agriculture and animal husbandry. Askar Akaev, its first president, initially garnered international support for his reformist rhetoric but later affirmed himself in power through patronage and authoritarian practices. The country's north-south divide and legacy of Soviet-era policies contributed to regional tensions that would later play a role in its political instability. Akaev had positioned himself as a reformist leader, introducing market-oriented policies and promoting democracy. Over time, however, his administration grew increasingly authoritarian. The aforementioned patronage networks and corruption undermined Akaev's credibility, and his government's inability to address poverty and inequality fuelled public discontent.[18]

[16] Copsey (2010, pp. 30–43).

[17] Companjen (2010, pp. 13–28).

[18] Lewis (2010, pp. 45–61).

8.9 Key Internal Actors and Strategies in the Colour Revolutions

The revolutions were often led by opposition figures who had been part of or closely associated with the ruling elite before shifting to opposition. For instance, Saakashvili in Georgia and Yushchenko in Ukraine were insiders, familiar with the political systems they sought to change.

Youth organizations also played critical roles in mobilizing protests. Kmara in Georgia, Pora in Ukraine, and KelKel in Kyrgyzstan emerged as prominent symbols of dissent. These groups were often supported by Western actors, including NGOs like George Soros' Open Society Institute, which provided funding and training initiatives that helped civil society groups organize and mobilize. Finally, election monitoring organizations like ISFED (Georgia), CVU (Ukraine), and CDCS (Kyrgyzstan) provided evidence of fraud, bolstering the credibility of opposition claims.

Protests in all three cases quickly escalated following the announcements of fraudulent results. Demonstrators used public squares as focal points for mobilization, such as Kiev's Maidan Nezalezhnosti during the Orange Revolution. The protests were largely peaceful, drawing on tactics of nonviolent resistance to pressure regimes into negotiations or resignations.

The regimes' responses to these acts varied. In Georgia and Ukraine, authorities were hesitant to use force against peaceful protesters, fearing international condemnation. In Kyrgyzstan, the government's attempts to suppress protests were less effective, partly due to the decentralized nature of the demonstrations.

8.10 External Actors: USA

Some portray the Colour Revolutions as US-backed coups aimed at installing pro-Western regimes. This perspective is particularly strong in Russian discourse, which views these events as a strategy to contain Russian influence amidst its neighbours. However, this view probably oversimplifies these events, ignoring the local dynamics and reducing them to proxy battles in the geopolitical arena. Another view holds that the US just played a limited, supportive role by funding civil society organizations, facilitating training programmes, and advocating for democratic principles. These actions, while influential, were not sufficient to independently trigger regime change.[19]

Following the collapse of the Soviet Union, the US prioritized supporting democratization and market reforms in Eastern Europe and the former Soviet republics. However, by the early 2000s, US attention shifted to the Middle East, with the wars

[19] McFaul (2007, p. 73).

in Afghanistan and Iraq overshadowing its post-Soviet agenda. The Bush administration continued to support democratic initiatives in the region, but its approach lacked the strategic focus seen in previous years. US interests in Georgia, Ukraine, and Kyrgyzstan included ensuring regional stability, promoting democracy, and countering Russian influence. However, these goals were often secondary to more immediate concerns for the US, like counterterrorism and energy security.

US-funded programmes helped build the capacity of civil society organizations and youth movements, which played pivotal roles in mobilizing protests. Examples include Georgia's Kmara, Ukraine's Pora, and Kyrgyzstan's KelKel. These groups adopted nonviolent resistance tactics, often drawing inspiration from successful movements in Serbia and Slovakia, which had received similar US support. The US facilitated exchanges between activists from different countries, fostering a sense of shared purpose and equipping them with tools to challenge authoritarian regimes. These efforts contributed to the transnational nature of the Colour Revolutions.

Democracy assistance programmes in the region were multifaceted, encompassing support for civil society organizations, election monitoring, and political party development. Key initiatives included funding for election monitors like the International Society for Fair Elections and Democracy (Georgia) and the Committee of Voters of Ukraine. Workshops and training sessions for political parties and activists were often facilitated by organizations like the National Democratic Institute (NDI) and the International Republican Institute (IRI).

While such programmes strengthened the capacity of opposition groups and civil society, their impacts were uneven across the three countries. Georgia and Ukraine benefited more significantly from these efforts than Kyrgyzstan, where democracy assistance was less present.

Therefore, democracy assistance programmes alone could not have led to the revolutions. These initiatives operated in many other countries without yielding comparable results, highlighting the importance of local conditions in shaping outcomes.

On the other hand, US diplomats and officials did actively advocate for free and fair elections—especially in Ukraine and Georgia—emphasizing their importance to democratic governance. In Georgia and Ukraine, this advocacy reinforced the credibility of opposition movements and amplified calls for electoral transparency.

By way of conclusions, it can be said that the perception of US involvement in the Colour Revolutions heightened tensions between Washington and Moscow. Russia viewed these events as direct threats to its sphere of influence, accusing the US of interfering with its geopolitical interests. The revolutions bolstered pro-Western leaders in Georgia and Ukraine, aligning these countries more closely with NATO and the European Union. This shift deepened the regional divide between Russia and the West.

8.11 External Actors: Russia

The Colour Revolutions in Georgia, Ukraine, and Kyrgyzstan alarmed the Kremlin, as these movements replaced authoritarian regimes with more pro-Western, democratic governments. Russia perceived these revolutions as part of a broader Western strategy to encircle and diminish Russian influence. Moscow viewed these events as precursors to potential democratic uprisings within its borders, raising fears of regime change engineered by external forces.[20]

Russia's historical ties to these countries intensified its reaction. Ukraine was seen as a critical part of the Slavic heartland and essential to Russia's identity and geopolitical strategy. Georgia's westward shift threatened Moscow's influence in the Caucasus, a region of symbolic and strategic importance.

Domestically, the Kremlin worked to insulate Russia from democratic contagion by consolidating authoritarian rule. This included restricting civil society, controlling media narratives, and ensuring loyalty within the political elite. Russia promoted an alternative model of governance emphasizing 'sovereign democracy', which prioritized state control and stability over Western-style democratic norms. This ideological framework served to delegitimize the narratives of democratization underpinning the Colour Revolutions.

The Kremlin saw the revolutions as Western-sponsored coups, accusing the US and European actors of meddling in Russia's backyard. This narrative was amplified through state-controlled media, reinforcing public scepticism of pro-democracy movements.

Russia provided financial and military support to allied regimes in the region, such as Belarus and Uzbekistan, to strengthen their resilience against democratic uprisings. In Kyrgyzstan, Moscow leveraged economic aid and energy subsidies to reassert influence following the Tulip Revolution.

The Kremlin actively funded pro-Russian political parties, supporting separatist movements, and exploiting ethnic divisions to destabilize pro-Western governments. Russia also collaborated with other actors to resist democratization collectively. Organizations like the Shanghai Cooperation Organization (SCO) emphasized state sovereignty and non-interference, countering the rhetoric of democracy promotion.

The Rose Revolution of 2003 in Georgia brought to power a leader openly hostile to Moscow. His pro-Western orientation and NATO ambitions exacerbated tensions. The 2008 Russia-Georgia War highlighted the Kremlin's willingness to use military force to counter what it perceived as threats to its regional influence.

The Orange Revolution of 2004 was a critical blow to Russian influence. The subsequent government established closer ties with NATO and the EU, challenging Moscow's vision of a Slavic union. Russia responded by leveraging energy politics and supporting pro-Russian politicians like Viktor Yanukovych, who eventually regained power in 2010.

[20] Wilson (2010, pp. 33–34).

The Colour Revolutions significantly strained US-Russia relations because Russia saw American democracy assistance programmes as tools of geopolitical interference, prompting laws restricting foreign-funded NGOs in Russia. The revolutions catalysed Russia's efforts to re-establish itself as a dominant regional power. This included expanding its diplomatic efforts, securing economic dependencies, and deepening ties with like-minded authoritarian regimes.

Finally, in the wake of the Colour Revolutions, Russia and other authoritarian regimes in the post-Soviet space developed sophisticated strategies to prevent future Colour Revolutions. These included restricting foreign-funded NGOs, tightening media control, and increasing surveillance and repression of opposition groups. Russia actively supported these counter strategies, both domestically and in allied states. The Kremlin view of the Colour Revolutions as Western-backed attempts to undermine its influence prompted it to respond by promoting its own version of election monitoring and governance norms through organizations like the CIS Election Monitoring Organization.

8.12 The Aftermath of the Colour Revolutions

The Rose Revolution in Georgia, led by Mikheil Saakashvili, initially brought optimism with its rhetoric of reform and democratic progress. Saakashvili's government embarked on significant anti-corruption measures and economic reforms, gaining international acclaim. However, over time, his government became increasingly authoritarian. Democratic backsliding was evident in events such as the violent crackdown on protests in November 2007 and the consolidation of power around the presidency.

Ukraine's Orange Revolution brought Viktor Yushchenko to power with promises of transparency and European integration. Despite some progress, the country struggled with political polarization, corruption, and institutional weaknesses. The inability to implement substantial reforms or maintain unity among the revolutionary leaders diminished public trust. By 2010, Viktor Yanukovych, the same figure ousted by the Orange Revolution, had returned to power by democratic means.

Kyrgyzstan's Tulip Revolution ousted Askar Akaev, but his successor, Kurmanbek Bakiyev, quickly adopted similar corrupt and authoritarian practices. The country's weak institutional framework hindered any meaningful democratic consolidation.

The pre-existing weaknesses in civil society, political institutions, and rule of law in these countries, significantly limited the scope for democratic consolidation after the revolutions. In Kyrgyzstan, the absence of a robust legislature or independent judiciary left the new government vulnerable to authoritarian tendencies. Similarly, Georgia and Ukraine struggled with entrenched corruption and oligarchic influence.

Leaders of the Colour Revolutions often prioritized state-building and economic reform over democratic governance. In Georgia, Saakashvili's authoritarian tendencies undermined the credibility of his reforms, while in Ukraine, infighting among revolutionary leaders eroded public trust.

Thus, while international support played a role in the success of the revolutions, external actors were less effective in ensuring democratic consolidation. Western governments often prioritized geopolitical considerations over the promotion of genuine democratic reforms.

The electoral breakthroughs that defined the Colour Revolutions proved insufficient for lasting democratic transformation. Overthrowing semi-democratic kleptocrats was easier than dismantling decades-old structures of power. Despite the dramatic nature of the revolutions, there was significant continuity in the political and economic structures of these countries. New leaders often perpetuated old practices, limiting the scope for meaningful reform. The weakness of grassroots civil society in these countries limited the potential for sustained democratic development. While civil society played a crucial role in mobilizing protests, it lacked the capacity to hold new governments accountable.

8.13 Exporting the Colour Revolutions

Activists from Serbia, Georgia, and Ukraine played instrumental roles in sharing their experiences with opposition groups in neighbouring countries. Western democracy assistance also played a significant role in facilitating this cross-national learning. NGOs, such as the National Endowment for Democracy (NED) and the Open Society Institute (OSI), provided funding and logistical support. This cross-national collaboration aimed to transfer the tactics and strategies that had worked to new contexts. However, the success of the Colour Revolutions proved to be the exception, rather than the rule.[21]

Failures in Belarus and Azerbaijan highlighted the challenges of applying a uniform strategy across diverse political environments. Such failures also proved that certain conditions were necessary for the success of a Colour Revolution. First, it was necessary that the revolution take place in a weak state. Successful revolutions occurred in semi-democratic states where the government was unable or unwilling to use force against demonstrators. Second, it was necessary that civil society was strong enough. A relatively free civil society and media environment were crucial for organizing protests and disseminating information. Third, other factors that helped in Georgia and Ukraine, such as relatively open media and less repressive government, were absent in many other states.

In Belarus, the authoritarian regime of Alexander Lukashenko effectively suppressed opposition through pre-election violence, media control, and the co-optation of civil society. Belarus' 'Denim Revolution' failed to gain traction, illustrating the limitations of the Colour Revolution model in highly repressive states. Similarly, in Azerbaijan, the government pre-emptively undermined the opposition's ability to mobilize. The failure to generate substantial Western pressure further weakened the opposition's efforts.

[21] Filin et al. (2022, pp. 465–474).

8.14 Kazakhstan and the Colour Revolutions: A Comparison

From the analysis presented above, it could be said that, for a Colour Revolution to be possible—albeit maybe not successful—there must be certain structural factors present, as well as certain agency factors, i.e. certain characteristics of the actors which take part. Among the structural factors we must mention the fact that the type of regime in place must be semi-democratic, i.e. the government is autocratic but its leader still feels the need to legitimize himself through elections overseen by a semi-independent judiciary, electoral authorities, and foreign election observers invited by the government to maintain good standing with the West.

Other important structural factors are the fact that the economy of the country must be largely in the hands of oligarchs, i.e. businessmen who have managed to amass most or a great part of the wealth of the country through a flawed and/or corrupt process of privatization which took place after the collapse of the former Soviet system. It is also common that, in the country where the Colour Revolution takes place, there are ethnic or territorial tensions, yet the opposition must have managed to unite if only to present a common front for the purpose of fighting against their common and undemocratic enemy.

Among what we can call agency factors there is the fact that the leaders of the opposition must be charismatic, and NGOs and democracy activists who have received training in peaceful protest tactics must be present. There must also be foreign funding, which may come from private, public, or semi-public foreign institutions with a strong interest in promoting democracy overseas. However, there may also be direct funding from foreign governments—e.g. Russia—which may also be intent on supporting the incumbent candidate and wary of the attempts by Western governments to increase their influence. This exposes an important factor in Colour Revolutions—namely that these events are also part of a larger political game to establish zones of influences, especially between the United States and Russia. Finally, and some scholars stress this very much, those who participate in Colour Revolutions will have been influenced by previous revolutions, which they are trying to emulate.[22] Not everyone agrees on the exemplary power of past revolutions, however.[23]

We can now try to summarize, referring to some of the structural and agency factors present, why the January events in Kazakhstan can probably not be described as a Colour Revolution.[24]

On the side of similarities, Kazakhstan is indeed a formerly socialist country which was part of the Soviet Union, like Georgia, Kyrgyzstan, and Ukraine. After the dissolution of the Soviet Union, the programme of privatization gave way to a system which can be labelled as authoritarian neoliberalism or patronal presidentialism, under which different clans of politicians, bureaucrats, and oligarchs share power

---

[22] Beissinger (2007, p. 264), Bunce and Wolchik (2009, pp. 69–73).

[23] Way (2008, p. 59).

[24] Rico (2010, pp. 196–216).

and economic assets. Corruption became rampant in many areas of everyday life, leading to increasing inequality and poverty after the initial period of growth. In Kazakhstan, this was then affected by the crisis in oil prices, several devaluations of the tenge, and the Covid-19 pandemic.

Despite these relative similarities with other formerly socialist countries where there have been Colour Revolutions, it can probably not be said that Kazakhstan is a semi-democratic state because, in addition to any flaws and fraud in the elections, there is simply no opposition worthy of that name. The government under President Nazarbayev (1991–2019) often engaged in the systematic harassment and sometimes imprisonment of opposition leaders. Thus, the disorganized and disunited groups that came together in January 2022 cannot be compared to the organized and disciplined political parties and civil society groups which managed to peacefully challenge their respective governments in the Colour Revolutions. Moreover, and most importantly, the January events did not take place in the context of an electoral race but were ignited as a result of a purely economic decision to raise the price of gas.

Therefore, rather than illustrating a new episode of Colour Revolution, the events of January 2022 in Kazakhstan should be studied within the framework of other relatively spontaneous protests that have taken place in the country in the course of the years: the Zhanaozen massacre of 2011, the protests of 2014 after the sharp devaluation of the national currency, the protests of 2016 after a land reform announcement, and the protests of 2019 after Tokayev succeeded Nazarbayev, albeit with Nazarbayev retaining important positions of power within the state. However, an important difference between this line of protests and the January 2022 events is that, in general, protests in Kazakhstan are poorly attended on account of how disorganized and weak the opposition is. Contrary to that, thousands of people took part in the January events. The extreme level of violence between the protestors and the security forces in the January events also marks a difference with the Colour Revolutions.

Another difference between the events in Kazakhstan and the Colour Revolutions is that, in the case of Kazakhstan, there were accusations of foreign intervention—the thousands of terrorists mentioned by Tokayev—but such accusations probably had no real basis. On the other hand, the Colour Revolutions were indeed the battleground between the influence of the West, especially the United States, and Russia.

A further, related difference is that the only case where there was a foreign military intervention was in Kazakhstan, with the entry of the peacekeeping troops of the CSTO. Moreover, the case of Kazakhstan was probably not the result of any interethnic clashes as was the case, to a certain extent, in Ukraine and Kyrgyzstan.

Notwithstanding the above, it may also be timely to remember that there may still be a lot we do not know about the complex line of events in Kazakhstan. The events may be properly seen as several crises or revolutions in one—the peaceful and the violent, an uprising to demand better economic conditions and more honesty, together with the dark and Machiavellian strategy to tip one governmental clique against another.

Once again, the danger of equating the January 2022 events in Kazakhstan with the Colour Revolutions lies in the fact that, if different political phenomena are bundled together, inadequate responses might be given, and the promotion of democracy and human rights will not be well served.

8.15 Conclusions: Misreading the Colour Revolutions and Misreading Kazakhstan

Western policymakers and media presented the Colour Revolutions as definitive democratic breakthroughs, portraying the ousting of entrenched leaders as triumphs of liberal democracy over authoritarianism. Leaders like Mikheil Saakashvili (Georgia) and Viktor Yushchenko (Ukraine) were celebrated as democratic heroes, while the systemic challenges in their respective countries were downplayed. The US assumed that the Colour Revolutions signalled a comprehensive embrace of democratic values by these nations. This assumption overlooked the structural issues, such as weak civil society, corruption, and fragmented political landscapes, which hindered sustainable democratization.

Post-revolution Georgia under Saakashvili faced significant criticism for authoritarian tendencies, including media restrictions and constitutional reforms that re-centralized power. These actions conflicted with the democratic promises made during the Rose Revolution. The US failed to hold Saakashvili accountable for these regressions, instead prioritizing strategic partnerships over democratic ideals.

In Ukraine, the Orange Revolution led to initial improvements in media freedom and civil liberties. However, persistent corruption and political infighting within the Orange coalition weakened governance and disillusioned the public. The US underestimated the challenges of unifying a deeply polarized country with entrenched regional divides, limiting the long-term effectiveness of the revolution's democratic gains.

Kyrgyzstan's Tulip Revolution was perhaps the weakest of the three, as it simply replaced one corrupt regime with another. The US's focus on maintaining its military base at Manas limited its ability to pressure the Bakiyev government for reforms, further undermining democratization efforts.

US policy overly relied on individual leaders, treating them as the primary agents of democratization while neglecting the broader institutional frameworks necessary for democracy. This approach backfired, particularly in Georgia, where Saakashvili's authoritarian tendencies were overlooked due to his pro-Western stance. The West's inability to adapt its democracy assistance programmes to the specific needs of each country limited their effectiveness.

The Colour Revolutions did not represent a clean break from the past. Instead, they marked the replacement of one political elite with another, often maintaining similar governance practices. The structural weaknesses that characterized the pre-revolutionary regimes persisted, undermining the potential for sustained democratic transformation and perpetuating cyclical phases of patronal presidentialism.[25]

[25] Gerlach (2014, pp. 30–31, 45).

Though initially celebrated as democratic breakthroughs, these movements ultimately revealed the resilience of semi-authoritarian regimes and the complexities of achieving systemic change.

Although the events of January 2022 in Kazakhstan must be studied as one more political process in the post-Soviet space, there is also the danger of misreading it in the same way that the Colour Revolutions may have been misread. Although the participants in the protests in Kazakhstan may have been motivated, at least in part, by a desire for democratic change, the West should not see the January 2022 events as a struggle between authoritarianism and a non-existent democratic civil society.

The motivations in the case of Kazakhstan have more to do with poor economic conditions and with the perception that such conditions were directly linked to the blatant corruption in the government. Similarly, regardless of the role of Russia in sending CSTO troops, it would be a mistake to see the quashing of the protests in Kazakhstan simply as the direct result of Russian intervention in a foreign country in order to secure the loyalty of that country in the present context of a second Cold War.

References

Baev PK (2011) A matrix for post-soviet "color revolutions": exorcising the devil from the details. Int Area Stud Rev 14(2):3–22

Beacháin Ó, Polese A (2010) The colour revolutions in the former Soviet republics. Successes and failures. Routledge, Abingdon-on-Thames

Beissinger MR (2007) Structure and example in modular political phenomena: The diffusion of bulldozer/rose/Orange/tulip revolutions. Perspect Polit 5(2):259–276

Bunce V, Wolchik S (2009) Debating the color revolutions. Getting real about "real causes". J Democr 20(1):69–73

Caron J (2023) Revolt in the steppe. Understanding Kazakhstan's january events of 2022. Palgrave Macmillan, London, pp 62–72

Collective Security Treaty of 15 May 1992, as amended by the Protocol of 10 December 2010. https://en.odkb-csto.org/documents/documents/dogovor_o_kollektivnoy_bezopasnosti/#loaded. Accessed on 10 June 2025

Companjen FJ (2010) Georgia. In: Beacháin Ó, Polese A (eds) The colour revolutions in the former Soviet republics successes and failures. Routledge, Abingdon-on-Thames, pp 13–28

Copsey N (2010) Ukraine. In: Beacháin Ó, Polese A (eds) The Colour Revolutions in the Former Soviet Republics Successes and Failures. Routledge, Abingdon-on-Thames, pp 30–43

Cornell SE (2022) Learning from Kazakhstan's january crisis. The Central Asia-Caucaus Analyst 18 April 2022. https://www.cacianalyst.org/resources/pdf/220418-FT-Kazakhstan.pdf. Accessed on 10 June 2025

Emtseva J (2022) Collective security treaty organization. Why are Russian Troops in Kazakhstan? Ejiltalk 13 January 2022. https://www.ejiltalk.org/collective-security-treaty-organization-why-are-russian-troops-in-kazakhstan/. Accessed on 10 June 2025

Radio Free Europe (2022) Top officials say Kazakhstan won't help Russian evade Western sanctions. Radio Free Europe Radio Liberty. 1 April 2022 https://www.rferl.org/a/kazakhstan-evade-sanctions-russia/31781750.html. Accessed on 10 June 2025

Filin N, Khodunov A, Koklikov V (2022) Serbian "Otpor" and the color revolutions' diffusion. In: Goldstone JA, Grinin L, Korotayev A (eds) Handbook of revolutions in the twenty-first century.

The new waves of revolutions, and the causes and effects of disruptive political change. Springer Nature, Berlin, pp 465–474
Gerlach J (2014) Color revolutions in Eurasia. Springer, Heidelberg, pp 33–39
Kudaibergenova D, Laruelle M (2022) Making sense of the January 2022 protests in Kazakhstan: Failing legitimacy, culture of protests, and elite readjustments. Post-Sov Aff 38(6):441–459
Lewis D (2010) Kyrgyzstan. In: Beacháin Ó, Polese A (eds) The colour revolutions in the former Soviet republics successes and failures. Routledge, Abingdon-on-Thames, pp 45–61
Libman A, Davidzon I (2023) Military intervention as a spectacle? Authoritarian regionalism and protests in Kazakhstan. Int Aff 99(3):1293–1312
Marat E, Tutumlu A (2022) Kazakhstan's protests aren't a Colour revolution. Foreign Policy. https://foreignpolicy.com/2022/01/11/kazakhstans-protests-arent-a-color-revolution/#cookie_message_anchor. Accessed on 10 June 2025
McFaul M (2007) Ukraine imports democracy. External influences on the Orange revolution. Int Secur 32(2):45–83
Mitchell LA (2012) The color revolutions. University of Pennsylvania Press, Philadelphia.
Mitchell LA. (2022) The color revolutions. Successes and limitations of non-violent protest. In: Goldstone JA, Grinin L, Korotayev A (eds) Handbook of revolutions in the twenty-first century. The new waves of revolutions, and the causes and effects of disruptive political change. Springer Nature, Berlin, pp 435–446
Niyazbekov N (2018) Is Kazakhstan immune to color revolutions? The social movements perspective. Demokratizatsiya: J Post-Sov 26(3):401–425
Rico I (2010) Kazakhstan. In: Beacháin Ó, Polese A (eds) The colour revolutions in the former Soviet republics successes and failures. Routledge, Abingdon-on-Thames, pp 196–216
Terzyan A (2022) Kazakhstan amid unrest and instability: Main implications. J Lib Int Aff 8(3):295–306
Way LA (2008) The real causes of the color revolutions. J Democr 19(3):55–69
Wilson JL (2010) The legacy of the color revolutions for Russian politics and foreign policy. Probl Post-Communism 57(2):21–36
Zhandayeva R, Rosenberg R (2022) Kazakhstan's bloody January: Digital repression on the "new silk road". Toda Peace Inst Policy Brief 140:4–7. https://toda.org/assets/files/resources/policy-briefs/t-pb-140_kazakhstans-bloody-january.pdf. Accessed on 10 June 2025

Part IV
Human Rights

Chapter 9
Labour Law Reforms in Central Asian Countries within the Context of International Labour Standards: A Comparative Analysis

Muslim Khassenov

Abstract Historically, labour legislation in Central Asian countries was influenced by the Soviet legacy and Russian Labour Law tradition. The situation began to change in 2015 when Kazakhstan became the first state to significantly liberalize the legislative framework around labour relations due to high pressure from lobbyist business groups. In 2016, 2023, and 2024, labour laws were reformed in Tajikistan, Uzbekistan, and Kyrgyzstan in less liberal ways. The political landscape in each country determines the level of freedom of trade unions and the right to strike. The governments have been subjected to harsh criticism by the ILO and other international institutions for serious violations of labour rights, especially in the field of freedom of association and forced labour. Comparative legal analysis shows that the labour relations framework in Central Asia noticeably falls behind international labour standards. The chapter covers an analysis of reforms in labour legislation and their compliance with ILO instruments, focusing on freedom of association, collective bargaining systems, collective labour dispute resolution, prohibition of discrimination in employment, and labour inspection systems, allowing for an evaluation of the possible impacts of political changes in Central Asian states on the transformation of labour law from a comparative perspective.

Keywords Labour law · Central Asia · International labour standards · Employment discrimination · Gender equality · Freedom of association · Collective bargaining · Labour inspection · Comparative legal analysis · Reforming labour legislation

---

M. Khassenov (✉)
Maqsut Narikbayev University, Astana, Kazakhstan
e-mail: m_khasenov@kazguu.kz; muslimkhassenov@fas.harvard.edu

Harvard University, Cambridge, MA, USA

S. Sayapin (ed.), *International Law, Politics and Security in Central Asia*,
https://doi.org/10.1007/978-3-032-17818-3_9

9.1 Overview of the Labour Law Landscape in Central Asia

9.1.1 Historical and Legal Background

The modern Central Asian countries (Kazakhstan, Kyrgyzstan, Tajikistan, Turkmenistan, and Uzbekistan) were established in 1991, following the collapse of the Soviet Union, under which they had existed as Soviet Socialistic Republics since the 1920s.

In the Soviet Union, the state provided universal welfare, engaging in multiple roles as an owner of the means of production, the main employer, and a provider of social protection. Following the collapse of the Soviet economy, the centralized social protection system was broken. The reorganization of national social protection in the 1990s included the introduction of privatization and insurance mechanisms instead of state-funded social benefits, elimination of subsidy programmes, and decentralization of health and education. The decline in production and the closure of many enterprises led to unemployment and a sharp contraction of labour demand.[1]

Deconstructing the socialistic welfare system forced independent Central Asian republics to revise their social security systems, which led to considerable reductions in social benefits and the weakening of social protection.

Labour relations in Soviet Central Asian countries were influenced by socialistic ideology for 70 years and are defined by the following characteristics.

Firstly, due to the lack of private property, the state (state-owned organizations) was the sole employer for all employees.[2] Moreover, labour was a universal right and duty; the centralization of labour management guaranteed absolute employment. Job avoidance, so-called *tuneyadstvo*, was criminally punishable and considered parasitism. Trade unions had monopolized power and were integral elements of the state machine, while employers' associations did not exist at all. Each dismissal required union approval.

Secondly, although collective agreements existed, collective bargaining was a mere formality as the state administration dictated the provisions of agreements. Collective agreements were concluded at the enterprise level and essentially contained only social matters, as wages were centrally fixed by the state. In addition, strikes could be regarded as a form of sabotage against socialist property, and strikers could be made liable to prosecution.[3]

Only in 1991, after the announcement of independence, did Central Asian republics begin to build market economies and democratic civil society. Since then, the independent countries have started developing labour laws oriented towards the demands of emerging economies.[4]

---

[1] Dugarova (2016, p. 7).

[2] Bronstein (2009, pp. 212–214).

[3] Ibid, pp. 214–215.

[4] See Khassenov (2022, p. 129).

The legal systems of the Central Asian republics are predominantly influenced by the Romanist-German legal tradition. The major sources of labour law in all countries of the region are legislation and collective bargaining agreements. Labour legislation comprises Constitutions, Labour Codes, other statutes, and normative legal acts. Codification of labour legislation is a common trend in all Central Asian countries. Each country has a Labour Code as well as separate laws on trade unions and the promotion of employment (except Kazakhstan, where the law on employment promotion is incorporated into the Social Code). However, Kyrgyzstan also has separate laws on occupational safety (2003) and collective agreements (2004). Although the importance of case law is recognized, it does not significantly influence labour relations; for example, the normative rulings of the Supreme Court contain explanations of judicial practice.

Approaches to systematization and organization of labour legislation vary from country to country, including the volume (size) of labour codes, adoption of other laws regulating relations in the labour sphere, etc. A comparative overview can be found in Table 9.1.

It can be clearly seen that the Kazakhstan Labour Code is the shortest code among those of the neighbouring countries. The shorter the Labour code, the fewer the guarantees it provides workers, and the more freedom employers have in employment relations. For more details about the liberalization of labour reform in Kazakhstan, see Sect. 9.1.3.1.

Nevertheless, all five countries legally provide the principle ‘in favorem’ in labour legislation as per Articles 10, 150, and 157 of the Labour Code of the Republic of Kazakhstan, Articles 4, 5, 8 of the Labour Code of the Kyrgyz Republic, Articles 10–12, 315 of the Labour Code of the Republic of Tajikistan, Articles 8, 14–16, 68, 86, 105 of the Labour Code of the Republic of Uzbekistan, and Article 2 of the Labour Code of Turkmenistan.

As we can see from Table 9.2, the most protective guarantees for employees are provided by the Labour Code of Uzbekistan, and the least protective are in Turkmenistan.

The essence of the ‘in favorem’ principle, or the favourability principle (‘toward improving the legal status of workers’) is that an act of the employer, employment contract, or collective agreement can only enhance or establish the same conditions but not worsen the employee’s position in comparison with the labour legislation. Labour legislation establishes a minimum level of rights and guarantees for workers, and unlike the Civil code, social partners and parties to employment relations cannot change them downwards (worsening the position of workers). Anything that worsens the position of employees will be recognized as invalid.[5]

This principle is the most important state guarantee that protects each worker from employer abuse and unfair treatment.

In addition, Kazakhstan’s legal system is also influenced by the Anglo-Saxon legal system: there is a special jurisdiction for the ‘Astana’ International Financial

[5] Khassenov (2023, pp. 95, 184).

Table 9.1 Comparative analysis of labour legislation systems in Central Asian countries

Country	Labour code	Law on trade unions	Other laws
Kazakhstan	Dated 23 November 2015, came into force on 1 January 2016 Contains 215 articles	Dated 27 June 2014	Social Code dated 20 April 2023
Kyrgyzstan	Dated 23 January 2025, came into force on 28 January 2025 Contains 265 articles	Dated 16 October 1998 The new law was adopted on 20 October 2021 by the Parliament but vetoed by the President and not in force	Law on occupational safety dated 1 August 2003, Law on promoting employment dated 3 August 2015
Tajikistan	Dated 23 July 2016, came into force after its official publication Contains 366 articles	Dated 2 August 2011	Law on promoting employment dated 1 August 2003
Turkmenistan	Dated 18 April 2009, came into force on 1 July 2009 Contains 410 articles	Dated 9 November 2013	Law on employment dated 18 June 2016
Uzbekistan	Dated 28 October 2022, came into force on 30 April 2023 Contains 581 articles	Dated 6 December 2019	Law on promoting employment dated 20 October 2020

Centre (AIFC), with its employment law (for more details about the AIFC regime, see Sect. 9.1.3.1).

International instruments traditionally have increased significance for labour law in the region. The Constitutions of the Central Asian countries, except for Turkmenistan, stipulate that legally binding (ratified) international treaties (recognized international legal acts in Tajikistan) are part of the national legal systems. In all countries except Kazakhstan and Kyrgyzstan, international treaties (recognized international legal acts in Tajikistan) have priority over the laws. In Uzbekistan and Turkmenistan, if an international treaty establishes other rules than those stipulated by the law, the rules of the international treaty shall apply (Article 15 of the Uzbekistan Constitution, Article 4 of the Turkmenistan Law on International Treaties).

Table 9.2 Comparative analysis of the 'in favorem' principle content in the labour legislation of Central Asian countries

Country	'In favorem' legal content
Kazakhstan	(1) Provisions of agreements of the parties to social partnership, collective agreement and employment contracts, acts of employers that worsen the position of employees in comparison with the labour legislation of the Republic of Kazakhstan are recognized as invalid and are not subject to application. (2) The collective agreement must not worsen the position of workers in comparison with the labour legislation of the Republic of Kazakhstan, general, sectoral, and regional agreements. Such provisions are recognized as invalid and are not subject to application. (3) In cases where employees are covered by several agreements simultaneously, the most favourable terms of the agreements for the employees shall be applied upon written applications from the employees
Kyrgyzstan	(1) In the event of a contradiction between the labour code and other regulatory legal acts containing provisions that worsen the situation of employees, the provisions of this code shall apply. (2) Local regulations that worsen the position of employees in comparison with labour legislation, collective agreements, agreements, or that are adopted without observing the procedure for coordinating with the representative body of employees provided by this code are invalid. In such cases, laws or other regulatory legal acts containing labour law standards shall apply. (3) Collective agreements, agreements, and employment contracts may not contain terms that worsen the rights and guarantees of employees established by labour legislation. If such terms are included in a collective agreement, agreement, or employment contract, they may not be applied
Tajikistan	(1) Acts of the employer that worsen the situation of employees in comparison with the labour code and other regulatory legal acts, the employment contract, agreement and collective agreements, are invalid and shall not be applied. (2) The provisions of agreements between the parties to social partnership, employment contracts, and collective agreements that worsen workers' legal status in comparison with this code and other regulatory legal acts are recognized as invalid and not subject to application. (3) The minimum level of labour rights and guarantees for employees is established by this code and other regulatory legal acts. General, sectoral (tariff), territorial (regional, city, district) agreements, employment contracts, and collective agreements may establish rights and labour guarantees not provided by this code and other regulatory legal acts. (4) The terms of the agreement and collective agreements that worsen the position of workers in comparison with the legislative and regulatory legal acts are invalid and are not subject to application

(continued)

Table 9.2 (continued)

Country	'In favorem' legal content
Turkmenistan	Collective agreements must not contain terms that reduce the rights and guarantees of workers established by the labour legislation of Turkmenistan. In the event of any contradictions between this code and other regulatory legal acts of Turkmenistan containing labour law provisions, and also if collective agreements contain terms that reduce the level of rights and guarantees of workers, then the provisions of this code shall apply
Uzbekistan	(1) No local act or individual legal act of the employer may worsen the employee's position in comparison with regulatory legal acts. It is prohibited to include provisions in sectoral and territorial collective agreements that worsen the position of employees compared to the general collective agreement. In cases where there is a discrepancy between the provisions of sectoral and territorial collective agreements, the provisions of the collective agreement that contain more favourable conditions for the employee shall apply. (2) It is prohibited to include in local acts rules that worsen the position of the employee in comparison with collective agreements. Local acts adopted by the employer in agreement with the trade union committee, as well as those adopted by the employer alone, must not contain rules that worsen the employee's position in comparison with the collective agreement. Local acts adopted by the employer unilaterally must not contain rules that worsen the employee's position compared to local acts adopted by the employer in agreement with the trade union committee. Failure to comply with these requirements shall entail the invalidity of those provisions of legal acts on labour that worsen the employee's position. (3) It is prohibited to include in an employment contract terms that worsen the employee's position compared to labour legislation and other legal acts on labour. Failure to comply with these requirements shall entail the invalidity of the terms of the employment contract that worsen the employee's position. The rules of legal acts on labour and the invalid terms of the employment contract shall not be applied. Such regulations and conditions shall be considered invalid from the moment of their adoption. (4) A collective agreement must not contain terms that worsen the position of employees compared to legislation or collective agreements that apply to these employees. If a collective agreement contains such terms, then such conditions are invalid. (5) Collective agreements must not contain terms that worsen the position of employees compared to labour legislation, as well as higher-level collective agreements that apply to these employees. If a collective agreement contains such, then such terms are invalid. (6) The terms worsening the employee's position in comparison with labour legislation and other legal acts on labour must not be included in the content of the employment contract. If they were included, they are recognized as invalid

Significant influence on the labour law landscape has come from the efforts of the International Labour Organization (ILO) through standard-setting and technical cooperation with the republics of the region. By ratifying ILO instruments, the states come under the ILO standards supervision system. All of the Central Asian countries are ILO members: Kyrgyzstan and Uzbekistan became members in 1992; Kazakhstan, Tajikistan, and Turkmenistan in 1993. Membership in the ILO assumes compliance with international labour standards, conventions, and recommendations.

Table 9.3 Statistics on the ratification of ILO conventions by Central Asian countries[6]

Country	Overall number of ratified ILO conventions	Fundamental conventions	Governance (Priority) conventions
Kazakhstan	26 of 190	10 of 10	4 of 4
Kyrgyzstan	55 of 190	8 of 10	3 of 4
Tajikistan	50 of 190	9 of 10	3 of 4
Turkmenistan	11 of 190	8 of 10	2 of 4
Uzbekistan	25 of 190	10 of 10	4 of 4

The primary indicator in this area is the number of conventions ratified by each country, as indicated in Table 9.3.

As we can see from Table 9.3, Kyrgyzstan has not yet ratified two fundamental conventions on occupational safety and health (No. 155 and 187) and one governance convention on labour inspection in agriculture (No. 129); Tajikistan has not ratified one fundamental convention on occupational safety and health (No. 187) and one governance convention on labour inspection in agriculture (No. 129); Turkmenistan has not ratified two fundamental conventions on occupational safety and health (No.155 and 187) and two governance conventions on labour inspections in agriculture (No. 81 and 129). Only Kazakhstan and Uzbekistan have ratified all the fundamental and governance conventions.

However, if we consider the overall scores on the ratification of ILO conventions, we can see that Kyrgyzstan and Tajikistan are leaders in the regions (55 and 50 conventions, respectively), while Kazakhstan and Uzbekistan have ratified half of these numbers (26 and 25 conventions, respectively). Turkmenistan's low number of ratified conventions (11 conventions) matches its reputation as one of the world's most closed-off and isolated countries.

Along with standard-setting and supervision, the ILO also provides technical assistance to countries to reorient their labour law and industrial relations systems. For example, in 2023, the ILO launched the RISE for Impact Project, which aims to enhance respect for fundamental principles and rights at work for a sustainable cotton supply chain in Uzbekistan (as well as India and Pakistan).[7]

Integration processes and supranational regulation also influence the labour relations systems in Kazakhstan and Kyrgyzstan. Both countries are members of the supranational Eurasian Economic Union and are bound by the Treaty on the Eurasian Economic Union (*Eurasian Treaty*) signed in 2014 in Astana by Belarus, Kazakhstan, and Russia (later acceded to by Armenia and Kyrgyzstan) which established a common economic market for capital, goods, and labour forces. Currently, this Treaty covers only labour migration issues and enforces a national regime for employees of the five member states. No other fields of supranational regulation of employment and collective labour relations are provided in the Eurasian Treaty. For example, in

---

[6] NORMLEX Information System on International Labour Standards [Electronic source] https://normlex.ilo.org/.

[7] International Labour Organization (2023b).

2023, the member states concluded an Agreement on mutual recognition of academic degrees in the Eurasian Economic Union States, and in 2019, the Pension Agreement for the Working Population of the Eurasian Economic Union Member States. The extension of the scope of integration into social security and academic affairs is explained by the fact that they are closely connected with the labour force movement.

We can see many common trends and approaches to labour market regulation in the Central Asian countries. However, each state has specific features in the reform process and is differentiated by the level of decentralization and liberalization of the labour framework. What also unites all countries is the widespread violations of human rights at work, limits on trade union freedoms, the persecution of civil society activists, and political arrests.

9.1.2 Human Rights in Central Asia in the Context of the Labour Sphere

Human rights at work have come a long way internationally towards being proclaimed as fundamental. Labour law emerged and developed originally to protect human rights at work. Human rights remain a core of labour law. In the human rights system, proclaimed by the International Covenant on Economic, Social and Cultural Rights of 1966, labour and trade union rights occupy a significant place.

Due to historical and cultural reasons, the human dimension of the labour market in the region faces serious challenges related to the confrontation between authoritarian political regimes and oligarchic groups, on the one hand, and civil society, including trade unions and unorganized workers' groups, on the other.

A study by Sayapin shows that thirty years after the dissolution of the Soviet Union, the Central Asian states are still learning to apply international human rights law and to communicate about it with external and domestic audiences.[8]

The current situation with human rights and civil freedoms is worsening. According to a new briefing paper from human rights organizations, civic space is increasingly restricted in Central Asia, and civil society representatives face unprecedented challenges across the region. The recent enactment of a foreign agent-style NGO law in Kyrgyzstan has raised particular alarm. It also sets a troubling precedent for other Central Asian countries, where civil society organizations (CSOs) receiving foreign funding already face enhanced government scrutiny and widespread suspicion. The recent move in Kazakhstan to publicly list foreign-funded CSOs has reinforced these concerns. In Tajikistan, several hundred CSOs have been forcibly closed or pressured to shut down since 2022, leading to a sharp decline in the civil society sector. In Uzbekistan, human rights groups continue to struggle to obtain compulsory state registration, while in Turkmenistan, no human rights monitoring or advocacy groups are registered or able to operate openly.[9]

---

[8] Sayapin (2023, p. 24).

[9] International Trade Union Monitoring Mission on Labour Rights in Central Asia (2024b).

According to the International Trade Union Confederation (ITUC) rating, Kazakhstan and Kyrgyzstan are included in the rating 5 category with 'no guarantees of rights'.[10] Other Central Asian countries are not rated in the Global Rights Index.

Noticeably, in 2024, Kyrgyzstan's rating worsened from 4 to 5 because trade unionists were arbitrarily detained over several weeks in 2023. The detentions were part of a successful fear-mongering campaign led by the government and state security committee. In September and October 2023, a ban on peaceful gatherings deemed 'political' was extended to Uzgen and the Chon-Alai district in the Osh region, marking a further shrinking of the space for freedom of expression, peaceful assembly, and association.[11]

Labour law scholar Lyutov pointed out that Kazakhstan is currently one of the most criticized countries in the world for its lack of compliance with international labour standards regarding freedom of association, the right to collective bargaining, the resolution of collective labour disputes, and the right to strike. Workers in Kazakhstan cannot legally and effectively resolve their conflicts with employers, which leads to a deterioration in their situation, the accumulation of conflict potential in society, the politicization of social and labour conflicts, and the growth of social instability.[12]

Conditions for creating and registering independent unions in Uzbekistan are still absent. Organized workers are forced to affiliate with state-controlled unions headed by government officials and employers. The restricted right to freedom of association discredits the attempted political reforms, making any positive changes precarious and reversible.[13]

In Tajikistan, trade unions are insufficiently active as organizations that are independent in their operations from the state and the employers, and capable of freely organizing workers and representing and protecting them without impediment.[14]

In Turkmenistan, the legal and political environment dominated by government-supported NGOs (GONGOs) is antagonistic to independent civic actors, who experience constant state-directed harassment, intimidation, and even persecution. In the meantime, the infrastructure supporting civil society is significantly underdeveloped. Poor coverage of civil society activities in the national media, apart from those of a few selected GONGOs, as well as an ongoing internet blockade, contribute to low public visibility. As a result, the public is left without effective mechanisms and channels to have their concerns and interests heard by the government.[15]

Freedom of association, the right to collective bargaining and to strike, and so-called collective labour rights are extremely violated in all republics.

One of the founders of Labour Law, Professor Kahn-Freund, emphasized that collective labour relations are organized in every country under the influence of strong political traditions. Decisions in particular cases are more highly political in this area

[10] International Trade Union Confederation (2024a).

[11] Ibid, p. 19.

[12] Lyutov (2024, p. 43).

[13] International Trade Union Monitoring Mission on Labour Rights in Central Asia (2021).

[14] Ibid.

[15] International Trade Union Monitoring Mission on Labour Rights in Central Asia (2024a).

than any other, so the importance of the constitutional allocation of decision-making power (whether to the court or government) assumes great significance. He referred to differences between political systems (communist and otherwise, democratic and dictatorial), differences in the allocation of power among the branches of government, and differences in the role of 'organized interests' in the making and the maintenance of legal institutions.[16]

Another aspect of human rights violations is the weakening of labour rights protections by state labour inspections.

According to Lyutov and Voitkovska, there is a clear trend towards downgrading the labour inspectorate for the sake of protecting the rights of employers from regulatory burdens, combating corruption, and limiting expenditure. In a series of instances, governments have given legal priority to protecting the rights of entrepreneurs from regulatory burdens over the need to maintain protections for workers' rights. In many cases the limitations on the powers of the labour inspectorate were conducted as part of structural reforms aimed at creating a more attractive environment for business that was coordinated, sponsored or encouraged by international financial institutions, such as the International Financial Corporation (IFC), the EBRD, the Organization for Economic Cooperation and Development (OECD), and others.[17] (For more detailed information about labour inspections, see Sect. 9.4).

Labour and union rights violations are consequences of the reforms and processes undertaken in each country within the context of the established political and socio-economic systems, as well as regulatory reforms.

9.1.3 Labour Law Reforms in Central Asian Countries

9.1.3.1 Kazakhstan

Kazakhstan became the first Central Asian country to radically reform labour legislation based on liberalization and deregulation.

The main reason for such a comprehensive revision of labour regulation was that, according to the government evaluation, the previous Labour Code did not encourage employers to create more jobs. This made it difficult to use the legal regulation mechanisms of labour relations which are successfully performed by countries with a stable market economy.[18]

In this regard, a new Labour Code (LC) was adopted in 2015 (Adilet 2015a). The LC limits the state's role by establishing minimum standards for participants in labour relations to enter into negotiations and conclude contracts and agreements.

In the new LC, the experts' community and legislative establishment are trying to find a solution to the problem of the flexibility of legal regulation of labour relations,

---

[16] Kahn-Freund (1974).

[17] Voitkovska, Lyutov (2021, p. 297–298).

[18] Khassenov (2015, p. 131).

the possibility of widely using not only standard labour contracts but also various contracts that regulate non-standard employment.

The LC is adapted to possible crisis phenomena; it has mechanisms to promote the increased stability of enterprises during economic instability (temporary relocation of staff to another employer with the suspension of the main labour contract, a simplified introduction of part-time work, etc.). The liberty of labour relations parties (employer and employees) has been extended considerably.[19]

As domestic scholars emphasize, Kazakh 'labour law' in a formal sense has very few advantages from the perspective of its application for achieving goals due to the liberalization of regulations of working relations to accelerate economic development.[20]

The key innovations of the LC are as follows[21]:

1. It introduces more flexible regulations on permanent contracts. In particular, it expands the grounds for fair dismissal, making it easier for employers to (fairly) dismiss workers.
2. It also liberalizes temporary contracts even further. More specifically, it allows employers to renew temporary contracts (for a maximum of two times).
3. The protection of some categories of vulnerable workers (such as youth and disabled persons) was abolished. The LC extends trial periods to all workers and abolishes the recent rule that employers can hire youth under temporary contracts only for a minimum of two years.
4. In addition, it gives more responsibilities to social partners to negotiate wages and labour standards. For example, before the reform in the LC, overtime work was paid at time and a half (during the working week) or double (on holidays and weekends) the wage. The new LC reduces pay for overtime work to 1.5 the wage and lets social partners negotiate higher overtime wages.

As reported by the OECD, the new LC gives more responsibilities to social partners to negotiate wages and labour standards. These steps go in the right direction because they reduce barriers to youth hiring.[22]

It should be noted that the primary lobbyist for labour reform was the National Chamber of Entrepreneurs of Kazakhstan, the nation-wide umbrella organization for all employers' associations. This highlights the current imbalances in the collective bargaining system, where employers' associations possess stronger and more influential positions.

A distinctive feature of the LC is that a significant number of articles (56) refer to collective agreements. Thus, the legislation lays the foundation for the autonomous regulation of labour relations with the agreement of employees and employers, thereby establishing a clear 'watershed' between the minimum social and labour

---

[19] Khassenov (2022, p. 138).

[20] Mukhamadiyeva et al. (2019).

[21] OECD (2017, pp. 83–84).

[22] Ibid., p. 19.

guarantees provided by the state and the guarantees established as a result of collective bargaining.[23]

The new LC's provisions aim to strengthen the collective-contractual method of regulating labour relations and the autonomy of the relations of employees, employers, and their representatives. The LC is qualitatively different from previous editions in that it enforces the transition to strengthening the parties' autonomy to form labour and collective agreements, provides for the expansion of the collective-contractual method of regulating social and labour relations, and allows for minimal interference by the state in the labour sphere.

In addition to weakening the individual rights of workers, the new Labour Code of Kazakhstan brought as its logical conclusion the 'reform' of collective labour law in terms of the procedure for conducting collective negotiations and resolving collective labour disputes, including the right to strike. Concerning conducting collective negotiations and conciliation procedures for resolving collective labour disputes, a system of forced monopoly is in effect. In the event of the existence of several workers' representatives, they are obliged to create a single representative body. Since the legislation does not contain any real guarantees to ensure the independence of workers' representatives from employers, in practice, this may lead to the relevant procedures being blocked by the employer by creating trade unions under its control to formally represent the majority of workers.[24]

This labour law liberalization was implemented along with the introduction of English law elements into the legal system of Kazakhstan. The newest example of the reception of foreign legal institutions, and in particular elements of English law, into the national legal system is the creation in Kazakhstan of a special jurisdiction, namely the Astana International Financial Centre (AIFC), which was designed to provide favourable and attractive conditions for the activities of its participants. To enable this, the acts of the AIFC bodies are based on the principles and norms of law in England and Wales, as well as the standards of the world's leading financial centres, in particular, the regulatory documents of the Dubai International Financial Centre (DIFC).

According to the Constitutional Law on the Astana International Financial Centre, the AIFC is a territory within Astana city with precisely defined borders determined by the President of the Republic of Kazakhstan (RK) in which a special legal regime is implemented in the financial sphere.[25]

The AIFC Court provides a common law court system based on the norms and principles of English law for the first time in Central Asia. It operates according to international standards to resolve civil and commercial disputes within the AIFC. It has exclusive jurisdiction over disputes arising out of the activities and operations of the AIFC and jurisdiction in the case of other disputes in which all parties agree to give the AIFC Court jurisdiction. The AIFC Court is separate and independent from Kazakhstan's judicial system. The AIFC Court has its own procedural rules

[23] Nurgaliyeva and Khassenov (2023, p. 84).

[24] Lyutov (2024, p. 45).

[25] Adilet (2015b).

modelled on the principles and procedures of English common law and standards applied by the world's leading financial centres.[26]

The AIFC bodies are entitled to adopt acts that regulate the issues arising between the Centre participants and (or) the Centre bodies, and (or) their employees relating to (1) civil relations; (2) civil procedure relations; (3) financial relations; (4) administrative procedures.

Although employment relations are not listed in the Constitutional Law as the subject of jurisdiction, in 2017, AIFC Employment Regulations were adopted. These Regulations apply to employees working in companies registered with the AIFC authority or whose employment contracts contain a reference to the AIFC Court jurisdiction. However, the Labour Code of Kazakhstan does not mention AIFC jurisdiction. In this regard, there is a unique situation of parallel existence of two separate labour law systems without any interaction.

Another trend in labour law reform is the trade union reform undertaken in 2014 after the tragic events in Zhanaozen in the western region of the republic.

The new trade union law adopted in 2014 was fundamentally different from the previous one, first of all, by strict regulation, it increased requirements for the charter and structure of trade unions. The law consolidated the vertical hierarchy of trade unions—a mandatory requirement was established for each trade union and each association of trade unions to be a member of a higher association of trade unions (mandatory membership of trade unions). The above norms were eliminated under pressure from international organizations only six years after the adoption of the law. In 2020, amendments to the labour legislation included the relevant changes to the law on trade unions. Nevertheless, the legislation still contains other contradictions to international labour standards and gaps in the legal status of trade unions.[27]

The most important consequence of the reactionary reform of labour legislation was the liquidation of many trade unions and direct repression of trade union activists. Criminal cases caused the most severe international reaction, alongside beatings of trade union activists and numerous refusals to register trade union associations.[28]

The ILO Committee on the Applications of Conventions and Recommendations has repeatedly criticized Kazakhstan's law criminalizing workers who strike. In a letter to the President of Kazakhstan, ITUC General Secretary Luc Triangle demanded that all sanctions against the striking workers be dropped and that all 'necessary measures be taken to ensure that this labour dispute is resolved through social dialogue and in line with the principle of freedom of association'.[29]

In Kazakhstan, independent union activists remain under considerable pressure. The legal restrictions hampering their activity are still in force, and unlawful court decisions against participants of peaceful actions continue. Threatened with criminal prosecution, workers of Kazakhstan express their frustration, with larger numbers

[26] Official website of the AIFC: www.court.aifc.kz/an-introduction. Accessed 16 March 2025.

[27] See Khassenov (2021).

[28] Lyutov (2024, p. 45).

[29] International Trade Union Confederation (2024b).

of them taking part in strike actions and staunchly demanding recognition of independent trade unions. Ten years after the Zhanaozen tragedy, the state has still failed to produce an adequate assessment of those events and compensate its victims. The state refuses to acknowledge its responsibility for failing to create conditions for a fair social dialogue and collective bargaining at the time, as well as for using firearms against the participants of the peaceful strike.[30]

In sum, Kazakhstan's current labour legislation has been in place for the past three decades and has been renewed significantly over the last ten years. The trend towards liberalization and borrowing from foreign legal institutes has spread throughout labour and employment relations.

9.1.3.2 Kyrgyzstan

The most recent labour law reform in the region has been undertaken in the Kyrgyz Republic, where a new Labour Code, dated 23 January 2025, was adopted 20 years after the adoption of the previous Labour Code (Centralized Data Bank of Legal Information of Kyrgyz Republic 2025).

According to the bill's justification, 'in connection with the development of economic and labour relations and the emergence of new forms of employment, there is a need to adopt a new Labour Code. The initiative to change the structure of the Labour Code was raised by representatives of the business community to increase the attractiveness of investment in the Kyrgyz Republic. This work was initiated, among other things, to further systematize the labour legislation with the aim of improving the logic and structure of organization to ensure more convenient application and understanding of labour law norms'.[31]

The Ministry of Labour also lists the main problems associated with the 2005 Labour Code. Stating that there was a gap between the theoretical norms of the Code and their actual implementation in practice: 'For example, the document provides for certain guarantees and rights for employees, such as the right to protection from discrimination, the right to leave, and others, but violations of these rights are quite common in real practice and employees may encounter difficulties in protecting their rights'. The current version contains shortcomings in the mechanisms for regulating labour relations, such as procedures for hiring and firing workers, determining working conditions, procedures for resolving labour disputes, and others.[32]

Analysis of the content of the new Labour Code adopted in Kyrgyzstan shows that this reform was not as liberal as that undertaken in Kazakhstan as the LC still provides more protection for workers than Kazakhstan's Labour code.

However, the trend towards liberalization was also inherent in previous labour law reforms. According to Ramankulov, labour legislation in the Kyrgyz Republic

---

[30] International Trade Union Monitoring Mission on Labour Rights in Central Asia (2021).

[31] Official website of the Parliament of the Kyrgyz Republic https://kenesh.kg/bills/651733. Accessed 30 March 2025.

[32] 24.kg (2024).

has significantly expanded employer powers regarding the dismissal of employees. In terms of the number of such grounds compared with the previous Labour Code (seven grounds, including additional ones), the current Labour Code (twelve grounds in total) has almost doubled, with a tendency for this list to continue to grow. The grounds for requiring prior written consent from the relevant authority upon dismissal have been significantly reduced.[33]

The most critical situation is connected with the attempt to reform trade union legislation in Kyrgyzstan. Kyrgyz President Sadyr Japarov has returned the adopted draft law on trade unions by deputies in October 2021 to the Parliament for the third time with his objections. Previously, this law was returned to Parliament in May and August 2021. The law violates the norms of the Constitution, ILO Conventions No. 87 and No. 98, and establishes strict frameworks and conditions for the activities of representative bodies of workers. Moreover, the bill includes an entire chapter defining fairly detailed conditions for forming governing bodies and the terms and procedure for electing the governing bodies of the Federation of Trade Unions of Kyrgyzstan and other trade union organizations. The charters of trade unions must establish these conditions. An absolute monopoly of the federation as the only trade union body—a social partner of the highest state authority of Kyrgyzstan—has thus been established. Many articles are vague and contradict each other.[34]

The President has not yet approved the new trade union law. This example of political struggle between lobbyist groups acting in the Parliament and independent trade unions and human rights organizations supported by the international community, and the Head of State demonstrates a higher level of maturity and development of civil society in the country in comparison with other countries of the region.

9.1.3.3 Tajikistan

The current Labour Code of Tajikistan[35] was adopted in 2016 and consolidates norms on occupational safety, social partnership, collective bargaining, and agreements.

Regarding remuneration issues, the Code provides that the employer independently decides on the choice of form, system, and amount of remuneration for employees. However, regular indexation of the employee's wages by the employer based on the inflation rate has been added. In addition, it is envisaged that employers will be granted the right to regulate the amount of compensation payments for work at night, on weekends, and on holidays, as well as overtime, through a collective labour agreement. The list of grounds for termination of an employment contract at the employer's initiative has been expanded: in the current Code, there were 13, and now there are 20.[36]

[33] Ramankulov (2019, p. 109).

[34] 24.kg (2021).

[35] Continent Online (2016).

[36] Asia—Plus (2016).

The most critical notes and recommendations from the ILO supervising bodies concern labour inspection activities. In 2024, the Committee of Experts on the Application of Conventions and Recommendations (CEACR) noted that the legal restrictions imposed under Law No. 1269 on the powers of labour inspectors were still in force, including regarding: (i) the frequency of inspections; (ii) the duration of inspections (sect. 26); (iii) the ability of labour inspectors to undertake inspection visits without previous notice; and (iv) the scope of inspections. In this regard, the Committee takes due note of the government's indication that two bills to amend the Labour Code and Law No. 1269, respectively, have been drafted at the initiative of the Ministry of Labour, Migration and Employment and are currently under consideration by the relevant ministries and authorities. The Committee also notes with deep concern the government's indication that, pending adoption of those bills, labour inspectors are to continue to carry out inspections by giving warnings to employers.[37]

In general, labour law has not undergone significant reforms in the last decade, and no reforms are planned. The current Labour Code has not significantly changed the balance between employers' and employees' interests.

9.1.3.4 Turkmenistan

The current Labour Code[38] was adopted in 2009 and is still in force.

The political regime in Turkmenistan, characterized by extreme absolutism, leaves no room for the emergence of independent unions, human rights organizations, or mass media. The use of forced labour in cotton harvesting, involving workers from various other sectors, also remains a common and systematic phenomenon.[39]

In this regard, there are mass violations of labour and trade unions rights in the country.

The provisions of the Labour Code concerning collective labour disputes does not refer to the right to strike; collective labour disputes are resolved through mediation or, failing this, in courts, and the parties cannot refuse to participate in these dispute resolution procedures. Compulsory arbitration, including through judicial proceedings, prevents strike action contrary to the right of trade unions to organize freely their activities and can only be justified in the public service for public servants exercising authority in the name of the state or in essential services in the strict sense of the term, that is, services the interruption of which would endanger the life, personal safety, or health of the whole or part of the population.[40]

In Turkmenistan, the most critical situation concerns widespread forced and child labour.

---

[37] International Labour Organization (2024b).

[38] Continent Online (2009).

[39] International Trade Union Monitoring Mission on Labour Rights in Central Asia (2021).

[40] NORMLEX (2022).

Forced labour of public sector employees in picking cotton was widespread and systematic in all regions monitored. Public sector employees were required to pick cotton, hire replacement pickers, or pay money to a supervisor for replacement pickers or other harvest expenses—a 'pick or pay' system. Child labour was used in the 2022 harvest, driven by poverty and the forced labour system. Turkmen News monitored and documented school-age children's mass, country-wide participation throughout the cotton harvest. While the state did not directly organize child labour, the state's policy of forcing adults to pick cotton or pay for a replacement appears to be the primary driver of child labour, since most children who picked cotton did so to earn money as replacement pickers or to replace a relative.[41]

ILO technical cooperation with Turkmenistan was limited. Because tripartite conditions for fuller cooperation were lacking, the ILO and constituents in Turkmenistan have not developed a Decent Work Country Program (DWCP), and there was no country-level development in 2018–2022. Representatives of tripartite constituents participated in a few regional capacity-building activities and, based on a request from the government, received technical guidance from the ILO on tools to assess labour market conditions during the COVID-19 pandemic. An ILO official participated in developing the UN Country Development framework, which included the ILO's concerns in its strategic document and in the second National Action Plan on Human Rights.[42]

In September 2023, the Government of Turkmenistan and the ILO signed a Memorandum of Understanding concerning the observation of working conditions during the 2023 cotton harvest. In accordance with the Memorandum, a delegation of ILO specialists, consisting of seven ILO teams, made phased visits to Turkmenistan in September–October 2023. During the visits, the ILO teams travelled to the country's regions to visit cotton harvest fields and met and held interviews with cotton harvest participants, tenants, farmer associations, and representatives of farms. An ILO report was prepared based on the results of the monitoring conducted within the framework of the road map and was discussed among stakeholders in February 2024. The report presented recommendations on continuing to improve legislation on the prevention and prohibition of forced labour, raising awareness of employers and local authorities on the prevention of the use of forced labour, including child labour, and on the mechanism for handling complaints and other recommendations.[43]

Therefore, the most conservative country in terms of the labour law reform process is Turkmenistan, with no significant changes or planned actions. Some legislative amendments have been made towards the recommendations of the ILO Committees, in particular, on forced labour elimination and labour inspections.

[41] Turkmen News and The Turkmen Initiative for Human Rights (2023, pp. 6, 22).

[42] International Labour Organization (2022, p. 31).

[43] International Labour Organization (2024d).

9.1.3.5 Uzbekistan

The current Labour code of the Republic of Uzbekistan was adopted in October 2022 and came into force on 20 April 2023, 27 years after the adoption of the previous one (LexUz Online 2022).

The adoption of the new code was the result of wide discussion in the country. Labour law scholar Gassanov believed that a more consistent reform of labour legislation would achieved simply through changes and additions to the labour code. It was thus necessary to adopt a new labour code that considered changes in all areas of the country.[44]

The new Labour Code introduces innovations in the regulation of individual labour relations and details the regulation of an extensive array of specific provisions of labour legislation. Changes to the employment agreement are supplemented by such grounds as changing the locality due to the employer moving and seconding the employee to another employer. The rules on termination of an employment agreement at the initiative of an employee are differentiated according to the subject composition (managers, seasonal workers, etc.) and the status of the enterprise/employer (micro firms, individual entrepreneurs, individuals using domestic workers). The new rules also supplemented the procedure for the termination of an employment agreement at the employer's initiative for a single gross breach of employment duties.[45]

The most vulnerable aspect of labour law in Uzbekistan concerns forced and child labour. ILO cooperation with Uzbekistan in the last decade was initially narrowly focused on eliminating child labour and forced labour but has become the most extensive country-level programme of work in Central Asia. Beginning in 2017, ILO activities broadened. The ILO began its technical cooperation with Uzbekistan in 2013 to support national efforts to eliminate child labour and forced labour in cotton production. Compulsory participation by school-aged children (some reportedly as young as 9 years old), university students, and public employees in the annual cotton harvest in Uzbekistan, a practice rooted in Soviet-era production quotas, had attracted international condemnation and a boycott of Uzbek cotton. The government of Uzbekistan requested ILO assistance to address the issue, which it provided starting in 2013. Since 2017, ILO–Uzbekistan cooperation broadened to include new areas of work, such as labour law reform, developing a national employment strategy, strengthening public employment services, advancing social protection, promoting gender equality in the labour market, and supporting tripartite social dialogue.[46]

According to ILO evaluation, while there is currently no systematic use of child and forced labour, isolated instances still occur. Government representatives, employers, trade unions, and civil society reviewing findings from independent monitoring of the 2024 cotton harvest agreed that such violations must continue to be tackled through ongoing monitoring and awareness-raising, as well as education campaigns, aimed at those involved in cotton cultivation and harvesting. One of the

[44] Ismailov (2023).

[45] Grata International (2022).

[46] International Labour Organization (2022, p. 31).

key recommendations from the 2024 Independent Monitoring Report was to enhance transparency in handling complaints. Providing clear information on how complaints are addressed and what actions are taken would increase public trust in the bodies responsible for protecting workers' rights.[47]

Monitoring by the Uzbek Forum showed that there was no widespread, systematic, government-imposed forced labour during the 2023 harvest. However, in interviews and across social media channels, monitors observed a distinct increase in reports of forced labour throughout the harvest. In the five regions where monitoring was conducted, monitors documented instances of the forced labour of employees of banks and state-owned organizations in picking cotton, revealing that, in the face of a shortage of pickers, government officials resorted to coercion to fulfil cotton production targets. These findings indicate a real risk that forced labour could again become widespread without the necessary civil and political changes that ensure reforms to eliminate forced labour do not backslide.[48]

An analysis of the legislation in Uzbekistan shows that, today, such terms as 'paid public works' and '*hashar*' are used. The lack of a clear definition of the term *hashar* in the legislation can lead to problems in terms of respect for the rights of persons involved in such activities. Only some legislation sets out the requirements for organizing *hashar*. The Uzbek dictionary defines the word *hashar* as 'voluntary, impartial participation of the majority in the performance of a task'. In this regard, the concept of *hashar* means the performance of any work on a voluntary basis. Based on the nature of social relations associated with the concept of *hashar*, for the practice of applying this concept in the legislation, it is expedient to define this concept as follows: '*Hashar* is work performed by a person voluntarily, necessary for the needs of the community to which he belongs, including the labour community, in strict compliance with the rules of labour protection and safety'.[49]

In this regard, along with the adoption of new labour legislation, Uzbekistan is continuing to resolve systematic challenges concerned with the elimination of child and forced labour, which remains one of the most complicated problems for the human dimension in the region.

9.2 Collective Labour Law

Freedom of association enjoys protection as a fundamental freedom guaranteed in the Constitutions of almost all Central Asian countries. However, this right is recognized only for citizens (Article 23 of the Constitution of Kazakhstan, Article 28 of the Constitution of Tajikistan, Article 39 of the Constitution of Uzbekistan), except for Kyrgyzstan, where it is the right of everyone (Article 36).

---

[47] International Labour Organization (2025).

[48] Uzbek Forum for Human Rights (2024, p. 5).

[49] Sulaymanov and Rasulov (2021, p. 1081).

The Constitution of Turkmenistan does not mention an individual's right to freedom of association or collective labour rights, including strikes. The Labour Code also does not provide the right to strike, which means it is prohibited by law. In Kazakhstan, as a result of the 2026 constitutional reform and the adoption of a new Constitution, the right to strike, which had previously been enshrined in the 1995 Constitution, was removed from the text of the Basic Law. This confirms, on the one hand, the general political course toward restricting civil rights and freedoms and, on the other hand, is intended to reduce social tensions at enterprises and improve the position of employers, for whom strikes pose a serious challenge to doing business.

Only the Constitution of Kyrgyzstan recognizes the right to strike. Other countries do not provide for this right in their Constitutions.

Several normative legal acts of Tajikistan prohibit the participation of public sector employees in strikes. Such prohibitions are established in the laws on 'Public Service' (2007), 'Police' (2007), 'Status of Servicemen' (2005), 'Courier Communications' (2002), and in the Customs Code (2005) and the law 'On the System of Execution of Criminal Punishment' (2004). National legislation also regulates procedural requirements for organizing and holding strikes. These procedures are established in the Labour Code (2016) and the law on 'Trade Unions' (2011). Restrictions on the organization and holding of strikes are established by the laws on 'Security' (2014) and 'Martial Law' (2019).[50]

Article 23 of the Constitution of Kazakhstan prohibits trade union membership of the Chairperson and judges of the Constitutional Court, the Supreme Court and other courts, the Chairperson and members of the Central Electoral Commission, the Supreme Audit Chamber, military personnel, employees of national security agencies, and law enforcement agencies. Article 8 of the Constitution of Kyrgyzstan prescribes trade unions and other public associations to ensure transparency of their financial and economic activities.

Despite the formal enshrinement of the right to freedom of association, its implementation is far from the normative model. Numerous critical reports and communications from international organizations, bodies, and NGOs confirm this.

Currently, the ILO Committee on Freedom of Association (CFA) is considering two active cases on freedom of association: one against Kazakhstan and one against Uzbekistan.

The case of Uzbekistan was initiated in November 2024 upon the complaint of the International Union of Food, Agricultural, Hotel, Restaurant, Catering, Tobacco and Allied Workers Associations (IUF), and the allegations are indicated as confidential.[51]

The case of Kazakhstan was initiated in May 2017 by a complaint from the International Trade Union Confederation (ITUC). The complainants allege obstacles to registration created by the 2014 Law on Trade Unions, ensuing dissolution of trade unions, and intimidation and prosecution of trade union leaders.[52]

[50] Abdulloeva (2021, p. 3).

[51] NORMLEX (2024a).

[52] NORMLEX (2017).

The CFA made the following recommendations upon this complaint: (a) the Committee expects that the Law on Trade Unions would be amended without further delay in consultation with social partners to ensure the right of workers to freely decide whether they wish to associate with or become members of a higher-level trade union structure and to lower threshold requirements to establish higher-level organizations. It requests the Government keep it informed of all progress made in this respect; (b) the Committee requests that the Government keep it informed of any developments regarding the case of Ms. Kharkova, and to indicate, should she decide to compensate six million tenge, how and to which entity these funds will be devolved; (c) the Committee draws the legislative aspects of this case to the attention of the Committee of Experts on the Application of Conventions and Recommendations (CEACR).[53] There has been no progress in this case; the relevant amendments have not been adopted, and no other steps have been taken to improve practice.

The ILO's activities in Kazakhstan were narrowly focused on improving social dialogue and reforming laws restricting freedom of association. Because of serious violations of freedom of association cited by the Committee on the Application of Standards (CAS) in 2015, 2016, and 2017, beginning in 2018, the ILO decided to limit technical cooperation activities in Kazakhstan until the government addressed the fundamental issues raised. The critical issue highlighted by the Governing Body was the legislative framework governing freedom of association for workers and employers in Kazakhstan, which established a system wherein effectively only one business organization and one workers' organization were authorized to engage in social dialogue with the government. Within the framework of recommendations made by the CAS, the government received a direct contact mission in September 2016, which resulted in the development of a roadmap for implementing the ILO's recommendations on freedom of association.[54]

According to the ITUC, the right to freedom of association in Kazakhstan is legally recognized but strictly regulated. The law prohibits anti-union discrimination but does not provide adequate means of protection against it. Prior authorization or approval by authorities is required to establish a union. The 2014 Trade Union Law imposes an obligation of registration as a legal entity on all trade union types except for primary (enterprise-level) trade unions. Yet, a primary trade union must become a local or industrial trade union member, which is obligated to register as a legal entity. The 2014 Trade Union Law imposes regulations on the trade union structure. For example, a territorial association may only be established at the level of one region, a city of national or regional significance, the capital, or a separate district.[55]

While the 2014 Trade Union Law allows trade unions to join international trade union organizations and cooperate, jointly organize, and hold events and projects, the Law on Public Associations of 1996 continues to prohibit the financing of trade unions by international and foreign organizations, subject to criminal liability provided in the Criminal Code.

---

[53] NORMLEX (2020).

[54] International Labour Organization (2022, p. 28).

[55] See: ITUC. Kazakhstan: Legal profile. https://www.ituc-csi.org/kazakhstan

A similar situation exists in Kyrgyzstan. The right to freedom of association is recognized by law but strictly regulated. The law does not explicitly protect workers from anti-union discrimination.[56]

Kyrgyzstan has also seen the most dramatic struggle for trade union rights and freedoms. Despite a veto by the President, on 30 June 2021 the Kyrgyz parliament adopted a new law on trade unions with provisions that breach ILO Conventions 87 and 98. According to international experts, the law would have seriously undermined freedom of association and deprived unions of their independence. The new law on trade unions states that the Federation of Trade Unions of Kyrgyzstan (FTUK) is the only social partner, giving it a monopoly, in clear violation of ILO Convention 87, as it deprives workers of creating another union confederation if workers choose to. The new law deprives unions of their independence by setting accountability to the government and employers and puts all unions in the country under the total control of the FTUK. Trade unions would be deprived of the right to independently determine their organizational structure, forms and types of associations, and charters and governing bodies.[57]

The range of workers' representatives in Central Asian countries is legally formalized. Two possible categories of workers' representatives exist: trade union bodies (their associations) and other elective representatives (associations of workers). In Uzbekistan, despite the possibility of non-union associations of workers, only the trade union committee is entitled to represent and protect the rights and interests of employees.

Therefore, the employees' representation system in the region is dominantly unionized, and non-union representatives remain subsidiary to trade unions. It should be mentioned that the scope of activities of trade unions and elected representatives is similar.

In all countries of the region except for Kazakhstan, students in educational institutions can be members of trade unions. In Kyrgyzstan, Tajikistan, and Turkmenistan, pensioners can also be members of trade unions. In Tajikistan, independent workers (self-employed), creative workers, and household workers can be members of trade unions. In Kyrgyzstan, it is also required that trade union members be citizens who have reached the age of 14; in Tajikistan and Uzbekistan, the age is 15. Kazakhstan's law on trade unions recognizes trade union membership exclusively for employees.

In all countries of the region except Kazakhstan, trade unions can be created by a minimum of three citizens; Kazakhstani legislation requires a minimum of ten citizens to establish a trade union.

The general trend is that only citizens have the right to create a trade union. Non-citizens may only become members of trade unions but cannot initiate or establish them.

In Kazakhstan, Tajikistan, and Turkmenistan the Laws on Trade Unions prescribe the structure of the trade union community, providing an exhaustive list of possible forms of trade union organizations. In Kazakhstan, there are five levels (forms) of

---

[56] ITUC. Kazakhstan: Legal profile. https://www.ituc-csi.org/kyrgyzstan

[57] IndustriALL Global Union (2021).

trade union hierarchy: (1) republican association of the trade unions; (2) territorial association of the trade unions, (3) sectoral trade union, (4) local trade union, (5) primary trade union organization. In Tajikistan, there are five levels (forms) of trade union hierarchy: (1) republican association of the trade unions, (2) sectoral trade union, (3) regional (oblast) trade unions, (4) municipal (city, district) trade unions, (5) primary trade union organizations. In Turkmenistan, there are four levels (forms) of trade union hierarchy: (1) republican association of the trade unions, (2) sectoral trade union, (3) territorial association of the trade unions, and (4) primary trade union organizations.

Such imperative and detailed regulation of trade union activities constitutes a gross violation of the freedom of association and the principles laid down in the ILO Convention 87.

Regarding the legal status of trade unions provided by labour legislation, there are two approaches to determining a trade union's role in worker-employer relations. In all countries except Kazakhstan, the trade union's opinion on a trade union activist's dismissal or disciplinary sanctions has mandatory legal force and consequences. Moreover, trade unions are entitled to initiate the dismissal of enterprise officials in some cases.

In Kyrgyzstan, dismissal at the employer's initiative of trade union committee chairpersons, members, and organizers who are not exempt from work is allowed only with the consent of a higher trade union body. Trade unions also have significant powers, especially in influencing the dismissal of state enterprise officials. According to the Law on trade unions,[58] at the request of the trade union body, the employer is obliged to terminate the employment contract with an official of a state enterprise or remove him/her from his/her position if he/she violates labour laws or does not fulfil the obligations under the collective agreement. If a violation of the labour law or infringement of an employee's labour rights is committed by an employer or an official of a non-state-owned enterprise, then, at the request of the trade union body, they can be suspended from their position for up to 6 months. Trade unions are also entitled to have their representatives in the collegial management bodies of enterprises.

Similar powers of trade unions are legitimized in Uzbekistan according to the Law on Trade Unions. Trade unions are entitled to implement public control, and based on its results, draft a final document that government bodies and employers must consider, with decisions to be based on it. State bodies and employers inform the relevant trade unions and their associations about the results of the report's consideration. Trade union officials enjoy legal protection from disciplinary sanctions and dismissals—they cannot be subject to disciplinary action or dismissal at the employer's initiative without the consent of the trade union body or the relevant trade union association; employees released from work as a result of election to elective positions in trade union bodies are provided with their previous job (position) after the end of their elective powers and, in its absence, another equivalent job (position)

[58] Centralized Data Bank of Legal Information of the Kyrgyz Republic (1998).

in the same or, with the consent of the employee, another organization. If it is impossible to provide employees elected to trade union bodies with the appropriate job (position), they enjoy benefits provided for by law and collective agreements.[59]

In Tajikistan, an employer may terminate an employment contract with employees elected as leaders or members of a trade union only with the prior consent of a higher trade union body. Trade union bodies have the right to demand the termination of an employment agreement (contract) with the head of an enterprise if he or she violates labour legislation, collective agreements, or agreements.[60]

In Turkmenistan, according to the Law on Trade Unions,[61] dismissal of employees elected to the elective body of a trade union at the employer's initiative is not allowed, except in cases related to the complete liquidation of the enterprise or the employee committing illegal actions.

Only in Kazakhstan are trade unions not entitled to provide consent for disciplinary sanctions or dismissal of the chairperson and members of trade union bodies. Their competence is restricted to providing a reasoned opinion of the trade union body, which is not obligatory for the employer to execute.[62] This means they can be dismissed or brought to disciplinary responsibility even after a negative opinion of the trade union. Employers are obliged to consider their opinion, not execute it. In this regard, we can see that the liberalized reform of labour legislation weakens trade unions significantly, depriving them of any influence on workers' protection.

The framework of collective labour relations in Central Asian countries is shaped by the tripartite commissions, which act as bodies of social partnership. The republican, sectoral, and regional commissions are constituted as permanently functioning bodies that ensure the coordination of interests of social partnership parties by conducting consultations and negotiations, which are formalized by appropriate decisions binding upon the parties.

According to the ILO technical brief, after the dissolution of the Soviet Union in 1991 and the subsequent independence of the former Soviet republics, each established national tripartite commissions, some relatively early (Kazakhstan and Kyrgyzstan between 1992 and 1994, respectively), others more recently (since 2008). The ILO often helped to strengthen or set up these institutions through policy advice to governments and social partners, capacity-building for its Member States, or technical cooperation projects (as in Tajikistan and Turkmenistan).[63]

All countries have a formal legal basis for their National Social Dialogue Institutions (NSDI). The tripartite commissions in Tajikistan, Turkmenistan, and Uzbekistan have a consultation, negotiation, and decision-making mandate, suggesting strong potential to influence social and labour policies in both design and implementation. In Kazakhstan and Kyrgyzstan, the mandate is limited to consultation functions only. Tripartite agreements and legal acts empower tripartite commissions

59 LexUz Online (2019).

60 Continent Online (2011).

61 Continent Online (2013).

62 Adilet (2014).

63 International Labour Organization (2024b, p. 4).

with a rather broad set of competencies, in the centre of which are labour market and employment issues and rights protections. Moreover, policy areas such as wages, income, living standards, social protection, and occupational safety and health play an important role in the agenda of the given institutions.[64]

Social dialogue is present in all countries at different stages of development. Accordingly, active participation and effective involvement of the social partners in crafting and shaping economic and social policies have seen differing rates of success. While some countries have advanced in establishing and implementing social dialogue, other countries are still in their early stages. The different sizes of, and the legal and administrative arrangements for, the tripartite commissions reflect a variety of possible approaches to social dialogue. Despite these differences, most countries have made progress in tripartite deliberations, although some areas offer themselves for reflection and improvement.[65]

Despite the formal regulation of social partnership bodies' status and activities, their effectiveness in practice, including their ability to prevent labour conflicts and spontaneous strikes, remains questionable.

For example, in 2023, strikes occurred at 15 enterprises in Kazakhstan. All strikes took place in a 'spontaneous manner', without observing the procedures for putting forward workers' demands established by the Labour Code—in connection with which five strikes were recognized as illegal by court decisions.[66] In 2024, strikes occurred at 18 enterprises.[67]

According to Lyutov and Voitkovska,[68] collective bargaining in post-socialist countries does not add much protection to statutory regulation, and trade unions cannot effectively substitute for the labour inspections carried out by the state.

An analysis of law enforcement practice shows that the institutions of social partnership and conciliation procedures do not work effectively in practice, trade unions are weak, and the existing channels of interaction between employees and employers cannot prevent labour conflicts.

Lyutov pointed out the essence of the problem of collective labour relations in Kazakhstan as being as follows: 'In a normal situation, collective labour law acts as a kind of safety valve that reduces tension in society and allows conflict situations to be resolved peacefully and strictly within the framework of discussing workers' socio-economic rights and legitimate interests. In conditions where officials "sweep the problem under the carpet", believing they can relieve social tensions through repression and prohibitions, they achieve the opposite goal. Problems and discontent accumulate, and when social discontent reaches a critical point at an unexpected moment for the state, mass protests occur, and conflicts become sharply radicalized and politicized'.[69]

---

[64] Ibid, p. 9.

[65] Ibid, p. 15.

[66] Ministry of Labour and Social Protection of the Republic of Kazakhstan (2023).

[67] Ministry of Labour and Social Protection of the Republic of Kazakhstan (2025).

[68] Voitkovska and Lyutov (2021, p. 270).

[69] Lyutov N (2024, p. 48).

In this regard, in 2024, the Research School for Labour Law at Maqsut Narikbayev University (Astana, Kazakhstan), led by professors Lyutov and Khassenov, initiated the reform of the collective labour law of Kazakhstan and prepared legislative amendments. The draft law was discussed in the Project Office of the Senate Parliament and a special working group comprising state bodies, trade unions, employers' associations, and experts. After wide debates and discussions, these legislative proposals were supported by some members of Parliament and were introduced as a bill in 2025, now being considered by the legislative body. This example of a bottom-up initiative confirms that there is hope for significant improvement in the status quo. Despite the resistance of the political regime and oligarchic groups, legal scholarship can be a driving force for change, activating social dialogue institutions and providing an evidence-based approach to the decision-making process.

The overall picture of the development of civil society in the region shows an extremely low level of implementation of civil rights, numerous restrictions on trade union freedoms, and violations of international labour standards. Authoritarian political regimes directly influence the functioning of collective labour law in Central Asian countries.

9.3 Employment Discrimination

The constitutions of all Central Asian republics proclaim the equality of each person before the law and court, gender equality, and the prohibition of discrimination on any grounds (Article 14 of the Constitution of Kazakhstan; Article 24 of the Constitution of Kyrgyzstan; Article 17 of the Constitution of Tajikistan; Articles 28–29 of the Constitution of Turkmenistan; and Articles 19, 42, 58 of the Constitution of Uzbekistan).

There are special laws on guarantees for gender equality adopted in all countries of the region: the Law of Kazakhstan on State Guarantees of Equal Rights and Opportunities for Men and Women (2009); the Law of Kyrgyzstan on State Guarantees of Equal Rights and Opportunities for Men and Women (2008), the Law of Tajikistan on State Guarantees of Equality of Men and Women and Equal Opportunities for Them (2005), the Law of Turkmenistan on State Guarantees of Equal Rights and Opportunities for Men and Women (2015), and the Law of Uzbekistan on Guarantees of Equal Rights and Opportunities for Men and Women (2019).

The modern concept of legal equality includes not only the existence of equal rights, but also the existence of equal opportunities, which the state is obliged to provide to vulnerable social groups so that they can actually take advantage of the rights proclaimed for all, as well as equal treatment by administrative, judicial and law enforcement authorities of all persons, regardless of whether they belong to minorities or socially vulnerable groups or not.[70]

[70] Dikman et al. (2009, pp. 7–8).

A list of professions prohibited for women has existed in Central Asia for many years. The ban was originally established in the 1930s when Soviet legislators argued that to 'ensure the protection of maternity and women's reproductive health', women should be banned from hundreds of jobs. At its height in 1978, the ban consisted of 431 prohibited occupations.[71]

The situation began to change in 2019 when Turkmenistan and Uzbekistan became the first states in the region to abolish formal prohibitions on women's work in certain professions.

However, in Uzbekistan, the ban on the use of women's labour in specific industries or professions, which the 2019 Decree abolished, has acquired a 'recommendatory character', leaving in practice inaccessible employment in professions 'not recommended' for women. Only in 2024 did the Cabinet of Ministers take particular measures to bring subordinate by-laws in line with the cancellation of the list. As a result, several professions in motor transport became accessible to women.[72]

An alternative report by ADC Memorial to the UN Committee on the Elimination of Discrimination against Women (CEDAW) indicated that, despite the abolition of the 'list of prohibited professions', in Turkmenistan—an authoritarian country with prevailing patriarchal traditions—a huge number of women are formally unemployed and engaged in unpaid domestic work or involved in the informal economy, which does not allow them to be financially independent or socially protected.[73]

In 2021, Kazakhstan entirely abolished the list of prohibited professions for women.[74] The lifting of the blanket ban without reservations over 'women's reproductive function' is a win against the framing of women exclusively as mothers and caregivers in Kazakhstan. It is an important milestone in challenging discrimination and gender stereotypes and has a potential for a trickle-down effect in the wider Central Asian region, where similar bans still exist. The grassroots mobilization of women has thus proved to be effective.[75]

In Kyrgyzstan, the list of professions prohibited for women was practically abolished in 2024, except for pregnant and breastfeeding women. According to Article 139 of the new Labour Code (2024), it is prohibited to use the labour of pregnant and breastfeeding women in heavy work, with harmful and (or) dangerous working conditions, in underground work (except for non-physical work or work on sanitary and household services), as well as in work associated with lifting and moving manually weights exceeding the maximum permissible norms for them.[76]

The reform of the Labour Code in Kyrgyzstan marks a shift from outdated employment restrictions, lifting a long-standing ban that prohibited all women from working

[71] Open Democracy (2021).

[72] Anti-Discrimination Center (2024d).

[73] Anti-Discrimination Center (2024c).

[74] Anti-Discrimination Center (2021).

[75] Open Democracy (2021).

[76] Anti-Discrimination Center (2024a).

in more than 400 professions deemed too arduous or dangerous. Now, job restrictions apply only to pregnant and breastfeeding women in hazardous environments, allowing greater access to various career opportunities.[77]

The only state with an existing list of banned professions is Tajikistan, whose Constitution prohibits heavy and underground work, and work with harmful working conditions, for women (Article 35).

However, in 2023, Tajikistan reduced the prohibited professions for women. A decree of the Government of the Republic of Tajikistan of 30 December 2023 approved a new List, reducing the number of prohibited profession from 334 to 194 in 22 economic sectors.[78]

Some scholars suggest that the abolition of this list is unlikely to significantly change the female sectoral structure of employment. This is primarily due to the negative attitude of women towards risk, due to their inclination for maternal responsibilities. Thus, realizing their differences in the physical plane and social roles, men and women are focused on various sectors of the economy.[79]

Open Democracy has emphasized that scrapping the ban is, arguably, only half the job. Women are still not being treated as equals at work. The country's obligation does not end by deleting a paragraph in the labour code—as much as its government would like it to. Eliminating women's remaining barriers to work is 'even more urgent today'.[80]

Although, formally, the principle of equal pay for men and women is prescribed by legislation, in practice, there is a large gap between their wages.

An empirical analysis of existing gender differentiation in labour income in Kazakhstan demonstrates that, in general, the scale of the gender gap in earnings in the Kazakhstani labour market is comparable to similar estimates obtained in other countries. The proportion of wages of women to men is 69 per cent. For the last 15 years, the reduction of difference in the salary by gender was caused by changes in the gender structure of employment. The results of the evaluation of the segregation indexes testify to the situation of the labour market in Kazakhstan. A decomposition of the distinction in annual average labour incomes between men and women, carried out by the method of Oaxaka-Blinder, showed that gender segregation explains more than a third of the observable differences in wages between men and women. The higher level of accumulated human capital of women does not offset this. However, 80 per cent of the gender distinctions in wages remain unexplained, apart from being related to the existing discrimination against women in the labour market in Kazakhstan.[81]

A recent study confirms this trend: men earn, on average, 30 per cent more than women. This situation has been observed since the 2000s. The most important reason for this is industrial segregation (also horizontal segregation). However, this applies

[77] Equality Now (2025).

[78] Anti-Discrimination Center (2024b).

[79] Lipovka (2016, pp. 205–211).

[80] Open Democracy (2021).

[81] Roshchin, Yemelina (2020, pp. 2, 20).

primarily in large cities like Astana and Almaty, where there is no pronounced industrial segregation, but the wage imbalance remains.[82]

According to Lipovka, the main reason for gender differences in the labour market of Kazakhstan is the insufficient use of women's human capital and the lack of demand for their individual abilities, for which certain favourable conditions are required from the state and the business community. Women have no less potential than men for entrepreneurial activity, as well as for occupying leadership positions in both public organizations and private companies.[83]

In Tajikistan, the government reported on the decreasing gender pay gaps in the agriculture sector, where the ratio of women's wages to men's went from 79.5 per cent in 2018 to 97.2 per cent in 2021; in the education sector, from 77 to 89 per cent; in healthcare, from 74.5 to 79.4 per cent; and in public administration and defence, from 77.2 to 87.4 per cent. However, according to information from the World Bank based on TajStat data, overall women earned 60 per cent of what men earned in 2018. According to the government, the pay gap persists due to the following factors: (1) there are more male managers in all sectors; (2) women are less likely to be involved in harmful working conditions, overtime, and night work, and are therefore not paid the corresponding supplements as part of their average wage; (3) in most cases, women work fewer hours; and (4) the total number of female workers is lower than the total number of male workers.[84]

We can observe a similar trend in Uzbekistan, but in a more extreme form. In 2018, more than two-thirds of women's total work time in Uzbekistan was spent on unpaid care and domestic work, compared to less than one-third of time spent by men. The gender gap in unemployment rates has widened significantly since 2018, with the women's unemployment rate almost double that of men in 2021.[85]

Employment discrimination also has another aspect concerning the rights of the male population in the context of family responsibilities.

An ILO report pointed out that, while recognizing *de jure* gender equality, in practice, women and men face difficulties in realizing their rights to decent work and equal opportunities. Maternity Leave Policy applies only to the reproductive role of women and does not apply to the participation of men in childcare, with the exception of cases where the mother is absent or ill. Today fathers can only take unpaid vacations and are not entitled to paid leave for the birth of a child.[86]

According to Kazakh scholars, there is an absence of judicial administrative practice in assigning responsibility not only for violation of the principle of equal pay for work of equal value but for violation of the principle of discrimination in the sphere of labour on any grounds.[87]

82 Kemelbayeva, Ospanov (2024, p. 7).

83 Lipovka (2016, pp. 205–211).

84 International Labour Organization (2024c).

85 International Labour Organization (2023a).

86 International Labour Organization (2021, p. 49).

87 Khamzina et al. (2022).

Indeed, the formal prohibition of discrimination in the legislation is not ensured by a reliable implementation mechanism, especially given the inevitability of responsibility and the 'zero tolerance' violence policy.

A person who has suffered discrimination generally has fewer avenues of legal recourse than the alleged perpetrator of the harm and, thus, does not have a fair chance in an ordinary civil dispute. Accordingly, at a minimum, there is a need for regulations detailing the prohibition of discriminatory behaviour, judicial, and administrative procedures that effectively provide victims of discrimination with opportunities to protect themselves and obtain compensation, and special structures capable of supporting victims of discrimination in a dispute with the alleged perpetrator of harm. These requirements are intended to be met by anti-discrimination legislation.[88]

In 2012, Tajikistan became the first country in the region to adopt a unified anti-discrimination law—the Law on Equality and Eliminating All Forms of Discrimination.[89] Currently, it is the only Central Asian state with comprehensive anti-discrimination legislation, while in other countries, there is long-term discussion on this matter. In particular, the law defines workplace harassment as any form of non-physical harassment in the workplace with repeated actions that have a humiliating effect on an individual and are intended to worsen the employee's working conditions or professional status.

In Kyrgyzstan, a draft Law on Ensuring the Right to Equality and Protection from Discrimination was registered on the website of the Parliament in 2023. It was, however, withdrawn by the initiator in 2024. Kyrgyzstan did become the first country in Central Asia and 41st country in the world to ratify the ILO Convention on Violence and Harassment of 2019 (No. 190) in June 2024. This was an important step towards reaffirming everyone's right to a safe and fair workplace free from violence and harassment.[90] The Convention entered into force for Kyrgyzstan on 03 Jun 2025. Other countries in the region have not yet ratified this Convention.

In Kazakhstan, several anti-discrimination draft laws have been developed by the human rights experts: the Kazakhstan International Bureau of Human Rights and Rule of Law[91] and Khassenov.[92] The consolidated idea of adopting a unified anti-discrimination law was proposed at the end of 2024 during the international conference organized by the Commissioner for Human Rights. The proposed law would define the types of discrimination; prohibit victimization, segregation, harassment, and incitement to discrimination; and guarantee the right to reasonable accommodation.[93]

Despite the absence of a unified anti-discrimination law in Uzbekistan, as well as the lack of ratification of ILO Convention 190, sexual harassment was criminalized

---

88 Dikman et al. (2009, p. 25).

89 Paragraph (2022).

90 International Labour Organization (2024a).

91 Kazakhstan International Bureau of Human Rights and Rule of Law (2024).

92 Commissioner for Human Rights in the Republic of Kazakhstan (2024).

93 Legal Media Center (2024).

in 2023. According to the Criminal Code, sexual harassment is the commission of a single rude or repeated action of a sexual nature against a person that is undesirable for him and humiliates his honour and dignity, expressed in a description of his appearance or physique, gestures, touching, provocation, or having a sexual inclination.[94]

Kazakhstan and Turkmenistan remain the countries without legal definitions of harassment and sanctions for this form of discrimination.

In sum, the situation with employment discrimination in Central Asia demonstrates progressive trends and achievements in comparison with other fields in the human rights dimension. Nevertheless, the practical implementation of anti-discrimination initiatives is still poor and requires the development of more effective law enforcement mechanisms.

9.4 Labour Inspections Activities

It is well known that labour inspections play a significant role in the implementation of labour legislation and the protection of workers' rights.

Considering that the violation of occupational safety and health (OSH) legal requirements often leads to accidents at work,[95] labour inspection is understood as an important instrument to promote the fundamental right to a safe and healthy working environment and, in this way, to prevent occupational accidents and diseases. Labour inspectorates play a central, indispensable, and critical role in the improvement of the working conditions at workplaces[96] by enforcing the law, working in partnership with other actors, and coordinating the implementation and evaluation of policy measures within the framework of a national system.[97]

Labour inspection is one of the core functions of a system of labour administration and has been the subject of international standard-setting since the ILO was founded, with references in the Treaty of Versailles and the ILO Constitution.[98]

The ILO Centenary Declaration for the Future of Work, 2019, underscores the importance of strengthening labour administration and inspection as a key aspect for further developing the ILO's human-centred approach to the future of work.

A recent study by the ILO identified some common challenges in the labour inspection systems of Tajikistan and Uzbekistan, some of which were already noted by the ILO CEACR in 2020 in its General Observation on The Application of The Labour Inspection and Labour Inspection (C81) in Agriculture (C129) Conventions. They include, most especially, the imposition of moratoria on inspection visits,

94 LexUz Online (2023).

95 Frick (2011).

96 Tõsine & Wedege (2013).

97 See Alli (2008), International Labour Organization (2006), International Labour Organization (2007), International Labour Organization (2011), Richthofen (2002), Takala (2005).

98 International Labour Organization (2023c).

including labour inspection visits, which is considered a serious violation of ILO C81 and C129, as well as the imposition of severe restrictions to the powers and activities of labour inspectors, including the limitation of their free initiative to carry out inspection visits, restrictions to their power to conduct inspection visits without previous notice, and limitations on the frequency, duration and scope of inspection visits.[99]

Almost all Central Asian countries have undertaken reforms of state control systems to improve their business climate and international ranking positions.

According to Lyutov and Voitkovska,[100] the primary reason for reform was, in many cases, to reduce the regulatory burden on business, based on the belief this would improve efficiency and make these countries more attractive to investment. It should come as no surprise that reducing costs by weakening protection for workers by limiting the scope of labour rights as well as by removing controls on compliance with established labour standards has resulted in what has been termed a ‘race to the bottom’ between developing countries.

It is especially troubling that, for many of the governments in the region, legislation and enforcement are guided by the priority given to the commercial interests and protection of entrepreneurial rights over the norms of labour legislation and workers’ rights. Labour inspection procedures are limited not by the norms of labour law but by means of business-friendly legislation concerning inspections in general, which take legal precedence over labour law, and labour legislation is applied only if it does not contradict these limiting norms.[101]

It should be noted that the ILO experts conducted an audit of labour inspection activities in Kazakhstan in 2018, which resulted in recommendations to strengthen labour inspection by transferring it to the subordination of the central executive body. In this regard, legislative amendments have been prepared to transfer state labour inspection from local executive bodies to the Ministry.[102] Thus, the most radical reforms were implemented in Kazakhstan in 2018–2022.

The ILO Committee notes with deep concern that the Entrepreneur Code still contains limitations to inspection powers, including with regard to: (i) the ability of labour inspectors to undertake inspection visits without previous notice; (ii) the free initiative of labour inspectors; and (iii) the ability of labour inspectors to carry out any examination, test, or enquiry which they may consider necessary to satisfy themselves that the legal provisions are being strictly observed.[103]

The Committee notes with concern that section 141 of the Entrepreneur Code still states that the frequency of inspections shall be no more than once a year for entities classified as high-risk, no more than once every two years for those of medium risk, and no more than once every three years for those of low risk. The Committee also notes the government’s indication in its report that, as of 1 August 2024, 4245

[99] International Labour Organization (2023c, p. 75).

[100] Voitkovska, Lyutov (2021, p. 271).

[101] Voitkovska, Lyutov (2021, p. 299).

[102] NORMLEX (2024b).

[103] NORMLEX (2024c).

inspections had been conducted, which represents an increase of 7.8 per cent in comparison to 2023. In its observations, the ITUC indicates that restrictions on the frequency and types of labour inspections are still in force. Under the current legislation, the frequency of scheduled inspections depends on the risk category assigned to employers. Consequently, there is no set frequency of inspections for low-risk employers who are, therefore, not subject to scheduled monitoring and inspection activities. The procedure for assessing the risk category assigned to an employer depends, among other criteria, on the number of employees: the higher the number of employees, the higher the probability of increasing the risk category. This reduces the likelihood of inspections of small and medium-sized enterprises, which have a significant risk of abuse by employers.

In Kyrgyzstan, the system of state inspections overseeing compliance with legislation in various areas was reformed in 2012 to reduce budget expenditures and corruption and administrative pressure on entrepreneurs. As a result, the labour inspectorate, which previously existed as an independent body under the Ministry of Labour and Social Development, was merged with several other specialized regulatory bodies within the framework of a single State Inspectorate for Environmental and Technical Safety under the government.[104]

According to the UNDP report, an unscheduled inspection is carried out according to a submitted application, i.e., a person working at the enterprise comes and writes a statement without fail that his legal rights have been infringed on. Based on his application, they receive an order from the Ministry of Economy and conduct an inspection. The outcome of this concludes with a control check. The violations detected during an inspection are addressed, with a follow-up check to determine whether these violations were eliminated and how so. A final report is made on the results of the control check. If a report has been received that an accident has occurred involving a person, the service begins an investigation.[105]

In Tajikistan, the first significant limitation on the activity of labour inspectorates was imposed by the Law of 25 December 2015, No. 1269, ‘On Inspections of Business Entities’ Activities’, which came into force in 2016. The law laid down rules concerning many state monitoring activities, including those of the labour inspectorate. Among other measures, the law introduced a more detailed risk-based approach towards inspections with further limitations on the frequency of inspections. It extended the existing obligation for inspectors to notify employers in advance from three to five working days while introducing additional rules on the limitations of the subject-matter of inspection and the questions contained in checklists, as well as shortening the maximum duration of inspections.[106]

The ILO CEACR expressed deep concern about the moratorium of 2018 and the limitations on the powers of labour inspections as representing serious infringements of the provisions of ILO Convention 81 in its Observations in 2018 and 2019.[107]

---

[104] Ramankulov (2019, p. 106).

[105] United Nations Development Program (2024).

[106] Voitkovska, Lyutov (2021, pp. 277–278).

[107] NORMLEX (2024d).

In Uzbekistan, the Presidential Decree of 2005 limited the power of labour inspectors to impose sanctions. Later, in 2018, there were enforced limitations on unscheduled inspections.[108]

It is thus common for Central Asian countries to breach international standards on labour inspectorates, particularly ILO Conventions 81 and 129.

The ILO has called for the repeal of moratoria on inspection visits and any bans to inspection visits to particular sets of employers or the removal of labour inspections from their scope of application, as well as for countries to refrain from imposing these in the future, entrusting labour inspectors (in law and in practice) with all the powers that they need to effectively discharge their duties; to cease the limitations to the frequency, scope, and duration of inspection visits; and to strengthen the coordination, supervision, and control of the labour inspection system by the central authority, including the consideration of the merger and incorporation of the trade union's labour inspectorate into the state inspectorate. Other ILO recommendations concern the status and conditions of service of the labour inspectors, their number, training, recruitment, performance appraisal, and remuneration, among others.[109]

Therefore, the system of protection of workers' rights has been weakened as a result of economic regulatory reforms and cannot prevent numerous abuses by employers. This situation indicates that states are not adequately fulfilling their social functions and protecting labour relations.

9.5 Conclusion

The study shows evident similarities between labour law and industrial relations systems in Central Asian countries. Firstly, the labour law landscape in the region is largely shaped by the Soviet socialist heritage and, more recently, by the influence of the ILO. Therefore, the main direction of labour law development in the republics tends to follow approaches formed in the industrialized world.

The historical background directly determines the level of industrial relations in all countries of the region. The Central Asian states share a period in history when collective bargaining and freedoms of association were totally eliminated: the Soviet era (1917–1991).

Industrial relations remains the most conservative sector in terms of labour law reforms in the Central Asian countries, and is influenced by the structure of governance and decision-making processes of their non-democratic political regimes.

At the same time, in Kazakhstan, the government has tended to liberalize labour laws significantly in the interest of economic growth and the creation of a favourable business climate. Common features of labour reforms in Kazakhstan are flexibilization and decentralization. Kazakhstan has undertaken a more radical liberalization reform of labour regulations, which has significantly affected the contours of

[108] Voitkovska, Lyutov (2021, p. 283).

[109] International Labour Organization (2023c, p. 75).

labour law; however, this has not been passed with extensive discussion. The current tendency exists due to an imbalance between employers and employee interests and bargaining powers. The removal of the right to strike from the new Constitution may further undermine the position of trade unions in defending the interests of workers. Nevertheless, emphasizing the role of bilateral relations between employer and employee representatives through state regulation has not reduced the significance and position of the government in tripartite bargaining. State authorities still promote and control national, sectoral, and regional agreements.

In contrast, the reform processes in Kyrgyzstan and Uzbekistan have followed a longer-term, more cautious, gradual route.

In all countries, collective agreements have a direct and binding effect on individual relationships between employers and employees and do not require the introduction of their provisions into employment contracts.

This model of collective bargaining constitutes an integral part of a tripartite partnership, covering all the matters concerning industrial relations (namely, social partnership).

The favourability principle for workers exists in all five countries, providing that any provisions of agreements or contracts (local acts) worsening employee rights and interests in comparison with the labour legislation shall be recognized as void and shall not be applied.

In sum, it seems clear that the complex picture of labour law reform in Central Asia has resulted from a mix of legal change, political resistance, and international pressure. The region remains significantly behind international labour standards, especially regarding freedom of association, labour inspections, and anti-discrimination enforcement. While reforms have occurred, they are often shaped by non-democratic governance structures and external economic interests rather than domestic rights-based advocacy. The literature suggests that any sustainable improvement in labour rights must be tied to broader political liberalization and institutional development.

References

24.kg (2021) Садыр Жапаров в третий раз отклонил закон о профсоюзах [Sadyr Japarov rejected the law on trade unions for the third time]. https://24.kg/vlast/216156_sadyir_japarov_vtretiy_raz_otklonil_zakon_oprofsoyuzah. Accessed on 25 March 2025

24.kg (2024) New labor code developed in Kyrgyzstan. https://24.kg/english/263395_New_Labor_Code_developed_in_Kyrgyzstan. Accessed on 25 March 2025

Abdulloeva N (2021) The right to strike in the public sector—Tajikistan. Country Fact Sheet. Edited by Markhaba Khalmurzaeva. European Public Service Union (EPSU). https://www.epsu.org/sites/default/files/article/files/Tajikistan%20-%20the%20right%20to%20strike%20in%20the%20public%20sector%202021.pdf

Adilet (2014) The law of the republic of Kazakhstan on trade unions. https://adilet.zan.kz/rus/docs/Z1400000211. Accessed on 10 Apr 2025

Adilet (2015a) Labour code of the republic of Kazakhstan. https://adilet.zan.kz/eng/docs/K1500000414. Accessed on 15 March 2025

Adilet (2015b) Constitutional law of the republic of Kazakhstan on Astana international financial centre. http://adilet.zan.kz/eng/docs/Z1500000438. Accessed on 16 March 2025

Alli B (2008) Fundamental principles of occupational health and safety, 2nd edn. International Labour Office

Anti-Discrimination Center (2021) Kazakhstan's list of "banned professions" for women to be abolished as of october 23, 2021. https://adcmemorial.org/en/news/kazakhstans-list-of-banned-professions-for-women-to-be-abolished-as-of-october-23-2021/. Accessed on 14 Apr 2024

Anti-Discrimination Center (2024a) The draft of the new Labour Code of Kyrgyzstan proposes to revise the prohibition of 446 professions for women. https://adcmemorial.org/en/news/the-draft-of-the-new-labour-code-of-kyrgyzstan-proposes-to-revise-the-prohibition-of-446-profes sions-for-women. Accessed on 14 Apr 2024

Anti-Discrimination Center (2024b) Tajikistan has reduced the list of professions prohibited to women. https://adcmemorial.org/en/news/tajikistan-has-reduced-the-list-of-professions-prohib ited-to-women/. Accessed on 14 April 2024

Anti-Discrimination Center (2024c) The UN CEDAW recommends Turkmenistan to provide equal opportunities for women in employment. https://adcmemorial.org/en/news/the-un-cedaw-rec ommends-turkmenistan-to-provide-equal-opportunities-for-women-in-employment/. Accessed on 14 Apr 2024

Anti-Discrimination Center (2024d) Uzbekistan has improved legislation on accessibility of the transport sector for women's employment. https://adcmemorial.org/en/news/uzbekistan-has-improved-legislation-on-accessibility-of-the-transport-sector-for-womens-employment/. Accessed on 14 Apr 2024

Asia—Plus (2016) Кодекс без широких обсуждений, или Когда размер не меняет суть [Code without broad discussions, or When size does not change the essence]. https://www.asiapl ustj.info/ru/news/tajikistan/society/20160702/kodeks-bez-shirokikh-obsuzhdenii-ili-kogda-raz mer-ne-menyaet-sut. Accessed on 5 Apr 2025

Bronstein A (2009) International and comparative labour law: Current challenges. International Labour Office

Centralized Data Bank of Legal Information of Kyrgyz Republic (2025) Labour code of the Kyrgyz Republic. https://cbd.minjust.gov.kg/3-45/edition/25298/ru. Accessed on 24 March 2025

Centralized Data Bank of Legal Information of the Kyrgyz Republic (1998) Law of the Kyrgyz republic on trade unions. https://cbd.minjust.gov.kg/4-125/edition/1250107/ru. Accessed on 10 Apr 2025

Commissioner for Human Rights in the Republic of Kazakhstan (2024) Уполномоченному по.правам человека представили промежуточные результаты исследования по противодействию дискриминации [The Human Rights Commissioner was presented with the interim results of the study on combating discrimination]. https://www.gov.kz/mem leket/entities/ombudsman/press/news/details/895550?lang=ru. Accessed on 12 Apr 2025

Continent Online (2009) Labour code of Turkmenistan. https://continent-online.com/Document/?doc_id=31348675#pos=15;-148. Accessed on 28 March 2025

Continent Online (2011) The law of the republic of Tajikistan on trade unions. https://continent-onl ine.com/Document/?doc_id=31051157#sub_id=380000. Accessed on 10 Apr 2025

Continent Online (2013) The law of Turkmenistanon trade unions, their rights and guarantees of activities. https://continent-online.com/Document/?doc_id=31473122. Accessed on 10 Apr 2025

Continent Online (2016) Labour code of the republic of Tajikistan. https://continent-online.com/Document/?doc_id=31960488. Accessed on 26 March 2025

Dikman S, Zhavoronkov R, Kudryavtseva O, Maranov R, Osipov A, Soboleva A, Timofeev M (2009) Защита личности от дискриминации: методические рекомендации для преподавателя [Protecting the individual from discrimination: methodological recommendations for teachers]. Novaya Justicia, Moscow

Dugarova E (2016) A new social protection model in the CIS countries: From social assistance to labour activation. In: International symposium 'social protection systems—Tying the knots', Bonn. https://www.researchgate.net/publication/307957025_A_new_social_protection_model_in_the_CIS_countries_from_social_assistance_to_labour_activation

Equality Now (2025) Kyrgyzstan lifts professional bans for women. https://equalitynow.org/news_and_insights/kyrgyzstan-lifts-professional-bans-for-women/. Accessed on 5 Apr 2025

Frick K (2011) Worker influence on voluntary OHS management systems—A review of its ends and means. Saf Sci 49(7):974–987

Grata International (2022) The labor code of the republic of Uzbekistan has been adopted in a new edition. https://gratanet.com/news/the-labor-code-of-the-republic-of-uzbekistan-has-been-adopted-in-a-new-edition. Accessed on 27 March 2025

IndustriALL Global Union (2021) Kyrgyzstan: New law on trade unions must comply with international labour standards. https://www.industriall-union.org/kyrgyzstan-new-law-on-trade-unions-must-comply-with-international-labour-standards Accessed on 27 March 2025

International Labour Organization (2006) Strategies and practice for labour inspection. International Labour Office

International Labour Organization (2007) Safe and healthy workplaces—Making decent work a reality. International Labour Office

International Labour Organization (2011) Labour administration and labour inspection, Report V to the 100th session of the international labour conference. International Labour Office

International Labour Organization (2021) Обзор национального законодательства и политики, связанных с охраной материнства и с работниками с семейными обязанностями [Review of national legislation and policy, related to maternity protection and with workers with family responsibilities]. ILO, Geneva, 2021

International Labour Organization (2022) High-level independent evaluation of ILO'S programme of work in Central Asia, 2018–2022. International Labour Office

International Labour Organization (2023a) ILO constituents to address root causes of gender inequality and discrimination in Uzbekistan. https://www.ilo.org/projects-and-partnerships/projects/rise-for-impact. Accessed on 31 March 2025

International Labour Organization (2023b) RISE for impact: Fundamental principles and rights at work in the cotton supply chain—A new phase, A new vision. https://www.ilo.org/projects-and-partnerships/projects/rise-for-impact. Accessed on 29 March 2025

International Labour Organization (2023c) Improving labour inspection system in Tajikistan and Uzbekistan through SSTC knowledge-sharing and peer-learning. ILO Decent Work Technical Support Team and Country Office for Eastern Europe and Central Asia. https://southsouthpoint.net/2023/08/10/improving-labour-inspection-system-in-tajikistan-and-uzbekistan-through-sstc-knowledge-sharing-and-peerlearning/

International Labour Organization (2024a) Kyrgyz parliament and ILO collaborate to implement the ILO convention on violence and harassment. https://www.ilo.org/resource/news/kyrgyz-parliament-and-ilo-collaborate-implement-ilo-convention-violence-and. Accessed on 29 March 2025

International Labour Organization (2024b) National social dialogue institutions in selected countries of Central Asia and the southern Caucasus closing the knowledge gap. Technical brief. International Labour Office

International Labour Organization (2024c) Observation of the Committee of Experts on the Application of Conventions and Recommendations (CEACR) on Tajikistan's implementation of Equal Remuneration Convention, 1951 (No. 100), 112nd ILC session. https://normlex.ilo.org/dyn/nrmlx_en/f?p=NORMLEXPUB:13100:0::NO::P13100_COMMENT_ID%2CP13100_LANG_CODE:4363959%2Cen

International Labour Organization (2024d) Observance of recruitment and working conditions in the cotton harvest in Turkmenistan. ILO, Geneva. https://www.ilo.org/sites/default/files/2025-03/2024%20Observance%20of%20recruitment%20in%20the%20cotton%20harvest%20in%20Turkmenistan.pdf

International Labour Organization (2025) Successful presentation on independent monitoring of 2024 cotton harvest held in Tashkent. https://www.ilo.org/resource/news/successful-presentation-independent-monitoring-2024-cotton-harvest-held. Accessed on 31 March 2025

International Trade Union Confederation (2024a) Global rights index. https://www.ituc-csi.org/global-rights-index. Accessed on 30 March 2025

International Trade Union Confederation (2024b) Kazakhstan: ITUC demands social dialogue and dropping of sanctions against striking workers. https://www.ituc-csi.org/Kazakhstan-ITUC-demands-sanctions-dropped. Accessed on 28 March 2025

International Trade Union Monitoring Mission on Labour Rights in Central Asia (2021) Final document fifth coordination meeting of the international labour rights monitoring mission for Central Asia. https://labourmission.org/en/news/final-document-fifth-coordination-meeting-international-labour-rights-monitoring-mission-for-central-asia/?sphrase_id=5787. Accessed on 26 March 2025

International Trade Union Monitoring Mission on Labour Rights in Central Asia (2024a) Civil society inside and outside Turkmenistan: Searching for meaningful engagement in the interest of the Turkmen public. https://labourmission.org/en/news/civil-society-inside-and-outside-turkmenistan-searching-for-meaningful-engagement-in-the-interest-of-the-turkmen-public/?f=9QpLXdfW. Accessed on 2 Apr 2025

International Trade Union Monitoring Mission on Labour Rights in Central Asia (2024b) Crackdown on civic freedoms in Central Asia: NGOs highlight alarming trend. https://labourmission.org/en/news/crackdown-on-civic-freedoms-in-central-asia-ngos-highlight-alarming-trend/. Accessed on 26 March 2025

Ismailov S (2023) Labour code of the republic of Uzbekistan: The law behind the practice is being improved. Galaxy Int Interdiscip Res J 11(8):376–380

Kahn-Freund O (1974) On uses and misuses of comparative law. Mod Law Rev 37(1):8–20

Kazakhstan International Bureau of Human Rights and Rule of Law (2024) Антидискриминационное законодательство в РК: предпосылки созданы, пути намечены [Anti-discrimination legislation in the Republic of Kazakhstan: prerequisites created, paths outlined]. https://bureau.kz/novosti/antidiskriminaczionnoe-zakonodatelstvo/. Accessed on 12 April 2025

Kemelbayeva S, Ospanov A (2024) Гендерная экономика: Что мы знаем о мире и Казахстане? [gender economics: What do we know about the world and Kazakhstan?]. MIND Analytical Report. Maqsut Narikbayev University, Astana, p 7

Khamzina Z, Buribayev Y, Taitorina B, Yessengazieva A, Kuttygalieva A (2022) Towards nondiscrimination and gender equality: The role of international labor standards. Sustainability, MDPI 14(9):1–14

Khassenov (2021) Профсоюзы Казахстана: проблемы и возможности [Trade unions in Kazakhstan: challenges and opportunities]. Research paper. Friedrich Ebert Foundation, Astana

Khassenov M (2015) Flexibilization of labour in Kazakhstan: New legal framework and institutional decisions. E-J Int Comp Labour Stud 5(1):130–139

Khassenov M (2022) Collective bargaining Systems in Germany and Kazakhstan. In: Central Asian yearbook of international law and international relations, Vol 1. Eleven.

Khassenov (2023) Трудовое право Республики Казахстан. В 3 томах. Том 1. Общая часть. Учебник [Labour Law of the Republic of Kazakhstan. In 3 volumes. Volume 1. General Part.]. Textbook, Smart University Press, Astana

Legal Media Center (2024) Закон о недискриминации предлагают принятьв Казахстане [Non-discrimination law proposed to be adopted in Kazakhstan]. https://lmc.kz/ru/news/zakon-o-nediskriminacii-predlagayut-prinyat-v-kazahstane. Accessed on 12 Apr 2025

LexUz Online (2019) Law of the republic of Uzbekistan on trade unions.. https://lex.uz/ru/docs/4631283. Accessed on 10 April 2025

LexUz Online (2022) Labour code of the republic of Uzbekistan. https://lex.uz/ru/docs/6257291. Accessed on 27 March 2025

LexUz Online (2023) The Law of the Republic of Uzbekistan on amendments and additions to some legislative acts of the Republic of Uzbekistan in connection with the further improvement of the system of reliable protection of the rights, freedoms and legitimate interests of women and children. https://www.lex.uz/acts/111457. Accessed on 11 Apr 2025

Lipovka A (2016) Гендерный потенциал экономики Казахстана в условиях глобальных изменений [Gender potential of the economy of Kazakhstan in the context of global changes]. Turan Univ Bull 4(72):205–211

Lyutov N (2024) Свобода объединения в Казахстане: есть ли надежда на сближение с международными трудовыми стандартами [Freedom of association in Kazakhstan: Is there hope for convergence with international labor standards]. Law State 4(105):43–53

Ministry of Labour and Social Protection of the Republic of Kazakhstan (2023) О принимаемых мерах по охране труда в Казахстане [On the measures taken for labor protection in Kazakhstan]. https://www.gov.kz/memleket/entities/enbek/press/news/details/656807?lang=ru. Accessed on 12 Apr 2025

Ministry of Labour and Social Protection of the Republic of Kazakhstan (2025) Отчет о реализации плана развития Министерства труда и социальной защиты населения Республики Казахстан на 2023–2027 годы за 2024 год [2024 Report on the implementation of the development plan of the Ministry of Labor and Social Protection of the Population of the Republic of Kazakhstan for 2023–2027]. https://www.gov.kz/memleket/entities/enbek/documents/details/798838. Accessed on 12 Apr 2025

Mukhamadiyeva G, Kalkayeva N, Bopabaev E, Sailibayeva Z, Khamzina Z, Buribayev Y (2019) Evolution of labor law in Kazakhstan: Overview and commentary on regulatory objectives and development. J Adv Res Law Econ 9(38):2664–2674

NORMLEX (2017) Information system on international labour standards. Committee on freedom of association (CFA), Case No 3283 (Kazakhstan)—Complaint date: 17-MAY-17. International Trade Union Confederation (ITUC)

NORMLEX (2020) Information system on international labour standards. Committee on freedom of association (CFA), effect given to the recommendations of the committee and the governing body—report no 392, October 2020. Case no 3283 (Kazakhstan)—Complaint date: 17-MAY-17—Follow-up

NORMLEX (2022) Information system on international labour standards. Observation (CEACR)—Adopted 2022, published 111st ILC session (2023). Freedom of association and protection of the right to organise convention, 1948 (no. 87)—Turkmenistan

NORMLEX (2024a) Information system on international labour standards. Observation (CEACR)—Adopted 2023, published 112nd ILC session (2024). Equal remuneration convention, 1951 (no. 100)—Tajikistan

NORMLEX (2024b) Information system on international labour standards. Observation (CEACR) adopted 2018, published 108th ILC session (2019) Labour Inspection Convention, 1947 (No. 81), Tajikistan (Ratification: 2009). ILO Normlex Database; Observation (CEACR) adopted 2019, published 109th ILC session (2021) Labour Inspection Convention, 1947 (No. 81)—Tajikistan

NORMLEX (2024c) Information system on international labour standards. Committee on freedom of association (CFA), case no 3487 (Uzbekistan)—Complaint date: 29-NOV-24. International Union of Food, agricultural, hotel, restaurant, catering, tobacco and allied workers' associations (IUF)

NORMLEX (2024d) Information system on international labour standards. Observation (CEACR)—Adopted 2024, published 113rd ILC session (2025). Labour inspection convention, 1947 (no. 81)—Tajikistan

Nurgaliyeva Y, Khassenov M (2023) Labour law and industrial relations in Kazakhstan. In: Hendrickx F (ed) International encyclopedia for labour law and industrial relations. Kluwer Law International, The Hague

OECD (2017) Building inclusive labour Markets in Kazakhstan: A focus on youth, older workers and people with disabilities. OECD Publishing, Paris, pp 83–84

Open Democracy (2021) Redefining 'women's work' in Kazakhstan. https://www.opendemocracy.net/en/odr/redefining-womens-work-in-kazakhstan/. Accessed on 12 Apr 2025

Paragraph (2022) *Law on equality and eliminating all forms of discrimination*. https://online.zakon.kz/Document/?doc_id=35098909. Accessed on 12 Apr 2025

Ramankulov K (2019) Проблемы трудового законодательства Кыргызской Республики в контексте современных реформ и международных трудовых стандартов [problems of labor legislation of the Kyrgyz Republic in the context of modern reforms and international labor standards]//Вестник Тюменьского государственного университета. Социально-Экономические И Правовые Исследования [Bulletin Tyumen State University Socio-Econ Leg Res] 5(1):103–120

Richthofen W (2002) Labour inspection: A guide to the profession. International Labour Office

Roshchin S, Yemelina N (2020) Gender differentiation in wages in Kazakhstan. Higher school of economics research paper no. WP BRP 240/EC/2020, pp 2, 20

Sayapin S (2023) Human rights in Central Asia—Challenges and perspectives. In: Mihr A, Wittke C (eds) Human rights dissemination in Central Asia. Springer briefs in political science. Springer, Cham, pp 15–29

Sulaymanov O, Rasulov J (2021) Abolition of forced labour: Case of Uzbekistan. Turk J Comput Math Educ 12(4):1078–1089

Takala J (2005) Introductory report: Decent work—Safe work. International Labour Office

Tõsine H, Wedege N (2013) Measuring performance of the occupational safety and health function—A handbook for labour inspectorates. International Association of Labour Inspection (IALI)

Turkmen News and The Turkmen Initiative for Human Rights (2023) Time For Change: Forced Labor in Turkmenistan Cotton 2022. https://tuatara-jaguar-29pr.squarespace.com/s/Forced_labor_Turkmenistan_2023_report-_LR.pdf

United Nations Development Program (2024) Contribution of the ministry of labor to the agenda of business and human rights. https://www.undp.org/kyrgyzstan/stories/contribution-ministry-labor-agenda-business-and-human-rights. Accessed on 27 March 2025

Uzbek Forum for Human Rights (2024) Uzbek cotton harvest 2023. Risk of forced labour remains high: Government officials use coercion to address shortage of pickers. Berlin.

Voitkovska I, Lyutov N (2021) Labour inspections in post-soviet countries: Reform or collapse? Int J Comp Labour Law Ind RelatS 37:269–300

Part V
International Criminal Law

Chapter 10
Uzbekistan's Experience in Combating Money Laundering

Farkhod Fazilov

Abstract This is an in-depth study within a larger work, focusing on the challenges of adapting criminal law norms to contemporary contexts. It specifically addresses the criminal liability associated with the legalization of illicitly gained revenue. The chapter critically examines Article 243 of the Uzbekistan Criminal Code, shedding light on judicial practices and legislative responses to these challenges. Its innovative approach offers fresh insights into the theory of criminalization and the practical application of criminal law in Uzbekistan, making it an essential read for researchers, legal practitioners, students, and anyone interested in the complexities of criminal law and efforts to combat the legalization of criminal proceeds.

Keywords Anti-Money Laundering (AML) legislation · money laundering · crime · predicate offenses · criminal law · criminal liability · legalization of criminal proceeds

10.1 The Fundamental Concept and Origins of Money Laundering Activities

10.1.1 Combating Money Laundering: A Strategic Approach to Legislative and Institutional Development in Uzbekistan

The legalization of criminal proceeds, commonly referred to as money laundering, represents a multifaceted and systemic phenomenon that requires a comprehensive and well-structured state strategy to effectively combat it. Recognizing the critical importance of this challenge, the Concept for the Improvement of Criminal and Criminal Procedure Legislation of the Republic of Uzbekistan, adopted on May 14, 2018, explicitly tasked state institutions with addressing this issue. This initiative aims

F. Fazilov (✉)
Tashkent State University of Law, Tashkent, Uzbekistan
e-mail: f.fazilov@tsul.uz

S. Sayapin (ed.), *International Law, Politics and Security in Central Asia*,
https://doi.org/10.1007/978-3-032-17818-3_10

to enhance legislative frameworks, strengthen enforcement mechanisms, and align domestic regulations with international standards to effectively deter and counter money laundering activities.

In line with the provisions of the document, it is imperative to conduct a thorough inventory of criminal legislation to ensure its unification and alignment with advanced international standards and best practices from foreign jurisdictions. This process is particularly critical for addressing transnational crimes, including money laundering, which involves the legalization of proceeds derived from criminal activities. By harmonizing domestic laws with global norms, the state aims to enhance its capacity to combat complex and cross-border criminal phenomena effectively.[1]

Since the adoption of the Law of the Republic of Uzbekistan 'On Countering the Legalization of Revenue Received from Criminal Activities, the Financing of Terrorism, and the Financing of the Proliferation of Weapons of Mass Destruction' on August 26, 2004,[2] the country has undertaken significant steps to establish a systematic state framework for combating these offenses. This framework has been designed to align with contemporary international standards, reflecting Uzbekistan's commitment to enhancing its legislative and institutional mechanisms to effectively address money laundering and associated financial crimes. This law serves as the foundation for a comprehensive strategy aimed at safeguarding the integrity of the nation's financial system while fulfilling its international obligations in combating transnational crime.

The law defines the legalization of revenue received from criminal activities as follows:

'Legalization of revenue received from criminal activity is a criminally punishable, socially dangerous act. It involves the transfer, conversion, or exchange of property obtained as a result of criminal activities, as well as the nondisclosure or concealment of the original nature, source, location, method of disposal, movement, or genuine rights related to the property or its ownership, provided that such property was obtained through criminal means.'

This definition underscores the multifaceted nature of the crime, combining both the physical handling of illicitly acquired assets and the deliberate efforts to obscure their unlawful origins. It aligns with international legal standards by emphasizing the socially dangerous nature of money laundering and its role in enabling further criminal activities while integrating illicit proceeds into the legitimate economy.

Under Article 243 of the Criminal Code of the Republic of Uzbekistan,[3] legalization of revenue received from criminal activities is a transfer, conversion, or exchange of property, which has been obtained in result of criminal activities, as well as nondisclosure or concealment of the original nature, source, location, way of disposal, movement, and genuine rights in relation to the property or ownership thereof in the instance if such property has been obtained as a result of criminal activities.

---

[1] LexUz Online 2018.

[2] LexUz Online 2004.

[3] LexUz Online 1994.

The Resolution of the Plenum of the Supreme Court dated February 11, 2011, titled 'On Some Issues of Judicial Practice in Cases on Legalization of Revenue Received from Criminal Activities,' provides a clear interpretation of the concept of legalization. It emphasizes that the legalization of criminal revenue involves the act of giving a legitimate appearance to the origin of property obtained through criminal activities.

In this context, any property recognized under Article 169 of the Civil Code as an object of ownership may qualify as the subject of legalization. Typically, the process of legitimizing such property occurs during financial transactions or other dealings involving money or assets. These activities are intended to obscure the illicit origins of the property and integrate it into lawful economic circulation.

The resolution further clarifies that the concept of 'legalization' is determined by analyzing both the method used to carry out the act and the specific purpose behind it. This dual focus ensures that the legal framework addresses not only the actions involved in concealing illicit proceeds but also the intent to legitimize their criminal origins. This approach aligns with international legal standards and enhances the ability of judicial systems to combat money laundering effectively.

10.1.2 The Dynamics of Money Laundering: Legal Definitions, International Frameworks, and Global Implications

In legal science, it is widely recognized that money laundering is characterized by a core feature: the aim to disguise the illicit origins of criminal proceeds and present them as legitimate income. We fully endorse this perspective, as it underscores the fundamental objective of money laundering processes.[4]

Historically, the term 'money laundering' first emerged in modern legal discourse in the late twentieth century in the United States, specifically in connection with the proceeds of drug trafficking. This initial context highlights the close association between money laundering and transnational organized crime, which continues to be a critical area of focus for contemporary legal and regulatory frameworks.[5]

In international law, the definition of legalization (laundering) of the revenue from criminal activities is given in Article 3 of the UN Vienna Convention against Illicit Traffic in Narcotic Drugs and Psychotropic Substances of December 19, 1988.[6]

The 1988 United Nations Vienna Convention formally recognized money laundering—specifically involving proceeds from drug trafficking—as a criminal offense. This landmark international treaty marked a significant step in the global fight against organized crime and established a legal framework for addressing the laundering of illicit funds.

[4] Larichev 2003, p. 100.

[5] Oswald 1997, p. 6.

[6] United Nations 1988.

The proceeds derived from criminal activities serve various purposes, which can be categorized as follows:

1. Covering Current Expenses: Supporting the operational costs of ongoing criminal enterprises.
2. Accumulation: Building reserves of illicit funds for future use.
3. Expansion of Criminal Activities: Financing the growth and diversification of illegal operations.
4. Investment in the Legal Economy: Introducing illicit funds into legitimate businesses or financial systems to create the illusion of legality and generate further profits.

This multifaceted use of criminal proceeds underscores the importance of robust legal and regulatory measures to identify, trace, and disrupt money laundering schemes, which often bridge the gap between the illicit and legitimate economies.

Considering these factors, the process of money laundering is a highly lucrative and efficient criminal enterprise. Within the framework of criminal law doctrine, the key characteristics of money laundering are identified as follows: the commission of a predicate offense, the legitimization and concealment of the illicit origins of proceeds, the creation of an appearance of legitimacy, and the subsequent integration of these proceeds into lawful business activities. This multifaceted approach underscores the sophistication of money laundering schemes and their capacity to undermine the integrity of financial and economic systems.

Bashyan identifies the organized legalization of proceeds from fraud as a specific form of economic criminal deception. This phenomenon encompasses a complex set of interrelated crimes carried out by organized groups, including criminal communities or organizations. It involves financial operations and transactions with money, property, or rights knowingly obtained through fraudulent activities by the offender or associated individuals. The ultimate aim is to confer a legitimate appearance on the possession, use, or disposal of such illicitly acquired assets. Additionally, this classification extends to the individuals orchestrating or participating in these criminal schemes, emphasizing the systematic and structured nature of such operations.[7]

Rustambayev identifies that the assets subject to laundering are those acquired through criminal activities, including theft, smuggling, extortion, illicit trafficking of narcotic drugs and psychotropic substances, arms trafficking, operating and maintaining brothels, and production or distribution of pornographic materials, among others.[8] This perspective is shared by Nematov, who concurs with Rustambayev's assessment.[9]

The Financial Action Task Force (FATF) has established a comprehensive list of predicate offenses associated with money laundering. These offenses encompass a broad spectrum of criminal activities, such as drug trafficking, human trafficking, bribery, fraud, and other illegal endeavors that generate substantial illicit

[7] Bashan 2008, p. 10.

[8] Rustambayev 2016.

[9] Ne'matov 2001, p. 3.

funds. Recognizing these predicate offenses is crucial for implementing effective anti-money laundering measures.

Understanding the range of predicate offenses is essential for developing robust anti-money laundering strategies. By identifying and addressing the underlying criminal activities that generate illicit proceeds, authorities can more effectively disrupt the money laundering process and enhance the integrity of financial systems.

Lavrov approaches the concept of legalization of criminal proceeds from a narrow perspective. He defines it as 'a specific form of participation in criminal activities' which is manifested through financial operations or other transactions involving money or property obtained through illegal means. Furthermore, he emphasizes the utilization of such proceeds in entrepreneurial ventures or other economic activities, underscoring the role of these transactions in integrating illicit funds into the legitimate economy. This interpretation highlights the transactional and economic dimensions of money laundering as a criminal act.[10]

Bukarev contends that the term 'laundering' as employed in international legal instruments to describe this crime is both more precise and appropriate. He critiques the use of the term 'legalization' for criminal proceeds, deeming it a terminological inaccuracy that requires legislative correction. According to Bukarev, 'laundering' should be adopted universally as it represents the most accurate, logical, and widely accepted term within international legal science and practice. This distinction reflects the need for consistency and clarity in legal terminology to better align domestic law with global standards.[11]

The opposite position is taken by Bosholov, who believes that the term 'laundering' should be excluded from the law as an unnecessary and disorienting practice.[12]

The German scholar Kerner defines money laundering as 'a set of operations aimed at concealing or obscuring the existence, origin, or intended purpose of material assets derived from criminal activity during the initial stage, with the ultimate goal of enabling the generation of regular income from these assets in subsequent stages.' This definition emphasizes the dual-stage process of money laundering, highlighting both the masking of illicit origins and the integration of such assets into legitimate economic activities to yield continuous profits.[13]

Scholar Bear defines money laundering as 'the process of converting illicitly obtained cash into another asset, obscuring the true origin or ownership of the property from which the funds were unlawfully acquired, and creating the appearance of legitimacy for both the source and the property.' This definition underscores the transformative and deceptive nature of money laundering, which aims to disguise the illegal origins of assets while integrating them into the legitimate economy.[14]

---

[10] Lavrov 2000, p. 39.

[11] Bukarev 2006, p. 154.

[12] Boskholov 2005, p. 38.

[13] Kerner & Dakh 1996, p. 6.

[14] Beare 1990, p.11.

German experts have made significant contributions to the discourse on combating money laundering, and their perspectives are often difficult to dispute. Kottke, for example, defines 'dirty' money by identifying its primary sources of acquisition, which he categorizes into two main domains: general criminal activities and tax-related offenses. He further asserts that the methods of laundering, despite their variations, represent cohesive and integral processes. This approach highlights the systemic nature of money laundering and the need for a comprehensive understanding of its mechanisms to effectively counter it.[15]

The legalization of criminal proceeds is often intertwined with the continuation and expansion of criminal activities, as highlighted in scientific literature. Notably, Aliyev observes that approximately one-third of illicit revenues are reinvested into the development of illegal enterprises, effectively sustaining and expanding unlawful operations. Additionally, around one-fifth of these proceeds are allocated to the acquisition of assets, further embedding the criminal gains into tangible property and potentially serving as a mechanism for laundering funds. This dual-purpose use of criminal proceeds highlights the complex strategies employed by offenders to perpetuate and legitimize their activities.[16]

This staged complex understanding of money laundering is also found in the model adopted by the FATF: phase 1—introduction of 'dirty money' into legal circulation; phase 2—dissolution of illegal funds in the legal flow; phase 3—investment in legitimate business.[17]

10.1.3 The Evolution of Money Laundering: Historical Roots, Legal Frameworks, and Modern Challenges

In academic literature, money laundering is often referred to as the 'dark side of globalization' or the 'illicit facet of the global economy.'[18] These descriptions emphasize its pervasive and transnational nature, fueled by the interconnectedness of global markets. Furthermore, money laundering is frequently characterized as a high-tech crime, leveraging sophisticated methods and technologies to obscure the origins of illicit funds and integrate them into legitimate financial systems. This perspective highlights the complexity of combating money laundering in a rapidly evolving globalized and digitized economic landscape.

In our view, a broader interpretation of the concept of legalization is more accurate, as reflected in the works of domestic scholars. A historical analysis of the practice of legalization reveals that attempts to obscure the criminal origins of wealth date back to ancient times. Offenders apprehended with stolen goods often sought to justify their possession by claiming lawful acquisition.

---

[15] Kottke 2005, p.14.

[16] Aliev 2001, p.6.

[17] Ivanov 2004.

[18] Dalla Chiesa 2012, p.11.

For instance, the laws of the Babylonian King Hammurabi (1792–1750 BCE) established procedures to verify the legitimacy of an item's origin, requiring the owner to provide testimony demonstrating good-faith acquisition. Similarly, legal principles addressing the verification of property origins were embedded in the *Arthashastra* of Kautilya in Ancient India (321–297 BCE) and the Laws of Solon in Ancient Greece (594–593 BCE). These historical precedents underscore the enduring challenge of countering the concealment of illicitly acquired assets, which continues to be a focus of modern legal systems.

However, until the twentieth century, the concept of legalizing criminal proceeds was absent from legislative frameworks, indicating that this socially dangerous phenomenon—centered on skillfully concealing the illicit origins of assets or funds—had not yet evolved into its modern form. This can be attributed to the underdevelopment of economic systems, the predominance of simplistic market structures, and the relatively low profitability of criminal activities during earlier periods.

In such contexts, the accumulation of substantial sums of money from unknown sources was rare and quickly attracted the attention of state authorities, often serving as a trigger for investigations. The absence of sophisticated economic mechanisms and financial instruments limited opportunities for integrating illicit proceeds into legitimate economic channels, thereby reducing the need for systematic legalization processes as understood today.

Article XLIII of the *Constitutio Criminalis Carolina* (1532 CE), titled 'Sufficient Suspicion of Theft,' introduced provisions for verifying the legal origin of property, placing the burden of proof on the suspect. The article states:

'If stolen property is found or discovered on a suspect, and if they possessed it in whole or in part, sold it, exchanged it, or gave it away, this constitutes sufficient evidence of a crime against them unless they can provide information on the source from whom they purchased or acquired the property. Furthermore, they must prove that the acquisition occurred not through criminal or punishable means but in good faith.'

This early legal precedent highlights a systematic approach to addressing the concealment of stolen property, emphasizing the necessity for suspects to substantiate the legitimacy of their possessions. Such provisions reflect the foundational principles of property law and the early efforts to combat the laundering of illicitly obtained assets.[19]

A retrospective analysis of criminal legislation addressing the legalization of proceeds derived from criminal activities reveals that, prior to the independence of the Republic of Uzbekistan, such offenses were not explicitly codified in the Criminal Codes of the Uzbek SSR. This absence reflects the historical context, where the legal and economic systems of the time were not structured to address complex financial crimes like money laundering. The underdeveloped financial infrastructure and limited market mechanisms during the Soviet era likely contributed to the lack of specific legislative provisions targeting the concealment and integration of illicitly obtained assets into the legitimate economy. This legislative gap underscores

[19] Krasheninnikova et al. 2017.

the need for comprehensive reforms in the post-independence period to align with international standards and effectively combat modern financial crimes.

This is primarily due to the fact that in the international legal arena, the concept of legalization of revenue from criminal activities appeared for the first time in the UN Convention 'On Combating the Illicit Transport of Drugs and Psychotropic Substances' only in 1988.

While the Soviet government had abolished private property, there was a rule in the Criminal Code of the Uzbek SSR of 1926 that to some extent similarly covered the laundering of illegally obtained income.

The Criminal Code of 1959 introduced a more generalized provision, stipulating penalties for the acquisition or sale of property knowingly obtained as a result of a criminal offense. This rule primarily addressed items associated with socialist property, often acquired through acts such as theft or other criminal offenses, including illegal logging or smuggling.

However, the application of this norm was inherently challenging as it required the establishment of the elements of the original crime through which the property was acquired. This dependency on proving the predicate offense significantly complicated the enforcement of the provision as it necessitated comprehensive evidence linking the suspect's actions to the prior unlawful act. Such limitations highlighted the need for more precise legal frameworks to address the complexities of criminal activities involving illicit property.[20]

In the Criminal Code of the Uzbek SSR of 1926, Chap. I, titled 'State Crimes,' included provisions analogous to the modern concept of concealing or misrepresenting illicitly acquired property. Specifically, Articles 81, 82, and 83 addressed offenses such as:

1. Concealment of Inherited or Donated Property**:** This includes acts of hiding property received through inheritance or donation, either in full or in part, or artificially reducing the property's value to circumvent laws on inheritance, donations, or related taxes.
2. Concealment or Misrepresentation of Taxable Items or Products**:** This involved organized efforts by mutual agreement to hide or falsify the quantities of goods or products subject to taxation or mandatory reporting.
3. Land Reform Related Concealment or Embezzlement**:** This included the concealment or inaccurate reporting of land size, livestock, and agricultural equipment during land reforms aimed at confiscation or forced redemption. It also addressed the theft or embezzlement of property already documented by local land commissions.

These norms highlight an early recognition of property-related offenses that involved misrepresentation or concealment, which can be seen as precursors to modern provisions addressing money laundering and the legal obfuscation of illicit property. While these provisions primarily aimed to protect state property and enforce tax and

[20] Radchenko et al. 1994.

land reform laws, they reveal a foundational approach to tackling crimes involving concealment and misrepresentation of assets.

In the Criminal Code of 1959, provisions addressing crimes analogous to modern money laundering were found in Chapters III-IV, titled 'Crimes Against Socialist Property' and 'Crimes Against the Personal Property of Citizens.'

Relevant articles include Article 121 on the 'Acquisition or sale of property knowingly obtained by criminal means, if the property belongs to the state or public entities,' and Article 132 on the 'Acquisition or sale of property knowingly obtained by criminal means, if the property has personal property rights.'

A comparison of the 1926 and 1959 editions of the Criminal Code reveals a shift in how such crimes were categorized and understood. In the 1926 Criminal Code, offenses akin to money laundering were classified as 'crimes against the management order,' emphasizing regulatory and administrative violations. By contrast, the 1959 edition placed greater focus on the property and economic dimensions of these crimes, recognizing their impact on socialist and personal property rights.

This evolution in classification reflects a growing awareness of the economic implications of property-related crimes. It also highlights a shift in legislative priorities, moving from administrative concerns to safeguarding economic systems. This approach continued to shape the treatment of such offenses in subsequent editions of the Criminal Code, aligning with the broader development of economic and criminal law.

In the USSR, where the market economy was reduced to a minimum, the legalization of criminal revenue was almost impossible, which significantly hindered the growth of economic crimes.[21]

In the Criminal Code of 1994, the offense of legalizing revenue from criminal activities was explicitly addressed in Article 243. Initially, this provision defined the crime as follows: 'Legalization of revenue received from criminal activities, which includes the transfer, transformation, or exchange of property obtained through criminal means, as well as the concealment or disguise of the true nature, source, location, disposition, movement, or actual rights associated with such property or its assets, provided that the property was obtained through criminal activities.'

This definition reflects a significant step forward in recognizing money laundering as a distinct and complex crime. By detailing both the acts of handling illicitly acquired property and the methods used to obscure its criminal origins, the article aligns with international standards in combating money laundering. The comprehensive nature of this provision highlights the growing importance of addressing the financial dimensions of crime and preventing the integration of illegal proceeds into legitimate economic systems.[22]

Article 243 of the Criminal Code of the Republic of Uzbekistan underwent significant revision with the adoption of Law No. 223 on September, 2009. The updated wording of the article refined the definition of the offense, stating:

---

[21] Ne'matov 2002, p. 162.

[22] LexUz Online 1994.

'Legalization of revenue received from criminal activities is the transfer, conversion, or exchange of property obtained as a result of criminal activities, as well as the nondisclosure or concealment of the original nature, source, location, method of disposal, movement, or genuine rights related to the property or its ownership, provided that such property has been obtained as a result of criminal activities.'

This amendment emphasized the broader scope of actions that constitute money laundering, reflecting an enhanced understanding of the complexities involved in disguising illicit proceeds. By explicitly including nondisclosure and concealment alongside physical actions like transfer and conversion, the revised article aligns more closely with international frameworks and underscores the importance of addressing both direct and indirect methods of laundering criminal revenues. This change represents a key step in strengthening the legislative foundation for combating financial crimes in Uzbekistan.

The primary goal of the revised version of Article 243 was to clarify that the offense of legalization must involve an attempt to give a legitimate appearance to the origin of illicit property. This distinction enables a clear separation between the simple handling of criminal proceeds and their legalization.

In criminal law theory, it is widely acknowledged that property obtained through criminal means can often be transferred or sold in some manner. However, such actions alone do not necessarily constitute money laundering. For an act to qualify as legalization under Article 243, the subjective intent to create the appearance of legitimacy for the criminal proceeds must be present. Without this specific intent, the actions remain within the realm of ordinary turnover of criminal revenue.

The Resolution of the Plenum of the Supreme Court of the Republic of Uzbekistan, titled 'On Certain Issues of Judicial Practice in Cases on the Legalization of Revenue Received from Criminal Activities' (February 11, 2011), further underscores this distinction. The resolution directs courts to differentiate between acts of legalization and the mere acquisition or sale of property obtained through crime. For instance, the acquisition or sale of stolen property, such as a car, does not constitute legalization if the property is not given the appearance of being legally obtained (e.g., through the use of forged documents like a passport or power of attorney for the car's sale).

This guidance reinforces the importance of establishing the subjective element of intent to legitimize criminal proceeds as a key criterion for distinguishing legalization from other criminal actions.

Depending on the specific circumstances of a case, particularly the intent behind transactions involving stolen property, such actions may be classified differently under the law. For instance, they could be regarded as complicity in theft (participation in the theft of someone else's property), or as acquisition or sale of property obtained by criminal means under Article 171 of the Criminal Code. Additionally, if relevant circumstances exist, such actions may also be classified as forgery of documents.

In conclusion, the process of unifying and aligning national criminal legislation with international standards, while incorporating modern criminal law doctrine, remains a critical priority for improving domestic legal frameworks.

The analysis of national and foreign legislation, international law, and doctrinal studies reveals a significant gap in the conceptual framework of money laundering (legalization of criminal proceeds). A unified definition and classification of this crime have yet to be established. Moreover, there is no consensus on the precise identification of its object and subject, which complicates its effective regulation and enforcement. Addressing these gaps is essential for developing coherent legislation that aligns with global best practices and effectively combats this category of socially dangerous acts.

10.2 Legal Analysis of the Legalization of Revenue Received from Criminal Activities in Uzbekistan

10.2.1 Objective Signs of Money Laundering in Uzbekistan

The defining elements of any crime are its object and its objective side. In the realm of domestic criminal law, the object of a crime is understood as socially significant and valuable relationships that are safeguarded by criminal legislation. These relationships are conceptualized in abstract terms as a purely social category. The commission of a crime disrupts these relationships, either causing or posing the risk of causing significant harm to their integrity and functioning.

From an analytical perspective, this interpretation highlights the central role of the object in distinguishing criminal acts from other forms of social misconduct. By focusing on the social relationships at risk, the law emphasizes the broader societal implications of criminal behavior. This approach aligns with the theoretical foundation of criminal law, which prioritizes the protection of key societal values and norms against actions that threaten their stability and cohesion. The recognition of harm, whether actual or potential, underscores the preventative and protective aims of criminal law in preserving the fabric of society.

The concept of the object of a crime has been interpreted differently by various legal scholars throughout history. For instance, Tagantsev describes the object of a crime as 'a legal norm in its real existence,'[23] while Khvostov argues that a crime infringes upon 'the authority of law and the state,'[24] and Margolin views it as an encroachment on 'the law-enforcement interests of individuals, citizens, society, and the state.'[25]

Some researchers, however, have expressed skepticism about the feasibility of precisely defining the concept of crime and, by extension, its object. This reflects the inherent complexity of identifying and categorizing the abstract and dynamic social relationships that criminal law seeks to protect.

---

[23] Tagantsev (2019)

[24] Khvostov (2016), p.138

[25] Margolin (1907), p.127

During the Soviet period, the object of a crime was predominantly conceptualized as *socialist social relations,* reflecting the ideological framework of the time. This perspective emphasized the protection of collective societal structures aligned with socialist principles, prioritizing state and collective interests over individual concerns.

These diverse interpretations highlight the evolving nature of the object of crime as a legal construct. While earlier theories often focused on abstract legal norms or state authority, contemporary perspectives recognize the object of a crime as socially significant relationships that criminal law protects. This shift underscores the increasing emphasis on the social dimension of legal protections and the adaptability of criminal law to changing societal values and structures.

Lopashenko identifies the object of legalization as social relations rooted in the principle of prohibiting criminal behavior in economic activities. This perspective underscores the legal and societal imperative to prevent the integration of illicit conduct into legitimate economic systems.[26]

Hun aptly emphasizes that recognizing public relations as the object of a crime is essential to understanding its societal danger. Without this recognition, critical questions remain unanswered: *Why is the act socially dangerous? What constitutes its public harm? And why does it necessitate criminal penalties?* These inquiries highlight the centrality of public relations in framing the rationale for criminalization and punishment.[27]

Naumov offers a complementary perspective, defining the object of any crime as public relations—encompassing interests and benefits—protected by criminal law which the crime either harms or poses an immediate threat to harm. This definition connects the harm caused by the crime to the necessity of legal intervention.[28]

In the theory of criminal law, the classification of crime objects traditionally follows a hierarchical framework:

1. General Object: The entirety of social relations protected by the criminal law.
2. Generic Object: A broad category of social relations protected by a specific group of legal norms.
3. Specific Object: A narrower subset of social relations protected by a particular article or set of articles.
4. Direct Object: The specific social relation directly impacted by the crime.

This classification system facilitates a structured analysis of criminal acts, aiding in the identification of the societal values and interests at stake. It also provides a theoretical foundation for assessing the harm and danger posed by various crimes, guiding legislative and judicial responses to criminal behavior.

Mikhailov argues that the direct object of money laundering, or the legalization of funds or property obtained through criminal means, is 'the legally established

[26] Lopashenko 1997, p.177.

[27] Hun 2004.

[28] Naumov 2018, p.98.

procedure for conducting financial transactions and other dealings involving money or property, as well as their use in entrepreneurial or other economic activities.'[29]

This perspective highlights the essence of money laundering as a crime that undermines the integrity of lawful financial and economic systems. By violating the prescribed legal frameworks, such activities distort the transparency and trust that underpin financial transactions and economic operations. Mikhailov's view underscores the critical need to protect these procedural norms, as their disruption not only facilitates further criminality but also erodes the stability of legitimate economic activities.

From this standpoint, money laundering can be seen as a dual-threat offense: it both conceals the origins of illicit proceeds and integrates them into the lawful economy, thereby corrupting the very systems designed to uphold fairness and legality in financial and economic transactions. This interpretation emphasizes the broader societal harm caused by money laundering and reinforces the importance of robust legal measures to prevent such activities.

Aslakhanov offers an intriguing perspective, identifying the direct object of money laundering, or the legalization of criminally acquired funds or property, as 'relations in the sphere of exchange.'[30] This interpretation focuses on the disruption of the economic and financial relationships that underpin the lawful exchange of goods, services, and capital.

Maximov articulates that the direct object of legalization (money laundering) is the *social relations that underpin legal property turnover in general and monetary circulation in particular.* This perspective emphasizes the fundamental role of lawful economic and financial systems in maintaining societal stability and economic fairness.[31]

Analyzing the structure of the crime of money laundering, it is evident that the offense can be qualified based on its objects. Melnikova offers a nuanced approach, noting that 'in some cases, sections are organized by generic object, and within these sections, chapters may be divided by specific object. In other cases, sections are distinguished by a complex or composite object, while chapters are defined by a generic object.'

A complex or composite object is formed by two or more generic objects that are interrelated, creating a cohesive unit of social relations. This classification aligns with the hierarchical division of crime objects into general, integrated, generic, specific, and direct categories. Such a vertical classification is especially appropriate when considering the structure of the Special Part of the Criminal Code, as it facilitates philosophical and logical comparability across criminal law concepts.

In this context, the general object of crime encompasses the entirety of public relations protected by criminal law, while the direct object represents the specific social relation targeted by a particular crime. For the offense of money laundering, this direct object is typically the lawful turnover of property and financial systems.

---

[29] Mikhailov 2002, p.80.

[30] Aslakhanov 1997, p.163.

[31] Gauchman 1998, p.182.

The direct object of this offense is more specific and pertains to public relations within the economic activity of the Republic of Uzbekistan, as well as the public relations ensuring public security. This dual nature highlights the societal and economic harm posed by the act of money laundering, where the infiltration of illicit proceeds undermines both financial stability and public trust in legal institutions.

The model law of the CIS countries, 'On Countering the Legalization (Laundering) of Illegally Obtained Revenue,' provides a comprehensive definition of financial transactions. These include all actions involving financial resources, regardless of their form or method of execution, connected to property rights, payments, or other related operations. Examples encompass import/export and domestic transfer of funds or property; international money transfers; loans and financial investments; non-commercial transfers such as wages, pensions, and inheritances; and transactions involving real estate, securities, or organizational capital investments. This broad definition reflects the complexity and diversity of financial activities potentially exploited for money laundering, capturing both commercial and non-commercial actions across borders.

An examination of foreign legislation reveals varying approaches to defining the object of money laundering offenses. While many jurisdictions recognize financial and economic systems as primary objects of protection, others emphasize the broader societal harm, such as the erosion of trust in public institutions and the rule of law.

The diversity in defining the object of money laundering offenses reflects the nuanced priorities of different legal systems. While Uzbekistan aligns its legal framework with international standards, such as the CIS model law, it also reflects domestic priorities by situating these crimes within the broader context of public security. This dual approach ensures that both the economic and societal impacts of money laundering are addressed, while also facilitating cooperation with global anti-money laundering initiatives.

Rustambayev emphasizes that the objective side of a crime comprises a collection of objective, socially, and legally significant features that define the external manifestation of a socially dangerous act directed against an object protected by criminal law. These features illustrate the degree of public danger posed by the criminal act. This view is supported by other scholars, including Usmonaliev,[32] Kabulov, and Otajonov,[33] who align with Rustambayev's interpretation.

This perspective highlights the critical role of the objective side in criminal law, as it provides a concrete basis for evaluating the harmful effects of the offense. It encompasses elements such as the physical action (or inaction), the causal link between the act and its consequences, and the resulting harm or threat to the protected object. By focusing on these external aspects, the analysis of the objective side enables a structured assessment of criminal behavior and its impact on public and social order.

The alignment of these scholars underscores the importance of this concept in determining the public danger and legal culpability of an offense. It also reflects the broader theoretical framework of criminal law, where the objective side serves as a

[32] Usmonaliev 2005.

[33] Kabulov and Otazhonov Kabulov et al. 2012.

critical component for distinguishing punishable acts from mere moral or social transgressions. This shared understanding contributes to the development of consistent and comprehensive legal practices aimed at addressing socially dangerous conduct.

The objective side of the legalization of revenue received from criminal activities is defined by actions such as the transfer, transformation, or exchange of property obtained through criminal means, as well as the concealment or nondisclosure of the true nature, source, location, disposition, movement, or actual rights associated with such property. These actions collectively aim to obscure the illicit origins of the property, integrating it into legitimate economic circulation.

As the objective side of a crime reveals the methods by which it is committed, the dissertation of Candidate of Legal Sciences Mirzaraimov[34] provides a comprehensive list of techniques and methods commonly employed in money laundering. These include:

1. Placement of funds in credit and financial institutions—depositing illicit funds to integrate them into the financial system.
2. Purchase of foreign currency—converting proceeds into different currencies to obscure their origin.
3. Postal money transfers—utilizing postal services for transferring illicit funds.
4. Money transfers—leveraging domestic or international financial transfers to disguise sources.
5. Export of funds by smuggling—physically transporting cash across borders to evade detection.
6. Transfer of funds to companies with foreign participation—using joint ventures to integrate illicit funds.
7. Transfer of funds to offshore companies—leveraging jurisdictions with minimal transparency for fund placement.
8. Payment of perceived contracts with foreign firms—masking proceeds through fictitious contracts.
9. Payment for services of foreign organizations—using service transactions as a veil for illicit funds.
10. Buying property abroad—investing in foreign real estate to launder criminal revenue.
11. Buying real estate in Uzbekistan—utilizing the domestic property market for fund placement.
12. Payment for household and other services—hiding illicit funds through payments for various services.
13. Declaring revenue as a win—misrepresenting criminal proceeds as gambling or lottery winnings.

This exhaustive categorization underscores the adaptability and complexity of money laundering methods. Each technique reflects an attempt to manipulate legal frameworks and financial systems to disguise the illicit nature of proceeds. Recognizing

---

[34] Mirzaraimov 2004, p.116.

these methods is essential for developing targeted countermeasures in financial monitoring, legal enforcement, and regulatory oversight, ensuring that such activities are detected and disrupted effectively.

In the theory of criminal law, the key characteristics of the legalization (laundering) of criminal revenue are identified as follows:

1. Purposeful process, not just a result:

Legalization is conceptualized as a purposeful and deliberate process rather than merely the achievement of a particular result. This distinguishes the act of laundering criminal revenue from other offenses, emphasizing its procedural nature rather than its outcome.

2. Integration and maintenance in legal economic circulation**:**

Legalization as a crime encompasses both the initial introduction of illicitly obtained funds or property (commonly referred to as 'dirty money') into legitimate economic circulation and the continued handling of these assets. This includes conducting financial transactions, maintaining possession, and transforming these assets within the framework of the legal economic system.

3. Process-oriented nature and moment of cessation:

Since legalization is a process rather than a one-time act, it has a distinct point at which the crime is considered complete. This cessation moment is critical in determining the scope of criminal liability, as it depends on the stage at which the laundering activities cease or are interrupted.

4. 'Dilution' of illicit property with legitimate assets:

Legalization often involves blending illicitly obtained funds or property with legitimate assets, a process referred to as 'dilution.' This tactic aims to obscure the criminal origin of the funds, making them more difficult to trace and allowing for their seamless integration into the legal economy.

If we analyze the norms, we can assume that there is a need to exclude the terms 'money' and 'other property' from the disposition of the crime under consideration and combine them with the term 'property,' which, according to international legal documents, as well as the Civil Code of the Republic of Uzbekistan, covers movable and immovable property, property, copyright, and other rights.[35]

It should be noted that the composition of Article 243 of the Criminal Code of the Republic of Uzbekistan is formal.[36]

The formal composition of a crime refers to a type of criminal offense where the mere act of committing the prohibited conduct (or its omission) is sufficient for it to be considered a punishable crime, regardless of whether any harmful consequences occurred.

---

[35] Yusupov 2011.

[36] Ne'matov 2002, p.162.

By establishing liability for money laundering and not requiring a sentence for a predicate offense to qualify an act, the legislator assumes that the predicate offense has taken place (been committed). This circumstance must be considered in light of the general provisions on the completed crime and stages of said crime. If a predicate crime has been committed and can be considered complete from the point of view of criminal law, there are no problems with the theoretical interpretation and practice of applying the rule on liability for legalization. Similarly, problems are absent if the predicate crime is interrupted due to circumstances beyond the control of the perpetrator and forms a preparation for a crime or an attempt to commit a crime (Article 25 of the Criminal Code) under which if, as a result of the commission of an unfinished crime, it was possible to acquire money or property, they should be considered received as a result of the commission of a crime or by criminal means.

10.2.2 Subjective Signs of Money Laundering in Uzbekistan

In the domestic science of criminal law, the subject of a crime is defined as a natural, sane individual who has committed an offense and has reached the minimum age of criminal responsibility as established by law. The presence of these elements is fundamental to the recognition of a subject of a crime.

The absence of any one of these elements—whether it be the natural personhood of the offender, their sanity at the time of the act, or their attainment of the legally prescribed age of responsibility—results in the absence of the subject of the crime. Consequently, this also negates the existence of the crime itself in legal terms.

This principle underscores the importance of establishing these essential characteristics during the legal assessment of criminal cases.

Natural personhood ensures that only human actors, not entities like organizations or corporations (unless specified by law), can be considered criminally liable.

Sanity is required to ascertain that the offender had the capacity to understand the nature and consequences of their actions.

Age of criminal responsibility reflects a societal and legal determination of when an individual is deemed capable of understanding and adhering to legal norms.

This approach not only provides a foundation for assigning criminal liability but also reflects the balance between protecting society and ensuring that only those capable of forming criminal intent are held accountable. It aligns with fundamental principles of justice by excluding from criminal liability those who cannot fully comprehend or control their actions due to youth or mental incapacity.

Moreover, this framework emphasizes the necessity of clear and precise legal definitions in criminal law to ensure fair and equitable application of justice, safeguarding both societal order and individual rights.

In the theory of criminal law, the subjects of crime are traditionally classified into the following types.

A general subject has all the characteristics specified in Article 17 of the Criminal Code of the Republic of Uzbekistan. A special subject of a crime is a person who, along with the general characteristics of the subject (reaching the age of criminal responsibility and sanity), also meets additional special features specified in the disposition of the articles of the Special Part of the Criminal Code, which are subject to mandatory establishment when qualifying and limiting the circle of persons who may be liable under this article. A special subject must be defined by criminal law.

Analyzing the corpus delicti of the legalization of revenue received from criminal activities, it is evident that the Criminal Code of the Republic of Uzbekistan does not define a special subject for this crime. This omission indicates that the subject of the crime is a general one, which, under the provisions of the Criminal Code, includes sane individuals who have reached the age of 16.

This interpretation aligns with the broader framework of criminal law, where the absence of a specific designation for a special subject suggests that the offense is accessible to any individual meeting the general criteria of criminal liability.

Analyzing the subjective side of the crime, it is evident that this aspect delves into the perpetrator's mental attitude toward their actions deemed criminal under the law. According to Rustambayev, the subjective side is characterized by four primary elements: guilt, motive, purpose, and emotions.

This perspective underscores that the subjective side is not merely about the physical commission of a crime but also about the internal state and intent of the perpetrator at the time of the offense. These elements play a pivotal role in determining the degree of responsibility and culpability.

The subjective side of a crime represents an internal characteristic that exists in relation to the objective side, reflecting the mental and emotional attitude of the perpetrator toward their socially dangerous act. In the scientific literature, it is commonly defined as the internal, psychological relationship of an individual to the offense they commit, encompassing elements such as motives, goals, emotions, and intent.

In fact, this author clearly defines the form of guilt as direct intent in all the comments to the relevant norms of the Criminal Code.

At present, the question of the subjective side of the crime prescribed in Article 243 of the Criminal Code of the Republic of Uzbekistan does not seem to be completely clear. The disposition of the Article does not contain an indication of the purpose of performing the actions provided in it despite the fact that the corresponding term legalization is used in its name. A person who is aware that he is making a financial transaction or other transaction cannot but wish to make this transaction (operation) of a legitimate nature. Criminal acts are committed on the intent of the person. That is, in my opinion, the direct intent of the occurrence of criminal consequences of legalization (namely, giving the received income the appearance of legal origin) should be covered by the intent of the subjects of the crime.

In light of this, it is important to examine the potential for committing a crime with indirect intent under Article 243 of the Criminal Code of the Republic of Uzbekistan. The essence of the offense, involving the legalization of proceeds from criminal activities, is inherently tied to financial and economic interests. In such cases, the mercenary aspect is evident; however, unlike crimes involving the theft of another's property, the legislator does not place significant emphasis on this component. Consequently, it becomes essential to refine the understanding of the concept of criminal motive, both in general and specifically concerning the offense in question.[37]

10.3 Conclusion

The analysis conducted highlights the need for further criminalization of money laundering and the establishment of criminal liability in all jurisdictions in accordance with the 40 Recommendations of the FATF.

It is proposed to simultaneously use the terms 'legalization' and 'money laundering' in the title of Article 243 of the Criminal Code and to replace the word 'property' in the article's disposition with the phrase 'funds and other assets,' while establishing the purpose as a mandatory element of the crime. It is also deemed appropriate to include qualifying elements in the disposition of Article 243 of the Criminal Code, specifically:

1. Legalization of funds or other assets in especially large amounts;
2. Legalization by an organized group of persons or in its interests, or in the interests of third parties;
3. Introducing 'an official' as a special subject of the crime.

It is further proposed to set the age of criminal liability for money laundering at 18 years, coinciding with the full attainment of civil legal capacity. Given the liberalization of economic crimes, this approach appears justified. A mandatory condition for qualifying the act is the existence of a special circumstance requiring that the perpetrator be lawfully empowered to conduct transactions. Only in such cases can criminally obtained property or funds be recognized as lawful.[38]

---

[37] Ibid.

[38] Building on the foregoing analysis, the following revised wording of Article 243 of the Criminal Code of the Republic of Uzbekistan ("Legalisation (money laundering) of the proceeds of crime") is proposed:

Legalization of the proceeds of crime, i.e., acts aimed at giving a lawful appearance to the origin of funds or other assets through their transfer, conversion, or exchange, as well as concealing or disguising the true nature, source, location, disposition, movement, ownership, or rights to such assets, provided that the assets were obtained through criminal activities, including the acquisition, possession, or use of such assets, shall be punishable by a fine of 100 to 200 base calculation units, corrective labour for up to three years, restriction of liberty for one to three years, or imprisonment for one to three years.

The same acts committed:

(a) On a large scale;

(b) By a group of persons by prior conspiracy;

(c) By abusing official powers,

shall be punishable by restriction of liberty for three to five years or imprisonment for three to five years.

The same acts committed:

(a) On an especially large scale;

References

Aliev V (2001) Теоретические основы и прикладные проблемы борьбы с легализацией (отмыванием) доходов, полученных незаконным путем [Theoretical foundations and applied problems of combating legalization (laundering) of illegally obtained income]. *Dissertation. Faculty of Law. Moscow*, 6.

Aslakhanov A (1997) Проблемы борьбы с преступностью в сфере экономики: криминологические и уголовно-правовой аспекты [Problems of combating crime in the economic sphere (criminological and criminal-legal aspects)]. *Dissertation. Faculty of Law. Moscow*, 163.

Bashan N (2008) Counteraction to organized legalization of revenue received from fraud: criminological and criminal-legal aspects. [Противодействие организованной легализации доходов от мошенничества: криминологический и уголовно-правовой аспекты]. *Dissertation abstract. Moscow State Law University (MSAL)*, 10.

Beare M (1990) Tracing of illicit funds: money laundering in Canada. Ottawa, p.11.

Boskholov S (2005) Criminal liability for legalization of cash or other property, acquired by criminal means. [Уголовная ответственность за легализацию денежных средств или иного имущества, приобретенных преступным путем]. Dissertation. Faculty of Law. Moscow, p.36–38.

Bukarev V (2006) Legalization (laundering) of revenue acquired by criminal means: the social danger and the question of qualification. [Легализация (отмывание) доходов, приобретенных преступным путем: общественная опасность и вопросы квалификации]. Dissertation. Moscow State Linguistic University, p.154.

Dalla Chiesa F (2012) *L'impresa mafiosa. Tra capitalismo violento e controllo sociale [The mafia enterprise: between violent capitalism and social control]* (p. 11). Cavallotti University Press.

Gauchman L (1998) *Maksimov S.V. Crimes in the sphere of economic activities. [Уголовная ответственность за преступления в сфере экономики]* (p. 182). YUrInfoR.

Hun A (2004) The object of criminal law relations: theoretical and law enforcement aspects. [Объект уголовно-правовых отношений: Теоретический и правоприменительный аспекты]. Dissertation. Faculty of Law. Krasnodar.

Ivanov E (2004) The system of international legal regulation of the fight against the legalization (laundering) of proceeds from crime. [Система международно-правового регулирования борьбы с легализацией (отмыванием) доходов, полученных преступным путем]. Dissertation. Faculty of Law.

Kabulov R, Otazhonov AA et al. (2012) Criminal law. General part: Textbook. 2nd ed., revised. [Уголовное право. Общая часть: Учебник]. Tashkent: Academy of the Ministry of Internal Affairs of the Republic of Uzbekistan.

Kerner H & Dakh E (1996) Money laundering. *Moscow*, 6.

Khvostov V (2016) General theory of law. Elementary essay. In *Общая теория права: Элементарный очерк* (p. 138). URSS.

Kottke K (2005) *"dirty" money – how to deal with it? Handbook on tax legislation* (9th German ed., pp. 13–14). Publishing House "Business and Service".

Krasheninnikova O & Lysenko V et al. (2017) History of state and law of foreign countries. [История государства и права зарубежных стран]. Textbook. Volume 1: The ancient world and the middle ages. 3rd ed., revised. Moscow: Legal norm, SIC INFRA-M, p.720.

Larichev V (2003) Improvement of legislation on combating the legalization of revenue received from criminal activities. [Совершенствование законодательства о борьбе с «отмыванием» денег, полученных преступным путем]. *State and Law, 2*, 100.

Lavrov V (2000) Criminal liability for the legalization (laundering) of money or other property acquired illegally. [Уголовная ответственность за легализацию (отмывание) денежных

(b) By an organized group or in its interests,
shall be punishable by imprisonment for five to ten years.

средств или иного имущества, приобретенных незаконным путем]. *Dissertation. Faculty of Law., N. Novgorod*, 39.

LexUz Online (2018) The concept of improving the criminal and criminal procedure legislation of the Republic of Uzbekistan https://lex.uz/docs/3734183. Accessed 10 April 2025.

LexUz Online (2019) Law of the Republic of Uzbekistan "On International Treaties of the Republic of Uzbekistan". https://lex.uz/docs/4193763. Accessed 10 June 2025.

Lopashenko N (1997) Crimes in the sphere of economic activity: concept, system, problems of qualification and punishment. [Преступления в сфере экономической деятельности: Понятие, система, проблемы квалификации и наказания].: SGAP Publishing House, pp.168–177.

Margolin A (1907) From the field of criminal law. The main features of the new criminal code. [Из области уголовного права. Основные черты нового Уголовного Уложения].: Tip. J.B. Neumann, p.127.

Mikhailov V (2002) Countering the legalization of revenue from criminal activities: Legal regulation, criminal liability, operational investigative measures and international cooperation. In *[Противодействие легализации доходов от преступной деятельности: Правовое регулирование, уголовная ответственность, оперативно-розыскные мероприятия и международное сотрудничество]. St* (p. 80). Legal Center Press.

Mirzaraimov I (2004) Criminal-legal and criminological measures to prevent the disclosure of proceeds of crime. [Уголовно-правовые и криминологические меры предупреждения раскрытия доходов, полученных преступным путём]. Dissertation. Faculty of Law. Tashkent, p.116.

Naumov A (2018) Russian Criminal Law: General part. [Российское уголовное право. Общая часть]. Course of lectures in 2 volumes. Vol. 1. 6th ed., revised.: Legal Literature, p.98.

Ne'matov J (2001) On the problem of international legal regulation countering legalization of criminal revenue. [К проблеме международно-правовой регламентации борьбы с легализацией преступных доходов]. Huquq-Pravo-Law. p.3.

Ne'matov J (2002) Criminal-legal law problems of international cooperation countering the legalization of revenue received from criminal activities. [Уголовно-правовые проблемы международного сотрудничества в борьбе с легализацией доходов, полученных от преступной деятельности]. Dissertation. Faculty of Legal Sciences. Tashkent, pp. 162, 54, 71–72.

Oswald K (1997) Die Implementation gesetzlicher Massnahmen zur Bekämpfung der Geldwasche in der Bundesrepublick Deutschland. In *Max-Planck-Institut für ausländisches und internationales Strafrecht* (p. 6).

Radchenko A Mikhlin A and Shmarov I (1994) Commentary on the Criminal Code of the RSFSR. [Комментарий к Уголовному кодексу РСФСР]. Moscow, p.386.

Rustambayev M (2016) Course of criminal law of the Republic of Uzbekistan. [Курс уголовного права Республики Узбекистан]. The special part. Vol. 4. Tashkent: Publishing house of the academy of the Ministry of Internal Affairs of the Republic of Uzbekistan.

Tagantsev N (2019) Russian criminal law in 2 volumes. [Российское уголовное право в 2 томах]. Part 1.: Yurayt Publishing House, p.414.

United Nations (1988) Vienna Convention against Illicit Traffic in Narcotic Drugs and Psychotropic Substances of 19 December 1988. https://www.unodc.org/pdf/convention_1988_ru.pdf. Accessed 26 March 2025.

Usmonaliev M (2005) Criminal law. General part: Textbook for universities. In *Уголовное право. Общая часть: учебник для вузов.* Yangi Asr Avlodi.

Yusupov N (2011) Criminal liability for the legalization (laundering) of property obtained from crime in the field of illicit trafficking in narcotic drugs, psychotropic substances or their analogues. [Уголовная ответственность за легализацию (отмывание) имущества, полученного от преступлений в сфере незаконного оборота наркотических средств, психотропных веществ или их аналогов]. Dissertation. Faculty of Legal Sciences.

Part VI
International Trade and Investment Law

Chapter 11
The Agreement on Fisheries Subsidies and Implications for Central Asian WTO Members as Landlocked Countries

Sherzod Shadikhodjaev

Abstract The issue of fisheries subsidies has garnered significant attention within the global community due to its multifaceted implications for both economic development and environmental sustainability. Adopted at the 12th Ministerial Conference of the Word Trade Organization (WTO) in 2022, a new Agreement on Fisheries Subsidies (AFS) aims to prevent governments from using certain subsidies that lead to unsustainable fishing practices. As the first WTO environmental agreement, the AFS differs from the existing WTO disciplines on industrial subsidies by focusing on environmental protection and preservation rather than countering trade distortions. Once in effect, the AFS is expected to also apply to the WTO members from Central Asia, all of which are landlocked countries. This chapter discusses the negotiation history and main provisions of the AFS as well as its relevance to the Central Asian and other landlocked country members. It concludes that, despite the limited direct impact of the AFS on these countries, their full participation will support global sustainability efforts and help meet their domestic demand for fish products.

Keywords Central Asia · landlocked countries · WTO · Agreement on Fisheries Subsidies (AFS) · Subsidies and Countervailing Measures (SCM) Agreement · UNCLOS · SDG · illegal, unreported, and unregulated (IUU) fishing · overfished stocks · regional fisheries management organization or arrangement (RFMO/A)

11.1 Introduction

The Food and Agriculture Organization (FAO) of the United Nations (UN) reports that fisheries and aquaculture production reached an all-time high of 223.2 million tons in 2022, contributing an estimated 20.7 kg of aquatic animal foods per capita. This accounts for nearly 15 percent of animal protein consumption globally and over 50 percent in some Asian and African countries, making fisheries a significant source

S. Shadikhodjaev (✉)
KDI School of Public Policy and Management, Sejong City, Republic of Korea
e-mail: sherzod1@kdischool.ac.kr

S. Sayapin (ed.), *International Law, Politics and Security in Central Asia*,
https://doi.org/10.1007/978-3-032-17818-3_11

of nutrients for many people worldwide.[1] In addition to direct consumption, fish is also used in the production of fish meal, fish oil, and various processed products widely utilized in the agricultural, cosmetics, and pharmaceutical industries.

Despite the growing importance of fisheries, scientists estimate that 75 percent of the world's fisheries are either fully exploited, overexploited, or have collapsed, with only 1 percent showing signs of recovery from depletion.[2] This overfishing has become a serious global problem with far-reaching sustainability implications. Environmentally, excessive fishing depletes ocean wildlife populations and disrupts marine ecosystems and biodiversity. Economically, it makes it harder for fish-dependent communities to sustain themselves, causing economic losses in fishing and related industries. Socially, it creates potential conflicts over fishing rights and threatens the cultural identities of coastal communities for whom fishing is a traditional way of life.

Overfishing is driven by, inter alia, government subsidies that fuel the build-up of excessive fishing capacity, like vessels and equipment, reduce fishing costs, or promote unsustainable fishing practices. Already in 1998, a World Bank study concluded that subsidies were a significant factor in undermining the sustainable use of marine resources and warned that, without corrective measures, including subsidy reforms, the sustainability crisis in world fisheries would become 'a chronic and intractable problem'.[3]

Since the launch of the Doha Round in 2001, the World Trade Organization (WTO) has been working on establishing new disciplines to constrain environmentally harmful fisheries subsidies. These negotiations have been particularly bolstered by the adoption of UN Sustainable Development Goal (SDG) 14 in 2015, which focuses on the conservation and sustainable use of the oceans, seas, and marine resources. SDG Target 14.6 explicitly urged the prohibition by 2020 of fisheries subsidies that contribute to overcapacity and overfishing and subsidies that contribute to illegal, unreported, and unregulated (IUU) fishing, and recognized that the WTO fisheries subsidies negotiations should include appropriate and effective special and differential treatment for developing and least developed countries.[4]

After nearly two decades of complex and challenging negotiations, the WTO finally approved an Agreement on Fisheries Subsidies (AFS) at the 12th Ministerial Conference in 2022. The AFS is remarkable for being the first WTO agreement with an environmental, rather than trade, focus as its priority[5] and as the second multilateral trade agreement (after the Agreement on Trade Facilitation) adopted since the WTO's

---

[1] FAO 2024, p. vii.

[2] Ocean Connections n.d.

[3] Milazzo 1998, pp. 79, 81.

[4] UN 2015, p. 24.

[5] The primary focus of the WTO-led multilateral trading system has typically been on liberalizing trade and maintaining fair trade conditions even though many WTO texts do contain environment-related provisions. The WTO subsidy rules initially envisaged a carve-out for certain environmental subsidies, but it expired after a five-year period following members' disagreement over its extension. For environmental policy space in trade law, see Shadikhodjaev 2024, pp. 34–45; Shadikhodjaev 2025, pp. 109–114.

establishment in 1995. By prohibiting harmful fisheries subsidies that affect living marine resources, the new disciplines will help preserve the sustainability of oceans and seas.

Among the five Central Asian countries, Kazakhstan, Kyrgyzstan, and Tajikistan are WTO members while Turkmenistan and Uzbekistan are currently in the process of acceding to the WTO (as of 1 July 2025).[6] The multilateral trading system allows its members to benefit from greater and fairer access to overseas markets and to use WTO instruments to protect their trading interests from adverse foreign measures. It also, however, reduces their freedom in trade and industrial policies as they must adhere to WTO norms.

As landlocked countries, the Central Asian WTO members do not have fisheries industries in maritime zones. However, they have not been indifferent to the issue of regulating marine fisheries subsidies under the WTO system. For example, Tajikistan, which has inland fisheries falling outside the AFS's scope, has nevertheless stressed the importance of the issue above due to the country's food security needs and its desire for better access to seafood nutrients.[7] In this connection, some recent data show that the average per capita animal protein intake for landlocked developing countries is much lower (17.2 g/day) than the average for developing regions (26.9 g/day), with the share of fish in their animal protein intake being less than half of the developing regions' average.[8]

This chapter proceeds as follows. Section 11.2 discusses the maritime law status of landlocked countries and the relevance of the AFS to them. Section 11.3 provides an overview of key developments in AFS negotiations, followed by Sect. 11.4 elaborating on the main provisions of the AFS and their implications for the Central Asian WTO members. Section 11.5 concludes this analysis.

11.2 Landlocked Countries and Relevance of the Fisheries Subsidies Issue

There are 43 landlocked countries—i.e., States with no seacoast[9]—out of which 32 are developing countries. The latter include all five Central Asian countries and 17 of the least developed countries, among others.[10] These 32 countries are classified by the UN as landlocked developing countries.[11] Of these, 26 are WTO members and six are observers.[12] The absence of territorial access to the sea places them

[6] See WTO n.d.b; Umirdinov et al. 2026.

[7] See WTO 2021f, paras. 4.57–4.60.

[8] FAO 2021, p. 6.

[9] UNCLOS 1982, Article 124.1(a).

[10] International Seabed Authority 2021, pp. 9–10.

[11] UN n.d.; UN Trade and Development n.d.

[12] WTO 2021g.

at a disadvantage compared to coastal States in terms of higher trade costs[13] and lower seafood accessibility. Meeting on the margins of the 13th WTO Ministerial Conference in Abu Dhabi in 2024, a Group of Landlocked Developing Countries—a negotiating coalition in the WTO—expressed concern that, although trade accounted for a greater share of their Gross Domestic Product than the world average, their share in global merchandise exports was just 1.1 percent, with their exports consisting mainly of primary commodities.[14]

This Group of Landlocked Developing Countries, which includes all the Central Asian WTO members,[15] expressed its full support for subsidy-constraining efforts in the WTO to prevent the depletion of global fishing stocks. In the course of negotiations, some members of this group submitted a joint proposal embedding the 'leaving no one behind' approach to safeguard the interests of landlocked developing countries, 'including the right of access to the sea, freedom of navigation, freedom of fishing, freedom of scientific research, among others'.[16] As a co-sponsor of this joint proposal, Mongolia stated in a WTO meeting:

> 'These [harmful fisheries] subsidies have a negative impact on Members' rights including the landlocked developing countries' rights and possibilities of fishing in the high seas and exclusive economic zones of coastal states as well as their right to exploit the living resources in these areas.
>
> Mongolia also believes that enhanced partnerships between the LLDCs [landlocked developing countries] and the coastal states, in cooperation with international and regional organizations such as the Regional Fisheries Management Organizations would improve the involvement of landlocked developing countries in fishing practices and help them exercise their rights to utilise fish stocks and other living resources in the exclusive economic zones of coastal states in an equitable manner'.[17]

Reflecting the joint proposal above, one of the initial drafts of the AFS guaranteed intactness of landlocked country members' rights under public international law.[18] Negotiations here discussed, inter alia, the scope of such rights and whether a provision on this issue was needed at all.[19] Another draft provision was about securing technical assistance to landlocked developing country members.[20]

However, the final AFS text removed specific references to landlocked countries as such and instead opted for more inclusive formulations. In particular, Article 11.3 of the AFS reads that '[n]othing in this Agreement shall be construed or applied in a manner which will prejudice the jurisdiction, rights and obligations of Members,

---

[13] According to WTO estimates, trade costs of landlocked developing countries are 1.4 times higher than those of coastal developing countries. See WTO 2021a, p. 100.

[14] WTO 2024c, p. 2.

[15] See the list of 'Land-locked Developing Countries' in WTO n.d.a.

[16] WTO 2021f, paras. 4.251–4.253; WTO 2020.

[17] WTO 2021b, p. 197.

[18] See WTO 2021c, Article 11.1; WTO 2021d, Article 11.1; Explanatory Note on Article 11.1 in WTO 2021e; WTO 2021f, para. 4.383.

[19] WTO 2021e, para. 106.

[20] See WTO 2021c, Article 7; WTO 2021d, Article 7.

arising under international law, including the law of the sea'. Article 7 provides for '[t]argeted technical assistance and capacity building assistance to developing country Members, including LDC [least developed country] Members' needed for the implementation of this agreement. For this purpose, a voluntary WTO funding mechanism was created in cooperation with the relevant international organizations.

Many landlocked developing countries, except the Central Asian countries, are parties to the 1982 UN Convention on the Law of the Sea (UNCLOS).[21] As seen above, the law of the sea is mentioned in Article 11.3 of the AFS, and the AFS negotiations discussed the maritime interests of landlocked countries. Therefore, it is also worth reviewing the main provisions of the UNCLOS concerning landlocked countries.

The UNCLOS recognizes that the achievement of its goals will contribute to the realization of a 'just and equitable international economic order' which takes into account, inter alia, the special needs and interests of developing countries, whether coastal or landlocked.[22] Under the UNCLOS, landlocked States have the right of access to and from the sea for the purpose of exercising the rights given by this convention, like the freedom of the high seas and the common heritage of mankind, and enjoy freedom of transit through the transit territory by all means of transport.[23] No customs duties, taxes, or other charges except specific service charges can be imposed on goods in transit.[24] Ships flying the flag of landlocked States enjoy equal treatment as other foreign ships in maritime ports.[25] All States, regardless of their geographic location, have the right to conduct marine scientific research, subject to the rights and duties of other States.[26] States must promote the development of the marine scientific and technological capacity, particularly of developing States including landlocked ones, concerning 'the exploration, exploitation, conservation and management of marine resources, the protection and preservation of the marine environment, marine scientific research and other activities in the marine environment compatible with this Convention'.[27] The UNCLOS also calls for technical cooperation for effective technology transfer in this field to States in need, including developing landlocked States.[28]

As for fishing activities, landlocked States have the right to participate, on an equitable basis, in the exploitation of an appropriate part of the surplus of the living resources of an exclusive economic zone (EEZ)—a maritime area extending up to 200 nautical miles from a national coastal baseline, beyond the territorial sea[29]—of a coastal State in the same sub-region or region. This right can be exercised taking

[21] See International Seabed Authority 2021, p. 10.

[22] UNCLOS 1982, Preamble.

[23] Ibid., Article 125.1.

[24] Ibid., Article 127.1. See also Shadikhodjaev 2013.

[25] UNCLOS 1982, Article 131.

[26] Ibid., Article 138.

[27] Ibid., Article 266.2.

[28] Ibid., Article 269(a).

[29] Ibid., Articles 55 and 57.

into account the relevant economic and geographical circumstances of all the States concerned, the right of the coastal State to determine the allowable catch of living resources in the EEZ, and its obligation to promote their optimum utilization.[30] The terms and modalities of such participation are determined by relevant bilateral, sub-regional, or regional agreements.[31] When a coastal State nears the capacity to harvest all allowable living resources in its EEZ, it must cooperate with other States to create equitable arrangements enabling developing landlocked States of the same (sub-)region to participate in resource exploitation under mutually satisfactory conditions.[32]

11.3 AFS Negotiation Developments in Brief

In the WTO, fisheries subsidies and their environmental impacts were initially discussed in the Committee on Trade and Environment in 1997–1999.[33] At that time, members differed in their views as to the role subsidies have played in the overexploitation of fish resources, with some, for example, pointing to the lack of sustainable fisheries management as a main cause of this problem.[34] As a result of these discussions, the Doha Ministerial Declaration (2001), launching a new round of multilateral trade negotiations, instructed negotiating members to 'clarify and improve WTO disciplines on fisheries subsidies, taking into account the importance of this sector to developing countries'. This issue was included in the WTO rules section of the negotiations, and this was reiterated in the trade-and-environment part of the same declaration.[35]

Meanwhile, the UN World Summit on Sustainable Development (2002) acknowledged that achieving sustainable fisheries required, inter alia, the elimination of subsidies that contribute to IUU fishing and overcapacity as well as the completion of WTO efforts to clarify and improve its disciplines on fisheries subsidies.[36]

The sixth WTO Ministerial Conference (2005) clarified the negotiating mandate for the Negotiating Group on Rules with respect to fisheries subsidies, specifying the scope of targeted subsidies to be banned and implications for developing countries:

> '[We] *recall* our commitment at Doha to enhancing the mutual supportiveness of trade and environment, *note* that there is broad agreement that the Group should strengthen disciplines on subsidies in the fisheries sector, including through the prohibition of certain forms of fisheries subsidies that contribute to overcapacity and over-fishing, and *call on* Participants promptly to undertake further detailed work to, *inter alia*, establish the nature and extent

[30] Ibid., Article 69.1.

[31] Ibid., Article 69.2.

[32] Ibid., Article 69.3.

[33] Scholaert 2022, p. 4.

[34] See, e.g., WTO 1998, paras. 48–60.

[35] WTO 2001, paras. 28, 31.

[36] UN 2002, para. 31(f).

> of those disciplines, including transparency and enforceability. Appropriate and effective special and differential treatment for developing and least-developed Members should be an integral part of the fisheries subsidies negotiations, taking into account the importance of this sector to development priorities, poverty reduction, and livelihood and food security concerns'.[37]

The overall stalemate in the Doha Round, which prevented it from being concluded, could not bypass the negotiations on fisheries subsidies. But the adoption of UN SDG 14.6 in 2015[38] gave a new impetus, highlighting the environmental importance of the global campaign concerning this issue. As a result, the 11th WTO Ministerial Conference (2017) set the goal of ending the related negotiations by the following Ministerial Conference[39]:

> 'Members agree to continue to engage constructively in the fisheries subsidies negotiations, with a view to adopting, by the Ministerial Conference in 2019, an agreement on comprehensive and effective disciplines that prohibit certain forms of fisheries subsidies that contribute to overcapacity and overfishing, and eliminate subsidies that contribute to IUU-fishing recognizing that appropriate and effective special and differential treatment for developing country Members and least developed country Members should be an integral part of these negotiations'.

With both advancements and failures in the negotiation process,[40] WTO members eventually reached a consensus on the finalized text of the AFS at the 12th Ministerial Conference in Geneva in 2022, co-hosted by Kazakhstan. This conference was originally scheduled to be held in Kazakhstan in 2020 but was postponed due to the COVID-19 pandemic. As mentioned below, some parts of the AFS draft were withdrawn from the final text to be discussed in the follow-up negotiations for eventual inclusion in the WTO regime. At the time of writing, these negotiations were still ongoing.

11.4 Main Provisions of the AFS

11.4.1 Scope of Application

The AFS prohibits three types of subsidies, namely subsidies contributing to IUU fishing, subsidies regarding overfished stocks, and subsidies for fishing in the unregulated high seas. Whether a particular measure is indeed a covered 'subsidy' is a threshold issue.

Pursuant to Article 1 of the AFS, this agreement applies to specific subsidies, within the meaning of the Subsidies and Countervailing Measures (SCM) Agreement,

[37] WTO 2005, Annex D, para. 9 (emphasis in original).

[38] See Sect. 11.1 of this chapter.

[39] WTO 2017, para. 1.

[40] See Scholaert 2022, pp. 6–8.

given to wild marine capture fishing and fishing-related activities occurring at sea.[41] Thus, the AFS follows the definition of a 'subsidy' under Article 1 of the SCM Agreement as a government-related financial contribution (or otherwise income or price support) conferring a benefit. A financial contribution by a government or a public body (or a private body through governmental entrustment or direction) includes direct transfers of funds, revenue foregone, and the provision of goods or services or purchases of goods.[42] The AFS clarifies that a subsidy is attributable to a subsidizing member 'regardless of the flag or registry of any vessel involved or the nationality of the recipient'. To fall within the AFS's scope, a subsidy must be what Article 2 of the SCM Agreement terms as 'specific' to an enterprise or industry (or a group of enterprises/industries) or a particular region, or be either an export subsidy or import-substitution subsidy, both of which are prohibited and deemed to be specific under the SCM Agreement.

The AFS does not extend to aquaculture and inland fisheries or to government-to-government payments under fisheries access agreements.[43] Thus, inland fisheries and

---

[41] AFS 2022, Article 2 provides the following definitions of certain terms:

For the purpose of this Agreement:

(a) 'fish' means all species of living marine resources, whether processed or not;

(b) 'fishing' means searching for, attracting, locating, catching, taking, or harvesting fish or any activity which can reasonably be expected to result in the attracting, locating, catching, taking, or harvesting of fish;

(c) 'fishing-related activities' means any operation in support of, or in preparation for, fishing, including the landing, packaging, processing, transshipping, or transporting of fish that have not been previously landed at a port, as well as the provisioning of personnel, fuel, gear, and other supplies at sea;

(d) 'vessel' means any vessel, ship of another type or boat used for, equipped to be used for, or intended to be used for, fishing or fishing-related activities;

(e) 'operator' means the owner of a vessel, or any person, who is in charge of or directs or controls the vessel.

[42] SCM Agreement 1994, Article 1 ('Definition of a Subsidy') reads:

1.1 For the purpose of this Agreement, a subsidy shall be deemed to exist if: (a)(1) there is a financial contribution by a government or any public body within the territory of a member (referred to in this Agreement as 'government'), i.e. where:

(i) a government practice involves a direct transfer of funds (e.g. grants, loans, and equity infusion), potential direct transfers of funds or liabilities (e.g. loan guarantees);

(ii) government revenue that is otherwise due is foregone or not collected (e.g. fiscal incentives such as tax credits) [footnote omitted];

(iii) a government provides goods or services other than general infrastructure, or purchases goods;

(iv) a government makes payments to a funding mechanism, or entrusts or directs a private body to carry out one or more of the type of functions illustrated in (i) to (iii) above which would normally be vested in the government and the practice, in no real sense, differs from practices normally followed by governments;

or

(a)(2) there is any form of income or price support in the sense of Article XVI of GATT 1994; and

(b) a benefit is thereby conferred.

For examples of industrial subsidies in practice, see Shadikhodjaev 2023, pp. 626–633.

[43] AFS 2022, footnotes 1 and 2.

(freshwater) aquaculture in the Central Asian countries, which do not have fisheries industries in maritime zones, are excluded from the scope of the AFS. However, because landlocked countries may still have ships flying their flags,[44] subsidies given to these vessels involved in fishing and fishing-related activities at sea are subject to the AFS disciplines. For example, the WTO Secretariat's trade policy review report on Kazakhstan indicates, quoting the local authorities, that this country had two licensed maritime fishing vessels in 2024.[45]

All subsidies prohibited by the AFS can be challenged through the WTO dispute settlement procedures and face multilateral remedies under Article 4 of the SCM Agreement designed for subsidies prohibited by the SCM Agreement.[46] Among other things, this means that, if WTO adjudicators find a challenged fisheries subsidy to be prohibited by the AFS, the subsidizing member must withdraw that subsidy without delay, or else a complaining member may take appropriate countermeasures as a last resort.

It should be noted that the SCM Agreement already covers all fisheries subsidies, meeting the parameters of this agreement, whether or not included by the AFS.[47] Under the SCM Agreement, members are entitled to counter foreign subsidies specific to the fisheries industry through the WTO dispute settlement procedures (the multilateral track) and/or domestic countervailing duty procedures (the national track) to tackle associated trade distortions.[48] With respect to its relationship with the SCM Agreement, Article 11.5 of the AFS states that the AFS 'does not modify or nullify any rights and obligations as provided by the SCM Agreement'. This provision appears to acknowledge the applicability of the SCM Agreement to both (i) fisheries subsidy aspects not specifically addressed by the AFS and (ii) overlapping matters. The first case includes, inter alia, those export subsidies and import-substitution subsidies in the fisheries sector which are already prohibited by the SCM Agreement but are not related to the AFS-banned categories. The second case is about where, for example, the AFS makes cross-references to the SCM Agreement and/or incorporates some of its parts where relevant. In addition, if the same subsidy simultaneously falls under the prohibitions of both the SCM Agreement and the AFS, the latter (in light of Article 11.5) will not preclude challenges under the SCM Agreement. Some legal uncertainty may emerge if the same fisheries subsidy qualifies as an 'actionable' subsidy under the SCM Agreement but a 'prohibited' subsidy under the AFS. Among other things, this could be true of certain overcapacity or overfishing subsidies that may become prohibited under the to-be-created additional AFS disciplines currently under negotiation.[49] Here, the parallel application of the SCM Agreement and the AFS, as implied by Article 11.5 above, can have different

[44] WTO 2021f, para. 4.253.

[45] WTO 2024d, para. 4.24.

[46] See AFS 2022, Article 10.

[47] For the SCM Agreement's application to fisheries subsidies and its implications for the AFS, see Lo & Wang 2021, pp. 172–174.

[48] See Shadikhodjaev 2018, pp. 90–93.

[49] See Sect. 11.4.7 of this chapter.

implications for such subsidies because the legal treatment of actionable subsidies under the SCM Agreement is more lenient (as they are not banned outright and hence usable) than that of prohibited subsidies under the AFS. The plain reading of Article 11.5 seems to suggest that it is up to the challenging member itself which agreement to invoke to counter the subsidy in this case. However, if only the SCM Agreement is invoked to neutralize trade-distortive effects of such subsidies,[50] this will undermine the AFS's environmental sustainability approach underlying the prohibition of the subject subsidies.

The AFS will be included in Annex 1A to the WTO Agreement—the list of multilateral agreements on trade in goods—and enter into force upon acceptance by two-thirds of WTO members.[51] In her speech at the FAO headquarters in Rome in 2023, WTO Deputy Director-General Angela Ellard urged governments to promptly accept the AFS and mentioned that this was 'important for landlocked countries as well because they need a sustainable source of fish protein'.[52] From Central Asia, only Kazakhstan has formally accepted the AFS as of 1 July 2025.[53] In this regard, the trade policy review report of Kazakhstan's government reads, in part:

> 'On 19 June 2024, Kazakhstan ratified the Agreement on Fisheries Subsidies. By joining this agreement, Kazakhstan aligns with global efforts to combat overfishing and the prohibition of subsidies related to illegal, unreported, and unregulated (IUU) fishing. Moreover, it contributes to the UN's Sustainable Development Goals, which are vital for ocean health, livelihoods, and food security'.[54]

Receiving the country's instrument of acceptance from the Kazakh ambassador in 2024, WTO Director-General Okonjo-Iweala commended 'Kazakhstan's commitment, even as a landlocked nation, to responsible fisheries resource management' which 'underscores the need for global cooperation in safeguarding the shared marine ecosystem upon which all of us depend'.[55]

11.4.2 Prohibition of Subsidies for IUU Fishing (AFS Article 3)

IUU fishing refers to activities that undermine sustainable fisheries management and conservation, as specified by relevant FAO standards.[56] These include, inter alia, fishing without a coastal State's permission in its waters, fishing activities un/

[50] SCM Agreement 1994, Article 7.8 suggests that a member providing an actionable subsidy, found to be WTO-inconsistent in a dispute, may comply with a WTO ruling, inter alia, by removing adverse trade effects of that subsidy (without withdrawing the subsidy per se).

[51] WTO 2022, para. 4.

[52] WTO 2023.

[53] WTO n.d.c.

[54] WTO 2024e, para. 7.4.

[55] WTO 2024a.

[56] FAO 2001 (providing the definition of IUU fishing, which is followed by AFS 2022).

misreported to the relevant authority, fishing activities in the area of the competence of a relevant regional fisheries management organization or arrangement (RFMO/A)[57] conducted by vessels flying the flag of a non-RFMO/A Member State.[58] According to recent UN estimates, one in five fish caught globally originates from IUU fishing, which significantly threatens marine ecosystems and fishing communities and causes annual losses of 11 to 26 million tons of fish, with an economic value of up to US$23 billion.[59] The FAO highlights the following negative aspects of IUU fishing[60]:

> 'IUU fishing takes advantage of corrupt administrations and exploits weak management regimes, in particular those of developing countries lacking the capacity and resources for effective monitoring, control, and surveillance (MCS). IUU fishing is found in all types and dimensions of fisheries; it occurs both on the high seas and in areas within national jurisdiction, it concerns all aspects and stages of the capture and utilisation of fish, and it may sometimes be associated with organized crime. Fisheries resources available to bona fide fishers are removed by IUU fishing, which can lead to the collapse of local fisheries, with small-scale fisheries in developing countries proving particularly vulnerable. Products derived from IUU fishing can find their way into overseas trade markets thus throttling local food supply. IUU fishing therefore threatens livelihoods, exacerbates poverty, and augments food insecurity'.

Article 3.1 of the AFS prohibits members from subsidizing a vessel or operator involved in IUU fishing or fishing-related activities supporting IUU fishing. A subsidizing member here will typically be the flag State (including a relevant landlocked country), but it is not ruled out that this will also be a coastal State subsidizing vessels carrying foreign flags (including landlocked countries' vessels if applicable) fishing in its waters.[61] IUU-related subsidies of developing country members provided within the EEZ are exempt from WTO dispute settlement challenges for two years from the AFS's entry into force.[62]

The Article 3.1 prohibition is triggered if an affirmative determination about a vessel's or operator's engagement in IUU activities is made by a coastal member (for activities in its waters), a flag State member (for vessels flying its flag), or an RFMO/A (for areas under its competence)[63] in line with certain evidence-related and procedural requirements.[64] Once the affirmative determination has been duly made, the subsidizing member must stop subsidizing for the period it establishes

[57] See ibid., para. 6(c) (defining an RFMO/A as 'an intergovernmental fisheries organization or arrangement, as appropriate, that has the competence to establish fishery conservation and management measures').

[58] See ibid., para. 3

[59] UN 2023, p. 41.

[60] FAO n.d.b.

[61] See Hoekman et al. 2023, p. 270 (n. 25). To recall, footnote 3 to Article 1 of the AFS 2022 explicitly states that 'for the purposes of this Agreement, a subsidy shall be attributable to the Member conferring it, regardless of the flag or registry of any vessel involved or the nationality of the recipient'.

[62] AFS 2022, Article 3.8.

[63] Ibid., Article 3.2.

[64] Ibid., Articles 3.2(c) and 3.3.

on its own, taking into account 'the nature, gravity and repetition of IUU fishing committed'. This is not, however, an entirely self-judging period, as the prohibition in Article 3.1 must apply at least as long as the sanction resulting from the affirmative determination remains in force or as long as the vessel/operator is listed by an RFMO/A, whichever is the longer.[65] While the affirmative determinations above trigger the Article 3.1 prohibition, a notification by a port State member about IUU fishing by a vessel in one of its ports triggers the obligation of a subsidizing member to 'give due regard to the information received and take such actions in respect of its subsidies as it deems appropriate'.[66]

Furthermore, Article 3.7 obligates each member to 'have laws, regulations and/or administrative procedures in place to ensure that subsidies referred to in Article 3.1, including such subsidies existing at the entry into force of this Agreement, are not granted or maintained'. As this obligation applies regardless of a member's maritime law status, whether coastal or landlocked, all Central Asian WTO members that have accepted the AFS will have to introduce such domestic rules/procedures. Moreover, each member, including those from Central Asia, will have to notify the WTO's Committee on Fisheries Subsidies of its laws, regulations, and administrative procedures under Article 3.7 within one year of the date of entry into force of the AFS, and promptly inform that Committee of any modifications thereafter.[67] Upon another member's request for additional information, a State must quickly respond in writing and in a comprehensive manner. If a member considers that a notification or information has not been provided, that member may bring the matter to the attention of the member concerned or to the Committee on Fisheries Subsidies.[68]

11.4.3 Prohibition of Subsidies for Overfished Stocks (AFS Article 4)

Article 4.1 of the AFS prohibits members from providing subsidies for fishing or fishing-related activities regarding stocks that are overfished. According to the FAO, over a third of the world's marine stocks are overfished[69]—that is exploited beyond their ability to regenerate. A fish stock is considered overfished if it is so recognized by a relevant coastal member or RFMO/A 'based on scientific evidence available to it'.[70] The Article 4.1 ban does not apply if a member's subsidies or other measures are implemented to rebuild the stock to a biologically sustainable level as determined by a relevant costal member based on applicable reference points (e.g., maximum

[65] Ibid., Article 3.4.

[66] Ibid., Article 3.6.

[67] Ibid., Articles 8.3 and 8.4.

[68] Ibid., Article 8.5.

[69] See FAO 2024, p. 43.

[70] AFS 2022, Article 4.2.

sustainable yield) or by an RFMO/A in charge.[71] This could include, for instance, government support for purchases of more selective fishing gear or improving fishers' catch monitoring.[72] As with the IUU case above, developing country members' subsidies here are exempt from dispute challenges in the WTO during a two-year grace period.[73]

11.4.4 Prohibition of Subsidies in the Unregulated High Seas and Other Disciplines (AFS Article 5)

Article 5.1 prohibits subsidies for fishing and fishing-related activities in areas beyond any coastal country's jurisdiction and an RFMO/A's competence, or in other words, in the unregulated high seas. This provision is introduced to address any risk of unsustainable fishing due to the lack of effective control in these areas. However, because the actual level of catches from the unregulated high seas has been marginal, Article 5.1 is expected to have a limited practical impact,[74] at least in the short run.

Separately from the prohibition above, Article 5 also mandates that members 'take special care and exercise due restraint' (i) when subsidizing vessels not flying their flag (hence, potentially including Central Asian vessels if any) or (ii) when subsidizing fishing or fishing-related activities concerning stocks whose status (on how far they are exploited) is unknown.[75] While not entailing a ban, the terms 'special care' and 'due restraint', albeit not defined, indicate a need for caution against subsidies in these situations. Subsidies for disaster relief are exempt from the Article 5 disciplines.[76]

11.4.5 Notification (AFS Article 8)

Article 25 of the SCM Agreement requires all members to regularly notify the WTO of their industrial subsidies which meet the parameters of 'subsidy' and 'specificity' under that agreement. Article 8.1 of the AFS obliges each member to add to their Article 25 subsidy notifications the information about the type of subsidized fishing activity and, 'to the extent possible', about the status of stocks in the subsidized fishery (whether overfished, sustainably fished, or underfished, etc.), conservation and management measures, fleet capacity in the subsidized fishery, name and identification number of subsidized vessels, and catch data in the subsidized

[71] Ibid., Article 4.3.

[72] Irschlinger & Tipping 2023, p. 12.

[73] AFS 2022, Article 4.4.

[74] Hoekman et al. 2023, p. 272.

[75] AFS 2022, Articles 5.2 and 5.3.

[76] See ibid., Article 11.1.

fishery. While being subject to this notification requirement, the Central Asian WTO members are likely to provide little to no substantive information about (most of) these items as these appear largely irrelevant to them. Moreover, the AFS permits developing country members accounting for less than 0.8 percent of global marine capture production to provide this additional information on fisheries every four years.[77] This lower-than-usual frequency of fisheries-related notification will most likely apply to the Central Asian WTO members as well.

Furthermore, each member must annually notify the WTO of vessels and operators that it has affirmatively determined as IUU engaged. If a Central Asian WTO member made such determination for vessels (if any) flying its flag, it must notify accordingly. In addition, each member (hence, including those from Central Asia) must, within one year of the AFS's entry into force, inform the WTO of its AFS-implementing measures and provide a description of its fisheries regime including laws, regulations, and administrative procedures.[78]

Members must also notify 'any RFMO/A' to which they are parties, along with the RFMO/A's foundation legal instrument, information about the area and species under its competence, the managed fish stocks' status, conservation and management measures, the rules and procedures for IUU fishing determinations, and updated lists of vessels/operators that it has determined as having been engaged in IUU fishing.[79] The reference to 'any' RFMO/A in the notification requirement above must be read together with the other parts of the AFS, including, inter alia, on the exclusion of aquaculture and inland fisheries from the scope of this agreement. Thus, RFMO/As not in charge of marine fisheries appear to fall outside the notification obligation. This is the case of, for example, the Central Asian and Caucasus Regional Fisheries and Aquaculture Commission—an RFMO dealing with fisheries management and conservation measures as well as sustainable development of aquaculture in the inland waters of Central Asia and the Caucasus.[80] Among the Central Asian countries, Kyrgyzstan and Tajikistan are members of this body.[81] While not obliged, these countries may still decide to voluntarily notify this RFMO to the WTO for transparency reasons.

To preclude any legal disadvantages for the notifying member from what it has notified, the AFS makes it clear that notifications under this agreement do not prejudice the nature of the notified measure, its legal status under WTO rules, or its effects under the SCM Agreement.[82]

[77] Ibid., footnote 13 to Article 8.1.

[78] Ibid., Articles 8.3 and 8.4.

[79] Ibid., Article 8.6.

[80] FAO n.d.a.

[81] Ibid.

[82] AFS 2022, Article 8.7.

11.4.6 Institutional Framework (AFS Article 9)

Like many other agreements in the WTO, the AFS will have its own specialized administrative body with some overseeing functions as envisaged in Article 9 of the AFS. In particular, the Committee on Fisheries Subsidies, composed of representatives from each member, will meet at least twice a year, and the Central Asian WTO members, like others, will be able to have their say in these meetings. The Committee is specifically tasked with facilitating consultations among members on any matter regarding the operation of this agreement, examining all information provided by members under the notification provisions, reviewing the AFS's implementation and operation, and maintaining close contact with the FAO and other relevant international organizations in this field.

11.4.7 Conditional Sunset Clause (AFS Article 12)

Article 12 of the AFS provides that, unless decided otherwise, this agreement will immediately terminate if comprehensive disciplines are not adopted within four years from the entry into force of this agreement. As background information for this sunset provision, the current AFS text does not address subsidies contributing to overcapacity (in essence, excessive fishing capacity above what is necessary to harvest an optimum yield)[83] and overfishing (collectively 'OCOF') that were initially included in the AFS negotiations but removed at the final stage because of the absence of consensus. The sunset clause was added to pressure members to finalize the unfinished work on OCOF subsidies. At the 13th Ministerial Conference (2024), WTO members failed to agree on the proposed additional disciplines, according to which OCOF subsidies would include subsidies for[84]:

- vessel construction, acquisition, maintenance, and modernization;
- the purchase or maintenance of machines and equipment for vessels;
- the purchase of fuel, ice, or bait;
- costs of personnel, social charges, or insurance;
- income support;
- price support of fish caught;
- at-sea support; and,
- operating losses of vessels or fishing or fishing related activities.

As long as the Central Asian countries' fisheries subsidies remain limited to aquaculture and inland fisheries, which are excluded from the AFS rules, these subsidies are unlikely to be affected by the future disciplines on OCOF subsidies.

[83] See Coastal Resources Center and Graduate School of Oceanography 2014, pp. 1–2.

[84] See WTO 2024b.

11.5 Conclusion

Despite the difficulties in consensus-building, WTO members managed to adopt the AFS in support of the UN SDG on the conservation of the oceans, seas, and marine resources. They still have to complete the second phase of negotiations dealing with OCOF subsidies. Unlike the SCM Agreement that regulates industrial subsidies due to their trade-distortive effects, the AFS disciplines fisheries subsidies to address their negative environmental impacts. This shift in regulatory focus is a clear indication of the growing integration of environmental sustainability into global trade policymaking.

Because the AFS prohibits marine fisheries subsidies, it will be of comparatively limited relevance to the Central Asian WTO members, which are landlocked countries. However, as this chapter has shown, the AFS does not make explicit exemptions for landlocked countries as such and obligates all members, whether coastal or landlocked, to adopt the necessary national laws and comply with the transparency requirements, among other obligations. Overall, the full participation of the Central Asian WTO members in the AFS will demonstrate their support for global sustainability efforts and help them meet their own needs for fish products.

References

AFS (2022) Agreement on fisheries subsidies. https://www.wto.org/english/docs_e/legal_e/legal_e.htm. Accessed 4 July 2025.

Coastal Resources Center and Graduate School of Oceanography (2014) Addressing the overcapacity issue in small-scale fisheries. University of Rhode Island.

FAO (2001) International plan of action to prevent, deter and eliminate illegal, unreported and unregulated fishing.

FAO (2021) Aquaculture growth potential in landlocked developing countries. WAPI factsheet. https://openknowledge.fao.org/server/api/core/bitstreams/e6a6f758-66e8-43b1-b33d-2d45f00d58ce/content.

FAO (2024) The state of world fisheries and aquaculture: Blue transformation in action.

FAO (n.d.-aa) Central Asian and Caucasus Regional Fisheries and Aquaculture Commission (CACFISH). https://www.fao.org/fishery/en/organization/cacfish. Accessed 4 July 2025.

FAO (n.d.-bb) Illegal, unreported and unregulated (IUU) fishing. https://www.fao.org/iuu-fishing/en/. Accessed 4 July 2025.

Hoekman B M, Mavroidis P. C, & Sasmal S. (2023) Managing externalities in the WTO: The agreement on fisheries subsidies. *Journal of International Economic Law, 26*, 266–284. https://doi.org/10.1093/jiel/jgad008

International Seabed Authority (2021) Landlocked developing countries and the law of the sea: an ocean of opportunity.

Irschlinger T. & Tipping A. (2023) *The WTO agreement on fisheries subsidies: A reader's guide.* International Institute for Sustainable Development.

Lo C & Wang T-K (2021) From addressing trade distortion to correcting environmental distortion: The fisheries subsidies negotiation as the turning point of the WTO'S task. *Asian Journal of WTO & International Health Law and Policy, 16*, 153–178. https://papers.ssrn.com/sol3/papers.cfm?abstract_id=3933674

Milazzo M (1998) Subsidies in world fisheries: A reexamination. World Bank Technical Paper No. 406 (Fisheries Series).
Ocean Connections (n.d.) Overfishing. https://www.oceanconnections.org/overfishing. Accessed 4 July 2025.
Scholaert F (2022) *WTO agreement on fisheries subsidies.* European Parliamentary Research Service.
SCM Agreement (1994) Agreement on Subsidies and Countervailing Measures. https://www.wto.org/english/docs_e/legal_e/legal_e.htm. Accessed 4 July 2025.
Shadikhodjaev S (2013) Duty drawback and regional trade agreements: Foes or friends? *Journal of International Economic Law, 16*, 587–611. https://doi.org/10.1093/jiel/jgt020
Shadikhodjaev S (2018) Industrial policy and the World Trade Organization: Between legal constraints and flexibilities. *Cambridge University Press, Cambridge.* https://doi.org/10.1017/9781316535172
Shadikhodjaev S (2023) Industrial policy in Asia-Pacific integration: Localization measures and subsidies in ASEAN countries. *Asia Pacific Law Review, 31*, 618–640. https://doi.org/10.1080/10192557.2023.2216418
Shadikhodjaev S (2024) Energy and the environment: Exploring the nexus under international economic law. *Cambridge University Press, Cambridge.* https://doi.org/10.1017/9781009042239
Shadikhodjaev S (2025) Foundations of the energy-environment nexus and international economic law. *Manchester Journal of International Economic Law*, *22*, 94–121. https://papers.ssrn.com/sol3/papers.cfm?abstract_id=5296533
Umirdinov A, Shadikhodjaev S, & Mukhitdinov M (2026) National implementation of international economic law: Uzbekistan. In Schefer KN Cottier T (eds) Elgar encyclopedia of international economic law. 2nd edn (expanded). https://doi.org/10.4337/9781800882324.cr.national.implementation.international.economic.law.uzbekistan
UN (2002) Report of the world summit on sustainable development. Johannesburg. South Africa. 26 August–4 September 2002. A/CONF.199/20. Plan of implementation of the World Summit on Sustainable Development.
UN (2015) Transforming our world: The 2030 agenda for sustainable development. Resolution adopted by the General Assembly on 25 September 2015, A/RES/70/1 (21 October 2015).
UN (2023) The sustainable development goals report 2023: Special edition.
UN (n.d.) What is a landlocked developing country? https://www.un.org/en/landlocked/about-landlocked-developing-countries. Accessed 4 July 2025.
UN Trade and Development (n.d.) List of LLDCs. https://www.un.org/ohrlls/content/list-lldcs. Accessed 4 July 2025.
UNCLOS (1982) United Nations Convention on the Law of the Sea. https://www.un.org/depts/los/convention_agreements/texts/unclos/unclos_e.pdf. Accessed 4 July 2025.
WTO (1998) Committee on Trade and Environment—Report of the meeting held on 19–20 March 1998—Note by the Secretariat. WT/CTE/M/17 (9 April 1998).
WTO (2001) Ministerial Conference—Fourth session—Doha, 9–14 November 2001—Ministerial declaration—Adopted on 14 November 2001. WT/MIN(01)/DEC/1 (20 November 2001).
WTO (2005) Ministerial Conference—Sixth session—Hong Kong, 13–18 December 2005—Doha work programme—Ministerial declaration—Adopted on 18 December 2005. WT/MIN(05)/DEC (22 December 2005).
WTO (2017) Ministerial Conference—Eleventh session—Buenos Aires, 10–13 December 2017—Fisheries subsidies—Ministerial decision of 13 December 2017. WT/MIN(17)/64, WT/L/1031 (18 December 2017).
WTO (2020) Negotiating group on rules—Unofficial room document—Fisheries subsidies—Draft proposal—Communication from the delegations of Afghanistan, Mongolia, Nepal and Paraguay. RD/TN/RL/130 (30 October 2020).
WTO (2021a) Easing trade bottlenecks in landlocked developing countries.

WTO (2021b) General Council—Minutes of meeting—Held in virtual format on 16–18 December 2020. WT/GC/M/188 (22 February 2021).
WTO (2021c) Negotiating group on rules—Fisheries subsidies—Revised draft text—Revision. TN/RL/W/276/Rev.2 (8 November 2021).
WTO (2021d) Negotiating group on rules—Fisheries subsidies—Revised draft consolidated chair text—Revision. TN/RL/W/276/Rev.1 (30 June 2021).
WTO (2021e) Negotiating group on rules—Fisheries subsidies—Revised draft consolidated chair text—Chair's explanatory note accompanying TN/RL/W/276/Rev.1—Addendum. TN/RL/W/276/Rev.1/Add.1 (30 June 2021).
WTO (2021f) Trade negotiations committee—Minutes of meeting—Held in virtual format on 15 July 2021, TN/C/M/41 (30 July 2021).
WTO (2021g) WTO examines progress in landlocked developing countries' trade performance. 26 April 2021. https://www.wto.org/english/news_e/news21_e/devel_26apr21_e.htm. Accessed 4 July 2025.
WTO (2022) Ministerial Conference—Twelfth session—Geneva, 12–15 June 2022—Agreement on fisheries subsidies—Ministerial decision of 17 June 2022. WT/MIN(22)/33, WT/L/1144 (22 June 2022). Attachment. Protocol amending the Marrakesh agreement establishing the World Trade Organization—Agreement on fisheries subsidies.
WTO (2023) DDG Ellard urges acceptance of fisheries subsidies agreement, progress on new disciplines. 13 June 2023. https://www.wto.org/english/news_e/news23_e/ddgae_13jun23_e.htm. Accessed 4 July 2025.
WTO (2024a) Kazakhstan formally accepts agreement on fisheries subsidies. 1 July 2024. https://www.wto.org/english/news_e/news24_e/fish_01jul24_e.htm. Accessed 4 July 2025.
WTO (2024b) Ministerial Conference—Thirteenth session—Abu Dhabi, 26–29 February 2024—Additional provisions on fisheries subsidies—Draft text. WT/MIN(24)/W/10 (16 February 2024).
WTO (2024c) Ministerial Conference—Thirteenth session—Landlocked developing countries (LLDCs) ministerial declaration—WTO ministerial meeting of the group of landlocked developing countries, 25 February 2024, Abu Dhabi, United Arab Emirates—Theme: 'unlocking the opportunities for LLDCs in global trade: The role of the multilateral trading system'. WT/MIN(24)/41 (5 March 2024).
WTO (2024d) Trade Policy Review Body—Trade policy review—Report by the Secretariat—Kazakhstan. WT/TPR/S/459 (21 August 2024).
WTO (2024e) Trade Policy Review Body—Trade policy review—Report by Kazakhstan, WT/TPR/G/459 (21 August 2024).
WTO (n.d.-aa) Groups in the negotiations. https://www.wto.org/english/tratop_e/dda_e/negotiating_groups_e.htm. Accessed 4 July 2025.
WTO (n.d.-bb) Members and observers. https://www.wto.org/english/thewto_e/whatis_e/tif_e/org6_e.htm. Accessed 4 July 2025.
WTO (n.d.-cc) Members submitting acceptance of agreement on fisheries subsidies. https://www.wto.org/english/tratop_e/rulesneg_e/fish_e/fish_acceptances_e.htm. Accessed 4 July 2025.

Chapter 12
Stabilization Clauses and Subsoil Use: Economic Development, Sovereignty, and International Law in Central Asia

Alberto Pecoraro

Abstract Stabilization clauses, which can be contract or legislation based, are meant to restrain a government from exercising its legislative and administrative powers to modify investment contracts it struck with mining companies. Their purpose is to assuage the investor's concerns that the state party may unilaterally nullify mining rights through legislation. From the viewpoint of national public law, the idea that a state could fetter its ability to legislate through contract is problematic. Such tension is well illustrated by an Israeli Supreme Court Decision from 27 March 2016, according to which stabilization clauses breach 'the general principle of administrative law regarding the prohibition of shackling the authority's ability to govern' since 'the government does not have the power not to decide and not to act.' Many questions arise concerning the effect of stabilization clauses in national and international law. These include: (1) whether stabilization clauses are compatible with national constitutions, (2) whether international law gives any effect to stabilization clauses even when they are incompatible with national law, (3) whether these clauses impede state regulation or merely create a duty to compensate the mining company. We will explore these three issues by analysing the contractual and legislative practice of Kazakhstan and Uzbekistan, referring to the not-so-consistent international case law on those issues.

Keywords Stabilization clauses · Investment agreements · Mining disputes · Permanent sovereignty over natural resources · International investment law

A. Pecoraro (✉)
Maqsut Narikbayev University, Astana, Kazakhstan
e-mail: a_pecoraro@kazguu.kz

S. Sayapin (ed.), *International Law, Politics and Security in Central Asia*,
https://doi.org/10.1007/978-3-032-17818-3_12

12.1 Stabilization Clauses and What they Are for

Investment projects concerned with the exploitation of natural resources are often vulnerable to regulatory risk. [1]Executed over a long period of time, and premised on several rights granted by national law, they can be affected by political and economic factors arising after the investor has decided to commit resources.[2] In this context, the state often plays a double role: as an economic actor—by being party to a mining development agreement or a production sharing agreement with the investor—and as a sovereign which maintains the ability and duty to regulate that investor's activities. Accordingly, changing circumstances, e.g. unforeseen windfall profits made by the investor or environmental pollution caused by extractive activities, may convince the host state that the initial bargain it struck with that investor must be changed. This may result in the termination of mining/petroleum rights, the imposition of new taxes, or other regulatory changes which may have extremely negative implications for investment projects. States are the masters of their internal laws and may, by constitutional, legislative, regulatory, or judicial measures, radically modify the legal environment where the investment is taking place.[3]

Stabilization commitments are commonly used to address such regulatory risk. These can be defined as 'legal devices to manage non-commercial (fiscal or regulatory) risk' which 'involve a contractual or legislative commitment by the host government not to alter the regulatory framework governing an investment project outside specific circumstances—such as the investor's consent.... and/or payment of compensation.'[4] Such clauses seek to stabilize the host state's actions to limit negative impacts on the economics of an investment project; however, their content and shape are heterogeneous.[5] These commitments come in different types. They may be contractual (contained in specific licenses or contracts granted by the state to contractors) or legislative (contained in general laws or regulations applicable to extractive activities).

A first category is that of classical 'freezing' clauses which fix national law at the time of the making of the investment agreement 'so as to make any subsequent changes to that particular law inapplicable to the investment.'[6] It can be said that they attempt to freeze time in regard to an investment project. An example of freezing clauses can be found in Article 19 of Uzbekistan's current Foreign Investment Law:

'If the subsequent legislation of the Republic of Uzbekistan worsens the investment conditions, the legislation in force on the date of investment is applied to investors within ten years from the date of investment. The investor has the right to apply those provisions of the new legislation that improve the conditions of his

[1] *The Movement for Quality Government in Israel v. Prime Minister*, paras 106, 107.

[2] Kabange Nkongolo, p.1.

[3] Weil (1974), p. 303.

[4] Cotula (2010), p.10.

[5] Umirdinov 2015, p. 460.

[6] Grenada Private Power Limited and WRB Enterprises, Inc. v. Grenada, ICSID Case No. ARB/17/13, Award of 29 March 2020, para 214.

investment at his own discretion. The guarantee of application for ten years of the legislation in force at the time of investment, in case of deterioration of investment conditions by subsequent legislation of the Republic of Uzbekistan, is applied in the following cases.'[7]

Another category is that of intangibility clauses, which require the consent of both parties to modify an investment contract.[8] Finally, economic equilibrium clauses provide that alterations to the contractual relationship are subordinate to a renegotiation of the contract to restore its original economic equilibrium or to the payment of compensation.[9] An example can be found in Kazakhstan's 1994 Law on Foreign Investments (FIL), under which:

'changes in the legislation of the Republic of Kazakhstan in the area of ensuring defence potential, national security, ecological safety and public health and morals. If a change in legislation adversely affects the position of a foreign investor in these areas, the foreign investor must be paid immediate adequate and effective compensation in the currency of the investment or in the foreign currency established by the foreign investor's agreement with the Republic of Kazakhstan.'[10]

There is also a wide variety concerning the subject matter of such clauses. Some are extremely broad and cover all matters except carve-outs in the field of environmental protection, industrial safety, worker health, and security. Others are more limited and cover only fiscal matters or matters of corporate governance. Overall, a correctly drafted stabilization commitment neither limits a state's bona fide public measures nor subjects investors to the pressure of arbitrary actions by the state.[11] Indeed, too sweeping stabilization commitments may unduly constrain action in social, fiscal, or environmental matters: the notion of sustainable development—which juggles economic, social, and environmental considerations—requires a level of regulatory flexibility that allows the state to adapt its legal framework to changing conditions.[12]

12.2 Stabilization Clauses in National Laws: Kazakhstan and beyond

May a state limit its regulatory action by contract or by law without violating its fundamental constitutional principles? As was stated by Sornarajah, '[t]he state, in theory, must act in the public good as it perceives it to be at any given time. It may not be possible, as a matter of constitutional theory, for a state to bind itself by a contract made with a private party, particularly a foreign party, to getter its

[7] Law of the Republic of Uzbekistan of 14.12.2019 No. 598 'On Investments and Investment Activity', article 19.

[8] Cotula 2008.

[9] Luttrell & Murphy 2019, p. 35.

[10] AES Corporation and Tau Power B.V. v. Republic of Kazakhstan, para 161.

[11] Umirdinov 2015, p. 460.

[12] Cotula 2010, p.10.

legislative power.'[13] Additionally, 'it is trite law that a legislature is not bound by its own legislation and the power to change it,' so that 'as a matter of constitutional theory, a stabilization clause may not be able to achieve what is sets out to do'[14] because national principles of law provide that the 'government does not have the power to decide not to act.'

Common law jurisdictions traditionally adhere to a principle of *non-fettering*, whereby, in the absence of an explicit legislative authorization to do so, a state may not limit by contract its ability to legislate.[15] For example, in 2007, the Federal High Court of Nigeria found unconstitutional a statute providing for the stability of an investment project because it interfered with the constitutional rules on the legislature's powers.[16] In Canada, the Supreme Court ruled in *Pacific National Investments Ltd v. Victoria (City)* that a contractual obligation to compensate a private contractor for the exercise of regulatory powers (in effect, what an economic equilibrium clause is about) was incompatible with the public law prohibition against fettering.[17] The plaintiff had argued that a contract for the construction of residential housing contained an implied term whereby construction would only be done in consideration of a certain zoning decision: consequently the municipality had to offset the re-zoning's financial impact through financial compensation.[18] However, the distinction between direct and indirect fettering suggested by the plaintiff was rejected by the Canadian Supreme Court. It considered that the ratio of the prohibition against fettering is to protect the legislative process from undue influence: in this regard direct and indirect fettering would have had the same effect on the exercise of those powers.[19]

Similarly, various civil law jurisdictions enshrine protections for the state's regulatory activity. For example, French law recognizes the existence of a separate category of administrative contracts whereby the state party is given a power of unilateral modification in the public interest (with, however, a corresponding duty to pay compensation).[20] For instance, French courts operate a balance of the different interests at play so that not any and all public purpose will justify derogating from a stabilization commitment. Accordingly, in 2014, France's supreme administrative court held that the goal of gaining more revenue for the public budget did not per se justify legislative amendments which would have upended prior promises of fiscal stability.[21]

---

[13] Sornarajah 2010, pp. 282–283.

[14] Ibid.

[15] Rederiaktiebolaget Amphitrite v. The King; see also Silly Creek Estate and Marina Company Ltd. v. Attorney General of Turks and Caicos Islands.

[16] Niger Delta Development Commission v. Nigeria Liquefied Natural Gas Company Limited, Suit Number FHC/PH/313/2005, Judgment of 14 July 2007, p.32.

[17] Pacific National Investments Ltd. v. Victoria (City) para 59.

[18] Ibid.

[19] Ibid.

[20] Wauters et al. Wauters & de Valkeneer 2018, p. 101.

[21] Conseil d'État 2014.

Analogous principles were at play in the Israeli Supreme Court ruling in *The Movement for Quality Government in Israel v. Prime Minister* where the Supreme Court struck down a freezing clause contained in a government plan for the development of natural gas deposits. This plan was not a contract, but the parties to the dispute agreed it amounted to a binding governmental promise.[22] Speaking for the majority, justice Rubinstein considered that, 'while governmental promises are binding, in exceptional cases governments may depart from them where changed circumstances justify it… However, governments are not allowed to refrain from using their discretion in order to decide whether such circumstances do exist,' which, he says, 'the Government has committed itself to doing in this case.'[23] That being said, justice Rubinstein distinguished between unacceptable freezing clauses and acceptable economic equilibrium clauses which granted more leeway to the government.[24] This point was seized by the only dissenting judge, Justice Sohlberg, who considered that there was no real fettering where the government could depart from the clause upon the payment of compensation to the promisee.[25]

Nevertheless, there are also national laws which are perfectly comfortable with the idea of stabilization commitments given by state bodies. In some rare cases, national constitutions explicitly grant to the state the right to freeze the law through contractual undertakings.[26] More commonly, it is ordinary legislation that contains stabilization commitments or at least authorizes the government to include stabilization clauses in investment contracts, and to be bound by them.

Such is the case in the Republic of Kazakhstan, where the sweeping stabilization guarantees in the 1994 FIL were abandoned in favour of a more nuanced approach. Currently, three different scenarios can be identified. Firstly, there is the guarantee of 36(7) of the Code on Subsoil and Subsoil use, under which:

'Amendments and additions to the legislation of the Republic of Kazakhstan that *worsen the results of entrepreneurial activities* of a subsoil user under subsoil use contracts shall not apply to the contracts concluded before making such amendments and additions. The guarantees established by part one of this paragraph *shall not apply to changes in the legislation* of the Republic of Kazakhstan *in the field of ensuring national security, defence capability, environmental safety, healthcare, taxation, customs regulation and protection of competition,* except for the case provided for by part three of this paragraph. The guarantees established by part one of this paragraph shall apply to changes in the legislation of the Republic of Kazakhstan in the field of customs regulation, which provides for temporary exemption from export customs

---

22 Frid de Vries 2017, p. 334.

23 Ibid, p. 336.

24 The Movement for Quality Government in Israel v. Prime Minister, paras 94–102.

25 Ibid, per Justice Sohlberg, at [8]–[39].

26 See Constitution of Peru, article 62: 'By means of contract law, the State may provide guarantees and grant security. These may not be modified legislatively, without prejudice to the protection provided in the preceding paragraph.'

duties on crude oil produced under a contract for the exploration and production or production of hydrocarbons under complex projects' [emphasis added].[27]

Article 36(7) is premised on a notion—the worsening of the results of entrepreneurial activities—which is not defined precisely. In the case of *AES v. Kazakhstan* this notion was precisely at the centre of the disputes between the parties: between 2001 and 2008 changes in national competition law led to the inclusion of claimant's companies among regulated monopolies, and sanctions were imposed on AES companies for violations of competition laws and abuse of market dominance.[28] The claimant argued that the adverse effects of these new rules were, on their own, sufficient to trigger the stabilization clause in Article 6 of the FIL (which had a similar language). The tribunal disagreed: the claimant's interpretation would 'not only be unmanageable but it would also create problems of transparency and predictability as to which provisions apply to a particular investor and which do not.'[29] Additionally, it held that Kazakhstan's legislative amendments had the goal of liberalizing the energy market and followed 'a common approach to the regulation of markets in the general public interest.'[30] Hence, the protections under the stabilization clause contained in the 1994 FIL had not been triggered. In other words, the fact that the application of a new rule may—in some cases—result in a greater financial burden is not sufficient.

Another important aspect is that Article 36(7) has an extremely broad carve out which includes taxation but also extremely broad concepts such as national security. Finally, the stipulations of this code do not foresee the existence of contractual economic equilibrium clauses—which are neither prohibited nor explicitly provided for. To the author's best knowledge, Kazakhstan's more recent mining licenses do not contain any additional stabilization guarantees.[31] However, it is very much possible that some of the older mining concessions contracts which included broader stabilization guarantees are still in force.[32]

A second scenario concerns a group of eleven Production Sharing Agreements (PSAs) concluded between the government of the Republic of Kazakhstan and

---

[27] Code on Subsoil and Subsoil Use of the Republic of Kazakhstan, article 36.

[28] AES Corp v. Kazakhstan, ICSID No. ARB/10/16, Award of 1 November 2013, paras 44–45.

[29] Ibid, para 272.

[30] Ibid, para 278.

[31] See, for example, Kazakhmys, Exploitation License 2019, section 9: "Исчисление налоговых обязательств по налогам и другим обязательным платежам в бюджет по деятельности, осуществляемой в рамках Контракта, производится в соответствии с налоговым законодательством, действующим на момент возникновения обязательств по их уплате. Исполнение налоговых обязательств по деятельности, осуществляемой в рамках Контракта, не освобождает Недропользователя от исполнения налогового обязательства по осуществлению деятельности в Республике Казахстан, выходящей за рамки Контракта, в соответствии с налоговым законодательством Республики Казахстан, действующим на дату возникновения налогового обязательства."

[32] See, for example, Contract No. 954 for the Exploration and Production of Hydrocarbons entered into between CCC and the MEMR on 27 May 2002, section 28.

various petroleum companies.[33] Among those PSAs, the most crucial are those which regulate the exploitation of the Karachaganak and Kashagan oil fields, concluded for a duration of forty years.[34] Currently, there is no specific legal instrument which regulates existing PSAs in Kazakhstan.[35] In 2010, the Kazakh legislator abandoned this form of contract. However, this did not affect the PSAs which had been previously negotiated with the companies involved in the exploitation of Kashagan and Karachaganak.[36] Given the strong bargaining power of major international oil companies in the late 1990s, it is probable that those PSAs contain broad tax and regulatory stabilization clauses. It is possible that there are economic equilibrium clauses protecting the initial contractual bargain should it be affected by regulatory changes. Unfortunately, those PSAs are not in the public domain.

A third scenario is that of investors benefiting from tax stabilization due to an investment agreement. This does not apply to subsoil use, so that—for our purposes—this legal regime is not particularly important. Here, it will suffice to say that Article 289 of the Entrepreneur Code grants legal stability from changes in 'the tax legislation of the Republic of Kazakhstan in accordance with the Code of the Republic of Kazakhstan "On Taxes and Other Obligatory Payments to the Budget" (Tax Code) and the "legislation of the Republic of Kazakhstan on migration of the population in the field of attracting foreign labour".'[37]

12.3 Stabilization Clauses in General International Law

One may wonder what international law has to do with stabilization commitments made by the state through national law. International law may intervene in different ways. First, when the contract incorporates explicitly or implicitly international law as part of its governing law. For instance, in the contract-based *Cambodia Power Company v. Kingdom of Cambodia* arbitration, the tribunal held that it could hear a claim based on customary international law because of the latter's incorporation in the law that governed that contract—English law.[38] Similarly, in *Penwell v. Kyrgyz* Republic the tribunal based itself on Article 6 of the then Constitution of Kyrgyzstan

---

[33] Perzadayeva and Amangeldy (2022).

[34] Ibid.

[35] Sahin (2020), p. 8.

[36] Ibid.

[37] Tax Code of the Republic of Kazakhstan, article 289.

[38] Cambodia Power Company v. Kingdom of Cambodia, para 333: 'The express choice of English law itself has the effect of including (rather than displacing) at least a body of customary international law, since customary international law (i.e. general practices of states followed by them from a sense of legal obligation) constitutes part of the Common law by a well-established doctrine of incorporation. When customary international law changes, the Common law also incorporates these changes, save to the extent that such changes conflict with domestic law.' See also Interocean Oil Development Company and Interocean Oil Exploration Company v. Federal Republic of Nigeria.

(referring to universally recognized rules of international law) to apply the international legal prohibition on corruption and exclude its jurisdiction over the claim.[39] Second, it may be that international law is part of the *lex arbitri:* for example, Article 42 of the International Centre for Settlement of Investment Disputes (ICSID) Convention grants to arbitral tribunals the inherent power to apply international law to a given dispute. When parties have selected national law, international law will still play a supplementary and corrective role vis à vis the contract.[40] This 'may result in not applying it where that [national] law, or action taken under that law, violates international law.'[41]

Even more importantly, international jurisprudence has generally recognized the validity of (contractual) stabilization clauses. Referring to the principles of party autonomy and *pacta sunt servanda,* arbitral case law has consistently held them to be an expression of state sovereignty rather than a violation of the principle of permanent sovereignty over natural resources. In *Texaco v. Libya* and *Revere Copper v. OPIC,* the arbitrators went as far as suggesting that international law was objectively applicable to the dispute because of the specific nature of the underlying contracts as 'economic development agreements.'[42] More recently, the *Grenada Private Power Limited and WRB Enterprises, Inc. v. Grenada* grounded the validity of a freezing clause (which excluded the application of rules of law incompatible with it) on Article 42 of the ICSID convention. By allowing parties to designate 'rules of law' rather than 'law,' it enables them to agree on a partial choice of law and select specific rules from a system of law.[43]

Case law has shown contrasting approaches regarding the effect of those clauses. An old investment contract arbitration, *Aminoil v. Kuwait,* assessed whether a contractual stabilization clause prevented the nationalization of an oil concession. The tribunal hinted that the principle of permanent sovereignty over natural resources requires a restrictive interpretation of those clauses:

'No doubt contractual limitations on the State's right to nationalize are juridically possible, but what that would involve would be a particularly serious undertaking which would have to be expressly stipulated for, and be within the regulations governing the conclusion of State contracts; and it is to be expected that it should cover only a relatively limited period. In the present case however, the existence of such a stipulation would have to be presumed as being covered by the general

---

[39] Penwell Business Limited (by MegaCom) v. Kyrgyz Republic, paras 331 et seq.

[40] Alvik (2011), p.60.

[41] Southern Pacific Properties (Middle East) Limited v. Arab Republic of Egypt, Award of 20 May 1992, para 84.

[42] Revere Copper and Brass Incorporated v. Overseas Private Investment Corporation, para 128.

[43] Grenada Private Power Limited and WRB Enterprises, Inc. v. Grenada, para 215. On a related note, Societe des Mines de Loulo S.A. c. La Republique du Mali, para 165 observed that 'the parties agreed, in their exchanges, that [a freezing clause in a mining contract] consecrates the supremacy of that agreement over Mali's national law.' Similarly in Eni Ghana Exploration and Production Limited and Vitol Upstream Ghana Limited v. Republic of Ghana and Ghana National Petroleum Corporation (GNPC), Ghana did not contest the validity and effect of a stabilization commitment incorporating freezing, intangibility, and economic equilibrium obligations.

language of the stabilization clauses, and over the whole period of an especially long concession since it extended to 60 years. *A limitation on the sovereign rights of the State is all the less to be presumed where the concessionaire is in any event in possession of important guarantees regarding its essential interests in the shape of a legal right to eventual compensation.*' [emphasis added].[44]

A more recent ICSID arbitration has given a broader reading to contractual stability commitments. In *Duke Energy v. Peru,* the claimant had hitherto benefited from tax benefits under Peru's Merger Revaluation Law. It had concluded a Legal Stabilization Agreement with Peru, which guaranteed that the foreign investor would not be subject to a higher taxation rate.[45] Its investment operations were negatively affected by a change in the interpretation of national tax law which rendered impossible the claimant's acquisition of a local company. No new regulation had been introduced by the state, rather the dispute concerned a novel interpretation of existing law. The tribunal held that stabilization commitments freeze not only the law but also its interpretation. Indeed, 'if, at the time when the guarantee was granted, the application of the existing rules resulted in a consistent interpretation, such interpretation must be deemed to be incorporated into the guaranteed stability.'[46] In the absence of such a stable interpretation, all the investor may expect is that the existing law not be interpreted or applied in a 'patently unreasonable or arbitrary manner.'[47]

Duke Energy v. Peru provides a comprehensive description of the legal effects of a stabilization clause pronounced by a tribunal pursuant to Peruvian and international law. However, generalizing its conclusions may be difficult. The first reason concerns the specific nature of Peru's legal system with its constitutional and legislative protection of legal stability for foreign investors. Peruvian law—Article 24 of the Investment Regulations—speaks of 'stability to *the legal system* in force at the time of execution of the agreement.' Secondly, establishing whether a prior interpretation is stable enough may alter radically the role of international tribunals which do not sit as 'appellate divisions' of national bodies. It requires those bodies to 'opine on the correctness of the relevant decision or interpretation' compared to a prior interpretation which the tribunal decides was sufficiently established.[48]

Thirdly, its definition of 'stable interpretation' may itself be unworkable. When does an interpretation of the law become sufficiently stable? The Duke Energy case speaks only of clear case law, well-established practice, or generally accepted legal

---

[44] The American Independent Oil Company v. The Government of the State of Kuwait, para 95.

[45] Article 10(a) of Peru's Foreign Investment Law: 'By virtue of the guaranteed stability of the tax regime, the foreign investor shall not be subject to a rate higher than the one established in the appropriate agreement for the purposes of the income tax payable by the company receiving the investment, and the tax assessing the profits attributed thereto and/or the dividends distributed in favor thereof; therefore, if the income tax payable by the company is increased, the rate applied to the foreign investor shall be reduced by the required amount so that the company's profits freely available thereto are at least equal to the guaranteed profits.'

[46] *Duke Energy International v. Republic of Peru, para* 218.

[47] Ibid, para 227.

[48] Ibid, para 215.

doctrines.[49] Let's suppose for example that Kazakhstan's Supreme Court decides that investment contract arbitral clauses are invalid because they place tariff disputes beyond the control of the Republic.[50] Would a stabilization clause protect foreign investors from the new 'correct' application of Kazakh law? Finally, more recent jurisprudence—such as *AES v. Kazakhstan*—has shown a more nuanced approach concerning the applicability of stabilization clauses to regulatory changes.

Rules of international law may also affect the enforceability of stabilization commitments which were granted in violation of the applicable national law. This is in keeping with their suppletory and corrective role *vis a vis* the applicable national law. In various instances, investment tribunals have applied general principles of law to reject a state's claim that stabilization commitments were void due to the violation of constitutional principles.[51] Two examples illustrate this point well. In *SPP v. Egypt*, an ICSID tribunal dealt with Egypt's argument that the investor's rights were void ab initio since the state could not legally alienate land in the pyramids' area. This did not convince the tribunal:

'These acts, which are now alleged to have been in violation of the Egyptian municipal legal system, created expectations protected by established principles of international law. A determination that these acts are null and void under municipal law would not resolve the ultimate question of liability for damages suffered by the victim who relied on the acts.... the practice of states has conclusively established the international responsibility for unlawful acts of state organs, even if accomplished outside the limits of their competence and contrary to domestic law.'[52]

More recently, in *Stans Energy v. Kyrgyz Republic* a tribunal based on the state's FIL ruled that the initial illegality of the investor's licenses was not opposable to the investor: the latter could trust that its licenses were lawful because 'the entire process was organized and controlled by the respondent and because the latter continued to cooperate with the investor for years as well as re-issuing the licenses.'[53]

Finally, international law also intervenes at the level of the consequences arising from a violation of a stabilization clause. One point where there is unanimity concerns the remedies that are open due to the violation of a stabilization commitment. International case law points to payment of compensation as the main legal effect of a breach: in other words, there is no rule of international law requiring that a state stop regulating because of a stabilization commitment.[54] This is in keeping with the principle of permanent sovereignty over natural resources, justifying a restrictive

[49] Ibid, para 220.

[50] Ust Kamenogorsk Hydrogen Plant JSC v. AES Ust Kamenogorsk Hydropower Plant LLP, para 8 summarizing the Kazakh Supreme Court Order of 8 January 2004.

[51] Grenada Private Power Limited and WRB Enterprises, Inc. v. Grenada, para 215.

[52] Southern Pacific Properties (Middle East) Limited v. Arab Republic of Egypt, paras 81, 86.

[53] Stans Energy Corp. and Kutisay Mining LLC v. the Kyrgyz Republic, para 646.

[54] AGIP S.p.A. v. People's Republic of Congo, ICSID Case No. ARB/77/1, Sentence du 30 Novembre, 1979, para 88. Indeed '[l]a référence faite au droit international suffit à démontrer le caractère irrégulier, au regard de ce droit, des mesures de nationalisation intervenues en la présente affaire. Il en résulte que le Gouvernement est tenu d'indemniser AGIP au titre des dommages résultant pour elle de la nationalisation, notamment en ce qui concerne la valeur de sa participation au

interpretation of those clauses.[55] Investment tribunals have very rarely granted forms of remedy other than compensation, holding that this is legally impossible 'where a State has, in the exercise of sovereign power put an end to a contract or a licence or any other foreign investor's entitlement.'[56]

12.4 Stabilization Clauses and Investment Treaties

Stabilization mechanisms have played a key role in investment treaty arbitration through their impact on the application of treaty rules such as the prohibition on expropriation and the state's duty to grant fair and equitable treatment to the investor. Different arbitral decisions have considered stabilization clauses as a stark limit to the state's ability to exercise its police powers. Thus, in *Parkerings v. Lithuania*—concerning a municipality's refusal to authorize the construction of a parking lot close to the historical centre—the tribunal held that '[a] state has the right to enact, modify or cancel a law at its own discretion. *Save for the existence of an agreement, in the form of a stabilization clause or otherwise,* there is nothing objectionable about the amendment brought to the regulatory framework existing at the time an investor [invested].'[57] In other words, a stabilization clause creates a promise not to regulate, on which an investor may legitimately rely.

Here, there is a close relationship with the principle of legitimate expectations: where specific actions or statements by a State induce a person to act, the State, as a general rule, should not be able subsequently to renege on those commitments without generating liability.[58] Various types of state conduct may create legitimate expectations,[59] but it is generally considered that the existence of a law favourable to a foreign investor does not create an expectation that it will not be changed.[60] This suggests that, on their own, statutory stabilization clauses do not create a legitimate expectation that the law will not be changed. This was emphasized in *Oxus Gold v. Uzbekistan*, where the claimant complained of the state's revocation of tax privileges in violation of a statutory stabilization commitment. The tribunal held that:

---

capital de la société et le montant payé par AGIP ou susceptible d'être exigé d'elle en qualité de garant correspondant à cette participation.'

[55] American Independent Oil Company v. The Government of the State of Kuwait, para 95.

[56] Bernhard von Pezold and Others v. Republic of Zimbabwe, paras 709, 726.

[57] Parkerings-Compagniet AS v. Republic of Lithuania, para 332.

[58] Biggs 2021, p.100.

[59] See ESPF Beteiligungs GmbH v. Italian Republic, para 513: 'Legitimate expectations are based on the investor's objective understanding of the legal framework within which the investor has made its investment or, in other words, what a reasonable investor at the time would have expected. Such legal framework includes the host state's domestic legislation and regulations, as well as its international law obligations, any contractual arrangements concluded between the investor and the state, and the specific representations or undertakings made by the state.'

[60] El Paso Energy International Company v. Argentine Republic, para 337.

'As far as stabilization clauses are concerned, it is the view of the Tribunal that such a clause in a law or a general regulation does not give a vested right to the investor, as the State can always modify its laws and general regulations. The situation is different when a stabilization clause is included in a contract, or a regulation specifically directed at the investor.'[61]

The same was not the case for various Decrees which expressly concerned the specific goldfields Joint Venture in which the investor was engaged.

A good illustration of the possible effect of stabilization clauses is provided by an Energy Charter Treaty (or ECT) case involving the Italian authorities' decision to lower the feed-in-tariffs which had been granted to investors in the renewable energies sector. In this case, Greentech argued that Italian legal, regulatory, and contractual instruments repeated a commitment that tariffs were awarded for a period of twenty years.[62] For the tribunal, 'given the specificity of the assurances Italy offered (Conto Energia decrees, statements and conduct of Italian officials, and individual GSE letters and GSE Agreements), those assurances bear the hallmarks of... an agreement, in the form of a stabilisation clause or otherwise.'[63] Interestingly, the tribunal also seemed to suggest that the violation of a stabilization clause is not per se sufficient to constitute a breach of the fair and equitable treatment (or FET) obligation. Indeed, it stated a balancing of the regulatory right against the host state's assurances implicates a reasonable and valid policy justification for the changes.[64] Two lessons can be drawn from Greentech: first, that the meaning of 'stabilization' may be quite broad; second, that a breach of a stabilization guarantee may not on its own be sufficient to impose international liability on the state.

On this point, it may be difficult to understand whether a legislative or contractual provision is actually a stabilization clause creating a reasonable expectation that the legal regime will not be amended and/or that compensation will be paid in case of regulatory changes. This point is illustrated by the *Belenergia v. Italy* decision which concerned facts nearly identical to those in Greentech. There, the tribunal held that the accumulation of contractual, regulatory, and legislative commitments did not stabilize the rules applicable to investors in the renewable energy sector. Indeed, according to the consistent case law of Italian courts, the GSE Conventions were administrative contracts which replicated the regulatory rules that were subject to change by national regulators and were not addressed specifically to the claimant. In this regard:

'Neither does the Tribunal agree that the contractual 20-year term originally applying to feed in tariffs or the prohibition on unilateral changes could be considered a stabilization clause. The subsidy (feed-in tariff) (1) amount and (2) duration components under the GSE Conventions on feed-in tariffs were replicated from the

---

61 Oxus Gold v. Republic of Uzbekistan, p. 332.

62 Greentech Energy Systems A/S, et al. v. Italian Republic, para 413.

63 Ibid, para 453.

64 Ibid, para 454: in that case the tribunal was not convinced by Italy's justification of lowering of prices on private consumers because the law was also addressed to industrial consumers and its effects did not lead to a significant reduction of electricity costs for consumers.

relevant legislation including the successive Energy Account Ministerial Decrees that automatically applied to Belenergia's PV plants depending on their date of start of operations as they equally applied to any other PV plants satisfying the pre-requisites for this subsidy. These two components were set forth in Italian legislation and were not personally addressed to Belenergia. The contractual prohibition on unilateral changes concerned the GSE and not the Italian legislator.'[65]

This suggests that the analysis of legitimate expectations must be broadened. Not any clause which promises stability is actually a stabilization commitment, and the violation of a stabilization commitment is not sufficient for finding that a state has committed an international wrong. One must also look at its relationship with rules that occupy a higher position in the hierarchy of national norms and may require a level of regulatory flexibility.

12.5 Some Conclusions

Foreign investors engaged in extractive activities have sought from host states assurances that regulatory changes will not affect the economic balance of their project. Numerous states, including those in Central Asia, have accordingly created exceptional legal regimes applicable to foreign investors. This has been done through contractual and legislative mechanisms to fetter state regulation. As seen above, the use of this type of mechanism can be violative of fundamental principles of constitutional law requiring the sovereign to regulate. Regardless of such norms, international law has generally recognized that stabilization clauses do have an effect—even when they are void under national law. Where international law is less clear, is the effect of those stabilization clauses—that is, which regulatory changes trigger them, which obligations they actually impose, and their relationship with investment treaty standards. For instance, international arbitral case law has tended to attribute more impact to contractual stabilization clauses as opposed to similar provisions contained in legislation. This is even though, under national laws, the position of contractual stabilization commitments is potentially much more tenuous.

References

AES Corp v Kazakhstan, ICSID No. ARB/10/16, Award of 1 November 2013.

AGIP S.p.A. v. People's Republic of Congo, ICSID Case No. ARB/77/1, Sentence du 30 Novembre 1979.

Alvik I (2011) Contracting with Sovereignty: State Contracts and International Arbitration, Hart Publishing Studies in International Law, volume 31.

American Independent Oil Company v. The Government of the State of Kuwait, Final Award of 24 March 1982.

---

[65] *Belenergia S.A. v. Italian Republic*, para 580.

*Belenergia SA*v *Italian Republic*, ICSID Case No. ARB/15/40, Award of 28 August 2019.
Bernhard von Pezold and Others v Republic of Zimbabwe, ICSID Case No. ARB/10/15, Award of 28 July 2015.
Biggs J (2021) The scope of investors' legitimate expectation under the FET standard in the European renewable energy cases. *ICSID Review—Foreign Investment Law Journal, 36*(1), 99–128.
Cambodia Power Company v Kingdom of Cambodia, ICSID Case No. ARB/09/18, Decision on Jurisdiction of 22 March 2011.
Code of the Republic of Kazakhstan on Subsoil and Subsoil Use dated December 27, 2017, No. 125-VI.
Code of the Republic of Kazakhstan on Taxes and Other Obligatory Payments to the Budget' dated October 29, 2015 No 375-V, LRK.
Conseil d'Etat avis n° 387959, *Projet de loi de pays en Nouvelle Calédonie*, Rapport Public 2014.
Contract No. 954 for the Exploration and Production of Hydrocarbons entered into between CCC and the MEMR on 27 May 2002, excerpts available at https://jusmundi.com/en/document/decision/en-caratube-international-oil-company-llp-and-devincci-salah-hourani-v-republic-of-kazakhstan-ii-award-wednesday-27th-september-2017. Accessed 20 August 2025.
Cotula (2008) Regulatory Takings, Stabilization Clauses and Sustainable Development (2008), OECD Global Forum on International Investment VII "Best Practices in Promoting Investment for Development") at https://www.iied.org/x00009. Accessed 20 August 2025.
Cotula L (2010) Pushing the boundaries vs striking a balance: The scope and interpretation of stabilization clauses in light of the Duke v. Peru award. *The Journal of World Investment & Trade, 1*, 27–43.
Duke Energy International v. Republic of Peru, ICSID Case No. ARB/03/28, 18 August 2008.
El Paso Energy International Company v. Argentine Republic, ICSID Case No. ARB/03/15, Award of 31 October 2011.
Eni Ghana Exploration and Production Limited and Vitol Upstream Ghana Limited v. Republic of Ghana and Ghana National Petroleum Corporation (GNPC), SCC Case No. U2021/114, Award of 8 July 2024.
ESPF Beteiligungs GmbH, ESPF Nr. 2 Austria Beteiligungs GmbH, and InfraClass Energie 5 GmbH & Co. KG v. Italian Republic, ICSID Case No. ARB/16/5, Award of 14 September 2020.
Frid de Vries R (2017) Stability shaken? Israeli high court of justice strikes down the stabilization clause in the Israeli government's gas plan. *Journal of World Investment & Trade, 18*(2), 332–341.
Greentech Energy Systems A/S, et al v. Italian Republic, SCC Case No. V 2015/095, Final Award.
Grenada Private Power Limited *and* WRB Enterprises, *Inc. v. Grenada*, ICSID Case No. ARB/17/13.
Interocean Oil Development Company and Interocean Oil Exploration Company v. Federal Republic of Nigeria, ICSID Case No. ARB/13/20, Award of 6 October 2020.
Kabange Nkongolo C La Revision par l'Etat des Contrats Conclus avec les Personnes Privees: Cas des Contrats Miniers en RD Congo, available at: https://www.leganet.cd/Doctrine.textes/Decon/Dcontrats/RevisiondescontratsminiersRDC.pdf Accessed 19 August 2025.
Kazakhmys Exploitation License 2019 https://resourcecontracts.org/countries/kz. Accessed 20 August 2025.
Legislative Decree No. 662 (Foreign Investment Law of the Republic of Peru).
Luttrell S & Murphy A (2019) *Stabilisation provisions in long-term mining agreements IN fry J and Bret LA* (p. 2019). The Guide to Mining Arbitrations.
Movement for Quality Government in Israel v. Prime Minister, HCJ 4374/15, Judgment, 27 March 2016.
Niger Delta Development Commission v. Nigeria Liquefied Natural Gas Company Limited, Suit Number FHC/PH/313/2005, Judgment of 14 July 2007.
Oxus Gold v *Republic of Uzbekistan*, UNCITRAL, Award of 17 December 2015/.
Pacific National Investments Ltd. *v. Victoria* (City) [2000] 2 SCR 919.

Parkerings-Compagniet AS *v. Republic of Lithuania*, ICSID Case No. ARB/05/8, Award of 11 September 2007.

Penwell Business Limited (by MegaCom) v. Kyrgyz Republic, PCA Case No. 2017–31, Final Award of 8 October 2021.

Perzadayeva S and Amangeldy S (2022) Production Sharing Agreements: Kazakhstan, 31 January 2022, at https://www.mondaq.com/oil-gas%2D%2Delectricity/1155354/production-sharing-agreements-kazakhstan. Accessed 20 August 2025.

Rederiaktiebolaget Amphitrite v. The King (1921) 3 KB 500 ((1921) All ER Rep 542.

Revere Copper and Brass Incorporated v. Overseas Private Investment Corporation, Arbitral Award in Dispute Involving U.S. Investment Guaranty Program.

Sahin H (2020) *Production sharing agreements in the Caucasus and.* A Contextual.

Silly Creek Estate *and Marina Company Ltd v. Attorney General of Turks and Caicos Islands* [2021] UKPC 9.

Societe des Mines de Loulo S.A. c. La Republique du Mali, Affaire CIRDI ARB/13/16, Sentence du 2 Juin 2016.

Sornarajah M (2010) The international law on foreign investment, Cambridge University Press 3rd edition.

Southern Pacific Properties (Middle East) Limited v. Arab Republic of Egypt, ICSID Case No. ARB/84/3, Award of 20 May 1992.

Stans Energy Corp. and Kutisay Mining LLC v. the Kyrgyz Republic, PCA Case No. 2015–32, Award of 20 August 2019.

Study of Azerbaijan and Kazakhstan. Transnational Dispute Management 17(1):493–508.

Umirdinov A (2015) The end of hibernation for stabilisation clauses in investment arbitration: Reassessing its contribution to sustainable development. *Denver Journal of International Law & Policy, 43*(4), 455–487.

Ust Kamenogorsk Hydrogen Plant JSC v. AES Ust Kamenogorsk Hydropower Plant LLP [2013] UKSC 35.

Wauters K de Valkeneer D Vanderburie A (2018) La modification unilatérale d'un contrat public In: Wauters K « La modification unilatérale du contrat », Anthemis 2018.

Weil P (1974) Les Clauses De Stabilisation Ou d'intangibilité Insérées Dans Les Accords De Développement Économique In La communauté internationale: Mélanges Oferts a Charles Rousseau, 301–328. Weil-P.-Droit-international-et-contrats-dEtat.pdf https://www.sfdi.org/wp-content/uploads/2020/04/Weil-P.-Droit-international-et-contrats-dEtat.pdf. Accessed 20 August 2025.

Part VII
International Environmental Law

Chapter 13
International Legal Standards of Animal Welfare

Maria Baideldinova

Abstract Animal welfare has been an issue of ever-growing interest worldwide over the last decades. It is discussed in connection with pets, stray population control measures, animals used for entertainment, and in great part with agricultural animals. As vast multidisciplinary research demonstrates, the welfare of agricultural animals is tightly connected with human health. Poor conditions on farms and intensive farming, low transportation standards, and certain husbandry and slaughter practices negatively affect the quality of products of animal origin. Many countries increase their demands towards animal welfare for the sake of food safety. While Members of the WTO follow the sanitary standards established by the organization, there are countries that set their own stricter rules of animal welfare in addition to these standards. Some Central Asian countries, such as Kazakhstan, Kyrgyzstan, and Tajikistan are members of the WTO. Others (Uzbekistan and Turkmenistan) have the status of observers. The purpose of this chapter is to analyse the WTO documents regarding animal welfare, both in their content and in their nature, and to determine to what extent these standards are obligatory for countries which are members of the organization and those which are not. The chapter discusses the issue of how animal welfare standards may influence international trade and vice versa to see if international trade may help to improve animal welfare standards for agricultural animals in the world. The author argues that the WTO needs to set higher standards of animal welfare, while Kazakhstan, as an important participant of international trade in products of animal origin, needs to adjust its internal legislation to meet international legal animal welfare standards.

Keywords Animal welfare · Husbandry · WTO · Animal health · Kazakhstan

[…] the wise man is one who never sets himself apart from other living things, whether they have speech or not […]

A Wizard of Earthsea by Ursula Le Guin

M. Baideldinova (✉)
Law School, KIMEP University, Almaty, Kazakhstan
e-mail: maria@kimep.kz

S. Sayapin (ed.), *International Law, Politics and Security in Central Asia*,
https://doi.org/10.1007/978-3-032-17818-3_13

13.1 Introduction

The severity of the impact of animal welfare on human life and on the environment, as well as the interconnection between all the living organisms, has received constant confirmation from research in the natural sciences. Whether they are wild or domesticated animals, livestock or pets, their health and well-being echoes in the health of other species of animals, including *homo sapiens*. This is particularly true for agricultural animals, given their numbers and the fact that they serve as a source of animal products in human diets.

The WTO is notably not an organization explicitly devoted to the protection of animals, but animal welfare standards, especially in the sphere of agricultural production, play an increasing role in it. Developing countries joined the WTO for reasons unrelated to animal welfare, but by doing so they unintentionally set themselves on a path that could lead to improvements in animal welfare standards, as well as other unanticipated aspects of life.

This chapter explains why and how the WTO and other international trade mechanisms positively affect animal welfare worldwide.

Most of the published research on this issue comes from developed countries. Although there are authors who express doubts or open criticism towards the international trade system as a hindrance to developed countries in their attempts to set higher animal welfare standards,[1] many current publications in this sphere are rather optimistic.[2]

Indeed, looked at from the perspective of countries where public awareness and sensitivity regarding animals have a decades-long if not centuries-long tradition, the international standards appear lower than their internal ones. Only recent jurisprudence allows for some optimism from the point of view of these countries.

This chapter shows the situation from the perspective of the Republic of Kazakhstan, which, like other developing countries, sees the establishment of international animal welfare standards through the international trade system as an effective incentive for improving the internal standards.

The chapter considers the General Agreement on Tariffs and Trade (GATT) provisions,[3] as well as the provisions about agricultural animals contained in these agreements. Further, it describes the evolution of animal-related decisions made by the Dispute Settlement Body of the WTO while also considering the development of

[1] See, for instance, Thomas (2007), Stevenson and White (2015), who consider the WTO free trade rules as 'a major impediment to the adoption of stronger animal protection legislation by the EU', and others.

[2] See, for instance, Cunningham and Vindedzis (2017), Nielsen (2007), Sykes (2016) and others.

[3] We limited our discourse to the GATT provisions as the most significant for the animal welfare debate and jurisprudence. We did not consider here side-agreements which indirectly affect animal welfare, and which also were cited in some of the animal-related cases in the WTO system. For instance, the Agreement on Technical Barriers to Trade (TBT), the Agreement on Agriculture (AoA), and the Agreement on the Application of Sanitary and Phytosanitary Measures (SPS) are the most relevant to animal welfare issues. However, these agreements primarily focus on food safety, agricultural subsidies, and technical regulations rather than on animal welfare.

Kazakhstan's internal legislation regarding agricultural animals in the same timeline. Finally, the chapter analyses the perspectives and possible future developments of animal welfare standards in Kazakhstan and other developing countries through the prism of international trade rules.

13.2 Why Agricultural Animal Welfare Matters

The spheres in which humans interact with animals[4] are multiple. Trading in pets and captive wild animals—including illegal trafficking—takes place extensively worldwide. This chapter limits itself to considering the welfare of agricultural animals. Agricultural animals make up one of the most numerous categories of animals. For comparison, registered pets in Kazakhstan as of February 2025 amount to 303,310 animals, out of which 215,135 are cats, 88,167 are dogs, and the rest are other pets (ferrets, rabbits, and other). The unofficial statistics claim that the registered animals constitute 15% of the total kept animals (Katasonova and Sotnikov 2023). Even if one considers these unofficial statistics on pets, the number of agricultural animals is still incomparably higher. Just the horses bred for agricultural purposes exceed 4 million (Bureau of National Statistics 2024). There are over 9 million cows, over 20 million sheep and goats, and over 45 million chickens reared annually for human consumption in Kazakhstan (Bureau of National Statistics 2024).

At the same time, the suffering of agricultural animals remains latent and public concern about their welfare appears insignificant. In addition, since animal-based products make up a significant portion of people's diets, the focus is often placed on production numbers rather than on the welfare of the animals.

The welfare of agricultural animals is notably directly linked to public health.[5] Certain agricultural practices, like intensive farming, exclude any consideration for animal welfare a priori. Combined with the immense quantity of animals in question, this constitutes an important reason for paying more attention to the issue of animal health and well-being.

Another reason this topic is important is the impact agriculture, especially animal husbandry, has on the environment. According to the Food and Agriculture Organization of the United Nations (FAO), animal husbandry is accountable for as much as '14.5% of global anthropogenic greenhouse gas emissions' (FAO 2017). Agriculture-dependent soil and water pollution also takes place worldwide. 'The livestock sector is one of the top three contributors to the most serious environmental problems, including water pollution, at every scale from local to global' (Mateo-Sagasta 2018).

---

[4] Here and after, when using the term 'animals' we mean all animals excluding humans. The terms 'animals' and 'non-human animals' are synonymous for the scope of this chapter.

[5] There is abundant research on this issue, and attention to this link is increasing. The OneHealth initiative, which is discussed later in this chapter, demonstrates that there is an understanding of the interconnection between the health of animals, humans, and the environment. Regarding the link between animal welfare and public health see, for instance, Akhtar (2012).

13.3 Why Consider the WTO in the Context of Animal Welfare

The Preamble of the Agreement Establishing the World Trade Organization indicates, among its other objectives, sustainable development. It states that the WTO seeks 'to protect and preserve the environment.' It is unclear whether at the time this language was used in the founding Agreement of the WTO there was a well-established understanding of the interconnection between a healthy environment and animal welfare. The WTO is not and has never been an animal protection organization. Moreover, for the international trade system animal welfare concerns often appear as an obstacle for the free circulation of goods, with an 'antagonistic relationship between animal law and trade law' (Anand 2023). At the same time, there are numerous organizations worldwide which set the protection of animals as their priority. Why, then, are we talking about the WTO in this context?

Firstly, the above-mentioned provisions of the Preamble are acquiring new nuances of meaning, leaning ever more towards the inclusion of animal welfare.

Secondly, the cooperation between the WTO and the World Organization for Animal Health (WOAH, founded as the OIE) gives the WTO members a scientifically reliable instrument for making their point in front of the Dispute Settlement Body should animal welfare cases be filed in future. Although these may still be considered as insufficiently fast progress, because WOAH standards are based on scientific results, which, in some cases, may fall behind the ethical standards of certain countries, it is still a powerful mechanism for improving and harmonizing these standards across the globe. As the researchers in this field affirm, for developing countries, where animal welfare concerns are still a novelty, 'debates on the international plane might operate as policy incentives on a national level' (Blattner 2015, p. 43).

Thirdly, the WTO is the only near-global organization which regulates trade issues, and the only organization of this influence with a dispute settlement mechanism having dealt with several animal welfare cases. Although the International Court of Justice also has considered cases regarding animal welfare, for instance the Whaling in the Antarctic Case (Australia v. Japan, New Zealand Intervening),[6] the WTO is increasingly engaging with agricultural animal welfare. Dispute settlement within the WTO is further acquiring growing significance for animal welfare in view of its latest decisions in the Seal Case,[7] which opens new horizons for animal protection.

[6] See, for instance in Rahman (2014).

[7] The Seal Case is discussed in more detail further in this chapter.

13.4 The Impact of the WTO on Animal Welfare Worldwide

13.4.1 Hindering Progress in Developed Countries

13.4.1.1 Principles of Non-Discrimination

The purpose of the existence of the global trade system is to remove all possible barriers to trade so that goods and services can freely circulate on the global market. The creation of obstacles to trade contradicts the system. To guarantee that the country members of the WTO uniformly understand and apply the approach of the organization, the WTO has established the principles of non-discrimination between the countries. There are two of these principles. The WTO inherited these principles from the GATT, which in the GATT Article I (1947) establishes the famous most-favoured-nation principle, which precludes a country from differentiating between its trade partners by providing preferable conditions only to some of them. It states that: 'any advantage, favour, privilege or immunity granted by any contracting party to any product originating in or destined for any other country shall be accorded immediately and unconditionally to the like product originating in or destined for the territories of all other contracting parties' (GATT 1947).

Another principle, which Thomas Kelch names 'the fundamental cornerstone of the GATT' (Kelch 2017, p. 224) and which played a significant—negative—role for animal welfare in the disputes described below, is the National Treatment principle. It is established by Article III of the GATT and provides that the goods produced inside the country or imported to it shall be treated equally in terms of charges, regulations, and other conditions.

> The products of the territory of any contracting party imported into the territory of any other contracting party shall not be subject, directly or indirectly, to internal taxes or other internal charges of any kind in excess of those applied, directly or indirectly, to like domestic products. (GATT 1947)

The concept of 'like-hood' of products is widely discussed and criticized by the doctrine.[8] The criticism can be summarized in two main points. Firstly, sometimes the products are called 'like' even if they are not in terms of their impacts on environment and human health.[9] Secondly, products may be considered 'like' independently of their methods of production, which include, among other things, inhumane practices of animal husbandry. Stevenson calls the latter 'the most damaging aspect of the GATT affecting animal welfare reform' (Stevenson 2002).

---

[8] See, for instance, Kelch (2017) and Stevenson (2002).

[9] For instance, in Asbestos Case WT/DS135/12. (https://www.wto.org/english/tratop_e/dispu_e/cases_e/ds135_e.htm) the decision of the Dispute Settlement Body did not take into account the adverse effect of asbestos on environment and human health and considered the ban of these products as not justified because they were considered products in terms of their use. Later this decision was successfully appealed.

These principles, intended to liberalize trade, do not promote the establishment of higher animal welfare standards. For the EU, for example, they represent a clear obstacle, hindering progress towards improving the lives of farm animals. If an imported animal-based product, produced under inhumane conditions, is treated the same as a domestic humanely produced one, it is highly likely that the imported product will be favoured due to its lower cost for the final consumer.

13.4.2 WTO and GATT Jurisprudence

WTO jurisprudence, at least until recent times, was criticized for not being supportive of the establishment of higher animal welfare standards. The most significant cases in this context primarily address environmental concerns, adopting an eco-centric approach to animal protection. They deal with wildlife protection and biodiversity conservation, but they indicate a trend in the consideration of animal welfare, which can extend to agricultural animals. These cases set a precedent suggesting that jurisprudence did not incentivize animal welfare reforms. The most recent Seal case gives hope for certain positive dynamics.

13.4.3 Tuna-Dolphin Cases I and II

The Tuna-Dolphin I case took place in 1991. It regarded an embargo set by the USA against tuna and tuna products coming from Mexico. The embargo was imposed as a consequence of the US Marine Mammal Protection Act.[10] In accordance with this act, aimed at the conservation of marine mammals, fishing yellowfin tuna in the eastern tropical Pacific Ocean required compliance with certain rules. These rules specifically mention a prohibition on the use of purse seine nets for capturing tuna as they lead to the bycatch of large numbers of dolphins, who often die or get injured in the process. These rules apply to internal as well as to foreign fisheries. Mexico failed to comply, and so the embargo was imposed. Mexico argued under the GATT procedures that these measures were unjustified. The US referred to the general exceptions listed in article XX of GATT. Namely, among the values, the protection of which would justify limitations of the circulation of goods, Article XX(b) indicates 'human, animal or plant life and health', and Article XX(g) 'conservation of exhaustible natural resources if such measures are made effective in conjunction with restrictions on domestic production or consumption.'

Sadly, the ruling of the panel fully satisfied Mexico's claim. To support its ruling the panel raised the so-called 'product' versus 'process'[11] issue and the issue of 'exterritoriality.' Precisely, the panel decided that a country cannot impose limits on

[10] Marine Mammals Protection Act of 1972, further referred to as MMPA.

[11] For more details see WTO Mexico etc. v. US: Tuna Dolfin.

trade on the basis of the process by which the product is produced but does have the right to regulate the quality of the product. If the product, like in the case of yellowfin tuna, is the same or largely the same, an embargo is not justified. The 'exterritoriality' referred to the fact that, as the panel ruled, a country cannot impose its own standards and rules onto other countries, whatever the goal. Moreover, the panel stated that, if the arguments of the US were accepted, this would open the door for potential abuses and the GATT 'would then no longer constitute a multilateral framework for trade among all contracting parties but would provide legal security only in respect of trade between a limited number of contracting parties with identical internal regulations' (Analytical Index GATT 2012).

Remarkably, apart from the concern of bio conservation, the MMPA utilizes the term 'humane' when referring to the ways marine mammals should be captured, explaining that this is necessary to guarantee '(A) the protection or welfare of the mammal, (B) the protection of the public health and welfare, or (C) the nonlethal removal of nuisance animals' (MMPA 1972). The ruling of the GATT ignored these considerations, as well as the argument of the US regarding the exception contained in Article XX(b). This had certain freezing effects on environmental and animal welfare reform in most member countries for several years.

The Tuna-Dolphin II case, which started in 1992 and on which the Panel ruled in 1994, did not contribute to improving the situation with animal welfare either.

13.4.4 The Shrimp-Turtle Case

Another case where a party trying to apply higher environmental and animal welfare standards ended up as a defendant under the GATT was the Shrimp-Turtle Case. Like in Tuna-Dolphin I, that country was the US, and just as previously, it was arguing that Article XX exceptions should be applied. The outcome of the case was also not favourable for the US; however, the Panel's argumentation differed from in the previous decision (Panel Report 1998). The message of the protests which preceded the Panel's decision led some authors to conclude that this case contributed to the understanding that 'animal welfare has been linked to international trade governance' (Anand 2023).

The case was initiated in 1997 and then appealed in 1998. The claimants, India, Malaysia, Pakistan, and Thailand, argued that the import ban on shrimp and shrimp products imposed by the US was not justified. These countries considered that the ban contradicted the WTO's principles of non-discrimination. The US, however, insisted on the ban for the necessity of protecting sea turtles, which often ended up as bycatch in the shrimp harvesting process. The population of sea turtles was endangered, so, apart from being inhumane, the traditional methods of catching shrimp could lead to the extinction of sea turtles. The US Endangered Species Act of 1973 prohibited the capturing the sea turtles and required all US trawlers to use a specific device ('turtle excluder devices (TEDs)') which excluded capturing of turtles when harvesting shrimp. The position of the US was that all imported shrimp and shrimp products should have a certification which would confirm compliance with the provisions of the US Endangered Species Act. In accordance with the Act, an importer eligible for this certification would be:

> (a) Any harvesting nation without any of the relevant species of sea turtles occurring in waters subject to its jurisdiction; (b) Any harvesting nation that harvests shrimp exclusively by means that do not pose a threat to sea turtles, e.g. any nation that harvests shrimp exclusively by artisanal means; (c) Any nation whose commercial shrimp trawling operations take place exclusively in waters subject to its jurisdiction in which sea turtles do not occur.

For non-certified importers the US imposed a ban. According to the US position, this was a clear case when the exception of Article XX(g) of GATT on conservation of exhaustible resources applied.

The Panel once again ruled in favour of the claimants. It stated that the US had violated the provisions of Article XI:1 of the GATT, and that this case did not fall under the exceptions to Article XX, which should be interpreted narrowly; thus it recognized the embargo illegitimate (WT/DS58/R 1998).

However, unlike in Tuna-Dolphin Cases, where the ruling indicated that a country cannot impose its domestic regulations on other countries, the Appellate Body Report recognized that this is possible under certain conditions. Thus, the exterritoriality issue was addressed in a different manner. The Appellate Body Report stated that: 'the United States measure, while qualifying for provisional justification under Article XX(g), fails to meet the requirements of the chapeau of Article XX, and, therefore, is not justified under Article XX of the GATT 1994' (Appellate Body 1998). In addition, to clarify its position, the Appellation Body added that:

'In reaching these conclusions, we wish to underscore what we have not decided in this appeal. We have not decided that the protection and preservation of the environment is of no significance to the Members of the WTO. Clearly, it is. We have not decided that the sovereign nations that are Members of the WTO cannot adopt effective measures to protect endangered species, such as sea turtles. Clearly, they can and should. And we have not decided that sovereign states should not act together bilaterally, plurilaterally or multilaterally, either within the WTO or in other international fora, to protect endangered species or to otherwise protect the environment. Clearly, they should and do' (Appellate Body 1998).

However, with some slight positive dynamics and with less indifference to environmental problems and animal welfare, the Shrimp-Turtle case still presented 'an immensely damaging impact on animal protection laws' (Stevenson 2002).

13.4.5 The Seal Case

In 2009, Norway and Canada presented their concerns regarding the EU ban on seal products, which later became known as 'the EU seal regime', and requested consultations in the WTO forum. In 2011, the case was brought before the Dispute Settlement Body, whose decision was then appealed by the claimants in 2014.

At first glance, one may notice similarity with the two previously cited cases: a ban, established in order to protect a population of animals captured in inhumane way, contested by an exporter. However, this time the argumentation of the parties and the outcome were different, which allowed animal lawyers worldwide to express moderate optimism.[12]

The ban originated in Council Directive 83/129/EEC of 1983 concerning the importation into Member States of skins of certain seal pups and products (Council Directive 1983) but was confirmed and expanded by Regulation (EC) No. 1007/2009 of the European Parliament and of the EC Council of 16 September 2009 on trade in seal products. Under this Regulation, seals were recognized as 'sentient beings that can experience pain, distress, fear and other forms of suffering' (Regulation 2009) and the ban was aimed at protecting these beings from the suffering which almost necessarily accompanies hunting. The Regulation established an exception for Inuit indigenous populations—'indigenous members of the Inuit homeland, namely those arctic and subarctic areas where, presently or traditionally, Inuit have aboriginal rights and interests, recognised by Inuit as being members of their people and includes Inupiat, Yupik (Alaska), Inuit, Inuvialuit (Canada), Kalaallit (Greenland) and Yupik (Russia)' (Regulation 2009). In accordance with the Regulation, 'The placing on the market of seal products shall be allowed only where the seal products result from hunts traditionally conducted by Inuit and other indigenous communities and contribute to their subsistence' (Regulation 2009, Art. 3:1).

The claimants argued that the ban violated the GATT principle of non-discrimination, as well as certain technical regulations under the WTO's TBT (Technical Barriers to Trade) Agreement. The EU argued that it was not in violation of the GATT norms and that 'any inconsistencies of the measure under the GATT 1994 should be justified under the general exceptions provisions of the GATT 1994, namely Articles XX(a) and XX(b), because the measure is necessary to protect public morals (regarding the welfare of seals) and to protect seals' health, respectively' (Panel Report 2013, para 7.3).

The Panel ruled, and the Appellate Body upheld the ruling, that the EU Seal Regime was inconsistent with GATT Article I (most-favoured nation) and with GATT Article III (national treatment). At the same time, it was decided that the EU Seal Regime was 'necessary to protect public morals', which constituted the exception mentioned in GATT Article XX(a) (WTO Dispute Settlement Body 2015). This exception would justify the violation of the principle of non-discrimination if the requirements of the 'chapeau' of Article XX were met. However, both the Panel and the Appellate Body established that these requirements were not met.

Although the EU Seal Regime was not upheld as a result of the case, it was a groundbreaking moment for the animal welfare debate. For the first time, the WTO considered a case based solely on animal welfare, rather than on environmental protection, and acknowledged the significance of the public morality argument in the protection of animals. The case acknowledged that 'that animal welfare, a moral issue which is distinguishable from animal species conservation, is an important issue

[12] See, for instance, Serpin (2016), Sykes (2021), Blattner (2015), Howse et al., (2015) and others.

in international trade discourse' (Anand 2023) and 'animals have certainly gained more visibility in international trade law' (Fitzgerald 2012).

The outcome of the Seal Case certainly represents a step towards international recognition of the importance of animal welfare. However, given the significance of the issue, the connection between animal welfare and public health, and the increasing public awareness and academic debate, the WTO's provisions and jurisprudence still fall short of contemporary demands, especially from the perspective of developed countries.

13.5 Fostering Progress in Developing Countries

From the perspective of developing countries, the situation appears different. These countries often struggle to meet the minimum animal welfare standards. Wars, past struggles, corruption, internal conflicts in society, scarcity of natural resources, and the inefficiency of governments are the most common reasons why a country may progress too slowly on its development path. This chapter does not analyse these reasons, does not assess them, and does not judge. It is taken as the basic notion that there are countries at different level of economic development and with different possibilities in pursuing higher animal welfare standards.

For countries where the internal momentum towards improving animal welfare is insufficient, international regulations serve as a driver, encouraging them to develop their domestic animal welfare legislation more rapidly, set clear goals, and work towards achieving these.

For these countries, the WTO is an instrument of progress, and a way to be integrated successfully into international trade. Being a member of the WTO provides unique market access opportunities, including to the markets with higher animal welfare standards for farm animals. In order to increase its attractiveness as a trading partner, a country must thus adopt better regulations.

The WOAH collaborates with the WTO in setting science-based, internationally recognized, animal welfare standards. Being a member of the WTO incentivizes the member countries to follow these.

13.5.1 Case Study: Kazakhstan

Kazakhstan is a rapidly developing country with a vast territory and high potential for development of husbandry. It is increasingly concerned about farm animal welfare issues. However, due to different factors, it has progressed rather slowly on the path towards improving animal welfare standards.

Kazakhstan's legislation on animals is vast.[13] Regulations on the welfare of farm animals are mostly found in veterinary legislation and in the recent Law on Responsible Treatment of Animals. Furthermore, Kazakhstan participates in regional agreements regulating animal husbandry. Below, it is shown how membership in the WTO has contributed to improving animal welfare standards in Kazakhstan.

13.5.2 Historical Perspective: Independence, EAEU, and WTO

The year 1991, when the Tuna-Dolphin I Case took place and debate in the international community on the importance of environmental and animal welfare issues received a significant boost, was a year of drastic political and economic change for Kazakhstan due to the collapse of the Soviet Union and the acquiring of independence. The following decade saw years of deep economic, social, and demographic distress, as well as legislative reform in all branches of law.

In 1993, Kazakhstan and the other 14 ex-Soviet republics signed an Agreement on Cooperation in the Sphere of Veterinary (Agreement 1993). The same year, Kazakhstan became a member of the OIE (now WOAH). In 1995, a Decree of the President of the Republic on Veterinary Medicine came into force (Law 1995). That was the period of transition from collective economy in agriculture to privately owned agricultural enterprises and farms. As the statistics shows (Bureau of National Statistics 2025), the inertia that kept the agricultural sector moving during the first years of independence slowed down by the mid-1990s, leading to a drastic decrease in agricultural production in 1995–1997. For Kazakhstan's agricultural sector, this was a period of struggle for survival. At that time, while the EU and the US already had a decades-long tradition in animal welfare legislation, Kazakhstan's veterinary legislation was necessarily fully anthropocentric and considered animal health—not yet welfare—exclusively from the perspective of its impact on the safety of the final product.

In 1996, Kazakhstan applied for WTO membership. It took 20 meetings of the Working Party before Kazakhstan actually became a member (WTO Accessions Kazakhstan).

In 2002, the Law on Veterinary Medicine came into force, replacing the previous Decree. However, it did not contribute to the development of animal welfare, still concentrated on the protection of animals against diseases which can affect human health and the quality of animal-derived food.

In the meantime, in 2004, the WTO conducted the first plurilateral meeting discussing the terms of Kazakhstan's accession. The first three plurilateral meetings were fully dedicated to agricultural issues. Overall, 20 out of 29 plurilateral

[13] More in Baideldinova and Dalpane (2013).

meetings conducted before Kazakhstan's accession to the WTO regarded agricultural issues and SPS measures (WTO Accessions Kazakhstan). Animal and plant health was at the centre of these discussions.[14]

In 2007, the Customs Union between Belarus, Kazakhstan, and Russia was founded. In the following years, the member states signed several documents harmonizing their strategies and policies regarding animal health. The Customs Union Agreement on Sanitary and Veterinary Measures, signed in 2010, contains references to the Terrestrial Animal Health Code and the Aquatic Animal Health Code—the fundamental documents of the WOAH—as well as to the TBT and SPS Agreements of the WTO. Remarkably, at that time, none of the members of the Customs Union was yet a member of the WTO.

In 2011, Kazakhstan requested to participate in the Veterinary Legislation Support Program (VLSP) of the WOAH. The following year, the Russian Federation became a member of the WTO. Since that period there has been increasing interest in Kazakhstan in the improvement of farm animal welfare standards.

In the meantime, the regional integration processes were becoming more intensive and, in 2014, resulted in the creation of the Eurasian Economic Union (EAEU). That same year the Eurasian Economic Commission signed a Memorandum of Understanding with the WOAH (Decision #299 2013).

On 30 November 2015, Kazakhstan became a member of the WTO.

In 2017, the 'Tentative Programme of activities to implement the Memorandum of Understanding between the OIE and the Eurasian Economic Commission (EEC) for the triennial period of 2018 to 2021' was adopted. That same year the Interparliamentary Assembly of the Commonwealth of Independent States adopted a Model Law on Responsible Treatment of Animals, which contained norms on animal welfare which were very progressive for the countries involved.

In 2018, the Parliament of Kazakhstan, the Ministry of Agriculture, and the Ministry of Natural Resources and Environment started drafting the Law on Responsible Treatment of Animals. The Law was adopted in December 2021 and was followed by the correspondent changes in the Criminal Code, the Code of Administrative Offences, and several normative acts related to animal welfare.

One can see a clear parallel between Kazakhstan's involvement with the WTO and the improvement of its animal health and animal welfare legislation. Throughout this period, however, public debate on animal welfare remained relatively muted. Although the number of animal protection NGOs and academic publications on animal welfare and related laws has grown, the issue remains underrepresented and has yet to achieve significant influence. As a result, while there have been some internal efforts to improve animal welfare in Kazakhstan, progress in ensuring better conditions for agricultural animals is largely driven by the incentives and the guidance provided by international cooperation.

---

[14] For instance, in the WTO Accessions (2005) 'Check-list of Illustrative Sanitary and Phytosanitary (SPS) Issues: Consistency of Acting Kazakh Legislation with the Norms of the WTO Agreement on the Application of SPS Measures' Kazakhstan confirms its commitment to adhere to international standards set by OiE.

13.6 Conclusion

We all agree that, in terms of trade, 'animals have historically been regarded and treated against … economic background' (Fitzgerald 2012). For a long time, there prevailed the opinion that protection of animal welfare and increasing wealth had opposing vectors. In the last decades, however, it is becoming ever clearer that animal welfare, human health, and environment are interconnected. Therefore, international organizations now pay increasing attention to farm animal welfare issues. The WTO, although not an organization aimed at animal protection, now also pays attention to animal welfare.

An analysis of WTO jurisprudence reveals clear progress in addressing environmental concerns and animal protection. A key factor in this advancement is the collaboration between the WTO and the OIE/WOAH. The WTO upholds animal welfare standards that are scientifically validated, while the OIE/WOAH, through its Terrestrial Animal Health Code, establishes these standards, which the WTO subsequently recognizes as scientifically proven. Although not legally binding, these standards create a strong presumption in favour of a positive outcome in cases alleging their violation.

Another key finding is that, after decades of impeding the development of animal welfare standards—particularly in developed countries—the WTO is now emerging as one of the most influential international forces driving improvements in animal welfare. While its impact on developed nations remains debatable, the fact that most WTO members are developing countries suggests that its overall contribution to global animal welfare is increasing. For Kazakhstan and other Central Asian countries, international animal welfare standards are high and require significant resources to meet. Therefore, for this region and other nations in similar or more challenging circumstances, the WTO serves as a crucial driver of progress in animal welfare standards.

Recent developments further indicate that the WTO is increasingly willing to consider animal welfare as an independent issue, separate from biodiversity, environmental protection, and even animal and human health. The organization recognizes that certain cruel practices should be abolished not based solely on their broader consequences but on moral grounds. In this way, the WTO is evolving into an institution that defines the ethical treatment of animals, even though it remains far from being an animal protection organization.

Additionally, while the WTO is the only body that regulates trade at the global level, multiple regional organizations also influence animal welfare—both positively and negatively. Furthermore, bilateral agreements between countries remain one of the most effective mechanisms for improving animal welfare standards.

Although developing countries often struggle to fully implement WTO standards, this does not mean that these standards should be lowered to accommodate slower adoption. As they are grounded in scientific research, WTO standards should continue evolving in line with the latest findings, remain as ambitious as possible, and incorporate ethical and moral considerations, as exemplified in the Seal Case.

Kazakhstan is gradually aligning its domestic animal welfare regulations with international expectations—primarily driven by trade considerations rather than internal policy initiatives. Continued international cooperation will incentivize Kazakhstan to uphold higher animal welfare and sustainability standards.

References

Akhtar A (2012) Animals and public health: Why treating animals better is critical to human welfare. Springer

Analytical Index GATT (2012) https://www.wto.org/english/res_e/booksp_e/gatt_ai_e/art20_e.pdf. Accessed 9 March 2026

Agreement (1993) On cooperation in the sphere of veterinary. https://adilet.zan.kz/rus/docs/H930000258_. Accessed 9 March 2026

Anand S (2023) The intersection of animal welfare with international trade law. Int J Law Manag & HumIties 6:3478–3483

Baideldinova M, Dalpane F (2013) Animal law in Kazakhstan: a survey. Glob J Anim Law 2. https://ojs.abo.fi/index.php/gjal/article/download/1298/1608. Accessed 9 March 2026

Blattner C (2015) Global animal law: hope beyond illusion: the potential and potential limits of international law in regulating animal matters. Mid-Atl J Law Public Policy 3(1):10–54

Bureau of National Statistics of the Agency of Strategic Planning and Reforms of the Republic of Kazakhstan (2025) Volumes of agricultural production in Kazakhstan in 1991–2024. https://view.officeapps.live.com/op/view.aspx?src=https%3A%2F%2Fstat.gov.kz%2Fupload%2Fiblock%2Ffbd%2Fszkoguz8bvbwh2iku7llqou6r82iqr1i%2F4.%2520%25D0%2598%25D0%25A4%25D0%259E%2520%25D1%2581%25D1%2585%25201990-2024%2520%25D1%%2580%25D0%25B5%25D0%25B3%25D0%25B8%25D0%25BE%25D0%25BD%25D1%258B.xls&wdOrigin=BROWSELINK. Accessed 9 March 2026

Bureau of National Statistics of the Agency of Strategic Planning and Reforms of the Republic of Kazakhstan. The Main Indicators of the Development of Livestock (2024) https://stat.gov.kz/ru/industries/business-statistics/stat-forrest-village-hunt-fish/publications/157407/. Accessed 12 Feb 2025

Council Directive (1983) 83/129/EEC concerning the importation into Member States of skins of certain seal pups and products derived therefrom. https://eur-lex.europa.eu/legal-content/EN/ALL/?uri=CELEX%3A31983L0129. Accessed 9 March 2026

Cunningham R, Vindedzis S (2017) Four legs good, two legs bad: animal welfare vs the world trade organization (featuring article xx of the general agreement on tariffs and trade and article of the technical barriers to trade). Adel Law Rev 38(2):311–350

Decision of the Eurasian Economic Commission #299 (2013) On Draft of Memorandum of Understanding between EAEU and WOAH. https://docs.eaeunion.org/upload/iblock/0e6/39uebfgsjmwp7e0ipamfytvhlpc8jkln/clcd_18122013_299_doc.pdf. Accessed 9 March 2026

Decree of the President of Kazakhstan having the force of law on Veterinary Medicine (1995) N 2376. https://adilet.zan.kz/rus/docs/U950002376. Accessed 9 March 2025

FAO (2017) Livestock solutions for climate change. https://www.fao.org/family-farming/detail/en/c/1634679/. Accessed 11 July 2025

Fitzgerald P (2012) International issues in animal law. Carolina Academic Press, p 171

General Agreement on Tariffs and Trade (GATT) (1947) https://www.wto.org/english/docs_e/legal_e/gatt47_e.htm. Accessed 9 March 2026

Howse R, Langille J, Sykes K (2015, April 1) Pluralism in practice: Moral legislation and the law of the WTO after seal products. 48 Geo Wash Int'l L Rev (2015), NYU School of Law, Public Law Research Paper No. 15–05, pp 81–150. Available at SSRN: https://ssrn.com/abstract=2588509

Kelch T (2017) Globalization and animal law: Comparative law, international law and international trade. Kluwer Law International BV, p 244

Katasonova T, Sotnikov A (2023, March) Zoomarket in Kazakhstan: Peculiarities and perspectives. https://zooinform.ru/business/articles/zoorynok-kazahstana-osobennosti-i-perspektivy/. Accessed 12 Feb 2025

Mateo-Sagasta J, Marjani Zadeh S, Turral H (2018) More people, more food, worse water? A global review of water pollution from agriculture. https://openknowledge.fao.org/handle/20.500.14283/ca0146en. Accessed 9 March 2026

Nielsen L (2007) The WTO, animals and PPMs, vol 8. Brill

Panel Report (1998) WT/DS58/R. https://www.wto.org/english/tratop_e/dispu_e/58r00.pdf. Accessed 9 March 2026

Panel Report (2013) WT/DS400/R#WT/DS401/R. https://docs.wto.org/dol2fe/Pages/FE_Search/FE_S_S009-DP.aspx?language=E&CatalogueIdList=125339,124826,124807,124760,123564,122179,122115,121006,121007,115881&CurrentCatalogueIdIndex=7&FullTextHash=&HasEnglishRecord=True&HasFrenchRecord=True&HasSpanishRecord=True. Accessed 9 March 2026

Rahman M (2014) Battle for whales in the Hague: analysis of ICJ judgment in Australia v. Japan. SSRN Electron J. https://doi.org/10.2139/ssrn.2418817

Regulation (2009) (EC) No 1007/2009 of the European Parliament and of the Council of 16 September 2009 on trade in seal products. https://eur-lex.europa.eu/legal-content/EN/TXT/?uri=CELEX%3A32009R1007. Accessed 9 March 2026

Serpin P (2016) The public morals exception after the WTO seal products dispute: Has the exception swallowed the rules. C Bus Law Rev, 217

Stevenson P (2002) The World Trade Organization rules: Legal analysis of their adverse impact on animal welfare. Anim Law 8:107–142

Stevenson P, White S (2015) The impact of the World Trade Organization rules on animal welfare. Compassion in World Farming

Sykes K (2021) Animal welfare and international trade law: the impact of the WTO seal case. Edward Elgar Publishing; Blattner CE (2021) Animal welfare and international trade law: the impact of the WTO seal case

Sykes K (2016) Globalization and the animal turn: how international trade law contributes to global norms of animal protection. Transnatl Environ Law 5(1):55–80

Thomas E (2007) Playing chicken to the WTO: Defending an animal welfare-based trade restriction under GATT's moral exception. Boston CollE Environ Aff Law Rev 34:605

United States Marine Mammals Protection Act (1972)

WT/DS58/R (1998) Panel's consultations with scientific experts. https://www.wto.org/english/tratop_e/dispu_e/58r01.pdf https://www.wto.org/english/tratop_e/dispu_e/58r01.pdf. Accessed 9 March 2026

WTO Accession (2005) Check-list of illustrative sanitary and phytosanitary (SPS) Issues: consistency of acting Kazakh legislation with the norms of the WTO agreement on the application of SPS measures. https://docs.wto.org/dol2fe/Pages/SS/directdoc.aspx?filename=q:/WT/ACC/KAZ64.pdf&Open=True. Accessed 9 March 2026

Евразийский экономический союз (ЕАЭС) https://www.eaeunion.org/. Accessed 9 March 2026

WTO Accessions Kazakhstan webpage. https://www.wto.org/english/thewto_e/acc_e/a1_kazakhstan_e.htm. Accessed 9 March 2026

WTO Appellate Body Report (1998) WT/DS58/AB/R. https://www.wto.org/english/tratop_e/dispu_e/58abr.pdf. Accessed 9 March 2026

WTO Asbestos case WT/DS135/12. https://www.wto.org/english/tratop_e/dispu_e/cases_e/ds135_e.htm. Accessed 9 March 2026

WTO Dispute Settlement Body (2015) DS401. https://www.wto.org/english/tratop_e/dispu_e/cases_e/ds401_e.htm. Accessed 9 March 2026

WTO Mexico etc v. US: Tuna Dolfin case at https://www.wto.org/english/tratop_e/envir_e/edis04_e.htm. Accessed 9 March 2026

Chapter 14
International Environmental Law in Central Asia: Implementation Challenges and Limitations

Kamila Mateeva, Kanykei Kasybekova, and Begaiym Esenkulova

Abstract This chapter is focused on international environmental law in Central Asia. It examines the current state of international environmental law in Kazakhstan, Kyrgyzstan, and Uzbekistan, and focuses on problems of its implementation as well as its limitations in these countries. Although the Central Asian states have ratified major international environmental agreements, they often prioritize economic interests over environmental problems and do not provide for the adequate implementation of these agreements at the national level. There is also a problem of a lack of effective cooperation with respect to addressing environmental problems at the regional level. This chapter concentrates on three major cases illustrating the problems with the implementation of international environmental law in Central Asia. It first discusses the issues related to the Western Tien Shan and the UNESCO World and Natural Heritage Lists. It then focuses on the problem of the Aral Sea and the case of the Taldykol lakes in Kazakhstan. While the problem of the Aral Sea dates back to the Soviet Union, the case involving the Taldykol lakes is recent, with the local administration deciding to drain part of the rich, biodiverse system for residential buildings. Cases like these, in which countries demonstrate a lack of true commitment to preserving the natural environment, illustrate the significant problems with the implementation of international environmental law in Central Asia. This chapter advances proposals for solving the above-mentioned environmental protection problems in Central Asia.

K. Mateeva
Law Division of the American University of Central Asia, Bishkek, Kyrgyzstan
e-mail: mateeva_k@auca.kg

K. Kasybekova · B. Esenkulova (✉)
AUCA Law Program Faculty, Bishkek, Kyrgyzstan
e-mail: esenkulova_b@auca.kg

K. Kasybekova
e-mail: kasybekova_k@auca.kg

K. Mateeva · K. Kasybekova · B. Esenkulova
American University of Central Asia Law Program, Bishkek, Kyrgyzstan

S. Sayapin (ed.), *International Law, Politics and Security in Central Asia*,
https://doi.org/10.1007/978-3-032-17818-3_14

Keywords Environmental Law · Natural Heritage · Aral Sea · Taldykol lake · International obligations · Implementation · Central Asia

14.1 An Overview of Environmental Problems in the Central Asian States

The Central Asian region has a specific geopolitical position as 'transcontinental highways of the past and the present pass-through central Eurasia'.[1] The Central Asian region is comprised of landlocked states with environments 'characterized as mountain-desert and steppe landscapes'.[2] It is well known that, when the Soviet Union collapsed, negotiations regarding border demarcation took some time, with water resources also coming under consideration during the demarcation process.

As noted by Angelini, 'these countries have common characteristics, but political and social geography is highly diverse and accordingly, the priority given to environmental constraints also varies'.[3] The Central Asian states face problems related to air pollution, hazardous waste, biodiversity and ecosystem production, use of water resources and hydropower, energy efficiency, the ineffective use of lakes and rivers, and many other environmental problems.[4] Air pollution is one of the most discussed problems, especially in winter time, as the heating systems in the states have not been modernized, with the UN reporting that the worst of the pollution is largely the result of residential winter heating and cooking using raw coal in Kyrgyzstan.[5] Hazardous waste is also a big problem in the region. Kazakhstan is noted as one of the largest producers of hazardous waste globally, with almost 100% of total generated waste classified as hazardous.[6] There are also significant problems with the loss of biodiversity and degradation of ecosystems.[7] As noted by experts, 'the loss of biodiversity and complexity of the network of protected natural areas within the region is a major challenge' in all discussed states of the region.[8] The use of water resources, lakes, and rivers is another much discussed topic, as the Central Asian states are all landlocked (though Kazakhstan and Turkmenistan have access to the Caspian Sea). The ineffective use of water resources, insufficient irrigation systems, and limitations on water resources from hydropower have been always observed within these states. This chapter focuses on Kazakhstan, Uzbekistan, and Kyrgyzstan only since data on Turkmenistan and Tajikistan is limited.

---

[1] Pobedinsky and Shestak (2020, p. 69).

[2] Pobedinsky and Shestak (2020, p. 69).

[3] Angelini, p. 7.

[4] Ibid.

[5] UNICEF (2023, para 1).

[6] Nugumanova et al. (2017, p. 3).

[7] Ibid.

[8] Gray et al. (2002, para 1).

14.2 National Legislation Related to Environmental Protection and International Environmental Law Obligations of Central Asian States

There are many issues that international environmental law attempts to regulate. When it comes to international treaties, one can conclude that 'the instruments of general international law are too abstract and therefore they are not adopted to the specific context of the region'.[9] However, the treaties established in the international arena do represent good instrumental support for states in regulating different environmental aspects through autonomous agreements that they may choose to enter of their own volition based upon interest and readiness.

Kazakhstan, Kyrgyzstan, and Uzbekistan have expressed their commitment towards international law as the foundation of their international relations with other states. They have thus entered into the major international environmental treaties. However, acceding to these international obligations is only a formal step towards resolution of the problems. The most important step is the implementation process, and the mechanisms of enforcement are, unfortunately, not working properly. Many problems have therefor arisen, including violations of international obligations, failures of implementation, and a lack of enforcement of state obligations. This is especially important when the distribution of the resources is not made even, and the interests of the population are not properly considered. Thus, when discussing environmental law problems in the region, one should also discuss the issues concerning environmental human rights. This allows for the interests of population to also be considered, something which is indicated expressly by the Constitutions of Kazakhstan and Uzbekistan (yet it is not mentioned in the law of Kyrgyzstan).

All three of the above-mentioned Central Asian states have national and international instruments that are built on respecting fundamental human rights and freedoms. This has been a practice of the majority of states across the globe since World War II when the regulations around respecting the rights and freedoms of individuals worldwide changed. The right to environment is generally understood to belong to the 'third generation of human rights' called 'collective rights', which a state should respect and observe. Looking to the domestic law of the states, there are provisions that directly and indirectly regulate this area. The Constitution of Kazakhstan (Article 31) states that the 'state aims at protection of environment favourable to human life and health'.[10] As for the Constitution of the Kyrgyz Republic, it states in Article 16 that the '[l]and and natural resources are used as the basis for the life and activities of the people of the Kyrgyz Republic; To preserve a unified ecological system and sustainable development, they are under the control and special protection of the state'.[11] Article 49 of the Constitution of Uzbekistan states that '[e]veryone

[9] Tolstykh (2023, p. 956).

[10] Constitution of Republic of Kazakhstan (1995).

[11] Constitution of the Kyrgyz Republic (2021).

has the right to a favourable environment and reliable information about its condition; The state, in accordance with the principle of sustainable development, implements measures to improve, restore and protect the environment, maintain ecological balance'.[12] Hence, the protection of an environment which is favourable to human life and health is a direct constitutional guarantee provided by the Republics of Kazakhstan and Uzbekistan. These provisions directly connect environmental protection to individual human rights. As for the Kyrgyz Republic, the state has a more general objective of preserving ecological system and sustainable development as whole. All three are united by the fact that they aim to protect the environment due to its close relation with human society. The above-mentioned provisions were incorporated in the Constitutions of the states in the light of their international obligations. Additionally, the states also passed relevant national legislation on environmental protection.

The aforementioned Central Asian countries have joined various multilateral environmental agreements (MEAs) on both international and regional levels since their independence in 1991.[13] For example, Kyrgyzstan has joined the following key agreements:

- **1995**: Convention for the protection of World Cultural and Natural Heritage 1972;
- **1996**: Basel Convention on the Control of Transboundary Movements of Hazardous Wastes 1989; Convention on Biological Diversity 1992;
- **1997**: UN Convention to Combat Desertification 1994;
- **2000**: Convention on Long-range Transboundary Air Pollution 1979; Vienna Convention for the Protection of Ozone Layer 1985; Montreal Protocol on Substances that Deplete the Ozone Layer 1987; UN Framework Convention on Climate Change 1992; Rotterdam Convention on the Prior Informed Consent Procedure for Certain Hazardous Chemicals and Pesticides in International Trade 1998;
- **2001**: Convention on Environmental Impact Assessment in a Transboundary Context 1991; Convention on Access to Information, Public Participation in Decision-Making and Access to Justice in Environmental Matters 1998;
- **2003**: International Plant Protection Convention 1951; Ramsar Convention on Wetlands of International Importance 1971;
- **2005**: Cartagena Protocol on Biosafety 2000;
- **2006**: Stockholm Convention on Persistent Organic Pollutants 2001;
- **2007**: Convention on International Trade in Endangered Species of Wild Fauna and Flora 1973;
- **2009**: International Treaty on Plant Genetic Resources for Food and Agriculture 2001;
- **2014**: Convention on Migratory Species 1979;
- **2020**: Paris Agreement on Climate Change 2015.[14]

---

[12] Constitution of Uzbekistan (1992).

[13] UN Treaty Collection.

[14] Ibid.

Similarly, Uzbekistan and Kazakhstan also ratified the major international agreements related to environmental protection. However, the main issue remains their compliance in good faith with their international obligations. If a state fails to observe its obligations in a transboundary case where a State A causes environmental damage to State B, there is an international institution that can accept the latter's judicial complaint. However, it is more challenging if the environmental damage takes place inside the territory of a single country in which the citizens have access only to the state court to file a complaint for the state's failure to fulfil its environmental law obligations. In other words, when a state fails to fulfil its international environmental law obligations within its own territory, there is often a lack of enforcement mechanisms in treaties. This can be contrasted against other areas of international law, such as international human rights law, where there are international enforcement mechanisms that allow, for example, an individual to file a complaint against the state in international institutions such as the Committee for the International Covenant on Civil and Political Rights or European Court on Human Rights. When there is violation of international environmental law, individuals suffering from the damage do not have access to any international institutions and, therefore, the only mechanism they can use is the internal domestic court system. The case of the Taldykol system of lakes (discussed below) is an example where local communities tried to preserve the environment using local (national) remedies that were not effective, with the state solely following its economic interests and ignoring its international environmental obligations. Civil society has continued trying to raise this issue, but they have no access to any international institutions to aid in the protection of an environment that is being damaged by their state. Similarly, the two other cases discussed in this chapter illustrate problems related to the enforcement of international legal obligations. These cases show that there are various problems related to both the legislative regulation of environmental protection and its enforcement. Among the problems are legislative and regulatory gaps and collisions, weak enforcement as well as non-enforcement of laws and regulations, and the issue of mild sanctions for their violation.

14.3 Case Study 1: Natural Heritage Protection and Recent Developments in the Central Asian Countries

In 2015, Kazakhstan, Kyrgyzstan, and Uzbekistan proposed the Western Tien Shan for inscription on the UNESCO World and Natural Heritage List.[15] As noted by the International Union for the Conservation of Nature (IUCN), these states expressed

[15] IUCN (2016, p. 27); Republic of Kazakhstan, Kyrgyz Republic, and Republic of Uzbekistan (2016).

willingness 'to work collaboratively with China on transboundary aspects of the Tian-shan Mountain Range which straddles all four countries'.[16] Following the proposal, and based on the Convention Concerning the Protection of the World Cultural and Natural Heritage to which the three mentioned countries are members, as well as on its Operational Guidelines, the IUCN evaluated the information presented by the states and provided an advisory report and recommendations.[17] During the 40th session of the World Heritage Committee (WHC) meeting in 2016 it was decided to 'inscribe Western Tien-Shan, Kazakhstan, Kyrgyzstan, and Uzbekistan, on the World Heritage List on the basis of criterion (x)'.[18] The recommendations included the essential need for 'transboundary cooperation' and the need to 'further develop collaboration between the States Parties in the framework of a to-be-signed tripartite Memorandum for management of the property', to address 'integrated protection and management measures including establishment of a joint steering committee', and to 'review and rationalize the boundaries and their buffer zones'.[19] The state parties were asked to submit a subsequent report for examination in the following year.

Since the initial recommendations in 2016, the states concluded the Memorandum in 2019, and only by 2023 were they able to set up the joint steering committee.[20] The WHC issued its subsequent decisions on the Western Tien Shan with its requests in 2018, 2021, and 2023.[21] The WHC repeatedly asked all state parties to 'review and rationalize the boundaries of the components of the property and their buffer zones to ensure that they fully correspond to criterion (x)', and also requested that certain states provide comments on certain specific concerns.[22] In particular, it requested that Kazakhstan comment on the boundary change in regard to 'excision of a substantial part of Sayram-Ugam National Nature Park in Kazakhstan from the property' and that Uzbekistan clarify the 'new protection status and protection regime' for the relevant territories. It also asked both states to comment on potential dangers in regard to the value and integrity of the region, and for Kyrgyzstan to address if any new threats existed.[23] The states were also urged to submit joint reports on the inscribed property.

[16] IUCN (2016, p. 27), The Xinjiang Tianshan was inscribed into to the World Heritage List in 2013, see more UNESCO World Heritage Centre, n.d.b.

[17] IUCN (2016, pp. 35–36).

[18] UNESCO World Heritage Committee Decision (2016, para 2). Based on the Operational Guidelines for the Implementation of the World Heritage Convention, the criteria (x) 'to contain the most important and significant natural habitats for in-situ conservation of biological diversity, including those containing threatened species of outstanding universal value from the point of view of science or conservation.'.

[19] UNESCO World Heritage Committee (2016, para 4).

[20] UNESCO World Heritage Committee (2021, para 3); UNESCO World Heritage Committee (2023, para 3).

[21] UNESCO World Heritage Centre n.d.a.

[22] UNESCO World Heritage Committee (2018, para 8); UNESCO World Heritage Committee (2021, para 7); UNESCO World Heritage Committee (2023, para 6).

[23] UNESCO World Heritage Committee (2018, para 6–7); UNESCO World Heritage Committee (2021, para 4–6); UNESCO World Heritage Committee (2023, para 4–5, 7).

The joint reports of 2020 and 2023 contained certain responses. The 2023 joint report addressed the creation of the Regional Committee and agreement on the joint Work Plan.[24] However, the 2023 Periodic Reporting Cycle 3 reflected information only on Uzbekistan's part of the property and included the following statement: 'An adequate legal framework exists for the broader setting of the World Heritage property and the buffer zone, but there are some deficiencies in implementation which undermine the maintenance of the Outstanding Universal Value (OUV) including conditions of Authenticity and/or Integrity of the property'.[25] Apart from this, as of the 2023 Periodic Report, the state parties had yet to enhance awareness-raising or ensure participation and cooperation of the various groups to maintain OUV of the property.[26] The 2024 executive summary report reemphasized the activities of the Regional Committee and the joint meetings between the member states, but with regard to the earlier WHC request for the joint revision of the boundaries, the state parties 'identified technical mistakes that occurred at the time of inscription',[27] necessitating further communication on the boundaries.

The 2025 Decision raised a number of concerns and further reflected the poor implementation examples. Specifically, the Kyrgyz Republic issued the geological exploration licenses for the activities in the protected reserves, whereas it is incompatible with the property with the World Heritage status.[28] The WHC requested 'the State Party [Kyrgyz Republic] to pursue the permanent cancellation of the licenses and to undertake rehabilitation of any degraded areas in line with the mission recommendations'.[29] To Kazakhstan WHC addressed that the development projects, as ski resorts or planned hydroelectric power projects, minimize impact on the environment, and 'any decision on implementing the project should not compromise the OUV of the property'.[30] The inclusion of the Western Tien Shan could arguably be a positive action in terms of the recognition of the environmental values from the Central Asian states. However, as noted by Song, the establishment of nature reserves or wildlife sanctuaries in Central Asia is 'inadequate to meet the needs of sustainable development'.[31] In addition, the changes to the boundaries of the protected territories and slow pace in addressing the concerns of the WHC may diminish the positive impacts resulting from their commitments to the Western Tien Shan.

---

[24] UNESCO World Heritage Centre (2023).

[25] UNESCO World Heritage Centre n.d.a.

[26] Ibid.

[27] Ibid.

[28] Convention concerning the Protection of World Cultural and Natural Heritage, Art. 6(3).

[29] UNESCO World Heritage Committee (2025, para 10–13).

[30] Ibid.

[31] Song et al. (2025, p. 2).

14.4 Case Study 2: The Aral Sea

The Aral Sea crisis is one of the most notorious man-made environmental catastrophes in the Central Asian region.[32] It originated from the decision of the Soviet Union to divert the two major rivers that flowed into the Aral Sea to the desert areas of the region to promote the growing of cotton and other crops.[33] As noted by experts, this decision 'devastated the Aral Sea' and, consequently, 'the increasingly salty water became polluted with fertilizer and pesticides'. The 'blowing dust from the exposed lakebed, contaminated with agricultural chemicals, became a public health hazard' leading to the degradation of soil.[34] Apart from this, the Aral Sea which constituted 'the largest fishery basin in Central Asia with an annual catch of up to 40,000 tons of fish' until the 1960s, lost its 'commercial fishing importance'.[35] The disappearance of the Aral Sea within the time of one generation has affected more than 60 million people in the region, as well as the general ecosystem, in a negative way.[36] This case illustrates the prioritization of economic interests over the goal of environmental protection.

The problem of the Aral Sea was not given proper consideration during the time of the Soviet Union. However, after the collapse of the Union, the Central Asian states began taking steps towards addressing this problem. Kazakhstan, Kyrgyzstan, Uzbekistan, Tajikistan, and Turkmenistan signed an agreement on cooperation in the field of the joint management of the use and protection of water resources from interstate sources in 1992.[37] Article 4 of the Agreement provided for the following:

> 'The parties shall carry out jointly works for the solution of the environmental problems connected with the drying of the Aral Sea and also establish amounts of sanitary release for each specific year, proceeding from water content of interstate sources. In exclusively shallow years concerning water supply of extremely scarce areas the special separate decision is made'.[38]

In addition to this, the Central Asian countries signed an Agreement on joint actions to solve the problem of the Aral Sea and the Aral Sea region, environmental rehabilitation, and ensuring the socio-economic development of the Aral region in

[32] Sayapin (2022, pp. 340–341); See also Sayapin (2021, pp. 198–199).

[33] Columbia University, The Aral Sea Crisis.

[34] NASA Earth Observatory World of Change: Shrinking Aral Sea.

[35] The Agency for the Management of Project Implementation of the Aral Sea Basin, The Aral Sea Crisis.

[36] The Agency for the Management of Project Implementation of the Aral Sea Basin, The Aral Sea Crisis.

[37] The Agreement between the Republic of Kazakhstan, the Republic Kyrgyzstan, the Republic of Uzbekistan, the Republic of Tajikistan, and Turkmenistan on Cooperation in the field of Joint Management of Use and Protection of Water Resources of Interstate Sources, 18 February (1992).

[38] The Agreement between the Republic of Kazakhstan, the Republic Kyrgyzstan, the Republic of Uzbekistan, the Republic of Tajikistan, and Turkmenistan on Cooperation in the field of Joint Management of Use and Protection of Water Resources of Interstate Sources, 18 February (1992).

1993.[39] The participating states agreed to establish an Interstate Council on the problems of the Aral Sea basin.[40] The Central Asian states also founded an International Foundation to Save the Aral Sea (IFAS) in the same year.[41] The IFAS was created 'with the aim of developing and funding environmental and applied research projects and programs in order to improve ecological situation in the areas affected by the Aral Sea catastrophe and address the socio-economic issues in the region'.[42] In addition, the Central Asian states established an Interstate Commission for the Water Coordination of Central Asia, which is the only interstate body authorized to make 'binding decisions on current and emerging issues related to interstate water allocation and use'.[43]

The Central Asian states also addressed the problem of the Aral Sea in the UN General Assembly. For example, in 1993 the President of Uzbekistan, Islam Karimov, called for the creation of a special UN Commission on the Aral Sea,[44] and in 2017 the President of Uzbekistan, Shavkat Mirziyoyev, asked for assistance to the residents of the Aral Sea area.[45] Similarly, in 2015 the President of Kazakhstan, Nursultan Nazarbayev, urged the taking of action on the problem of the Aral Sea, noting that the problem threatened not only the Central Asian region but also Europe and Antarctica, as the 'the wind annually raises to 75 million tons of dust and poisonous salt [from the Aral Sea], which are already found in Europe and Antarctica'.[46]

Apart from this, chief administrative officers of the UN visited the area of the Aral Sea, emphasizing the need to tackle the problems that had appeared due to the drying up of the sea. The former UN Secretary-General Ban Ki-moon visited the Aral Sea upon invitation by Uzbekistan's President and described the Aral Sea crises as 'clearly one of the worst environmental disasters of the world'.[47] Similarly, current UN Secretary-General Antonio Guterres visited the Aral Sea area, noting the following: 'Let the Aral Sea be a symbol of the destruction of the planet by humanity, and let this be a lesson for all of us to mobilize the entire international community in the implementation of the Paris agreement on climate… that the tragedies, similar to that I saw in Uzbekistan, haven't repeated'.[48]

When it comes to the regional level, the Central Asian states have adopted a number of declarations and signed agreements to address the Aral Sea Problem.

---

[39] Agreement on Joint Actions to Solve the Problem of the Aral Sea and the Aral Sea Region, Environmental Rehabilitation and Ensuring the Socio-Economic Development of the Aral Region.

[40] Ibid.

[41] International Fund for Saving the Aral Sea.

[42] International Fund for Saving the Aral Sea.

[43] Interstate Commission for Water Coordination of Central Asia; By-law of the Interstate Commission for Water Coordination of Central Asia (1992).

[44] United Nations, General Assembly Plenary Meeting Records, Speech of Islam Karimov, 1993.

[45] The Permanent Mission of the Republic of Uzbekistan to the United Nations, Address by H.E. Mr. Shavkat Mirziyoyev, the President of the Republic of Uzbekistan at the UNGA-72 (2017).

[46] Agency of IFAS, Crises of the Aral Sea.

[47] United Nations, Shrinking Aral Sea underscores need for urgent action on environment (2010).

[48] Agency of IFAS, Crises of the Aral Sea.

Among the notable declarations are the 1995 Nukus Declaration (emphasizing the importance of regional establishments in addressing the Aral Sea problem and the need for international assistance),[49] the 1997 Almaty Declaration (noting the need to develop a 'Convention on the steady development of the pool of the Aral Sea'),[50] the 2001 Ashgabat Declaration (highlighting the importance of increasing funding to address the problem of the Aral Sea and implementing projects on the social protection of people in the area),[51] and the 2002 Dushanbe Declaration (calling for the establishment of a special UN commission on the Aral Sea problem).[52] The Central Asian states have also concluded the following key agreements: the Agreement on Cooperation in the Field of Joint Management on Utilization and Protection of Water Resources from Interstate Sources,[53] Agreement on Joint Activities in addressing the Aral Sea and the Zone around the Sea Crisis, Improving the Environment, and Enduring the Social and Economic Development of the Aral Sea Region,[54] the Agreement about the Status of the IFAS and Its Organizations,[55] and others.

The Central Asian states have also taken some action in addressing the Aral Sea Problem. Kazakhstan has focused its efforts on restoring the North Aral Sea. As of 2025, the volume of water in the North Aral Sea had increased 'by 42% to 27 billion cubic meters'.[56] The revival of the North Aral Sea has been possible with the help of concrete actions taken by Kazakhstan. In particular, Kazakhstan completed the building of the Kok-Aral Dike and Dam in 2005, thereby preventing the flow of water into the South Aral Sea and helping restore the water level of the North Aral Sea.[57] The country took other measures to address the problem of the Aral Sea as well, including the planting of saxaul[58] and agricultural reforms.[59] Unfortunately, the situation in the South Aral Sea is not the same. Unlike Kazakhstan, Uzbekistan has focused its efforts on 'mitigating the consequences of the Aral disaster' by way

---

[49] Nukus Declaration (1995).

[50] Almaty Declaration (1997).

[51] Ashgabat Declaration (2001).

[52] Dushanbe Declaration (2002).

[53] Agreement between the Republic of Kazakhstan, the Kyrgyz Republic, the Republic of Tajikistan, Turkmenistan, and the Republic of Uzbekistan on Cooperation in the Field of Joint Management on Utilization and Protection of Water Resources from Interstate Sources (1992).

[54] Agreement between Republic of Kazakhstan, Kyrgyz Republic, Republic of Tajikistan, Turkmenistan, and Republic of Uzbekistan on Joint Activities in addressing the Aral Sea and the Zone around the Sea Crisis, Improving the Environment, and Enduring the Social and Economic Development of the Aral Sea Region (1993).

[55] The Agreement between the Government of Republic of Kazakhstan, the Government of the Kirghiz Republic, the Government of Republic of Tajikistan, the Government of Turkmenistan, and the Government of the Republics Uzbekistan about the status of IFAS and its organizations (1999).

[56] Sergey Kwan, Kazakhstan Increases Water Levels in North Aral Sea by 42%, The Times of Central Asia.

[57] Maksym Sushchuk, The Aral Sea's Rebirth: Hope Blooms.

[58] Salmukhanbetova et al. (2021, pp. 128–157).

[59] Musabekov et al. (2018, p. 178).

of 'planting saxaul, saltbush and tamarix to tamp the soil down and prevent its spread through dust storms'.[60]

Despite the actions taken to address the crisis of the Aral Sea, the problem is, unfortunately, far from solved. Although there have been many grant projects, events, meetings, and discussions regarding the Aral Sea crisis, the Aral Sea has not been restored. Experts argue that the states must thus undertake further steps to address the problem of the Aral Sea.

First, on the general level, priorities should be switched from focusing solely on economic development to a concentration on environmental protection. Yet, this is problematic. As noted by Musabekov, Nurasheva, and Mergenbaeva, the question now may be 'not so much...[about]...the fate of the Aral Sea as with the natural reserves of the region' with companies searching for oil and gas reserves in the area.[61] There are steps forward in that direction, with the Central Asian countries adopting the SDGs and engaging in international projects aimed at addressing the Aral Sea problem. One example is the World Bank funded project on 'Climate Adaptation and Mitigation Program for Aral Sea Basin'.[62] In this regard, the Central Asian states may take steps to hold the next COP in the region and draw attention to the Aral Sea problem.[63]

Second, it is clear that states should continue cooperating on issues related to the Aral Sea. As rightfully noted by experts, the water sector in the Central Asian states is '[e]ntirely dependent on regional cooperation'.[64] This is challenging in practice since the states have divergent interests when it comes to water resources, with the upstream countries focused on hydroelectric power projects and the downstream states concentrated on receiving sufficient water resources to develop their agriculture and other sectors.[65] As observed by Voloshin, despite the activities undertaken by the International Fund for saving the Aral Sea, 'little progress has been made up to this day, mainly because Uzbekistan continues to divert the waters of two rivers—the Amu Darya and Syr Darya—for agricultural purposes'.[66] Similarly, one cannot but agree with Tolstykh, who notes that 'saving the Aral Sea relies on implementing radical reforms that transition to rational models of water use and alter the economic specialization of the region', yet 'all states in the region continue to promote ... [irrigated agriculture as a "vital source of budget funding"], despite public expressions of environmental concerns'.[67] The current cooperation mechanisms of the Central Asian states are not sufficient. Steps should be taken to create stronger

---

[60] Aibarshyn Akhmetkali, Uzbekistan's Saxaul Plantation Initiative at Aral Sea Serves as Beacon of Hope.

[61] Musabekov et al. (2018, p. 179).

[62] World Bank Group, Climate Adaptation and Mitigation Program for Aral Sea Basin; See also Poberezhskaya and Bychkova (2022, p. 905) (discussing Kazakhstan's role in this project).

[63] Kudinov (2023, p. 38).

[64] Sharipova and Chemayeva (2022, p. 4).

[65] See generally Nanni (1996, pp. 132–133); Park et al. (2021, p. 1132).

[66] Voloshin (2011, p. 86).

[67] Tolstykh (2023, p. 969).

mechanisms of collaboration between these states. It is important to do this not only among the states of Kyrgyzstan, Kazakhstan, Tajikistan, and Uzbekistan, but also to integrate Afghanistan in this process,[68] especially considering the building of the Qosh Tepa Canal supported by the Taliban.[69] One way of solidifying cooperation efforts is to adopt a Convention on the Aral Sea. In particular, as stated by Sergey Sayapin, such a convention 'would be based on relevant scientific data, place limits on the use of the Amu Darya and Syr Darya Rivers for irrigation and other purposes, regulate cooperation in the areas of healthcare, the economy, and environmental protection, and establish an international expert monitoring mechanism'.[70] Such an option would benefit the countries willing to address the problem of the Aral Sea by focusing on the goals of environmental protection instead of concentrating solely on the objectives of economic growth. This having been said, the mere fact of adoption of an international convention without actions aimed at implementation will not help with addressing the problem. It can be demonstrated by the case of the Teheran convention on the Caspian Sea. Although it was adopted in 1998, it did not help in addressing the problems of the Caspian Sea.[71]

Thus, while the Central Asian states have taken some measures to address the problem of the Aral Sea, the measures taken have not resulted in the actual solution of the problem. Therefore, this case illustrates that the Central Asian states should work on reassessing their policies and prioritizing environmental protection over economic development to come up with lasting solutions to such problems. If there is a shift towards policies favouring environmental protection, then it may be possible to come up with appropriate legal responses.

14.5 Case Study 3: Taldykol Lakes

The Taldykol lake system, located in Astana, the capital of Kazakhstan, has been under threat due to local authorities' decision to use this area for development and urbanization. The Taldykol lake system 'consists of lakes Bolshoe Taldykol, Olmes, Maly Taldykol (group of lakes) and Tassuat'.[72] The lake system has more than 160 diverse species, some of which are included in the Red Book of the Republic of Kazakhstan.[73] It is also characterized by a wide range of plant species, with a total of 98 identified.[74] The Taldykol lakes form a stable eco system with rich biodiversity. Furthermore, wetlands such as those in the lake system are very important for the ecosystem of every state, including that of Kazakhstan.

---

[68] For a detailed analysis of the role of Afghanistan see Giritlioglu and Tsoy (2024, pp. 113–137).

[69] The Washington Post, Taliban Bringing Water to Afghanistan's Parched Plains via Massive Canal.

[70] Sayapin (2022, p. 341).

[71] Vadim Ni.

[72] Vigano, Birdlife International (2022, para 3).

[73] Baigaliyeva et al. (2024, p. 2).

[74] Ibid.

However, this system of lakes has been and continues to be affected by urbanization, which accelerated after 1997 when Astana became the country's capital city.[75] In 2020, Astana authorities approved a city development plan that included turning Kishi Taldykol (Small Taldykol, a section of the Taldykol lake system closest to the city core) into a residential neighbourhood with shops and business buildings.[76] This was put into the plan through the drainage of the lake, after which construction was initiated in the area.

There were some lakes which drained partly naturally, and others which were drained artificially. According to experts, 'as wetlands, these lakes require specific conservation and management practices in line with the Ramsar Convention's principles for the sustainable use of natural resources'.[77] However, this was ignored by the state bodies, 'where local authorities justified their actions, citing unpleasant odours, dirty water, and mosquitoes, claims refuted by nearby residents, moreover their justification included that these wetlands cause harm to health of citizens',[78] which was never proven nor was any independent authoritative commission decision made. In fact, the Kazakhstan Association for the Preservation of Biodiversity noted that 'the wetlands are critical to the local watershed around Astana, and that draining them could increase groundwater levels in the city and harm rare flora and fauna'.[79]

It is evident that the local administration has an economic interest in the urbanization of the city. However, the construction project in the area of Taldykol negatively effects the natural environment, most notably the biodiversity. While economic development is important for the development of a state, polluted environments and lack of pure water put biodiversity and the well-being of residents at risk. The media reported that local state administration promised to leave the system of lakes untouched, and that it should have been preserved. Yet, this did not happen in practice, leading to protests. As noted in the media, 'active development of the capital has been accompanied in recent years by the protests of urban residents calling on authorities to stop issuing licenses for the construction of high-rise buildings'.[80] Similarly, it has been observed that 'the desire of authorities to develop the district was so strong that licenses for the construction of high-rise buildings were issued despite overcrowded schools and polyclinics, and overloaded sewerage systems'.[81] There was concern raised by the civil society representatives and local community in Astana, which initiated legal action in the courts.[82] Regrettably, the Supreme Court 'took the side of property developers and future residents of the houses that are being built on the territory of the lake', even though it acknowledged 'wrongdoing on part of

---

[75] Baigaliyeva et al. (2024, p. 2).

[76] Utepov et al. (2021, p. 212).

[77] Akbayeva et al. (2022, p. 267).

[78] Malakshinova (2020, para 3).

[79] Kumenov (2021, para 6).

[80] Bekbasova (2024); Central Asian Bureau for Analytical Reporting, para 2.

[81] Bekbasova (2024); Central Asian Bureau for Analytical Reporting, para 2.

[82] Iskakova (2023, para 2).

the capital city administration regarding its zoning plans'.[83] Despite the fact that the case of the Taldykol lakes demonstrated the failure of the administration to observe its international environmental obligations, the state prioritized its economic interests. The court also prioritized construction interests over citizens' rights, upholding the Astana administration's failure to establish water protection zones. Eco-activists view this decision as unjust.[84]

The analysis of the Taldykol lakes case leads us to the following conclusions. It can be argued that Kazakhstan did not meet its obligations under the UNECE Convention on Access to Information, Public Participation in Decision-making and Access to Justice in Environmental Matters of 1998 (Aarhus Convention), which Kazakhstan acceded to in 2001. It failed to provide its citizens with access to environmental information, thereby depriving them from meaningful public participation in environmental matters, and failed to ensure judicial remedies for those who sustained harm through environmental decisions. In particular, several articles of the Aarhus Convention were not fulfilled. Articles 3 and 4 of the Convention require state-actors to provide the public with access to environmental information, including public participation in decision-making and access to justice.[85] However, information about draining part of the Taldykol lakes was never communicated to the public before the plan was put in action. As for Article 6(4), it states that '[e]ach Party shall provide for early public participation, when all options are open and effective public participation can take place'.[86] When the general public tried to challenge the state administration's decision in court, the Supreme Court of Kazakhstan supported the state administration's decision and ignored the public's concern.[87] Environmental specialists as well as the residents of Astana city collected evidence on what was happening to the lake system during the process of draining.[88] The local state administration never communicated information about the procedure and the decision that was made, which resulted in the draining of one part of the Taldykol lake system and its wetlands.

Another international environmental treaty that Kazakhstan did not fully observe in this case is the Ramsar Convention of 1971 (Kazakhstan became a party in 2007). Articles 1 and 4 of the Convention are aimed at protecting wetland resources.[89] 'For the purpose of this convention, waterfowls are birds that ecologically dependent on wetlands'.[90] The Ramsar Convention only allows for the removal of a wetland in cases of national interest. Specifically, Article 4(2) states 'Where a Contracting Party in its urgent national interest, deletes or restricts the boundaries of a wetland included in the list, it should as far as possible compensate for any loss of wetland resources,

[83] Moldagali (2024, para 2).

[84] Ibid.

[85] Aarhus Convention (1998).

[86] Aarhus Convention (1998).

[87] Tengri News (2023, para 11).

[88] Iskakova (2023, para 21).

[89] AARHUS Convention (1998).

[90] Ramsar Convention (1971).

and in particular it should create additional nature reserves for waterfowl'.[91] General guidance for interpreting 'urgent national interests' under Articles 2.5 and 4.2. of the Convention states that the determination of 'urgent national interest' lies solely with the state.[92] The guidelines include what can be taken into account to justify 'urgent national interest' by the state including: threat to national interests, decision made based on national policies, transboundary effects, proposed action offers greater benefits, immediate action is required to avert a significant threat or endangered species are threatened, and others.[93] None of the aforementioned reasons took place with the construction project at Taldykol. In addition, nothing was created to maintain the original habitat or the biodiversity in that part of the wetland as required by the convention. Specifically, the Astana state administration removed the Small Taldykol Lake and did not compensate for it or create an additional nature reservoir for waterfowl, ignoring its promise to make a recreation zone by the end of June 2025. However, Article 4 of the Ramsar Convention does not impose an imperative obligation as 'the wording of the pertinent provision [of Article 4.2] ("should create" as opposed to "shall create") seems, indeed, too weak to warrant such a conclusion'.[94] Therefore, the restoration and enforcement protection mechanisms for wetlands do not offer much support in the Taldykol case.

The draining of Small Taldykol resulted in the loss of many plants, with birds and other species losing their place of habitat.[95] Kazakhstan thus also failed to comply with the Convention on Biological Diversity of 1992 (which Kazakhstan ratified in 1994). Article 6 of the Convention requires 'conservation and sustainable use of biological diversity'[96] in the state, which was not observed with Taldykol.

The failure of Kazakhstan extended beyond its international obligations as it also violated the provisions of its own national legislation.[97] The Constitution of Kazakhstan, in Article 31, defines the state's objective as to 'protect an environment favourable to human life and health'.[98] This provision was also integrated in other statutes. In particular, the Water Code of the Republic of Kazakhstan 2003, Article 108(4) of which states that 'inhabitant endangered species of animals and other objects of flora and fauna shall be protected by local executive bodies that may limit the development of the coastal strip of water resources and perform other actions that worsen the condition of water bodies or parts thereof'.[99] However, as mentioned above, local state bodies allowed for the initiation of construction at the Taldykol lakes, which are an object of environmental protection.[100] This action was

---

[91] Ramsar Convention (1971).

[92] Resolution III.20 of the Ramsar Convention (2002).

[93] Resolution III.20 of the Ramsar Convention (2002).

[94] Ferrajolo (2011, p. 245).

[95] Baigaliyeva et al. (2024, p. 2).

[96] The Convention on Biological diversity (1992).

[97] Iskakova (2023, para14).

[98] Constitution of Republic of Kazakhstan (1995).

[99] Water Code of Republic of Kazakhstan (2003).

[100] Iskakova (2023, para 13).

taken in clear violation of the Environmental Code of the Republic of Kazakhstan. The Environmental Code of Kazakhstan, in Article 7, states that 'the environment is considered favourable for human life and health if its quality ensures environmental safety and natural balance of the natural environment, including the sustainable functioning of ecological systems, natural and natural-anthropogenic objects, and natural complexes, as well as the preservation of biodiversity'.[101] In this article, the Code explains how Article 31 of the Constitution of Kazakhstan should be considered. It outlines, among other things, that the natural balance of the environment, preservation of biodiversity, and sustainable functioning of ecological systems should be guaranteed—which is important in the present case.

Article 9 of the Environmental Code defines the objects that fall under environmental protection. It reads in its first paragraph that, '[a]ll components of the natural environment, biodiversity, gene pool, and genetic resources of living organisms, natural and natural-anthropogenic objects should be protected against destruction, degradation, depletion, damage, pollution, or other harmful effects'.[102] This article explicitly states the importance of the environmental protection of all components of the natural environment, biodiversity, natural objects, and others against any type of damage. With careful consideration of the facts of this case, it can be concluded that the Taldykol system is qualified to be protected under the provisions of environmental protection in Articles 7 and 9 of the Environmental Code. Article 10 of the Code highlights actions that are considered harmful to the environment, among which are those actions that bring negative changes to the environment in the forms of depletion or degradation of the natural environment components, destruction or disturbance of the sustainable functioning of natural objects, loss or reduction of biodiversity, reduction of aesthetic value of the natural environment, and obstacles to the use of the natural environment, its resources and properties for recreational and other purposes.

The case of Taldykol demonstrates the state's violations of its international environmental law obligations. While such problems do not only appear in Kazakhstan, the case highlights the ineffectiveness of many international environmental treaties. Many of these have weak sanctions and non-binding provisions. None of the treaties has an individual complaint mechanism, limiting local voices of individuals and community. However, in modern international law jurisprudence it was noted that cases like the Taldykol dispute, which involves environmental degradation and local community concerns, can increasingly be addressed within the framework of operation of human rights bodies, including the UN Human Rights Committee. One relevant example is Portillo Cáceres et al. v. Paraguay, which was decided by the Human Rights Committee in 2016. In January 2011, Rubén Portillo Cáceres and 22 family members in Colonia Yerutí, Paraguay, fell ill due to pesticide spraying from neighbouring soybean fields. Rubén died while others suffered symptoms including vomiting, diarrhoea, respiratory distress, and skin issues.[103] The Committee found

[101] Environmental Code of Kazakhstan (2021).

[102] Environmental Code of Kazakhstan (2021).

[103] Human Rights Committee, Portillo Caceres et.al. v. Paraguay, Comm. No.2751/2016.

that Articles 6 and 17 of the ICCPR were linked with environmental pollution,[104] and found that government inaction was responsible and made decision in favour of applicant after the exhaustion of all internal remedies. There are also other cases under Committee consideration linking ICCPR provisions with environmental issues. For example, in Billy et al. v. Australia (2022), climate inaction was linked to the harming of Indigenous life.[105] Recent developments in the practice of both universal and regional mechanisms for the protection of human rights dealing with issues at the intersection of international human rights law and environmental protection are finding solution to hold states responsible for their inaction or violations of environmental law.[106] We believe this is a way out and at the same time a crucial point in contemporary international law. Therefore, one can conclude that, while most environmental international agreements lack individual protection enforcement mechanisms, a growing body of jurisprudence demonstrates that individuals and communities are increasingly turning to human rights mechanisms to seek redress for environmental harm. In the Taldykol case, the local community is searching now for an individual to initiate legal proceedings; however, potential complainants have been unwilling to take an action due to the political nature of the case and probable personal risks associated with their involvement. Such reluctance demonstrates a challenge for the community in terms of access to justice when the case has a political context in environmental disputes. This case illustrates a pattern of institutional non-compliance with municipal legal norms, as construction activities continue without any regard to apparent violations of environmental and administrative laws, thereby undermining environmental governance.

14.6 Conclusion and Ways Forward

First, as the examination of the above cases has shown, although Central Asian states are officially committed to the advancement of sustainable development goals, in practice, they often prioritize economic development over environmental protection. The region of Central Asia is rich in natural resources, most of which are not even touched. Kyrgyzstan is rich in water resources,[107] while Kazakhstan and Uzbekistan have a lot of unexplored oil and gas deposits.[108] This prompts these states to focus on short-term interests related to gaining economic benefit from these resources without long-term planning.[109] It also affects their regional cooperation. As noted by Al-Fati, 'regional cooperation in Central Asia...should be strengthened and focused more on environmental protection and the rational use of natural resources instead of solely

[104] ESCR-Net (2020, para 9).

[105] Human Rights Committee, Billy et.al. v. Australia, Comm. No. 3624/2019.

[106] Diego Mejía-Lemos (2022, p. 2).

[107] Bankwatch.

[108] Dou et al. (2024).

[109] Himes (2017, p. 16).

looking at pressing economic interests'.[110] It is true that the idea of economic development has been consistently advanced by states as one of the priority objectives. The post-1945 period stressed the various concerns around the economic development of developing countries and self-determination of colonized peoples.[111] The developing countries emphasized the importance of the use of natural resources, which was reflected among other things in the UN Resolution on 'Permanent Sovereignty over Natural Resources'.[112] Importantly, the developing countries saw the environmental protection as proposed by the developed countries as going against their priorities in economic development.[113] Nonetheless, the approach that is currently taken is that 'economic development, social development and environmental protection are deemed the "interdependent and mutually reinforcing pillars" of sustainable development'.[114] Currently, the idea of sustainable development has reflection in Sustainable Development Goals and the 2030 Agenda for Sustainable Development.[115] These goals were adopted by the Central Asian states, albeit with challenges related to their implementation.[116] The official recognition of SDGs means that the Central Asian states should demonstrate their commitment to their implementation by providing a balanced approach and should not prioritize economic development over environmental protection.

The latest stance (at least, the official one) of the Central Asian states on the correlation between economic development and environment protection can be seen during the voting of the General Assembly on the Resolution Recognizing a Clean, Healthy, Sustainable Environment as Human Right.[117] Both Kazakhstan and Uzbekistan voted in favour of the resolution, whereas Kyrgyzstan, along with eight other states, abstained.[118] At the same time, the Central Asian states advanced the 2022 Draft Resolution on the Zone of Peace, Trust and Cooperation of Central Asia, which among others things calls upon 'all States of the Central Asian region to promote further regional cooperation, *inter alia*, for economic and social development, the protection of the environment and the conservation of living resources'.[119] The positive outcome of such official stances taken by Central Asian states is that there is a formal recognition of the importance of the balance between economic development and environmental protection, which in and of itself is important. Yet, considering the huge number of environmental problems in the region, it is high time for the Central Asian states to start balancing economic development and environmental protection in reality and to come up with sustainable solutions to these problems.

---

110 Al Fati (2008, p. 164).

111 Schrijver (2013, pp. 95–102).

112 UN General Assembly 1962.

113 Atapattu and Carmen (2015, pp. 9–12).

114 Handl (2012, p. 5).

115 UN General Assembly (2015).

116 Hasanova et al. (2020, pp. 11–18).

117 UN (2022).

118 UN Digital Library (2022).

119 UN General Assembly (2022).

They should thus reassess their policies and do their best to promote a balanced approach by improving their national environmental legislation and implementing international environmental conventions. One concrete example is environmental impact assessment. Both Kyrgyzstan and Kazakhstan acceded to the Convention on Environmental Impact Assessment in a Transboundary Context.[120] It is a required standard which is based on the principles of international environmental law as noted by the ICJ in its Pulp Mills decision.[121] It states that state parties shall minimally address the information to ensure transparent decision-making, taking into account all relevant circumstances to minimize the adverse impact. The Central Asian states should remember the importance of environmental protection in all of the policies they pursue, laws that they adopt, and measures that they implement.

Second, it is important to work on the actual implementation of international environmental law. Domestic legal systems have compliance because they have enforcement institutions. Without such institutions, the law would not be obeyed in domestic legal systems.[122] The international arena does not have the same type of enforcement institutions as domestic systems but practice shows overall that states do generally follow international law. There are certainly inconsistencies with the practice of states and their deviations from rules, but we still observe state compliance with international obligations, especially where there are reciprocal duties of states' rights to sovereignty, territorial integrity, prohibition on the use of force, etc. In international law, 'compliance theories are linked with general international law; for instance, in terms of the question of the use of countermeasures in compliance control and material breach of treaties'.[123] If non-compliance related to such issues takes place, there are international institutions that states can use to protect their rights. Such institutions include the International Court of Justice, International Criminal Court, Dispute Settlement Understanding, and others. Most of these institutions consider cases where there is a conflict between states. However, what if the state does not have a conflict with another state, but rather decides not to comply with its international environmental law obligations within its own jurisdiction? In this case, it is unfortunate that there is no international legal institution to which individuals can apply against the state for non-compliance of international environmental legal norms. Such institutions do exist related to human rights protection. Current international law jurisprudence shows that individuals can use this mechanism to protect their environmental rights as well, and this could be a good solution for individual and local communities faced with environmental issues when the scenario is touches on or violates individuals' rights covered under the International Covenant on Civil Political Rights of 1966 and other such treaties. Another option is a consistent reflection on monitoring and reporting mechanisms. This, however, would reflect a general picture rather than a specific situation.[124]

[120] Convention on Environmental Impact Assessment in a Transboundary Context (1991).

[121] International Court of Justice (2010).

[122] O'Connell (1995, p. 49).

[123] Gray et al. (2002, p. 1833).

[124] Sacharew (1991, p. 31).

The chapter has focused on international environmental law in Central Asia. It has examined the current state of international environmental law in Kazakhstan, Kyrgyzstan, and Uzbekistan and has concentrated on problems of its implementation as well as its limitations in these countries. The chapter has concentrated on three major cases illustrating the problems with the implementation of international environmental law in Central Asia, and has provided possible solutions to address the outlined problems.

References

Aarhus Convention (1998) https://treaties.un.org/doc/treaties/1998/06/19980625%2008-35%20am/ch_xxvii_13p.pdf. Accessed 15 June 2025

Agency of IFAS, Crises of the Aral Sea. https://aral.uz/en/crisis/. Accessed 15 March 2025

Agreement between the Republic of Kazakhstan, the Kyrgyz Republic, the Republic of Tajikistan, Turkmenistan, and the Republic of Uzbekistan on Cooperation in the Field of Joint Management on Utilization and Protection of Water Resources from Interstate Sources (1992) http://www.icwc-aral.uz/statute1.htm. Accessed 15 April 2025

Agreement between Republic of Kazakhstan, Kyrgyz Republic, Republic of Tajikistan, Turkmenistan, and Republic of Uzbekistan on Joint Activities in addressing the Aral Sea and the Zone around the Sea Crisis, Improving the Environment, and Enduring the Social and Economic Development of the Aral Sea Region (1993) http://www.icwc-aral.uz/statute13.htm. Accessed 15 April 2025

Agreement on Joint Actions to Solve the Problem of the Aral Sea and the Aral Sea Region, Environmental Rehabilitation and Ensuring the Socio-Economic Development of the Aral Region. efaidnbmnnnibpcajpcglclefindmkaj/https://faolex.fao.org/docs/pdf/mul67055.pdf. Accessed 15 March 2025

Aibarshyn Akhmetkali, Uzbekistan's Saxaul Plantation Initiative at Aral Sea Serves as Beacon of Hope. https://astanatimes.com/2023/12/uzbekistans-saxaul-plantation-initiative-at-aral-sea-serves-as-beacon-of-hope-video/. Accessed 15 April 2025

Akbayeva L, Meldeshova A, Makazhanov Y (2022) Anthropogenic impact on the Taldykol lake system in the city of Nur-Sultan. RUDN J Ecol Life Saf 30:266–279

Al-Fati I (2008) Environmental developments and report Kazakhstan. East Central Eur J Environ Law 12:1–203

Almaty Declaration (1997) http://cawater-info.net/library/eng/almaty_declaration.pdf. Accessed 15 April 2025

Angelini S (2010) Environmental Issues in Central Asia. https://www.univiu.org/vecchio-sito/117-ten-publications/372-working-papers-1. Accessed 31 June 2025

Ashgabat Declaration (2001) http://cawater-info.net/library/eng/ashgabat_declaration.pdf. Accessed 15 April 2025

Atapattu S, Carmen GG (2015) The North-south divide in international environmental law: framing the issues. In: Alam S, Atapattu S, Gonzalez CG, Razzaque J (eds) International environmental law and the global south. Cambridge University Press. https://doi.org/10.1017/CBO9781107295414

Baigaliyeva M, Atakhanova Z, Kairat A (2024) Spatiotemporal variations in urban wetlands in Kazakhstan: a case of the Taldykol Lake System in Astana City. Sustainability 16:1–26. https://www.mdpi.com/2071-1050/16/16/7077. Accessed 5 Dec 2024

Bankwatch. https://bankwatch.org/sites/default/files/briefing-KGmining.pdf. Accessed 15 March 2025

Bekbasova A (2024) Central Asian Bureau for analytical reporting, SOS Taldykol: why is it important for Kazakhstan to protect Lakes in Astana. https://cabar.asia/en/sos-taldykol-why-is-it-important-for-kazakhstan-to-protect-lakes-in-astana. Accessed 10 Jan 2025

By-law of the Interstate Commission for Water Coordination of Central Asia (1992)https://faolex.fao.org/docs/pdf/mul215835.pdf. Accessed 15 March 2025

Columbia University, The Aral Sea Crisis https://www.columbia.edu/~tmt2120/introduction.htm. Accessed 15 March 2025

Constitution of Republic of Kazakhstan (1995)https://www.akorda.kz/ru/official_documents/constitution. Accessed 5 Dec 2024

Constitution of the Kyrgyz Republic (2021)https://cbd.minjust.gov.kg/1-2/edition/1202952/ru. Accessed 10 Dec 2024

Constitution of Uzbekistan (1992)https://constitution.uz/ru/clause/index#section2. Accessed 10 Dec 2025

Convention concerning the Protection of World Cultural and Natural Heritage (1972) https://whc.unesco.org/en/conventiontext/. Accessed 10 Feb 2025

Convention on Biological diversity (1992) https://www.cbd.int/convention/articles/default.shtml?a=cbd-06. Accessed 15 Jan 2025

Convention on Environmental Impact Assessment in a Transboundary Context (1991) https://treaties.un.org/pages/ViewDetails.aspx?src=TREATY&mtdsg_no=XXVII-4&chapter=27&clang=_en. Accessed 10 Feb 2025

Dou L, Wen Z, Wang Z (2024) Distribution of oil and gas resources in Central Asia. In: Global oil and gas resources: potential and distribution. Springer, New York. https://doi.org/10.1007/978-981-97-4756-6_9. Accessed 15 March 2025

Dushanbe Declaration (2002) http://cawater-info.net/library/eng/dushanbe_declaration.pdf. Accessed 15 April 2025

Environmental Code of Kazakhstan (2021)https://online.zakon.kz/Document/?doc_id=39768520&pos=641;-44#pos=641;-44. Accessed 5 Dec 2024

ESCR-Net International Network for Economic, Social and Cultural Rights (2020) https://www.escr-net.org/caselaw/2020/portillo-caceres-and-others-v-paraguay-ccprc126d27512016-communication-27512016/?utm_source=chatgpt.com. Accessed 29 June 2025

Ferrajolo, O. (2011). State obligations and non-compliance in the ramsar system. J Int Wildl Law Policy 14:243–260

Giritlioglu S, Tsoy N (2024) Water security and regional stability in Central Asia: the case of Uzbekistan and Afghanistan. Euras Res J 6(2)

Gray C, Hill S, Newbold T, Hudson L, Borger L, Contu S, Hoskins A, Ferrier S, Purvis A, Guzman A (2002) A compliance-based theory of international law. Calif Law Rev 90:1823–1883

Handl G (2012) Declaration of the United Nations Conference on the Human Environment (Stockholm Declaration), 1972 and the Rio Declaration on Environment and Development, 1992. United Nations Audiovisual Library of International Law. https://legal.un.org/avl/pdf/ha/dunche/dunche_e.pdf. Accessed 20 Nov 2024

Hasanova S, Hasanov R, Assaubayeva D, Azhigaliyeva D, Wong P, Margaux M (2020) SDG drivers framework for North and Central Asia. https://unece.org/sites/default/files/2020-12/Background_paper_-_SDG_Drivers_Framework_for_North_and_Central_Asia.pdf. Accessed 3 July 2025

Himes K (2017) Promoting water security in Central Asia through international research partnerships. Seton Hall J Dipl Int Relat 18(1):15–24

Human Rights Committee, Billy et al. v. Australia, Comm. No. 3624/2019, U.N.Doc.CCPR/C/135/D/3624/2019 (2023) https://juris.ohchr.org/casedetails/3855/en-US?utm_source=chatgpt.com. Accessed 30 June 2025

Human Rights Committee, Portillo Caceres et.al. v. Paraguay, Comm. No.2751/2016, U.N.Doc. CCPR/C/ 126/D/2751/2016 (2019)https://tbinternet.ohchr.org. Accessed 30 June 2025

International Court of Justice (2010) Pulp Mills on the River Uruguay (Argentina v. Uruguay) https://www.icj-cij.org/case/135. Accessed 10 Feb 2025

International Fund for Saving the Aral Sea. https://ecifas.kz/en/. Accessed 15 March 2025
International Fund for Saving the Aral Sea. http://www.icwc-aral.uz/ifas.htm. Accessed 15 March 2025
Interstate Commission for Water Coordination of Central Asia. http://www.icwc-aral.uz/mandate.htm. Accessed 15 March 2025
Iskakova B (2023) Верховный суд вынес решение по делу о Малом Талдыколе [Supreme Court ruled on the Small Taldykol case], Kapital.kz. https://kapital.kz/gosudarstvo/117568/verkhovnyy-sud-vynes-resheniye-po-delu-o-malom-taldykole.html. Accessed 10 Jan 2025
IUCN (2016) IUCN World Heritage Evaluations 2016: IUCN Evaluations of Nominations of Natural and Mixed Properties to the World Heritage List. https://whc.unesco.org/document/141704. Accessed 10 Oct 2024
Kumenov A (2021) Kazakhstan capital to drain treasured wetlands, breaking promise, Eurasianet. https://eurasianet.org/kazakhstan-capital-to-drain-treasured-wetlands-breaking-promise. Accessed 10 Dec 2024
Kudinov A (2023) The Aral Sea: a global solution to a Regional problem. Russ Juridical J Electron Suppl (2)
Maksym Sushchuk, The Aral Sea's Rebirth: Hope Blooms. https://eos.com/blog/the-aral-seas-rebirth-hope-blooms/. Accessed 15 April 2025
Malakshinova A (2020) Кто самовольно застраивает озеро Малый Талдыколь в Нур-Султане? [Who is putting construction buildings at self-will at the places of Small Taldykol in Nursultan?], Informburo. https://informburo.kz/stati/kto-samovolno-zastraivaet-ozero-malyy-taldykol-v-nur-sultane-reportazh-informburokz.html. Accessed 3 Dec 2024
Mejía-Lemos D (2022) The protection of the environment through international human rights litigation: taking stock of challenges and opportunities in the Inter-American System. Hum Rights Law Rev 22:1–16
Moldagali B (2024) Malyi Taldykol: "A WildlifePark with a Parking Lot", Vlast media. https://vlast.kz/english/58735-malyi-taldykol-a-wildlife-park-with-a-parking-lot.html. Accessed 10 Jan 2025
Musabekov K, Nurasheva K, Mergenbayeva A (2018) Problems and Prospects of regulation of water resources of the Aral Sea Basin. J Adv Res Law Econ 9(1):178
Nanni M (1996) The Aral Sea Basin: legal and institutional issues. Rev Eur Comp Int Environ Law 5(2)
NASA Earth Observatory World of Change: Shrinking Aral Sea. https://earthobservatory.nasa.gov/world-of-change/AralSea. Accessed 15 March 2025
Nugumanova L, Frey M, Yemelina N, Yugay S (2017) Environmental problems and policies in Kazakhstan: air pollution, waste and water. Leibniz Institute for East and Southeast European Studies. https://www.econstor.eu/bitstream/10419/162150/1/889804818.pdf. Accessed 10 Feb 2025
Nukus Declaration (1995) http://cawater-info.net/library/eng/nukus_declaration.pdf. Accessed 15 April 2025
O'Connell M (1995) Enforcement and the success of international environmental law. Indiana J Glob Legal Stud 1:47–64
Park J, Adibayeva A, Saari D (2021) Contestation and collaboration for water resources: comparing the emerging Regional Water Governance of the Aral Sea, Irtysh River, and Mekong River. J Asian Afr Stud 56(6)
Pobedinsky V, Shestak V (2020) Improving environmental legislation in Central Asia. Environ Policy Law 50(1–2):69–80
Poberezhskaya M, Bychkova A (2022) Kazakhstan's climate change policy: reflecting national strength, green economy aspirations and international agenda. Post-Communist Econ 34(7)
Ramsar Convention (1971) https://www.ramsar.org/sites/default/files/documents/library/current_convention_text_e.pdf. Accessed 15 Jan 2025

Republic of Kazakhstan, Kyrgyz Republic, and Republic of Uzbekistan (2016) Proposal for Inscription on the UNESCO world cultural and natural heritage list. https://whc.unesco.org/uploads/nominations/1490.pdf. Accessed 1 Oct 2024

Resolution III.20 (2002) of the Ramsar Convention. https://www.ramsar.org/sites/default/files/documents/pdf/guide/guide-urgent.pdf. Accessed 30 June 2025

Sacharew K (1991) Promoting compliance with international environmental legal standards: reflections on monitoring and reporting mechanisms. Yearb Int Environ Law 2:1–52

Salmukhanbetova Z, Imanalinova A, Dimeyeva L, Zverev N (2021) State of saxaul plantations in Kazakhstan's section of the Aral Sea Region. Central Asian J Water Res 7(1):128–157

Sayapin S (2021) The Aral Sea. In Lee S, Lee HE, Haque ME, Sayapin S, Ravindran RB, Seifi J, Seneviratne W (eds) Encyclopaedia of Public International Law in Asia, Volume III: Central & South Asia

Sayapin S (2022) International law in Central Asia: practices and doctrines. Rev Central East Eur Law 47

Schrijver N (2013) Self-determination of peoples and sovereignty over natural wealth and resources. In: Realizing the right to development, pp 95–102. https://www.un-ilibrary.org/content/books/9789210559720s006-c002. Accessed 5 Oct 2024

Sergey Kwan, Kazakhstan Increases Water Levels in North Aral Sea by 42%, The Times of Central Asia. https://timesca.com/kazakhstan-increases-water-levels-in-north-aral-sea-by-42/%23%3A%7E%3Atext%3DKazakhstans%20efforts%20to%20restore%20the,have%20risen%20to%208%2C000%20tons. Accessed 15 April 2025

Sharipova B, Chemayeva N (2022) Adaptive water governance in Central Asia: un-puzzling the concept. Central Asian J Water Res 8(2)

Song S, Chen X, Zan C, Zhang H, Wang C, Hu Z, Li Y (2025) Integrated spatial priority assessment in Central Asia: bridging biodiversity, ecosystem services, and human activities. Geogr Sustain 6(2):1–15. https://doi.org/10.1016/j.geosus.2024.08.010

Tengri News (2023) Верховный суд поставил точку по озерам Малый Талдыколь (Supreme court finalized the case on Small Taldykol). https://tengrinews.kz/kazakhstan_news/verhovnyiy-sud-postavil-tochku-po-ozeram-malyiy-taldyikol-505484/. Accessed 15 Jan 2025

The Agency for the Management of Project Implementation of the Aral Sea Basin, The Aral Sea Crisis. https://aral.uz/en/crisis/. Accessed 15 May 2025

The Agreement between the Government of Republic of Kazakhstan, the Government of the Kirghiz Republic, the Government of Republic of Tajikistan, the Government of Turkmenistan, and the Government of the Republics Uzbekistan about the status of IFAS and its organizations (1999) http://www.icwc-aral.uz/statute3.htm. Accessed 15 April 2025

The Agreement between the Republic of Kazakhstan, the Republic Kyrgyzstan, the Republic of Uzbekistan, the Republic of Tajikistan and Turkmenistan on Cooperation in the field of Joint Management of Use and Protection of Water Resources of Interstate Sources, 18 February (1992) https://cis-legislation.com/document.fwx?rgn=5674. Accessed 15 March 2025

The Permanent Mission of the Republic of Uzbekistan to the United Nations, Address by H.E. Mr. Shavkat Mirziyoyev, the President of the Republic of Uzbekistan at the UNGA-72, 2017. https://www.un.int/uzbekistan/statements_speeches/address-he-mr-shavkat-mirziyoyev-president-republic-uzbekistan-unga-72. Accessed 14 March 2025

The Washington Post, Taliban Bringing Water to Afghanistan's Parched Plains via Massive Canal. https://www.washingtonpost.com/world/2023/08/20/afghanistan-taliban-canal-amu-darya/. Accessed 15 April 2025

Tolstykh V (2023) International law in Central Asia: factors, challenges, and prospects. Law Sci 2(4):955–982

UN (2010) Shrinking Aral Sea underscores need for urgent action on environment. https://news.un.org/en/story/2010/04/334402. Accessed 15 March 2025

UN (2022) With 161 Votes in Favour, 8 Abstentions, General Assembly Adopts Landmark Resolution Recognizing Clean, Healthy, Sustainable Environment as Human Right|Meetings Coverage and Press Releases. https://press.un.org/en/2022/ga12437.doc.htm. Accessed 20 Sept 2024

UN Digital Library (2022) The human right to a clean, healthy and sustainable environment: resolution/: Adopted by the General Assembly. https://digitallibrary.un.org/record/3982659. Accessed 5 Oct 2024

UN General Assembly (1962) Resolution 1803 (XVII) "Permanent Sovereignty over Natural Resources." https://www.ohchr.org/en/instruments-mechanisms/instruments/general-assembly-resolution-1803-xvii-14-december-1962-permanent. Accessed 5 Oct 2024

UN General Assembly (2015) Resolution 70/1 transforming our world: the 2030 agenda for sustainable development. https://docs.un.org/en/A/RES/70/1. Accessed 5 Oct 2024

UN General Assembly (2022) Draft Resolution zone of peace, trust and cooperation of Central Asia. https://digitallibrary.un.org/record/3983155?ln=en&v=pdf. Accessed 20 Sept 2024

UN, General Assembly Plenary Meeting Records, Speech of Islam Karimov (1993) https://documents.un.org/doc/undoc/gen/n93/866/17/pdf/n9386617.pdf. Accessed 15 Mar 2025

UNESCO World Heritage Centre (n.d.a) Western Tien-Shan—Documents. https://whc.unesco.org/en/list/1490/documents/. Accessed 31 Jan 2025

UNESCO World Heritage Centre (n.d.b) Xinjiang Tianshan. https://whc.unesco.org/en/list/1414/. Accessed 6 Dec 2024

UNESCO World Heritage Centre (2023) UNESCO World Heritage Centre—State of Conservation (SOC 2023) Western Tien-Shan (Kazakhstan, Kyrgyzstan, Uzbekistan). https://whc.unesco.org/en/soc/4496/. Accessed 31 Jan 2025

UNESCO World Heritage Committee (2016) Decision—40 COM 8B.9. https://whc.unesco.org/en/decisions/6788. Accessed 15 Oct 2024

UNESCO World Heritage Committee (2018) Decision—42 COM 7B.69. https://whc.unesco.org/en/decisions/7298. Accessed 15 Oct 2024

UNESCO World Heritage Committee (2021) Decision—44 COM 7B.95. https://whc.unesco.org/en/decisions/7811. Accessed 15 Oct 2024

UNESCO World Heritage Committee (2023) Decision—45 COM 7B.85. https://whc.unesco.org/en/decisions/8263. Accessed 15 Oct 2024

UNESCO World Heritage Committee (2025) Decision—47 COM 7B.8. https://whc.unesco.org/en/decisions/8732. Accessed 23 Oct 2025

UN Treaty Collection. Multilateral Treaties Deposited with the Secretary-General. https://treaties.un.org/Pages/Treaties.aspx?id=27&subid=A&clang=_en. Accessed 21 Nov 2024

UNICEF (2023) Air pollution in Kyrgyzstan causes major health impacts for children. https://www.unicef.org/eca/stories/air-pollution-kyrgyzstan-causes-major-health-impacts-children. Accessed 5 Dec 2024

Utepov A, Jumabayev S, Skakova A, Salmanova R, Kuandykov N (2021) The economic evaluation of water ecosystem services in urban planning in Nur Sultan, Kazakhstan. Public Policy and Administration 20:205–219

Vadim Ni. https://savethecaspiansea.com/tpost/f8pmocipo1-o-merah-po-sohraneniyu-kaspiiskogo-morya. Accessed 15 April 2025

Vigano M, Birdlife International (2022) Kazakh people are fighting to preserve the natural lakes of Nur-Sultan. https://www.birdlife.org/news/2022/01/17/kazakh-people-are-fighting-to-preserve-the-natural-lakes-of-nur-sultan. Accessed 5 Dec 2025

Voloshin G (2011) The struggle for resources in Central Asia: a curse or an opportunity? Yale J Int Aff 6(2):81–89

Water Code of Republic of Kazakhstan (2003) https://online.zakon.kz/Document/?doc_id=1042116&pos=2216;13#pos=2216;13. Accessed 5 Dec 2024

World Bank Group, Climate Adaptation and Mitigation Program for Aral Sea Basin. https://projects.worldbank.org/en/projects-operations/project-detail/P151363. Accessed 2 April 2025

Part VIII
International Law as an Academic Discipline

Chapter 15
The Two Worlds of Teaching International Law in Central Asia

Julia Emtseva

Abstract Discussions on the geographies and methods of teaching international law have become mainstream, to the extent that several edited volumes appeared on the topic in 2023 and 2024. The conversation is undoubtedly important; it is also vital to fill the gaps that exist in current published scholarship. This chapter, therefore, looks at how international law is taught in Central Asia. This is a topic that has been examined by scholars from the region, but instead of focusing on the doctrines taught and the space they occupy in the Central Asian international law curriculum, this chapter maps the structure of syllabi, teaching methodologies, and textbooks used in Central Asian private and public universities. The goal is to show that the landscape of international legal education is not monolithic in the region; it is very much dependent on the broader educational structures and university politics. The contribution of this chapter, therefore, lies in unveiling the diversity in international law education in Central Asia, the implications of which might also have relevance for other regions and jurisdictions.

Keywords International law pedagogy · Central Asia · Public/private education · Diversity · University politics

I Would Like to Thank Artur Simonyan for His Insightful Feedback; His Expertise in International Law in the Eurasian Region Has Enriched This Text. I Am Also Particularly Grateful for All the Colleagues From Kyrgyzstan, Kazakhstan, and Uzbekistan for Sharing Their Syllabi With Me to Conduct This Study.

J. Emtseva (✉)
HEC Paris, Paris, France
e-mail: emtseva@hec.fr

S. Sayapin (ed.), *International Law, Politics and Security in Central Asia*,
https://doi.org/10.1007/978-3-032-17818-3_15

15.1 Introduction

The ways in which public international law (PIL) is taught in different parts of the world and in different contexts have recently become a popular object of study among scholars in the field. Practicing reflexivity[1] is now becoming common when international lawyers discuss not only the epistemologies of international law but also how it is depicted in books, taught to university students, and spoken about in different academic and global forums. In the year 2024 alone, three edited volumes with the title *Teaching International Law* were published by different publishing houses.[2] Yet, none of these touched upon an often-neglected but actually very interesting region for such study, Central Asia.

The region represents a distinct historical, geopolitical, and educational landscape for studying how international law has developed within the law faculties of local universities. Its Soviet legacy shaped a legal tradition that partly diverged from Western-centric international law, emphasizing collective ideological frameworks, such as socialist internationalism.[3] Nevertheless, since gaining independence around 30 years ago, Kazakhstan, Kyrgyzstan, Tajikistan, Turkmenistan, and Uzbekistan have witnessed some quite foundational transformations, including in the education sector. Independence opened the region to new opportunities, such as the establishment of private universities, often supported by Western donors, which introduced globalized and liberal curricula that mimicked how education is designed in the West.

Central Asia,[4] thus, appears to be somewhat unique within the Commonwealth of Independent States (CIS) with regard to the variety of universities that differ in nature. While Russia, for instance, lacks a comparable landscape of private universities offering English-language programs with Western-style accreditation, several institutions in Central Asia have successfully positioned themselves as regional leaders in international education. Such Western-oriented universities offer English-language programs, which enjoy higher prestige and stronger international recognition than their counterparts operating in Russian or local languages. These institutions attract international faculty, charge higher tuition fees, and adopt globally competitive curricula, positioning themselves as regional hubs for transnational legal education. Thus, I focus here solely on private universities offering programs in English for the study of international law and the ways in which they pose a contrast to public universities.

Geopolitically (though not necessarily geographically), the region is positioned at the crossroads of Russia, China, and the West, creating a dynamic interplay of influences that challenge any singular pedagogical approach. The combination of

---

[1] Emtseva (2022).

[2] Diehl and Ku (2024); Gauci and Sander (2024); Hilpold and Nesi (2024.

[3] Cherviatsova and Yarmysh (2017).

[4] Similar trends can be observed in the South Caucasus as well, where the presence of private institutions directly supported by Western states is also strong. Nevertheless, given the tighter regulation of higher education, the number of private universities in the South Caucasus is smaller than in Central Asia.

Soviet-era influences, emerging Western frameworks, and local traditions makes Central Asia a unique site for examining the tension between competing epistemologies and the broader implications for decolonizing and contextualizing international law education.

This chapter brings Central Asia into the broader discourse on teaching international law. More than that, it seeks to highlight the region's unique position in these discussions by illustrating the existence of two distinct pathways for the training of international lawyers. The first produces graduates of private, Western-oriented universities whose education is shaped by globalized curricula and English-language instruction. The second produces graduates trained in large, public universities, where legal education continues to reflect highly centralized and state-controlled study programs. My aim in this chapter is to test the hypothesis that private universities in Central Asia adopt a more Eurocentric approach to teaching international law, while public universities retain a Soviet-introduced curriculum.

To accomplish this, I review ten different public international law (PIL) syllabi from public and private universities across the region. I examine how educators navigate (if at all) the interplay between local traditions, post-Soviet legal legacies, and the imperatives of Western or 'globalized' legal discourse. Additionally, I pay special attention to the materials used to teach international law. I examine the local textbooks and the literature students are advised to read to explore the field. And, while the course structures and sources are important, I believe that we cannot detach the person from the curriculum. By studying the biographies of those who teach international law in Central Asia, I attempt to show that individual choices also matter in the systematic examination of the teaching of international law.

This chapter not only highlights the divergent approaches to legal education across the region but also contributes to broader discussions on the international law curriculum in various jurisdictions. Much of the existing scholarship on this topic operates under the assumption that there is a single, coherent approach to teaching PIL within a given jurisdiction, often focusing on the portrayal of PIL in textbooks and syllabi. This chapter challenges that assumption by demonstrating that multiple, sometimes competing, perceptions of PIL can coexist within the same jurisdiction. These differences are shaped by various factors, including the institutional status of law schools, the language of instruction, and the professional backgrounds of educators. This plurality of perspectives might influence how students engage with international law, complicating any attempt to draw definitive conclusions about societal perceptions more broadly. Ultimately, the perception of PIL within a society is not only a function of legal education but also contingent on broader domestic and foreign policy shifts, which evolve over time and differ across governments.

In Sect. 15.2, I expand on the significance of studying international law curricula in Central Asia, drawing on my own experiences as both a law student and lecturer in Kyrgyzstan. This discussion builds upon existing scholarship, particularly comparative insights from colleagues working on legal education in other regions, such as Latin America. Section 15.3 outlines the study's methodology, detailing the selection and analysis of syllabi, as well as the challenges encountered during the research process. Section 15.4 is structured in three parts, presenting findings from the examination of (1) syllabi, (2) textbooks and other reading materials, and (3) the educational and professional trajectories of international law educators. The concluding section reflects on the broader implications of these findings for the invisible and divisible colleges of international law.

15.2 Why Study PIL Curricula in Central Asia?

Researching how international law is taught around the globe has occupied many scholars. Calls for the exposure of the epistemological roots of and biases transmitted through the education of international law have become louder, and rightly so. A recent event, organized by the Centre for International Law (CIL) at the National University of Singapore, is an example of these calls reaching the region of Central Asia.[5] A report based on the online event, organized jointly by KIMEP University (Almaty, Kazakhstan) and CIL, highlights the important challenges of teaching PIL in the region: the scarcity of resources or access to them; the variety of languages within the region, but with Russian still the dominant language in most public universities; and the irrelevance of PIL as a discipline for students who wish to practice law.[6] While the report gives valuable insights into how PIL is taught and researched in the region, my intention is to bring the analysis further and study the syllabi of PIL courses at Central Asian universities.

My motivation to focus on the distinction between private and public universities stems from my own experience as a law student in Kyrgyzstan. I pursued my first law degree at the American University of Central Asia (AUCA), a private institution modeled on the American liberal arts system. Established in the late 1990s during Kyrgyzstan's early years of independence, AUCA was supported financially by the US government and George Soros' Open Society Foundation. Its law program, titled 'International and Business Law,' stands apart from the more traditional programs at public universities, which typically emphasize civil, criminal, and public law.

Many readers will be familiar with the liberal arts university model; a defining feature of AUCA against other universities in Kyrgyzstan is the flexibility to choose non-core courses, allowing law students to focus more on either international law or business law. In contrast, my friends who decided (or had no other opportunities but) to pursue their law studies at public universities experienced a rigid curriculum with predesigned programs that left little room for choice and experimentation. International law in particular occupied a marginal role in these public universities' law curricula. Nevertheless, almost all students, regardless of institution, were required to take at least one course in PIL.

[5] Anghie and Valdez (2023).

[6] Ibid.

The differences extended beyond curriculum design to the materials and teaching approaches. At AUCA, I studied PIL in English, using English-language materials. Meanwhile, my peers in public universities encountered a different set of resources and course structures. The PIL courses were mainly taught in Kyrgyz or Russian (depending on the university); the materials provided were respectively in these languages. Reflecting on these divergent experiences, I became increasingly curious about how the institutional structures of universities shape the teaching of international law.

The divergent epistemological orientation and faculty composition of public and private universities in Central Asia also influence the contrasting approaches to teaching PIL. Private universities, often influenced by Western educational models, tend to adopt a more internationalized orientation, frequently employing professors with Western training or international academic backgrounds. By contrast, public universities predominantly rely on locally trained faculty, whose teaching approaches and materials are often rooted in regional and national perspectives. While there is growing global scholarship on tailoring international law education to a 'global classroom' and integrating critical or decolonial approaches,[7] less attention has been paid to the unique challenges of teaching PIL in such divided contexts. This includes the experiences of Western-trained scholars teaching in non-Western institutions or their counterparts adapting locally grounded methodologies in public universities.

Moreover, as pointed out by colleagues who have studied PIL textbooks, such an exercise is crucial in understanding how the next generation of international lawyers in the region is being shaped.[8] Textbooks do more than just provide knowledge—they construct boundaries of what is included or excluded in the teaching of a particular subject.[9] In the context of international law, they can reveal implicit biases, defining what is presented as 'core' international law versus what is relegated to niche or peripheral status, and they often omit critical perspectives that interrogate the global power structures underpinning legal norms.[10] Besides this, my inquiry probes the extent to which PIL curricula in Central Asia perpetuate state-centric, idealist, or institutionalist narratives that usually dominate traditional European approaches to international law. Moreover, my analysis of the syllabi allows for an assessment of whether the materials used and cited in these courses reflect a diversity of voices, or if they predominantly privilege the works of white European men, as is often critiqued in international law scholarship.

In Central Asia, where educational institutions are influenced by both local traditions and Western pedagogical imports, examining the usage of textbooks can thus hint at whether two different sets of international laws are taught in the region.

This disparity sparked my motivation to examine whether such differences reflect broader regional patterns in Central Asia and beyond. My hypothesis is that private

[7] Schwöbel-Patel (2013); Burgis-Kasthala and Schwobel-Patel (2022); Al Attar and Abdelkarim (2023); Odermatt (2024).

[8] Bernardino (2021).

[9] Apple and Christian-Smith (1991).

[10] Bernardino (2021).

and public universities not only approach the teaching of international law differently but also potentially reproduce distinct epistemologies, shaped by their funding sources and institutional priorities. By investigating these dynamics, I hope to contribute to a deeper understanding of how institutional contexts influence what is taught, how it is taught, and whose perspectives are prioritized in the classroom. Studying these contrasts is not merely an academic exercise; it sheds light on the power structures and ideological underpinnings that shape the formation of legal professionals and the dissemination of international legal norms.

15.3 Methodology

While the teaching of international law in Central Asia has been examined in part, notably in Rustam Atadjanov's article published in the Indonesian Journal of International Law, my study seeks to advance this discourse by going deeper into the pedagogical frameworks employed in the region. While Atadjanov's piece provides a valuable overview of the challenges in teaching PIL in Central Asian universities, my work diverges in both scope and focus. Atadjanov's analysis centers on broad, systemic questions such as the delivery of PIL education, the contextual factors affecting it, and general challenges like limited resources, the impact of COVID-19, and local doctrinal influences.[11] While these questions are significant and align with themes I explored in my earlier work on reflexivity,[12] my current study shifts the emphasis toward the specifics of what is taught, how, and by whom.

As a methodological inspiration for this study, I am particularly grateful to colleagues from Latin America who study the issue of international law education, the results of which inspire this and other examinations of the issue around the globe.[13] This chapter thus builds on the methodology offered by Luíza Leão Soares Pereira and Fabio Costa Morosini from the Federal University of Rio Grande do Sul in Brazil in their European Journal of International Law piece on international law textbooks, in which they unveil the role of textbooks as 'powerful sites for shaping knowledge and the discipline.'[14]

Pereira and Morosini combined textual and empirical analysis when examining ten major Brazilian international law textbooks, which they selected based on their widespread use and representativeness in Brazilian legal education; their focus was on the authors' biographies, topics covered, and references cited.[15] Moreover, to address questions beyond the scope of textual analysis, they conducted semi-structured interviews with the living textbook authors, exploring themes such as professional

---

[11] Atadjanov (2022).

[12] Emtseva (2022).

[13] Betancur Restrepo and Prieto-Ríos (2017); Bernardino (2021); Leão Soares Pereira and Morosini (2024).

[14] Leão Soares Pereira and Morosini (2024).

[15] Ibid.

networks, audience considerations, and editorial influences.[16] My exploration of international law curricula in Central Asia is less ambitious for several reasons. First, there is only a handful of textbooks authored by scholars from the region; second, as I attempt to study the divergent approaches in public versus private universities, I focus only on a limited number of international law courses offered at the few universities I was able to reach out to; and third, given the rich studies produced by colleges from other regions, it is worth determining if these patterns also apply to Central Asia, even if illustrated only in the low number of syllabi studied.

Like Pereira and Morosini, who examined the biographies of textbook authors by documenting their educational backgrounds, academic affiliations, and professional practices outside academia, I similarly investigate the social markers such as academic background, career path, and social networks of those who teach international law in Central Asia, namely professors and instructors. My analysis focuses on the institutions where they obtained their degrees, their career trajectories, and the extent to which their academic and professional experiences shape their teaching. I also pay attention to 'structural questions about international law (such as whether there are substantive themes of "national" interest that are repeated in the textbooks, whether there are privileged sources among their citations and what are the patterns of nationality and gender among the authors of secondary works cited) and questions about the agency of the authors of these textbooks (how do the textbooks reflect the authors' professional histories, geographic location, academic background and positionality?).'[17] I also explore the topics these educators prioritize in their syllabi, assessing how their choices reflect broader influences, such as regional legal traditions, international funding sources, and the interplay between global and local perspectives in shaping the curriculum.

To conduct this study, I focused on a selected sample of universities in Central Asia that offer PIL courses. The selection includes big public universities with law programs or law-specific academies and private universities that are known for their Western orientations and reputations as good educational institutions. Similarly to the approach used by Restrepo and Prieto-Rios in their studies of international law education in Bogotá through PIL programs and syllabi, I acknowledge that the information derived from syllabi is inherently constrained,[18] offering only a partial view of teaching practices. Curricula across institutions vary widely, and the syllabi themselves may not fully reflect the actual delivery of the course or the informal aspects of teaching that influence students' understanding of PIL. Furthermore, syllabi often omit 'hidden' or 'silenced' curricula—unwritten, informal, or implicit elements of instruction—that may play a significant role in shaping how PIL is taught and understood.[19]

I examine ten PIL syllabi from universities in Kazakhstan, Kyrgyzstan, and Uzbekistan, covering both private and public institutions. The selection includes

[16] Ibid.

[17] Ibid.

[18] Betancur Restrepo and Prieto-Ríos (2017).

[19] Ibid.

syllabi from four private universities: KIMEP University (Kazakhstan), the American University of Central Asia (AUCA, Kyrgyzstan), Westminster University Tashkent (Uzbekistan), and Ala-Too International University (Kyrgyzstan), and six public universities: the Kyrgyz Russian Slavic University (Kyrgyzstan), Toraighyrov University (Kazakhstan), Ablai Khan University of International Relations and World Languages (Kazakhstan), the Kyrgyz State Law Academy (Kyrgyzstan), the University of World Economy and Diplomacy (UWED, Uzbekistan), and Tashkent State University (Uzbekistan). All syllabi date from 2019 to 2025.

Access to these syllabi was obtained through two main channels: direct sharing by colleagues who teach PIL at the law faculties of these universities or searches on departmental websites. The choice of universities was also highly dependent on who responded to my requests and kindly sent me their study programs. There were, however, many who did not. While I tried to reach many more colleagues, I acknowledge that the number of studied syllabi might not be representative of the whole region. I hope, however, that some patterns are applicable to the general context of international legal education in the region. The language of instruction varies across institutions. In the private universities I sampled for this study, PIL is taught exclusively in English, whereas in the public universities, syllabi are available in Russian and local languages, including Kazakh, Kyrgyz, and Uzbek.

A significant limitation of this study is the lack of data from Turkmenistan and Tajikistan. Despite much effort, I was unable to establish contact with colleagues from these countries or locate publicly available information about PIL programs at their universities. This gap underscores a broader challenge in mapping legal education across Central Asia. However, it is hoped that this study will encourage scholars in Turkmenistan and Tajikistan to undertake similar examinations, contributing to a more comprehensive understanding of how PIL is taught across the region. Despite these limitations, my hope is that this analysis may serve as an initial diagnostic tool, laying the groundwork for further exploration into the nuances of teaching PIL in Central Asia and offering a foundation for further discussion among educators and scholars to refine and develop teaching practices that address both regional needs and global epistemic perspectives.

15.4 Public–Private Divide

As noted in the introduction, Central Asia presents a distinctive educational landscape within the CIS region. However, due to my limited knowledge of educational systems beyond the former Soviet space, I cannot confidently assess whether the differences between public and private universities in Central Asia are more pronounced than in other regions. In the jurisdictions I have studied, such a stark division was not as evident, at least not to me. For instance, in Germany, the majority of universities are public, whereas in the US, private institutions dominate. While variations certainly exist, even among institutions of the same legal status, studying these differences might need a more nuanced approach, as identifying them often requires examining a broader set of indicators.

From my personal experience in Kyrgyzstan, I can say that the education provided in public and private universities is quite different. The division between public and private universities in Central Asia might be rooted in the region's historical and socioeconomic transformations following the dissolution of the Soviet Union. During the Soviet era, higher education was exclusively state-controlled, with a uniform curriculum designed to serve the ideological and practical needs dictated by the central authorities.[20] After independence, the newly formed Central Asian states sought to diversify and modernize their higher education systems.[21] This led to the emergence of private universities alongside the established public institutions. Moreover, these private institutions were also freer to adopt rhetoric aligned with Western ideologies, emphasizing the democratization, decentralization, liberalization, pluralism, and humanization of learning.[22] Despite some cracks in the liberal narratives and the rising disappointment with Western standards (seen not only in education), the ideological division between public and private universities remains strong.

Public universities, which continue to dominate higher education, are generally state-funded and follow traditional, often rigid, curricula that prioritize conformity and state oversight. These institutions are heavily influenced by post-Soviet governance structures, which limit academic freedom, restrict innovation, and maintain a hierarchical approach to teaching and administration. As a result, public universities are often characterized by bureaucratic inertia and limited flexibility in adapting to global educational trends.

In contrast, private universities have arisen as more flexible alternatives, aiming to cater to a growing demand for specialized and globally oriented education. These institutions tend to adopt Western-style teaching methods, emphasize English-language instruction, and often attract faculty with international training or experience. They are also less constrained by state control, allowing for greater autonomy in designing curricula and pedagogical approaches. However, private universities in the region face their own challenges, including inconsistent quality standards, limited access to resources, and, in some cases, issues with accreditation and recognition of their diplomas.[23]

Another important factor to consider is that private education, especially in well-established private universities such as AUCA or KIMEP, is much more expensive than in public universities. Not surprisingly, this also reflects broader socioeconomic divides, with private universities often catering to wealthier students or those seeking international exposure, while public universities remain the primary option for the majority of the population. While there are options for receiving financial aid and

20 Silova and Niyozov (2020).

21 Ibid.

22 Ibid.

23 Atadjanov (2022).

scholarships, private education remains an option only for those who can afford to pay several thousand dollars for an academic year.[24]

The following subsections explain the findings from the studied syllabi: (1) focuses on the themes that are covered in the studied syllabi; (2) looks at the textbooks that are assigned as reading materials in the syllabi and what these textbooks can tell us; (3) briefly looks at the social markers of those who drafted these syllabi.

15.4.1 Themes Covered and Teaching Methodologies

The comparative analysis of the PIL syllabi from the four private universities in Central Asia (Ala-Too International University, AUCA, KIMEP, and Westminster International University in Tashkent) reveals a shared foundation in core PIL principles, including treaties, customary international law, and general principles. All syllabi address sources of international law, subjects of international law, international organizations, international human rights law, and international criminal law. All courses last for about 15 weeks (12 weeks at the Westminster University of Tashkent).

Of course, there is some divergence among these syllabi. For instance, the study program from Ala-Too University emphasizes treaty law and diplomacy; KIMEP covers international trade and the World Trade Organization as well as the positioning of non-state actors within international law; Westminster University integrates individual criminal responsibility with moot court training; and syllabi from AUCA and Ala-Too University put a special emphasis on the interplay between municipal law and international law. The AUCA syllabus, unlike the others, does not mention the use of force or dispute settlement mechanisms (probably because the law program has two mandatory PIL classes).

Interestingly, the syllabus from KIMEP University is unique in incorporating a regional perspective, situating international law within the Central Asian context. This is quite telling when referring to the standardization of study programs, which most probably often reproduce each other from year to year; the topic of international law in Central Asia became a point to study only quite recently. The syllabus from Westminster University is the only one to mention the historical developments of international law (though KIMEP has a session on the future of international law).

There is also quite strong coherence within the assigned readings among the syllabi. All of the documents include the PIL textbook authored by Malcolm Shaw. This textbook enjoys very wide usage around the globe. As a bachelor student at AUCA and an LLM student in the US, I had Shaw's textbook as a core reading for my PIL courses. Many universities most probably use it as a core text as it aligns with standard international law curricula and provides a solid doctrinal foundation.

[24] The average cost for an academic year in a bachelor program at AUCA is around US$7,500; at KIMEP, US$9,250.

Yet, the reason for such a widespread 'obsession' with this textbook is not entirely clear to me.

There are also plenty of supplementary reading materials assigned in the studied syllabi. For instance, the KIMEP syllabus also suggests Peter Malanczuk's Akehurst's Modern Introduction to International Law, the Encyclopaedia of Public International Law in Asia, and Gerhard Werle and Florian Jessberger's Principles of International Criminal Law. Westminster University of Tashkent incorporates works by James Crawford and Rebecca Wallace, and AUCA emphasizes case law and treaties by using Larry Damrosch's textbook and Anthony Aust's Handbook of International Law.

Pedagogical methods also present an interesting object of study. All four universities emphasize interactive learning through discussions and case studies. Ala-Too University and AUCA employ traditional mid-term and final exams, KIMEP includes take-home assignments alongside in-person exams, and Westminster University prioritizes practical engagement through moot courts. Westminster University's focus on moot court exercises stands out as a hands-on approach to applying theoretical knowledge, preparing students for the practical challenges of international legal practice.

Overall, the syllabi from the private Western-oriented universities seem rather similar in content and in the teaching materials used. These similarities might be explained first by the requirements from the ministries of education on the content of the courses, and second by the content of the textbooks used. The differences within these study programs could point to the individual preferences of the instructors and their backgrounds. To see if similar findings can be traced within teaching PIL in public universities, let us turn now to the examination of the other set of syllabi.

A comparative analysis of PIL syllabi from public universities in the region (the Kyrgyz State Law Academy, Ablai Khan University, Toraighyrov University, the Kyrgyz Russian Slavic University, UWED, and Tashkent State University) reveals, similarly to private universities, both commonalities in foundational international legal education and significant divergences in specialization, pedagogical methods, and curricular emphases. A defining feature across all the syllabi is the comprehensive coverage of PIL's core principles. Each program provides instruction on state sovereignty, sources of international law, treaty law, dispute resolution mechanisms, and international security frameworks. Thematic modules consistently address human rights, international criminal law, and the legal status of international organizations, ensuring that students gain a strong doctrinal foundation—a rather similar set of topics to those taught at private universities in the region.

However, the depth and breadth of specialized topics vary considerably, reflecting the unique institutional priorities of each university. Ablai Khan University, for instance, places greater emphasis on comparative international law, arbitration, and European legal systems, aligning its curriculum with Kazakhstan's international economic and diplomatic engagements. In contrast, Toraighyrov University adopts a positivist, state-centric approach, focusing on Kazakhstan's treaty obligations and institutional participation in global governance mechanisms. Meanwhile, the Kyrgyz State Law Academy integrates a legal-methodological approach, prioritizing case law analysis and statutory interpretation, albeit with limited practical applications. The Kyrgyz Slavic State University dedicates several sessions to how international law is integrated into Kyrgyz and Russian domestic legislation.

A significant point of divergence from private universities lies in the pedagogical methodologies employed. All universities rely on traditional examinations and theoretical lecturing, emphasizing doctrinal instruction, with assessments primarily based on memorization. The presence of oral exams as well as the use of the 'ticket' system (*экзаменационные билеты*) shows that the traditional legal education model is still persistent at public universities, having survived in the region for many decades.

The choice of reading materials, expectedly, varies from the syllabi for the PIL courses taught in English at private universities. While foundational texts such as the United Nations Charter, the Vienna Conventions, and major International Court of Justice rulings are occasionally assigned, the selection of mandatory literature is quite similar. The syllabi feature a selection of texts, with repeated reliance on authors such as Lukashuk, Zvekov, Ushakov, and Ignatenko, all scholars with a Russian or Soviet background. Lukashuk stands out as the most widely referenced author across multiple syllabi. Additionally, the syllabi include supplementary readings by Kolosov and Kuznetsov, further cementing the dominance of Russian legal doctrine in public legal education in the region. The only syllabi that assign textbooks written by local scholars as primary reading material are those from the Kyrgyz Slavic State University (Borubashov), UWED (Rasulov et al.), and Tashkent State University (Yuldasheva, Umirdinov et al.). Yet, they all also include materials authored by Russian scholars (and in some instances, also materials in English—mainly chapters from Shaw's textbook). This empirical pattern reveals a clear dependence on Russian academic sources, with limited integration of non-Russian literature. The continued predominance of these specific texts might point to the deep-rooted influence of Russian legal scholarship in Central Asian legal education.

Ultimately, the study of PIL in Central Asian private and public universities reveals a dual tension: one between state-centered legal positivism and the demands of an increasingly transnational legal order, and another between traditional doctrinal teaching and the need for greater practical engagement in legal education.

What unites all the syllabi, however, is the limited engagement with critical scholarship in the teaching of PIL. This phenomenon is simultaneously not surprising and surprising. It is not surprising because critical approaches have not yet penetrated PIL curricula on a big scale in any jurisdiction in the world. It is surprising given that the Soviet scholarship was highly critical of Eurocentric international law, yet there is no mention of Soviet legal scholars like Pashukanis, Kozhevnikov, or Korovin, even in the study programs of public universities.

However, as previously stated, Central Asia is not a unique region with regard to the nonintegration of critical approaches to international law in the syllabi across law schools. This could find reflections in the challenges observed in similar contexts in postcolonial states. Following independence, Central Asian legal education largely remained Soviet-heavy (or perhaps, more correctly, Russian-heavy), as many academics who taught at the newly established universities in the independent states were professors educated in the Soviet system themselves. Perhaps an interesting comparison can be made with postcolonial India. B.S. Chimni noted that, after India's independence, Indian international lawyers sought to learn international law from Western institutions, with many prominent figures pursuing advanced degrees in elite law schools in the UK and US.[25] Even now, despite the rise of critical approaches to PIL such as Third World Approaches to International Law (TWAIL), the international law curriculum remains quite Eurocentric.[26]

Even in regions where critical traditions have been created and elaborated on, traditional Eurocentric international law remains mainstream. The situation is similar in Central Asia. While Soviet or Russian approaches have remained mainstream in public universities, European approaches have penetrated private universities, and the region has yet to develop a robust, localized critique of international law. Central Asian states often perceive themselves as peripheral in the global hierarchy of knowledge production, which reinforces the dominance of Russian scholarship in legal education. This reliance could similarly be shaped by what Chimni described as a 'postcolonial mindset,' which views Russian-authored works as more authoritative and rigorous than locally produced scholarship.[27] The absence of a strong tradition of Central Asian legal scholarship, coupled with limited resources and infrastructure, perpetuates this dynamic, leaving international law curricula heavily influenced by Russian perspectives and sidelining the development of localized or regional approaches.

15.4.2 Textbooks

As mentioned in the CIL report, there are some challenges too when it comes to PIL textbooks in Central Asia. Sergey Sayapin noted that Russian-language materials, often authored by Russian scholars and reflecting Russian perspectives, still dominate the teaching of PIL courses. This is also confirmed by my analysis of the syllabi from public universities.[28] While some law schools incorporate mainstream English-language textbooks, such as Shaw's, many teach exclusively in Russian or Central Asian languages, bypassing these English texts.[29] A few localized textbooks exist, focused on regional materials, and translation efforts have yielded Kazakh and Uzbek versions of mainstream English texts; however, there remains no comprehensive textbook that addresses regional priorities and the role of Central Asian states in shaping international law.[30]

While I cannot carry out a comprehensive examination of the large number of textbooks used in law schools across the region (as in the aforementioned study

[25] Chimni (2010).

[26] Ibid.

[27] Chimni (2010).

[28] Anghie and Valdez (2023).

[29] Ibid.

[30] Ibid.

conducted by the Brazilian team and another by Anthea Roberts), in order to assess substantive differences in the PIL curricula in Central Asian universities, I can offer some insights into two interesting examples of PIL textbooks produced in the region. The Contemporary International Law: Materials and Cases textbook, compiled by a group of legal scholars from Kyrgyzstan from AUCA and the Kyrgyz State Law Academy, came out in 2012; it is the first open-access English and Russian compilation of study materials collectively produced in Kyrgyzstan. The International Law (latest edition, 2018) textbook by Borubashov, a professor of law at the Kyrgyz Slavic State University, is another example of a locally produced work in the Russian language, with two editions.

Both textbooks adhere to a, perhaps, conventional framework, covering the essential aspects of international law such as the concepts, sources, principles of international law, state responsibility, diplomatic protection, and so forth. The first textbook offers a broad and analytically rich perspective. It integrates discussions on contemporary challenges, such as the role of private actors and transnational governance, which better reflects a more dynamic and evolving view of international law. It is incredibly rich in different cases and excerpts from international treaties, yet it lacks explanatory text, albeit possibly as this lies outside its intended scope.

By contrast, the second textbook follows a more traditional and systematic approach, structured around core doctrinal categories: sources, principles, subjects, and key legal mechanisms. It is comprehensive but leans toward a descriptive rather than analytical style, focusing on legal fundamentals with an emphasis on codified norms and historical evolution. It does, however, include a dedicated section on the implementation of international law in Kyrgyzstan, which, I believe, might be helpful for Kyrgyz students.

The big divergence between these two textbooks is in the referenced literature. The Materials and Cases textbook cites mostly primary sources such as treaties and international court and UN treaty body decisions but also incorporates short excerpts from articles written by (mostly) Western experts published in English-speaking journals and publishing houses.[31] Although there is a Russian-language version of this textbook, there is no mention of the works of colleagues from the CIS region, even though there are many references to judicial decisions that involve Kyrgyzstan.

The bibliography of Borubashov's textbook primarily consists of works by Russian and Soviet scholars. It also has a strong emphasis on historiographical and legal traditions within the Soviet and post-Soviet academic frameworks. Many references are drawn from disciplines beyond law, including history, ethnography, and political science. For instance, the inclusion of historical and ethnographic studies,

[31] From the acknowledgment section: The Editors thank the authors, scholars, and publishers who agreed to contribute their work in gratis to this book which will be provided at no cost to university faculty and students of Kyrgyzstan in support of their legal education, including David Weissbrodt and Fionnuala Ni Aolain, Ashfaq Khalfan and Marie-Claire Cordonier Segger, Dinah Shelton, Richard Lillich, Hurst Hannum, and James Anaya, Vyacheslav V. Gavrilov, Andrew Clapham, Sir Franklin Berman, Noemi Gal-Or, Alison MacDonald, Louis-Philippe Rouillard, Oxford University Press, Aspen Publishers, The American Bar Association, New Zealand Armed Forces Law Review, Santa Clara University Law Review, and the United Nations.

such as those by Bartold, Bernshtam, and Radlov, suggests that the author was concerned with the origins and evolution of the Kyrgyz people; yet, the authors of these works present quite a Russia-centric view on how the non-Russian nations from the Soviet Union developed their own national and legal systems. This literary selection showcases how legal education in Kyrgyzstan still reflects methodological and ideological influences coming from the Soviet period that shaped scholarship on statehood, territorial integrity, and legal theory in the region.

Perhaps there is little point in even mentioning that references to female international lawyers, scholars, and authors writing on non-mainstream approaches to international law are almost entirely absent. This is not surprising at all, given that there is unlikely to be much attention paid to these concerns in the region. It is possible that knowledge—regional, universal, Eurocentric, or other—is constantly reproduced; if all textbooks historically have been written excluding, or more passively unconcerned with, these categories of scholars and legal practitioners, it is more likely that these patterns will be repeated. Textbook writing is a complicated process that is influenced by many factors: promotion-seeking, relevance to educational programs set by ministries of education, or simply to elevate one's reputation among colleagues—both those who have written other textbooks and those who will validate new ones. All these peculiarities have their influence on why we have such results when we look at how international law is taught, and why so few things change.

15.4.3 Social Markers of PIL Teachers

Studying the biographies of PIL instructors is crucial if we are to understand the intellectual and educational frameworks shaping the teaching of the discipline. As Anthea Roberts argues, while elite law schools in states like the US, UK, France, China, and Russia often attract international student bodies, the degree to which their PIL instructors are internationalized through foreign legal education varies significantly.[32] This has been the case for many decades in the field of international law. Back in the 1970s, Oscar Schachter was already emphasizing the 'transnational movement of professors' as a marker of the global network of international lawyers.[33] However, such educational migration often follows predictable patterns, reflecting nationalizing, denationalizing, and Westernizing influences.[34] In Central Asia, where legal education lacks a consolidated 'elite' system, studying the educational diversity (or homogeneity) of PIL instructors reveals how these broader influences manifest in the region's academic and legal networks.

The biographies of the colleagues who kindly provided their syllabi for the current study present very rich and diverse backgrounds; I focus on the common features

---

[32] Roberts (2017).

[33] Schachter (1977).

[34] Roberts (2017).

that are present in their career trajectories, with the hope that this can also tell us something about the decisions to design syllabi the way they are.

At private universities in Central Asia, the majority of PIL lecturers hold advanced degrees from prestigious institutions in the US or Europe. This is what Anthea Roberts calls 'outbound diversity'; it often entails completing master's or doctoral programs abroad before returning to teach in a home country.[35] The international exposure of these academics could also play a big role as a denationalizing influence on their teaching, as their training immerses them in Western legal traditions, methodologies, and materials. These lecturers tend to prioritize universalist principles of international law, globalized debates, and emerging transnational challenges, such as climate change and global governance. Their curricula, as we saw, frequently incorporate internationally recognized textbooks, case law from global tribunals, and theoretical frameworks from Western academia. Perhaps such a strong Western influence might also lead to a disconnection from local contexts, as less emphasis is placed on the application of international law within the specific geopolitical and legal realities of Central Asia. Indeed, we saw that only the syllabus from KIMEP University puts special emphasis on the role of international law for the region.

In contrast, PIL lecturers at public universities in Central Asia predominantly hold degrees from domestic institutions, with occasional regional mobility for professional training or postgraduate studies in neighboring states. These academics contribute to a 'nationalizing' perception of international law, as their education is deeply rooted in local legal systems and traditions.[36] Thus, courses at public universities are also focused on the international legal obligations of the countries in question, as well as their participation in regional organizations, nurturing 'epistemic nationalism,' as argued by Anne Peters.[37] This divergence between Western-trained and domestically trained academics in Central Asia aligns quite well with the broader global patterns of core-periphery dynamics in legal education studied by Anthea Roberts. The limited educational diversity among public university lecturers might also point to the historical and structural barriers to studying abroad, such as financial constraints, language limitations, and the enduring dominance of the Russophone core.

15.5 Implications for the Invisible and Divisible Colleges of International Law in Central Asia

In this chapter, I have shown that the approaches taken in the teaching of international law might differ within regions and individual jurisdictions. I have not challenged the important research that has been done in relation to examining how international law is differently taught in different parts of the world; instead, I complement the

[35] Roberts (2017).

[36] Ibid.

[37] Peters (2017).

existing scholarship by arguing that there are nuances in the educational landscapes that should also be taken into account.

Studying ten different syllabi from ten different private and public universities across the region highlights the distinct educational and pedagogical divides between institutions. This reflects broader global trends in the internationalization and localization of legal education. These differences, shaped by the backgrounds of educators, curricular foci, and institutional priorities, have significant implications for the legal professionals these institutions produce and their roles in regional and global legal contexts.

There are, however, some caveats to keep in mind while looking at the results of the current study. First, public universities educate the majority of students in Central Asia, producing large cohorts of lawyers who will primarily serve in domestic institutions such as courts, ministries, and local law firms. In contrast, private universities, with their smaller student bodies, are more likely to produce graduates who enter global networks, taking roles in international diplomacy, transnational corporations, or NGOs. These dynamics might also inspire important questions about the 'soft power of legal education,' such as questions of what kind of professionals Central Asian states need, and whether their ministries of foreign affairs and other key institutions value the global perspectives of Western-trained graduates or the pragmatic, local expertise of those educated in public universities.

Thus, the implications of these findings go beyond the current study. Perhaps this chapter could inspire future research that would explore the trajectories of graduates from both types of institutions, examining where they find themselves professionally and how their education shapes their contributions to international and domestic law. Such investigations could reveal much about the interplay between education, legal practice, and state preferences in shaping regional legal cultures.

More broadly, these findings contribute to discussions about the globalization of legal education and the ongoing tension between pluralism and universality in international law. The educational backgrounds of international law academics profoundly shape the 'divisible college' of international lawyers, reinforcing asymmetries in the production and dissemination of legal knowledge. Private universities in Central Asia, with their Western-trained faculty, bring denationalizing influences to a historically Russophone legal sphere. In contrast, public universities maintain nationalizing traditions, perpetuating a more localized (or Russian) perspective of PIL. Do these divides present something problematic? Do these divergent approaches need reconciliation?

We all learn to celebrate diversity. Yet, perhaps in order to strengthen international legal education in the region and spark interest in international law among the region's youth, we need to encourage more cross-institutional collaboration, foster greater educational mobility, and integrate localized and globalized perspectives into the curricula of both types of educational institutions. Such efforts would not only enrich the regional study of PIL but also contribute to the broader challenge of creating a pluralistic yet universal international legal order, one that respects diversity while equipping students with the tools to engage meaningfully across borders.[38]

References

Al Attar, M., & Abdelkarim, S. (2023). Decolonising the curriculum in international law: Entrapments in praxis and critical thought. *Law and Critique, 34*, 41–62. https://doi.org/10.1007/s10978-021-09313-y

Anghie, T., & Valdez, A. I. (2023). *Teaching and researching international law in Asia: Central Asia Report*. NUS Centre for International Law.

Apple, M., & Christian-Smith, L. (1991). *The politics of the textbook* (1st ed.). Taylor and Francis.

Atadjanov, R. (2022). Teaching public international law in Central Asia: Major challenges, problematic issues, coping strategies and useful methods. *Indonesian Journal of International Law, 20*, 1–19.

Bernardino, A. L. (2021). Going by the book: What international law textbooks teach us not to know. In A. Bianchi & M. Hirsch (Eds.), *International Law's invisible frames* (1st ed., pp. 293–308). Oxford University Press.

Betancur Restrepo, L., & Prieto-Ríos, E. (2017). Educación del derecho internacional en Bogotá: Un primer diagnóstico a partir de los programas de clase y su relación con las epistemologías de no conocimiento. *Rev Derecho Estado*. https://doi.org/10.18601/01229893.n39.04

Burgis-Kasthala, M., & Schwobel-Patel, C. (2022). Against coloniality in the international law curriculum: Examining decoloniality. *The Law Teacher, 56*, 485–506. https://doi.org/10.1080/03069400.2022.2057755

Cherviatsova, A., & Yarmysh, O. (2017). Soviet international law: Between slogans and practice. *Journal of the History of International Law, 19*, 296–327. https://doi.org/10.1163/15718050-19231034

Chimni, B. S. (2010). International law scholarship in post-colonial India: Coping with dualism. *Leiden Journal of International Law, 23*, 23–51. https://doi.org/10.1017/S092215650999032X

Diehl, P. F., & Ku, C. (2024). *Teaching international law*. Edward Elgar Publishing.

Emtseva, J. (2022). Practicing reflexivity in international law: Running a never-ending race to catch up with the western international lawyers. *German Law Journal, 23*, 756–768. https://doi.org/10.1017/glj.2022.46

Gauci, J.-P., & Sander, B. (Eds.). (2024). *Teaching international law: Reflections on pedagogical practice in context*. First published. Taylor & Francis Group.

Hilpold, P., & Nesi, G. (Eds.). (2024). Teaching international law.

Leão Soares Pereira, L., & Morosini, F. C. (2024). Textbooks as markers and makers of international law: A Brazilian case study. *European Journal of International Law, 35*, 25–62. https://doi.org/10.1093/ejil/chae007

Odermatt, J. (2024). Decolonising the international law curriculum: A critical literature review. *SSRN Electronic Journal*. https://doi.org/10.2139/ssrn.4857916

Peters, A. (2017). International legal scholarship under challenge. In J. d'Aspremont, T. Gazzini, A. Nollkaemper, & W. Werner (Eds.), *International law as a profession* (pp. 117–159). Cambridge University Press.

Peters, A. (2019). Multiperspectivism in and on international law. *Völkerrechtsblog*. https://doi.org/10.17176/20190115-100404-0

Roberts, A. (2017). *Comparing international law academics*. Oxford University Press.

Schachter, O. (1977). The invisible college of international lawyers. Northwest Univ Law Rev.

[38] Peters (2019).

Schwöbel-Patel, C. E. J. (2013). 'I'd like to learn what hegemony means': Teaching international law from a critical angle. *Recht En Methode Onderz En Onderwijs, 3*, 67–84. https://doi.org/10.5553/ReM/221225082013003002006

Silova, I., & Niyozov, S. (2020). *Globalization on the margins: Education and post-socialist transformations in Central Asia* (2nd ed.). Information age publishing Inc.

MIX
Papier aus verantwortungsvollen Quellen
Paper from responsible sources
FSC® C105338

If you have any concerns about our products,
you can contact us on
ProductSafety@springernature.com

In case Publisher is established outside the EU,
the EU authorized representative is:
Springer Nature Customer Service Center GmbH
Europaplatz 3, 69115 Heidelberg, Germany

Printed by Libri Plureos GmbH
in Hamburg, Germany